D1100391

Exploring cognition: Damaged brains and neural networks

Readings in cognitive neuropsychology and connectionist modelling

edited by

Gillian Cohen
Open University, UK

Robert A. Johnston
University of Birmingham, UK

Kim Plunkett
University of Oxford, UK

WITHDRAWN FROM THE LIBRARY

UNIVERSITY OF WINCHESTER

Ψ Psychology Press
Taylor & Francis Group

HOVE AND NEW YORK

Publis /ersity

KA 0341880 4

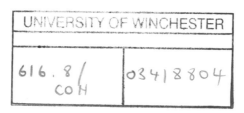

UNIVERSITY OF WINCHESTER

616.8/
CO H

03418804

First published 2000 by Psychology Press
27 Church Road, Hove, East Sussex BN3 2FA

http://www.psypress.co.uk

Simultaneously published in the USA and Canada
by Taylor & Francis Inc.
270 Madison Avenue, New York NY 10016

Reprinted 2005

Psychology Press is part of the Taylor & Francis Group

© 2000 by The Open University

All rights reserved. No part of this book may be reprinted or
reproduced or utilised in any form or by any electronic,
mechanical, or other means, now known or hereafter invented,
including photocopying and recording, or in any information
storage or retrieval system, without permission in writing from
the publishers.

British Library Cataloguing in Publication Data

A catalogue record for this book is available from the British Library

ISBN 1-84169-217-4 (Hbk)
ISBN 1-84169-218-2 (Pbk)

Cover design by Jim Wilkie
Typeset in 10/12pt Times by Graphicraft Limited, Hong Kong
Printed and bound in Great Britain by Biddles Ltd, King's Lynn, Norfolk

What is the true value of knowledge? That it makes our ignorance more precise

Anne Michaels

Contents

Preface

This book analyses the contribution made by two methodologies, cognitive neuropsychology and connectionist modelling. Both are currently at the cutting edge of research on cognitive psychology and can be employed, both separately and jointly, to shed light on the nature of the brain mechanisms involved in cognitive processes. Bringing together the evidence from both damaged brains and neural nets constitutes an innovative approach which leads to re-examination and re-evaluation of traditional theories. So, for example, interpretation of the functioning of the damaged brain is tested against the functioning of the "lesioned" model. The book is designed primarily as a text for students at postgraduate level but will be of interest to all researchers working in these areas. Rather than trying to cover a broad range of topics in a superficial fashion, the book focuses on a limited number of topics and treats these in depth so that students can gain a deeper level of understanding and develop the ability to evaluate the material. The topics that have been selected represented the most important areas where there has been a fruitful intersection of cognitive neuropsychology and connectionist modelling and where lively debates are currently in progress.

The Introduction outlines the main features of the two methodologies and evaluates their power, scope and limitations. The rest of the book is divided into two main sections, Studies in Visual Recognition, and Studies in Language Processes. Each section begins with an introduction that provides a context for the articles included in that section. The main themes are highlighted and conceptual issues are explored. Some of the same themes recur in different sections. The conflict between modular and interactive accounts is a thread that runs through all the studies. In visual recognition, different explanations are explored for the phenomenon of category specificity both in the case of living versus nonliving things and in the case of faces versus objects. The underlying mechanism for covert recognition is investigated in the context of both face recognition and word recognition. The question of whether some language processes require symbolic rule-based operations or whether they can be handled by a nonsymbolic connectionist network is debated with reference to learning past tense forms and to reading regularly spelled words. Evidence from both neuropsychological cases and connectionist models is brought to bear on each issue. Both approaches are integrated in studies where connectionist models are lesioned to simulate the impaired performance of the damaged brain. Finally, the Overview provides an overall assessment of research based on damaged brains and on neural networks in the light of the articles that have been included.

Gillian Cohen has been Professor of Psychology at the Open University, producing courses on cognitive psychology. Her research has focused on ageing, on naming faces, and on memory. Her most recent book, *Memory in the Real World* (Hove, UK: Psychology Press, 1996), reflects her interest in everyday life applications of memory.

Robert Johnston is Senior Lecturer in Psychology in the School of Psychology at the University of Birmingham. He has researched and published extensively on models of face recognition and object recognition including both clinical and computational approaches. Kim Plunkett is Professor of Cognitive Neuroscience in the Department of Experimental Psychology at the University of Oxford. His main interest is in connectionist modelling and he recently co-authored the seminal textbook *Introduction to Connectionist Modelling of Cognitive Processes* (P. McLeod, K. Plunkett, & E. T. Rolls, Oxford University Press, 1998). Nick Braisby is a Lecturer in Cognitive Psychology at The Open University. His research focuses on concepts and categorisation, and language acquisition. Peter Naish is also a lecturer in Cognitive Psychology at The Open University. His research focuses on attention and hypnosis. Professor Glyn Humphreys of the University of Birmingham has acted as advisor to the editors and as external assessor of the MSc Open University Psychology course DS871 (Exploring Cognition: Damaged Brains and Neural Networks). This book is the main text for the course.

Chapter acknowledgements

Chapter 1
Forde, E. M. E., & Humphreys, G. W. (1999). Category-specific recognition impairments: A review of important case studies and influential theories, *Aphasiology, 13*, 169–193. Reprinted with permission.

Chapter 2
Farah, M. J., & McClelland, J. L. (1991). A computational model of semantic memory impairment: Modality specificity and emergent category specifity, *Journal of Experimental Psychology: General, 120*, 339–357. Copyright © 1991 by the American Psychological Association. Reprinted with permission.

Chapter 3
Joseph T. Devlin, Laura M. Gonnerman, Elaine S. Anderson and Mark Seidenberg, 'Category-Specific Deficits in Focal and Widespread Brain Damage: A Computational Account'. *Journal of Cognitive Neuroscience*, 10:1 (January, 1998), pp. 77–94. Copyright © 1998 by the Massachusetts Institute of Technology.

Chapter 4
McNeil, J. E., & Warrington, E. K. (1993). Prosopagnosia: A face-specific disorder, *Quarterly Journal of Experimental Psychology, 46A*, 1–10. Reprinted by kind permission of the Experimental Psychology Society.

Chapter 5
Young, A. W., Hellawell, D., & De Haan, E. H. F. (1988). Cross domain semantic priming in normal subjects and a prosopagnosic patient, *Quarterly Journal of*

Experimental Psychology, 40, 561–580. Reprinted by kind permission of the Experimental Psychology Society.

Chapter 6
Reprinted from: *Cognition*, Vol. 39, pp. 129–166, Burton, A. M., Young, A. W., Bruce, V., Johnston, R. A., & Ellis, A. W., Understanding covert recognition, 1991. With permission of Elsevier Science.

Chapter 7
Farah, M. J., O'Reilly, R. C., & Vecera, S. P. (1993). Dissociated overt and covert recognition as an emergent property of a lesioned neural network, *Psychological Review, 100*, 571–588. Copyright © 1993 by the American Psychological Association. Reprinted with permission.

Chapter 8
Burton, A. M., & Young, A. W. (1999). Simulation and explanation: Some harmony and some discord. *Cognitive Neuropsychology, 16*, 73–79. Reprinted with permission.

Chapter 9
Virginia A. Marchman, 'Constraints on Plasticity in a Connectionist Model of the English Past Tense'. *Journal of Cognitive Neuroscience*, 5:2 (Spring, 1993), pp. 215–234. Copyright © 1993 by the Massachusetts Institute of Technology.

Chapter 10
Reprinted from: *Trends in Cognitive Sciences*, No. 11, pp. 428–435, Marslen-Wilson, W. D., & Tyler, L. K., Rules, representations and the English past tense, 1991. With permission of Elsevier Science.

Chapter 11
From: Juola, P., & Plunkett, K. Why double dissociations don't mean much. *Proceedings of the 20th Annual Conference of the Cognitive Science Society, 1–6*, 1998. Copyright Cognitive Science Society, Incorporated, used by permission.

Chapter 12
Recovery in deep dysphasia: Evidence for a relation between auditory-verbal STM capacity and lexical errors in repetition, by Martin, N., Saffran, E. M., & Dell, G. S., from *Brain and Language*, Volume 52, 83–113, copyright © 1996 by Academic Press, reprinted by permission of the publisher. All rights reserved.

Chatper 13
Coltheart, M., Curtis, B., Atkins, P., & Haller, M. (1993). Models of reading aloud: Dual route and parallel distributed processing approaches, *Psychological*

Review, 100, 589–608. Copyright © 1993 by the American Psychological Association. Reprinted with permission.

Chapter 14

From Hinton, G. E., Plaut, D. C., & Shallice, T. (1993). Simulating brain damage. *Scientific American*, October, 58–65. Copyright © (1993) by Scientific American, Inc. All rights reserved.

Chapter 15

Mayall, K., & Humphreys, G. W. (1996). Covert recognition in a connectionist model of pure alexia. In J. A. Reggia, E. Ruppin & R. S. Berndt (Eds.) Neural Modeling of Brain and Cognitive Disorders, 229–247. Singapore: World Scientific. Reprinted with permission of World Scientific Publishing Co Pte Ltd.

Introduction

Robert A. Johnston and Nick Braisby

How should cognition be studied? Perhaps the most straightforward answer is provided by the experimental approach. Empirical studies should be conducted, yielding evidence of the normal, typical functioning of the mind. Hypotheses should be generated, and theories constructed. These processes should cycle, so that new studies are devised to evaluate hypotheses and theories, and these should be improved in the light of the evidence.

This book explores two approaches to the study of the mind that are complementary to this more straightforward one. The first, cognitive neuropsychology, reflects the view that normal, typical cognition can be studied by examining patterns of intact and impaired performance in brain-damaged individuals. The second, connectionist modelling, assumes that cognition can be studied through the development and testing of "brain-like" computer models. Later sections of the book explore specific topics to illustrate how the application of these approaches supplements the "toolbox" of experimental, laboratory-based cognitive psychology, and to enable the reader to judge their potential utility.

In this introduction we set out the rationale and methodology behind cognitive neuropsychology and connectionist modelling and offer a brief account of how these approaches have arisen, their advantages and shortcomings.

COGNITIVE NEUROPSYCHOLOGY: THE STUDY OF DAMAGED BRAINS

Cognitive neuropsychology focuses on the errors produced by people who have suffered some type of brian damage. These errors are likely to be longer lasting and more serious than the everyday ones that characterise normal, typical cognition.

But talk of "errors" should not lead one to conclude that people with brain damage behave "incorrectly" and that others behave "correctly". It is not inconceivable that brain damage might allow certain tasks to be performed better or more quickly than might otherwise be possible. So, to be more precise, cognitive neuropsychology is the study of the patterns of changed and preserved abilities in the brain-damaged individual. According to Ellis and Young (1988) it has two central aims: (1) to draw conclusions about normal, intact cognitive processes from the patterns of impaired and intact capabilities seen in brain-injured patients, and (2) to explain the patterns of impaired and intact performance seen in brain-injured patients in terms of damage to one or more of the components of a theory or model of normal cognitive functioning.

Cognitive neuropsychology is also characterised by a commitment to a number of assumptions, developed in the following sections, concerning the organisation of the mind and the nature of the empirical studies required to investigate it. These are the notion that the mind is broadly modular, that functional structures are localised within the brain, that dissociations in performance imply modular organisation, and that single case studies may be as appropriate as group studies, if not more so. However, all these assumptions are open to challenge.

Modularity

Cognitive neuropsychology's commitment to the assumption of modularity is something of an article of faith—if it proves to be substantially incorrect it may well be that the aims of cognitive neuropsychology would be seen as intractable. In its simplest terms the modularity thesis is the view that the processes that make up the cognitive system are organised in a modular fashion, such that there are independent systems for different cognitive activities. Perhaps there is a module for face recognition that is entirely independent from the module for word recognition. Such modular organisation would make it possible that a selective form of brain damage could impair an individual's ability to recognise faces while leaving their ability to recognise words intact. An extensive account of modularity has been provided by Fodor (1983) who suggested that modules be characterised by nine properties relating to the nature of their processing. For our purposes, the following five are key:

- *Informational encapsulation.* Processing within modules is unaffected by the information processed elsewhere in the system, i.e., modules are not interactive in their processing.
- *Domain specificity.* Each module is specialised to process input from only one kind of stimulus domain.
- *Mandatoriness.* Modules process *whenever* they receive input, and this processing must continue until completion.
- *Innateness.* Modules are not formed through learning but are inborn.

- *Fixed neural architecture.* Modules are associated with dedicated neural hardware, so different modules tend to call on different physical resources within the brain.

Fodor's suggestions have been very influential, but are not all accepted without reservation (e.g., Marslen-Wilson & Tyler, 1987). Many people are particularly concerned about the suggestion that modules are innate. For example, if reading were subserved by modular processing, then it would seem unlikely that such modules could be innate given that this skill has only been acquired relatively recently and is not universal among humans. However, a possible counter argument might be that modules that were originally specialised for some other task subserve reading. Indeed, support for this position might be seen in Chialant and Caramazza's (1998) suggestion that impairments in reading may arise from degraded transfer of information between visual and language processing systems.

In spite of the controversies, Fodor's view of modularity suggests both that cognitive neuropsychology can play a vital role within cognitive psychology, and that there is a limit to its utility. Just as modularity allows for the possibility that brain damage might lead to selective functional impairments, so observations of such patterns of intact and impaired performance can be seen to support explanations of normal functioning in terms of modularity. Fodor's claims of modularity were most forcefully made for input systems such as visual perception and language processing, and so it is in studying systems such as these that cognitive neuropsychology might play a critical role. It may enable us to evaluate the claims of modularity and investigate putative modules further. But Fodor distinguishes such systems from non-modular, central systems involved in thinking, reasoning, and problem solving. Central systems are neither informationally encapsulated nor domain specific and so the utility of cognitive neuropsychology in explicating the nature of these systems may be open to question. In fact, Fodor goes further and questions the success of any of the cognitive sciences in providing explanations for the nature of central systems.

Regardless of how these debates are resolved, modern cognitive neuropsychology follows the largely pragmatic approach of adopting the following assumption:

- *Modularity.* Cognitive functions are largely, though not completely, characterised by the features of modularity suggested by Fodor (1983). Informational encapsulation may be a matter of degree, so that functions are not completely encapsulated and show a degree of interactivity in processing.

According to this assumption, whereas modularity may provide a reasonable description of the mind's organisation, it remains unclear as to just how much of the mind is modular. This pragmatic stance with respect to modularity as a whole is also mirrored in a flexible stance towards the assumption that different functional processes are localised differently, that is, rooted in different anatomical locations.

Localisation

In 1861, Broca described the patient Leborgne who although capable of under-standing language had no meaningful speech. Broca proposed that language processing could be damaged selectively leaving other cognitive processes intact. Following a post-mortem of Leborgne, despite a large amount of neural damage, Broca surmised that the most likely site of the lesion was the third frontal convolution of the left hemisphere (which continues to be labelled as Broca's area). A decade later Wernicke (1874) described several cases where individuals exhibited the opposite form of disturbance to that shown by Leborgne, that is they could speak fluently but were unable to comprehend what was said to them. A post-mortem investigation of one of these patients revealed substantial damage in the primary convolution of the left hemisphere. These findings suggested that language comprised at least two sub-components that were located in different areas of the brain. In an early "model" of language, Wernicke proposed that these represented an articulatory centre and an auditory centre, and that damage to either would cause a specific and different form of aphasia. Going beyond this mere cataloguing of deficit, Wernicke predicted a third manifestation of aphasia, which he labelled "conduction aphasia", which should arise when there is damage to the link between these two sites.

This type of theorising certainly foreshadows cognitive neuropsychology in its firm embrace of modularity, but also differs from it in a substantial way which was to be the downfall of a group of early neuropsychological researchers whom Shallice (1988) refers to as the "diagram makers". The diagram makers were largely neurologists and neuroanatomists who carried out detailed examina-tions of individual patients and constructed elaborate drawings or diagrams to illustrate their accounts of the brain's organisation. They were preoccupied with localisation. When subsequent re-analysis by critics and opponents was able to demonstrate weaknesses in the accuracy of their anatomical claims, then the psychological foundation of these models crumbled too.

Contemporary cognitive neuropsychology has a more varied attitude to the importance of localisation. We can understand this relationship by examining what may be seen as an extreme viewpoint within this approach, a viewpoint Shallice (1988) calls ultra cognitive neuropsychology. There are three aspects of this perspective that are most relevant to the approach we take in this volume. These comprise (1) a reduced concern with localisation, (2) a move from a con-sideration of group studies to a focus on individual cases, and (3) a diminished interest in the clinical aspects of the case. In the remainder of this section, and the next one, we focus on the first two characteristics.

The demise of the diagram makers was due partly to their inability to defend anatomical claims, so a reduced emphasis on localisation might have been pre-dicted. Nevertheless, the diagram makers produced figures that look remarkably similar to those used in contemporary cognitive neuropsychology. However, the lines that connect "boxes" in contemporary diagrams are information processing channels rather than the specified neural pathways of the diagram makers. Indeed, because the connections are functional, contemporary models are not so dependent on precise localisation. The assumption of isomorphism (that there is a meaningful correspondence between the organisation of the brain and that of the cognitive system—literally that they share the same shape) remains widely accepted within cognitive neuropsychology. Thus, even though functional models do not make predictions about neurological organisation, they need to be consistent with such evidence.

A complete rejection of localisation would also deny the role that increasingly sophisticated techniques can play in identifying the brian activities associated with particular functional processes. Techniques such as Positron Emission Tomography (PET), Computerised Axial Tomography (CAT), Magnetic Resonance Imaging (MRI), and Functional MRI (fMRI) all raise the possibility of identifying regions of activity in the brain that are linked to the information processing required for different tasks (such as reading or speaking). MRI and fMRI are particularly exciting because they are less intrusive in terms of the preparation of participants and allow repeated investigations of the same person.

For reasons such as these, cognitive neuropsychologists tend to adopt the following working assumption:

- *Localisation*. There is some degree of localisation within the brain, such that distinct functional processes tend to be implemented in different physical locations.

Although our current state of knowledge concerning information processing in the brain prevents very precise predictions concerning localisation, different researchers will have differing degrees of conviction in this assumption, just as they may disagree as to what counts as "distinct".

Studying groups or individuals

The second characteristic of ultra cognitive neuropsychology is its emphasis on individual case studies rather than group studies. Given the way in which experimental psychologists typically engage in research, it may come as a surprise to learn that some researchers believe cognition can be studied through the use of individual case studies. However, cognitive psychologists working with non-damaged participants assume that they have a *homogeneous* population, whereas this cannot be assumed in brain-injured individuals. By simply grouping patients together on the basis of a similar deficit and then averaging their performance, cognitive neuropsychologists would leave themselves open to the criticism that the average masks important information about individual impairments. Indeed, the pattern of deficit represented by average group performance may not be found in any individual: there may be no such thing as an average neuropsychological patient.

One way of addressing this difficulty involves grouping patients on the basis of syndromes (e.g., Robertson, Knight, Rafal, & Shimamura, 1993). This ensures greater homogeneity in the group because individuals share co-occurring symptoms. Naturally, the appropriateness of such syndrome-based groups will depend on how precisely the syndrome has been defined. This situation is further complicated by the co-occurrence of symptoms that are functionally unrelated, but which arise through the impairment of processes that, although functionally distinct, happen to be localised in adjacent areas of the brain. Consequently both activities will tend to be impaired by damage to that region. In view of these difficulties several cognitive neuropsychologists have suggested that the best way to proceed is with individual case studies (e.g., Caramazza, 1986). Shallice (1988) argues that many of the objections raised about group studies are not valid, but he does agree that there are practical obstacles that are difficult to overcome. These include the time required to collect and study enough individuals who are sufficiently well matched. Perhaps the most important outcome of this debate is the recognition that patients need to be intensively tested using a range of neuropsychological assessments in order to establish robust baseline data (e.g., Shallice, 1979). In practice, cognitive neuropsychology makes use of data from both group and single case studies.

Dissociations

In cognitive neuropsychology patterns of preservation and loss can take the form of dissociations and associations. Associations are detected when several different functions are similarly affected by brain damage. If impairments in face recognition always occurred in conjunction with impaired object recognition, the two functions would be associated. Dissociations occur when impairment to one function occurs together with preservation of another. If a patient showed impaired face recognition, but intact object recognition, the two functions would be dissociated. If another patient manifested the opposite pattern—intact face recognition but impaired object recognition—then the two functions would be doubly dissociated. Dissociations are usually far more informative than associations. Associations may arise because the associated functions are related to one another, but there is also a strong possibility that their co-occurrence might arise due to the processes being localised in areas of close anatomical proximity. The interpretation of dissociations is much more straightforward. A patient who is unable to recognise faces and yet can recognise objects may be seen to provide evidence for the modularity of the processes for face and object recognition. However, the true picture may be more complicated. It could be that a single set of processes had been damaged to the extent that the harder task of discriminating among faces is impaired while the relatively easier task of discriminating among objects is left intact. Thus, task difficulty rather than modular organisation might explain the dissociation. A more sturdy position is attained when double dissociations can be demonstrated. If complementary patients can be identified (one can do task A but not task B, another can do task B but not task A) the processes underlying each activity seemingly must be independent of one another. Again, there are difficulties with this explanation. Some researchers (e.g., Glymour, 1994; see also Juola & Plunkett, this volume) argue that double dissociations can be explained without invoking modularity. In practice, however, cognitive neuropsychology tends to proceed by assuming the usefulness of modular explanations.

Transparency

A further assumption that is made within cognitive neuropsychology is what Caramazza (1986) calls the transparency assumption (also referred to as the assumption of subtractivity). In effect, this is the assumption that the result of brain damage is a constellation of intact and normal functions and impaired ones. The assumption that the unimpaired functions are normal is important if cognitive neuropsychology is to succeed in its aim of shedding light on normal information processing. Nonetheless, there are shades of opinion as to the strength of this kind of assumption. Farah (1994) characterises the related locality assumption:

- *Locality.* This is the assumption that non-damaged components of the mind's structure continue to operate normally in patients with brain damage.

This strong assumption follows from a commitment to Fodor's view of modules as localised and informationally encapsulated. According to Farah it is characteristic of cognitive neuropsychology. However, there are weaker variants of this assumption. One such is offered by Caramazza's (1992) transparency assumption:

- *Transparency.* This is the assumption that interaction between damaged and non-damaged components may lead the latter to behave differently from normal, but that their aberrant behaviour will remain understandable in terms of their normal processing.

Despite disagreement concerning the strength of the assumption made, cognitive neuropsychology assumes that, by and large, there is no substantial reorganisation of, or other modification to, the processing of unimpaired modules. Clearly this assumption depends on the possibilities for rehabilitation following brain injury. If rehabilitation significantly modifies the way in which preserved processes operate, then it may not be possible to draw conclusions about normal cognition from evidence concerning these processes in patients.

So far, we have seen that cognitive neuropsychology offers a valuable role in understanding cognition. However, in addition to its largely empirical methods, other researchers have sought to understand the mind by building and evaluating computational models of the mental processes that may underlie particular tasks.

COGNITIVE MODELLING: SYMBOLIC SYSTEMS AND NEURAL NETWORKS

It is a general characteristic of science to make use of metaphors. Essentially, this will involve discussing novel or difficult ideas in the language of another domain that is more familiar or better understood. Psychology has frequently made use of this device and the metaphors used to understand different mental activities have taken several forms; often these reflect the current level of technology. By way of libraries, hydraulic systems, and telephone switchboards, to list but a few examples, the most often adopted metaphor for the mind is currently one based on computers. The attraction of this metaphor is obvious. At heart, computers are systems that manipulate, transform, and compare symbols and this is very much the way cognitive psychology characterises the mind. The diversity of computer hardware that can generally run the same software highlights the distinction between process and the structures that the process is implemented upon. This distinction between brain and cognition is a reassuring one for researchers needing to investigate mental processes in the absence of a complete knowledge of neurology. The existence of computers themselves is a vindication of the notion that very complex end products can be formed from very simple primitives—provided many of these are combined in a flexible manner. Computers also have the property of universality—if appropriately programmed and provided with sufficient time and memory, digital computers are thought to be capable of computing any function that can be computed.

The use of the computer metaphor also forms the basis for cognitive modelling —the use of computer modelling of information processing tasks to shed light on normal cognitive functioning. For present purposes, there are two clear benefits to such a strategy. The first is that representing a theory as a program requires that the theory be specified fully and precisely, and typically more precisely than might normally be achieved in words. Thus, modelling provides a means by which ambiguity within a model can be identified and then reduced or eliminated, perhaps by unpacking some of the existing theoretical assumptions, or perhaps by conducting further empirical study of the task involved. In other words, constructing computational models compels theorists to be explicit and precise in a way that they need not be in merely verbal statements of a theory, or even using other devices such as box–arrow diagrams. A corollary of this precision is that computer models are required to be internally consistent—otherwise they would not work. So, while consistency is not always transparent in the case of theories expressed in other ways, a successful model computer *must* be consistent.

The second clear benefit arising from cognitive modelling is that the models can become quite complex without becoming unmanageable. While it is acceptable to represent a theory by many different means, and prose sentences are one way of doing this, they are not always equally useful. An early device for representing theories was the "box–arrow" diagram. These have the utility of representing quite complex ideas and interactions in a relatively transparent way and can allow a theory to be more easily understood. However, as theories become even more complex the nature of the interactions between different components within a theory will become harder to predict. Representing theories as computer programs allows these complexities to be more easily dealt with and predictions to be derived from complex interactions among different components of the theory.

It is important to recognise that none of this means that computer models are "better" than verbally expressed theories or box–arrow diagrams. For instance, the fact that a computer model may be successfully constructed does not guarantee that it provides a correct account of cognition. There are many algorithms for completing a particular task so we cannot know we have selected the one that the cognitive system happens to employ. Nonetheless, by building computer models of existing cognitive theories we can subject the theories to additional tests—on their completeness and on their consistency.

Symbolic models

Traditionally, computer models have followed a position elaborated during the very early days of computing, and during the time at which researchers were beginning to notice a link between minds and computers. According to this tradition, computers are symbol processors that work by manipulating the symbols that they receive as input. They can manipulate symbols through such processes as reading, writing, deleting, comparing, shifting, copying, and out-putting among others. Combinations of these basic symbol manipulations can produce highly complex information processing. Indeed, any function that could in principle be computed can be computed via combinations of these simpler processes. These properties led researchers such as Alan Turing to conjecture that the computer and the mind are fundamentally alike—that any information a mind could process could also be processed by a digital computer. Given the apparent power of computers, and the belief that all information processing could be understood in terms of symbol manipulation, it was perhaps only natural that researchers soon sought to understand the mind in symbolic terms. Newell and Simon (1976) gave the most concrete expression to this programme of enquiry. They coined the Physical Symbol Systems Hypothesis—the hypothesis that symbol manipulation is necessary for general intelligent thought and action—claiming that the symbol is to cognition what the cell is to biology and what the atom is to physics.

The physical symbol systems hypothesis is contentious, although a number of important arguments have been advanced as to why we might expect cognition to be a matter of symbol manipulation. Nevertheless, the likening of minds to symbol systems raises the issue of how exactly the computer metaphor is to be interpreted. Turing suggested that computers might be indistinguishable from people in terms of their behaviour. The work of Newell and Simon suggests that minds and computers might be similar in terms of how they operate, i.e., via manipulating symbols. Certainly, minds and computers are not alike in terms of their physical instantiation—there is little similarity between the neurons of the brain and the transistors of digital computers. These three possibilities for relating minds and computers are illustrations of Marr's (1982) levels. At level 1, the computational level, minds and computers are compared in terms of what they do, that is, their input–output behaviour. At level 2, the algorithmic level, they are compared in terms of how they do what they do, that is, in terms of the style of information processing (e.g., symbol manipulation). At level 3, the implementation level, they are compared in terms of their physical instantiation, that is, the physical basis of their information processing.

Given this framework, we can understand cognitive modelling and symbolic models more clearly. Cognitive modelling is predicated on the belief that at level 1, *the computational level,* there are no fundamental differences between people and appropriately programmed computers. The task for cognitive psychologists, therefore, is to discover the appropriate kinds of computer program that most closely resemble human performance. It is an article of faith that there must be such programs. Symbolic models are then a specific variety of cognitive model, predicated on the further hypothesis that the mind is a symbol manipulator, and hence that the programs being sought will be couched exclusively in terms of symbols and operations over them. They therefore purport to explain cognition at level 2, *the algorithmic level.*

Despite the success of work within the "mind as symbol manipulator" tradition, since the early to mid-1980s an alternative conception has emerged, based on the view that better cognitive models of the mind can be built provided that they are based on more "brain-like" views of computation.

Connectionist models

Connectionist models, or artificial neural networks, are particular kinds of computer model. The key intuition that has guided their development and use in cognitive modelling has been the belief that cognitive models require a more "brain-like" view of computing. Connectionist models also attempt to explain cognition at level 2, but do so by invoking algorithms that are more clearly related to level 3, *the implementational level.*

It is not clear which was the first connectionist model, but probably all have their roots in the work of McCulloch and Pitts (1943). They showed how simple neuron-like units, when combined into equally simple networks, could compute functions similar to the logic circuits of digital computers. Also at this time Hebb (1949) proposed a mechanism for explaining how learning could take place in networks of interlinked neurons ("cell assemblies") relating stimuli and responses. He suggested that when two neurons tend to be active at the same time the connections between them are modified so as to make them mutually excitatory. Hebb's proposal was relatively easy to formulate as an algorithm for learning in artificial neural networks. Rosenblatt (1962) then showed how very simple networks called perceptrons could spontaneously learn to group inputs according to their similarity. In other words, perceptrons could learn to classify their inputs. This rate of progress in developing an understanding of "brain-like" computation was then significantly slowed by the work of Minsky and Papert (1969). In a formal analysis, they proved that certain functions could not be computed by perceptrons. The negativity of this result led many researchers to be disenchanted with the idea of building neural networks. However, Minsky and Papert's results only held for certain kinds of very simple neural network and interest in rather more complicated neural networks has subsequently revived.

In general, connectionist networks consist of a number of simple, interconnected "neuron-like" computing elements. Each unit possesses a certain level of activation and can pass its activation to other units to which it is connected. Units can also receive input from outside the neural network (usually set by the modeller). For example, a modeller might evaluate the performance of a network that simulates spoken word recognition by specifying inputs corresponding to particular acoustic-phonetic features. The connections between units represent the degree of association between those units, and have a sign and a strength that is encoded in what is called the connection weight. A large positive weight means that an active unit will tend to cause its connected unit to increase its activation also. A small negative weight means that an active unit will tend to suppress the activity of its connected unit, although this effect will be small. Depending on the nature of the influence between units, which in turn depends on the sign and the size of the weight, excitatory and inhibitory links between neurons can be modelled.

Often the entire collection of units will be organised into groups or layers. A common configuration is for units to be organised into a three-layer network. One layer is designated the input layer and one the output layer, with the interposing layer being called the hidden layer. The hidden layer is particularly important, as it represents a level of processing interposed between input and output. For some, it is this kind of layer that renders explanations in terms of connectionist networks truly cognitive. Researchers often scrutinise the hidden layers, on the view that these encode the means by which the network represents the classes of input with which it is presented. As such they could provide clues as to the kinds of internal representation required to perform particular functions.

In three-layer networks, the weights are often constrained to be unidirectional —that is, activation can pass from the input to the hidden to the output layer, but not from the output to the hidden or from the hidden to the input layer. Such a configuration is known as feed-forward. Other models (interactive models) incorporate feedback. So, for example, the hidden layer might pass activation to the input layer. In general, there are a large number of possibilities for the configuration of connectionist networks, an issue to which we will return later. However, all operate on the principle that activation is passed from unit to unit according to the nature of the connections between them.

The output provided by connectionist networks is simply the pattern of activation of the network. Of course, in general, activation will flow continually in such a network, and so the modeller may have to make an *a priori* decision as to the time at which the network's activation pattern will be taken to represent its output. Sometimes, only the activation of some units will be of interest. For instance, units in an output layer may represent particular properties or features of interest, and so it may be that only these are considered as the network's output.

So far, we have considered networks where the connection strengths are already established, and the modeller observes the behaviour of the network in response to some input. However, an even more interesting class of networks are those that are capable of learning. Hebb suggested a form of learning in which connection strengths would increase if the units connected were both strongly active, and variants of this suggestion inform connectionist modelling today. What these variants have in common is that they all propose rules for changing the weights between units depending on properties of those units, such as their activation. One learning algorithm, back-propagation, similar to means–ends analysis, introduces changes in weights so as to reduce the difference between the actual output and the intended output. Consider, for example, a network that learns to associate acoustic-phonetic features with words. Presented with an input pattern representing acoustic-phonetic input it will generate an output that should represent the corresponding word. If there is an error in the output pattern, the nature and magnitude of this will lead to changes in the weights leading from any interconnected units. The output units may become more sensitive to the activation of some units and less sensitive to others. The back-propagation algorithm is designed so that these changes in the weights will tend to increase the chances of the network generating the correct output given the same input pattern again. Very many repeated applications of the algorithm to all of the units in the network can help the network to learn the required associations.

The learning that occurs in connectionist networks also varies according to the degree of autonomy that the network possesses. The back-propagation algorithm just described requires the network to be given some help or supervision during learning. The supervisor of the learning (usually the modeller) needs to specify the particular output pattern that the network should achieve given a particular input, and may have to do this for a large number of input patterns. However, the objection is sometimes made that this kind of learning is not learning at all, as the network is merely being adjusted so as to compute what the modeller indicates ought to be computed. Certainly, much human learning occurs under the influence of a supervisor, although it is rare that the supervision is so directive. However, presumably just as much, if not more, learning occurs unsupervised, and so research has been directed towards networks that appear to learn autonomously. For example, competitive learning algorithms operate in hierarchical, feed-forward networks. The algorithm shifts a fixed total amount of weight strength for a unit from connections with inactive neighbours to connections with active neighbours. It enables a network with no previous structure to its weights to learn to detect and respond to particular structures of the input patterns (e.g., Rumelhart & Zipser, 1985).

A further dimension on which connectionist networks can be located concerns the nature of the representations they incorporate. In some networks, each processing unit is considered to represent a particular feature. For example, if you were building a network to retrieve information about people, you might want a unit to encode information about someone's profession. That is, you might introduce a unit that represents the profession "politician". This kind of representation is known as localist, because the representation remains local to one processing unit (not to be confused with the assumptions of localisation and locality made within cognitive neuropsychology). However, the same information could be represented differently. A modeller could decide to represent the profession "politician" as a pattern of activation over a collection of units. In this case, the representation would be distributed, as the collection of units as a whole would represent the information. Indeed, it would be unclear what, if anything, each individual unit represented. Connectionist models with distributed representations are sometimes known as Parallel Distributed Processing (PDP) models. Few networks, however, embody completely distributed representations. That is, most networks use clusters of units to represent particular kinds of information (even though representation within those clusters may be distributed). For example, in modelling word recognition, a cluster of units could represent letter-level information, while another could represent different lexical items. Within such a scheme, both letters and words could be represented in a distributed fashion, but over distinct sets of units. A consequence of this type of organisation is that units tend not to be involved in representing *all* kinds of information. Networks can be thought of as consisting of clusters or sub-networks dedicated to the processing of distinct kinds of information. Thus there is, in general, no incompatibility between the use of distributed representations within connectionist modelling and the cognitive neuropsychological view that cognitive functions are localised.

There has been considerable debate concerning the merits of connectionist networks and the extent to which they offer a genuine alternative to symbolic models. However, for present purposes, we will focus on some relatively undisputed claims concerning the properties that network computation appears to possess.

- *Graceful degradation*. There are two ways in which connectionist networks exhibit graceful degradation. First, they appear to perform sensibly with ill-formed input. That is, with inconsistent or degraded input, networks are capable of producing an output that appears appropriate. Second, some networks, even when damaged, seem capable of performing reasonably well. For example, when some connections or units are removed, the computation of the network may only be mildly affected. Such smooth or graceful degradation is not characteristic of symbolic models, in which error in the input or damage to the model can lead to complete failure to compute, but is more similar to the kind of performance shown by humans with brain damage.
- *Content addressability*. Content addressability refers to the ability to retrieve information from only a partial specification of its content. Much of human memory appears content addressable: Sometimes we can retrieve a large amount of information about someone from a specification of only a single one of their properties. Connectionist networks appear capable of retrieving information in a content-addressable manner. Given a partial input, networks may retrieve all the output that is normally associated with that input. Again, symbolic models are typically not content addressable.
- *Constraint satisfaction*. Much of cognition involves the simultaneous satisfaction of multiple constraints. In the complex action of typing this sentence, I (Nick Braisby) am co-ordinating (at least) visual, haptic, and auditory information, and actively considering linguistic, semantic, and conceptual issues. Each typing action results from the interplay of a number of different systems. This integrating of multiple constraints appears to be a characteristic feature of connectionist networks. If the activation of units is taken to represent information, then the network computes by balancing a large amount of possibly competing information.
- *Generalisation*. Connectionist networks typically represent information about particular input patterns. For instance, a network may learn (through supervision) to give different outputs to different kinds of input. An interesting feature is that networks can behave as though they represent information about different *categories* of input pattern, even though their learning has taken place in response only to *particular* patterns. For instance, networks can respond appropriately when they are presented with completely novel inputs (provided these are sufficiently similar to input patterns in the learning set).
- *Emergent properties*. The striking feature of these properties of connectionist networks is that, in some sense, they "come for free". The guiding intuition behind the construction of connectionist networks was that the computing elements should bear some resemblance to neurons. It would be unsurprising if content addressability were a property of a system that was designed to be content addressable. But, in large part, this is not true of connectionist networks. They have not been designed to possess these properties. Rather, these properties emerge naturally from the computational properties of the units and

their combination. Indeed, that they can give rise to such emergent properties is another interesting feature of connectionist networks.

- *Interconnectivity.* Although not a defining feature of connectionist networks, most exhibit a high degree of interconnectivity among their component units. This interconnectivity among units tends to support interactivity in terms of information processing, or non-modularity. So, although it is possible to engineer connectionist networks to support strictly modular or sequential processing (e.g., modelling bottom-up or top-down processes), many researchers exploit the interconnectivity of networks to simulate processing of a more interactive nature (e.g., where top-down and bottom-up influences are exerted simultaneously). In general, however, the interconnectivity of units within a network is not uniform. Some units will be more connected than others; some will be connected only to units within a cluster. By choosing different patterns of interconnectivity, researchers can design networks to support more or less interactivity in processing (and by extension, more or less modularity).

There is considerable debate concerning the proper treatment of connectionism. Some researchers (e.g., Fodor & Pylyshyn, 1988) maintain that connectionism is only informative as to how cognitive theories might be implemented in neuron-like hardware. Others (e.g., Smolensky, 1988) argue that connectionism offers a truer account of most information processing than the symbolic view. Still other researchers argue that symbolic and connectionist views of cognition are not only compatible but complement one another in offering a more complete account of the mind. However these debates are settled, the intriguing features of connectionist networks (such as those outlined earlier) suggest that it may be possible to build more accurate cognitive models more readily using connectionism.

Outstanding questions

This introduction to the background and rationale behind cognitive modelling, as well as some of the key technical aspects of the different kinds of model, will equip you for exploring the rest of this book. However, there are many outstanding questions regarding the claims attached to cognitive modelling. Some of these concern the debate about symbolic and connectionist approaches. As this book explores the connectionist perspective, we have paid more attention to the remaining questions that concern the nature of connectionist networks. Throughout this book, in approaching the sections as well as particular articles, you may find it helpful to return to some of these questions and consider to what extent they could alter your views of the issues raised.

- *Are connectionist networks really symbolic systems?* The answer to this question will depend on the extent to which one can identify elements of connectionist networks with symbols and symbol structures. If individual units represent features or aspects of the input, perhaps they are really symbols for that aspect of the input. However, if a representation is distributed over a collection of units, then do the individual units represent anything? If they do, then the network might really be a symbol system, but if they do not the network may genuinely be non-symbolic.

- *What are the constraints on designing connectionist networks?* This is not an easy question to answer. In practice, experienced modellers will have considerable "feel" for how a network should be designed, but it is not clear that this translates into a set of transparent design principles. In building a model, decisions will have to be taken concerning the numbers of units, their inter-connectedness, and their configuration into layers as well as the number of layers. If distributed representations are to be used, the modeller must have in mind over how many units the representations can be spread. Further, as networks provide output by settling into particular patterns of activation, questions arise as to the stability of such patterns. If the patterns are not stable over time, then a time point must be decided at which the current activation is taken as the network's output. Again, deciding when this point occurs is not straightforward.
- *Are connectionist networks sufficiently brain-like?* Although connectionist networks are inspired by views of neural computation, there are significant dis-analogies between neurons and connectionist units. There are many different kinds of neuron, and each appears specialised for a different kind of purpose. Connectionist units, by and large, are of one and the same type. The inter-connectedness of real neurons is enormous: Some neurons may be connected with more than 100,000 others. The interconnectedness of connectionist units is usually much, much less—often considerably less than 100. These and other dissimilarities between real neural networks and artificial neural or connectionist networks raise the question of whether connectionist networks would behave in the same way if they were made more realistic. They also raise questions concerning the notion of introducing lesions in connectionist networks. If networks are not terribly brain-like, and so perhaps describe cognition at a more functional level, then what sense can we make of such lesions?

COGNITIVE NEUROPSYCHOLOGY AND CONNECTIONIST MODELLING: THE INTERFACE

Cognitive neuropsychology and connectionist modelling represent departures from the orthodox methodological assumptions of cognitive psychology. Cognitive neuropsychology makes assumptions concerning modularity and transparency for example. Although there are debates concerning the appropriateness of these assumptions, none, as yet, has been shown to be in error. Moreover, there are often independent reasons for wishing to make such assumptions. Not least of these is the potential usefulness of neuropsychological evidence in placing an additional and often crucial constraint on cognitive theorising. Neuropsychological evidence can enable one to choose between competing models or theories. Indeed, it may be that only neuropsychological evidence could distinguish certain very similar models.

Connectionist modelling also represents a departure from the orthodox assumptions of cognitive psychology. Connectionist modellers tend to view the mind as being non-symbolic or at least as having aspects that are not best explained in symbolic terms. Connectionism assumes that there are virtues in offering functional accounts of the mind that are expressed in terms of computations similar to those that may be performed by the brain. Although not uncontentious, making these assumptions opens the way to a style of computational modelling that has proved remarkably successful in modelling cognitive processes.

While expanding on each of these approaches to cognitive psychology, this book focuses on the link between them. One question that arises concerns their compatibility. As each makes assumptions concerning the mind, one may ask whether these assumptions are all mutually consistent. Indeed, Farah (1994) uses connectionist models as a source of alternative explanation to those promoted from within cognitive neuropsychology. Specifically, she suggests that the interactive style of processing found in many connectionist networks violates the assumption of informational encapsulation, and so ultimately violates the view that damage to components of a system leaves the non-damaged components behaving normally. However, as we noted earlier, within both cognitive neuropsychology and connectionism there are different strengths of commitment to assumptions such as localisation and modularity. Farah herself suggests that her work implies that cognitive neuropsychology need not be strongly committed to informational encapsulation (and hence modularity). So, tensions between connectionism and cognitive neuropsychology may certainly arise, but they may in fact be helpful in informing existing debates within the two approaches.

Connectionism and cognitive neuropsychology can also help to support the cognitive explanations that the other provides. This is most clearly seen in the case of the artificial lesioning of connectionist networks. In spite of the uncertain relation between brain computation and connectionist computation, the lesioning technique appears to offer a further means of choosing between competing models. By subjecting connectionist models to damage and looking for patterns of degraded performance that mirror those seen in brain-damaged patients, researchers hope to be able to make more reliable inferences as to the nature of normal cognitive processing.

The technique raises a number of questions. In particular, we may ask to what extent the connectionist models that are lesioned offer functional as opposed to physical descriptions of the brain's activity. If networks offer functional explanations then we might ask how the lesioning of such a network is intended to provide a model for physical damage to the brian. Equally, the technique of lesioning connectionist networks appears to make most sense when different units play somewhat different roles. Does the technique then presuppose a localist form of representation, either at the level of individual units or of clusters of units? Answering questions such as these will require a detailed knowledge of cognitive neuropsychology as well as a detailed knowledge of connectionism. Only by evaluating these twin research endeavours will we truly be able to determine the usefulness, as well as the difficulties, of techniques such as this. Nevertheless, lesioning illustrates how research into the mind is likely to be enhanced through relating neuropsychological and connectionist approaches. Each approach independently offers constraints on what counts as a good cognitive theory or model. When the approaches are combined, not only must a good cognitive theory satisfy all of the constraints of the separate approaches but also further constraints can be generated, such as that provided by lesioning.

CONCLUSION

This introduction has attempted to introduce two interconnected strands of thinking within cognitive psychology. Cognitive neuropsychology introduces a set of methods and assumptions that enable the study of brain-damaged patients to yield insights into the nature of normal information processing. Cognitive modelling allows researchers to refine and evaluate theories by comparing the predictions drawn from very precise statements of the theories to data drawn from human participants. Connectionist modelling offers a further advantage in that the very architecture in which connectionist networks are built seems to embody important features of cognition. The rest of this book is predicated on the view that, in exploring cognition, researchers can greatly deepen our understanding of the mind through combining the study of damaged brains with the study of neural networks.

REFERENCES

Broca, P. (1861). Remarques sur le siège de la faculté de langage articulé suivies d'une observation d'aphémie (perte de parole). *Bulletin Société Anatomique, 36*, 330–357.

Caramazza, A. (1986). On drawing inferences about the structure of normal cognitive systems from the analysis of patterns of impaired performance: The case for single patient studies. *Brain and Cognition, 5*, 41–66.

Caramazza, A. (1992). Is cognitive neuropsychology possible? *Journal of Cognitive Neuroscience, 4*(1), 80–95.

Chialant, D., & Caramazza, A. (1998). Perceptual and lexical factors in a case of letter-by-letter reading. *Cognitive Neuropsychology, 15*(1–2), 167–201.

Ellis, A. W., & Young, A. W. (1988). *Human cognitive neuropsychology.* Hove, UK: Lawrence Erlbaum Associates Ltd.

Farah, M. J. (1994). Neuropsychological inference with an interactive brain: A critique of the "locality" assumption. *Behavioral and Brain Sciences, 17*(1), 43–104.

Fodor, J. A. (1983). *The modularity of mind.* Cambridge, MA: MIT Press.

Fodor, J. A., & Pylyshyn, Z. (1988). Connectionism and cognitive architecture: A critical analysis. *Cognition, 28*, 3–71.

Glymour, C. (1994). On the methods of cognitive neuropsychology. *British Journal for the Philosophy of Science, 45*, 815–835.

Hebb, D. O. (1949). *The organisation of behaviour*. New York: Wiley.

Marr, D. (1982). *Vision*. San Francisco, CA: Freeman.

Marslen-Wilson, W., & Tyler, L. K. (1987). Against modularity. In J. L. Garfield (Ed.), *Modularity in knowledge representation and natural-language understanding*. Cambridge, MA: MIT Press.

McCulloch, W. S., & Pitts, W. (1943). A logical calculus of the ideas immanent in nervous activity. *Bulletin of Mathematical Biophysics*, *5*, 115–133.

Minsky, M., & Papert, S. (1969). *Perceptrons*. Cambridge, MA: MIT Press.

Newell, A., & Simon, H. A. (1976). Computer science as empirical enquiry: Symbols and search. *Communications of the Association for Computing Machinery*, *19*.

Robertson, L. C., Knight, R. T., Rafal, R., & Shimamura, A. P. (1993). Cognitive neuropsychology is more than single case studies. *Journal of Experimental Psychology: Learning, Memory and Cognition*, *19*, 710–717.

Rosenblatt, F. (1962). *The principles of neurodynamics*. New York: Spartan.

Rumelhart, D. E., & Zipser, D. (1985). Feature discovery by competitive learning. *Cognitive Science*, *9*, 75–112.

Shallice, T. (1979). Case-study approach in neuropsychological research. *Journal of Clinical Neuropsychology*, *1*, 183–211.

Shallice, T. (1988). *From neuropsychology to mental structure*. New York: Cambridge University Press.

Smolensky, P. (1988). On the proper treatment of connectionism. *Behavioral and Brain Sciences*, *11*, 1–74.

Wernicke, C. (1874). *Der Aphasische Symptomenkomplex*. Breslau: Cohn & Weigart.

STUDIES IN VISUAL RECOGNITION

Robert A. Johnston

WHAT IS RECOGNITION?

Visual recognition comprises many complex interacting processes that transform the rich and detailed information in the environment into high-level concepts. This section is concerned with the higher-level stages that interpret an image at the conceptual level rather than with low-level visual processing of the image. Studies of visual recognition traditionally include recognition of objects, faces, and events, but neuropsychologists have concentrated on recognition of objects and faces. This section brings together studies that explore some of the most puzzling and theoretically controversial aspects of recognising objects and faces.

Recognising a familiar object, like a chair or a cat, is an activity that most people perform so fluently and automatically that its complexity is not apparent. We are usually able to recognise a particular object instantly in spite of seeing it from different viewpoints and in different contexts. There are some occasions where identification may be delayed or mistaken, for example when an object is seen at a distance or in poor light. However, we would probably attribute these failures to deficiencies in the visual system rather than to a faulty component at the conceptual level within the object recognition system.

Even at the higher level, the act of recognising an object or a face is not a single process but can be decomposed into several sub-processes or stages. Although recognition usually includes naming, this stage may not be accessed. Animals recognise people and objects without being able to label them and humans may recognise objects for which they do not know the name or have forgotten it. We have all probably experienced occasions when it was possible to recognise an object but not be able to name it, or to know someone is familiar but not be able to remember their name. Fortunately, while this experience is not uncommon, it usually temporary. In most cases the name will eventually become accessible again. In fact, the object recognition process can be divided further into even more components than just recognising and naming. For example, objects may be classified at different categorical levels such as Rover, an alsatian, a dog, an animal, or a living thing. We may need to identify an individual item or simply to recognise it as a member of a particular class. However, it is open to question whether we can deliberately limit our level of identification or whether all the information automatically becomes available when our recognition system is functioning properly. In general, we are more likely to need to identify faces as individuals, whereas it may sometimes be sufficient to categorise an object as a member of a class. This difference in the habitual level of identification is an important distinction between recognising objects and recognising faces.

MODELS OF RECOGNITION

Investigation of object recognition and face recognition in the laboratory suggests that in both cases information becomes available to people in a consistent order. Structural information is accessed first, then semantic information, and lastly name information. The findings from laboratory experiments investigating the time required to perform various face identification and object identification tasks conform to this sequence and are reflected in a hierarchical model of sequential stages. If recognition involves the passage through such a hierarchy, the process might be expected to get "stuck" and break down at particular points. In other words, people might show a consistent pattern of errors in identifying objects that can be predicted by this sequence of access. Examining the problems experienced by normal people can offer useful clues to understanding cognition, but the relatively few occasions on which errors occur with normal subjects makes the systematic study of these phenomena more difficult. The study of people who have suffered brain injury represents a potential way of circumnavigating this limitation. People who have experienced brain damage may make some errors more frequently or they may experience them in a more permanent fashion. In addition, in some cases they may even show pathologies that have no analogue at the mundane level. Can we assess the problems faced by such individuals and explain them in a manner that is coherent with a theory of object recognition?

Recognising objects

The study of impaired object recognition has a long history. Lissauer (1890) describes a patient, GL, as having visual agnosia. GL appeared to have normal visual acuity, as estimated from his ability to draw copies of objects, but was unable to recognise these objects by sight. On the other hand he was able to signal his knowledge of these items if given them to handle or if they had characteristic sounds (e.g., he could recognise a whistle if it was blown). Lissauer was aware of different types of agnosia and proposed a distinction between apperceptive and associative agnosia. Apperceptive agnosia involves disruption of the perceptual process, while associative agnosia is present when perceptual processing is intact but has become disconnected from the semantic system. The studies in this section are concerned with disorders arising at the higher conceptual level of recognition and would therefore be classed as associative agnosias. However, while this distinction still has some relevance nowadays, it is known that object recognition can fail in more ways than this.

The study of impaired individuals can provide evidence for sequentially organised stages of the identification process. We can identify people suffering from anomia who can recognise an object, and describe or mime its use, but cannot retrieve its name. However, there are also individuals with agnosia whose difficulty means they cannot even retrieve the semantic information. These people can see the object perfectly well, many would be able to describe it in terms of its components, some might even be able to produce an accurate drawing, but they would not be able to describe its purpose.

Such cases provide evidence for a very coarse-level decomposition of the object identification process into independent modules. Some patients are able to see an item but cannot say what it is, and so have a problem located between the structural level and the semantic level. Other patients can recognise what an object is for but cannot name it, and so have the locus of their difficulty between the semantic and phonological levels. These examples represent support for a very simple model of the process of object recognition in which a structural analysis module is followed by retrieval of semantic information about what it is and its function from a semantic module, which in turn is followed by access to its name from the phonological module.

Current theories of object recognition do not all conform to the strictly hierarchical model outlined here. From studies with uninjured people, Humphreys, Riddoch, and Quinlan (1988) have constructed a cascade model of picture naming which differs from the traditional form of object recognition. The cascade model retains the same order in which information about objects is accessed (structural $\rightarrow$ semantic $\rightarrow$ phonological), but unlike the traditional account it does not demand that processing at a later stage can only begin when processing at an earlier stage has been resolved. In a cascade model, information is transmitted continuously between the different levels following the onset of activation at the previous level. The organisation is therefore not strictly modular, as the levels interact with each other. This means that the stored representations of many items can become activated in parallel due to direct connections between individual items at different levels of representation. In such an arrangement, it would be necessary for a mechanism to prevent inappropriately activated representations forming the output. This could be achieved if representations at the same level inhibit one another.

To give an example, when the item presented for naming is visually similar to many related items (e.g., an apple is visually similar to oranges, peaches, pears) the structural representations of these related items will also be activated and all these structural-level representations will pass activation onward to the semantic level. As that stage starts to be activated, further activation will proceed down to the phonological, or naming, level. The first consequence of this activation is a large amount of noise in the system. In order for the system to respond correctly with "apple" this noise must be dampened down and this is the purpose of activations inhibiting one another at the same level. At the naming stage, for the system to yield a correct response, the apple phonology must win out over its competitors. In pathological cases, patients might tend to produce incorrect names—or even no name at all—if the system is noisy and the noise cannot be dampened so that no single phonological representation can win out.

Section I.I and the studies reported in Chapters 1, 2, and 3 explore one particular issue in the study of object recognition that might not even be noticed if we restricted ourselves to examining normal people—the proposition that the representation of objects is category-specific. This hypothesis arises from our observations that some people after brain damage have difficulties with quite specific categories of objects. Humphreys' cascade model, just described, has been used to offer a possible explanation of the mechanism underlying category-specific deficits.

However, numerous questions have not yet been answered by models of object recognition. How incomplete is semantic identification? Do the models apply to all objects or just some types? Do all patients fit the same pattern? Can any patients retrieve names but not semantic information? These are all questions that must be answered before we could claim to have a comprehensive account of object recognition. By their very nature, some of these issues will not be amenable to study by looking at normal individuals and so psychologists must turn to the other methods of enquiry developed in this volume: (1) looking at people with damaged brains, and (2) constructing computational models.

In cognitive neuropsychology, research is limited to individuals who have accidentally suffered damage in a relevant way. Such examples as not always forthcoming and are, in fact, relatively rare. Ideally, we would have many patients available with accurate knowledge about the date, location, and extent of their lesions. It would also be desirable to have detailed measures of their premorbid abilities. In practice, these criteria are very far from being fulfilled.

One solution may be offered by building computer models of the processes that are believed to underlie the cognitive activities we are studying. By constructing computational models we are free to test the validity of our theorising by lesioning models and observing how the lesion affects performance. The location, extent, and nature of these deliberately inflicted lesions can be systematically varied. In this way, a sample of "brain-injured" models can be created to order. In the field of object recognition connectionist models that employ massively parallel interactive processing rather than a sequence of independent modules are currently being developed. These are posing challenges to the established theories and opening up new possibilities.

Recognising faces

Section I.II focuses on face recognition. Initially, our treatment of face recognition must establish that this is a separate activity from merely recognising objects. On the one hand, it might be thought that face recognition simply labels one specific type of object recognition ability—faces are arguably a subset of objects. However, it may be the case that faces represent a group of objects that have such significance for us, and which require such an unusually fine level of interstimulus discrimination, that our cognitive systems have evolved a separate module with special mechanisms to deal with these items. In this situation, double dissociations provide a useful form of evidence. If there are people whose problem is specific to faces and not objects, and others who have problems with objects but not faces, this supports the "separate modules" view.

The identification of a familiar face is another activity that naively we might think of as a single act or operation. However, yet again this is a process that appears to be decomposable into several substages. We might reach this conclusion from examining people's performance in the laboratory where we are able to measure how much time is required to recognise a face as familiar, to recall semantic details about the person, and to remember the name. Additional evidence comes from the kind of face recognition failures in everyday life that are sometimes temporarily experienced by normal people. Alternatively, it can also be useful to examine the difficulties of brain-injured people who experience pathological difficulties with face recognition.

Models of face recognition are concerned with mapping out routes to recognition. That is, trying to establish the way that information is represented about familiar people and how, and in what order, this information is accessed when a familiar face is seen. The modular hierarchical model of object recognition outlined earlier proposed a sequential access route to different types of stored information: structural, semantic, and then phonological. Research on face recognition has also examined how we access different information from faces and suggests a similar pattern of access, which researchers generally refer to as familiarity information, semantic or biographical information, and names. The correspondence between these stages and those proposed in object recognition should be immediately apparent. While it is sometimes possible to forget the name of an object temporarily, the incidence of this problem appears exaggerated in face naming. When a face is seen, semantic, biographical information may be readily available while the name remains inaccessible, and this raises questions about the route by which we access different types of information. The section on face recognition examines different approaches, both neuropsychological and computational, to mapping out this route.

As in the case of object recognition, connectionist models have challenged the modular sequential models which assume that, once a face has been structurally encoded, it is matched against stored structural representations of known faces by a module known as an FRU (face recognition unit). In connectionist models there are no stored templates. Instead the incoming activation settles into a stable pattern which corresponds to the perceived identity of the face. Both faces and objects can be recognised by parallel distributed processing systems which contain no stored structural representations.

As noted, patterns of impaired object recognition may reveal evidence of category-specificity. Recognition of some categories (for example, living things) is impaired, while others (e.g., non-living things) are intact. Dissociations are also found between recognition of objects and recognition of faces, and between recognition of human faces and animal faces. These dissociations also reflect a kind of category-specificity although in the latter case both categories are living things. Different explanations are outlined in Chapters 1, 2, and 3. There are two basic types of explanation. One suggestion is that the dissociated categories are represented in separate independently functioning modules. The other possibility is that both categories are processed within the same module but involve different levels of difficulty with the impaired category being in some way more difficult. The "separate modules" account depends on the existence of double dissociations between face and object recognition, but it is important to bear in mind that "pure" double dissociations of face and object recognition are extremely rare. Farah (1990) carried out a meta-analysis of 99 cases of associative agnosia in which patients were tested for ability to recognise faces, objects, and words. In 97 of these cases there was some degree of impairment in all three. That is, prosopagnosia was accompanied by some degree of impairment in object and word recognition. This evidence is more compatible with the "differential difficulty" view.

In Section I.II several chapters focus on the phenomenon of covert recognition, sometimes known as "recognition without awareness". Some brain-damaged patients cannot consciously recognise faces. Shown a particular face they may be unable to name it and cannot say anything about the person. Yet it can be shown that, below the level of conscious awareness, they do have some knowledge. For example, they may find it easier to learn the true name for the face than to learn a false name. The mechanism that underlies covert recognition is a controversial issue. One view is that the face processing module is intact but has become disconnected from consciousness. Alternatively, covert recognition is interpreted as being the residual functioning of a damaged face processing system. Both the performance of brain-damaged patients and the performance of lesioned connectionist models are brought to bear on this issue in Chapters 5, 6, and 7.

REFERENCES

Farah, M. J. (1990). *Visual agnosia*. Cambridge, MA: MIT Press.

Humphreys, G. W., Riddoch, M. J., & Quinlan, P. T. (1988). Cascade processes in picture identification. *Cognitive Neuropsychology, 5*, 67–103.

Lissauer, H. (1890). A case of visual agnosia with a contribution to theory. *Archiv für Psychiatrie und Nervenrankheiten, 21*, 220–270.

Object recognition: Opening boxes

Robert A. Johnston

CATEGORY-SPECIFIC IMPAIRMENTS

A central issue within the study of object recognition concerns whether the representations of some types of object are more vulnerable to damage, and hence loss, than others. This is a difficulty that is unlikely to be observed with normal subjects, but there are a number of reported case studies which seem to suggest that some patients experience quite specific impairments. When these studies are viewed as a group, the findings suggest that there are some people who are no longer able to recognise living things and other people who are no longer able to recognise non-living things. This division is typified by a double dissociation between two patients described by Warrington (1981). JBR could only recognise 2 out of 48 living things, but could recognise 45 out of 48 non-living things, whereas VER showed the opposite pattern and had difficulty with non-living things.

Explaining category-specific impairment

The first question to ask is whether the appearance of a category-specific deficit is real or whether it could be due to an artefact. It is well established that factors such as the familiarity and frequency of items used in tests affect the ease with which they can be named, and have not always been equated across categories. For example, it is easier to name a chair than an aardvark, but this may be because chairs are more familiar and frequently encountered rather than because they are members of the non-living category. However, further work has shown conclusively that category-specific impairment persists even when these factors are controlled. Hillis and Caramazza (1991) found a double dissociation between two patients using exactly the same stimuli: PS had a deficit for the living items and JJ for the non-living things. This result is very unlikely to be an artefact. Other researchers have re-analysed the data from earlier studies and confirmed that, when confounding factors have been controlled, category-specific impairments persist. It appears that, in general, recognition of living things is more vulnerable to brain damage than recognition of non-living things. However, the division between living and non-living items is not always clear-cut. JBR (described above) can reliably name body parts (living things) but experiences problems with musical instruments and precious stones (non-living things). Why should this be? Exceptions that do not fit neatly into the living/non-living distinction pose a problem for several explanations. In Chapter 1, Forde and Humphreys review the main theories.

The domain-specific organisation hypothesis

It has been suggested that category-specific impairments reflect the underlying architecture of semantic memory. Perhaps the conceptual knowledge system is organised into two modular semantic categories, living things and non-living things, that are functionally and anatomically separate. Caramazza and Shelton (1998) have argued that such an organisation would have evolutionary advantages as, in the natural world, the categories require very different kinds of response. However, most researchers have been unconvinced and this hypothesis does not have much support.

The sensory/functional hypothesis

A more widely accepted idea is that the dissociation between recognition of living and non-living things actually reflects another property of the category members which broadly correlates with the living/non-living distinction. In other words, the pattern of impairment does not arise from the semantic distinction between animate and inanimate, but rather from some characteristic that is generally true of each type of category. Warrington and Shallice (1984) took such a position. They argued that the distinction is based on the relative importance of different types of semantic information. Functional properties are important for non-living objects, whereas for living things, sensory information about physical features may be more important. According to this view, JBR's difficulty would be explained in terms of a problem in processing sensory features. Patients who experience difficulties with artificial objects would be seen as having a problem with processing functional features. In other words, what looks superficially like a distinction between living and non-living items is really a surface manifestation of a quite different dissociation.

This approach can accommodate the exceptions that pose problems for the living/non-living distinction. Although JBR had difficulty with most living things, he was able to identify body parts successfully. On the other hand he was impaired in his recognition of musical instruments. These exceptions are difficult to incorporate into an account based on a strict living/non-living distinction, but are compatible with one based on a dissociation between sensory features and functional attributes. Body parts are something we use and so are represented mainly in terms of function, whereas people who are not musicians might represent musical instruments mainly in terms of their visual appearance.

The multi-modal hypothesis

Further discrepancies can be explained by suggesting that there are subcategories within the broad division between sensory and functional information. Different kinds of sensory information, such as visual, auditory, and tactile, are differently weighted for different items. In addition, some items are relatively complex in that they have more component parts while others may be recognised more holistically. Some items are more frequently encountered or more directly handled so that different kinds of information acquire different degrees of significance. For example, experience of handling objects would make their function more salient. Intuitively, a sensory/functional distinction is more reasonable than a living/ non-living one. There is other evidence to support this position. In Chapter 2, Farah and McClelland point out that separate brain areas are used to represent information from sensory and motor channels, and suggest that the latter might be the site of functional knowledge.

Category structure: The structural similarity hypothesis

Humphreys, Riddoch, and Quinlan (1988) have emphasised the importance of the relationship between the exemplars that make up a category. If we consider the category of furniture and the category of animals, we can start to identify a different sort of relationship among the exemplars. It is not hard to imagine a prototypical animal template that can be used to store representations and against which "animal input" could be compared. It would be very hard to think of a similar template for the category "tools". Cats, polar bears, and zebras all share a similarity of form and have roughly the same outline, and hence are vulnerable to being confused with one another. Hammers, chisels, and saws are not structurally similar. Humphreys et al. suggest we can divide most categories of items up in terms of the structural similarity of its members. They describe categories like animals, birds, fruit, and insects as being structurally similar (SS) and categories like furniture, tools, and vehicles as being structurally distinct (SD). This division of categories in terms of the visual characteristics of their exemplars largely breaks down across the same divide that other researchers have labelled as living/non-living or structural/functional. Indeed, in respect of the living/ non-living taxonomy, the SS/SD characterisation may capture some of the exception items (e.g., body parts, unlike most living items, are an SD category). The structural similarity hypothesis explains the greater vulnerability of living things that is typical of category-specific impairment.

Category structure: The correlated features hypothesis

Another aspect of category structure is the extent to which features of category members are correlated. Certain features tend to co-occur. For example, wings and feathers, leaves and flowers, legs and feet go together. It has been suggested that living things have more of these intercorrelated features than non-living things and that these are represented in the brain in dense clusters. It follows that damage to a particular area might affect a larger number of the features necessary for recognition of living things. On the other hand, if damage was only slight, intercorrelated features could support each other. The effects will also depend on whether the damaged features are distinctive ones. A category structure with features that are not closely correlated may be more resistant to damage if the isolated features are highly distinctive. If these distinctive features escape damage they can provide easy identification. As Forde and Humphreys make clear in Chapter 1, it is difficult to map the predictions from category features onto the living/non-living distinction very precisely.

COMPUTATIONAL MODELLING OF CATEGORY-SPECIFIC IMPAIRMENTS

The Farah and McClelland model

Another contemporary approach to understanding category-specific impairments makes use of distributed representations to capture category-specific effects. In Chapter 2, Farah and McClelland adopt the sensory/functional hypothesis proposed by Warrington and Shallice (1984) but contend that there is a problem with it. Farah and McClelland suggest that it means patients with a deficit for living things, like JBR, should still show a good knowledge of their functional attributes. So, although JBR might not be able to describe a parrot, he should still have been able to retrieve facts, such as it is often kept as a pet. Conversely, patients with a deficit for non-living items should still have access to their sensory attributes. However, an examination of patients' performance has suggested that, in most cases, both sensory and functional knowledge has been lost.

Farah and McClelland have a solution for this discrepancy which they think supports the sensory/functional hypothesis and at the same time accounts for the contradiction just outlined. The simulations described by Farah and McClelland represent only visual and semantic information and they do this by making use of distributed representations in a nonmodular interactive system. These are representations that code semantic information using several units where the micro-feature specified by each individual unit will not necessarily correspond to a feature that can be linguistically labelled. In their Experiment 1, Farah and McClelland employed undamaged normal subjects to investigate the visual and functional attributes that we store for living and non-living things. They found

visual and functional properties were listed in a ratio of 7.7 : 1 for living things, whereas for non-living objects the ratio was 1.4 : 1. On this basis they constructed their model with three times as many visual semantic units as functional semantic units. The living and non-living items learned by the model were represented as random patterns across these semantic units which maintained the ratios just noted. By means of lesioning their models, Farah and McClelland were able to simulate the effects of brain damage. When visual semantic memory units were damaged there was a larger detrimental effect on naming living things, whereas when the functional semantic memory units were damaged this had more impact on naming non-living items.

As originally formulated by Warrinton and Shallice, their account could not explain why people impaired on sensory characteristics of living things are also impaired at accessing functional attributes. However, Farah and McClelland's model is a nonmodular interactive system. A feature of the interactivity of distributed representations is that the different parts of the representation provide mutual support for one another. This is believed to be a strength of such representations as it means that they will be less vulnerable to damage. However, there is a limit to the amount of damage that can be compensated. Farah and McClelland talk about this in terms of a "critical mass" that the representation might need in order to become activated. When damage is widespread among the visual semantic memory units of living things there may be too few functional units to provide this critical activation even if the units themselves may remain intact. This explains why recognition based on functional properties is also affected when units representing visual properties are damaged.

The Devlin et al. model

Most explanations of category impairments have been based on data from patients with focal brain damage arising from injuries or strokes, and suggest that information about categories is topographically represented so that either sensory or functional information can be predominantly affected. In Chapter 3 Devlin et al. describe a connectionist model that shows how category-specific deficits can also arise from the diffuse widespread brain damage that occurs in Alzheimer's disease. Gonnerman et al. (1997) reported two Alzheimer patients who, taken together, showed a double dissociation between living and non-living items.

The Devlin et al. model is based on the assumptions that:

1. Sensory and functional features are topographically represented.
2. The ratios of each differ for living and non-living items.
3. Living things have fewer distinctive features than non-living things.
4. Living things have more highly correlated features than non-living things.

The model predicts that, at low levels of damage, intercorrelated features will interact to provide mutual support and compensate for the damage, so protecting

the living things categories. With mild damage, the non-living categories with fewer intercorrelated features will suffer most, especially if distinctive features are lost. At a high level of damage, however, compensation from intercorrelation is no longer possible; the effect will be catastrophic and recognition of living things will suffer. Summarising, Devlin et al. state "the degree of damage interacts with the structure of semantic representations to produce a double dissociation over time" (i.e., as the disease progresses and damage increases). Behavioural evidence from patients confirms that, when the disease is still mild, non-living things will be relatively more affected; as it progresses, recognition of living things will become severely impaired; finally the deficit will spread to all categories.

Devlin et al. treated each simulation as one "subject" and modelled longitudinal performance. Although the short supply of homogeneous patients is a serious difficulty for cognitive neuropsychology, this technique allows many more "subjects" to be tested. The model maps information between semantic and phonological representations using attractor networks. (These are explained in Section II.II, p. 363.) The representations were designed to conform to the four assumptions listed earlier and the model was lesioned so as to mimic the neuropathology of Alzheimer's. Accordingly, connections between features were removed so as to have a graded effect; damage was randomly spread through the network to simulate diffuse effects and was increased progressively. The results conformed to the predictions. A further simulation using one-shot, rather than progressive, lesioning, modelled the effects of focal brain damage and replicated the results of Farah and McClelland.

Devlin et al.'s study is important because it overcomes the shortcomings of cognitive neuropsychology, where it is often the case that only small numbers of patients may be tested, their pathologies are unlikely to be identical and their performance may not be followed up over time. More generally, computational modelling of cognitive deficits such as category-specific impairment provides insight into the micro-structure of the phenomenon. Connectionist models are supplying evidence against which the competing theories outlined earlier can be evaluated.

REFERENCES

Caramazza, A., & Shelton, J. R. (1998). Domain specific knowledge systems in the brain: The animate–inanimate distinction. *Journal of Cognitive Neuroscience, 10*, 1–34.

Gonnerman, L. M., Andersen, E. S., Devlin, J. T., Kempler, D., & Seidenberg, M. S. (1997). Double dissociation of semantic categories in Alzheimer's disease. *Brain and Language, 57*, 254–279.

Hillis, A., & Caramazza, A. (1991). Category specific naming and comprehension impairment: A double dissociation. *Brain and Language, 114*, 2081–2094.

Humphreys, G. W., Riddoch, M. J., & Quinlan, P. T. (1988). Cascade processes in picture identification. *Cognitive Neuropsychology, 5*, 67–103.

Warrington, E. K. (1981). Neuropsychological studies of verbal semantic systems. *Philosophical Transactions of the Royal Society of London, 295*(1077 Series B), 4121–4123.

Warrington, E. K., & Shallice, T. (1984). Category specific semantic impairments, *Brain, 107*, 829–854.

CHAPTER ONE

Category-specific recognition impairments: A review of important case studies and influential theories

Emer M. E. Forde
University of Aston, Birmingham, UK

Glyn W. Humphreys
University of Birmingham, Birmingham, UK

Patients with category-specific recognition impairments for living and non-living things have played a crucial role in developing current theories of semantic memory and object recognition. This paper reviews a number of the classic cases and discusses the theories that have been developed to account for these impairments. The first reports of patients with category-specific recognition impairments for living and non-living things were documented by Nielsen, who argued that they arose because living and non-living things were stored in functionally (and anatomically) separate systems. Although this hypothesis has been reiterated in some recent papers, the most widespread view has been that they emerge because living and non-living things have contrasting processing demands. The latter accounts include those which stress the relative importance of: the "weighting" of sensory and functional features associated with living and non-living things; the role of structural similarity between objects; the role of direct experience with objects; direct links between perceptual and functional features; and category structure. These theories are reviewed before outlining our own view on why category-specific recognition impairments emerge following brain damage.

Aphasiology, 1999, Vol. 13, No. 3, 169–193.

INTRODUCTION

Patients with selective cognitive impairments have often provided invaluable clues into the normal functioning of the human brain. This paper will review one intriguing class of patients, those with recognition problems restricted to one category of object, and how these patients have motivated new theories of semantic memory will be examined. Although there is now a voluminous literature on category-specific impairments, the first report in the literature was only about 50 years ago (Nielsen, 1946). Nielsen (1946) published cases of two patients with category-specific recognition problems: one patient had particular problems recognizing living things and the other non-living things. Nielsen reported that the first patient, Flora D., had visual agnosia for animate objects but not for inanimate objects. For example, she was able to recognize a pen-knife, a watch and a pencil but was unable to recognize her family and friends. The second patient, C.H.C., had "visual agnosia for inanimate objects while recognition and revisualization of animate objects was retained" (p. 176). C.H.C. was unable to identify a hat, a telephone or a car but was able to identify people and other living things such as flowers. Flora D. and C.H.C. also had different patterns of neurological damage. Flora D.'s lesion included damage to the left occipital lobe and C.H.C. to the right temporal and right occipital lobes and, consequently, Nielsen argued that "one occipital lobe may serve in recognition of animate objects while the other serves for inanimate ones" (p. 186). In particular, he suggested that the right occipital lobe would be involved in recognizing inanimate objects and the left occipital lobe in recognizing animate objects.

Nielsen's general hypothesis, that living and non-living things are represented in functionally and anatomically separate systems, is still one important view today (Sartori & Job, 1988; Caramazza & Shelton, 1998), although the anatomical areas he outlined have been shown to be incorrect by more detailed patient analysis (Gainotti et al., 1995; Gainotti & Silveri, 1996) and functional imaging (Damasio et al., 1996; Martin et al., 1996; Price et al., 1996; see Humphreys & Forde, 1999). This paper provides a review of the neuropsychological literature on category-specificity since Nielsen's original report. The vast majority of the neuropsychological reports of category-specific impairments have been for living things (e.g., Warrington & Shallice, 1984; Basso et al., 1988; Sartori & Job, 1988; Silveri & Gainotti, 1988; Sheridan & Humphreys, 1993; De Renzi & Lucchelli, 1994; Forde et al., 1997; Forde, 1998), although there have also been a few reports of patients with the reverse pattern (Hillis & Caramazza, 1991; Sacchett & Humphreys, 1992; Warrington & McCarthy, 1983, 1987, 1994).

THE SENSORY/FUNCTIONAL DISTINCTION

Nielsen's descriptions of Flora D. and C.H.C. make interesting reading but they are relatively anecdotal case reports. The first empirical study of patients with category-specific impairments was by Warrington and Shallice (1984) who investigated four patients with category-specific impairments in recognizing living

things. The discussion in this review will focus on one patient, J.B.R., who has been studied in some detail, though the findings generalize to the other three patients. J.B.R. was a 23 year old undergraduate student when he suffered from herpes simplex encephalitis that left him with bilateral temporal lobe damage. Following his illness, J.B.R. had profound difficulties recognizing living things, such as animals, fruit and vegetables, despite relatively normal recognition of non-living things, such as furniture, tools and clothing. For example, when given coloured photographs of living (animals and plants) and non-living things, he was only able to name, or give responses that demonstrated identification, 6% of the living things, compared to 90% of non-living things. His problem in naming living things did not appear to result from a "low level" visual/perceptual deficit since: (a) it was restricted to living things; (b) he performed normally on visual/ perceptual processing tasks, such as matching objects presented in usual and unusual views (Humphreys & Riddoch, 1984; Warrington & James, 1986); and (c) he was unable to access information about living things from other modalities. For example, although he was able to give precise definitions of non-living things, his definitions of living things were very impoverished. He defined a briefcase as a "small case used by students to carry papers" and a compass as "tools for telling direction you are going" but for parrot he said "don't know" and for daffodil he only knew that it was a plant. Due to the "central" nature of this deficit, Warrington and Shallice suggested that J.B.R.'s problem was with stored semantic representations of living things. They argued that J.B.R.'s semantic representations for living things were degraded so that he could only access very general superordinate information about most items: in contrast, his semantic representations for non-living things were relatively intact.

However, when Warrington and Shallice extended the range of categories tested, they found that J.B.R. also performed poorly with food items, precious stones, musical instruments and types of cloth, indicating that his impairment did not conform to a neat dichotomous dissociation between living and non-living things. As a result, Warrington and Shallice suggested that his problem did not reflect an impairment to a neuronal system dedicated to recognizing living things (as proposed by Nielsen, 1946). Instead, they argued that category-specific impairments arose because different types of information are needed to recognize different categories of object. In particular, they argued that sensory information is primarily important in differentiating between living things, whereas functional information (e.g., information about how objects are used) is important in differentiating between non-living things. As an example, they suggested that to distinguish between a raspberry and a strawberry, one needs to access detailed information about the colour, shape, size and texture of the items. In contrast, the important feature that distinguishes between chalk, a crayon and a pencil is the writing surface that is appropriate for each item. Warrington and Shallice suggested that "a semantic system based on functional specifications may have evolved for the identification of inanimate objects" (p. 849) and that this semantic system would be independent from a sensory semantic system.

According to this account there are two functionally independent semantic systems: one storing sensory information; and the other storing functional information.

MULTI-MODAL MODEL

Subsequent to Warrington and Shallice's original paper, Warrington and McCarthy (1987) reported a case of a patient who showed a dissociation within the category of non-living things. Warrington and McCarthy consequently modified the visual/functional dichotomy to account for this more fine-grained impairment (see also, McCarthy & Warrington, 1994; Warrington & McCarthy, 1994). The patient, YOT, was globally aphasic so picture–word matching tasks were used to assess her ability to recognize objects from different categories. She was significantly worse at picture–word matching for non-living things compared to flowers, animals or food items. However, further testing revealed that within the general category of non-living things she was significantly worse at picture–word matching for small manipulable objects (e.g., hairdryer, fork, cup, pencils) compared to large outdoor objects (e.g., ship, house, bridge, tanker).

To explain this more refined category-specific impairment, Warrington and McCarthy (1987) drew upon Lissauer's (1890) account of object recognition and semantic memory. His account emphasized that one not only has stored semantic information about the visual and functional properties of an object, but also about the sound, the smell, the taste, the characteristic motor pattern associated with it, etc. Lissauer used the example of a violin to illustrate his ideas: "there exist a number of recollections associated with its image, its name, its sound, the sensation, and tactile experiences which go along with handling it. In addition there will be the mental image of a violinist in his characteristic pose. It is only when the linkage between the percept of the instrument and such associated recollections occur promptly in consciousness that the individual will be able to interpret the object as a musical instrument, differentiate it from other instruments, and thus categorise it" (p. 182). Warrington and McCarthy suggested that these different types of semantic knowledge (visual/perceptual features, the sound of an object, the action pattern associated with it, etc.) might be stored in different modality-specific "channels", and that one's semantic representation of an object would be the sum of the activity across all of these channels. They proposed that the channels could be relatively fine-grained so, for example, there could be a number of functionally independent channels for different types of visual information (e.g., colour, shape and size). They suggested that the pattern of activity across these channels would differ for different categories, and in keeping with the ideas outlined by Warrington and Shallice (1984), living things would tend to have high weightings in the sensory channels whereas non-living things would tend to have high weightings in the motor channels (see Figure 1). This model can account for relatively fine-grained category-specific impairments because individual categories (e.g., animals, tools, fruit, musical instruments) would have different patterns of activity across all the channels. To account for YOT's data,

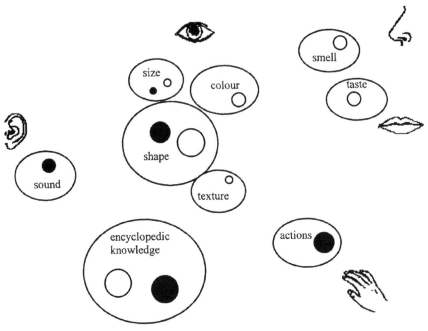

verbally acquired
knowledge

Figure 1. Multi-modal distributed semantic knowledge (Warrington & McCarthy, 1987). Specialized channels store information that was primarily acquired through a particular modality. Living things, such as fruit and vegetables (open circles), will have larger weightings in sensory regions, whereas non-living things, such as tools (filled circles), will have larger weightings in regions storing functional information.

Warrington and McCarthy (1987) suggested that visual information would be important for differentiating between large outdoor objects, whereas motor and somatosensory information was more important for small manipulable objects. YOT's fundamental problem would therefore be in accessing information in motor and/or somatosensory channels, which would lead to her particular impairment in recognizing small manipulable objects. In contrast, since the channels storing sensory information were intact all categories (living things and large outdoor objects) represented primarily in these channels would be spared.

THE IMPORTANCE OF VISUAL/PERCEPTUAL INFORMATION AND THE PROCESSING OF PARTS

The view of category-specificity outlined by Warrington and co-workers predicts that category-specific impairments for living things should co-occur with problems accessing the visual and sensory properties of objects. Consistent with this, several

investigators have subsequently noted that patients with poor identification of living things can be particularly impaired at retrieving visual knowledge about those items—for instance, in naming to visual as opposed to functional definitions (Silveri & Gainotti, 1988; Forde et al., 1997; Humphreys et al., 1997). Problems even gaining visual access to stored perceptual information was documented by Sartori and Job (1988). They reported a case study of a patient, Michelangelo, who had a category-specific impairment in naming living things following herpes simplex encephalitis. Michelangelo not only had problems in naming living things but he also had problems in retrieving visual/perceptual information about these items from vision. For example, he performed poorly in an object decision task requiring discrimination between pictures of real objects and non-objects (Riddoch & Humphreys, 1987a, b). His problem was greater for animals, compared to artifacts, and he made many false positive responses to non-objects formed by substituting parts between animals. On a second test he was shown pictures of animals which were complete or had one part missing (e.g., the tail), and he was asked to judge if the picture was complete. If it was not complete, he was asked to draw the missing part. He was unable to judge whether the picture of the animal was complete or not and was also unable to draw the correct missing part. He made three types of error when drawing the missing part. The first was to draw a generic part, rather than the specific shape of the missing part for that particular animal. For example, he added wings to birds and tails and horns to certain mammals, but he did not appear to be able to recall what shape the tail or horns were for a particular mammal (e.g., he drew rhino horns on a picture of a deer). The second type of error was to misplace the part and the third was to add a part to an animal that was already complete. In summary, he appeared to know the generic, prototypical shapes of animals but had problems in accessing the correct shape of parts for particular animals and, on occasions, the correct location of the part.

Sartori and Job (1988) suggested that Michelangelo's impairment was specifically in accessing stored visual or structural knowledge about animals because he was able to judge their ferocity, what sound they made and he could access superordinate information from their names. In addition, he was able to make correct judgements about their size (see also Forde et al., 1997, for evidence of preservation of size when other types of structural knowledge are degraded). The results are consistent with Warrington and McCarthy's (1987) account of category-specificity, since an impairment in recognizing living things co-occurred with problems in accessing visual/structural information; according to Warrington and McCarthy (1987), visual/structural knowledge should be strongly weighted for the recognition of living things. However, Sartori and Job (1988) offered an alternative explanation for the data. Their explanation differed in two ways from that offered by Warrington and McCarthy. First, they distinguished between a pre-semantic structural description system, which would store the visual properties of objects, and a "central" semantic memory system concerned with associative

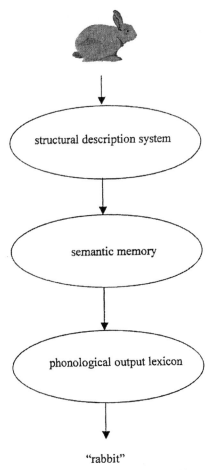

Figure 2. Stages involved in naming objects.

and functional knowledge about objects (Figure 2) (see Riddoch & Humphreys, 1987a, b; Humphreys et al., 1988 for this distinction). Sartori and Job (1988) suggested that Michelangelo's problem may be to the pre-semantic structural description system, rather than to the central semantic memory system. This is consistent with their finding that Michelangelo could not even judge whether an object was visually familiar in object decision, a task that does not necessarily require the patient to access any semantic information (see Riddoch & Humphreys, 1987a, b; Sheriden & Humphreys, 1993; Hillis & Caramazza, 1995 for evidence on access to structural but not semantic knowledge about objects). Secondly, Sartori and Job (1988) argued that Michelangelo's fundamental deficit was category-specific, rather than attribute-specific. This implies that the "pre-semantic"

structural description system must be categorically organized. They argued for category-specificity rather than attribute-specificity for two reasons. Firstly, when Michelangelo was given the names of two visually similar items and asked to judge what the difference was between them, he was significantly worse with animals compared to non-living things. Sartori and Job argued that, on a purely visual or structural level, these questions would be equally difficult for living and non-living things (though this was not verified empirically). Secondly, Michelangelo showed no difference in naming typical and atypical living things; here Sartori and Job assumed that typical things were more likely to be visually similar, so if the fundamental problem was in differentiating between visually similar items he should be worse with typical exemplars. The difficulty with this last argument, however, is that visual similarity within a category may trade-off against familiarity; typical things tend to be more familiar in addition to (perhaps) being more visually similar to other category members.

One of the most interesting features of Michelangelo's impairment was his ability to access the generic shape of animals, relative to his inability to access information about the parts for particular animals (e.g., as in the object decision task where non-objects preserved the overall shape of objects but inter-changed their parts). A number of authors have suggested that visual processing of parts may be fundamentally different for living and non-living things. Sacchett and Humphreys (1992) suggested that non-living things tend to contain the same local parts and are distinguished from one another by the spatial relationships between the parts. For example, a cup and a bucket contain the same two parts and they are differentiated by the position of the handle (see Biederman, 1987). In contrast, living things (particularly animals) tend to have the same parts (heads, legs, tails etc.) in the same spatial location, and it is rather subtle differences in the relative size and shape of the parts that differentiates items. Category-specific impairments for living things could then emerge in patients who have problems in accessing detailed information about the size and shape of parts. This is consistent with the data from Michelangelo, who was able to access generic information about parts of animals, but unable to access more fine-grained information. According to this account, category-specific impairments for non-living things may emerge in patients who are able to access detailed information about the shape of individual parts, but unable to judge the spatial locations of these parts on the target item (e.g., thereby confusing a cup and a bucket).

Farah (1991) also suggested that the representation of parts may be fundamentally different for different classes of object. Some parts may be relatively simple while others may be more complex, and may even be regarded as objects in their own right. In addition to a distinction between simple and complex parts, some objects will be decomposed into more parts than others, and indeed some objects may not be decomposed at all. Farah suggested that face recognition depends on recognizing one complex part, since decomposing a face into its constituent parts may be computationally difficult and less useful than using

some direct image-based representation (see also Biederman & Kalocsai, 1997). In contrast to face recognition, word recognition may depend largely on accessing a number of elementary parts (letters) in the correct spatial arrangement. Farah suggested that there may be two functionally independent visual processing systems—one which is specialized for representing complex parts (e.g., faces) and one which is specialized for representing multiple parts (e.g., letters in words). Living and non-living things may depend to differing degrees on these two systems. Animals (like faces) share the same basic parts and can only be differentiated from one another by rather subtle changes in the scaling of these parts. In contrast, individual parts of non-living things are more diagnostically useful and may even uniquely specify the target object (e.g., the dial of a phone, the end of a hammer). Farah suggested that if a patient's ability to represent complex parts is mildly impaired they will present with prosopagnosia—if more impaired they will also have problems recognizing other categories of object with complex parts (e.g., animals). Only objects with relatively simple parts will be recognized. In contrast, if a patient's ability to recognize single parts (simple and complex) is intact, but the ability to represent multiple parts is impaired, visual word recognition will be poor. Patients with this impairment may also have problems in recognizing non-living objects with numerous parts (although, objects with multiple parts may be recognized if one part uniquely specifies the object).

However, the contrasting role of parts in recognizing different categories of object cannot on its own account for all the category-specific impairments reported in the literature, as it does not capture dissociations which can include poor identification of fruit and vegetables along with other living things (e.g., animals). Unlike animals, fruit and vegetables tend to have very few parts, and their parts tend to be very simple shapes. Consequently, it is unlikely that a problem with fruit and vegetables can be accounted for by an impairment in representing complex parts. Furthermore, Farah's account fails to accommodate the different levels of recognition deficit that can occur. On this account, recognition deficits are linked to a problem in one of two distinct visual processing systems. Since object recognition depends on the same recognition systems as faces and words, a patient should not be agnosic for objects without additionally having either alexia or prosopagnosia. Against this are patients who are documented as having impaired object recognition along with intact face and word recognition, with the deficit contingent on damage to stored visual-structural knowledge (and to a lesser degree impaired functional knowledge) about objects (Rumiati et al., 1994; Humphreys & Rumiati, 1998). Interestingly, at least one such patient was also selectively impaired at identifying living relative to non-living things, though face identification was good (Rumiati et al., 1994). This is contrary to the proposal that the problem with living things is necessarily linked to a deficit in representing complex parts, though this remains possible in other patients.

DEPTH OF PROCESSING AND
STRUCTURAL SIMILARITY

Although Sartori and Job (1988) argued for a categorically organized structural description system, it is possible that Michelangelo had problems in recognizing living things because he could not access detailed information about the parts of objects, and this ability is particularly important for living things (as discussed above). In a later paper, Sartori et al. (1993a) appeared to move away from the view that the structural description system was categorically organized and towards the view that category-specific impairments can emerge because categories of objects differ in the specificity of visual processing required for recognition. Sartori et al. (1993a) suggested that impairments to a structural description system might affect living things significantly more than non-living things because living things are more structurally similar to one another. They draw upon Marr's (1982) model of object recognition, in which knowledge about the visual attributes of an object is stored in a hierarchy that becomes progressively more detailed. Sartori et al. suggested that, since living things are more structurally similar to one another, they are represented by "deeper" hierarchies than non-living things. If information at the deepest, or most specific, level of the hierarchy was impaired, living things would be differentially affected compared to non-living things. This view of the structural description system, and their account of category-specific impairments for living things, is consistent with work on normal subjects (Humphreys et al., 1988; Gaffan & Heywood, 1993) and animal studies (Gaffan & Heywood, 1993).

Humphreys et al. (1988) similarly suggested that patients may find living things more difficult to recognize because these objects tend to belong to categories where there are large numbers of structurally similar exemplars. In contrast, non-living things within a particular category tend to be structurally dissimilar from one another. The important point here is that although two or three non-living things from a particular category may be structurally similar to one another, living things belong to categories where there are significantly more structurally similar exemplars (for example, as measured by the number of parts in common and the level of overlap in their overall shapes, Humphreys et al., 1988). There may be several consequences of this on visual object identification. One is that a more fine-grained visual analysis may need to be computed to identify living things relative to non-living things. Another is that, during their identification, representations of more visual and semantic competitors will be activated for living things. This will create difficulty when responses are contingent on representations for individual objects being activated (e.g., in naming compared to superordinate categorization). Competition will also increase for naming relative to perceptually based responses (e.g., in object decision, operating at a structural description level, see Figure 2) due to semantic competition playing a greater role in naming. Consistent with these proposals, pictures of

living things are named more slowly than pictures of non-living things by normal subjects (Humphreys et al., 1988), and the difference between living and non-living things is larger in naming than in object decision (Lloyd-Jones & Humphreys, 1997). A wider range of visual and semantic errors are also made to living things when normal subjects name pictures to a response deadline (Vitkovitch et al., 1993). Again, consistent with these proposals, Forde et al. (1997) reported a case of a patient (S.R.B.) with a category-specific impairment for living things who showed a more pronounced category difference in naming pictures than in object decision. Regression analysis showed that S.R.B.'s naming performance was more affected by a measure of structural similarity than by category and his impairment extended to non-living things when he was asked to distinguish between a set of structurally similar items (naming different types of cars). These data support the hypothesis that category-specific impairments for living things emerge because more detailed visual processing is required to distinguish between exemplars from these categories.

Furthermore, Gaffan and Heywood (1993) showed that even monkeys find it more difficult to learn to discriminate between line drawings of living things compared to non-living things. Monkeys were first taught to discriminate between eight pictures, then 16 and eventually 128 (the number of stimuli doubling in each phase). Gaffan and Heywood (1993) reported that even with eight stimuli, monkeys made more errors when required to distinguish between living things. However, as the number of items increased in the set there was a dramatic increase in the number of errors to living things, but not to non-living things. Since monkeys are non-verbal animals, any differences in their ability to discriminate between exemplars from these categories cannot arise from linguistic factors (or learned taxonomic categories) but must reflect differences in visual discriminability (or structural similarity) between the items. Gaffan and Heywood argued that category-specific recognition impairments for living things observed in patients emerge because these items belong to "visually crowded" (or "structurally similar") categories. It is inherently more difficult to visually distinguish between living compared to non-living things and, as a result, patients with impairments forming detailed visual representations of objects will have more problems identifying living things.

CONFOUNDING FACTORS IN CATEGORY-SPECIFICITY

The review to date has emphasized that factors that co-vary with different categories of object can be important in accounting for category-specific recognition deficits, especially for living things. These factors include the different contrasting "weights" assigned to particular forms of information and the degree of visual differentiation required to identify objects from categories varying in structural similarity. These factors, whilst co-varying with category information,

are intrinsic to the different categories. However, Funnell and Sheridan (1992) and Stewart et al. (1992) raised the possibility that category effects reflect co-varying factors that are not necessarily intrinsic to living things, such as familiarity, frequency, age of acquisition of the object's name and visual complexity. Could "category-specific impairments" be little more than a failure to control for these factors when patients are tested? These factors are not intrinsic to living and non-living things since it is possible to match different categories on these variables. On the other hand, visual-perceptual information may always be strongly weighted for living things, and living things will always belong to categories with structurally similar exemplars irrespective of the particular items chosen for a study.

Criticisms concerning the control of factors such as familiarity form an important reminder of the need for methodological rigour in neuropsychology; nevertheless, robust category-specific impairments have been documented in subsequent studies. The confounding effects of familiarity, frequency and visual complexity have been controlled by: (1) matching sets of living and non-living things on these factors (see Sartori et al., 1993b); and/or (2) by regression analysis (Farah et al., 1996; Forde et al., 1997; Kurbat, 1997; Kurbat & Farah, 1998). For example, Kurbat (1997) showed that living/non-living was still a significant predictor of the naming ability of patients, when visual complexity, familiarity, similarity to other objects, image agreement, name specificity, name frequency, amount of internal detail, proportion of straight contours and name length were controlled.

Furthermore, Funnell and de Mornay-Davies (1996) re-assessed J.B.R.'s naming performance 16 years after he was originally tested to examine the stability of his performance, and found that, in more carefully controlled experiments, he still showed a category-specific impairment. J.B.R. was presented with line drawings of 54 living things and 54 non-living things that were matched for familiarity and word frequency. Funnell and de Mornay-Davies (1996) found that J.B.R. still found it significantly harder to name living (30%) compared to non-living things (54%). However, on closer examination of the data, the category-specific impairment only emerged for low familiarity items (11% correct for living and 44% correct for non-living things). For highly familiar items there was no difference in naming performance for living (67%) and non-living (72%) things. J.B.R.'s pattern of errors also tended to differ across the two categories. When he was unable to name a living thing he tended to give the superordinate label, indicating that he knew the category to which the item belonged. In contrast, with non-living things he tended to make visual and visual/semantic errors. However, although J.B.R. still showed a category-specific impairment for living things, Funnell and de Mornay-Davies (1996) argued that the interaction between familiarity and category could not be easily accounted for by the sensory/functional hypothesis. Furthermore, they suggested that the familiarity of the

item, rather than the category, might be the most important factor influencing his performance. This review discusses the role of familiarity in semantic memory in more detail in the section below.

One further point to note is that confounding factors such as familiarity and name frequency, favouring non-living things, cannot account for the opposite pattern of category-specific impairment that has been documented in the literature, where patients are impaired at identifying non-living things (Warrington & McCarthy, 1983, 1987; Hillis & Caramazza, 1991; Sacchett & Humphreys, 1992; Warrington & McCarthy, 1994). For example, patient C.W. reported by Sacchett and Humphreys (1992) was significantly worse at naming non-living things even when they were matched for name frequency, more familiar and less visually complex than non-living things. Furthermore, Hillis and Caramazza (1991) documented a double dissociation between naming living and non-living things when the two patients were given the same set of pictures, indicating that category-specific impairments do not simply reflect uncontrolled confounding factors.

As alluded to in this paper's Introduction, one rather striking feature of the neuropsychological literature on category-specificity is that the vast majority of cases have been patients with impairments for living things. There have been comparatively few patients with category-specific impairments for non-living things. Again, this may reflect experimenters' failure to control for confounding factors such as familiarity, frequency and complexity. As noted above, the non-living things selected in many studies have tended to be more familiar, less visually complex and have a higher name frequency. Consequently, genuine category-specific impairments for non-living things may have been masked by experimenters choosing sets of non-living things that were disproportionately easier to name compared to the sets of living things. For example, Lambon Ralph et al. (1998) reported a case of a patient who initially appeared to have no category-specific impairment, but when regression analysis controlled for the effects of frequency and familiarity a category-specific impairment for non-living things emerged. Future work will show whether this asymmetry in the number of category-specific impairments for living and non-living things has been an artefactual finding, or if it reflects some interesting difference between living and non-living things. Our suggestion is that living things are genuinely more vulnerable to brain damage because: (1) exemplars from these categories tend to be more structurally similar to one another than non-living things. Consequently, more detailed processing is required to identify individual items, as discussed above; (2) Non-living things may be represented in more sensory and motor modalities, thereby protecting them when damage is to one specific type of attribute (e.g., visual attributes); and (3) some information, about the associated action and consequently, associated function, can be accessed directly from visually presented non-living things. We discuss these ideas in more detail in the next two sections.

THE IMPORTANCE OF DIRECT EXPERIENCE
WITH EVERYDAY OBJECTS

Funnell and de Mornay-Davies (1996) found that J.B.R.'s performance was significantly affected by the familiarity of the item, where "familiarity" was defined as "the degree to which you come in contact with or think about the concept" (Snodgrass & Vanderwart, 1980). It seems intuitively correct, and perhaps rather obvious, to suggest that highly familiar objects will be less vulnerable to brain damage. For instance, in many connectionist accounts of learning, more familiar objects will tend to develop more stable representations (involving larger weights between units) than less familiar objects (see Ellis & Humphreys, 1998). When weights are reduced by damage, or noise added to the connections, such representations will be more robust. However, examining what is really meant by "familiarity" and thinking about why familiar objects are less vulnerable is an interesting issue. What are the important factors that protect the semantic representations of highly familiar objects? Is it the sheer amount of information one has about such objects? Is it because these objects have some special importance for us (and therefore possibly have representations linked to the limbic system)? Might familiar everyday objects be experienced in more modalities (vision, touch, sound, etc.) than less familiar objects? Of course, these are not mutually exclusive alternatives, a number of them may be correct, and all would have consequences for the identification of living and non-living things. For instance, in addition to developing more robust representations within a single modality, there may be variations in the weighting for different modalities for highly familiar, relative to less familiar, objects. Funnell and Sheriden (1992) argued that although living things, such as animals, are not uncommon, one tends to learn about them by watching them or by reading about them. In contrast, one picks up and uses non-living things and so may process their physical features (e.g., their constituent parts) more precisely and/or gain direct sensory experience across a number of modalities. Funnell and Sheriden suggested that because one can pick up, manipulate and view man-made objects from different angles one may have developed richer "perceptual and conceptual representations" for them.

The importance of direct experience with objects has been emphasized in a number of other studies. A similar view was proposed by Temple (1986) to account for a case of a 12 year old boy who had a category-specific impairment for animals. The child, John, developed normally until he was 3 years 5 months, when he had a generalized epileptic seizure. He had another seizure when he was 5 years 7 months, and EEGs showed abnormalities over the right central area, bilateral posterior regions and the left temporal region (though a CT scan was normal). When tested at age 12 years old, John was significantly better at naming non-living things (85%) compared to animals (38%), and this did not appear to be a developmental lag, as control children showed the opposite pattern. Further testing a year later showed that his difficulty in naming animals

compared to other categories of object persisted. He was also unable to name animals when given definitions, or to provide definitions himself. For example, he defined a donkey as "he walks and goes out and finds something" and when asked what it looks like, he said "straight nose and he's got some horns at the top". Temple suggested that John often attempted to define animals in terms of functional information rather than describing their appearance, and when asked specifically to describe their appearance he often generated inaccurate information (e.g., a donkey has horns). In contrast, John's identification of non-living things may have been better because he had day-to-day experience with them: "they are involved in his actions. He acts upon them and they have functional significance for him. In this sense he may have motor programs for certain actions in which they are involved." (Temple, 1986). In contrast, John was impaired at naming animals (and also flowers and faces) which have no associated motor programmes.

Both Temple (1986) and Funnell and co-workers (Funnell & Sheriden, 1992; Funnell & de Mornay-Davies, 1996) argued that non-living things may be relatively spared because one has direct day-to-day experience with them. According to Funnell's account this means that one has richer representations of non-living things. Temple's account is somewhat different. She argued that "memories for actions are laid down, stored or recalled in a different way at an anatomically different site from memories for semantic facts". Preserved action patterns associated with non-living things may therefore help maintain the semantic representations of these items. In contrast, living things do not have any associated action patterns and so do not benefit from the links between motor engrams and semantic knowledge. The potential beneficiary links between actions and semantic knowledge has also been suggested by De Renzi and Lucchelli (1994) and Sirigu et al. (1991).

THE ROLE OF FUNCTIONAL INFORMATION IN RECOGNIZING NON-LIVING THINGS

In contrast to the sensory/functional hypothesis outlined by Warrington and Shallice (1984), De Renzi and Lucchelli (1994) proposed that the crucial difference between living and non-living things was in the links between perceptual and functional features, rather than the overall weighting of each type of feature. They argued that, since non-living things have been designed to perform a particular function, there would be direct links between their perceptual and functional features; in contrast, no analogous links would exist between the perceptual and functional features of living things. Note that, according to this account, the functional properties linked to the visual attributes of non-living things may be relatively abstracted (e.g., used for cutting), and are not necessarily laid down as motor engrams (as suggested by Temple, 1986). De Renzi and Lucchelli (1994) presented a case study of a patient, Felicia, who had difficulty

in naming living things, and who additionally, had difficulty in describing the perceptual differences between two living things, in performing object decisions and in drawing them from memory. One interesting feature of this patient was that she also had problems with non-living things when asked to retrieve their associated colour or name them from sound. De Renzi and Lucchelli suggested that her category-specific naming impairment emerged from an overall cognitive impairment in accessing the perceptual features of objects (both living and non-living things; cf., Sartori & Job, 1988; Silveri & Gainotti, 1988). However, for non-living things the close links between visual and functional features provided an alternative route to accessing the perceptual features of the object, thereby allowing the item to be recognized. De Renzi and Lucchelli also suggested that Felicia's inability to access the colour and sound of both living and non-living things was consistent with this hypothesis since there are no direct links between these perceptual features and function. However, De Renzi and Lucchelli (1994) acknowledged that "it remains to be explained how the function of an object can be inferred from its visual appearance, if this has not been recognized or retrieved from memory" (p. 19). Nevertheless, they suggested that, for non-living things, stored visual knowledge and stored functional knowledge could interact, so that "functional cues help to specify hypothesis on the nature of the stimulus that are left undefined by visual processing" (p. 20). For living things this compensatory route would be unavailable since there are few links between perceptual and functional features. The argument that functional or action information can be accessed directly from stored visual knowledge is supported by optic aphasic patients who can generate correct actions even when they cannot activate detailed associative/semantic knowledge (Riddoch & Humphreys, 1987b; Hillis & Caramazza, 1995). Nevertheless, it remains unclear how action or functional information may be used to resolve ambiguities concerning the structural representation of an object in the manner suggested by De Renzi and Lucchelli. One model that may be able to provide a mechanism to account for how the links between visual and functional properties can aid object recognition is the OUCH model of semantic memory (Caramazza et al., 1990). According to this model, in addition to the stored structural description of the whole object, salient parts of the object can directly activate the corresponding perceptual and functional attributes in semantic memory. For example, the perceptual features of a fork (e.g., the prongs and handle) can activate the corresponding functional attributes (i.e., about lifting and holding). Consequently, even if the stored structural description of the whole object is degraded, the pattern of semantic activation generated directly from the parts may be sufficient to identify the item.

Sirigu et al. (1991) provided an alternative explanation of how functional information could be used to identify non-living things. They distinguished between the correct manipulation of an object and the ability to identify its precise function or the context in which it is used. They proposed that non-living things "afford" actions which patients can make without being able to access any

semantic knowledge, and use to help activate the appropriate semantic representation. They argued that a category-specific impairment for living things
could arise from a general impairment to the structural description system or to
semantic memory. For non-living things, however, patients could compensate
for their impairment through activation of specific action patterns that could help
generate hypotheses about the function of the object, and then ultimately what
the object might be. However, this system could only be used for objects that have
very specific (maybe unique) action patterns; many objects have quite similar
action patterns but dissimilar names (e.g., axe and hammer, pen and pencil, jug
and teapot etc.) and others have no particularly characteristic action patterns
(e.g., plate, saucer, television). It therefore seems unlikely that activation of
associated actions could lead to preserved naming of a wide range of non-living
things in patients with impaired identification of living things. It also fails to
account for an association between impaired recognition of living things and
musical instruments which has been reported in a number of cases, since individual musical instruments do tend to have very characteristic motor patterns
(Warrington & Shallice, 1984).

THE IMPORTANCE OF FUNCTIONAL
KNOWLEDGE FOR LIVING AS WELL AS
NON-LIVING THINGS

Tyler, Moss and colleagues have also suggested that the difference between
living and non-living things is not in the amount of perceptual and functional
information stored in semantic memory, but in the links between perceptual and
functional features (Moss et al., 1997; Tyler & Moss, 1997). In contrast to both
the sensory/functional hypothesis proposed by Warrington and Shallice (1984),
and to accounts stressing the protective value of motor information for non-
living things (Sirigu et al., 1991), Moss, Tyler and colleagues argue that functional information may be salient, and spared relative to perceptual information
following brain damage, for living as well as non-living things. However, the
type of "functional" information that is salient will differ across categories: for
living things, this will concern biological functions (e.g., eating and moving),
whereas for non-living things it refers to the usage of the object. Also, for living
things, salient perceptual features (e.g., legs, mouth) will be common across
exemplars and linked to common biological functions (e.g., moves, eats). In
contrast, for non-living things, salient perceptual features are closely linked to
features specifying the use of the individual object, since such objects are
designed to perform a particular task. In this sense, perceptual features are diagnostic of the functional properties of individual non-living things. Tyler, Moss
and colleagues suggest that the close coupling between form and function for
both living and non-living things will protect these attributes following brain
damage, but the consequences will differ for different categories. For non-living

things, preservation of these form–function relationships will be sufficient to uniquely identify many items. However, preservation of the form–function relationships for living things will only provide access to common functional and superordinate knowledge. These form–function links may allow patients with category-specific impairments for living things to categorize correctly exemplars that they cannot name (e.g., Forde et al., 1997), but they do not enable individual identification to take place. According to this account, the fundamental difference between living and non-living things is in the nature of the relations between their perceptual and functional features. Even with general and non-specific damage to this system, differences between living and non-living things could emerge. This proposal differs from accounts stressing a distinction between sensory and functional representations for living and non-living things, where damage would have to affect each form of representation selectively to impair either living or non-living things (see Farah & McClelland, 1991, for a simulation). The model outlined by Moss, Tyler and colleagues also leads to the expectation that superordinate/functional information should be retrieved particularly efficiently for living things since it is supported by common perceptual features. This prediction is similar to that made by accounts stressing the role of visual/structural similarity in category differences (e.g., Humphreys et al., 1988). High levels of structural similarity between exemplars should lead to fast access to common functional information, though individual identification may then be slowed by competition. Empirical data on normal picture categorization and naming support these predictions (Humphreys et al., 1999).

THE IMPORTANCE OF LINKS BETWEEN FEATURES AND OF CATEGORY STRUCTURE

The idea that correlational links between features may differ for living and non-living things was also examined in some detail by McRae et al. (1997), though these authors stress correlations between different perceptual or different functional features, rather than correlations between perceptual and functional properties. McRae et al. (1997) asked normal subjects to generate lists of the important features associated with exemplars from categories of living and non-living things. The features generated were classified into five sets: aspects of a concrete entity (e.g., ⟨has a handle⟩), functional information (e.g., ⟨used for carpentry⟩), classification (e.g., ⟨is a fruit⟩), information related to a situation in which an object takes part (e.g., ⟨grows on trees⟩) and people's related cognitions (e.g., ⟨is fun⟩). Consistent with the accounts stressing the importance of functional information for non-living things, McRae et al. (1997) found that subjects generated significantly more functional information for non-living things; however, there was no significant difference between living and non-living things on any of the other classifications. McRae et al. not only examined the pattern of responses in terms of individual features but also in terms of the number of

Naming performance

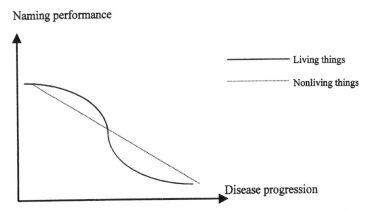

Figure 3. Schematic drawing of predicted naming performance for living and non-living things in patients with Alzheimer's disease (Gonnerman et al., 1998).

correlated feature pairs (i.e., features that are activated together for a number of concepts and do not often occur without the other). For example, the feature ⟨has fur⟩ is intercorrelated with ⟨has claws⟩, since the two features are activated together for a number of animals, and one does not often occur without the other. McRae et al. found that there were significantly more intercorrelated features for living compared to non-living things. This is consistent with the idea that the representations of living things are more densely interconnected and tend to cluster together more closely in "semantic space" than non-living things (Keil, 1987). McRae et al. suggested that these correlated features may protect processing systems against small degrees of damage, since linked features will help the recovery of each other. When greater degrees of damage are sustained, however, correlated features may tend to become impaired together leading to a catastrophic decrease in performance. Relating this to the distinction between living and non-living things, under small levels of generalized damage non-living things should be expected to suffer most. Under higher levels of damage, living things should be more impaired.

Some data along these lines have been reported in patients with Alzheimer's disease by Gonnerman et al. (1997) (see Devlin et al., 1998, for a simulation). Gonnerman et al. (1997) reported that, although, as a group, patients with Alzheimer's disease were not significantly worse at naming living or non-living things, individual patients showed category-specific impairments. Interestingly, Gonnerman et al. noted that the patients whose naming performance was good overall tended to have more difficulty naming non-living things; in contrast, the patients who were more generally impaired at naming tended to have more difficulty naming living things (see Figure 3). To explain this cross-over effect, Gonnerman emphasized the importance of intercorrelated features (McRae et al., 1997) and also "distinguishing features" (see also, Lambon Ralph et al., 1998).

Distinguishing features were defined as attributes that "occur almost exclusively for one item within a category and serve to conspicuously differentiate that item from related ones" (p. 270). For example, ⟨has black and white stripes⟩ would be a distinguishing feature for a zebra, since it differentiates it from other visually similar animals (such as a horse or a donkey). Consistent with Warrington and Shallice's (1984) sensory/functional hypothesis, Gonnerman et al. suggested that the distinguishing features for living things tend to be perceptual whereas for non-living things they tend to be functional. However, in contrast to the sensory/functional hypothesis, Gonnerman et al. suggested that category-specific impairments in patients with Alzheimer's disease did not necessarily reflect damage to areas storing perceptual or functional attributes, but could arise from random and diffuse damage to all kinds of semantic features. They argued that, since non-living things tend to be represented in terms of isolated features (rather than interconnected features), random semantic degradation could immediately damage distinguishing features, and lead to impaired recognition of some of these items. They predicted that as the disease progressed and semantic degradation increased, recognition of non-living things would be impaired in a linear fashion. However, small amounts of (random) damage to semantic information would initially have little impact on the recognition of living things, because the intercorrelations between features could help compensate for damage to individual features. Once the semantic degradation reached a critical point, though, the intercorrelated representations would no longer be able to activate a sufficient number of features, and all the exemplars in that category would be affected. Gonnerman et al. (1997) argued that "because there are many more features that participate in intercorrelations within biological kinds, the probability is higher that random damage will affect a feature in an intercorrelation. Therefore it is much less likely in this domain than in artifacts that a small amount of damage will affect a distinguishing feature and in this way wipe out a particular biological kind item" (p. 273). However, by definition, distinguishing features will not be highly correlated with other attributes, and assuming the number of distinguishing features is matched across categories, it is unclear how the more densely intercorrelated structure for living things can help protect these critical features. In addition, group studies on patients with Alzheimer's disease have not all been consistent with Gonnerman et al.'s predictions. Some studies have shown a significant category-specific impairment for living things across the group (Silveri et al., 1991; Montanes et al., 1995) and Garrard et al. (1998) found no significant interaction between the direction of category-specific impairments found in patients and the severity of their dementia (as measured by the MMSE). Garrard et al. (1998) challenged Gonnerman et al.'s proposal that category-specific impairments in DAT can arise from generalized and non-specific damage and, instead, argued that they reflected selective damage to particular areas of the brain. In particular, they argued that category-specific impairments for living and non-living things reflect damage to areas storing perceptual (temporal lobes)

and functional (frontoparietal areas) information, respectively (as suggested by Warrington & McCarthy, 1987).

SEMANTIC KNOWLEDGE IS ORGANIZED CATEGORICALLY IN THE BRAIN

This paper has reviewed a somewhat disparate set of accounts of why category-specific impairments arise following brain damage, but one common thread has been that category-specific impairments *emerge* because different categories have contrasting processing demands, or have come to have different forms of representation due to some co-varying factor (structural similarity, weightings of perceptual and functional knowledge, etc.). Only two accounts have maintained that *category* per se is a principle organizing factor (Nielsen, 1946; Sartori & Job, 1988). Nevertheless, perhaps this remains the most obvious and straightforward proposal. Sheridan and Humphreys (1993), for example, suggested that "true" category-based organization might hold for semantic knowledge but not for other forms of more perceptual stored knowledge (e.g., the structural description system); this has also been argued more recently by Coltheart et al. (1998). These suggestions have been elaborated by Caramazza and Shelton (1998). They reviewed a number of the influential reports of category-specific impairments and argued that support for the claim that visual information is particularly important for living things and functional information for non-living things is empirically weak. For example, they showed that experimenters often failed to match the relative difficulty of the questions designed to tap the patients' knowledge of visual and functional information. This makes it impossible to ascertain whether patients with category-specific impairments for living things do find it more difficult to retrieve visual information because this is selectively impaired (thereby causing the problem with living things), or if all semantic information is impaired; patients may perform more poorly with the visual questions because these are intrinsically more difficult than the functional questions used. In addition, they argued that, when experimenters have matched the difficulty of the visual and functional questions, patients with category-specific impairments for living things have found it equally difficult to retrieve information about both visual and functional properties of living things (Laiacone et al., 1993; Samson et al., 1998).

Caramazza and Shelton (1998) outlined a "domain specific knowledge" hypothesis and proposed that "evolutionary pressures have resulted in specialized mechanisms for perceptually *and* conceptually distinguishing animate and inanimate kinds . . . leading to a *categorical* organization of this knowledge in the brain" (p. 17). For example, evolutionary pressures could have lead to the separation of knowledge about animals, plant life and artifacts, and so it should be possible to find patients with selective category-specific impairments for any one of these three categories. They argued that "the empirically observed tripartite

distinction of category-specific deficits follows directly from the assumption that these, and only these, three categories form the basis for the organization of conceptual knowledge" (p. 32). Caramazza and Shelton also suggested that within each of these three functionally independent systems (for animals, plant life and artifacts) information about visual and functional properties would be stored for each category. Thus, and in contrast to the sensory/functional hypothesis (Warrington & Shallice, 1984), they argued that category-specific impairments should not be linked to impairments retrieving particular types of knowledge. Indeed, Caramazza and Shelton (1998) not only suggest that semantic information about living and non-living things might be stored in functionally independent systems, but also that it would be advantageous for lower-level perceptual systems to be specialized for recognizing animals, plants and artefacts.

Caramazza and Shelton's (1998) argument for categorically organized perceptual and semantic systems is primarily driven by patients with category-specific impairments for living things who have problems accessing visual *and functional* attributes about objects. However, this review suggests that these patients are only problematic for accounts stressing the importance of sensory information for living things and functional/motor information for non-living things, if the type of visual and functional information used in patient testing is itself matched across categories (see also Humphreys & Forde, 1999). However, this is intrinsically difficult to do since the type of "functional" information one stores about living and non-living things is qualitatively different. Stored "functional" information about non-living things generally concerns their use, and living things do not have a "function" in the same sense. Questions tapping "functional" information about living things range greatly, from those about where the item grows and how it moves to those about what it tastes like and whether it is eaten raw or not (Laiacona et al., 1993; Samson et al., 1998). Consequently, patients with deficits for living things may perform poorly with "functional" questions about the affected items, and not with "functional" questions about non-living things because the questions are tapping completely different types of knowledge. Furthermore, to answer some of these "functional" questions about living things we might need to draw on the sensory knowledge that is strongly weighted and in some sense, provides the "core" of the representation for these items. Consider a patient who has degraded visual/perceptual knowledge and no longer knows that an elephant is grey, has a trunk, is very heavy and has large, flapping ears. This paper suggests that this patient may well have difficulty answering a "functional" question, such as "do elephants appear in a circus?" because the properties ⟨is grey⟩, ⟨has a trunk⟩, ⟨is heavy⟩ and ⟨has large, flapping ears⟩ are crucially important for knowing what an elephant is. This hypothesis has been supported by functional brain imaging work, which shows that subjects access visual/perceptual knowledge even when answering questions about the "functional" attributes of living things. Visual/perceptual knowledge did not appear to be important when answering "functional" questions about non-living things (Thompson-Schill et al., 1999).

In addition, in our view, a tripartite distinction between animals, plants and manmade objects has not been reliably documented in the literature. The most common pattern is an impairment with all kinds of living things (animals and plant life) and there are relatively few cases of category-specific impairments for non-living things (Warrington & McCarthy, 1983, 1987; Hillis & Caramazza, 1991; Sacchett & Humphreys, 1992). The model outlined by Caramazza and Shelton (1998) would predict relatively equal numbers of each type of impairment. Even more problematic for their account, however, are category-specific impairments that are more fine-grained than a distinction between animals, plants and manmade artifacts (e.g., Warrington & McCarthy, 1987).

However, although there may not be an innate and fundamental distinction between living and non-living things, or between animals, plants and manmade objects, we suggest that exemplars from the same category will be represented closely in "semantic space". Thus semantic memory may *appear* to be categorically organized—but this only reflects the fact that exemplars from the same category tend to share more features with each other than with items from other categories (Allport, 1985; Warrington & McCarthy, 1987). Our view of semantic memory, and our ideas on why category-specific impairments arise, are rather similar to those outlined by Damasio and colleagues (Damasio, 1989, 1990; Damasio et al., 1996; Tranel et al., 1997). We review their account of semantic memory before concluding with our own proposals.

INTERACTIVE SEMANTIC REPRESENTATIONS

The emphasis of the model of semantic memory outlined by Damasio and colleagues is similar to the multi-modal model first proposed by Warrington and McCarthy (1987) (see also, Lissauer, 1890; Allport, 1985). Damasio and colleagues also stressed the importance of different types of sensory and sensorimotor information in our stored semantic representations: "an entity (e.g., a given individual or object) generates a multiplicity of representations *within* the sensory cortices of the same modality (for vision, examples are shape, colour, texture, motion) and *across* cortices of other sensory modalities (e.g., auditory, somatosensory, olfactory)" (Damasio, 1990, p. 95). In Damasio's model, modality-specific representations of an object's properties are stored in "sensory feature fragments" and "motor feature fragments". These feature fragments are stored in the corresponding sensory and motor cortices, which leads to a very distributed semantic system. For example, stored feature fragments for the smell of an item would be stored in olfactory cortex, for the colour or the shape of an item in visual cortex, and so on. Damasio argued that separate neural regions, termed "convergence zones" specify the codes that bind information across the different sensory modalities. These convergence zones occur in higher-level, association cortex. So if an object is visually presented, feature fragments in olfactory or auditory cortex (specifying the smell or sound of the object, respectively) can

only be activated via the convergence zone. Recognizing (and naming) an object requires the activation of a sufficient number of feature fragments, though Damasio (1990) suggested that the particular feature fragments that are activated could vary from one occasion to another—as long as a sufficient number are activated the object will be recognized. Following brain damage, patients might be able to activate some feature fragments but not enough to recognize objects explicitly. For example, visual agnosic patients may be able to access the appropriate sensorimotor feature fragments, and so gesture the correct action, but be unable to access any further information, as we have noted earlier (see also Riddoch & Humphreys, 1987b).

Consistent with the literature we have reviewed in this paper, Damasio (1990) has also suggested that a number of additional factors determine how different categories are represented. (1) The proportions of each type of feature fragment (representing colour, motion or smell, etc.) stored for items will vary across categories. (2) The hand (and eye) movements associated with an object will be represented. (3) The number of structurally similar exemplars within a category will affect recognition. (4) The emotional importance and the familiarity of the entity will be represented. According to this account, there is no fundamental distinction between living and non-living things, but exemplars from the same category tend to be encoded in terms of the same types of features.

HIERARCHICAL INTERACTIVE THEORY

Damasio's (1990) view, then, builds upon distinctions between different forms of knowledge (e.g., sensory, functional) and emphasizes the varying contributions of these different forms of knowledge to the identification of different categories. In addition, it suggests that there exist further distinct structures abstracted from modalities, "convergence zones", that serve to bind together different forms of perceptual knowledge. However, to provide a full account of the disorders we have reviewed, several further factors may need to be taken into consideration including: the role of correlated features, the relations between perceptual features and both common and distinctive features of objects, and the way that these factors contribute to different tasks. It is this last point that we now consider.

We have noted that, both in normal subjects and patients, the category of the object impacts differently depending on the task. For instance, the advantage for non-living over living things in normal subjects can be larger in naming than in object decision, and it can be reversed in classification tasks. These results fit with the idea that object naming is hierarchically organized; competition to select an individuating response to an object (e.g., its name) increases as information is passed from earlier to later stages. As a consequence, there is exacerbated competition for living things due to structural similarity, correlated features and common perceptual-functional features. Patients can also manifest category-specificity in some but not all tasks. Though naming can be impaired for living

things, superordinate classification can often be preserved, and patients can succeed on difficult object decisions for the living things that cannot be named (Sheridan & Humphreys, 1993). These results indicate that there can be breakdowns at different levels of the recognition system, with each producing a form of category-specific deficit. To account for this hierarchical breakdown, we have recently presented a Hierarchical Interactive Theory (HIT) which maintains that object naming required transmission of information through a series of hierarchical, but interactive, stages (Humphreys & Forde, 1999). The hierarchical nature of this model means that patients may access perceptual knowledge from a given input modality even when they have impaired access to other forms of knowledge. This accounts for patients who show good object decision performance but poor associative or functional matching from vision (Riddoch & Humphreys, 1987b; Hillis & Caramazza, 1995). Similar dissociations may also be expected for other modalities. The interactive nature of this theory, however, means that different forms of knowledge would be drawn upon both for particular objects and for particular tasks. The degree to which a particular form of knowledge would be drawn upon should be a function of its weighting in the overall representation of the object. In general terms, perceptual knowledge will be more strongly weighted for living things, and functional knowledge for non-living things (as suggested originally by Warrington & Shallice, 1984, and many authors thereafter). Thus, visual knowledge, represented in a structural description system, may be drawn on even to answer some "functional" questions for living things. Similarly functional knowledge may be drawn on when answering "perceptual" questions about non-living things. Particular forms of functional knowledge may be differentially weighted for contrasting non-living things (e.g., small objects manipulable by hand versus large vehicles). This helps account for patients with deficits with sub-classes of non-living things (Warrington & McCarthy, 1987). Particular forms of perceptual knowledge may also be differentially weighted for contrasting living things. For example, some patients have problems naming fruit and vegetables but not animals (Hillis & Caramazza, 1991) while others show the reverse pattern (Hart & Gordon, 1992).

In addition to accounting for neuropsychological impairments for both living and non-living things, HIT correctly predicts differences in the efficiency with which normal subjects perform various tasks with particular classes of object—for instance, fast categorization of living things but slow naming. "Category-specificity", therefore, is not solely a consequence of neuronal damage but is an emergent property of the normal object recognition system.

ACKNOWLEDGEMENTS

This work was supported by grants from the Medical Research Council, the European Union and the Human Frontier Science programme. The ideas have benefited from discussion with many people but we especially thank Jane Riddoch and Cathy Price.

REFERENCES

Allport, D. A. (1985). Distributed memory, modular systems and dysphasia. In S. K. Newman & R. Epstein (Eds.), *Current perspectives in dysphasia* (pp. 32–60). Edinburgh: Churchill Livingstone.

Basso, A., Capitani, E., & Laiacona, M. (1988). Progressive language impairment without dementia: A case study with isolated category-specific semantic defect. *Journal of Neurology, Neurosurgery and Psychiatry, 51,* 1201–1207.

Biederman, I., & Kalocsai, P. (1997). Neurocomputational bases of object and face recognition. *Philosophical Transactions of Royal Society of London, Series B—Biological Sciences, 352,* 1203–1219.

Caramazza, A., Hillis, A. E., Rapp, B. C., & Romani, C. (1990). The multiple semantics hypothesis: Multiple confusions? *Cognitive Neuropsychology, 7,* 161–189.

Caramazza, A., & Shelton, J. R. (1998). Domain specific knowledge systems in the brain: The animate-inanimate distinction. *Journal of Cognitive Neuroscience, 10,* 1–34.

Coltheart, M., Inglis, L., Cupples, L., Michie, P., Bates, A., & Budd, B. (1998). A semantic system specific to the storage of information about the visual attributes of animate and inanimate objects. *Neurocase, 4,* 353–370.

Damasio, A. R. (1989). Time-locked multiregional retroactivation: A systems-level proposal for the neural substrates of recall and recognition. *Cognition, 33,* 25–62.

Damasio, A. R. (1990). Category-related recognition defects as a clue to the neural substrates of knowledge. *Trends in Neuroscience, 13,* 95–98.

Damasio, H., Grabowski, T. J., Tranel, D., Hitchwa, R. D., & Damasio, A. R. (1996). A neural basis for lexical retrieval. *Nature, 380,* 499–505.

De Renzi, E., & Lucchelli, F. (1994). Are semantic systems separately represented in the brain? The case of living category impairment. *Cortex, 30,* 3–25.

Devlin, J., Gonnerman, L., Anderson, E., & Seidenberg, M. (1998). Category specific semantic deficits in focal and widespread brain damage: A computational account. *Journal of Cognitive Neuroscience, 10,* 77–94.

Ellis, R., & Humphreys, G. W. (1998). *Connectionist psychology.* Hove, UK: Psychology Press.

Farah, M. J. (1991). Pattern of co-occurence among the associative agnosias: Implications for visual object representation. *Cognitive Neuropsychology, 8,* 1–19.

Farah, M. J., & McClelland, J. L. (1991). A computational model of semantic memory impairment: Modality specificity and emergent category specificity. *Psychological Review, 120,* 339–357.

Farah, M. J., Meyer, M. M., & McMullan, P. A. (1996). The living/nonliving dissociation is not a artifact: Giving an a priori implausible hypothesis a strong test. *Cognitive Neuropsychology, 13,* 137–154.

Forde, E. M. E. (1998). Category specific recognition impairments. In G. W. Humphreys (Ed.), *Case studies in the neuropsychology of vision.* Hove, UK: Psychology Press.

Forde, E. M. E., Francis, D., Riddoch, M. J., Rumiati, R., & Humphreys, G. W. (1997). On the links between visual knowledge and naming: A single case study of a patient with a category-specific impairment for living things. *Cognitive Neuropsychology, 14,* 403–458.

Funnell, E., & de Mornay-Davies, P. D. (1996). JBR: A re-assessment of concept familiarity and a category specific disorder for living things. *Neurocase, 2,* 461–474.

Funnell, E., & Sheridan, J. (1992). Categories of knowledge? Unfamiliar aspects of living and nonliving things. *Cognitive Neuropsychology, 9,* 135–153.

Gaffan, D., & Heywood, C. A. (1993). A spurious category-specific visual agnosia for living things in normal human and nonhuman primates. *Journal of Cognitive Neuroscience, 5,* 118–128.

Gainotti, G., & Silveri, M. C. (1996). Cognitive and anatomical locus of lesion in a patient with a category-specific semantic impairment for living beings. *Cognitive Neuropsychology, 13,* 357–389.

Gainotti, G., Silveri, M. C., Daniele, A., & Giustolisi, L. (1995). Neuroanatomical correlates of category-specific semantic disorders: A critical survey. *Memory, 3,* 247–264.

Garrard, P., Patterson, K., Watson, P. C., & Hodges, J. (1998). Category specific semantic loss in dementia of Alzheimer's type: Functional-anatomical correlations from cross-sectional analyses. *Brain, 121,* 633–646.

Gonnerman, L. M., Anderson, E. S., Devlin, J. T., Kempler, D., & Seidenberg, M. S. (1997). Double dissociation of semantic categories in Alzheimer's disease. *Brain and Language, 57,* 254–279.

Hart, J., & Gordon, B. (1992). Neural subsystems for object knowledge. *Nature, 359,* 60–64.

Hillis, A. E., & Caramazza, A. (1991). Category-specific naming and comprehension impairment: A double dissociation. *Brain, 114,* 2081–2094.

Hillis, A. E., & Caramazza, A. (1995). Constraining claims about theories of semantic memory: More on unitary versus multiple semantics. *Cognitive Neuropsychology, 12,* 175–186.

Humphreys, G. W., & Forde, E. M. E. (1999). Category-specific deficits: A major review and presentation of the Hierarchical Interactive Theory. *Aphasiology, 13,* 169–193.

Humphreys, G. W., Price, C., & Riddoch, M. J. (1999). From objects to names: A cognitive neuroscience approach. *Psychological Research, 62*(2–3), 118–130.

Humphreys, G. W., & Riddoch, M. J. (1984). Routes to object constancy: Implications from neurological impairments of object constancy. *Quarterly Journal of Experimental Psychology, 36A,* 385–415.

Humphreys, G. W., Riddoch, M. J., & Price, C. (1997). Top-down processes in object identification: Evidence from experimental psychology, neuropsychology and functional anatomy. *Proceedings of the Royal Society, Series B, 352,* 127–128.

Humphreys, G. W., Riddoch, M. J., & Quinlan, P. T. (1988). Cascade processes in picture identification. *Cognitive Neuropsychology, 5,* 67–103.

Humphreys, G. W., & Rumiati, R. (1998). Agnosia without prosopagnosia or alexia: Evidence for stored visual memories specific to objects. *Cognitive Neuropsychology, 15,* 243–277.

Keil, F. (1987). Conceptual development and category structure. In U. Neisser (Ed.), *Concepts and conceptual development: Ecological and intellectual factors in categorisation* (pp. 175–200). New York: Cambridge University Press.

Kurbat, M. A. (1997). Can the recognition of living things really be selectively impaired? *Neuropsychologia, 35,* 813–827.

Kurbat, M. A., & Farah, M. J. (1998). Is the category-specific deficit for living things spurious? *Journal of Cognitive Neuroscience, 10,* 355–361.

Laiacona, M., Barbarotto, R., & Capitani, E. (1993). Perceptual and associative knowledge in category specific impairment of semantic memory: A study of two cases. *Cortex, 29,* 727–740.

Lambon Ralph, M., Howard, D., Nightingale, G., & Ellis, A. W. (1998). Are living and nonliving category-specific deficits causally linked to impaired perceptual or associative knowledge? Evidence from a category-specific double dissociation. *Neurocase, 4,* 311–338.

Lissauer, H. (1890). Ein Fall von Seelenblindheit nebst einem Beitrag zur Theorie derselben. *Archiv fur Psychiatrie, 21,* 222–270. [Edited and reprinted in translation by Jackson, M. 1988, Lissauer on agnosia. *Cognitive Neuropsychology, 5,* 157–192.]

Lloyd-Jones, T. J., & Humphreys, G. W. (1997). Perceptual differentiation as a source of category effects in object processing: Evidence from naming and object decision. *Memory and Cognition, 25,* 18–35.

Marr, D. (1982). *Vision: A computational investigation into the human representation and processing of visual information.* San Francisco: W. H. Freeman.

Martin, A., Wiggs, C. L., Ungerleider, L. G., & Haxby, J. V. (1996). Neural correlates of category-specific knowledge. *Nature, 379,* 649–652.

McCarthy, R., & Warrington, E. K. (1994). Disorders of semantic memory. *Philosophical Transactions of the Royal Society of London, 346,* 89–96.

McRae, K., de Sa, V. R., & Seidenberg, M. S. (1997). On the nature and scope of featural representations of word meaning. *Journal of Experimental Psychology, General, 126,* 99–130.

Montanes, P., Goldblum, M. C., & Boller, F. (1995). Naming colour and black-white pictures from living and nonliving things in Alzheimer's disease. *Journal of the International Neuropsychological Society, 1,* 39–48.

Moss, H. E., Tyler, L. K., & Jennings, F. (1997). When leopards lose their spots: Knowledge of visual properties in category-specific deficits for living things. *Cognitive Neuropsychology, 14*, 901–950.

Nielsen, J. M. (1946). *Agnosia, apraxia, aphasia: Their value in cerebral localization* (2nd Edn.). New York: Hoeber.

Price, C. J., Moore, C. J., Humphreys, G. W., Frackowiak, R. S. J., & Friston, K. J. (1996). The neural regions sustaining object recognition and naming. *Proceedings of the Royal Society of London, Series B, 263*, 1501–1507.

Riddoch, M. J., & Humphreys, G. W. (1987a). Picture naming. In G. W. Humphreys & M. J. Riddoch (Eds.), *Visual object processing: A cognitive neuropsychological approach* (pp. 107–143). Hove, UK: Lawrence Erlbaum Associates Ltd.

Riddoch, M. J., & Humphreys, G. W. (1987b). Visual object processing in optic aphasia: A case of semantic access agnosia. *Cognitive Neuropsychology, 4*, 131–185.

Rumiati, R., Humphreys, G. W., Riddoch, M. J., & Bateman, A. (1994). Visual object agnosia without prosopagnosia or alexia: Evidence for hierarchical theories of visual recognition. *Visual Cognition, 1*, 181–226.

Sacchett, C., & Humphreys, G. W. (1992). Calling a squirrel a squirrel but a canoe a wigwam: A category-specific deficit for artefactual objects and body parts. *Cognitive Neuropsychology, 9*, 73–86.

Samson, D., Pillon, A., & De Wilde, V. (1998). Impaired knowledge of visual *and* nonvisual attributes in a patient with a semantic impairment for living entities: A case of a true category-specific deficit. *Neurocase, 4*, 273–290.

Sartori, G., & Job, R. (1988). The oyster with four legs: A neuropsychological study on the interaction of visual and semantic information. *Cognitive Neuropsychology, 5*, 105–132.

Sartori, G., Miozzo, M., & Job, R. (1993a). Category-specific naming impairments? Yes. *Quarterly Journal of Experimental Psychology, 46*, 489–504.

Sartori, G., Job, R., Miozzo, M., Zago, S., & Marchiori, G. (1993b). Category-specific form-knowledge deficit in a patient with herpes simplex encephalitis. *Journal of Clinical and Experimental Neuropsychology, 15*, 280–299.

Sheridan, J., & Humphreys, G. W. (1993). A verbal-semantic category-specific recognition impairment. *Cognitive Neuropsychology, 10*, 143–184.

Silveri, M. C., Daniele, A., Giustolisi, L., & Gainotti, G. (1991). Dissociation between knowledge of living and nonliving things in dementia of the Alzheimer type. *Neurology, 41*, 545–546.

Silveri, M. C., & Gainotti, G. (1988). Interaction between vision and language in category-specific semantic impairment. *Cognitive Neuropsychology, 5*, 677–709.

Sirigu, A., Duhamel, J., & Poncet, M. (1991). The role of sensorimotor experience in object recognition. *Brain, 114*, 2555–2573.

Snodgrass, J. G., & Vanderwart, M. (1980). A standardised set of 260 pictures: Norms for name agreement, familiarity, and visual complexity. *Journal of Experimental Psychology: General, 6*, 174–215.

Stewart, F., Parkin, A. J., & Hunkin, N. M. (1992). Naming impairments following recovery from herpes simplex encephalitis. *Quarterly Journal of Experimental Psychology, 44A*, 261–284.

Temple, C. (1986). Anomia for animals in a child. *Brain, 109*, 1225–1242.

Thompson-Schill, S. L., Aguirre, G. K., D'Esposito, M., & Farah, M. J. (1999). A neural basis for category and modality specificity of semantic knowledge. *Neuropsychologia, 37*, 671–676.

Tranel, D., Damasio, H., & Damasio, A. (1997). A neural basis for the retrieval of conceptual knowledge. *Neuropsychologia, 35*, 1319–1327.

Tranel, D., Logan, C. G., Frank, R. J., & Damasio, A. R. (1997). Explaining category-related effects in the retrieval of conceptual and lexical knowledge for concrete entities: Operationalization and analysis of factors. *Neuropsychologia, 35*, 1329–1339.

Tyler, L., & Moss, H. (1997). Functional properties of concepts: Studies of normal and brain-damaged patients. *Cognitive Neuropsychology, 14*, 511–545.

Vitkovitch, M., Humphreys, G. W., & Lloyd-Jones, T. (1993). On naming a giraffe a zebra: Picture naming errors across different categories. *Journal of Experimental Psychology: Learning, Memory and Cognition, 19*, 243–259.

Warrington, E. K., & James, M. (1986). Visual object recognition in patients with right hemisphere lesions: Axes or features? *Perception, 15*, 355–366.

Warrington, E. K., & McCarthy, R. (1983). Category-specific access dysphasia. *Brain, 106*, 859–878.

Warrington, E. K., & McCarthy, R. (1987). Categories of knowledge: Further fractionations and an attempted integration. *Brain, 110*, 1273–1296.

Warrington, E. K., & McCarthy, R. (1994). Multiple meaning systems in the brain: A case for visual semantics. *Neuropsychologia, 32*, 1465–1473.

Warrington, E. K., & Shallice, T. (1984). Category-specific semantic impairment. *Brain, 107*, 829–854.

A computational model of semantic memory impairment: Modality specificity and emergent category specificity

Martha J. Farah and James L. McClelland
Carnegie Mellon University, Pittsburgh, USA

It is demonstrated how a modality-specific semantic memory system can account for category-specific impairments after brain damage. In Experiment 1, the hypothesis that visual and functional knowledge play different roles in the representation of living things and nonliving things is tested and confirmed. A parallel distributed processing model of semantic memory in which knowledge is subdivided by modality into visual and functional components is described. In Experiment 2, the model is lesioned, and it is confirmed that damage to visual semantics primarily impairs knowledge of living things, and damage to functional semantics primarily impairs knowledge of nonliving things. In Experiment 3, it is demonstrated that the model accounts naturally for a finding that had appeared problematic for a modality-specific architecture, namely, impaired retrieval of functional knowledge about living things. Finally, in Experiment 4, it is shown how the model can account for a recent observation of impaired knowledge of living things only when knowledge is probed verbally.

How is semantic memory organized? Two general answers to this question have been proposed. One is that semantic memory is organized by taxonomic category, such that different parts of the system represent knowledge about objects from different categories. Alternatively, semantic memory could be subdivided by modality of knowledge, such that one component is responsible for visual information about objects, another for auditory information, and so on.

Journal of Experimental Psychology: General 1991, Vol. 20, No. 4, 339–357.

Patients with selective losses of knowledge after brain damage appear to provide a direct source of evidence on the organization of semantic memory. Unfortunately, this evidence yields conflicting answers. In most cases, the losses appear to be tied to specific modalities, resulting in impaired recognition of objects in just one modality (e.g., visual or auditory agnosia) or in impaired manipulation of objects with specific uses, despite intact recognition of them (apraxia; e.g., a key might be pulled, rather than turned). These observations are consistent with recent neurophysiological data showing that most cortical neurons are modality-specific, even in regions that were traditionally viewed as supramodal association areas (e.g., Sereno & Allman, 1991). In some cases, however, brain damage seems to cause category-specific losses of knowledge, which cut across different modalities. Specifically, there are patients who seem to have lost their knowledge of living things, and others who seem to have lost their knowledge of nonliving things. These observations suggest that the architecture of semantic memory incorporates at least two general, taxonomically defined subsystems, for representing knowledge of living and nonliving things.

In this article, we attempt to resolve the apparent conflict between these two types of neuropsychological evidence. After reviewing the neuropsychological evidence for category specificity in semantic memory, we present a parallel distributed processing (PDP) model in which the architecture distinguishes only between modalities of knowledge, but when damaged, displays category specificity similar to that of the patients described in the neuropsychological literature.

IMPAIRMENTS IN KNOWLEDGE OF LIVING AND NONLIVING THINGS

The most commonly observed semantic memory dissociation is between impaired knowledge of living things with relatively preserved knowledge of nonliving things. In the first report of this phenomenon, Warrington and Shallice (1984) described 4 patients who were much worse at identifying living things (animals, plants) than nonliving things (inanimate objects). All 4 of these patients had recovered from herpes encephalitis, and all had sustained bilateral temporal lobe damage. Two of the patients were studied in detail and showed a selective impairment for living things across a range of tasks, both visual and verbal. Table 1 shows examples of their performance in a visual identification task, in which they were to identify by name or description the item shown in a colored picture, and in a verbal definition task, in which they were to provide definitions when the names of these same items were presented auditorily. Examples of their definitions are also shown in Table 1.

Farah, McMullen, and Meyer (1991) studied 2 head-injured patients whose knowledge of living things appeared to be selectively disrupted. We examined their picture recognition performance as a function of the living–nonliving distinction as well as many other possibly confounded factors that might influence

TABLE 1

Performance of two patients with impaired knowledge of living things on various semantic memory tasks

Case	Living thing	Nonliving thing
Picture identification		
JBR	6%	90%
SBY	0%	75%
Spoken word definition		
JBR	8%	79%
SBY	0%	52%
Examples of definitions		
JBR	Parrot: don't know	Tent: temporary outhouse, living home
	Daffodil: plant	Briefcase: small case used by students to carry papers
	Snail: an insect animal	Compass: tools for telling direction you are going
	Eel: not well	Torch: hand-held light
	Ostrich: unusual	Dustbin: bin for putting rubbish in
SBY	Duck: an animal	Wheelbarrow: object used by people to take material about
	Wasp: bird that flies	Towel: material used to dry people
	Crocus: rubbish material	Pram: used to carry people, with wheels and a thing to sit on
	Holly: what you drink	Submarine: ship that goes underneath the sea
	Spider: a person looking for things, he was a spider for his nation or country	Umbrella: object used to protect you from water that comes

performance, including complexity, familiarity, name frequency, name specificity (i.e., basic object level or subordinate level), and similarity to other objects. A regression analysis showed that even with all of these factors accounted for, the living–nonliving distinction was an important predictor of recognition performance.

Other cases of selective impairment in knowledge of living things include additional postencephalitic patients described by Pietrini et al. (1988), Sartori and Job (1988), and Silveri and Gainotti (1988); a patient with encephalitis and strokes described by Newcombe, Mehta, and de Haan (1994); and a patient with a focal degenerative disease described by Basso, Capitani, and Laiacona (1988). In all of these cases, there was damage to the temporal regions, known to be bilateral except in Case 2 of Farah et al. (1991), Case 1 of Pietrini et al., and the case of Basso et al., in which there was evidence only of left temporal damage.

The opposite dissociation—namely, impaired knowledge of nonliving things with relatively preserved knowledge of living things—has also been observed. Warrington and McCarthy (1983, 1987) described 2 cases of global dysphasia, after large left-hemisphere strokes, in which semantic knowledge was tested in a series of matching tasks. Table 2 shows the results of a matching task in which the subjects were asked to point to the picture, in an array, that corresponded to a spoken word. Their performance with animals and flowers was reliably better

TABLE 2
Performance of two patients with
impaired knowledge of nonliving things
on various semantic memory tasks

Case	Category		
	Animal	Flower	Object
Spoken word–picture matching			
VER	86%	96%	63%
YOT	86%	86%	67%
Picture–picture matching			
YOT	100%	—	69%

than with nonliving things. One of these subjects was also tested with a completely nonverbal matching task, in which different-looking depictions of objects or animals were to be matched to one another in an array, and showed the same selective preservation of knowledge of animals relative to inanimate objects.

IMPLICATIONS OF THE LIVING–NONLIVING DISSOCIATIONS FOR MODELS OF NORMAL SEMANTIC MEMORY

The most straightforward interpretation of the double dissociation between knowledge of living and nonliving things is that these two bodies of knowledge are represented by two separate category-specific components of semantic memory. This interpretation is consistent with the view that semantic memory is organized along taxonomic lines, at least as far as the distinction between living and nonliving things is concerned. However, Warrington and colleagues (e.g., Warrington & McCarthy, 1983, Warrington & Shallice, 1984) suggested an alternative interpretation, according to which semantic memory is fundamentally modality-specific. They argued that selective deficits in knowledge of living and nonliving things may reflect the differential weighting of information from different sensorimotor channels in representing knowledge about these two categories. More specifically, they pointed out that living things are distinguished primarily by their sensory attributes, whereas nonliving things are distinguished primarily by their functional attributes. For example, knowledge of an animal, such as a leopard, by which it is distinguished from other similar creatures, is predominantly visual. In contrast, knowledge of a desk, by which it is distinguished from other furniture, is predominantly functional (i.e., what it is used for). Thus, the distinctions between impaired and preserved knowledge in the cases reviewed earlier may not be living–nonliving distinctions per se, but rather sensory–functional distinctions.

The sensory–functional hypothesis seems preferable to a strict living–nonliving hypothesis for two reasons. First, it is more consistent with what is already known

about brain organization. As mentioned earlier, it is well known that different brain areas are dedicated to representing information from specific sensory and motor channels. Functional knowledge could conceivably be tied to the motor system. In any case, there is prior evidence for the selective vulnerability of knowledge of functional attributes after left-hemisphere damage: Goodglass and Baker (1976) found that left hemisphere-damaged aphasic patients had particular difficulty relating a named object to a word describing its use compared with words describing its sensory qualities or words denoting other objects in the same category. A second reason for preferring the sensory–functional hypothesis to the living–nonliving hypothesis is that exceptions to the living–nonliving distinction have been observed in certain cases. For example, Warrington and Shallice (1984) reported that their patients, who were deficient in their knowledge of living things, also had impaired knowledge of gemstones and fabrics. Warrington and McCarthy's (1987) patient, whose knowledge of most nonliving things was impaired, seemed to have retained good knowledge of very large outdoor objects, such as bridges or windmills. It is at least possible that knowledge of these aberrant categories of nonliving things is primarily visual.

Unfortunately, there is a problem with the hypothesis that living things impairments are just impairments in sensory knowledge and nonliving things impairments are just impairments in functional knowledge. This hypothesis seems to predict that cases of living things impairment should show good knowledge of the functional attributes of living things and cases of nonliving things impairment should show good knowledge of the visual attributes of nonliving things. The evidence available in cases of nonliving things impairment is limited to performance in matching-to-sample tasks, which does not allow one to distinguish knowledge of visual or sensory attributes from knowledge of functional attributes. However, there does appear to be adequate evidence available in cases of living things impairment, and in at least some cases, it disconfirms these predictions.

KNOWLEDGE OF NONVISUAL ATTRIBUTES OF LIVING THINGS IN CASES OF LIVING THINGS IMPAIRMENT

Consider the definitions of living and nonliving things given by Warrington and Shallice's (1984) 2 cases (Table 1). Although the definitions of nonliving things may be somewhat skimpy on visual detail, in keeping with the sensory–functional hypothesis, the definitions of living things do not show preserved functional knowledge. If these subjects have lost just their visual semantic memory, they should be able to retrieve the functional attributes of living things; for example, parrots are kept as pets and can talk, daffodils are a spring flower, and so on.

In the other cases of living things impairment, visual and functional knowledge have been compared directly, and functional knowledge of living things ranges from mildly to severely impaired. Newcombe et al. (1994) presented their

subject with triads of words, with the instruction to group together two of the words according to either the visual similarity of the words' referents or some factual commonality (e.g., normally found in the United Kingdom). When the words named nonliving things, their subject performed within normal limits. However, when the words named living things, their subject performed significantly worse than control subjects, even when the grouping was based on factual, rather than visual, properties. Silveri and Gainotti (1988) assessed the ability of their patient to identify animals on the basis of two kinds of spoken definition: visual descriptions of the animal's appearance, such as "an insect with broad, colored, ornate wings" for *butterfly*, and nonvisual descriptions, of either metaphorical verbal associations to the animal, such as "king of the jungle" for *lion*, or functions of the animal, such as "the farm animal that bellows and supplies us with milk" for *cow*. Although the subject was worse at identifying animals from visual descriptions than from nonvisual descriptions, he performed poorly with both and identified only 58% of the animals on the basis of nonvisual descriptions (which control subjects had rated *easy*). A patient of Basso et al. (1988) also appeared to be better at retrieving nonvisual information, but nonvisual information was not intact. These different types of knowledge were tested by naming a word and then asking a multiple-choice question about it. The question tapped categorical information, such as "is it a bird, mammal, fish or reptile?"; functional information, such as "does it live in Italy or the desert?"; or visual information, such as "does it have a smooth back or is it hump-backed?" The patient performed at chance on the categorical as well as on the visual questions and performed less than perfectly with the functional questions (35 out of 42). (It should be noted that not all of the words denoted living things. Basso et al. tested the patient with words he had failed to match with pictures; most of these were living things. The results for living and nonliving things were not separately reported.)

Similarly, Sartori and Job (1988) found better performance in their case in tests tapping nonvisual, rather than visual, knowledge of animals, but their subject nevertheless appeared mildly impaired in nonvisual tasks. For example, in defining living and nonliving things, the subject made numerous factual errors about nonvisual characteristics of animals and vegetables, twice as many as were made about nonliving things. The subject also made occasional errors in identifying animals with their characteristic sounds or environments, although in the absence of normative data it is difficult to interpret these results. Farah, Hammond, Mehta, and Ratcliff (1989) tested the ability of one of the head-injured patients described earlier (Farah et al., 1991, Case 1) to retrieve visual and nonvisual knowledge about living and nonliving things and compared the subject's performance to age- and education-matched normal subjects. The patient's performance fell outside of normal limits only for visual knowledge of living things. However, whereas he performed at an average level in retrieving nonvisual information about nonliving things, he performed below-average in retrieving nonvisual information about living things, and the discrepancy between the two levels

of performance with these two kinds of question was larger than for any of the 12 control subjects. Unpublished observations of Case 2 of Farah et al. (1991) are that the subject was impaired at retrieving functional information about animals, such as knowing which animal provides wool, as well as at recognizing animal sounds. When given the test designed by Farah et al. (1989), she performed at chance on the questions concerning visual as well as nonvisual properties of living things, whereas she performed far-above-chance with nonvisual properties of nonliving things.

In sum, the sensory–functional hypothesis seems more attractive then the living–nonliving hypothesis because it is more in keeping with what is already known about brain organization. However, it does not seem able to account for all of the data. In particular, it does not seem able to account for the impaired ability of these patients to retrieve nonvisual information about living things.

The goal of our model is to demonstrate that the sensory–functional hypothesis is sufficient to account for these semantic memory impairments when it is taken together with a certain conception of mental representation; specifically, the idea of active, distributed representations, in which the activation of the representation depends on mutual support among different parts of the representation. This idea is common to a wide range of recurrent PDP models (e.g., Anderson, Silverstein, Ritz, & Jones, 1977; McClelland & Rumelhart, 1985). We show that a model of semantic memory with active distributed representations consisting of just two types of semantic information, visual and functional, can be lesioned to produce selective impairments in knowledge of living things and nonliving things. More important, we show how such a model can account naturally for the impairment of both visual and functional knowledge of living things after damage confined to visual semantics. Finally, we also show how this model can account for a recently described case in which knowledge of living things was impaired only when probed verbally, which had initially been interpreted as evidence that semantic memory is subdivided not only by category of knowledge but also by modality of access.

Before presenting the simulation model and the results of lesioning the model, we describe an experiment that tests the basic assumption of the sensory–functional hypothesis, namely, that living things are known primarily by their sensory features and that nonliving things are known primarily by their functional features.

EXPERIMENT 1

In this experiment, normal subjects read dictionary definitions of living and nonliving things and underlined all occurrences of visual and functional descriptors. This tested whether there is a difference in the importance of sensory (specifically, visual) and functional properties for the meaning of living and nonliving things and provided us with a quantitative estimate of the ratio of

visual to functional features for the representations of living and nonliving things in the model.

Method

Materials. The lists of living and nonliving things were taken from Warrington and Shallice's (1984) Experiment 2. Definitions were copied from the *American Heritage Dictionary* (1969) and printed in a random order.

Procedure. Subjects read for either visual descriptors or functional descriptors. If they read for visual descriptors, they were told to underline all occurrences of words describing any aspect of the visual appearance of an item. If they read for functional descriptors, they were told to underline all occurrences of words describing what the item does or what it is for.

Subjects. Forty-two undergraduate students from Carnegie Mellon University participated in exchange for course credit. Half read for visual descriptors, and half for functional descriptors.

Results and discussion

Subjects who read for visual desriptors underlined an average of 2.68 visual descriptors for each living thing and 1.57 for each nonliving thing. Subjects who read for functional descriptors underlined an average of 0.35 functional descriptors for each living thing and 1.11 for each nonliving thing. The resultant ratios of visual to functional features are 7.7 : 1 for living things and 1.4 : 1 for nonliving things. Thus, these data confirm the hypothesis that visual attributes are more important than functional attributes for defining living things, but do not support the converse hypothesis that functional attributes are more important than visual attributes for defining nonliving things: Subjects found more visual descriptors than functional descriptors in the definitions of nonliving things, but did not find more functional than visual descriptors for nonliving things. One of the interesting conclusions of the simulation to be described is that a large difference in the number of visual and functional attributes for living things, with a much smaller difference in the *same* direction for nonliving things, is sufficient to account for both the living things impairments and the nonliving things impairments. The overall ratio of visual to functional features, combining living and nonliving things, is 2.9 : 1.

THE MODEL

In PDP systems, a representation consists of a pattern of activation across a network of highly interconnected neuron-like units (Anderson et al., 1977; Hinton, McClelland, & Rumelhart, 1986; McClelland & Rumelhart, 1985). The units can

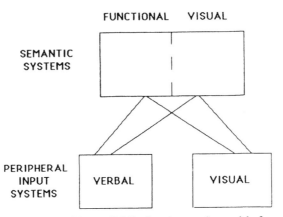

Figure 1. Schematic diagram of the parallel distributed processing model of semantic memory.

be thought of as each representing some aspect of the entity being represented by the pattern (although these aspects need not be nameable features or correspond in any simple way to our intuitions about the featural decomposition of these concepts). For example, in the case of living and nonliving things, some of the units would represent aspects of the visual qualities of the item, and other units would represent aspects of the item's functional roles. The extent to which activation in one unit causes activation in the other units to which it is connected depends on the connection strengths, or *weights*, between the units. Presenting a stimulus to the network results in an initial pattern of activation across the units, with some units being activated and others not. This pattern then begins to change as each unit receives activation from the other units to which it is connected within the network. Eventually, a stable pattern results, with each unit holding a particular activation value as a result of the inputs it is receiving from the other units to which it is connected.[1]

Figure 1 shows the architecture of the model. There are three main pools of units, corresponding to verbal inputs or outputs (name units), visual inputs or outputs (picture units), and semantic memory representations. The semantic memory units are divided into visual units and functional units. There are bi-directional connections between units both within and between pools, with the exception that there are no direct connections between the name and picture units. There are 24 name units; 24 picture units; and 80 semantic memory units, divided into 60 visual semantic and 20 functional semantic units, according to the roughly 3 : 1 ratio obtained in Experiment 1.

The specific processing assumptions of this model are the same as for the distributed memory model of McClelland and Rumelhart (1985). In brief, units can take on continuous activation values between −1 and +1. The weights on the connections between units can take on any real values (positive, negative, or zero). There are no thresholds in the model, and the influence of each unit on the

input to each other unit is just the activation of the influencing unit multiplied by the strength of the relevant connection. Processing is synchronous; that is, on each cycle the total input to each unit is calculated on the basis of the activation levels of the units to which it is connected and the weights on those connections, and the activation levels of all units are then updated simultaneously. Activation levels are updated according to a nonlinear activation function, which keeps activations bounded between −1 and +1. Inputs are presented for 10 cycles.

Ten living and 10 nonliving things were represented as randomly generated patterns of −1 and +1 over all three pools of units. The representation of each item included the full 24 name units and picture units, but only subsets of the semantic memory units to capture the different ratios of visual and functional information in living and nonliving things. Living things were represented with an average of 16.1 visual and 2.1 functional units, and nonliving things were represented with an average of 9.4 visual and 6.7 functional units. All patterns contained both types of semantic memory unit.

A simple error-correcting learning procedure was used to train the network to produce the correct semantic and name pattern when presented with each picture pattern, and the correct semantic and picture pattern when presented with each name pattern. On each training trial, the name of the picture corresponding to one of the living or nonliving things was presented to the name or picture input units, and the network was allowed to settle for 10 cycles. The weights among the units were then adjusted using the delta rule (Rumelhart, Hinton, & McClelland, 1986) to minimize the difference between the resultant activation of each unit and its correct activation.[2] To distribute the work of producing the desired outputs over as much of the network as possible, the weights were all multiplicatively reduced by 2% of their value at the end of each training epoch (i.e., each pass through the full set of 40 training trials). This procedure, known as *weight decay*, tends to keep individual weights from growing large, thereby forcing the network to distribute the associations across a larger number of connections. This results in networks that are more resistant to partial damage. Training was continued for 100 epochs. From the point of view of the training procedure, there are no hidden units, so back-propagation is not necessary.

To assess the generality of results obtained with this model, 4 variants of the model were also tested. The first 2 variants consisted of the exact same architecture and training procedure for setting weights, but with training terminated after 50 and 200 epochs. Although both of these variants were trained sufficiently well that they performed perfectly before damage, the different final patterns of weights might be expected to respond differently to damage. The third variant consisted of the same architecture with a different training procedure. In this case, there was no weight decay, and the network was therefore expected to show less resistance to damage. A fourth variant consisted of the original architecture and training procedure, but with a different proportion of visual and functional semantic units in the model. Because one group of subjects in Experiment 1

identified visual attributes used in defining living and nonliving things, and the other group identified functional attributes used in defining living and nonliving things, the ratio of visual to functional semantic units obtained in Experiment 1 was computed from different subjects' data. Instead of using the results of Experiment 1 to set this ratio in the model, in the third variant, we arbitrarily set the numbers of visual and functional semantic units to be equal (i.e., 40 semantic units of each type). We used the data of Experiment 1 only to set the ratios of visual units in the representations of living and nonliving things and of functional units in the representations of living and nonliving things, which were ratios obtained within subjects. In this version of the model, living things were represented with an average of 10.6 visual and 4.0 functional units, and nonliving things were represented with an average of 6.2 visual and 12.8 functional units. The effects of lesions on the performance of the basic model and its variants were then explored.

EXPERIMENT 2

The goal of this experiment is to test the hypothesis that selective impairments in knowledge of living and nonliving things can be explained by selective damage to visual and functional semantic memory representations, respectively. We test this hypothesis by lesioning the model and observing its performance at associating pictures and names of both living and nonliving things. Picture-naming is a kind of picture–name association task, in which the picture is given and the name must be produced. In this model, picture-naming consists of presenting the picture portion of a pattern in the picture units, letting the network settle, and then reading the resultant pattern in the name units. Matching-to-sample, as used by Warrington and McCarthy (1983, 1987), is another kind of picture–name association task, in which the name is given and the correct picture must be selected from among a choice set. In this model, it consists of presenting the name portion of a pattern in the name units, letting the network settle, and then reading the resultant pattern in the picture units. In each case, the model's performance on each pattern was scored as correct if the resulting pattern matched the correct pattern more closely than any of the other 19 possible patterns.

Method

Twelve types of simulation were run, corresponding to 0%, 20%, 40%, 60%, 80%, and 99% damage to the visual and the functional semantic memory units. The different degrees of damage were brought about by subjecting each unit of the relevant pool of semantic memory units to a 0, .2, .4, .6, .8, or .99 chance of being damaged. Each of the 12 simulations was damaged five times each, with the damage being reapplied to an intact network each time. For each of these simulations, 40 picture–name association trials were run: 20 picture-naming

TABLE 3

Performance of the basic model as measured by probability of correctly associating names and pictures, for living and nonliving things, after different amounts of damage to visual and functional semantic units

	Probability correct for nonliving things		Probability correct for living things	
Amount of damage[a]	M	SE	M	SE
Damage to visual semantic memory				
0	1.00	0	1.00	0
20	0.97	.02	0.98	.02
40	0.91	.04	0.86	.05
60	0.88	.05	0.70	.07
80	0.80	.06	0.22	.06
99	0.73	.06	0.05	.03
Damage to functional semantic memory				
0	1.00	0	1.00	0
20	1.00	0	1.00	0
40	0.93	.04	1.00	0
60	0.88	.05	1.00	0
80	0.87	.05	1.00	0
99	0.73	.06	1.00	0

[a] Amount of damage refers to the percentage of visual or functional semantics units destroyed.

trials, in which each of the picture patterns was presented to the network and the resultant name patterns were scored, and 20 matching-to-sample trials, in which each of the name patterns was presented to the network and the resultant picture patterns scored. This procedure was applied to the original model and to the four variants described earlier.

Results and discussion

Table 3 shows the results from the simulations of visual and functional semantic memory damage to the basic model. When visual semantic memory units are damaged, the effect is greater on the naming of living things than nonliving things. As can be seen in Figure 2, the greater the damage, the greater the dissociation between performance with living and nonliving things. When functional semantic memory units are damaged, the only effect is on nonliving things, and this effect also increases with increasing damage.

The pattern of results obtained with the four variants of the model was similar, as shown in Figures 3–6. Figure 3 shows the results of visual and functional semantic memory damage when learning was terminated after half as many trials as in the basic model. Figure 4 shows the results of lesioning visual and functional

Basic model

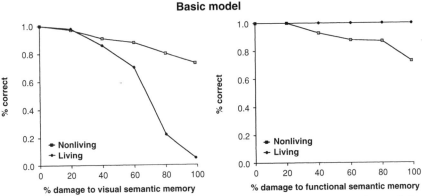

Figure 2. Performance of the basic model, as measured by probability of correctly associating names and pictures, for living and nonliving things, after different amounts of damage to visual and functional semantic units. (Experiment 2.)

Training stopped after 50 cycles

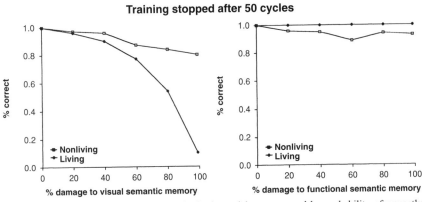

Figure 3. Performance of one variant of the basic model, as measured by probability of correctly associating names and pictures, for living and nonliving things, after damage to visual and functional semantic units, with training stopped after 50 epochs. (Experiment 2.)

semantic memory when learning continued for twice as long as in the basic model. In both variants, visual semantic memory damage affects performance with living things more than with nonliving things, and functional semantic memory damage affects performance with nonliving things more than with living things. Figure 5 shows the effects of semantic memory damage on the model trained without weight decay. Damage has a much larger effect overall on the performance of this model, consistent with the tendency of weight decay to produce more distributed and thus more robust representations. However, as in the previous models, damage to visual semantics impairs performance on living things more than on nonliving things, and damage to functional semantics has the opposite

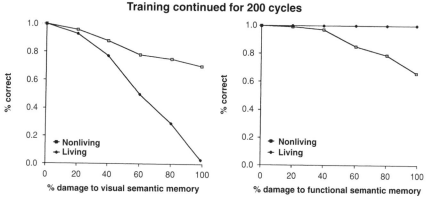

Figure 4. Performance of one variant of the basic model, as measured by probability of correctly associating names and pictures, for living and nonliving things, after damage to visual and functional semantic units, with training continued for 200 epochs. (Experiment 2.)

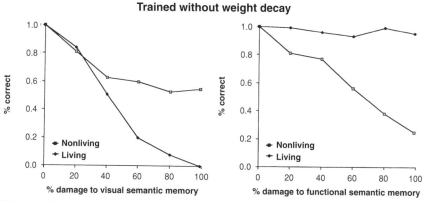

Figure 5. Performance of one variant of the basic model, as measured by probability of correctly associating names and pictures, for living and nonliving things, after damage to visual and functional semantic units, trained without weight decay. (Experiment 2.)

effect. Figure 6 shows the results of lesioning a model in which the overall numbers of visual and functional semantic memory units were arbitrarily set to be equal, with the ratios of each type of semantic memory attribute in the representations of items being set by the within-subjects data from Experiment 1, as before. As in the previous models, lesioning visual semantics causes disproportionate impairment of performance with living things, and lesioning functional semantics causes disproportionate impairment of performance with nonliving things.

Another way of assessing the effects of damage to either visual or functional semantics on the network's knowledge of living and nonliving things is to compare the pattern of activation obtained in the semantic units after damage

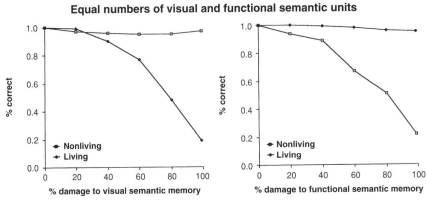

Figure 6. Performance of one variant of the basic model, as measured by probability of correctly associating names and pictures, for living and nonliving things, after damage to visual and functional semantic units, with equal numbers of visual and functional semantic units. (Experiment 2.)

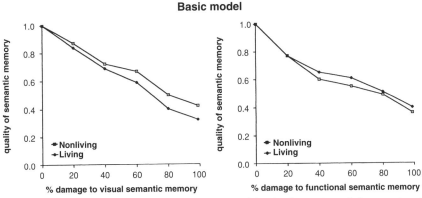

Figure 7. Performance of the basic model, as measured by the dot product of the correct and obtained semantic patterns, for living and nonliving things, after different amounts of damage to visual and functional semantic units. (Experiment 2.)

when a picture or name is presented with that obtained before damage. One way to quantify this comparison is using the dot product of the pattern obtained and the target pattern. The bigger the dot product, the better the match. Table 4 and Figure 7 show the average dot products, normalized to 1 for the undamaged network, for the semantic memory patterns after different degrees of damage to visual and functional semantics for the basic model. Figures 8–11 show the same information graphically for the four variants of the basic model. The dot product indicate that damage to visual semantics impairs the semantic representation of living things more than nonliving things and damage to functional semantics has the opposite effect.

TABLE 4
Performance of the basic model, as measured by the dot
product of the correct and obtained semantic patterns, for
living and nonliving things, after different amounts of
damage to visual and functional semantics units

	Scaled dot product of semantic units for nonliving things		Scaled dot product of semantic units for living things	
Amount of damage[a]	M	SE	M	SE
Damage to visual semantic memory				
0	1.00	0	1.00	0
20	0.87	.02	0.84	.02
40	0.72	.02	0.69	.02
60	0.67	.02	0.59	.02
80	0.50	.01	0.40	.02
99	0.42	.01	0.32	.01
Damage to functional semantic memory				
0	1.00	0	1.00	0
20	0.77	.02	0.77	.02
40	0.60	.02	0.65	.02
60	0.55	.02	0.61	.02
80	0.49	.02	0.51	.02
99	0.36	.01	0.40	.01

[a] *Amount of damage* refers to the percentage of visual or functional semantic units destroyed.

In summary, the basic prediction of the sensory–functional hypothesis was borne out: Damage to visual semantic memory impaired knowledge of living things to a greater extent than nonliving things, and damage to functional semantic memory impaired knowledge of nonliving things to a greater extent than living things. This result was general across five different implementations of the model and across two different ways of measuring model performance.

EXPERIMENT 3

Earlier it was noted that at least some cases of living things impairment are impaired at accessing functional as well as visual information about living things. On the face of things, this phenomenon seems to disconfirm the sensory–functional hypothesis and requires that the model incorporate into its architecture an explicit distinction between knowledge of living and nonliving things. The goal of this experiment is to find out whether the model can account for impaired access to functional information about living things after damage to visual semantic memory units.

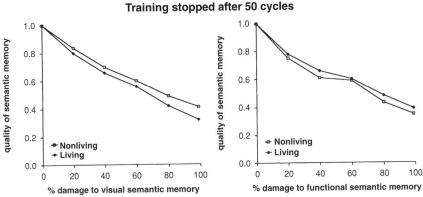

Figure 8. Performance of one variant of the basic model, as measured by the dot product of the correct and obtained semantic patterns, for living and nonliving things, after damage to visual and functional semantic units, with training stopped after 50 epochs. (Experiment 3.)

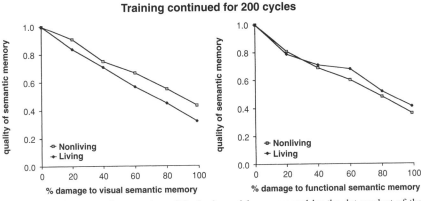

Figure 9. Performance of one variant of the basic model, as measured by the dot product of the correct and obtained semantic patterns, for living and nonliving things, after damage to visual and functional semantic units, with training continued for 200 epochs. (Experiment 3.)

If it were the case that representations need a certain "critical mass" to become activated—so that even if a portion of the representation were spared by brain damage, it could not be accessed in the absence of other parts of the representation —then the sensory–functional hypothesis could explain the apparent across-the-board impairments in knowledge of living things as follows: Given that most of the semantic memory features in the representations of living things are visual features, and they have been destroyed, then those few functional features associated with the representation might lack the critical mass to become activated. In fact, most PDP models display just this critical mass effect. The effect arises because the ability of any given unit to attain and hold its proper activation value

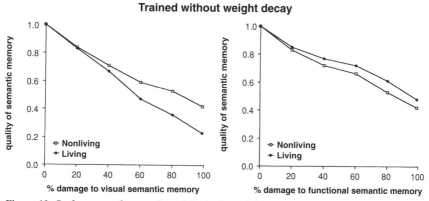

Figure 10. Performance of one variant of the basic model, as measured by the dot product of the correct and obtained semantic patterns, for living and nonliving things, after damage to visual and functional semantic units, trained without weight decay. (Experiment 3.)

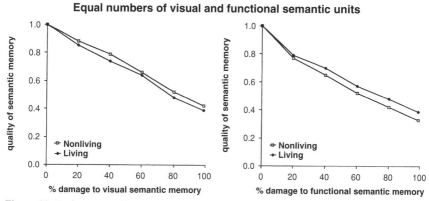

Figure 11. Performance of one variant of the basic model, as measured by the dot product of the correct and obtained semantic patterns, for living and nonliving things, after damage to visual and functional semantic units, with equal numbers of visual and functional semantic units. (Experiment 3.)

depends on collateral connections with other units in the network. Although PDP systems are robust to small amounts of damage, if a large proportion of the units participating in a given representation are destroyed, the remaining units will not receive the necessary collateral inputs to achieve their proper activation values.

Method

Rather than elaborate the model with additional pools of input and output units to represent questions and answers, for the purpose of simulating question-answering tasks, we have assessed the availability of functional semantic memory

TABLE 5

Performance of the basic model for functional knowledge of
living and nonliving things, as measured by the dot product
of the correct and obtained functional semantic patterns, after
different amounts of damage to visual semantic units

Amount of damage[a]	Scaled dot product of functional semantic units for nonliving things		Scaled dot product of functional semantic units for living things	
	M	SE	M	SE
0	1.00	0	1.00	0
20	0.95	.02	0.92	.03
40	0.91	.02	0.84	.02
60	0.89	.02	0.80	.03
80	0.84	.02	0.70	.03
99	0.81	.02	0.65	.03

[a] *Amount of damage* refers to the percentage of visual semantic units destroyed.

information in the model directly: Input patterns (names or pictures) were pre-sented, the network was allowed to settle, and the resultant patterns of activation in the functional semantic memory units were recorded. As in the previous experiment, the quality of the semantic memory representation was measured by a normalized dot product, in this case, in just the functional semantic memory units. The procedures for training and damaging the model were the same as for Experiment 2.

Results and discussion

Table 5 and Figure 12 show the average scaled dot products of the obtained and correct functional semantic memory patterns for living and nonliving things, at each degree of damage to the visual semantic memory units. As predicted, damage to visual semantic memory impairs access to functional semantic memory disproportionately for living things. As can be seen in Figure 13, essentially the same results were obtained for the four variants of the basic model described earlier. The different variants display the effect to different degrees, but all show the same qualitative pattern, namely, impaired activation of functional semantic memory, more so for living than nonliving things, after visual semantic memory damage.

Although damage to visual semantic memory impairs retrieval of functional knowledge of living things, it affects functional knowledge of living things less than visual knowledge. This can be seen by comparing Figures 7–11, which show the dot products of the obtained and correct pattern over all of semantics after

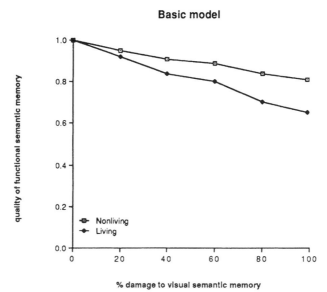

Figure 12. Performance of the basic model for functional knowledge of living and nonliving things, as measured by the dot product of the correct and obtained functional semantic patterns, after different amounts of damage to visual semantic units. (Experiment 3.)

visual semantic damage, to Figures 12 and 13, which show the dot products for functional semantics in particular. This pattern is consistent with the behavior of the patients reviewed earlier, whose impairments in knowledge of living things tend to be more obvious in the visual than in the functional domain.

EXPERIMENT 4

A third type of dissociation involving living and nonliving things was recently described by McCarthy and Warrington (1988). They described a patient with progressive aphasia and left temporal hypometabolism of unstated etiology. This subject's knowledge of living things appeared to be impaired only when tested verbally. As shown in Table 6, he was able to identify pictures of both living and nonliving things and to define nonliving things that were named aloud to him. However, he was impaired at defining living things that were named aloud. Table 6 also shows examples of his responses to visually and verbally probed animals.

In their discussion of this patient, McCarthy and Warrington (1988) suggested that the pattern of impaired and preserved performance implies that semantic memory may be subdivided by both category and modality of access. According-ing to this interpretation, there is one store of knowledge about living things for access by verbal systems, another store of knowledge about living things for

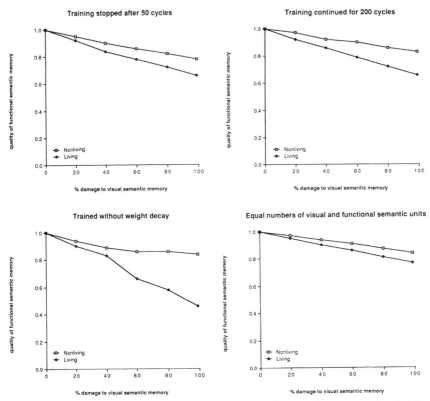

Figure 13. Performance of the four variants of the basic model for functional knowledge of living and nonliving things, as measured by the dot product of the correct and obtained functional semantic patterns, after different amounts of damage to visual semantic units. ([top left] Training stopped after 50 epochs. [top right] Training continued for 200 epochs. [bottom left] Trained without weight decay. [bottom right] Equal numbers of visual and functional semantic units.) (Experiment 3.)

TABLE 6
Performance of a patient whose semantic memory impairment was
confined to knowledge of living things when probed verbally

Probe	% of living things identified	% of nonliving things identified
Spoken word	33%	89%
Picture	94%	98%

Examples of identifications of living things include *rhinoceros* (spoken word: "animal, can't give you any functions"; picture: "enormous, weighs over 1 ton, lives in Africa") and *dolphin* (spoken word: "a fish or a bird"; picture: "dolphin lives in water ... they are trained to jump up and come out ... In America during the war they started to get this particular animal to go through to look into ships."

access by visual systems, a store of knowledge about nonliving things for verbal access, and so on. The goal of this experiment was to simulate the behavior of McCarthy and Warrington's case with the present model, which does not have separate knowledge stores either for living and nonliving things or for different input modalities. This was accomplished by damaging the connections between the name units and the visual semantics units.

Method

The model was damaged by destroying the connections that go from the name units to the visual semantics memory units. Six different simulations were run, corresponding to different degrees of damage to these connections: destruction of 0%, 20%, 40%, 60%, 80%, and 100% of the connections between name and visual semantics units, randomly chosen. As in Experiment 2, the performance of the network after damage was tested in two ways. First, we scored the percentage of trials on which, given a picture, the correct name could be selected or, given a name, the correct picture could be selected. Second, we calculated the normalized dot product between the obtained and target semantic memory patterns when either a picture or name was presented.

Results and discussion

Table 7 and Figure 14 show the percentage correct for name–picture association after different degrees of damage to connections from name units to visual semantics units in the basic model. Like the case of McCarthy and Warrington (1988), the impairment of the model has both category specificity and modality specificity. The model is by far the most impaired with living things presented verbally, next most impaired with nonliving things presented verbally, and least impaired with pictures of either living or nonliving things. One curious aspect of the model's performance is the better comprehension of the names of nonliving things when the connections between names and visual semantics are entirely destroyed than when they are 80% destroyed. The poor performance at 80% disconnection is interpretable as a kind of interference caused by the extremely noisy patterns of activation entering the semantics units from the name units. The 20% remaining connections evidently produce inappropriate patterns of activation in the visual semantics units, thereby interfering with the ability of collateral connections from functional semantics to activate the correct patterns in visual semantics.

Figure 15 shows the performance of the four variants of the model when damaged and then tested as just described. The same qualitative pattern of results is found in each case, with the worst performance by far found for named living things.

Table 8 and Figure 16 show the average normalized dot products of the obtained and correct semantic memory patterns for living and nonliving things,

TABLE 7

Performance of the basic model, as measured by probability
of correctly associating names and pictures, for living and
nonliving things, probed verbally and pictorially, after
different degrees of damage to the connections linking
name units to visual units

Amount of damage[a]	Probability correct for nonliving things		Probability correct for living things	
	M	SE	M	SE
Picture				
0	1.00	0	1.00	0
20	1.00	0	1.00	0
40	1.00	0	1.00	0
60	1.00	0	1.00	0
80	1.00	0	1.00	0
99	1.00	0	1.00	0
Name				
0	1.00	0	1.00	0
20	0.98	.02	0.92	.04
40	0.92	.04	0.90	.04
60	0.76	.06	0.56	.07
80	0.66	.07	0.30	.07
99	0.80	.06	0.00	0

[a] *Amount of damage* refers to the percentage of name–visual semantic connections destroyed.

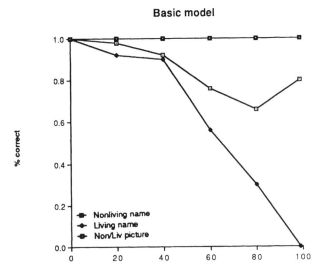

Basic model

Figure 14. Performance of the basic model, as measured by probability of correctly associating names and pictures, for living and nonliving things, probed verbally and pictorially, after different degrees of damage to the connections linking name units to visual units. (*Non/Liv* indicates nonliving or living.)

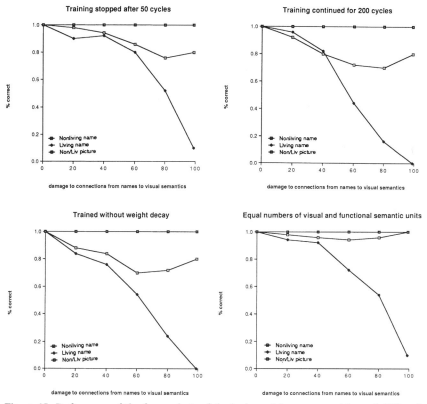

Figure 15. Performance of the four variants of the basic model, as measured by probability of correctly associating names and pictures, for living and nonliving things, probed verbally and pictorially, after different degrees of damage to the connections linking name units to visual units. ([top left] Training stopped after 50 epochs. [top right] Training continued for 200 epochs. [bottom left] Trained without weight decay. [bottom right] Equal numbers of visual and functional semantic units. *Non/Liv* indicates nonliving or living.) (Experiment 4.)

presented as names and pictures, for the basic model. Figure 17 shows the same measures for the four other versions of the model. The dot products reveal essentially the same qualitative pattern of performance as the percentage correct measure. The activation of semantic memory by pictures is relatively unimpaired at all levels of damage in this model, whereas the activation of semantic memory by names is impaired, particularly for the names of living things.

In summary, we have shown that the behavior of McCarthy and Warrington's (1988) patient can be accounted for in a relatively parsimonious way, by postulating damaged connections between name units and visual semantics units. One possible objection to this account is based on McCarthy and Warrington's observation that the patient's performance was consistent, in terms of specific items failed, from testing session to testing session. It has been proposed (Shallice,

TABLE 8

Performance of the basic model, as measured by the dot
product of the correct and obtained semantic patterns for
living and nonliving things, probed verbally and pictorially,
after different degrees of damage to the connections linking
name units to visual units

	Scaled dot product in semantic units for nonliving things		Scaled dot product in semantic units for living things	
Amount of damage[a]	M	SE	M	SE
Picture				
0	1.00	0	1.00	0
20	0.98	.01	0.98	.01
40	0.96	.01	0.96	.01
60	0.94	.01	0.94	.01
80	0.92	.01	0.92	.01
99	0.90	.01	0.90	.01
Name				
0	1.00	0	1.00	0
20	0.94	.01	0.91	.01
40	0.87	.01	0.79	.02
60	0.76	.02	0.63	.02
80	0.68	.01	0.46	.03
99	0.58	.02	0.23	.03

[a] *Amount of damage* refers to the percentage of name–visual semantic connections destroyed.

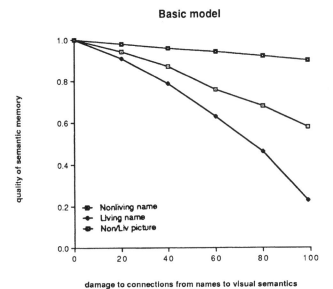

Figure 16. Performance of the basic model, as measured by the dot product of the correct and obtained semantic patterns for living and nonliving things, probed verbally and pictorially, after different degrees of damage to the connections linking name units to visual units. (*Non/Liv* indicates nonliving or living.)

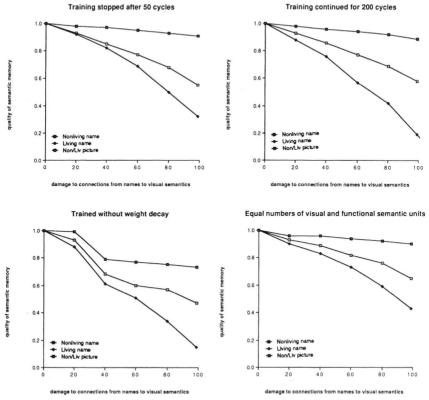

Figure 17. Performance of the four variants of the basic model, as measured by the dot product of the correct and obtained semantic patterns for living and nonliving things, probed verbally and pictorially, after different degrees of damage to the connections linking name units to visual units. ([top left] Training stopped after 50 epochs. [top right] Training continued for 200 epochs. [bottom left] Trained without weight decay. [bottom right] Equal numbers of visual and functional semantic units. *Non/Liv* indicates nonliving or living.) (Experiment 4.)

1987) that consistency implies damage to representations, whereas impaired access to representations should lead to variable performance. It is certainly true that some types of access disorders would lead to variable performance (e.g., noise in a telephone line). However, in the context of the present model, it can be seen that there is no necessary relation between disorders of representation versus access, on the one hand, and damage to units versus connections, on the other. Damage to connections in this model leads to high consistency in items failed. This is because certain connections are more important for activating some representations than others, and so whenever a given subset of connections is destroyed, the subset of representations that is most dependent on those connections will always suffer.

GENERAL DISCUSSION

The existence of selective impairments for knowledge of living and nonliving things would seem to imply that the architecture of semantic memory consists of at least some taxonomically defined components. However, we have shown that a simple model of semantic memory with only modality-specific components can account for all three types of category-specific semantic memory impairment that have been observed with patients. Let us examine some of the general implications of these findings for cognitive psychology and neuropsychology as well as some cautions that should be borne in mind while interpreting the results of our model.

Limitations of the present model

The model we have presented here is a simple one, designed to test some very general principles concerning the relations between modality-specific and category-specific knowledge. Our goal was to determine whether these principles could account for certain general findings that have emerged across a number of different studies of patients with different impairments in semantic memory. We have not attempted to provide a detailed account of the ways that semantic memory is used in naming pictures, defining words, and so on, or of the precise nature of the damage in cases of semantic memory impairment.

For example, the model has only two kinds of semantic memory representations: visual and functional. We could have added semantics derived from other perceptual modalities (e.g., auditory, tactile), and we could have subdivided the fairly general concept of *functional* semantic memory into more specific components. Whereas such elaborations of the model might change the sizes of the dissociations found here, they would probably not change the basic qualitative patterns (unless the proportions of added semantic units were negatively correlated with the visual and functional units in terms of the numbers participating in the representations of living and nonliving things).

Another way in which the model is simplified and unrealistic is that there is no difference between name and picture representations in the kinds of relations they have with semantic memory. For example, it might be expected that the perceptual representations of pictures would have a closer (more systematic, more robust, or both) set of connections with the visual semantic representations than the name representations have. If we had included this difference in the model, differences between the size of the dissociation found in picture-naming compared with purely verbal tasks, such as definitions, might have been found. Specifically, one might expect the effects of damage to visual semantics to be more pronounced in tasks involving picture processing. There is a hint of such a difference in the patients' data shown in Table 1.

For simplicity's sake, we have also assumed that the effects of brain damage can be simulated by destroying the neuron-like units or the connections between such units. However, the effects of herpes encephalitis, head injury, and stroke

on neural functioning may be more fully captured by the combined effects of destroying units and connections as well as by other changes to the network, such as adding noise to the connection strengths or to the activation levels of the units, changing the maximal activation values of the units, or changing the rate at which activation decays. These different ways of damaging the network would be expected to have slightly different effects on its performance after damage. For example, adding noise to a certain pool of units would lead to low consistency in the particular test items failed from one test to another, whereas destroying units or connections would lead to high consistency. Nevertheless, these differences would not change the basic patterns concerning the category specificity and modality specificity of the deficits reported here.

A final word of caution in relating our simple model to patient behavior is that the measures of performance that we have used with the model are not the same as those that have been used with patients. The 20-alternative, forced-choice picture–name association task is somewhat similar to the picture-naming and matching-to-sample tasks that have been used with patients, but reading the dot product of the actual and expected semantic memory patterns is quite an abstraction from the question-answering tasks used with patients. This problem is, however, not unique to comparisons between computer simulations and patients. Different patients have been studied with different tasks, which makes precise interpatient comparisons impossible as well. However, the difficulties with neither precise interpatient nor simulation–patient comparisons prevent us from generalizing about common qualitative patterns of impairment and their possible underlying causes.

We also wish to note that the present model is not intended to account for category-specific impairments in cognitive systems other than semantic memory. Selective dissociations have been documented within the visual recognition system, affecting just face recognition or just printed-word recognition (e.g., Farah, 1991) and, within the lexical system, affecting name retrieval for categories as specific as colors, letters, or body parts (e.g., Goodglass, Wingfield, Hyde, & Theurkauf, 1986). From the point of view of the present model, these impairments would be located in the "visual" and "verbal" input systems, which we have not attempted to model with any verisimilitude. Our results are relevant to these other category-specific phenomena only in a very general way: They alert us to the fact that every neuropsychological dissociation need not have a corresponding distinction in the cognitive architecture.

General implications

Having enumerated some of the ways in which the present model may be incomplete or inaccurate in detail and some neuropsychological phenomena that it is not intended to explain, we now review the general principles that the model has been successful in demonstrating. First, the model has shown how category-

specific impairments can arise after damage to a system that has no category-specific components. Specifically, it has shown how impairments in knowledge of living things and nonliving things—and even impairments in knowledge of living things when just probed verbally—can be accounted for without postulating a semantic memory system with any inherently category-specific components. Instead, these impairments can all be accounted for by a relatively simple semantic memory architecture, in which there are just two components of semantic memory, which differ from one another by modality and not by category.

The ability of a modality-specific semantic memory architecture to account for category-specific semantic memory impairments depends, of course, on there being a correlation between modality of knowledge and category of knowledge. In this case, this ability depends on the fact that living things are known primarily through their visual attributes, which was suggested years ago by Warrington and her colleagues, and which we verified in Experiment 1. One way of describing the relation between the living–nonliving distinction and the visual–functional distinction is that they are confounded, in the same way that we might speak of confounded factors in an experiment. However, such a description does not fully capture the degree to which the impairments are category-specific. In patients with impaired knowledge of living things, knowledge about functional properties of living things is also impaired. This is true of the model as well and can be explained in terms of a very general property of distributed representations, in which the different parts of the representation provide mutual support for one another. Although such representations are robust to small amounts of damage, larger amounts will deprive the intact parts of the representation of needed support. As a result, even those intact parts will be unable to attain their proper activation levels. Thus, category specificity is an emergent property of the network under certain kinds of damage.

Figure 1 is a box-and-arrow outline of our model, showing the different types of representations involved in semantic memory and their relations to one another. This is the level of description at which most models are cast in cognitive neuropsychology. In many cases, this level of detail has been sufficient, and many cognitive impairments have been successfully interpreted as the simple deletion of a box or an arrow. However, the semantic memory impairments discussed here provide an example of the limitations of this approach and of the need to understand what goes on within the boxes. As discussed earlier, it is not apparent why damage to the visual semantic memory component of the model would result in impaired access to functional semantic memory knowledge about living things. To explain this, in the context of the model shown in Figure 1 at any rate, one must describe the system at a more detailed level of analysis, which includes the internal workings of the boxes. The effect of visual semantic memory damage on functional knowledge of living things can be explained in terms of the kinds of representations and computations taking place inside the outlined components in Figure 1. In more general terms, the macrostructure of

the system's behavior—what categories or modalities of knowledge are spared or impaired—does not just depend on the macrostructure of the system: for example, what different categories or modalities of knowledge there are and which has access to which other. It also depends on the microstructure of the system: how items are represented within each box and how representations in one box activate representations in other boxes.

The question of whether PDP models accurately reflect the microstructure of human cognition is a controversial one, which cannot be settled on the basis of any single result. Nevertheless, the present results suggest that two very general properties of PDP models are explanatory of some otherwise puzzling phenomena and hence provide some degree of confirmation for the psychological reality of at least these properties of PDP. The first property is the involvement of all parts of a network, directly or indirectly, in the computations that intervene between an input in one part of the system and an output in another part. This property accounts naturally for the effects of damage localized to one part of semantic memory on the ability to associate names and pictures of items that are represented in still-intact parts of semantic memory. At the macroscopic level of analysis, it is not clear why eliminating one of two or more possible routes from pictures to names (such as pictures to functional semantics to names) should result in impaired ability to associate pictures with their names, so long as another possible route (such as pictures to visual semantics to names) is still intact. The second of these properties is the need for collateral support in activating one portion of a representation from other parts of the same representation. This property accounts naturally for the effects of damage to visual semantics on the retrieval of functional information about living things. Again, at the macroscopic level of analysis, it is not clear why loss of knowledge of the appearance of something would affect the ability to access knowledge of its functions. Thus, the explanatory power of the model presented here depends on it having these properties of PDP models. The PDP mechanisms are not an incidental aspect of the model's implementation; rather, they play a crucial explanatory role.

ACKNOWLEDGEMENTS

This research was supported by Office of Naval Research Grant NS0014-89-J3016, National Institute of Mental Health (NIMH) Grant R01 MH48274, National Institutes of Health Career Development Award K04-NS01405, NIMH Career Development Award MH00385, and National Science Foundation Grant BNS 88-12048. We thank Robin Rochlin for assistance in data collection.

NOTES

1. Many recent connectionist models, such as the models of spelling-to-sound translation of Rosenberg and Sejnowski (1986) or Seidenberg and McClelland (1989), have used only unidirectional connections from input by way of internal units to output and have computed activations in a single, feed-forward pass. At least in the latter case, the use of a feed-forward architecture was a

simplification adopted for the sake of tractability and did not represent a change of principle in favor of feed-forward information processing.

2. Note that the training procedure is not meant to simulate the process by which people acquire semantic memory knowledge. It is merely a tool for creating a pattern of connection strengths that embodies the assumed associations between patterns in the different pools of units.

REFERENCES

American Heritage Dictionary. (1969). New York: American Heritage Publishing Co.

Anderson, J. A., Silverstein, J. W., Ritz, S. A., & Jones, R. S. (1977). Distinctive features, categorical perception and probability learning: Some applications of a neural model. *Psychological Review, 84*, 413–451.

Basso, A., Capitani, E., & Laiacona, M. (1988). Progressive language impairment without dementia: A case with isolated category specific semantic defect. *Journal of Neurology, Neurosurgery and Psychiatry, 51*, 1201–1207.

Farah, M. J. (1991). Patterns of co-occurrence among the associative agnosias: Implications for visual object representation. *Cognitive Neuropsychology, 8*, 1–19.

Farah, M. J., Hammond, K. H., Mehta, Z., & Ratcliff, G. (1989). Category-specificity and modality-specificity in semantic memory. *Neuropsychologia, 27*, 193–200.

Farah, M. J., McMullen, P. A., & Meyer, M. M. (1991). Can recognition of living things be selectively impaired? *Neuropsychologia, 29*, 185–193.

Goodglass, H., & Baker, E. (1976). Semantic field, naming, and auditory comprehension in aphasia. *Brain and Language, 3*, 359–374.

Goodglass, H., Wingfield, A., Hyde, M. R., & Theurkauf, J. C. (1986). Category-specific dissociations in naming and recognition by aphasic patients. *Cortex, 22*, 87–102.

Hinton, G. E., McClelland, J. L., & Rumelhart, D. E. (1986). Distributed representations. In D. E. Rumelhart & J. L. McClelland (Eds.), *Parallel distributed processing: Explorations in the microstructure of cognition* (pp. 77–109). Cambridge, MA: MIT Press.

McCarthy, R. A., & Warrington, E. K. (1988). Evidence for modality-specific meaning systems in the brain. *Nature, 334*, 428–430.

McClelland, J. L., & Rumelhart, D. E. (1985). Distributed memory and the representation of general and specific information. *Journal of Experimental Psychology: General, 114*, 159–188.

Newcombe, F., Mehta, Z., & de Haan, E. F. (1994). Category specificity in visual recognition. In M. J. Farah & G. Ratcliff (Eds.), *The neuropsychology of high-level vision: Collected tutorial essays*. Hillsdale, NJ: Lawrence Erlbaum Associates Inc.

Pietrini, V., Nertimpi, T., Vaglia, A., Revollo, M. G., Pinna, V., & Ferro-Milone, F. (1988). Recovery from herpes simplex encephalitis: Selective impairment of specific semantic categories with neuroradiological correlation. *Journal of Neurology, Neurosurgery, and Psychiatry, 51*, 1284–1293.

Rosenberg, C. R., & Sejnowski, T. K. (1986). *NETtalk: A parallel network that learns to read aloud* (EE & CS Tech. Rep. No. JHU/EECS-86/01). Baltimore, MD: Johns Hopkins University.

Rumelhart, D. E., Hinton, G. E., & McClelland, J. L. (1986). A general framework for parallel distributed processing. In D. E. Rumelhart & J. L. McClelland (Eds.), *Parallel distributed processing: Explorations in the microstructure of cognition* (pp. 45–76). Cambridge, MA: MIT Press.

Sartori, G., & Job, R. (1988). The oyster with four legs: A neuropsychological study on the interaction of visual and semantic information. *Cognitive Neuropsychology, 5*, 105–132.

Seidenberg, M. S., & McClelland, J. L. (1989). A distributed, developmental model of word recognition and naming. *Psychological Review, 96*, 523–568.

Sereno, M. I., & Allman, J. M. (1991). Cortical visual areas in mammals. In A. G. Leventhal (Ed.), *The neural basis of visual function* (pp. 160–172). London: Macmillan.

Shallice, T. (1987). Impairments of semantic processing: Multiple dissociations. In M. Coltheart, G. Sartori, & R. Job (Eds.), *The cognitive neuropsychology of language*. Hove, UK: Lawrence Erlbaum Associates Ltd.

Silveri, M. C., & Gainotti, G. (1988). Interaction between vision and language in category-specific semantic impairment. *Cognitive Neuropsychology, 5*, 677–709.

Warrington, E. K., & McCarthy, R. (1983). Category specific access dysphasia. *Brain, 106*, 859–878.

Warrington, E. K., & McCarthy, R. (1987). Categories of knowledge: Further fractionation and an attempted integration. *Brain, 110*, 1273–1296.

Warrington, E. K., & Shallice, T. (1984). Category specific semantic impairments. *Brain, 107*, 829–854.

Category-specific semantic deficits in focal and widespread brain damage: A computational account

Joseph T. Devlin, Laura M. Gonnerman, Elaine S. Andersen, and Mark S. Seidenberg
University of Southern California, USA

Category-specific semantic impairments have been explained in terms of preferential damage to different types of features (e.g., perceptual vs. functional). This account is compatible with cases in which the impairments were the result of relatively focal lesions, as in herpes encephalitis. Recently, however, there have been reports of category-specific impairments associated with Alzheimer's disease, in which there is more widespread, patchy damage. We present experiments with a connectionist model that show how "category-specific" impairments can arise in cases of both localized and widespread damage; in this model, types of features are topographically organized, but specific categories are not. These effects mainly depend on differences between categories in the distribution of correlated features. The model's predictions about degree of impairment on natural kinds and artifacts over the course of semantic deterioration are shown to be consistent with existing patient data. The model shows how the probabilistic nature of damage in Alzheimer's disease interacts with the structure of semantic memory to yield different patterns of impairment between patients and categories over time.

INTRODUCTION

Semantic memory impairments can be caused by several types of neuropathology, including Alzheimer's disease (e.g., Nebes, 1989), herpes simplex encephalitis (e.g., Warrington & Shallice, 1984), and cerebrovascular accidents (e.g., Hart & Gordon, 1990). A goal of research on such impairments is to understand them in terms of damage to the normal semantic system. Connectionist modeling has

Journal of Cognitive Neuroscience, 10:1 pp. 77–94.

provided a useful tool in pursuing this goal. This approach involves implement-ing semantic networks using the units, weights, learning algorithms, and other components of the connectionist approach (Rumelhart & McClelland, 1986). Semantic memory impairments can then be simulated by introducing anomalies in the computational model (e.g., Hinton & Shallice, 1991; Plaut & Shallice, 1993). Such simulations can provide important clues concerning the organization of semantic memory and the bases of semantic impairments. Although these models have as yet incorporated only very general neurobiological constraints, they represent a step along the path toward understanding how semantic informa-tion is represented and processed in the brain.

An example of this approach is provided by recent work on category-specific semantic impairments. Warrington and her colleagues (Warrington & McCarthy, 1983, 1987; Warrington & Shallice, 1984) observed a striking double dissocia-tion in the residual semantic abilities of six subjects after focal brain injury. Two were impaired in their ability to recognize pictures of artifacts compared to pictures of food and animals. Four others displayed the opposite pattern: They were impaired at naming pictures of animals and food compared to pictures of artifacts. The authors interpreted this double dissociation as indicating that arti-facts and natural kinds could be preferentially affected by brain damage. Certain categories proved problematical for this division, however. One patient, JBR, suffered from a natural kinds deficit but was also impaired on musical instruments, gemstones, and fabrics. He also had preserved knowledge of body parts, which might be considered a natural kinds category. Patient YOT, on the other hand, had an artifacts deficit that included body parts but not musical instruments, gemstones, or fabrics. This pattern led Warrington and McCarthy to recast the distinction between artifacts and natural kinds as one between functional and perceptual features as follows (Warrington & McCarthy, 1987, p. 1275):

> We have ... argued for a refinement of the animate/inanimate dichotomy and suggested that a distinction cast in terms of the relevant salience of processing functional/physical (also termed sensory) attributes might account for these dissociations. Thus similar items from the broad category of objects are primarily comprehended in terms of their core functional significance, physical attributes being of less importance for their differentiation. ... Food and living things by contrast are differentiated primarily in terms of their physical attributes.

This pattern of results has now been observed several times (see Saffran & Schwartz, 1994, for a review). Artifact categories such as musical instruments pattern with natural kinds categories such as animals because musical instru-ments, which have similar functions, are largely distinguished from one another on the basis of perceptual properties. Conversely, body parts are natural entities that may pattern with artifacts because their functions are highly relevant to distinguishing among them. Category-specific impairments can then be seen as secondary to selective damage to different types of features.[1]

Farah and McClelland (1991) developed a connectionist model based on these insights. They derived an empirical estimate of the relative frequency of the two types of features, which yielded a 3:1 ratio of visual to functional features overall. More significantly, this ratio varied from 7.7:1 for natural kinds to 1.4:1 for artifacts. Thus, both types of features are relevant to both domains, but for the natural kinds, perceptual features are much more important than functional ones, whereas for the artifacts they are more equally important. Farah and McClelland incorporated these observations about the proportions of featural types in a connectionist model that took a representation of either a picture or a word as input and generated its semantic representation as output. The trained model was then damaged in differing degrees by eliminating either visual or functional semantic features. Damage to visual features yielded a selective impairment for natural kinds, while removing functional features resulted in a deficit specific to artifacts. In both cases the severity of the deficit was correlated with an increase in semantic damage. Thus, the model produced category-specific deficits even though its semantic representation was not organized by category. "Category specificity" was seen as an emergent property of the semantic system arising from the underlying distribution of perceptual and functional semantic features.

In addition to reproducing the basic patterns of impaired behavior, the Farah and McClelland (1991) model explained the additional finding that several subjects with natural kinds deficits also exhibit impaired functional knowledge on the same items (Basso, Capitani, & Laiacona, 1988; Sartori & Job; 1988; Silveri & Gainotti, 1988). For example, Silveri and Gainotti described a patient with a severe natural kinds deficit who had difficulty naming animals from visual descriptions (e.g., "a black-and-white striped wild horse" for zebra; 11% correct) and from nonvisual descriptions (e.g., "the farm animal which bleats and supplies us with wool" for sheep; 58% correct). Farah and McClelland argued that the deficit in functional knowledge was a secondary result of damage to perceptual features. In their view, the conjunction of visual and functional features that forms an object's semantic representation constitutes a single stable pattern such that without a "critical mass" of activated features the integrity of the entire representation suffers. Their model demonstrated that damage to perceptual features had secondary effects on the activation of functional features because of the connections between them. For instance, having removed 40% of the model's visual features, they found a degraded pattern of activation over the functional features for natural kinds.

Category-specific impairments in Alzheimer's disease

The work of Warrington and colleagues (Warrington & McCarthy, 1983, 1987; Warrington & Shallice, 1984) and of Farah and McClelland (1991) speaks directly to the structure of the normal semantic system, suggesting that information

must be topographically organized such that focal brain damage can preferentially affect either perceptual or functional features. Given that we accept a topographically organized system, it is not obvious how nonfocal neuropathologies, such as the widespread, patchy damage found in Alzheimer's disease (AD), could produce the same kinds of semantic impairments. It is therefore of considerable theoretical interest that there have been two recent reports of category-specific impairments associated with Alzheimer's disease (Mazzoni, Moretti, Lucchini, Vista, & Muratorio, 1991; Silveri, Daniele, Giustolisi, & Gainotti, 1991).

Both studies examined the behavior of subjects with probable AD and found selective deficits in natural kinds compared to artifacts. The authors noted that the AD subjects were impaired in the same domain, natural kinds, as were herpes simplex encephalitis (HSE) patients who have been reported to have category-specific impairments (e.g., Pietrini, Nertempi, Vaglia, Revello, Pinna, & Ferro-Milone, 1988), despite significant differences in the etiologies. Both Silveri et al. (1991) and Mazzoni et al. (1991) drew inferences from these deficit patterns about the localization of perceptual and functional information in the brain. Perceptual information was said to be localized in the temporo-limbic areas of the brain, and functional information in the fronto-parietal regions, a hypothesis that is receiving increasing support from both neuropsychological studies and imaging studies with normals (Damasio, Grabowski, Tranel, Hichwa, & Damasio, 1996; Martin, Haxby, Lalonde, Wiggs, & Ungerleider, 1995; Martin, Wiggs, Ungerleider, & Haxby, 1996; Perani et al., 1995). The researchers suggested that both HSE and Alzheimer's patients show natural kinds impairments because early in the course of the disease, AD affects temporo-limbic areas in much the same way HSE does.

There are a number of reasons to be cautious about this explanation, however. Gonnerman, Andersen, Devlin, Kempler, and Seidenberg (1997) conducted studies examining category-specific impairments in two groups of AD subjects. Both studies assessed the lexical semantic knowledge of 15 mild to moderate AD subjects using black-and-white line drawings of natural kinds and artifacts, as in the Silveri et al. (1991) research. In both of Gonnerman et al.'s studies, analyses of the group data did not yield an overall deficit for natural kinds. However, two individuals did present a double dissociation involving artifact and natural kind domains. The first subject, GP, displayed a natural kinds deficit similar to those reported in Silveri et al. (1991) and Mazzoni et al. (1991) on three tasks: picture-naming, superordinate comprehension, and word–picture matching; the second subject, NB, showed the opposite pattern: selective impairment on artifacts on all three tasks while performing at ceiling on natural kinds. If early AD affects the brain in much the same way that HSE does, it is unclear why two separate groups of mild to moderate AD subjects failed to yield an overall natural kinds deficit. It is even less clear how such a hypothesis can explain the artifact deficit of NB.

Finally, it may be misleading to equate herpes simplex encephalitis and mild Alzheimer's disease in terms of their neuropathological effects. HSE acutely affects the hippocampus and proximal cortical regions (Damasio & Van Hoesen,

1985). AD, a progressive disease, presents a more complicated pattern. Although there is substantial evidence that early AD strongly affects the hippocampal formation (e.g., Hyman, Van Hoesen, Damasio, & Barnes, 1984), this early stage does not include neocortical temporal regions affected in HSE. As the disease progresses, its effects become widespread and include the association cortices, among other regions (Pearson, Esiri, Hiorns, Wilcock, & Powell, 1985). One hypothesized scenario is that AD spreads transynaptically out of the hippocampal formation via cortico-cortical fibers (see DeLacoste & White, 1993, for a review). If this is correct, the neocortical temporal regions and fronto-parietal areas would be affected simultaneously as both regions receive hippocampal afferents. Thus AD pathology is thought to affect the hippocampal formation first and then spread to association cortices. This is quite different from HSE, which simultaneously affects the hippocampus, the anterior temporal regions, and the orbito-frontal cortex. This account provides little basis for expecting early AD to preferentially affect perceptual information.

The research described below evaluates possible computational bases of category-specific impairments resulting from both focal (e.g., HSE) and widespread (AD) types of neuropathology. Our primary goal was to determine whether the similar patterns of behavioral impairment resulting from different etiologies could be explained within a single, unified semantic system. The structure of the paper is as follows. First, we describe a theory of semantic representation in which category-specific impairments can arise from both focal and diffuse types of damage. This approach was outlined by Gonnerman et al. (1997) and is developed further here. Second, we describe an implementation of the theory within a connectionist model of semantic memory. Simulations examine the effects of different types and degrees of damage within this semantic memory system. We then assess some predictions of the model concerning the interaction between type of damage, degree of damage, and semantic category with respect to case reports in the literature.

Category-specific impairments: Type and degree of damage

In connectionist models of semantic memory (e.g., Farah & McClelland, 1991; Hinton, 1981; Small, Hart, Gordon, & Hollard, 1993), concepts such as DOG or BOAT are represented as patterns of activation distributed over computational units encoding semantic primitives. These features can include perceptual (e.g., *has-fur*), functional (e.g., *guards-house*), and encyclopedic (e.g., *man's-best-friend*) information, among others; they are simplified localist representations of knowledge that is assumed to be encoded by larger pools of neurons in the brain. Such models do not entail the claim that all semantic knowledge is reducible to simple features; in fact there is good evidence from both child development and adult performance concerning the use of nonfeatural forms of knowledge (e.g., Keil, 1989; Murphy & Medin, 1985). Rather, the claim is that important aspects

of semantic knowledge relevant to tasks such as word or object naming are captured by featural representations. McRae, de Sa, and Seidenberg (1997) provide evidence that early, rapid, automatic aspects of word processing make use of featural representations, whereas later, slower, more intentional aspects of processing draw on other forms of knowledge. When a word or picture is presented in a connectionist model, a pattern of activation is computed over these semantic units. Farah and McClelland's (1991) model made two additional assumptions: (1) perceptual and functional features are topographically distinct and (2) the ratios of perceptual and functional features differ in natural kinds and artifacts. Category-specific impairments due to focal lesions could then be explained in terms of damage to different types of semantic features.

Our account of category-specific impairments due to diffuse damage turns on two additional properties of semantic representation. The first is that features differ in terms of how informative they are about the concepts in which they participate. Variants of this idea have been developed by Rosch (1975), Rosch and Mervis (1975), Smith, Shoben, and Rips (1974), Tversky (1977), Warrington and Shallice (1984), and others. For our purposes, we need to incorporate the minimal assumption that features differ in the degree to which they help distinguish among concepts. Thus, some features are more relevant (i.e., informative, distinguishing, defining) than others with respect to categorizing an entity as an instance of a given type. For example, the feature *has-fur* provides little identifying information at the basic level that most mammals are named. The conjunction of *has-fur* and *has-claws* provides some additional constraint but not enough to identify the animal. Knowing that the referent *has-fur* and *has-stripes*, however, greatly increases the likelihood that the entity is a tiger. *Having-stripes*, then, is more informative about the object's identity within the animal category than is *having-fur* or *having-claws*. In part this is because *fur* co-occurs with several other features in many animal concepts, while *stripes* occurs less often and is not strongly correlated with other features (e.g., it co-occurs with *fur* in TIGER but *hair* in ZEBRA). Similarly, *having-red-breast-marking* is important in distinguishing a ROBIN from a BLUEJAY, which both share *having-feathers, having-a-beak*, and *having-claws*. Such features do not provide necessary or sufficient information for identifying an object; rather, they tend to be more informative on a probabilistic basis. As Warrington and Shallice observed, artifacts tend to be distinguished in terms of functional features and natural kinds in terms of perceptual, but these generalizations are not inviolable (Malt & Johnson, 1992).

The second important aspect of semantic representation is the existence of intercorrelations among features and differences in the distribution of these intercorrelated features across natural kinds and artifacts. Many people have observed that semantic features are often correlated with one another, especially for natural kinds concepts (Keil, 1987, 1989; Malt & Smith, 1984). For example, an animal that has fur is also likely to have claws, whiskers, and a tail. Evidence that people encode such intercorrelations is provided by McRae et al. (1997).

McRae et al. gathered feature norms that indicated that the features that subjects listed for natural kinds such as TIGER were more highly correlated with one another than the features listed for artifacts such as CHAIR. Moreover, for natural kinds, the extent to which words overlapped in terms of correlated features predicted the magnitude of semantic priming effects in behavioral experiments. For artifacts, in contrast, overlap in terms of simple features predicted priming effects. McRae et al. developed a connectionist model of natural kinds and artifact categories that acquired knowledge of these relationships among features and simulated the results of several experiments. Such correlated features play a central role in our account of category-specific deficits in AD; they provide the basis for catastrophic loss of categories without focal damage to perceptual or functional types of features. The models described below acquire information about the informativeness of features and the correlations among them on the basis of exposure to concepts. Acquiring this statistical knowledge can be seen as an important aspect of concept development.

These two additional aspects of semantic representation were implicit in earlier models such as Farah and McClelland's (1991), but did not figure directly in their account of the phenomena that were the focus of attention. The distributions of correlated features across natural kind and artifact categories and the fact that features differ in terms of how much they serve to distinguish one object from others derive from facts about the nature of objects in the world. Thus, we would expect these characteristics to be represented in any model that encodes the relevant sorts of featural primitives for a sufficiently large sample of objects and has the capacity to represent relations among features.

Within this framework we derive category-specific impairments in AD as follows. We assume that damage to the semantic system affects random features by reducing the degree to which they are activated. Whether features that fail to become active should be considered "lost" or merely "inaccessible" (Rapp & Caramazza, 1990; Shallice, 1988) is not relevant to this account.[2] What matters is that some features become unavailable due to damage. When these include informative features that happen to distinguish between two entities (e.g., *having-stripes* distinguishes TIGERS from LIONS), errors occur in naming these objects. The more informative a particular feature is to a given object, the more likely that object will be misnamed when the feature is damaged. Conversely, losing a feature that is uninformative has little behavioral consequence. Consider the following example. *Has-fur* is less informative than *barks* because many animals have fur but only a few animals, such as dogs, seals, and hyenas, bark. When damage makes *has-fur* unavailable, a patient might still produce the word DOG (although be unable to verify whether dogs have fur). If *barks* were unavailable, however, the remaining semantic features might afford more than one response (e.g., DOG *or* CAT), increasing the likelihood of an overt naming error. Thus the behavioral consequence of damage is significant relative to the informativeness of the lost feature.

Because features that occur across many items are less informative than those occurring in only a few items and because natural kinds tend to share more features across items, natural kinds have relatively fewer informative features than do artifacts. Although damage to these features can lead to errors on individual natural kind items, the behavioral effect of damage to informative features will be stronger for artifacts (i.e., more artifacts will be misnamed) because they have proportionally more informative features than natural kinds.

The intercorrelations among features figure in the category-specific impairments as follows. We assume that the architecture of the semantic system permits the encoding of these correlations. At low levels of damage features that participate in these correlations are more resistant to random damage than other features because of strong collateral support within a set of intercorrelated features. In a highly interactive architecture it will be possible to complete a semantic pattern despite moderate damage affecting individual features. As damage becomes more severe, however, the feedback excitation among intercorrelated features will itself be reduced until it can no longer provide compensation. At that point, the loss of individual features within an intercorrelated set can have catastrophic effects, reducing the activation of other features in the set. This may in turn cause the other features to fall below threshold levels of activation and become inactive, yielding a cascade of lost features. Thus, an entire set of intercorrelated features can be impaired together (see Ruppin & Reggia, 1995, for a discussion of catastrophic loss in associative memory systems).

The predicted behavioral effect of this damage scenario is an inability to name all of the items that rely on the affected intercorrelated features. Natural kind categories tend to include many items with such features, creating their tendency to show "category-specific" impairments. Artifact categories tend to entail fewer of these intercorrelated features; therefore individual items will typically be impaired as features that are highly informative about their identities are lost. These predictions must be modulated by two further observations. First, items within natural kind categories differ in terms of the extent to which they entail intercorrelated features; thus not all members of a category will necessarily be equally affected (compare lemons, limes, and oranges, which share several intercorrelated features, with pineapples or tomatoes). We therefore predict a simultaneous loss of many items that share feature structure. Idiosyncratic items within such categories that do not entail the correlated features (such as tomato) should behave more like typical artifacts: They should be more susceptible to mild damage and lost on an item-by-item basis rather than en masse. Second, there will be natural kind and artifact categories that deviate from these predictions because they have distributions of features that are more typical of categories in the other domain (e.g., musical instruments resemble natural kinds more than they do other artifact categories). This is consistent with our view that semantic memory is structured in terms of distributions of types of features, not categories per se.

To summarize, nonfocal damage yields different progressions for different categories depending on their featural properties. Categories with many informative features and few intercorrelated ones, which tend to be artifacts, lose individual items as random damage affects relevant informative features. Loss of items is predicted to be roughly linear with the amount of damage. On the other hand, categories with many intercorrelated features, which tend to be natural kinds, should follow a nonlinear trajectory, with exemplars initially resistant to minor damage and then clusters of items simultaneously affected by the loss of shared sets of features. The net result is that the degree of damage interacts with the structure of semantic representations to produce a double dissociation over time. An initial, mild difficulty with artifacts compared to natural kinds is predicted to yield to much more severe, catastrophic impairment of natural kinds as damage to the semantic system increases. In the most severe phase of semantic impairment, of course, patients may become globally impaired.

Behavioral evidence

Gonnerman et al. (1997) presented cross-sectional studies of the picture-naming performance of two groups of probable AD subjects that supported this hypothesized progression. In the first study, 15 clinically diagnosed AD subjects named 36 black-and-white line drawings of common objects, including both natural kinds and artifacts. They found that subjects with the best overall performance showed a slight disadvantage for artifacts and that most of the more impaired subjects showed more difficulty with natural kinds. To determine if this finding would replicate, a second study was conducted with a different group of 15 AD subjects who named 72 black-and-white line drawings of common objects. The results for subjects in the second study are shown in Figure 1. Three of the five subjects with the best performance had more difficulty with artifacts than with natural kinds, with the other two subjects performing equally well on items from both domains. The ten remaining subjects did poorly on natural kinds relative to artifacts, with the size of the difference increasing as overall performance declined. In general then, the data from both studies are consistent with the hypothesized progression of an early, mild difficulty with artifacts over natural kinds, which becomes a definite natural kinds deficit as semantic deterioration increases.

THE MODEL

We developed a connectionist computational model of the proposed semantic system to explore three questions: (1) whether diffuse, progressive damage to the model's semantic system would yield the effects observed by Gonnerman et al. (1997), (2) whether the model could explain reported variation among AD subjects (e.g., why only some studies observed a natural kinds deficit for groups of AD subjects), and (3) whether the same model could account for category-specific deficits arising from both AD and focal brain damage. In addressing

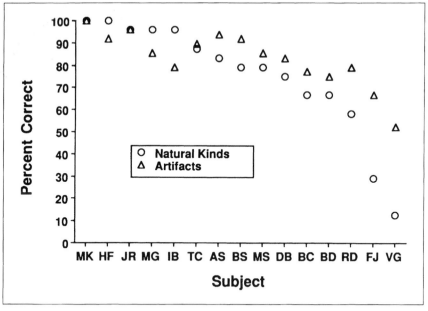

Figure 1. Performance of 15 Alzheimer's subjects on a picture-naming task. Percentage correct scores for natural kinds and artifacts are plotted for each subject, ordered according to degree of impairment on natural kinds. From Gonnerman et al. (1997).

these questions we exploited two aspects of the modeling approach. First, if each simulation is considered an artificial "subject," we can create and evaluate longitudinal data from many more subjects than traditional neuropsychological methods permit in a comparable time period. Second, because each simulation begins with an identical semantic system, we can control for premorbid differences across subjects and thus observe the effects of different pathologies without this confound.

We implemented a hetero-associative memory network that mapped between semantic and phonological representations. The model was one of a general class of models called *attractor networks*, where patterns of activity form stable points in processing space called *attractors* (Amit, 1989; Hopfield, 1982). Each attractor develops a region surrounding it, called a *basin of attraction*, such that activity in this region will eventually settle into the attractor (see Plaut, 1991; Plaut & Shallice, 1993, for more extensive discussion). In our model the attractor states corresponded to the phonological and semantic patterns for words.

Architecture

The network consisted of four layers, a phonological layer, a semantic layer, and two hidden layers, as shown in Figure 2.[3] One hidden layer was fully connected to the phonological layer, the other, to the semantic layer; these are labeled

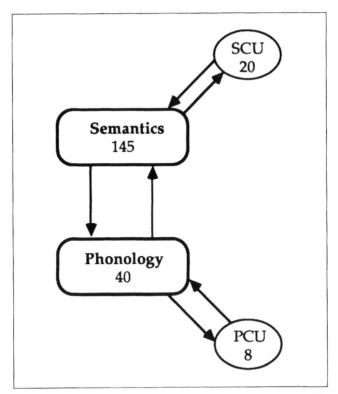

Figure 2. Model architecture: An attractor network with four layers: Semantics, Phonology, and two layers of clean-up units. The numbers in each oval indicate the number of units in that layer, and arrows indicate full connectivity between groups.

Phonological Clean-Up units (PCU) and Semantic Clean-Up units (SCU), respectively (cf., Plaut, 1991). In addition, the phonological and semantic layers were fully connected to each other, but units within a layer were not. The model contained 18,040 weighted connections.

Input to the model was either a phonological or a semantic pattern of activation. To model comprehension, a phonological input was provided and the associated semantic pattern was computed. To model production, a semantic input was provided and the corresponding phonological output was computed. The focus of the present work was on the production task.

Representations

The training set included 60 words, half of them natural kind terms and half artifacts. Categories included animals (15 items), fruits and vegetables (15), vehicles (10), clothing (10), and tools (10). Phonological patterns were random

binary vectors of length 40 with a mean of 12.9 phonological features ($SD = 3.9$) active per word. A vector served only as a unique identifier for a word. This representation captured the fact that the mapping between phonology and semantics is essentially arbitrary for monomorphemic words; however, because this code did not represent an actual phonological structure, any errors that were made were not phonologically meaningful.

The semantic representations were designed to implement properties that our theory suggests are relevant to explaining category-specific impairments: (1) the different proportions of perceptual and functional information in the natural kind and artifact domains, (2) the greater numbers of correlated property pairs in natural kinds compared to artifacts, and (3) the fact that features differ in informativeness. Semantic representations were developed on the basis of feature norms collected from 30 undergraduate subjects. Subjects were given a word such as BOOK and asked to list perceptual and functional properties of the item. This collection of feature lists was used as a guide in constructing the semantic representations, with the most frequently named features included in them.[4] Each of the 60 words was represented as a binary vector over 145 semantic units; a 1 indicated the presence of a feature and a 0, its absence. On average each word had 8.2 active semantic features with a standard deviation of 1.0. A one-way analysis of variance revealed no significant difference in the mean number of features by category, although there was a trend toward more features in natural kinds than artifacts ($F(4, 55) = 3.54$, $p < 0.10$). Of the 145 semantic features, 88 were perceptual and 57 functional. A feature was considered perceptual if it described a visual, auditory, or tactile property of a concept (e.g., *has-wheels*). Functional features were those describing what an item does or what it is used for (e.g., *used-for-driving*). Attributes that met neither of these criteria, such as encyclopedic knowledge (e.g., *found-in-Africa*), were not included.

Each word was represented by both perceptual and functional properties. Table 1 shows the distribution of features by categories. Overall the model had a 1.5:1 ratio of perceptual to functional features; the ratio for natural kinds was 3.0:1, whereas the ratio for artifacts was only 1.4:1. Our ratios do not exactly match Farah and McClelland's (1991), but the distributions are similar in so far as natural kinds have more perceptual features than do artifacts, whereas artifacts have greater numbers of functional features than do natural kinds.

Having constructed representations for the 60 words based on these principles, we then examined the extent to which features were correlated. Such correlations must exist in the representations of concepts if they are to be encoded by the network during training. Following McRae et al. (1997), the Pearson product moment correlation was computed for all pairs of semantic features. Of the 10,440 possible correlations, only 416 were significant ($r > 0.216$, $p < 0.05$). Figure 3 shows the mean number of correlations by category. Natural kinds had reliably more correlated features (mean = 18.3, $SD = 8.5$) than did artifacts (mean = 13.8, $SD = 5.8$), $F(4, 55) = 5.59$, $p < 0.05$. Examples of correlated property pairs are

TABLE 1
Feature distributions across categories

	Number of words	Total number of features/word	Number of perceptual features/word	Number of functional features/word
Natural kinds				
Fruits & vegetables	15	8.3	6.1	2.2
(*SD*)		(0.88)	(0.70)	(0.41)
Animals	15	8.6	6.6	2.0
(*SD*)		(1.30)	(1.12)	(0.76)
Artifacts				
Vehicles	10	7.9	4.6	3.3
(*SD*)		(0.88)	(0.70)	(0.48)
Clothing	10	7.9	4.5	3.4
(*SD*)		(1.00)	(0.97)	(0.52)
Tools	10	8.0	5.0	3.0
(*SD*)		(0.94)	(0.67)	(0.67)

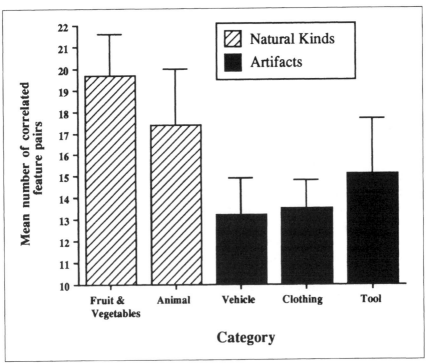

Figure 3. Mean number of correlated property pairs by category with 95% confidence error bars. Natural kinds have reliably more intercorrelations than artifacts.

TABLE 2
Examples of correlations in the semantic
representations

Correlated property pairs	Pearson r
High correlation	
is-sharp—used-for-cutting	1.000
has-a-handle—used-manually	0.927
is-juicy—is-sour	0.809
made-of-wool—is-soft	0.809
is-tasty—is-sweet	0.718
Medium correlation	
keeps-body-warm—made-of-cloth	0.688
used-for-transportation—has-wheels	0.528
has-buttons—has-a-zipper	0.483
eats—has-a-tail	0.417
made-of-wood—made-of-metal	0.348
Low correlation	
has-4-legs—is-gentle	0.288
has-legs—has-a-long-tail	0.287
east—has-4-legs	0.279
is-small—has-fur	0.247
pollutes-the-air—has-an-engine	0.245

shown in Table 2. The highly interactive nature of the architecture allowed these correlations to be stored as connection strengths within the semantic system (i.e., the semantic and SCU layers of the model and the connections between them).

Earlier it was hypothesized that damaging highly informative features would affect naming behavior by making similar objects less distinguishable and thus harder to name. A simple measure of feature informativeness is given by 1 over the number of objects the feature occurs in. For example, in our corpus the feature *barks* occurred only in the word DOG and consequently *barks* was highly informative. Conversely, the feature *eaten-by-people* occurred in 18 words giving it an information score of 0.056, thus not a very informative feature.

Because artifacts have fewer intercorrelated features, their features tend to be more informative than those in natural kinds. We calculated the mean feature information score (mean = 0.298) and labeled all features with scores above the mean as "informative." Artifacts within the model had reliably more informative features per word (mean = 3.4) than natural kinds (mean = 2.4), $t = 2.53, p < 0.05$. Consequently random damage is more likely to strike an informative feature in an artifact object than in a natural kind object and thus increase the likelihood of misnaming that item. It is important to note that random damage will affect both artifacts and natural kinds, but with limited damage it will affect artifacts more heavily. Later, once sets of intercorrelated features are lost, many items from categories relying on those intercorrelations will be impaired.

The informativeness of features necessarily depends on both the set of words in the chosen corpus and the set of features used to represent these words. Consequently, while the values we have calculated are exact in the context of the model, they should be taken as only rough approximations of how informative individual semantic features really are. The feature representations used in the model were based on empirical norms reflecting subjects' knowledge of all concepts, not merely those included in the model, suggesting that these relationships should be preserved in larger-scale models. We should note, however, that the semantic representations maintained some of the limitations of the empirical norms from which they were derived. Subjects only listed the features they found most salient for each concept; thus, the fact that *has-an-engine* was not listed for BUS and the fact that *has-a-mouth* was only listed for HIPPO are reflected in the model's representations for these concepts. Thus, the model representations capture only the most salient features of concepts, not everything a subject might know about them.

Training

The goal of the training procedure was to obtain a set of weights that allowed the model to perform two functions: It had to encode the essentially arbitrary mappings between semantics and phonology and it had to learn attractor states for each word's semantic and phonological patterns. The implications of this training are twofold. First, there was only a single phonological system for both production and comprehension, as opposed to separate lexicons for phonological input and output (cf., Hillis & Caramazza, 1991). This system, consisting of the phonology units, phonological clean-up units, and the connections between them, encoded phonological regularities and processed both phonological input and output representations. Such a system is capable of producing dissociations between errors of productions and comprehension, although a discussion of this behavior is outside the scope of this paper (Devlin, 1998). Second, individual words corresponded to attractor states in a dynamic processing space as opposed to static nodes in a mental lexicon. Thus, although features are instantiated as individual units, words are not. The meaning of a word was its pattern of activation over semantic features, whereas its phonological form was its pattern of activation over phonological features. Both of these claims, that there is only one phonological system and that words correspond to attractor states, are not consequences of the modeling but rather are substantive claims about the normal cognitive system.

The model was trained using the recurrent back-propagation algorithm with conjugate gradient descent and a line search technique to determine step sizes (cf., Hassoun, 1995). The network began in a random state with all connection strengths initialized to values in the range [−1 to +1] with a random uniform distribution. Two exemplars per word were then presented to the net, one providing

phonology as input and expecting semantics as output (P→S), the other providing semantics as input and expecting phonology as output (S→P). The 120 exemplars (60 S→P, 60 P→S) constituted one epoch. Weights were updated after each epoch. Training ended when the activation of all output units was within 0.2 of the target values. Training took 210 epochs.

During training each exemplar was active for 10 time steps. A pattern of activation was clamped over the input units for the first three time steps until activity had spread to all layers of the net. Then the input units were unclamped for seven time steps, and during this time target values existed for every unit in the input and output groups. The net had to learn to compute the appropriate output given an input and to correctly maintain an input pattern without external assistance.

To illustrate, given the P→S AIRPLANE training exemplar, a phonological input pattern was clamped over the phonology units to begin a training trial. At the next time step, activation spread to the semantic layer and to the PCU. During the third time step, it spread further to the SCU. From the fourth to the tenth steps, the phonological units were unclamped (i.e., no external input was provided) but were expected to maintain their current levels of activation, whereas the semantic units were expected to display activation of properties such as *has-wings, flies, made-of-metal*, etc. Similarly, the S→P AIRPLANE training exemplar mapped in the opposite direction by presenting the semantic features of AIRPLANE and computing the phonological pattern for the word.

EXPERIMENT 1: MODELING ALZHEIMER'S DISEASE

Connectionist models are often described as *neurally inspired* because they capture general properties of neural computation, such as distributed representation and massively parallel processing, while typically abstracting away from neurophysiological details (Rumelhart & McClelland, 1986). Most models incorporate some general biological constraints and are broadly compatible with others. The principal goal of first-generation attempts to simulate effects of brain injury was to account for nontransparent aspects of the behavioral data (e.g., Hinton & Shallice, 1991; Patterson, Seidenberg, & McClelland, 1990). However, recent models of normal and disordered cognition have begun to incorporate more specific neurophysiological constraints (Cohen & Servan-Schreiber, 1992; Horn, Ruppin, Usher, & Herrmann, 1993). Our goal was to simulate the behavioral effects of two different types of brain damage using mechanisms that capture basic features of these neuropathologies. Thus, the etiology of the disease constrained the manner in which the model was damaged.

A large literature exists concerning the neuropathology of AD, with research ranging from the molecular biological level (e.g., Yankner & Mesulam, 1991) to the anatomical level (e.g., Price, Davis, Morris, & White, 1991; see Henderson

& Finch, 1989, for a review). We focused on three elements: (1) regional distributions of histopathological markers involving association cortices early in the disease (Pearson et al., 1985; Rogers & Morrison, 1985), (2) cortical synaptic loss as a major pathological component of AD correlated with degree of cognitive impairment (DeKosky & Scheff, 1990; Gibson, 1983; Scheff, DeKosky, & Price, 1990; Terry et al., 1991), and (3) AD as a dynamic process of progressive degeneration. These properties all constitute general, noncontroversial, well-established aspects of AD that can be plausibly incorporated in a connectionist framework, in so far as they can be related to basic properties of such nets. The fact that AD is characterized by relatively diffuse damage to most regions of association cortex suggests that even if perceptual and functional features are localized in different parts of the cortex (e.g., temporal vs. fronto-parietal), both types of features are likely to be affected by AD. Moreover, the primary histopathological markers of AD, neuritic plaques and neurofibrillary tangles, are correlated with a loss of synaptic junctures, the primary site of neuronal communication (Masliah, Hansen, Mallory, & Terry, 1991; Masliah, Terry, Mallory, Alford, & Hansen, 1990; Terry et al., 1991). Within our model, the best analogy to this pathology is provided by removing connections between units. The intent here is not to suggest that features in the model map directly onto individual neurons or that connections between features correspond to synapses. Rather, the information represented as a single semantic feature in the model is assumed to be represented in the brain by a large number of neurons with complex interactions. Thus the loss of synapses in AD would presumably have a graded effect on the ability to use the information from a single feature. Therefore removing a feature within the model is too abrupt a form of damage. Instead, removing connections causes features to gradually decay in efficacy as their input degrades. To simulate the widespread effects of AD, connections within the semantic system involving both perceptual and functional features were randomly chosen and removed. Finally, because AD is a degenerative disease, damage to the model was applied progressively. Again, this procedure is intended to capture a basic characteristic of the disease process, while abstracting away from more specific details.

In the AD simulations, damage was limited to connections within the semantic system, namely, those between the Semantic and SCU units. Because the association cortices affected by AD presumably play an integral role for both phonology and semantics, this was not an anatomical constraint. Instead, it was based on the fact that while AD consistently impairs semantic processing, there is little evidence that AD directly affects phonological processing (but see Patterson, Graham, & Hodges, 1994, and Patterson & Hodges, 1992, for evidence of indirect phonological impairment in AD). Consequently, connections directly affecting phonological computations were spared in these simulations, and those affecting both perceptual and functional semantic information were randomly chosen and removed.

Testing

Testing focused on the equivalent of a picture-naming task. Naming a black-and-white line drawing normally begins with analysis of the input by the visual system, which activates perceptual semantic features corresponding to elements present in the image (Caramazza, Hillis, Rapp, & Romani, 1990; Shallice, 1993). As these visual features increase in activation, they begin to activate features associated with properties of the object not present in the visual image. For instance, a picture of a school bus might activate the semantic features *has-wheels, is-large*, and *is-long*, which would in turn activate other properties of buses not present in the image, such as *is-yellow, has-an-engine*, and *used-for-transportation*. As the semantic pattern builds, it activates a corresponding phonological pattern. Partial activation in the phonological system may itself feed back on semantics. Once the phonological pattern is sufficiently specified, the subject can initiate production of the object's name. Damage to the semantic system interferes with this process, causing activation of incorrect semantic representations that can produce naming errors.

In our simulation, we activated an item's semantic pattern as input and clamped it for three time steps, placing the model in the trained attractor state corresponding to the word's semantics and phonology. Randomly distributed damage within the semantic system affected processing in three ways: (1) A semantic pattern was severely disrupted such that the wrong output was produced, (2) a semantic pattern included some incorrect features, or failed to activate some correct features, and yet was still close enough to the veridical pattern to produce the correct phonology, or (3) a given item was not affected at all. Although the process of picture naming in the model did not directly correspond to that of subjects (i.e., the model began with a correct semantic pattern and drifted away as a result of damage, whereas subjects presumably begin with only visual features and fail to generate the rest of the correct pattern), we assume that the final computed patterns are roughly equivalent.

To simulate the progressive nature of the disease, the model was lesioned cumulatively. Initially the lesions were in small increments that gradually grew larger as damage accumulated. A lesion consisted of removing a percentage of the 5800 weights between the semantic layer and the SCU. The first lesion randomly deleted 1% of the connections, or 58 weights. This procedure was repeated until 20% of the connections were gone. Lesions then occurred in 5% increments until the 50% damage level was reached. Finally, all remaining lesions were in 10% increments. After each lesion, the model was evaluated on the above task for all 60 S→P exemplars. The pattern of activation over the phonological units was considered the output vector.[5] An output was judged correct when the Euclidean distance from the output vector to the target phonology was closer than the distance between the output and the phonological pattern of any other word. One consequence of this evaluation scheme is that no matter how distorted a phonological output pattern was, it was judged one of the 60 "words." One

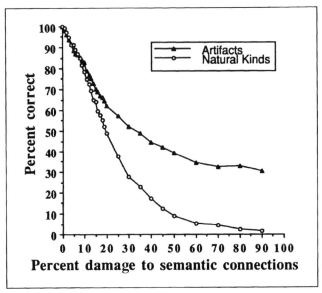

Figure 4. The model's performance averaged over all 50 trials. As damage increased a preferential impairment in natural kinds arose.

complete simulation consisted of 30 lesions (1%, 2% . . . , 20%, 25%, . . . , 50%, 60%, . . . , 90%). Each simulation was repeated 50 times.

Results and discussion

Figure 4 presents the results averaged over all 50 simulations. For the averaged scores of the entire set, the general pattern is one where increasing damage led to a preferential impairment of natural kinds over artifacts. Figure 5 displays the same data separated into the two main subpatterns of performance. In Figure 5a, the modal pattern is shown. In 38 out of 50 simulations, low levels of damage led to more errors on artifacts than natural kinds, with increasing damage producing a crossover to more errors on natural kinds than artifacts. In Figure 5b, the model's performance is shown averaged over 11 simulations that displayed only a natural kinds deficit throughout the entire progression.

Thus, in most cases (76%) the model displayed the expected progression of an initial mild selective difficulty for artifacts that crossed over into a preferential impairment of natural kinds as damage accumulated. Interestingly, 22% of the simulations resulted in more difficulty with natural kinds that persisted throughout the simulation. The remaining one simulation was both aberrant and intriguing. It had initial problems with natural kinds, which then reversed into an artifacts deficit as the damage increased, before finally turning into an equal impairment for both domains. We return to this case later.

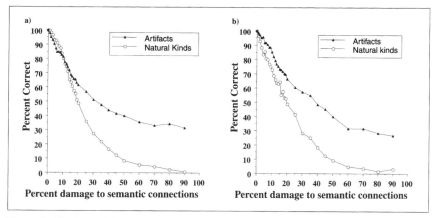

Figure 5. (a) The model's performance averaged over the 38 trials displaying the most frequently observed progression. Low levels of damage led to more errors on artifacts than natural kinds, with increasing damage producing a crossover to more errors on natural kinds than artifacts. (b) The model's performance averaged over the 11 trials where the model made consistently more errors on natural kinds.

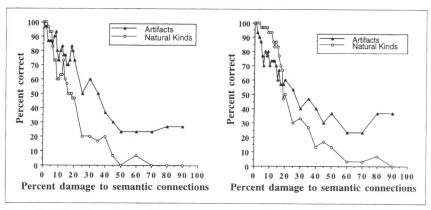

Figure 6. (right) The model's performance on simulation 22. On this trial the initial artifacts deficit is relatively clear, and the crossover point does not occur until 18% damage. (left) The model's performance on simulation 18. On this trial the initial difficulty with artifacts was quite mild, as it was in most cases.

The model exhibited considerable variability across simulations. This is evident when comparing the two patterns discussed above, but also within each pattern. For example, among the 38 trials in which the model experienced greater diffi-culty with artifacts before crossing over into a natural kinds impairment, both the magnitude of the initial artifacts deficit and the point of crossover varied (see Figure 6). In most of these trials the effect of low levels of damage on artifacts

was only mildly greater than its affect on natural kinds (e.g., Figure 6, left). On a few trials, however, the initial artifacts impairment was quite large; one such trial is shown in Figure 6, right. Similarly, the crossover point between an artifact and natural kinds deficit ranged from 3 to 20% damage across simulations. Consequently, the strong nonlinear deterioration of natural kinds (the result of a set of intercorrelated features failing en masse) is clearly seen in individual simulations, such as in Figure 6, but less pronounced when averaged together (see Figure 5).

The variability in the effects of damage of performance in the modeling results is consistent with the variability observed among AD subjects and helps to explain some seeming inconsistencies in the behavioral literature. Recall that two studies found a category-specific deficit for natural kinds in groups of mild to moderate AD subjects (Mazzoni et al., 1991; Silveri et al., 1991), while one found no overall effect of category (Gonnerman et al., 1997). It seems clear from Figure 4 that the sampling of subjects in a group study will play a critical role in determining the observed findings. Silveri and Mazzoni's subjects could simply have tended to be further along the progression than those in the Gonnerman et al. study. Indeed, the picture-naming scores from individual subjects as displayed in Mazzoni et al.'s Figure 4b indicate that those subjects scored in the 80 to 100% correct range for artifacts but in the 30 to 80% correct range for natural kinds, a larger overall impairment than observed by Gonnerman et al. In fact, most of Gonnerman et al.'s subjects appeared to be relatively close to their hypothesized crossover points, whereas the two subjects who exhibited a pronounced deficit on natural kinds would be more like the subjects in the Silveri and Mazzoni studies.

The modeling data are also consistent with Gonnerman et al.'s (1997) two case studies of subjects NB and GP, who displayed a double dissociation with regard to semantic domain. The higher-functioning subject, NB, made fewer errors overall and had more difficulty with artifacts than with natural kinds. Indeed her errors were evenly spread across all artifact categories, as one would expect if this deficit were the result of damage striking individual distinguishing features. GP made more errors overall and displayed a preferential impairment of natural kinds, as we would expect for a subject further along in the progression. The only surprising result from these subjects was the magnitude of NB's artifact deficit. The model typically produced a much smaller artifacts deficit; however, it should be noted that the model did produce a more pronounced initial artifacts impairment on occasional trials, such as the one in Figure 6, right. Thus NB may represent a rare case in terms of the size of her impairment, but she nonetheless fits within the range of patterns observed in the model.

Finally, recall the simulation that produced an aberrant pattern (Figure 7): There was an initial natural kinds deficit followed by an artifacts deficit before global anomia. Most of the initial natural kind errors were in the fruits and vegetables category, whereas very few were in animals. The artifact errors, on

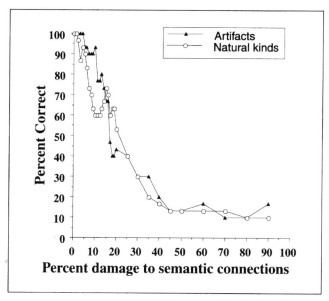

Figure 7. Performance of the model on simulation 7 where the model displayed an initial natural kinds deficit, then an artifacts deficit, and finally a global deficit.

the other hand, were distributed more equally across the tools, clothing, and vehicles categories. Thus, the random damage initially struck the intercorrelations underlying fruits and vegetables enough to preferentially affect that category. That particular pattern of damage, however, was not enough to cause a catastrophic loss of the intercorrelations underlying animals, and consequently animals were relatively spared. With fewer intercorrelations, items from the artifact categories were gradually lost as damage increased and distinguishing features were affected. Thus the immediate loss of many fruits and vegetables produced a relative impairment of natural kinds that gradually crossed over into an artifact deficit as individual artifacts continued to be lost. Finally, enough damage accumulated that the intercorrelations among the animals were lost, affecting many items from this category and leaving the model generally impaired.

In summary, these results parallel those observed in AD subjects, namely, that on average a small artifact deficit will precede a larger preferential impairment of natural kinds when the semantic system suffers progressive, diffuse damage. Although the majority of simulations show this pattern, the number of artifacts on which they initially err is usually small; such deficits may not reach statistical significance for individual subjects and may therefore easily escape notice. Indeed, mean performance from groups of subjects would probably reveal only the more pronounced deficit, the natural kinds impairment. These simulations illustrate how a probabilistic account of damage yields a variety of impairment patterns,

including the small initial artifact deficit, no initial artifact deficit, and an initial artifact advantage in rare cases. All of these patterns have the same computational basis, however. These results highlight the importance of understanding the factors that give rise to individual differences among subjects, a point to which we return in the "General Discussion."

EXPERIMENT 2: MODELING AD AS UNIT LOSS

In the first experiment AD was modeled as a progressive loss of connections within the semantic system on the assumption that this form of damage was most closely analogous to the neuropathology of AD. It might be argued, however, that motivating the type of damage to the model by analogy to the actual neuropathology was meaningless because the model is so far removed from neurobiological reality. If this is correct, one might expect other forms of damage to produce similar effects. To address this question, we conducted another experiment in which AD was modeled as a progressive loss of semantic units. If the type of damage to the semantic system is relevant, we would expect both that different types would yield different results but also that the one that matches the neuropathology more closely would provide a better account of the behavioral data.

Testing

Damage was applied progressively to semantic units. Each "lesion" consisted of removing a certain percentage of semantic features randomly selected from both perceptual and functional units. The first lesion removed 1% of the units, or 1.5 units on average, and was repeatedly applied until 10% of the units were removed. Lesions then occurred in 5% increments until the 50% damage level was reached. All subsequent lesions were in 10% increments. One complete simulation consisted of 22 lesions (1%, 2%, . . . , 10%, 15%, . . . , 50%, 60%, . . . , 90%). At each level of damage the model was evaluated on its performance for all 60 S→P exemplars. Each simulation was repeated 50 times.

Results and discussion

Figure 8 presents the overall results of the 50 simulations. The data demonstrated a small natural kinds deficit for relatively low levels of damage that then faded into a global anomia as the model became severely impaired.

The most striking aspect of the data was the variability of individual simulations. Although the overall result was a natural kinds impairment followed by a more equal distribution of errors across domains, only 15 of the 50 trials showed this pattern. An additional 9 trials followed the overall pattern found in Experiment 1 with more difficulty for artifacts at low levels of damage followed by a natural kinds deficit and finally a more global impairment. The majority of simulations did not conform to either of these patterns. Twenty-six simulations

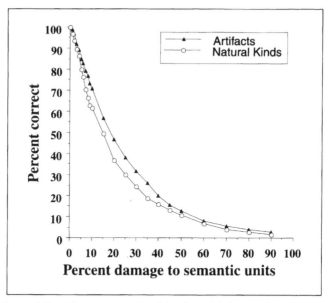

Figure 8. The model's performance over 50 trials when Alzheimer's disease is modeled as progressive loss of semantic features. The data show a natural kinds deficit for low levels of damage that becomes a more global deficit as the damage increases in severity.

presented a variety of results including selective deficits for artifacts (4) or natural kinds (4), equal distributions of errors across domains (2), and a host of more complicated patterns that varied with the degree of damage (16).

Thus, the different types of damage introduced into the model were associated with different behavioral results, with the form of damage that more closely resembles the pathological affects of AD providing a much better fit to the subject data. Whereas the simulations in Experiment 1 yielded two main deficit patterns that could be related to behavioral data in a straightforward way, the simulations in Experiment 2 yielded a broader range of patterns, including ones not observed in any AD subjects.

EXPERIMENT 3: MODELING FOCAL BRAIN DAMAGE

Because category-specific deficits are more typically associated with focal brain damage, any explanatory model would have to demonstrate how the same behavioral deficit could arise from different pathologies. In the third experiment, therefore, we attempted to do so by replicating Farah and McClelland's (1991) findings with our model, using methods that closely approximated theirs. Farah and McClelland removed only visual or only functional semantic units, depending on the trial, based on the assumption that focal brain damage could preferentially affect either type of semantic information across subjects. In order to capture the

TABLE 3
Performance of the model when either perceptual or functional
semantic units are removed

Amount of damage[a]	Probability correct for artifacts	Probability correct for natural kinds
Damage to perceptual features		
0	1.00	1.00
10	0.80	0.71
20	0.67	0.50
30	0.56	0.34
40	0.42	0.24
50	0.33	0.18
60	0.28	0.11
70	0.20	0.07
80	0.14	0.06
90	0.10	0.04
99	0.04	0.03
Damage to functional features		
0	1.00	1.00
10	0.87	0.88
20	0.73	0.76
30	0.58	0.67
40	0.47	0.56
50	0.38	0.53
60	0.32	0.46
70	0.23	0.37
80	0.16	0.36
90	0.13	0.34
99	0.07	0.30

[a] *Amount of damage* refers to the percentage of perceptual or functional semantic units destroyed.

effects of a distinct neuropathological episode as in a CVA or in herpes encephalitis, damage was introduced on a one-shot, rather than cumulative, basis.

Testing

Twenty types of simulations were run corresponding to 10, 20, 30, 40, 50, 60,
70, 80, 90, and 99% unit loss of either perceptual or functional semantic units.
On each trial the perceptual or functional units of an intact model were subjected
to either a 0.1, 0.2, 0.3, 0.4, 0.5, 0.6, 0.7, 0.8, 0.9, or a 0.99 chance of being
removed. The same criteria from the previous experiments were used to evaluate
the model's performance. Each condition was repeated 50 times.

Results and discussion

Table 3 shows the results from these simulations. When damage was applied
exclusively to perceptual units, the model displayed a selective deficit for natural
kinds. Conversely, damage to functional units yielded an artifacts impairment. In

both cases, as the level of damage increased, so did the severity of the impairment. These results clearly replicate the basic findings of Farah and McClelland (1991).

GENERAL DISCUSSION

In this paper we have used a connectionist model to demonstrate how category-specific deficits resulting from two types of brain injury can arise in a single semantic system without explicit category representations. Our findings indicate that the following four properties of the semantic system are relevant to category specific deficits: (1) perceptual and functional features, which are more important to natural kinds and artifacts, respectively, (2) topographic organization of the two types of features, (3) variation in the informativeness of features, and (4) more intercorrelations among features in natural kinds than artifacts. The first two properties have been used by Warrington and Shallice (1984), Farah and McClelland (1991), and others to explain how focal brain damage, such as herpes encephalitis or cerebrovascular accident, can preferentially impair perceptual or functional semantic information, yielding a natural kinds or artifacts deficit, respectively. This work extends those claims by making use of the third and fourth properties and demonstrates that in widespread, progressive damage, such as in Alzheimer's disease, the degree of damage interacts with the structure of the semantic system to yield a progression from an initial mild difficulty with artifacts to a definite natural kinds impairment. This account not only provides an integrated explanation of category-specific deficits in different types of brain damage but also helps to explain inconsistencies in reported behavioral data.

Garrard et al. (1998) have recently taken issue with our account, arguing that we "accept an anatomical account of category specificity in HSV encephalitis and MCA territory infarction, but reject it for DAT" and implying that our account is therefore unparsimonious. They suggest that the neuropathology of AD may be more focal than we have assumed, allowing all cases of category specificity to be explained in terms of focal damage. What is at issue here is a question of fact rather than parsimony. There is considerable debate about the pathogenesis of AD, as summarized in the "Introduction." Our theory is consistent with the majority of this evidence, which suggests that AD and HSE are associated with different types of neuropathology, as reflected in our simulations.

Our work is closely related to two other computational models of double dissociations, Farah and McClelland's (1991) model of category-specific semantic impairments and Plaut's (1995) model of selective impairments of either concrete or abstract nouns. In our work, as in theirs, words were represented as attractor states in a semantic space composed of perceptual and functional features, processing was highly interactive, and the behavior was an emergent property of a system not explicitly organized along category lines. The important difference between these models and ours lies in the way double dissociations were produced.

In each of their models, damage localized to a single component of the semantic system yielded one-half of the double dissociation. In order to produce the other half, a different component was damaged in a separate simulation. The double dissociation relied on a comparison between these simulations. In our model, however, the double dissociation relied on the progression of damage, which affected the entire semantic system. Thus within a single simulation, both sides of the double dissociation are observed at different points in time.

Aside from explaining detailed aspects of behavioral data, our model makes a number of testable predictions. The first arises from the single aberrant simulation in Experiment 1. Recall that by chance the initial damage in that simulation was specific enough to effectively remove the intercorrelated features underlying fruits and vegetables while leaving all other categories largely unaffected, in essence creating a "pure" category-specific deficit with very narrow scope. This outcome should only occur in categories with strong intercorrelations, which typically are natural kinds categories (though not natural kinds such as body parts) but may also include some unusual artifact categories such as musical instruments or gemstones. Interestingly, there are four such pure deficits in the literature: two were specific to animals, leaving plants and artifacts spared (Hart & Gordon, 1992; Hillis & Caramazza, 1991), and two affected plants specifically with a relative sparing of animals and artifacts (Hart, Berndt, & Caramazza, 1985; Pietrini et al., 1988). There are no reported cases of a specific artifact category being selectively affected by brain damage. Such a case could be accommodated within the current model only if it were one of the atypical artifact categories such as gemstones whose semantic features are highly intercorrelated.

A more obvious prediction relates to the behavioral progression that individual AD subjects should display. The model predicts that a majority of AD subjects will display an initial mild difficulty with artifacts over natural kinds that will eventually cross over into a natural kinds impairment as the degree of semantic impairment increases. It is not crucial to this claim that all subjects follow this hypothesized progression. Because of the variability in the disease process, not all subjects will begin at the same point or follow an identical pattern of deterioration. More specifically we would expect that (1) a large minority of cases might never display an initial artifacts deficit, (2) cases like NB with significant artifacts deficits would be rare, (3) preferential impairments to artifacts would only occur in subjects at the beginning of the progression, and (4) no subject would initially display a natural kinds deficit and then cross over into an artifacts deficit unless the initial deficit was specific to a single natural kinds category. To date our model is consistent with the existing behavioral literature, but these data are only suggestive. The modeling results make specific predictions about the interaction of degree of damage and the type of impairment that need to be evaluated in further, longitudinal AD studies.

Our model provides a detailed illustration of why it is important to examine data from individual patients. As Caramazza and his colleagues have argued

(Caramazza, 1986; Caramazza & McCloskey, 1988), averaging subjects may obscure important aspects of the data. In Experiment 1, for example, averaging across simulations masked the fact that on a majority of the trials there was a small initial artifact deficit that developed into a natural kinds deficit, as well as the fact that the deterioration followed two distinct trajectories. On the other hand, it may also be necessary to examine large numbers of patients rather than relying solely on individual case studies in order to identify subtle effects, such as the initial artifact deficit, that may not be statistically reliable in any single case. Our model addresses both of these concerns: It explains the manifest variability in individual subjects while still capturing the group profile.

Although there is widespread agreement that it is necessary to examine individual patient data, there is less agreement about how to explain the variability that is observed. Differences in the patterns of impairment exhibited by patients are typically assumed to reflect different types of underlying deficits. Our modeling results, in common with the research described by Plaut (1995), strongly call into question the validity of this assumption (see also Seidenberg, 1988, and Farah, 1994). We have shown that a given type of etiology (e.g., loss of connections) can give rise to qualitatively different patterns of behavioral impairment. The fact that the different impairment progressions observed in Experiment 1 all derived from the same type of underlying deficit could not have been deduced from the behavioral data alone. These findings suggest that it is important not only to examine individual patient data but also the bases of different deficit patterns. In light of the simulations we have reported, it would be naive to assume that all differences in deficit patterns among patients necessarily reflect different types of underlying pathology. Computational models of the sort we have described provide a way to understand how probabilistic aspects of neuropathology interact to produce different behavioral deficits.

ACKNOWLEDGEMENTS

This work was supported in part by NIA Grants AG10109-01, 2T32AG00037, and AGO 5142-10 and by NIMH grants MH47566 and 01188. We thank Daniel Kempler and Victor Henderson for helpful discussions about the behavioral data and neurological implications, respectively.

NOTES

1. The word *category* has been used in this literature to refer to both narrower categories such as animals, tools, and vehicles and broader categories such as natural kinds or artifacts. We will use *category* in the former sense and *domain* in reference to the latter.
2. The cited authors have debated criteria for deciding between loss of a representation vs. loss of access to it, but these criteria do not capture the range of effects that are observed in connectionist networks. For example, damage to connections might result in a given feature never being activated even though its unit ("representation") remains intact.

3. All simulations were performed on an HP730 using the Xerion simulator developed by Tony Plate, Drew van Camp, and Geoff Hinton at the University of Toronto.
4. Our semantic representations are available upon request.
5. It is important to note that after damage more time was necessary for the model to settle into stable patterns. Whereas 10 time steps were enough to form stable patterns during training, the damaged model needed up to 38 time steps until activity settled. Consequently the phonological pattern of activation at time = 38 was used as the output vector.

REFERENCES

Amit, D. (1989). *Modeling brain function: The world of attractor neural networks.* Cambridge: Cambridge University Press.

Basso, A., Capitani, E., & Laiacona, M. (1988). Progressive language impairment without dementia: A case study with isolated category specific semantic deficit. *Journal of Neurology, Neurosurgery, and Psychiatry, 51,* 1201–1207.

Caramazza, A. (1986). On drawing inferences about the structure of normal cognitive systems from the analysis of patterns of impaired performance: The case for single-patient studies. *Brain and Cognition, 5,* 41–66.

Caramazza, A., Hillis, A. E., Rapp, B. C., & Romani, C. (1990). The multiple semantics hypothesis: Multiple confusions? *Cognitive Neuropsychology, 7,* 161–189.

Caramazza, A., & McCloskey, M. (1988). A case for single patient studies. *Cognitive Neuropsychology, 5,* 583–623.

Cohen, J., & Servan-Schreiber, D. (1992). Context, cortex, and dopamine: A connectionist approach to behavior and biology in schizophrenia. *Psychological Review, 99,* 45–77.

Damasio, H., Grabowski, T., Tranel, D., Hichwa, R., & Damasio, A. (1996). A neural basis for lexical retrieval. *Nature, 380,* 499–505.

Damasio, A., & Van Hoesen, G. (1985). The limbic system and the localization of herpes simplex encephalitis. *Journal of Neurology, Neurosurgery, and Psychiatry, 48,* 297–301.

DeKosky, S., & Scheff, S. (1990). Synaptic loss in frontal cortex biopsies in Alzheimer's disease: Correlation with cognitive severity. *Annals of Neurology, 27,* 457–464.

DeLacoste, M.-C., & White, C. (1993). The role of cortical connectivity in Alzheimer's disease pathogenesis: A review and model system. *Neurobiology of Aging, 14,* 1–16.

Devlin, J. (1998). Unpublished doctoral dissertation, Department of Computer Science and Neuroscience Program, University of Southern California.

Farah, M. (1994). Neuropsychological inference with an interactive brain: A critique of the "locality" assumption. *Behavioral and Brain Sciences, 17,* 43–104.

Farah, M., & McClelland, J. (1991). A computational model of semantic memory impairment: Modality specificity and emergent category specificity. *Journal of Experimental Psychology: General, 120,* 339–357.

Garrard, P., Patterson, K., Watson, P., & Hodges, J. (1998). Category-specific semantic loss in dementia of Alzheimer's type: Functional-anatomical correlations from cross-sectional analyses. *Brain, 121,* 633–646.

Gibson, P. (1983). EM study of the numbers of cortical synapses in the brains of ageing people and people with Alzheimer-type dementia. *Acta Neuropathologica, 62,* 127–133.

Gonnerman, L. M., Andersen, E. S., Devlin, J. T., Kempler, D., & Seidenberg, M. S. (1997). Double dissociation of semantic categories in Alzheimer's disease. *Brain and Language, 57,* 254–279.

Hart, J., Berndt, R., & Caramazza, A. (1985). Category specific naming deficit following cerebral infarction. *Nature, 316,* 439–440.

Hart, J., & Gordon, B. (1990). Delineation of single-word semantic comprehension deficits in aphasia, with anatomical correlation. *Annals of Neurology, 27,* 226–231.

Hart, J., & Gordon, B. (1992). Neural subsystems for object knowledge. *Nature, 359,* 60–64.

Hassoun, M. (1995). *Fundamentals of artificial neural networks.* Cambridge, MA: MIT Press.

Henderson, V., & Finch, C. (1989). The neurobiology of Alzheimer's disease. *Journal of Neurosurgery, 70,* 335–353.

Hillis, A., & Caramazza, A. (1991). Category specific naming and comprehension impairment: A double dissociation. *Brain and Language, 114,* 2081–2094.

Hinton, G. (1981). Implementing semantic networks in parallel hardware. In G. Hinton & J. Anderson (Eds.), *Parallel models of associative memory* (pp. 161–188). Hillsdale, NJ: Lawrence Erlbaum Associates Inc.

Hinton, G., & Shallice, T. (1991). Lesioning an attractor network: Investigations of acquired dyslexia. *Psychological Review, 98,* 74–95.

Hopfield, J. (1982). Neural networks and physical systems with emergent collective computational abilities. *Proceedings of the National Academy of Science, USA, 79,* 2554–2558.

Horn, D., Ruppin, E., Usher, M., & Herrmann, M. (1993). Neural-network modeling of memory deterioration in Alzheimer's disease. *Neural Computation, 5,* 736–749.

Hyman, B., Van Hoesen, G., Damasio, A., & Barnes, C. (1984). Alzheimer's disease: Cell-specific pathology isolates the hippocampal formation. *Science, 235,* 1168–1170.

Keil, F. (1987). Conceptual development and category structure. In U. Neisser (Ed.), *Concepts and conceptual development.* Cambridge, UK: Cambridge University Press.

Keil, F. (1989). *Concepts, kinds, and cognitive development.* Cambridge, MA: MIT Press.

Malt, B., & Johnson, E. (1992). Do artifact concepts have cores? *Journal of Memory and Language, 31,* 195–217.

Malt, B., & Smith, E. (1984). Correlated properties in natural categories. *Journal of Verbal Learning and Verbal Behavior, 23,* 250–269.

Martin, A., Haxby, J., Lalonde, F., Wiggs, C., & Ungerleider, L. (1995). Discrete cortical regions associated with knowledge of color and knowledge of action. *Science, 270,* 102–105.

Martin, A., Wiggs, C., Ungerleider, L., & Haxby, J. (1996). Neural correlates of category-specific knowledge. *Nature, 379,* 649–652.

Masliah, E., Hansen, L., Mallory, M., & Terry, R. (1991). Immunoelectron microscopic study of synaptic pathology in Alzheimer's disease. *Acta Neuropathologica, 81,* 428–433.

Masliah, E., Terry, R., Mallory, M., Alford, M., & Hansen, L. (1990). Diffuse plaques do not accentuate synapse loss in Alzheimer's disease. *American Journal of Pathology, 137,* 1293–1297.

Mazzoni, M., Moretti, P., Lucchini, C., Vista, M., & Muratorio, A. (1991). Category-specific semantic disorders in Alzheimer's disease. *Nuova Rivista di Neurologia, 1,* 77–85.

McRae, K., de Sa, V., & Seidenberg, M. S. (1997). On the nature and scope of featural representations of word meaning. *Journal of Experimental Psychology: General, 126,* 99–130.

Murphy, G. L., & Medin, D. L. (1985). The role of theories in conceptual coherence. *Psychological Review, 92,* 289–316.

Nebes, R. (1989). Semantic memory in Alzheimer's disease. *Psychological Bulletin, 106,* 377–394.

Patterson, K., Graham, N., & Hodges, J. (1994). The impact of semantic memory loss on phonological representations. *Journal of Cognitive Neuroscience, 6,* 57–69.

Patterson, K., & Hodges, J. (1992). Deterioration of word meaning: Implications for reading. *Neuropsychologia, 30,* 1025–1040.

Patterson, K. E., Seidenberg, M. S., & McClelland, J. L. (1990). Connections and disconnections: Acquired dyslexia in a computational model of reading processes. In R. G. M. Morris (Ed.), *Parallel distributed processing: Implications for psychology and neuroscience* (pp. 131–181). London: Oxford University Press.

Pearson, R., Esiri, M., Hiorns, R., Wilcock, G., & Powell, T. (1985). Anatomical correlates in the distribution of the pathological changes in the neocortex in Alzheimer's disease. *Proceedings of the National Academy of Sciences, USA, 82,* 4531–4534.

Perani, D., Cappa, S., Bettinardi, V., Bressi, S., Gornotempini, M., Matarrese, M., & Fazio, F. (1995). Different neural systems for the recognition of animals and man-made tools. *Neuroreport, 6,* 1637–1641.

Pietrini, V., Nertempi, P., Vaglia, A., Revello, M., Pinna, V., & Ferro-Milone, F. (1988). Recovery from herpes simplex encephalitis: Selective impairment of specific semantic categories with neuroradiological correlation. *Journal of Neurology, Neurosurgery, and Psychiatry, 51,* 1284–1293.

Plaut, D. (1991). *Connectionist neuropsychology: The breakdown and recovery of behavior in lesioned attractor networks.* Unpublished doctoral dissertation, Carnegie-Mellon University.

Plaut, D. (1995). Double dissociation without modularity—Evidence from connectionist neuropsychology. *Journal of Clinical and Experimental Neuropsychology, 17,* 291–321.

Plaut, D., & Shallice, T. (1993). Deep dyslexia—a case study of connectionist neuropsychology. *Cognitive Neuropsychology, 10,* 377–500.

Price, J., Davis, P., Morris, J., & White, D. (1991). The distribution of tangles, plaques and related immunohistochemical markers in healthy aging and Alzheimer's disease. *Neurobiology of Aging, 12,* 295–312.

Rapp, B., & Caramazza, A. (1990). On the distinction between deficits of access and deficits of storage: A question of theory. *Cognitive Neuropsychology, 10,* 113–141.

Rogers, J., & Morrison, J. (1985). Quantitative morphology and regional and laminar distributions of senile plaques in Alzheimer's disease. *Journal of Neuroscience, 5,* 2801–2808.

Rosch, E. (1975). Cognitive representations of semantic categories. *Journal of Experimental Psychology: General, 104,* 192–233.

Rosch, E., & Mervis, C. (1975). Family resemblances: Studies in the internal structure of categories. *Cognitive Psychology, 7,* 573–605.

Rumelhart, D., & McClelland, J. (1986). *Parallel distributed processing: Explorations in the microstructure of cognition.* Cambridge, MA: MIT Press.

Ruppin, E., & Reggia, J. (1995). A neural model of memory impairment in diffuse cerebral atrophy. *British Journal of Psychiatry, 166,* 19–28.

Saffran, E., & Schwartz, M. (1994). Of cabbages and things: Semantic memory from a neuropsychological perspective—A tutorial review. In C. Umiltà & M. Moscovitch (Eds.), *Attention and performance* XV: *Conscious and nonconscious information processing* (pp. 507–536). Cambridge, MA: MIT Press.

Sartori, G., & Job, R. (1988). The oyster with four legs: A neuropsychological study on the interaction of visual and semantic information. *Cognitive Neuropsychology, 5,* 103–132.

Scheff, S., DeKosky, S., & Price, D. (1990). Quantitative assessment of cortical synaptic density in Alzheimer's disease. *Neurobiology of Aging, 11,* 29–37.

Seidenberg, M. S. (1988). Cognitive neuropsychology and language: The state of the art. *Cognitive Neuropsychology, 5,* 403–426.

Shallice, T. (1988). *From neuropsychology to mental structure.* Cambridge: Cambridge University Press.

Shallice, T. (1993). Multiple semantics: Whose confusions? *Cognitive Neuropsychology, 10,* 251–261.

Silveri, M.-C., Daniele, A., Giustolisi, L., & Gainotti, G. (1991). Dissociation between knowledge of living and nonliving things in dementia of the Alzheimer type. *Neurology, 41,* 545–546.

Silveri, M.-C., & Gainotti, G. (1988). Interaction between vision and language in category-specific semantic impairment. *Cognitive Neuropsychology, 5,* 677–709.

Small, S., Hart, J., Gordon, B., & Hollard, A. (1993). Performance variability in a diffusely lesioned model of semantic representation for object naming. *Neurology, 43,* 404.

Smith, E., Shoben, E., & Rips, L. (1974). Structure and process in semantic memory: A featural model for semantic decision. *Psychological Review, 81,* 214–241.

Terry, R., Masliah, E., Salmon, D., Butters, N., DeTeresa, R., Hill, R., Hansen, L., & Katzman, R. (1991). Physical basis of cognitive alterations in Alzheimer's disease: Synaptic loss is the major correlate of cognitive impairment. *Annals of Neurology, 30,* 572–580.

Tversky, A. (1977). Features of similarity. *Psychological Review, 84,* 327–352.

Warrington, E., & McCarthy, R. (1983). Category specific access dysphasia. *Brain, 106,* 859–878.

Warrington, E., & McCarthy, R. (1987). Categories of knowledge: Further fractionations and an attempted integration. *Brain*, *110*, 1273–1296.

Warrington, E. K., & Shallice, T. (1984). Category specific semantic impairments. *Brain*, *107*, 829–853.

Yankner, B., & Mesulam, M. (1991). Seminars in medicine of the Beth Israel Hospital, Boston. Beta-amyloid and the pathogenesis of Alzheimer's disease. *New England Journal of Medicine*, *325*, 1849–1857.

Face recognition: Mapping routes

Robert A. Johnston

ARE THERE SEPARATE FACE AND OBJECT RECOGNITION SYSTEMS?

Although faces are arguably a subset of visual objects, many researchers have suggested that humans have special cognitive processes that are dedicated to the recognition of faces. This issue is one that is unlikely to be resolved by investigating normal people recognising faces and other objects. An examination of people who have face-specific or object-specific impairments is more likely to be illuminating. Bodamer (1947) was the first to provide a detailed account of face recognition problems which he considered might be a sub-category of agnosia, and this condition has since been labelled prosopagnosia. However, it might be argued that a face recognition impairment simply reflects a mild form of object recognition difficulties. In the laboratory, it has been demonstrated that there are many similarities in the way that objects and faces are processed, but De Renzi (1986) presented evidence that the two processes are separate. He described a patient who could not recognise familiar faces, but who could complete a number of finely detailed object tasks. For example, he could distinguish Italian coins from other foreign coins, discriminate different breeds of cat, and recognise his own possessions from those of other people (e.g., his wallet). However, it is possible to argue that these tasks are still easier than the face recognition one. It seems essential to be able to investigate tasks that involve within-category discriminations such as recognising individual animals. Bruyer et al. (1983) describe a prosopagnosic patient who could still recognise his own cows and dogs, and double dissociations between recognising human and animal faces have been reported.

In Chapter 4, McNeil and Warrington describe a patient, WJ, who became prosopagnosic as a result of a stroke, and after his accident retired to become a sheep farmer. WJ was very impaired in his recognition of familiar faces and also on a number of other face processing tasks such as judging sex or facial expression. In trying to show that WJ's problem was specific to faces it is useful to show that his recognition of objects was not impaired.

The current fluency of his sheep recognition skills has been demonstrated by showing an equivalent performance to other retired sheep farmers, and superior performance to age matched controls who have had no experience with sheep. In contrast, both these groups of controls are able to recognise or learn faces much better than WJ. Before his stroke, WJ was unfamiliar with sheep and so his sheep recognition abilities must have been learnt since then. McNeil and Warrington concluded that his problem is face-specific, given this evidence of his being able to process other visually difficult and confusable stimuli.

WHY ARE PEOPLE'S NAMES SO VULNERABLE TO LOSS?

Research on face recognition has examined how we access different information from familiar faces and suggests a pattern of access that might be labelled familiarity, semantic, and name information. That is, people first decide that a face is familiar, then retrieve biographical/semantic information about the person, and finally recall the name. Although it is sometimes possible to temporarily forget the name of an object, this problem seems more prevalent in face naming where tip-of-the-tongue (TOT) states appear to occur more frequently. The profusion of reported name retrieval blocks has focused attention on the route by which we access information that is stored about familiar faces.

The Bruce and Young (1986) model remains the most exhaustive account of face processing (see Chapter 6, Figure 1). This model includes many aspects of face processing, but this section is concerned only with how we recognise familiar faces. As in the case of object recognition, although identifying a familiar face will often seem immediate and complete it is possible to decompose the process into a set of stages. A key feature of the Bruce and Young account of the recognition of familiar faces is that information becomes available in a specified order and that there is no direct link between the representation of a person's face and the representation of their name.

In the laboratory this sequence of stages is reflected in the response times of normal people. It is faster to judge that a face is familiar than to access biographical information such as occupation, and this in turn is faster than naming (e.g., Young, McWeeny, Ellis, & Hay, 1986). In everyday life, this pattern is occasionally reflected in errors. We sometimes see a face that seems familiar to us, but we cannot say who it is. This generally occurs when a person is seen out of their usual context. Another type of error occurs when we know who someone is

but cannot retrieve their name. We may recognise an actor or a politician and access biographical facts such as nationality, films starred in, speeches made, and scandals implicated in. The phenomenon is intriguing because of the extent of semantic information that can be available during a name block, and because of the relationship between names and faces. There is nothing in the surface appearance of a face to indicate that it belongs to a politician or an actor. To determine correctly the occupational category of a presented face we must have accessed a uniquely identifying cognitive representation of that person's identity —but somehow that representation does not necessarily give access to the name. This decomposition of the face identification process is again more apparent when we examine individuals whose face identification problems are of a pathological kind.

There are case studies of patients who have problems that appear to be occurring at different places along the face recognition route. De Haan, Young, and Newcombe (1991) reported the case of ME who could reliably decide whether faces were familiar or not, but who could not retrieve any semantic information about the person, and other patients have been reported who could access extensive semantic information, but not retrieve names. The patterns of error observed in patients taken together with patterns that do not occur—no-one has found a patient who can name faces but not retrieve semantic information—have led theorists to suggest that complete face identification entails a traversal of a route through these sources of information.

CAN NAMES BE IMPAIRED WHILE SEMANTICS ARE PRESERVED?

Generally, the data obtained with prosopagnosic patients have been amenable to explanation by the Bruce and Young account, but, in recent years, evidence has been uncovered that is less compatible with the proposal of a strict sequential model. In these cases the performance of brain-damaged subjects has forced theories to evolve and in part this process has been aided by trying to build computer simulations of these face recognition models.

Young, Hellawell, and De Haan (1988) described such a case. PH is a prosopagnosic patient who is unable to recognise faces that were once familiar to him. On the other hand PH shows preserved semantic information about people when shown their names. This would be explained by the Bruce and Young (1986) account in terms of damage to Face Recognition Units (FRUs). However, PH belongs to a class of prosopagnosic patients who show what is termed covert recognition and he exhibits what has been termed covert priming. These abilities are harder for the model to explain.

The phenomenon of covert recognition is shown when galvanic skin responses are greater to familiar compared to unfamiliar faces, even though the familiar faces cannot be overtly recognised. Covert recognition is also shown by the fact

that patients may be able to learn the correct name for a face that they cannot overtly recognise better than they can learn an incorrect name. PH makes use of this covert recognition ability to show covert priming. Semantic priming has been shown to occur with many stimuli including words, pictures, and faces. It is facilitation that arises in processing due to the earlier presentation of an item that has a related meaning. Thus naming a presented picture of a dog would be primed by previously seeing a picture of a cat. Semantic priming also occurs with faces, although the relationship is generally restricted to associates (like Charles and Diana) rather than simply people drawn from a similar category.

Semantic priming can cross modalities and operate across names and faces. Thus while a familiarity decision to the face of Dawn French would be faster if the face of Jennifer Saunders had just been viewed, it is also the case that a familiarity decision to Dawn French's name would be speeded up after seeing the face of Jennifer Saunders. PH is unable to recognise most familiar faces overtly, but he is able to recognise the names of familiar people and access quite complete biographical details. PH also shows covert face–name semantic priming even though he cannot (overtly) recognise the presented face. This pattern is not consistent with the sequential route proposed by Bruce and Young.

In order to attempt an explanation of covert prosopagnosia, Young and De Haan (1988) proposed a discontinuity between a properly functioning input stage (face recognition) and the cognitive system, but where these systems could still interact with each other via other input recognition systems. In their model, they represent this account by introducing new associative links between face recognition units and name recognition units (see Chapter 6, pp. 173–174). These links would allow an explanation of PH's covert priming, but the explanation is less satisfactory because the nature of these connections would have to be very different from all the other links in the model. This account also weakens a central assumption of the Bruce and Young account that there is no direct link between face and name representations. An alternative approach is offered by computational models which have attempted to understand covert recognition in terms of the architecture of the system representing the information.

COMPUTATIONAL MODELLING WITH DISCRETE, LOCALIST REPRESENTATIONS

One explanation for the pattern of impairments exhibited by patients like PH was proposed by Burton, Young, Bruce, Johnston, and Ellis in a paper reproduced here in Chapter 6, an account developed from their IAC (Interactive Activation and Competition) model of face recognition. They suggested that it was necessary to unpack the coarser model represented by Bruce and Young (1986) and examine the micro-architecture of the face recognition system. In order to achieve this they built an IAC model of the face recognition system where structures like FRUs and PINs (Person Identity Nodes) are represented as active units, collected

in separate pools, that are connected by modifiable links. IAC models have a connectionist architecture as they comprise active units connected by modifiable links. However, they make use of localist rather than distributed representations. Although the possible variations of such models are manifold, there are some central aspects of the architecture that are common to all variants.

Active units at the same level of representation are grouped together in pools where they are linked by inhibitory links. Related units at different levels of representation are linked by facilitatory connections. When activation is introduced into the system it passes across the excitatory and inhibitory links causing the changes in the activation of connected units. With passage of time, the activation within the system tends to stabilise, favouring a particular configuration of units whose activation is balanced by its inhibition.

Although the IAC model was based on the Bruce and Young framework, in order to construct it many aspects of the Bruce and Young account needed to be more finely specified. In Chapter 6, Burton et al. use the modified model to show how the behaviour of PH could be easily explained. This is described on pages 178–185. Essentially, the IAC model explains semantic priming on the basis of residual activation from the prime face persisting in the system. This reduces the time the target face needs to exceed its recognition threshold. In covert prosopagnosia, the FRU–PIN links have become attenuated rather than disconnected. This means that, while the presented face never reaches its own threshold of identification at the PIN, there is enough activation passing into the system to facilitate the recognition of a related name and covert recognition of a face.

Computational modelling that compels us to attend to the micro-structure of theories has liberated us from the straitjacket of single sequential routes, but some models still employ this approach. The model of face recognition by Farah, O'Reilly, and Vecera reprinted here in Chapter 7 is sequential although it employs a connectionist architecture.

COMPUTATIONAL MODELLING WITH DISTRIBUTED REPRESENTATIONS

The Farah et al. model differs from the Burton et al. account in a number of important ways. They suggested that "face and name units are not directly connected, but rather they send activation to one another through hidden and semantic units" (p. 211) so that semantics must be accessed before names can be accessed. Their model is essentially sequential, whereas in the Burton et al. model names and semantics are accessed in parallel.

The Farah et al. model employs five pools of distributed units. Two of these pools comprise hidden units which are intended to improve the learning of association between the other three layers of units that represent face input units, semantic units, and name units (see Chapter 7, Figure 2). The model learned to associate the faces, occupations and names of 40 individuals. Farah and colleagues

simulated a number of face processing activities, however, it is the work reported in the section of Chapter 7 entitled Simulation 4 that is most relevant here.

In this simulation Farah et al. lesioned their model so that it showed both covert recognition and semantic priming. The model was able to re-learn correct name–face associations faster than incorrect ones and could categorise a presented name faster when it was preceded by an "unrecognised" face drawn from the same category. Farah et al. proposed that covert and overt prosopagnosics are not two distinct disorders, but instead represent different points along a continuum of face recognition impairment. Whereas the Burton et al. account suggests that covert recognition arises due to an intact visual recognition system becoming partially disconnected from the rest of the system, Farah et al. consider that covert recognition can be explained by an impairment in visual recognition.

CAN THESE TWO APPROACHES BE RECONCILED?

It can been seen from the preceding discussion that there are two competing models of face recognition which both appear to allow the simulation of many face processing activities including covert recognition by prosopagnosics. It is interesting to consider what overlap there is between these two approaches and explore differences that exist between them. This analysis leads to a consideration of the wider benefits of computational modelling for accounts of cognitive neuropsychological phenomena.

Farah et al. list two important differences between their model and that of Burton et al. First, their account employs distributed representations while that of Burton and colleagues uses local ones. Second, they distinguish their model by its ability to learn the representations it uses, whereas the Burton et al. model is hard-wired and does not learn. However, these differences might have been thought to arise largely through convenience. The lack of learning in IAC models means they provide "snapshots of cognition" and Burton (1994) has shown it is possible for IAC models to learn. Learning is simply more easily implemented with distributed representations. The issue of type of representation might also turn out to be unimportant. On the one hand, IAC models could be implemented with distributed rather than local representations. More contentiously, it could be claimed that the Farah et al. model also employs a form of local representation in the way that occupation units are interpreted.

However, the greater importance of the differences between these two approaches to modelling face recognition was brought into sharp focus in a special issue of the journal *Cognitive Neuropsychology* (Kanwisher & Moscovitch, 2000). Both camps have been able to extend their accounts and comment on differences between these rival models both in terms of their construction and also with reference to their success in modelling various face processing activities. Not surprisingly, these explorations leave many of the differences unresolved, but

the exercise was very instructive in delineating precisely where those differences lie. In Chapter 8, Burton and Young summarise the issues that still divide the models.

So far, the differences between the models have been viewed as differences in their construction. Burton and Young, however, cast these differences in terms of the researchers' philosophy. O'Reilly and Farah (1999) claim that their model shares such similarities with real neural networks that it can be considered as a model of a brain, and hence they eschew any difference between psychological and neurophysiological levels of explanation. Burton and Young are unable to accept this level of identification. On the one hand, they point out that, while it is likely that the brain uses distributed representations, it cannot be assumed that these are the same type of distributed representations that happen to be chosen by modellers. Specifically, they propose that the brain probably uses coarse coded distributed representations while the Farah et al. model codes across all units at a particular level. Burton and Young are also unhappy about the use of learning algorithms that bear little resemblance to those employed by human cognitive systems. O'Reilly and Farah shrug off such technicalities as theory-irrelevant, but Burton and Young contend that the type of learning employed will determine the representations that are formed. They consider the "mere presence of learning in connectionist models is of little value if that learning is unlike human learning". The identification of such fundamental differences in perspective illustrates how attempts to model a quite circumscribed process such as face recognition can inform our discussion of the utility of neuropsychological and computational approaches to understanding the cognitive system.

REFERENCES

Bodamer, J. (1947). Die Prosop-Agnosie. *Archiv für Psychiatrie und Nervenkrankheiten, 179*, 6–53.

Bruce, V., & Young, A. W. (1986). Understanding face recognition. *British Journal of Psychology, 77*, 305–327.

Bruyer, R., Laterre, C., Seron, X., Feyereisen, P., Strypstein, E., Pierrard, E., & Rectem, D. (1983). A case of prosopagnosia with some preserved covert remembrance of familiar faces. *Brain and Cognition, 2*, 257–284.

Burton, A. M. (1994). Learning new faces in an interactive activation and competition model. In V. Bruce & G. W. Humphreys (Eds.), *Object and face recognition* [Special issue of *Visual Cognition*, Vol. 1, No. 2/3, pp. 313–348]. Hove, UK: Lawrence Erlbaum Associates Ltd.

Burton, A. M., Bruce, V., & Johnston, R. A. (1990). Understanding face recognition with an interactive activation model. *British Journal of Psychology, 81*, 361–380.

De Haan, E. H. F., Young, A. W., & Newcombe, F. (1987). Faces interfere with name classification in a prosopagnosic patient. *Cortex, 23*, 309–316.

De Haan, E. H. F., Young, A. W., & Newcombe, F. (1991). A dissociation between the sense of familiarity and access to semantic information concerning familiar people. *European Journal of Cognitive Psychology, 3*(1), 51–67.

De Renzi, E. (1986). Current issues in prosopagnosia. In H. D. Ellis, M. A. Jeeves, F. Newcombe, & A. W. Young (Eds.), *Aspects of face processing* (pp. 243–252). Dordrecht, Netherlands: Martinus Nijhoff.

Kanwisher, N., & Moscovitch, M. (Eds.). (2000). The cognitive neuroscience of face processing [special issue of *Cognitive Neuropsychology*, *17*(1/2/3), 1–296]. Hove, UK: Psychology Press.

O'Reilly, R. C., & Farah, M. J. (1999). Simulation and explanation in neuropsychology and beyond. *Cognitive Neuropsychology*, *16*, 49–72.

Young, A. W., & De Haan, E. H. F. (1988). Boundaries of covert recognition in prosopagnosia. *Cognitive Neuropsychology*, *5*, 317–336.

Young, A. W., Hellawell, D., & De Haan, E. H. F. (1988). Cross-domain semantic priming in normal subjects and a prosopagnosic patient. *Quarterly Journal of Experimental Psychology*, *40A*, 561–580.

Young, A. W., McWeeny, K. H., Ellis, A. W., & Hay, D. C. (1986). Naming and categorizing faces and written names. *Quarterly Journal of Experimental Psychology*, *38A*, 297–318.

CHAPTER FOUR

Prosopagnosia:
A face-specific disorder

Jane E. McNeil and Elizabeth K. Warrington
National Hospital, London, UK

A follow-up study of a patient, WJ, with a very severe prosopagnosia is reported. After a stroke he became a farmer and acquired a flock of sheep. He learnt to recognize and name many of his sheep, and his performance on tests of recognition memory and paired-associate learning for sheep was significantly better than on comparable tests using human face stimuli. It is concluded that in some instances prosopagnosia can be a face-specific disorder.

Experimental studies of face perception have shown a double dissociation between the ability to perceive unknown faces and the ability to recognize familiar faces (Tranel, Damasio, & Damasio, 1988; Warrington & James, 1967). However, one of the continuing controversies is whether or not prosopagnosia, the inability to recognize familiar faces, is specific to faces. Bodamer (1947) first described the syndrome as a specific disorder of the face recognition system, but more recent authors have suggested that the deficit may also apply to other within-category discriminations. Damasio, Damasio, and Van Hoesen (1982) suggested that prosopagnosia was not specific to human faces, but would be found for all "visually ambiguous stimuli whose recognition depends on contextual memory evocation" (p. 331).

Recent studies have suggested that prosopagnosia itself may not be a unitary disorder. De Renzi (1986; De Renzi, Faglioni, Grossi, & Nichelli, 1991) has proposed two distinct types of prosopagnosia. The first he terms "perceptual" or "apperceptive prosopagnosia" and the second "mnestic" or "associative prosopagnosia". He also proposes that it is among patients with the associative form

The Quarterly Journal of Experimental Psychology, 1993, *46A*(1) 1–10.

that a face-specific disorder is most likely to be observed. Indeed Case 4 from his 1986 paper appeared to be a case of the associative form of prosopagnosia, a deficit that was selective for faces. He was unable to recognize close friends or relatives but could identify his own belongings from others of the same category, sort foreign from Italian coins, and pick out particular breeds of cats from photographs. However, it could be argued that these types of tasks are easier than distinguishing between two faces.

In our alternative classification (McNeil & Warrington, 1991) we have treated apperceptive difficulties as an associated deficit and would wish instead to emphasize the presence or absence of covert recognition. So, rather than distinguishing between apperceptive and associative forms, we suggested that the two forms could be seen as being due to either a disconnection of the face recognition units or damage to the units themselves. However, this issue of face specificity still exists.

Davidoff (1986) has argued that visual stimuli need to be equated for familiarity and difficulty of discrimination before a selective deficit for faces can be inferred. At the very least, within-category discriminations for other visually difficult categories should be tested.

There are a few papers in the literature that have attempted to test prosopagnosic patients' abilities to make other within-category discriminations by using animals that were previously familiar to them. Bornstein (1963) reported the case of a bird watcher who could no longer identify birds, and Bornstein, Sroka, and Munitz (1969) describe a prosopagnosic farmer who was no longer able to recognize his own cows. Bruyer et al. (1983) provide a clinical description of a farmer (Mr W) who could not recognize faces but who could identify his own cows and dogs. A further case by Assal, Favre, and Anderes (1984) showed the converse pattern. They describe a farmer, MX, who was initially impaired at recognizing human faces and his livestock (cows). However, when he was retested after 6 months, he had recovered the ability to recognize faces but was still unable to recognize his cows.

These studies provide some evidence that prosopagnosic patients can be unimpaired on other visually similar and confusable stimuli and therefore do appear to have a face-specific disorder. The aim of the present study is to describe our further observations of a very severe case of prosopagnosia, who had a stable and longstanding impairment for recognizing very familiar people but who nevertheless learnt to identify a flock of sheep.

CASE REPORT

WJ was a 51-year-old right-handed professional man with a history of at least 3 vascular episodes. On examination he was found to have a profound prosopagnosia, normal visual acuity, and a dense right homonymous hemianopia with a relative scotoma in the upper left quadrants. A CT scan showed low-density

lesions in the left occipital lobe and left frontal and temporal lobes. There was also low attenuation in the right occipital lobe.

Neuropsychological investigation

WJ showed a significant impairment on the Performance scale of the WAIS but was unimpaired on the Verbal scale (PIQ = 116, VIQ = 143). He had a selective visual memory impairment, scoring at a chance level on the visual version of the Recognition Memory test but in the average range on the verbal version (Warrington, 1984). He had excellent naming skills, and he achieved a high score (24/30) on a proper names test (McKenna & Warrington, 1980). He performed normally on tests of shape detection and shape discrimination. He was impaired on some perceptual tests including unusual views and object silhouettes. However, his most marked impairments were on tasks that required the perception and recognition of faces. He was able to identify only 2 out of 12 very well-known faces, and it seemed that even for the faces that he correctly identified he was performing the task through the use of deductive strategies rather than by actually recognizing them. He was also unable to judge the age, sex, or facial expression of faces and was impaired on tests of face matching, including the Benton and Van Allen (1968) test (WJ's score = 36/54, which is in the moderately impaired range). (For further details, see McNeil and Warrington, 1991, Case 1.)

EXPERIMENTAL INVESTIGATION

1. Famous face familiarity

Our aim in this experiment was to confirm WJ's poor face recognition abilities and to replicate our original observations of covert recognition of faces. This test consisted of 30 arrays of three faces: one famous face and two unfamiliar distractors, which were similar in appearance (see Figure 1 for an example of the stimuli used). The famous faces were all contemporary personalities (this is an

Figure 1. An example of face familiarity stimuli.

TABLE 1
Scores on famous face familiarity tests

	Date tested	
	10 June 1991	*31 Oct. 1991*
Face only	10/30	13/30
Face and name	20/30	25/30

updated version of the original test material used by Warrington & McCarthy, 1988). The patient was merely required to pick out the famous face from the two unfamiliar distractor stimuli. WJ was administered this test on two occasions (6 months apart). His results were close to chance on both occasions (see Table 1).

The same test stimuli were re-presented together with the name of the famous face. So, rather than being asked, "which is the famous face?" he was asked, "which is Michael Aspel?". The number correct on each occasion was significantly greater than when he was merely pointing to the famous face: sign tests, $n = 16$, $x = 4$ and $n = 18$, $x = 3$, 1-tailed $p < 0.05$. WJ maintained that he was guessing on this task, even though his performance dramatically improved.

These findings provide a very robust replication of our original observations and suggest that WJ has covert face recognition abilities.

2. Sheep identification

Our earlier study did not address the issue of face specificity. We reported that WJ was able to name 9/10 famous buildings, 7/7 breeds of dog, 7/7 makes of car, and 14/15 flowers. But although these tasks test within-category discrimination, they do not test identification of unique individual exemplars within a category, as is the case for faces. The following experiments will attempt to test this by looking at WJ's abilities to recognize sheep.

WJ had recently (2 years previously) acquired a flock of 36 sheep, which he kindly photographed for the purposes of these experiments. Each of the 36 sheep had a number (ranging from 1 to 59) which was written on a tag in its ear, so that they could be individually identified. A sub-set of 16 sheep photographs was re-photographed so that only the face of each sheep, without a tag, was visible. WJ's first task was to tell us the number label of each of the sheep. He was able to identify, by number, 8/16 sheep; however, this is probably an underestimate of his actual knowledge of his sheep, as in several instances he would say things like, "I know that sheep very well, she's the one that had three lambs last year, but I can't remember her number". Obviously all answers like this had to be scored as incorrect as there was no way to check his answers. Nevertheless, WJ still shows a striking ability to recognize his sheep.

Figure 2. Examples of "known" sheep.

3. Recognition memory for sheep

To eliminate the need for WJ to recall the number labels of the sheep, a Yes/No recognition test was devised: 8 of the photographs of sheep faces were presented singly at a 3-sec presentation rate (see Figure 2). An orienting task was used, in which WJ had to say whether he thought the sheep was pleasant/not pleasant. Recognition memory was then tested by presenting the 8 stimuli and 8 distractors in a random order. WJ was required to say whether or not each item had been in the stimulus list.

Two subjects, in the same age range, who had also recently retired (4 years) and acquired a flock of sheep, were tested as controls; 5 age- and profession-matched controls were also tested.

Two further versions of this recognition memory test were devised. The first used a different breed of sheep that were unknown to WJ, and the second photographs of unknown human faces (with the hair masked). In each test there were again 8 stimuli and 8 distractors, and in each a pleasant/not pleasant orienting test was used. Both recognition memory tests were administered to WJ and the control subjects using the same Yes/No recognition procedure. The percentage correct for each test for WJ and the mean percentage correct (and range) for the control subjects are shown in Table 2.

The pattern of test scores for WJ is the opposite to that obtained by the control subjects. The profession-matched controls were significantly better at the unfamiliar face version than the unfamiliar sheep version: Wilcoxon test, $N = 5$, $T = 0$, $p < 0.05$. The two subjects with experience with sheep performed within the range of the profession-matched control group. However, WJ obtained significantly higher scores on both the familiar and unfamiliar sheep versions of this test than on the face version: $\chi^2 = 7.27$ and 9.6, respectively, $p < 0.05$. It is

TABLE 2
Recognition memory for faces of sheep and people

	WJ	Controls	
		Profession matched	Sheep experienced
Familiar sheep	87	66 (44–81)	59 (44–75)
Unfamiliar sheep	81	69 (56–81)	63 (44–81)
Faces	50	89 (75–100)	100

Mean percentage correct (range)

worth noting that the control subjects' performance was very similar on the tests using WJ's sheep and those using the sheep unfamiliar to WJ; it therefore seems reasonable to assume that WJ's sheep are not particularly easy to recognize.

4. Paired associate learning for sheep and faces

This test was a modification of a paired-associate learning task originally used by De Haan, Young, and Newcombe (1987) to demonstrate covert knowledge of faces. It consisted of 6 photographs of unknown sheep faces, which were paired with 6 plausible sheep "names" (e.g., "Frisky"). Figure 3 shows an example of

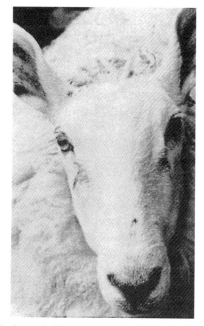

Figure 3. Examples of "unknown" sheep.

TABLE 3
Paired associate learning for sheep and people

| | | Mean percentage correct | |
| | | Controls | |
	WJ	Profession matched	Sheep experienced
Faces	23	71	78
Sheep	57	41	55

the sheep stimuli used. The 6 photographs were presented one at a time, and WJ was told the name that was to be associated with each face. He was then tested on his ability to recall the name for each sheep face photograph. The faces were presented in a different random order on each trial, and incorrect answers and no responses were corrected immediately by giving the correct answer. A second version of this task was devised using human faces, which were paired with similar descriptor names matched for frequency (e.g., "Friendly"). Five learning trials were given on each version of the test. The number of names correctly recalled across all the trials by WJ and the control subjects is given in Table 3.

The control subjects were significantly better at paired-associate learning of names for human faces than for sheep faces: Wilcoxon test, $N = 5$, $T = 0$, $p < 0.05$. An identical pattern was observed in the two subjects with experience of sheep. However, WJ did not show this normal human face advantage. His pattern of performance was the converse of that obtained by the control subjects, so that he was significantly better at learning sheep faces: $\chi^2 = 5.625$, $p < 0.05$.

This pattern of results is the same as that obtained on the recognition memory tests and indicates that WJ is unimpaired on tests involving sheep but performs poorly on learning and memory tasks involving human faces.

DISCUSSION

It has been shown that WJ continues to exhibit a profound prosopagnosia. In contrast, however, he has a remarkable ability to recognize another group of visually and easily confusable stimuli, the faces of sheep. He was able to identify his own sheep and claimed to recognize them more easily than faces. But, perhaps more surprisingly, he was also able to perform recognition memory tasks using photographs of sheep that were unfamiliar. It seems difficult to explain these results in terms of difficulty of discrimination, as the profession-matched controls found the sheep stimuli incredibly difficult to recognize (subjects complained that they "all looked the same"). It also cannot be explained in terms of familiarity with sheep, as the sheep-experienced controls were only marginally better. Unlike the other previously reported cases, WJ had no experience of sheep

before he developed his prosopagnosia. His current abilities to recognize sheep must have been learnt since his stroke, added to which it would seem implausible that he was now more familiar with sheep than with faces. It therefore seems as if WJ does in fact exhibit a face-specific recognition problem whilst remaining able to recognize other visually difficult and confusable stimuli.

According to De Renzi's classification, WJ should be termed a perceptual or apperceptive prosopagnosic (as he is severely impaired on tests of face perception) and should therefore be less likely to show a face-specific impairment. However, WJ does appear to have a face-specific deficit, as he can perform recognition memory tasks involving visually difficult stimuli other than faces. It seems implausible that his perceptual difficulties are only relevant for the recognition of faces, as the sheep stimuli used were just as perceptually demanding as faces. This seems further reason to suppose that his perceptual difficulties are insufficient to explain his prosopagnosia and should be seen as an associated deficit.

How WJ has learnt to recognize sheep is a matter for debate. It is possible that he has developed a sheep "prototype", which enables the effective encoding of sheep facial features. What is quite surprising, however, is the extent to which his abilities appear to generalize to other visually dissimilar breeds of sheep. Perhaps the more remarkable finding is that WJ has been totally unable to overcome his prosopagnosia. He has been seen in the department regularly over the past three years, and he is no better at recognizing faces now than when first seen in 1988. He seems unable to utilize the sorts of strategies he has learnt to use for sheep. This would suggest that his damaged face recognition system is actually still operating to such an extent that it prevents him from developing new strategies for use with faces. Previously we interpreted his performance on tests of face familiarity and famous face/name matching with reference to the Bruce and Young (1986) model of face perception and suggested that for WJ the problem lay at the output from the face recognition units to the person identity nodes and could be considered a disconnection. The units themselves are undamaged but are disconnected from the person identity nodes. It is possible that the existence of intact but disconnected face recognition units prevents the development of alternative methods of perceptual encoding.

Our patient provides further evidence that prosopagnosia can occur as a face-specific deficit. Other visually complex and difficult-to-discriminate stimuli were processed normally, indicating that prosopagnosia cannot be seen as a more general impairment for within-category discriminations. For some cases, at least, prosopagnosia appears to be a face-specific impairment.

ACKNOWLEDGEMENTS

We are grateful to Ms Anne-Marie Regan for supplying us with photographs of Irish sheep. Thanks are also due to Dr Gordon Plant for providing facilities to carry out this investigation.

REFERENCES

Assal, G., Favre, C., & Anderes, J. P. (1984). Non-reconnaissance d'animaux familiers chez un paysan: Zooagnosie ou prosopagnosie pour les animaux. *Revue Neurologique, 140*, 580–584.

Benton, A. L., & Van Allen, M. W. (1968). Impairment in facial recognition in patients with cerebral disease. *Cortex, 4*, 344–358.

Bodamer, J. (1947). Die Prosop-Agnosie. *Archiv für Psychiatrie und Nervenkrankheiten, 179*, 6–53.

Bornstein, B. (1963). Prosopagnosia. In L. Halpern (Ed.), *Problems of dynamic neurology*. Jerusalem: Hadassah Medical School.

Bornstein, B., Sroka, M., & Munitz, H. (1969). Prosopagnosia with animal face agnosia. *Cortex, 5*, 164–169.

Bruce, V., & Young, A. W. (1986). Understanding face recognition. *British Journal of Psychology, 77*, 305–327.

Bruyer, R., Laterre, C., Seron, X., Feyereisen, P., Strypstein, E., Pierrard, E., & Rectem, D. (1983). A case of prosopagnosia with some preserved covert remembrance of familiar faces. *Brain and Cognition, 2*, 257–284.

Damasio, A. R., Damasio, H., & Van Hoesen, G. W. (1982). Prosopagnosia: Anatomic basis and behavioral mechanisms. *Neurology, 32*, 321–341.

Davidoff, J. B. (1986). The specificity of face perception: Evidence from psychological investigations. In Bruyer, R. (Ed.), *The neuropsychology of face perception and facial expression*. Hillsdale, NJ: Lawrence Erlbaum Associates Inc.

De Haan, E. H. F., Young, A. W., & Newcombe, F. (1987). Face recognition without awareness. *Cognitive Neuropsychology, 4*, 385–415.

De Renzi, E. (1986). Current issues in prosopagnosia. In H. D. Ellis, M. A. Jeeves, F. Newcombe, & A. W. Young (Eds.), *Aspects of face processing* (pp. 243–252). Dordrecht: Martinus Nijhoff.

De Renzi, E., Faglioni, P., Grossi, D., & Nichelli, P. (1991). Apperceptive and associative forms of prosopagnosia. *Cortex, 27*, 213–221.

McKenna, P., & Warrington, E. K. (1980). Testing for nominal dysphasia. *Journal of Neurology, Neurosurgery and Psychiatry, 43*, 781–788.

McNeil, J. E., & Warrington, E. K. (1991). Prosopagnosia: A reclassification. *Quarterly Journal of Experimental Psychology, 43A*, 267–287.

Tranel, D., Damasio, A. R., & Damasio, H. (1988). Intact recognition of facial expression, gender and age in patients with impaired recognition of face identity. *Neurology, 38*, 690–696.

Warrington, E. K. (1984). *Recognition memory test*. Windsor, UK: NFER-Nelson Publishing Co. Ltd.

Warrington, E. K., & James, M. (1967). An experimental investigation of facial recognition in patients with unilateral cerebral lesions. *Cortex, 3*, 317–326.

Warrington, E. K., & McCarthy, R. A. (1988). The fractionation of retrograde amnesia. *Brain and Cognition, 7*, 184–200.

Cross-domain semantic priming in normal subjects and a prosopagnosic patient

Andrew W. Young and Deborah Hellawell
Lancaster University, UK

Edward H. F. De Haan
MRC Neuropsychology Unit, Radcliffe Infirmary, Oxford, UK

Cross-domain semantic priming of person recognition (from face primes to name targets at 500 msecs SOA) is investigated in normal subjects and a brain-injured patient (PH) with a very severe impairment of overt face recognition ability. Experiment 1 demonstrates equivalent semantic priming effects for normal subjects from face primes to name targets (cross-domain priming) and from name primes to name targets (within-domain priming). Experiment 2 demonstrates cross-domain semantic priming effects from face primes that PH cannot recognize overtly. Experiment 3 shows that cross-domain semantic priming effects can be found for normal subjects when target names are repeated across all conditions. This (repeated targets) method is then used in Experiment 4 to establish that PH shows equivalent semantic priming to normal subjects from face primes which he is very poor at identifying overtly and from name primes which he can identify overtly. These findings demonstrate that automatic aspects of face recognition can remain intact even when all sense of overt recognition has been lost.

Usually, our ability to recognize the faces of people we know operates automatically; we cannot look at a familiar face and decide not to recognize it. Under some circumstances, however, normal people may experience recognition failures or mistakes (Young, Hay, & Ellis, 1985) and in prosopagnosia, an unusual neurological condition, more or less permanent failure to recognize familiar faces overtly can occur.

A central question concerns the level(s) in the face recognition system at which errors can arise (Hay & Young, 1982; Young et al., 1985; Bruce & Young, 1986;

The Quarterly Journal of Experimental Psychology, 1988, 40A(3) 561–580.

H. Ellis, 1986a, b). A particularly interesting finding in this respect has been that prosopagnosic patients, who no longer recognize familiar faces overtly, may none the less exhibit "covert" recognition. Bauer (1984), for instance, found that electrodermal responses were greater to the correct name than to an incorrect name when his patient was viewing a familiar face that he could not recognize overtly, and Tranel and Damasio (1985) found that electrodermal responses were greater to familiar (but not overtly recognized) than to unfamiliar faces.

Covert recognition of familiar faces can also be demonstrated with behavioural (rather than electrophysiological) measures. De Haan, Young, and Newcombe (1987a, b) found that, despite being unable to identify overtly the faces used, the prosopagnosic patient PH was faster at matching the identities of simultaneously presented familiar than unfamiliar faces, learnt true names to familiar faces more easily than untrue names (for example, learning the name "Neil Kinnock" to Neil Kinnock's face more easily than he learnt the name "Roy Hattersley" to Cyril Smith's face), and showed interference from unrecognized distractor faces when performing name classification tasks. De Haan et al. (1987a, b) used these findings to argue that in certain types of prosopagnosia much of the processing of familiar faces can remain intact despite absence of awareness that recognition has occurred.

One way to conceptualise the disorder shown by such patients would be to consider that automatic aspects of face recognition mechanisms remain intact but disconnected from awareness (Young, 1988). This conception has the advantage that it allows prosopagnosia to be related to other types of neurological impairment that also seem to reflect the breakdown of different aspects of awareness (Schacter, McAndrews, & Moscovitch, 1988). The purpose of the present paper is to explore this idea by comparing PH's preserved face recognition abilities with aspects of recognition that seem to operate automatically in normal subjects.

Especially valuable techniques for examining automatic aspects of recognition mechanisms have involved priming effects. In particular, repetition priming (Bruce & Valentine, 1985; Young, McWeeny, Hay, & Ellis, 1986; A. Ellis, Young, Flude, & Hay, 1987) and semantic priming (Bruce, 1983, 1986; Bruce & Valentine, 1986) of face recognition have been investigated.

Repetition priming studies look at the influence of previous exposure to a particular stimulus on subsequent recognition. The effects found are reasonably long-lasting (measurable across minutes, hours, or even days) but usually specific to a particular type of stimulus material. Thus, seeing Ronald Reagan's face facilitates subsequent recognition of Reagan's face, but reading the name "Ronald Reagan" has no effect on subsequent recognition of Reagan's face (Bruce & Valentine, 1985; A. Ellis et al., 1987). This domain-specificity of repetition priming effects is found even within a task that might be considered to involve visual recognition of familiar people; seeing a familiar person's body does not prime later recognition of that person's face (A. Ellis et al., 1987). When cross-domain repetition priming effects have been found (between word and object recognition),

they are typically less marked than within-domain effects (Durso & Johnson, 1979; Kirsner, Milech & Stumpfel, 1986).

Semantic priming studies investigate the effect of having seen a related stimulus—for instance, the effect of seeing Nancy Reagan's face on recognition of Ronald Reagan's face. Substantial priming effects are found, but, in contrast to repetition priming effects, they dissipate rapidly (Dannenbring & Briand, 1982; Bruce, 1986). Thus it seems that semantic priming effects may arise in a different way from repetition priming (Young, 1988; Young & Ellis, 1989a). It has not been established whether or not semantic priming effects in person recognition will cross stimulus domains (e.g., from seeing Nancy Reagan's face to recognizing Ronald Reagan's name), but cross-domain semantic priming is found for recognition of other visually presented stimuli, such as words and objects (Sperber, McCauley, Ragain, & Weil, 1979), so that this might be expected.

Semantic priming effects are often investigated using a prime-target paradigm in which a prime stimulus (to which no response is made) precedes the target to which subjects make their response (Neely, 1976, 1977). The advantages of this technique are that by allowing the possibility of using a neutral prime stimulus, it permits examination of whether the priming effects obtained arise from facilitation of responses to targets preceded by related primes or inhibition of responses to targets preceded by unrelated primes (or both), and that it is possible to investigate the effects of stimulus onset asynchronies (SOAs) between the prime and target stimuli. In terms of Posner and Snyder's (1975) influential two-process theory of expectancy, automatic aspects of semantic priming will produce facilitation even at short SOAs, whereas conscious anticipatory effects will be more evident at longer SOAs and will also lead to inhibition of unrelated targets.

Using the prime-target paradigm, Bruce and Valentine (1986) found facilitation between related pairs of prime and target faces, even at SOAs as short as 250 msec, and no inhibition between unrelated prime and target faces. For name primes and name targets Bruce and Valentine (1986) also found facilitatory effects even at their shortest (250 msec) SOA, but there was also some evidence of inhibition. Bruce and Valentine (1986) did not examine cross-domain priming effects between face primes and name targets, or between name primes and face targets.

In the present paper we use the prime-target paradigm to look at cross-domain semantic priming effects in normal subjects and the prosopagnosic patient PH. We begin by determining whether or not cross-domain semantic priming between faces and names can be found for normal subjects, and whether such cross-domain effects are comparable to within-domain semantic priming. This then allows us to examine cross-domain and within-domain semantic priming for PH. Because PH is prosopagnosic, he cannot, of course, recognize most faces explicitly. Our interest in PH is thus in whether or not he shows semantic priming from face primes onto target names, and in comparing priming effects from unrecognized faces with those obtained to name primes that he *is* able to recognize overtly.

We begin, in Experiment 1, by establishing the presence of cross-domain priming effects from face primes to recognition of name targets for normal subjects, and comparing these to within-domain semantic priming effects from name primes to recognition of name targets.

EXPERIMENT 1

Method

Subjects.   Twenty-four students and staff of Lancaster University acted as subjects. All had normal or corrected-to-normal vision. All were paid. Of the subjects, 12 (6 male, 6 female) were allocated to the face/name condition and 12 (6 male, 6 female) to the name/name condition.

Stimuli and procedure.   Subjects were asked to make familiarity decisions to a series of printed names presented on back-projected slides (familiar name or unfamiliar name). An exposure duration of 2.5 sec was used for each name, and manual responses made by pressing one of two horizontally located buttons (one button for familiar names, one for unfamiliar names) were timed from target stimulus onset.

Each name target stimulus was preceded by a prime presented for 250 msec, which subjects were instructed to look at but make no response, and then a 250 msec blank interval (to produce on SOA of 500 msec). Our reason for the choice of 500 msec SOA was simply that this was the median SOA used by Bruce and Valentine (1986). In one experimental condition (name/name) primes were printed names, but in the other experimental condition (face/name) primes were black-and-white slides of people's faces. For familiar name targets, three different types of prime were used: related (prime person and target person both familiar and often associated with each other), neutral (the prime was the face of an unfamiliar person, or the name of an unfamiliar person), or unrelated (prime person and target person both familiar, but not associated with each other). Unrelated pairs of people were, in fact, created by scrambling potentially related pairs that were not used in the related condition for a particular subject, and the same unfamiliar face prime or unfamiliar name prime was used for all neutral trials.

Three sets of 10 related pairs (listed in Appendix 1) were used to create familiar target names for related, neutral, and unrelated conditions. These sets were matched on rated familiarity (determined by six independent raters) of the names to be used as targets, and the use of any particular set of pairs in related, neutral, or unrelated conditions was rotated across subjects. When the members of a related pair were not equally familiar, we chose the more familiar (to us) person as target and the less familiar as the prime (for example, Ronald Reagan was used as a target and Nancy Reagan as a prime). This was done to reduce the variance of reaction times to targets by making them as familiar as possible. Bruce

and Valentine (1986) have already shown that the order in which related pairs appear as primes or targets does not influence the semantic priming effect itself.

Half the target names were those of unfamiliar people (obscure actors and politicians, invented aristocrats, etc.). Two-thirds of these were preceded by familiar primes, and one third by the neutral prime stimulus, in order to balance the proportions of familiar (related + unrelated) and neutral primes preceding familiar or unfamiliar targets. Trials involving unfamiliar or familiar names and related, neutral, or unrelated pairs occurred in an unpredictable order. The session began with several practice trials involving stimuli not used in the main experiment. Stimuli (faces or names) subtended a horizontal visual angle of approximately 6°.

In summary, then, manual reaction times were measured to familiar target names preceded by related, neutral, and unrelated primes at an SOA of 500 msec. For half the subjects prime stimuli were faces, and for half the subjects prime stimuli were names. None of the target stimuli were repeated during the experiment, and of the prime stimuli only the "neutral" ones were repeated.

Results

Mean reaction times for correct responses to familiar targets preceded by related, neutral, and unrelated primes, and to unfamiliar targets, are presented in Table 1. Mean percentage error rates are also presented in Table 1 for inspection but will not be considered further.

A two-factor analysis of variance of the reaction times for correct responses to familiar target names was carried out, to determine the effects of prime domain (faces or names) and prime type (related, neutral, or unrelated; repeated measure). The only significant effect was that of prime type, $F(2, 44) = 44.44$,

TABLE 1

Reaction times for correct responses of normal subjects and error rates for familiarity decision to name targets preceded by related, neutral, or unrelated face or name primes

	Primes						Overall mean (msec)
	Face			Name			
Targets	Mean (msec)	SD (msec)	Errors (%)	Mean (msec)	SD (msec)	Errors (%)	
Familiar							
Related prime	692	101	5.0	698	122	4.2	695
Neutral prime	753	112	5.8	798	132	8.3	776
Unrelated prime	794	126	4.2	836	179	9.2	815
Unfamiliar	822	92	1.9	943	264	2.2	883

$p < 0.001$; there was no effect of prime domain ($F < 1$), and no prime domain $\times$ prime type interaction, $F(2, 44) = 1.40$, $p > 0.1$.

Newman–Keuls tests ($\alpha = 0.05$) were used to analyse the effect of prime type. These showed that reaction times for familiar targets preceded by related primes were faster than those for familiar targets preceded by neutral primes, and that these were in turn faster than those for familiar targets preceded by unrelated primes.

An items analysis was also carried out to determine whether or not these findings held generally across the set of items used in Experiment 1. This again revealed an effect of prime type, $F(2, 58) = 25.58$, $p < 0.001$, with no prime domain $\times$ prime type interaction, $F(2, 58) = 1.36$, $p > 0.1$. Planned comparisons showed that responses to familiar target names preceded by related primes were faster than responses to target names preceded by neutral primes, $F(1, 29) = 25.12$, $p < 0.001$, but the difference between the reaction times to target names preceded by neutral primes or by unrelated primes did not reach statistical significance, $F(1, 29) = 3.57$, $0.1 > p > 0.05$.

The items analysis thus confirms the principal findings of the analysis of subject means, namely an effect of prime type with no prime domain $\times$ prime type interaction. In the analysis by subjects, however, both facilitatory (related < neutral) and inhibitory (neutral < unrelated) components of the effect of prime type were found, whereas in the items analysis only the facilitatory component reached significance.

Discussion

The results show a semantic priming effect in which both facilitatory (related < neutral) and inhibitory (neutral < unrelated) components are present in the analysis of subject means, but only the facilitatory component is significant on items analysis. There is no prime domain $\times$ prime type interaction for subject or items analyses, so the semantic priming effect on name recognition is the same from face primes as from name primes. Thus there is evidence of cross-domain (face/name) semantic priming, and these cross-domain priming effects are as marked as within-domain (name/name) semantic priming effects.

Although significant facilitation of responses to familiar target names preceded by related primes was found both for analyses by subjects and by items, inhibition of responses to targets preceded by unrelated primes was found only to reach statistical significance in the analysis by subject means. It is possible that only a proportion of the related pairs are easily predictable across the relatively brief (500 msec) prime-target interval. We note that in analyses of subject means in their experiments Bruce and Valentine (1986) found priming effects in the form of facilitation without inhibition for face/face pairs, but facilitation and inhibition for name/name pairs. The explanation of those inconsistent inhibitory effects is not, however, of central importance to the present paper, for which the key point is that facilitation is consistently found.

Having established that normal subjects show semantic priming from face primes onto name targets, we now examine whether or not the same will be true for PH.

EXPERIMENT 2

Method

Subject.   PH has been unable to recognize familiar faces overtly since suffering a severe closed head injury in an accident in 1982, when he was 19 years old. On formal tests he recognized none of 20 highly familiar and 20 moderately familiar faces (De Haan et al., 1987a) and performed at chance level at discriminating familiar from unfamiliar faces in free choice (18/31—De Haan et al., 1987b) or forced choice (65/128—Young & De Haan, 1988) tasks. Thus he experiences no sense of overt familiarity to well-known faces. He is also unable to assign faces overtly to semantic categories (politician, television personality, etc.) at above-chance levels (De Haan et al., 1987a, b). In contrast, he is able to read, and continues to be able to recognize familiar people from their names (29/32 correct on familiarity decision to individually presented names—De Haan et al., 1987b; 118/128 correct on forced-choice familiarity decision—Young & De Haan, 1988).

PH's language abilities are relatively well preserved, and he performs normally on immediate memory tests, but he shows impairments on tests of long-term memory. Further details of ophthalmological and neuropsychological assessments are given by De Haan et al. (1987b).

Stimuli and procedure.   PH was asked to carry out a familiarity decision task to familiar and unfamiliar printed name targets, each of which was preceded by a face prime presented for 450 msec followed by a 50 msec blank interval (giving an SOA of 500 msec between prime and target). He was asked to look at the prime faces but otherwise pay no attention to them. Manual responses were made by moving a vertically mounted lever toward his body for familiar names and away from him for unfamiliar names, using his left arm (he had lost his right arm in the accident). Reaction times were recorded from the onset of each target name. Because PH's responses are usually slower than those of normal subjects (De Haan et al., 1987b), target names were each presented for 4 sec instead of the 2.5 sec used in Experiment 1.

Eighteen familiar target names were used, 9 of these preceded by faces of related people (close associates, or a person from the same semantic category) and 9 by unrelated faces derived from scrambling related pairs. . . . each set of 9 pairs had been matched on rated familiarity of the names and faces to normal subjects of comparable age to PH. The unfamiliar target names were all preceded by primes consisting of faces of famous people not otherwise used in the experiment.

Other details of procedure were as for Experiment 1. The reason for the absence of a neutral condition was that photographs of the faces of a sufficient

number of stimulus pairs were not available at the time when Experiment 2 was carried out. Our principal interest was, of course, in whether or not PH would show semantic priming from faces at all, given that he cannot recognize them overtly.

In order to provide a more stable estimate of PH's reaction time to each target name, the experiment was repeated later in the same day. A post-test was also given, in which PH was shown the face primes from the related and unrelated conditions with unlimited exposure) and asked to identify them.

Results

In the post-test PH did not recognize overtly any of the prime faces from the related or unrelated conditions. Mean reaction times for correct responses to unfamiliar and familiar target names preceded by related or unrelated face primes are given in Table 2, together with error rates.

Four of PH's six errors to familiar name targets preceded by related face primes involved failure to accept the names of Christopher Dean and Robert Redford as familiar, and when we discussed this with him afterwards he clearly did not know (or did not remember) these people; thus his mean reaction time for correct responses for this cell has been derived from the remaining seven target names.

In order to determine whether or not there was a significant difference between PH's correct reaction times to familiar target names preceded by related or by unrelated face primes, we used the uncorrelated t test to compare his mean reaction times to each of the seven target names to which correct responses were made in the related condition to his mean reaction times to the nine target names used in the unrelated condition (treating each name as if it were a separate subject). A significant difference was found, $t(14) = 2.23$, $p < 0.05$.

Discussion

Although he could not recognize any of the face primes overtly, PH none the less showed semantic priming from these faces onto name recognition at a quite short (500 msec) SOA. We were not, however, able to include a neutral

TABLE 2
Mean reaction times and error rates for
PH's correct responses to unfamiliar
and familiar target names preceded by
related or unrelated face primes

Targets	Mean (msec)	Errors
Familiar		
Related prime	1597	6/18
Unrelated prime	2023	2/18
Unfamiliar	1853	1/36

condition in the experiment, because we did not have access to a sufficiently large number of photographs of the faces of related pairs of people at the time when it was carried out. Thus although we have established that PH shows semantic priming from "unrecognized" faces, it is not certain whether this priming facilitates the recognition of related targets or inhibits recognition of unrelated targets.

Although PH's responses were, with the exception of the two names he did not recognize at all, reasonably accurate, they were slow compared with normal subjects. Slow reaction times have been found for several tasks performed by PH (De Haan et al., 1987a, b) and can be attributed to the generalized response slowing that often follows closed head injury (Van Zomeren & Deelman, 1978). The key point is that PH continues to show semantic priming.

In order to design an experiment in which a neutral condition could be included for PH, the simplest solution seemed to us to be to use the same set of stimulus pairs in related, unrelated (scrambled related pairs), and neutral (one member of pair as target + neutral prime) conditions. This would have the additional advantage that it would allow direct comparison of PH's reaction times to each target name in each condition. However, such a procedure has, to our knowledge, not been used in a prime-target semantic priming paradigm, and it might potentially confound repetition and semantic priming effects. We considered this particular risk to be slight because of the evidence (see Introduction to this paper) that repetition and semantic priming effects are different in nature, and especially that semantic priming effects dissipate within seconds (Dannenbring & Briand, 1982; Bruce, 1986). However, in order to confirm that a paradigm in which target stimuli were repeated across conditions would produce cross-domain (face/name) semantic priming, a further experiment was run with normal subjects.

EXPERIMENT 3

Method

Subjects.   Twelve staff and students of Lancaster University (6 male, 6 female) were subjects. All had normal or correct-to-normal vision. All were paid.

Stimuli and procedure.   Ten pairs of associated people were used as familiar stimuli. . . . Each of these 20 people was used once as a familiar target name preceded by the appropriate related face prime, once as a familiar target name preceded by a neutral (unfamiliar) face prime, and once as a familiar target name preceded by an unrelated face prime (unrelated pairs were made by scrambling the related pairs). A further 60 trials involving target names of unfamiliar people were also run, in which 20 unfamiliar targets were each twice preceded by each of the possible familiar face primes and once by the neutral prime; in this way, each of the primes could have no cue value in signalling that a familiar or an unfamiliar target name would follow ($p = 0.5$, for each prime).

As in Experiment 1, primes were presented for 250 msec, followed by a blank interval of 250 msec, to create SOAs of 500 msec. Target names were

presented for 2.5 sec each. Subjects were asked to decide whether or not each target name was that of a familiar person, and manual reaction times to the target names were recorded from stimulus onset. Faces and names subtended visual angles of approximately 6°, and trials with unfamiliar and familiar names and related, neutral, or unrelated face primes were arranged into an unpredictable order subject to the constraint that any particular stimulus person did not occur as face or name on two successive trials.

Results

Mean reaction times for correct responses to names of unfamiliar and familiar people preceded by related, neutral, or unrelated face primes are shown in Table 3. Error rates were less than 4% for all cells and will not be considered further.

A one-factor analysis of variance of reaction times for correct responses to familiar name targets was carried out, to determine the effect of prime type (related, neutral, or unrelated; repeated measure). This was found to be statistically significant, $F(2, 22) = 7.53$, $p < 0.01$, and Newman–Keuls tests ($\alpha = 0.05$) showed that reaction times to familiar names preceded by related face primes were faster than reaction times to familiar names preceded by neutral or by unrelated face primes, which did not differ from each other.

An items analysis confirmed the pattern of findings obtained in the analysis of subject means, with faster reaction times to familiar name targets preceded by related than by neutral face primes, $F(1, 19) = 4.71$, $p < 0.05$, and no difference between reaction times to familiar name targets preceded by neutral or by unrelated face primes ($F < 1$).

Discussion

The results of Experiment 3 show the classical "automatic" pattern of facilitation (related < neutral) without inhibition (neutral = unrelated). Thus it is clear that repeating the faces and names used across conditions does not abolish cross-domain (face/name) semantic priming in normal subjects. The absolute size of

TABLE 3
Reaction times for correct responses of normal subjects to familiar and unfamiliar name targets preceded by related, neutral, or unrelated face primes

Targets	Mean (msec)	SD (msec)
Familiar		
Related prime	627	118
Neutral prime	664	98
Unrelated prime	657	94
Unfamiliar	737	105

the priming effect looks smaller than that found in Experiment 1, but the reaction times are faster. More importantly, perhaps, there was no sign of any inhibitory priming component in the results of Experiment 3, which might also lead to a somewhat smaller-looking overall priming effect.

We are not certain why there should be evidence of an inhibitory component for Experiment 1 (though only in the analysis of reaction times by subjects in this experiment), but not from Experiment 3. In terms of Posner and Snyder's (1975) theory, this, of course, implies that both intentional strategies and automatic priming were operative in Experiment 1, but only automatic priming in Experiment 3. One possible reason for this might be that the faster reaction times produced by the repeated targets preclude conscious anticipation of which targets might follow particular primes in Experiment 3. Alternatively, Becker (1980) has argued that the use of a predictable (in this case a small) set of related pairs will lead to facilitatory priming.

In Experiment 4 the method of repeating stimuli across conditions was used to examine cross-domain semantic priming in PH. In addition, a condition was also run in which names were used as primes instead of faces, so that semantic priming could be compared for PH across faces (which he cannot recognize overtly) and names (which he recognizes overtly).

EXPERIMENT 4

Method

Subject.   PH (as for Experiment 2).

Stimuli and procedure.   A practice session was given, in which PH was shown the target names from Experiment 3 and asked to classify them as familiar or unfamiliar. He did this accurately. Four separate test sessions were then run, spread at intervals across a day.

In the first (face/name) session PH carried out Experiment 3, but with the procedural variations that a lever was used for responses (as in Experiment 2), face primes were presented for 450 msec, followed by a 50 msec blank interval (maintaining the SOA at the 500 msec used in Experiment 3, but increasing the presentation time of the faces a little), and target names were presented for 3 sec each (slightly longer than Experiment 3, to allow for the slower responses we expected). In the second (name/name) session the face primes were replaced by primes consisting of these people's printed names, and the experiment was repeated. Sessions 3 and 4 were repeats of Sessions 1 and 2, respectively.

Thus, at the end of the day, PH had heroically done the task twice with face primes and name targets, and twice with name primes and name targets. He was then shown all of the face primes one at a time (with unlimited exposure), told that these belonged to the familiar people whose names he had been classifying, and asked to identify them.

Results

PH made few errors (less than 4% for all cells of the design). His mean reaction times for correct responses to the target names are shown in Table 4.

Mean correct reaction times for each familiar name in each condition were calculated and submitted to a two-factor analysis of variance, to determine the effects of prime domain (faces or names; repeated measure) and prime type (related, neutral, or unrelated; repeated measure). There were significant effects of prime domain, with faster reaction times to target names preceded by name primes, $F(1, 19) = 4.57$, $p < 0.05$, and of prime type, $F(2, 38) = 4.01$, $p < 0.05$. There was no prime domain × prime type interaction ($F < 1$).

Newman–Keuls tests ($\alpha = 0.05$) were used to assess the effect of prime type. These showed that reaction times to familiar names preceded by related primes were faster than reaction times to familiar names preceded by neutral or by unrelated primes, which did not differ from each other.

In the post-test, PH was able to correctly identify two of the face primes: Ronnie Corbett and Margaret Thatcher. He has previously managed to identify Margaret Thatcher overtly on a few occasions (although he has also failed to recognize her overtly in other tests), but never Ronnie Corbett. This may have been a lucky guess, as he had encountered the names of the familiar people we had been using several times during the day. He did not, however, use these successfully to identify any of the other faces, maintaining that they were un-familiar. But the main point is that 18/20 of the familiar face primes were still unrecognized, yet the priming effect was found when measured across all the stimuli used. Inspection of the data revealed no differences between the pattern for names primed by Ronnie Corbett's or Margaret Thatcher's faces and the pattern for names primed by the other faces.

TABLE 4

Mean reaction times (in msec) for PH's correct
responses to target names of familiar and
unfamiliar people preceded by related, neutral,
or unrelated face or name primes

	Primes		
Targets	Face	Name	Overall
Familiar			
Related prime	1016	945	981
Neutral prime	1080	1032	1056
Unrelated prime	1117	1048	1083
Unfamiliar	1480	1265	1373

Discussion

PH's reaction times were again slow compared with those of normal subjects (Experiment 3), but he made few errors, and, more importantly, the *pattern* of his RTs to the different types of prime is the same as that found for normal normal subjects: facilitation of responses to targets preceded by related primes, without inhibition of responses to targets preceded by unrelated primes. This pattern did not differ between name primes, which he could recognize overtly, and face primes, of which the large majority could not be recognized overtly. Like the normal subjects of Experiment 1, cross-domain (face/name) semantic priming was as great as within-domain (name/name) semantic priming for PH.

A curious incidental result is that PH's responses were faster overall to name targets preceded by name primes than to name targets preceded by face primes. We suspect, however, that this may be explicable in terms of the fact that PH did the four blocks of trials in the order face primes, name primes, face primes, name primes. We noticed that his responses continued to get faster throughout these blocks, so that the faster RTs to name primes may only reflect a practice effect.

GENERAL DISCUSSION

Our experiments demonstrate that for normal subjects semantic priming effects on person recognition can cross stimulus domains (from face primes to name targets), and that this happens under conditions in which targets are repeated (Experiment 3) or not repeated (Experiment 1) during the course of the experiment. Experiment 1 also showed that cross-domain semantic priming effects for normal subjects did not differ from within-domain semantic priming (from name primes to name targets).

These findings from normal subjects are themselves of interest, but it is remarkable that the same pattern can be demonstrated for PH, a brain-injured patient who has seldom managed to recognize anyone overtly from their face during the last five years. PH showed semantic priming from faces to name targets in Experiment 1, in which he did not recognize overtly any of the faces employed, and in Experiment 4, in which he could not recognize overtly 90% of the faces. Yet in Experiment 4, PH produced exactly the same pattern of semantic priming effects (facilitation without inhibition) as found for normal subjects, and he showed as much priming from faces (which he was very poor at recognizing overtly) as from printed names (which he could recognize overtly).

We will consider the implications of these findings for two issues: recognition and awareness, and the nature of face recognition impairments.

Recognition and awareness

Some recent studies have sought to demonstrate that semantic priming effects can operate without awareness (e.g., Fowler, Wolford, Slade, & Tassinary, 1981; Marcel, 1983), but this has led to debate about several issues of method, and

especially the appropriate techniques for establishing presence or absence of awareness (Purcell, Stewart, & Stanovich, 1983; Cheesman & Merikle, 1984, 1985; Holender, 1986). Our own findings do not address these issues directly, because what Fowler et al. (1981) and Marcel (1983) sought to demonstrate was that semantic priming could operate even when subjects were not aware of seeing anything. PH, in contrast, is quite well aware of the faces he looks at, and he can comment on age, sex, hairstyle, etc.; his loss of awareness is thus confined to loss of awareness of recognition itself, as the faces that he sees seem to him to be those of unfamiliar people.

What is of interest about PH, then, is that semantic priming can operate *without awareness of recognition*. Our findings thus form a parallel to studies that have demonstrated semantic priming effects for normal subjects at presentation times that allow stimuli to be seen but are too brief for conscious identification (McCauley, Parmelee, Sperber, & Carr, 1980; Carr, McCauley, Sperber, & Parmelee, 1982). Thus there is converging evidence from normal subjects and from the effects of PH's brain injury to indicate that certain types of meaning can be extracted from visual stimuli without conscious identification.

The nature of face recognition impairments

The demonstration of semantic priming effects for PH parallels other findings that "automatic" aspects of recognition can be preserved in prosopagnosic patients (Bauer, 1984; Tranel & Damasio, 1985; De Haan et al., 1987a, b). There is also a parallel to work on aphasia, where automatic semantic priming onto lexical decision can be found in patients with severe language impairments (Milberg & Blumstein, 1981).

As Schacter et al. (1988) emphasize, a key feature of these demonstrations is that the effects of recognition are demonstrated *implicitly*; when such patients are asked to make explicit use of their impaired capacities, performance is poor. In the test phases of Experiments 2 and 4, for instance, PH was not required to try to recognize the face primes; he was only asked to respond to the name targets. On post-tests demanding explicit recognition of the faces from Experiments 2 and 4, PH performed very poorly (0% correct, and 10% correct).

In attempting to account for such dissociations between implicitly and explicitly tested abilities, De Haan et al. (1987b), Schacter et al. (1988) and Young (1988) suggested that what may happen is that recognition mechanisms can continue to operate normally but have become disconnected from the mechanisms that sustain awareness. An intriguing disorder of awareness may then arise, in which there is no global disturbance of consciousness, but the patient loses awareness of a *specific* aspect of human experience (in PH's case, recognition of familiar faces). The semantic priming effects found for PH are consistent with this type of conception, as the pattern of his reaction times across the different experimental conditions corresponds to that found for normal subjects, despite the overall slowing.

Although PH no longer achieves awareness of recognition for most familiar faces, then, there is evidence from implicit tests that some form of recognition continues to take place. In addition, the existence of a normal pattern of interference (De Haan et al., 1987a, b) and semantic priming effects demonstrates preserved interaction between face and name recognition abilities. Explaining the nature of this interaction presents an interesting theoretical challenge. Our current view (Young & De Haan, 1988) is that such effects may be primarily dependent on associative interconnections. It may be useful to build up associations that would allow us to recognize Ronald Reagan more readily after we have seen Nancy Reagan, or to recognize his photograph in a newspaper more quickly if we have just read Nancy Reagan's name. Such associations would serve the purpose of making the recognition system prepared for what it is likely to encounter next (Fodor, 1983).

We do not, however, claim that all cases of prosopagnosia will turn out to involve impairments similar to PH's. It seems more likely that there are different potential causes of loss of ability to recognize familiar faces, and that investigations of covert recognition may help in distinguishing these various causes. At least two other patients, for whom prosopagnosia arose in the context of a more general impairment of "higher-order" visual perceptual abilities, have been found *not* to show covert recognition on the types of implicit test used with PH (Young & Ellis, 1989b; Young, De Haan, & Newcombe, 1987).

We find, then, that semantic priming of person recognition can cross stimulus domains both in normal subjects and in the prosopagnosic patient PH. The semantic priming effects shown by PH exhibit the pattern of facilitation without inhibition thought to characterize automatic aspects of normal recognition. This finding has important implications for understanding the nature of prosopagnosia, semantic priming, and recognition itself.

ACKNOWLEDGEMENTS

This work was supported by MRC grants G 8519533 and PG 7301443. We are grateful to the Press Association for help in finding suitable photographs for use as stimuli.

REFERENCES

Bauer, R. M. (1984). Autonomic recognition of names and faces in prosopagnosia: A neuropsychological application of the guilty knowledge test. *Neuropsychologia, 22,* 457–469.

Becker, C. A. (1980). Semantic context effects in visual word recognition: An analysis of semantic strategies. *Memory and Cognition, 8,* 493–512.

Bruce, V. (1983). Recognizing faces. *Philosophical Transactions of the Royal Society, London, B302,* 423–436.

Bruce, V. (1986). Recognising familiar faces. In H. D. Ellis, M. A. Jeeves, F. Newcombe, & A. Young (Eds.), *Aspects of face processing* (pp. 107–117). Dordrecht: Martinus Nijhoff.

Bruce, V., & Valentine, T. (1985). Identity priming in the recognition of familiar faces. *British Journal of Psychology, 76,* 373–383.

Bruce, V., & Valentine, T. (1986). Semantic priming of familiar faces. *Quarterly Journal of Experimental Psychology, 38A*, 125–150.

Bruce, V., & Young, A. W. (1986). Understanding face recognition. *British Journal of Psychology, 77*, 305–327.

Carr, T. H., McCauley, C., Sperber, R. D., & Parmelee, C. M. (1982). Words, pictures, and priming: On semantic activation, conscious identification, and the automaticity of information processing. *Journal of Experimental Psychology: Human Perception and Performance, 8*, 757–777.

Cheesman, J., & Merikle, P. M. (1984). Priming with and without awareness. *Perception and Psychophysics, 36*, 387–395.

Cheesman, J., & Merikle, P. M. (1985). Word recognition and consciousness. In D. Besner, T. G. Waller, & G. E. Mackinnon (Eds.), *Reading research: Advances in theory and practice, Vol. 5* (pp. 311–352). New York: Academic Press.

Dannenbring, G. L., & Briand, K. (1982). Semantic priming and the word repetition effect in a lexical decision task. *Canadian Journal of Psychology, 36*, 435–444.

De Haan, E. H. F., Young, A., & Newcombe, F. (1987a). Faces interfere with name classification in a prosopagnosic patient. *Cortex, 23*, 309–316.

De Haan, E. H. F., Young, A., & Newcombe, F. (1987b). Face recognition without awareness. *Cognitive Neuropsychology, 4*, 385–415.

Durso, F. T., & Johnson, M. K. (1979). Facilitation in naming and categorizing repeated pictures and words. *Journal of Experimental Psychology: Human Learning and Memory, 5*, 449–459.

Ellis, A. W., Young, A. W., Flude, B. M., & Hay, D. C. (1987). Repetition priming of face recognition. *Quarterly Journal of Experimental Psychology, 39A*, 193–210.

Ellis, H. D. (1986a). Processes underlying face recognition. In R. Bruyer (Ed.), *The neuropsychology of face perception and facial expression* (pp. 1–27). Hillsdale, NJ: Lawrence Erlbaum Associates Inc.

Ellis, H. D. (1986b). Disorders of face recognition. In K. Poeck, H. J. Freund, & H. Ganshirt (Eds.), *Neurology: Proceedings of the 13th World Congress of Neurology* (pp. 179–187). Berlin: Springer-Verlag.

Fodor, J. (1983). *The modularity of mind.* Cambridge, MA: MIT Press.

Fowler, C. A., Wolford, G., Slade, R., & Tassinary, L. (1981). Lexical access with and without awareness. *Journal of Experimental Psychology: General, 110*, 341–362.

Hay, D. C., & Young, A. W. (1982). The human face. In A. W. Ellis (Ed.), *Normality and pathology in cognitive functions* (pp. 173–202). London: Academic Press.

Holender, D. (1986). Semantic activation without conscious identification in dichotic listening, parafoveal vision, and visual masking: A survey and appraisal. *Behavioral and Brain Sciences, 9*, 1–66.

Kirsner, K., Milech, D., & Stumpfel, V. (1986). Word and picture identification: Is representational parsimony possible? *Memory and Cognition, 14*, 398–408.

McCauley, C., Parmelee, C., Sperber, R., & Carr, T. (1980). Early extraction of meaning from pictures and its relation to conscious identification. *Journal of Experimental Psychology: Human Perception and Performance, 6*, 265–276.

Marcel, A. J. (1983). Conscious and unconscious perception: Experiments on visual masking and word recognition. *Cognitive Psychology, 15*, 197–237.

Milberg, W., & Blumstein, S. E. (1981). Lexical decision and aphasia: Evidence for semantic processing. *Brain and Language, 14*, 371–385.

Neely, J. H. (1976). Semantic priming and retrieval from lexical memory: Evidence for facilitatory processes. *Memory and Cognition, 4*, 648–654.

Neely, J. H. (1977). Semantic priming and retrieval from lexical memory: Roles of inhibitionless spreading activation and limited-capacity attention. *Journal of Experimental Psychology: General, 106*, 226–254.

Posner, M. I., & Snyder, C. R. R. (1975). Facilitation and inhibition in the processing of signals. In P. M. A. Rabbitt & S. Dornič (Eds.), *Attention and performance, V* (pp. 669–682). London: Academic Press.

Purcell, D. G., Stewart, A. L., & Stanovich, K. K. (1983). Another look at semantic priming without awareness. *Perception and Psychophysics, 34*, 65–71.

Schacter, D. L., McAndrews, M. P., & Moscovitch, M. (1988). Access to consciousness: Dissociations between implicit and explicit knowledge in neuropsychological syndromes. In L. Weiskrantz (Ed.), *Thought without language*. Oxford: Oxford University Press.

Sperber, R. D., McCauley, C., Ragain, R. D., & Weil, C. M. (1979). Semantic priming effects on picture and word processing. *Memory and Cognition, 7*, 339–345.

Tranel, D., & Damasio, A. R. (1985). Knowledge without awareness: An autonomic index of facial recognition by prosopagnosics. *Science, 228*, 1453–1454.

Van Zomeren, A. H., & Deelman, B. G. (1978). Long-term recovery of visual reaction time after closed head injury. *Journal of Neurology, Neurosurgery and Psychiatry, 41*, 452–457.

Young, A. W. (1988). Functional organisation of visual recognition. In L. Weiskrantz (Ed.), *Thought without language*. Oxford: Oxford University Press.

Young, A. W., & De Haan, E. H. F. (1988). Boundaries of covert recognition in prosopagnosia. *Cognitive Neuropsychology, 5*, 317–336.

Young, A. W., De Haan, E., & Newcombe, F. (1987). *Object agnosia and prosopagnosia without covert recognition*. EPS meeting, Nottingham.

Young, A. W., & Ellis, H. D. (1989a). Semantic processing. In A. W. Young & H. D. Ellis (Eds.), *Handbook of research on face processing*. Amsterdam: North Holland.

Young, A. W., & Ellis, H. D. (1989b). Childhood prosopagnosia. *Brain and Cognition, 9*, 16–47.

Young, A. W., Hay, D. C., & Ellis, A. W. (1985). The faces that launched a thousand slips: Everyday difficulties and errors in recognising people. *British Journal of Psychology, 76*, 495–523.

Young, A. W., McWeeny, K. H., Hay, D. C., & Ellis, A. W. (1986). Access to identity-specific semantic codes from familiar faces. *Quarterly Journal of Experimental Psychology, 38A*, 271–295.

CHAPTER SIX

Understanding covert recognition

A. Mike Burton
University of Nottingham, UK

Andrew W. Young
University of Durham, UK

Vicki Bruce and Robert A. Johnston
University of Nottingham, UK

Andrew W. Ellis
University of York, UK

An implementation of Bruce and Young's (1986) functional model of face recognition is used to examine patterns of covert face recognition previously reported in a prosopagnosic patient, PH. Although PH is unable to recognize overtly the faces of people known to him, he shows normal patterns of face processing when tested indirectly. A simple manipulation of one set of connections in the implemented model induces behaviour consistent with patterns of results from PH obtained in semantic priming and interference tasks. We compare this account with previous explanations of covert recognition and demonstrate that the implemented model provides the most natural and parsimonious account available. Two further patients are discussed who show deficits in person perception. The first (MS) is prosopagnosic but shows no covert recognition. The second (ME) is not prosopagnosic, but cannot access semantic information relating to familiar people. The model provides an account of recognition impairments which is sufficiently general also to be useful in describing these patients.

Cognition, 39 (1991) 129–166.

INTRODUCTION

A functional model of face recognition

The last decade has seen considerable progress in understanding the processes by which we recognize faces. A number of broadly similar functional models have been proposed which highlight the sequential nature of the stages involved in identifying people from their faces, and the relationship between face recognition and other uses made of facial information (Bruce & Young, 1986; Ellis, Young, & Hay, 1987; Ellis, 1986; Hay & Young, 1982). The most complete account is that offered by Bruce and Young (1986), reproduced here as Figure 1. The route shown to the right of the figure represents the processes involved in *identifying* a face. The parallel routes shown to the left show the independent routes (as suggested by evidence reviewed by Bruce & Young, 1986) for the processing of facial expression, lip reading ("facial speech") and for the deliberate scrutiny of faces in certain tasks involving face matching ("directed visual

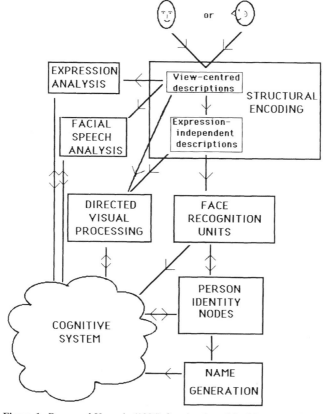

Figure 1. Bruce and Young's (1986) functional model of face recognition.

processing"). In this paper, we are concerned only with the processing of facial identity, and so we will concentrate on the route shown to the right of Figure 1.

After initial structural encoding, the Bruce and Young (1986) model posits three distinct sequential stages involved in identifying a face. The "face recognition units" (FRUs) store the visual structural descriptions which allow a particular known face to be discriminated from other faces, known or unknown. There is one FRU for each known face, and the model proposes that this unit becomes active when any (recognizable) view of the appropriate face is presented. The activation of an FRU also leads to activation of a "person identity node", or PIN. These units allow access to semantic information about the individual, for example their occupation, their relationship with the perceiver and so on. Unlike the FRUs, a PIN may become active as a result of input other than a face. Although not shown in Figure 1, it is assumed that there are other routes into the PIN store, through channels processing someone's voice, written or heard name. The PINs, then, represent the level of classification of a "person", rather than their particular face. Finally, Bruce and Young propose a stage of "name generation", which can only occur after activation of an appropriate PIN.

The Bruce and Young (1986) model has proved useful in research on face recognition in a number of ways. First, it provides a framework which gives an account of many empirical findings obtained in experiments with normal adults, or through observations of the patterns of impairment of face processing that may arise as the result of brain injury. This framework has served to point to new research directions in this field and is capable of generating new empirical hypotheses (e.g., see Bruce, 1988, and Young & Bruce, 1991, for accounts of how this framework has acted to guide research in this area). It has stood up remarkably well to rigorous experimental test. For example, Brennen, Baguley, Bright, and Bruce (1990) induced tip-of-the-tongue states (TOTs) by reading subjects semantic information about familiar people and waiting for occasions when subjects felt the name of the described person was on the "tip of their tongue". They argued that presentation of a face should not help to resolve these TOTs, since according to the model there is no direct link between FRUs and the name generation stage. Brennen et al.'s (1990) findings supported this counterintuitive prediction.

Although the Bruce and Young (1986) model of face recognition has been useful in guiding new research, it is underspecified in two particular areas which are important for the developments we present here. First, it was assumed by Bruce and Young (1986) that feelings of "familiarity" to a face arose from the level of the face recognition units themselves: "When a face is seen, the strength of the recognition unit's signal to the cognitive system will be at a level dependent on the degree of resemblance between its stored structural description and the input provided by structural encoding" (pp. 311–312). This signal was thought to be that used in determining the face's familiarity. However, no clear mechanism for translating such patterns of activation into explicit decisions about the

familiarity of the face was described. This was not possible, in part, because of a second element of underspecification in the model. Bruce and Young were unclear about whether the PINs *store* semantic information about people, or *allow access to* this information. Because this was not clearly spelled out it had to be assumed that familiarity decisions were made at the earlier stage of the FRUs. A common error in face recognition is the "familiar only" error, in which a person is recognized as familiar, but no further information is available (Young, Hay, & Ellis, 1985). If it is maintained that semantic information might be stored *at* the PIN, then clearly a familiarity decision has to be made before this stage of processing.

The lack of specification was thus responsible for the location of familiarity decisions at the FRU level. This in turn made it difficult for the model to accommodate the detailed pattern of effects arising from experiments on priming familiarity decisions. A great deal of the empirical work which has been performed on normal subjects has used the "face familiarity decision task" introduced by Bruce (1983); for example, see Bruce and Valentine (1985, 1986), Young, Hay, McWeeny, Ellis, and Barry (1985), Valentine and Bruce (1986), Young, McWeeny, Hay, and Ellis (1986a), Ellis, Young, Flude, and Hay (1987), and Brunas, Young, and Ellis (1990). In this task subjects are asked to respond "yes" or "no" according to whether they recognize a person's face as familiar. The procedure was developed in order to provide a measure of recognition uncontaminated by the additional (and sometimes difficult) process of name retrieval (Yarmey, 1973; Young, Hay, & Ellis, 1985; Young, McWeeny, Ellis, & Hay, 1986). Using this task it was shown that face recognition, like word recognition, gives rise to semantic priming[1] (Bruce & Valentine, 1986) and repetition priming[1] effects (Bruce & Valentine, 1985; Ellis, Young, Flude, & Hay, 1987). It was assumed by Bruce and Young (1986) that repetition priming resulted from the direct raising of activation at FRU level through previous exposure, while semantic priming resulted from activation of FRUs indirectly via the PIN/cognitive system. The problem with this assumption is that it fails to account for the different nature of repetition and semantic priming effects. For example, the time courses of these effects are quite different: semantic priming of faces does not survive an intervening item (Bruce, 1986), while repetition priming remains robust for at least 20 minutes after first presentation (Ellis, Young, Flude, & Hay, 1987). Furthermore, semantic priming crosses input domains; that is, names prime the faces of semantic associates, and faces prime names (Young, Hellawell, & De Haan, 1988). However, the longer-lasting repetition priming effect does not cross input domains. It has been difficult to deal with such findings within the Bruce and Young (1986) model. Young and Ellis (1989a) comment as follows on this issue: "The problem created by different time courses of semantic priming and repetition priming effects is that it is thus implausible to attribute both effects to a common mechanism in the form of increased activation of face recognition units. This problem is not insuperable, but it will require a more detailed knowledge of the

properties of semantic and repetition priming effects, and some revision of existing models, before an effective solution can be proposed" (p. 247).

As we describe below, Burton, Bruce, and Johnston (1990) implemented the
Bruce and Young (1986) model using an interactive activation architecture,
within which it was made explicit that PINs formed modality-independent
gateways to semantic information about identity, rather than themselves containing semantic information. (In fact, this assertion was not without precedent; see
Young, Hay, & Ellis, 1985, p. 517.) If semantic information is accessed via the
PIN, then familiarity decisions could be taken at PIN level, rather than solely on
the basis of activation passed from FRUs. Burton et al. (1990) describe how
such an implementation enables the separation of the locus of effects of semantic
and repetition priming, thus removing one apparent difficulty within the original
Bruce and Young framework. Briefly, semantic priming is taken to affect activation levels at the PINs, while repetition priming is taken to affect the strengths of
connections between FRUs and PINs. A direct consequence of this is that semantic
priming will cross input domains; that is, names will prime the faces of semantic
associates, and faces will prime names. Burton et al. (1990) discuss this proposition (and other consequences of the characterization of semantic and repetition
priming) at length, and we will return to a more detailed description of semantic
priming below.

In recent years a phenomenon has been reported in the neuropsychological
literature which seems to require more radical revision of the face recognition
model. The particular phenomenon of concern here is that of *covert* recognition
of faces by prosopagnosic patients. Here we review the basic phenomena of
prosopagnosia before introducing the details of covert recognition. We describe
how attempts were made to explain covert recognition in terms of a substantial
modification of the original framework. Finally, we show how an interactive
activation implementation of the original architecture can in fact accommodate
the phenomenon of covert recognition without major modification of the Bruce
and Young model.

Prosopagnosia and covert recognition

Prosopagnosic patients are unable to recognize the faces of familiar people.
Even the most familiar faces are affected, such as friends, family, and the patient's
own face when seen in a mirror (Hécaen & Angelergues, 1962). Prosopagnosic
patients remain able to see faces, and can point to the eyes, nose, mouth, etc. In
some cases the processing of expression, age and sex from facial appearance
remains well preserved, even though ability to identify familiar faces overtly is
very severely impaired (Bruyer et al., 1983; Tranel, Damasio, & Damasio, 1988).
The condition can occur despite preserved ability to recognize people from
non-facial cues, such as their voices or names. These widely reported observations demonstrate that prosopagnosia can involve a problem of face *recognition*,

rather than a more general face-processing impairment, and that there need not be any corresponding impairment affecting the patient's knowledge of familiar people.

Prosopagnosia was first identified as a distinct neuropsychological problem by Bodamer (1947). The underlying pathology involves lesions affecting occipito-temporal regions of cerebral cortex. Usually these are bilateral lesions (Damasio, Damasio, & Van Hoesen, 1982; Meadows, 1974), but several cases involving unilateral lesions of the right cerebral hemisphere have been reported in the more recent literature (e.g., De Renzi, 1986; Landis, Cummings, Christen, Bogen, & Imhof, 1986; Sergent & Villemure, 1989).

Recent attempts to account for the patterns of deficit found in prosopagnosic patients have focused on the functional nature of the disorder. This trend has occurred in parallel with (and has strongly influenced) the development of detailed functional models of normal face recognition (Bruce, 1988; Bruce & Young, 1986; Bruyer, 1987; Ellis, 1986; Ellis, Young, & Hay, 1987; Hay & Young, 1982; Young, 1988). There is now a body of work which suggests that prosopagnosic symptoms may occur for a variety of reasons, each reflecting breakdown at particular stages in the functional architecture of the recognition system (e.g., De Haan, Young, & Newcombe, 1987a, b; De Renzi, 1986; Hay & Young, 1982; Newcombe, Young, & De Haan, 1989; Sergent & Poncet, 1990; Sergent & Villemure, 1989; Young & De Haan, 1988; Young & Ellis, 1989b; Young, Hellawell, & De Haan, 1988).

Covert recognition represents one of the most challenging findings in the literature on prosopagnosia. Patients with no overt recognition of faces, and who have no more than chance ability to sort familiar from unfamiliar faces, may nevertheless show recognition when tested indirectly. This has now been demonstrated with a number of different types of measure including skin conductance (Bauer, 1984; Tranel & Damasio, 1985), evoked potentials (Renault, Signoret, DeBruille, Breton, & Bolgert, 1989), eye movements (Rizzo, Hurtig, & Damasio, 1987), face-name learning (Bruyer et al., 1983; De Haan et al., 1987a, b; Sergent & Poncet, 1990; Young & De Haan, 1988), and matching, priming and interference techniques derived from experimental psychology (De Haan et al., 1987b; Young et al., 1988).

In order to make sense of the pattern of findings in studies of covert recognition in prosopagnosia, it is useful to draw a distinction between direct and indirect tests of recognition (Young & De Haan, 1991). Direct tests will enquire about the ability of interest (e.g., "whose face is this?", "which face is familiar?"), whereas in an indirect test the ability in question is introduced as an incidental feature of a task that ostensibly measures something else (e.g., effects of familiarity on face *matching*, effects of different types of face prime on *name* recognition). In demonstrations of covert recognition of familiar faces in prosopagnosia, face recognition is usually tested indirectly. When this is done, the pattern of performance of prosopagnosic patients can show a "normal" influence of face

familiarity, even though performance on direct tests *with the same faces* is at chance level (Young & De Haan, 1988; Young et al., 1988). These findings are consistent with reports of preserved abilities on indirect tests deriving from a range of neuropsychological conditions (Schacter, McAndrews, & Moscovitch, 1988; Young & De Haan, 1988). More importantly, they cause us to fundamentally re-examine our conception of at least one form of prosopagnosia, since it is clear that at least some aspects of recognition remain intact, even though there is no awareness of recognition. To account for these effects Schacter et al. (1988) have suggested that the problem can be considered one of access to consciousness from the otherwise intact recognition system. In what follows, we shall propose a mechanism for an alternative account: that the recognition system can be damaged in such a way as to preserve covert effects, and yet cause loss of overt recognition. We will show that this is possible without recourse to theorizing about the processes which signal awareness.

It is important to point out that not all prosopagnosic patients show covert recognition (Bauer, 1986; Newcombe et al., 1989; Sergent & Villemure, 1989; Young & Ellis, 1989b). This observation is, of course, consistent with the view that prosopagnosia as a *symptom* can arise from more than one functionally separable *cause*.

In this paper, we will concentrate particularly on evidence provided by De Haan, Young, and Newcombe (1987a, b) and Young, Hellawell, and De Haan (1988). These studies are a result of detailed investigations of one prosopagnosic patient, PH. We will now present a brief case history of this patient and review some of the previous attempts to account for the puzzling effects which his case demonstrates.

PH: Case summary

Because our intention is to examine crucial aspects of PH's performance in tasks involving covert processing of familiar faces, we will summarize pertinent details of his case here. A full description of ophthalmological and neuropsychological assessments is given in De Haan et al. (1987b).

PH suffered a severe closed head injury in an accident in 1982, when he was 19 years old. His language skills are well preserved (verbal IQ = 91; consistent with his previous education), and he is still able to read without difficulty.

PH's main spontaneous complaint concerns his inability to recognize faces in everyday life. On formal tests he recognized none of 20 highly familiar and 20 moderately familiar faces (De Haan et al., 1987a) and performed at chance level at discriminating familiar from unfamiliar faces in free choice (18/36; De Haan et al., 1987b) or forced choice (65/128; Young & De Haan, 1988) tasks. Thus he experiences no sense of overt familiarity to well-known faces. He is also unable to assign faces overtly to semantic categories (politician, television personality, etc.) at above chance levels (De Haan et al., 1987a, b). In contrast, he continues

to be able to recognize familiar people from their names (De Haan et al., 1987b; Young & De Haan, 1988). It should be noted, though, that PH's recognition of familiar names (118/128) in forced-choice is not completely normal, but at 92% correct it is very much better than his chance-level (51% correct) recognition of familiar faces in the equivalent task.

On tests that require him to match views of unfamiliar faces or to identify expressions PH performs less well than control subjects, but is none the less well above chance level (De Haan et al., 1987b). However, like several other prosopagnosic patients he experiences severe problems in identifying individual members of other visually homogeneous categories such as cars (3/33) or flowers (0/26) (De Haan et al., 1987b).

In "short-term" memory tasks PH's performance is normal for both verbal and non-verbal material, but his performance of "long-term" memory tasks is impaired. This memory impairment is not typical of other prosopagnosic cases, and it is not considered to be the cause of PH's face recognition problems, since he can recognize most people from their names; that is, he has not forgotten who they are.

Despite his severe impairment of overt face recognition ability, PH shows a remarkable degree of covert access to face identity in indirect tasks. He matches photographs of different views of familiar faces more quickly than photographs of unfamiliar faces (De Haan et al., 1987b). When taught to associate a name with a photograph, he learns "true" pairings more readily than "untrue" pairings (De Haan et al., 1987b; Young & De Haan, 1988). Furthermore in semantic priming and interference tasks PH shows effects of non-target faces (which he cannot identify overtly) on the processing of target names (De Haan et al., 1987a, b; Young et al., 1988). So, he is faster to recognize a name if it is preceded by the face of a semantic associate; and when asked to decide to which of two semantic categories a name belongs, he is slower if the name is presented simultaneously with the face of a person in the alternative category. In the present paper we demonstrate that it is possible to simulate the last two types of effect (semantic priming and interference from "unidentified" faces) using an interactive activation model. We will describe these effects in more detail, and present the results of experiments with the simulation.

Previous accounts of covert recognition

Accounting for covert recognition in prosopagnosia has not proved easy. Bauer (1984, 1986) proposed that neurologically dissociable information-processing routes are involved in overt recognition and orienting responses to emotionally salient stimuli. Although theoretically elegant, this proposal suffers from the problem that covert recognition effects can be found even to faces of people who seem to have little "emotional" importance to the patient. Tranel and Damasio (1985) suggested that "facial templates" are intact in patients who show covert

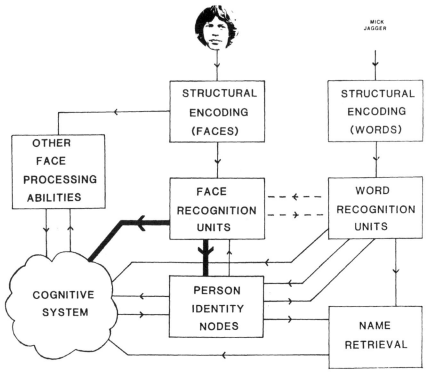

Figure 2. Young and De Haan's (1988) functional model of components involved in face and name recognition. Outputs from FRUs are highlighted to draw attention to the proposed account of PH's deficit.

recognition, but that the processes required for the "activation of multimodal associations" from the face are defective. However, evidence from other studies has shown that if this is the case, then these processes cannot be completely lost. The findings of Bruyer et al. (1983), De Haan et al. (1987a, b), Young et al. (1988), Young and De Haan (1988) and Sergent and Poncet (1990) all imply that *some* multimodal associations *are* implicated in covert recognition, since in all of these reports a defining characteristic of covert *face* recognition was its ability to influence *name* processing. In order to account for this fact, Young and De Haan (1988) offered an explanation in terms of the Bruce and Young (1986) model (as shown in Figure 1).

Young and De Haan (1988) proposed that the patterns of deficit observed in PH could be due to a disconnection of the *outputs* of the FRUs. Figure 2 illustrates this proposal: the FRU outputs are highlighted to draw attention to them. Damage to the pathways between FRUs and the cognitive system, and between FRUs and PINs, would prevent overt recognition being achieved despite normal activation at the recognition unit level. Furthermore, damage to the pathway

between FRUs and PINs would also prevent retrieval of any semantic information associated with the presented face. As we discussed above, Bruce and Young (1986) conceive of routes into the PINs through other modalities. So, for example, there will be an analogous "structural encoding" phase for written names, feeding information into a "word recognition unit" store which serves the same function as FRUs, but for the written names of people (see Figure 2). If this word/name recognition system is intact, but FRU outputs are eliminated, there should be no deficit in deciding the familiarity of names, or in retrieving appropriate semantic information from names.

This account in terms of disconnected FRUs appears satisfactory in explaining what PH cannot do (i.e., the breakdown of overt recognition of familiar faces). However, as Young and De Haan (1988) noted, it is still necessary to account for how the disconnected face recognition system can influence the word/name recognition system in indirect tasks. To achieve this Young and De Haan (1988) proposed that there is some rudimentary "semantic" organization in the form of associative links between input systems at the recognition unit level. They argued that it may be useful to build up associations that allow us to recognize Raisa Gorbachev more readily after we have seen Mikhail Gorbachev, or to recognize her photograph in a newspaper more quickly after we have read Mikhail Gorbachev's name. Such associations would serve the purpose of making the recognition system prepared for what it is likely to encounter next. This mechanism would allow semantic priming and interference effects from seen faces, with the patterns of priming and interference reflecting the rudimentary semantic organization present.

Although this proposal has some attractive features, it is not completely satisfactory. In particular, the status of associative links within the input systems must be assumed to be very different from the status of other links in the model (this is represented by the dashed lines in Figure 2). These "input system organization links" must not serve directly to trigger *firing* of an associated recognition unit. If such a function were possible, prosopagnosic patients could use the FRU to word-recognition-unit links in order to forge a route from face inputs into the cognitive system and the PINs. Young and De Haan (1988) therefore propose that these links have the effect of lowering the decision thresholds for associated people, and hence produce automatic associative effects without producing alternative routes through the system.

We have seen, then, that attempts have been made to use the Bruce and Young (1986) model to account for covert recognition. However, Young and De Haan's explanation is rather complex, and introduces radically new mechanisms. In the following we will show how the "IAC" computer implementation of Bruce and Young's (1986) model provides a much simpler account of covert recognition in prosopagnosia. Implementation of this model has led to a clearer characterization of its "microstructure", and this has suggested an alternative account to that described above. We show how this implementation may be used to understand

patterns of recognition in intact and lesioned systems, and demonstrate that it can simulate and thus provide an account of the basic pattern of interaction between face and name input systems observed in cases of prosopagnosia with covert recognition.

THE INTERACTIVE ACTIVATION MODEL OF PERSON RECOGNITION

The interactive activation model of person recognition (Burton et al., 1990) is based on Bruce and Young's (1986) functional model described above. It is implemented in the terms of McClelland and Rumelhart (1981), who have used a similar model to study word recognition. This architecture is connectionist in that it comprises units joined by connections of potentially variable strength. However, there are no distributed representations within the simulation—each unit has a discrete referent.

The model comprises a number of distinct pools of units. All the units within a pool are connected to each other with inhibitory links. Units may be connected across pools by excitatory links. Figure 3 shows the overall structure of the model. Following Bruce and Young (1986) we propose a number of pools of units corresponding to the following functional distinctions. FRUs become active when the system is presented with any recognizable view of a person's face. In the current simulation, these units receive input which is subsequently passed around the system. This input is arbitrary for the purposes of the demonstrations

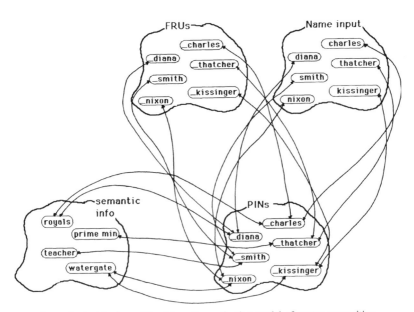

Figure 3. Architecture of the interactive activation model of person recognition.

presented here. However, it is assumed to represent the output of visual processing by the perceptual system (structural encoding). PINs are essentially domain and modality-free gateways into semantic information. They may be accessed through any input domain (face, name, voice, etc.), and provide access to information about that person. Semantic information units (SIUs) are simply units on which is coded particular semantic information. Name input units (NIUs) represent the same level of abstraction as FRUs, providing a route into the system for the names of known individuals. Though not represented in the present implementation, it is assumed that separate clusters of NIUs would be needed for seen or heard names (see Bruce & Young, 1986).

The configuration of these clusters is shown in Figure 3. Input to the model is made by exciting the activation of an FRU or a name input unit. Time is modelled here in terms of a number of processing cycles, after each of which activation at units is updated. The effect of this is that activation is passed along excitatory links into different pools, thus increasing the activation levels of associated units. Note that connections are all bidirectional, in keeping with McClelland and Rumelhart's original conception of the interactive activation architecture, and the Bruce and Young (1986) model (see Figure 1). In all such models there is also a global decay function which forces units towards a resting activation. After input to the system, units tend to stabilize when the effect of input activation is balanced by the effect of decay. McClelland and Rumelhart (1981, 1988) give details of the equations for governing transfer of activation and decay in these nets, and the Appendix gives the details of the particular parameters used here.

In this model, we propose that familiarity decisions are taken at the PINs. As discussed above, this is a departure from Bruce and Young (1986), who placed familiarity decisions at the interface between FRUs and the cognitive system. As we discussed earlier, this was largely because the relationship between PINs and semantic information was not clearly addressed by Bruce and Young, which forced familiarity decisions to a different locus. These authors thus implied that separate familiarity decision mechanisms must be taken for faces, names, voices and so forth. However, here the familiarity decision is assumed to be based on "person familiarity", as the same decision is taken at PINs whether they are activated through either FRU input or NIU input. This now seems to us a more plausible account. In daily life one is often presented with information about a person across more than one modality (e.g., we may see someone's face at the same time as hearing their voice). It would be parsimonious for these various inputs to feed to a single central pool of units at which familiarity judgements can be taken (Burton et al., 1990). It is important to note that this conception still allows for the common daily error in which one may recognize a person as familiar, but be unable to retrieve any semantic information about them (Young, Hay, & Ellis, 1985). We have here explicitly separated PINs and semantic information, and hence in theory it should be possible to access PINs (and hence

achieve a sense of familiarity) without accessing semantic information. One situation in which this might occur is if, for some reason, the connections between the PINs and the SIUs were abolished or attenuated. We will develop this idea in detail below.

The mechanism for decisions in the present model, unlike standard logogen models, is comparison of activation of units against a *constant* threshold. So, in familiarity decision, an arbitrary threshold is set for the pool of PINs, and any unit which reaches the threshold level is taken to be recognized as familiar. Note that this proposal has nothing to say about the *phenomenal experience* of awareness. We simply characterize a *familiarity judgement* as occurring when a PIN crosses a threshold. We do not offer any account of introspective awareness here.

Burton et al. (1990) have shown that this (Figure 3) conceptualization can account for a number of effects in the literature on normal face recognition, including semantic (associative) priming, repetition (identity) priming and distinctiveness effects. The different time courses of semantic and repetition priming are explained by proposing that semantic priming affects activation levels at the PINs while repetition affects the strength of the connections between FRUs and PINs.

The mechanism by which semantic priming takes place is of particular importance here, and so we will describe it using an illustrative example from the architecture shown in Figure 3. After input to a particular FRU (say Prince Charles), the "Prince Charles" PIN becomes active. As activation at this unit rises, it in turn passes activation along the excitatory links to the relevant semantic information units (say, "royal"). Now, as this unit rises in activation, excitatory activation is passed back into the PIN pool, to the "Princess Diana" PIN, which is connected to some of the same semantic information units as "Prince Charles". Hence, it is possible for several units within the same pool to rise in activation level, even though all units within a pool actually inhibit each other. During the scenario presented here, the Charles PIN will quickly rise above the threshold for a positive familiarity decision. However, because there is some cost involved in passing information, the Diana PIN will rise, but stabilize below this threshold. Now, on subsequent activation of the "Diana" FRU, the "Diana" PIN will quickly rise to threshold. Because the "Diana" PIN is already above its resting activation, it will take a shorter time to reach threshold than if it started at rest. This is the model of semantic priming. When we come to describe experiments with the model, we will present data from exactly this scenario (see Figure 4 on p. 181).

It is important to note that in this model semantic priming will take place across input domains. Because its mechanism is the excitation of PINs, subsequent input may come from any system which feeds into these PINs. So, for example, if a PIN has previously become active through presentation of a face, then subsequent presentation of a name will also be facilitated, since the appropriate PIN is already above resting activation. Cross-domain semantic priming

of this type is found for normal subjects, as well as in some prosopagnosics (Young et al., 1988). We will present demonstrations of these effects below, and a more detailed analysis of semantic and other priming effects may be found in Burton et al. (1990).

Implementation

The model as described here was developed using McClelland and Rumelhart's (1988) *iac* program. This is a small software environment for exploration of connectionist models. In the Appendix we present a detailed list of the parameters associated with the current implementation, in order that readers may replicate these simulations.

As a simplifying assumption in the model, all excitatory links have the same weight. Similarly, all inhibitory links have the same weight, though this is smaller than the excitatory links (see Appendix). The assumption of equality of weights does not correspond to the real situation. We are taking connection strength as an analogue of "degree of association" within the system. However, there will almost certainly be faces which are better known than others (i.e., by analogy, will have stronger connections between FRU and PIN), and there will also be varying degrees of association between PINs and SIUs (e.g., "Prince Charles is a member of the royal family" will be a strong link, whereas "Prince Charles studied in Cambridge" will be a weak link for most people). The commitment to equality of connection strengths within the implemented model serves to simplify the assumptions made here. In short, we aim to show that the behaviour exhibited by the model is a consequence of a *general* architecture, and not due to local manipulation of particular parameters.

Finally, note that this is not a simulation of learning. Unlike many connectionist models (see, for example, Hinton & Anderson, 1981; McClelland & Rumelhart, 1986; Rumelhart & McClelland, 1986), we do not modify the values of connection strengths in the simulations presented here. Instead the model is intended to implement a particular state of the face recognition system. As such, it has the same status as many other functional models, though as we will show below it allows for examination of a number of hypotheses which are hidden from view in unimplemented systems.

OUR ACCOUNT OF COVERT RECOGNITION

We now turn to the simulation of effects observed in the prosopagnosic patient, PH. We begin by noting that PH can match different views of faces (De Haan et al., 1987b, Tasks 1 and 2) and that he shows an advantage in reaction time (RT) for matching different views of familiar over unfamiliar faces, despite the fact that he denies recognizing any of the faces. The pattern of faster matching of familiar than unfamiliar faces is also found for normal subjects (Young, McWeeny, Hay, & Ellis, 1986b) and, like normal subjects, PH only shows this

phenomenon of faster matching of familiar faces when the match must be based on the face's internal features (eyes, nose, mouth) as opposed to external features (hair, face shape, chin) (De Haan et al., 1987b, Task 2; Young, Hay, McWeeny, Flude, & Ellis, 1985, Experiment 1).

As has been noted in previous studies, these effects of familiarity in face-matching tasks provide evidence that there is no gross impairment affecting the structural encoding of seen faces (including configural processing) sufficiently to prevent recognition by PH, and that FRUs themselves remain intact (De Haan et al., 1987b; Young & De Haan, 1988). Any impairment for PH cannot be located at this level.

In terms of the Burton et al. (1990) implementation of the Bruce and Young (1986) model, we therefore propose that the functional impairment lies in the *connection strengths* between the pool of FRUs and the pool of PINs. We propose that PH suffers attenuated connection strengths between these two pools. Hence, while *some* excitation is passed from an active FRU to its associated PIN, the weak connection strengths mean that this activation is small compared to an intact system. The result of this is that the appropriate PIN is active, but below threshold. This activation at the PIN can be passed to the connected SIUs in the normal way, and subsequently on to any associated PIN. The only difference between this and the intact system is that the levels of activation will be smaller.

We make this proposal to account for the fact that despite being unable to recognize faces overtly, PH displays some effects which are affected by structure deep in the face recognition system. A plausible account of these effects is that some activation is passed into this system, but that this is sufficiently attenuated to destroy the ability to make overt judgements of familiarity. To demonstrate that this is a plausible account, we now consider and simulate two of these effects: semantic priming and interference from "unrecognized" faces.

Semantic priming

We will begin the exploration with an account of covert recognition in pros-opagnosic patients as demonstrated by semantic priming from "unrecognized" faces. In normal subjects, presentation of the face of a familiar person as a prime stimulus facilitates a subsequent familiarity decision to the target face of a close semantic associate. So, for example, it is known that subjects are faster to respond positively to Oliver Hardy's face if it has been preceded by Stan Laurel's face, than if it has been preceded by an unrelated familiar face (e.g., Ronald Reagan) or by an unfamiliar face (Bruce & Valentine, 1986).

Semantic priming effects have been shown to cross stimulus input domains (Young et al., 1988). That is, Oliver Hardy's *face* primes recognition latency for Stan Laurel's *name*. This cross-domain semantic priming effect provides a technique for examining covert recognition in prosopagnosia, since it allows

TABLE 1
Cross-domain (face primes) and within-domain
(name primes) semantic priming of familiar name
recognition for PH (data are reaction times in
milliseconds from Young, Hellawell, & De Haan,
1988, Experiment 4)

Prime type	Related	Neutral	Unrelated
Face primes	1016	1080	1117
Name primes	945	1032	1048

the influence of a face prime to be investigated in the task of making familiarity decisions to name targets. Although PH is unable to recognize face primes overtly, he can readily identify most name targets, and thus carry out the task. Young et al. (1988) report that prior presentation of (for example) Eric Morecambe's face facilitates PH's recognition of Ernie Wise's name (these being a famous English comedy duo).

Table 1 shows data from Young et al. (1988, Experiment 4) for cross-domain (face prime and name target) and within-domain (name prime and name target) semantic priming of name recognition by PH. Notice that although PH cannot recognize face primes overtly but can recognize name primes overtly, the priming effect is equivalent across the different prime domains. In both cases there is facilitation of responses to targets preceded by related primes, and no significant inhibition from unrelated primes. Thus, presence or absence of overt recognition of the primes does not modify semantic priming. Although PH's reaction times are slower than those of normal subjects, the *pattern* of his performance across conditions remains the same (i.e., facilitation of responses to targets preceded by related primes, and equivalent cross-domain and within-domain effects; Young et al., 1988).

Figure 4 shows the effects of cross-domain and within-domain semantic priming in the intact Burton et al. (1990) model. These data come from a small net of 18 people (each with an FRU, PIN and NIU) and 9 SIUs. Figure 4(a) shows the effect of a related face prime on name recognition, Figure 4(b) shows the effect of a related name prime on name recognition, and Figure 4(c) shows the unprimed name recognition cycle. We have previously shown that unprimed (equivalent to "neutral condition" here) and unrelated prime conditions produce almost

---

Figure 4. Activation at PINs after input to FRUs and NIUs in the intact net, showing the effect of semantic priming. (a) Cross-domain semantic priming; the "Charles" FRU is activated for 80 cycles, followed by a 20-cycle rest period, followed by activation of the "Diana" NIU for 80 cycles. (b) Within-domain semantic priming, from a name prime ("Charles") to a second name input ("Diana"). (c) An "unprimed" comparison in which the "Diana" NIU is activated with no previous input.

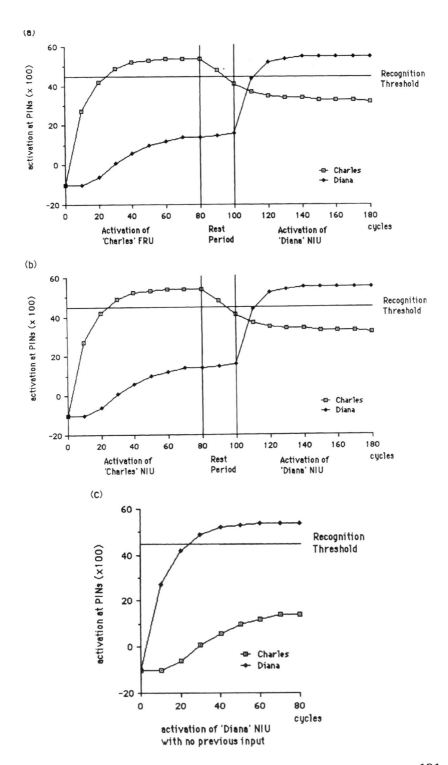

identical patterns of activation (Figures 3 and 5 in Burton et al., 1990). We therefore present only one of these controls in the diagrams given here.

The diagrams show activation at two PINs. In Figure 4(a) input is made to an FRU (Prince Charles), and the model is allowed to run for 80 cycles with this FRU activated to its maximum level. During this time, the Prince Charles PIN increases in activation until stabilizing at a particular value. Furthermore, the PIN of a semantic associate also rises in activation, through the route described above. What is happening here is that activation at the "Charles" PIN is passing activation to the "Royal" SIU, which is in turn passing activation to the "Diana" PIN. Both PINs tend to stabilize after a number of cycles, though the semantic associate achieves a lower activation level than the prime itself. So, in this case, the "Charles" PIN crosses the (arbitrarily set) threshold for a positive familiarity decision to be taken. While the "Diana" PIN becomes active, it remains below this threshold.

The system is then given a "rest period" of 20 cycles in which it is allowed to run with no external input; that is, the FRU activation is discontinued. This corresponds to the "inter-stimulus interval" used in experimental studies. During this time, units tend to decay. Note that the "Charles" PIN quickly drops below threshold. In this case, the "Diana" PIN continues to rise by a small amount, although if given more cycles it too would begin to decay (see Burton et al., 1990).

During the final 80-cycle period, the NIU for "Diana" is activated. As the "Diana" PIN remains above its resting position, the time taken for it to reach threshold is shorter than would normally be the case. To see this, Figure 4(c) shows the effect of activating the "Diana" NIU with no previous priming. In the primed case, the name "Diana" produces a familiarity decision after around 10 cycles, whereas in the unprimed condition it requires over 20 cycles. Of course we do not intend these thresholds to have any special meaning—they are chosen arbitrarily. For this reason Burton et al. (1990) discuss the fact that the model may make only ordinal predictions. However, the point of interest is that *wherever a threshold is set* the primed condition produces an advantage over the unprimed.

We should note here that this effect is not due to our choice of the number of cycles for which the model is allowed to run. We have chosen to illustrate an 80-cycle presentation and a 20-cycle inter-stimulus interval (ISI) in order to demonstrate the fact that the units tend to stabilize. Figure 4(a) shows that priming would exist over much shorter presentation times, and over all longer presentation times. Furthermore, the effect exists over a very large range of ISIs, including zero ISI. Given sufficiently large ISI, both active units will decay to resting activation (hence eliminating priming), though this takes many hundreds of cycles (Burton et al., 1990).

Figure 4(b) shows the effects of a name prime ("Charles") on subsequent activation in response to a related name ("Diana"). This is equivalent to within-domain semantic priming. As is found for normal subjects, the effect is closely comparable to that observed following a face prime—Figure 4(a); cross-domain

semantic priming. Having demonstrated these effects in the intact net, we now turn to the simulation of PH.

We mentioned earlier that our view of PH is that the FRU–PIN links have been affected by his brain injury. Figure 5 shows a replication of the experiments shown in Figure 4, but this time the connection strengths between all FRUs and PINs have been halved to represent our conception of PH's impairment. In Figure 5(a) activation of the "Charles" FRU does not cause the "Charles" PIN to reach the threshold for familiarity. However, both it and the semantic associate (Diana) PINs are active (above resting position) at the end of the rest period. This means that subsequent presentation of the "Diana" NIU causes the "Diana" PIN to rise more quickly to threshold than would usually be the case. For comparison, Figure 5(c) shows the rise in activity of the "Diana" PIN when the "Diana" NIU is activated, but there has been no previous priming. Once again, we see that there is an advantage for a primed person.

In this way we can account for the semantic priming observed in PH. Although the patient is unable to reach threshold recognition at the PIN level for a presented face, these PIN units are nevertheless active. This activity can be passed around the system and produce the semantic priming effects on name recognition observed in empirical studies.

Figure 5(b) shows the effect of name-to-name (within-domain) semantic priming in the simulation of PH. It can be seen that the effect of priming—i.e., the comparison with Figure 5(c)—is present whether the prime is an (unrecognized) face or a (recognized) name. This is the pattern observed in data from PH (Table 1). Of course, the main effect of *prime type* seen in Table 1 is not reflected in the simulation. The empirical data for PH show that, in general, names which have been primed by other names are recognized faster than names which have been primed by faces. However, as Young et al. (1988) note, this may simply reflect the order in which PH was given the different blocks of trials. In addition, the present model does not attempt to simulate the configural processing necessary for FRUs or NIUs to become active in the first place. The important point to note is that priming delivers an *advantage* to name recognition whether the prime is a name or a face, and that this can happen for primes which remain below the threshold for recognition at the PIN level. In these ways the simulation provides a close parallel to the findings with PH.

An interesting (and unintended) emergent property of this simulation is that comparing Figures 4(c) and 5(c) shows a general deficit in the attenuated model. Despite the fact that the only connection strengths to have been weakened are those between FRUs and PINs, the "lesioned" model takes longer to reach a familiarity judgement to *name* input than the intact model. This is a consequence of the fact that all links are bidirectional. When a PIN becomes active through name input, it will pass activation on to the FRU (and vice versa). This in turn passes activation back to the PIN, and these units tend mutually to increase each other's activation level. So, wherever links are attenuated in this model, there

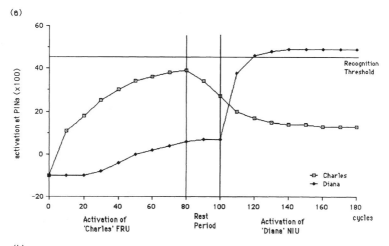

(a)

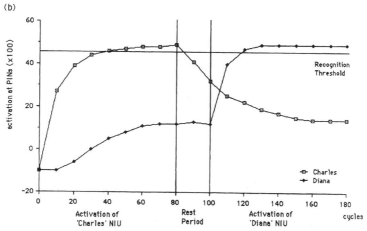

(b)

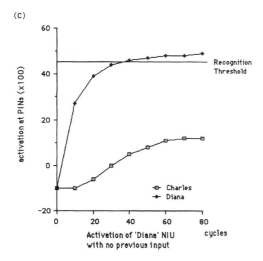

(c)

184

will be a general decrease in performance throughout the system. In fact, this decrease in performance is also shown by PH (compared to controls). Of course, there are many reasons why a patient with neurological damage may show a general slowing of RT, but the results described here provide one possible mechanism for the effect. What is lost is the facility for related units to bolster each other's activation in the system.

Finally, we should note that for the same reasons that it can simulate PH's preserved semantic priming from faces that do not reach recognition threshold, the Burton et al. (1990) model provides a general account of semantic priming under conditions in which stimuli do not reach threshold for normal subjects, such as when visual masking is introduced before overt recognition has occurred (e.g., Carr, McCauley, Sperber, & Parmelee, 1982; McCauley, Parmelee, Sperber, & Carr, 1980). The parallel between these findings and those obtained for PH had been made by Young et al. (1988), so it is reassuring that a similar account can be given.

Interference effects

In common with normal subjects, PH shows interference from distractor faces onto the semantic classification of simultaneously presented target names (De Haan et al., 1987a, b). The paradigm for this investigation comes from Young, Ellis, Flude, McWeeny, and Hay (1986). If subjects are asked to make a semantic decision about the names of familiar people (e.g., "is this a politician or a pop star?") there is an inhibitory effect when the name is presented simultaneously with the face of someone in the opposite semantic group. So, the decision that the name "Mick Jagger" is that of a pop star is made more quickly when the name is presented on its own, or when it is accompanied by the face of another pop star, than when it is presented simultaneously with the face of Neil Kinnock (a politician).

The same effect was observed in PH (De Haan et al., 1987a, b), even though his performance at explicitly classifying face stimuli into semantic categories was very poor. Once again, this suggests that this particular case of prosopagnosia has its roots deeper than any inability to extract configural information. The face recognition system is being activated in a way that invalidates this option.

In the following simulation we have copied the experimental design of Young, Ellis, Flude, McWeeny, and Hay (1986, Experiment 2) and of De Haan et al. (1987b, Task 3). The net is presented with the name of a person (i.e., the NIU is

---

Figure 5. Activation at PINs after input to FRUs and NIUs in the simulation of PH. (a) Effect of 80 cycles input to the "Charles" FRU, followed by a 20 cycles rest, followed by 80 cycles input to the "Diana" NIU. This corresponds to cross-domain semantic priming. (b) Effect of 80 cycles activation of the "Charles" NIU, followed by 20 cycles rest, followed by 80 cycles activation of the "Diana" NIU; corresponding to within-domain semantic priming. (c) Effect of activating the "Diana" NIU with no previous input, to provide an "unprimed" comparison.

activated). This is done in one of four conditions: (1) name input together with the face of the person whose name it is (equivalent to Young et al.'s SAME PERSON condition); (2) name input alone (Young et al.'s NAME ONLY condition); (3) name input together with the face of a person from the same category (Young et al.'s RELATED condition); (4) name input together with the face of a person from the opposite category (Young et al.'s UNRELATED condition). For this simulation, a net was assembled containing 18 people, 9 of whom were linked to one SIU (say "pop star"); and the remaining 9 to a second SIU (say "politician"). Both Young, Ellis, Flude, McWeeny, and Hay (1986) and De Haan et al. (1987b) found no significant differences between RTs in the first three conditions, but the unrelated face presentation caused a decrement in performance.

In order to simulate these experiments, it is necessary this time to examine the semantic information units rather than the PINs. By analogy with the person familiarity task (which is assumed to have its locus at the PINs) it seems reasonable to propose that the categorization decision occurs due to the appropriate semantic unit reaching some threshold value. Figure 6 shows the activation of the SIU associated with the *name* input, for each of the four conditions. This is in keeping with the experiments we are simulating, as the experimental task is to make a semantic judgement to the presented name. Figure 6(a) is for the intact net, while Figure 6(b) shows effects of the net in which FRU–PIN links have half the normal weight. For comparison, the RT means (in milliseconds) for normal subjects (Young, Ellis, Flude, McWeeny, & Hay, 1986, Experiment 2), and for PH (De Haan et al., 1987b, Task 3), are presented in Table 2.

In both Figures 6(a) and 6(b), it can be seen that presentation of an unrelated face in conjunction with the target name provides the slowest route to any threshold one cares to set. This is consistent with the data in Table 2. None of the remaining three conditions showed significant differences in empirical work. However, it is clear in Figure 6 that for the simulation there is a trend for the name only (no distractor) condition to be slower than the related name and same person conditions. This pattern is observed in Table 2, though the differences are not statistically significant. There is also a nonsignificant trend in the empirical data for the same person condition to produce faster responses than the related name condition. This is not found to be the case in the simulation presented here. Of course, it is not strictly appropriate to compare a non-significant trend from empirical data with output from the model. (Though note that the levels of activation from the same person and related name conditions are similar, and in fact cross in experiments from the model; see Figure 6.) We therefore do not take this difference to be fatal for the model. In fact, any possible facilitative effects from related or same face conditions will depend crucially on the semantic associativity between people. So, for example, in the real situation, famous people will have many SIUs, some of these shared within groups, and some unique. We cannot hope to capture such richness in a simple model of the type

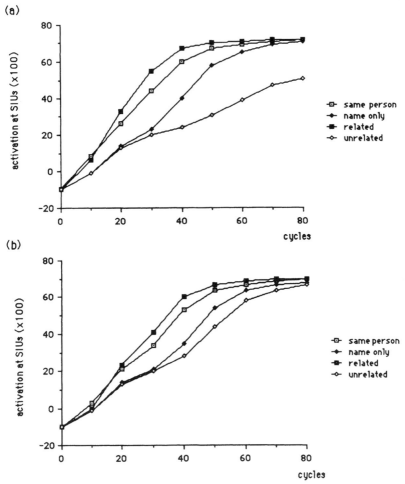

Figure 6. Activation at SIUs after input to FRUs and NIUs. The traces shown are the activations for the SIU associated with name input in each of the four conditions. (a) Data from the intact net. (b) Repetition of the same experiment with the simulation of PH.

TABLE 2

Mean reaction times (in milliseconds) for name classification with different types of face distractors by normal subjects (Young, Ellis, McWeeny, & Hay, 1986, Experiment 2), and PH (De Haan, Young, & Newcombe, 1987b, Task 3)

Type of face distractor	Same person	None	Related	Unrelated
Normal subjects	789	821	815	875
PH	1502	1565	1560	1714

used above. However, the situation is clearer in the inhibitory case: when the system is presented with inputs which do not share SIUs in common, the within-pool inhibition built into IAC models will ensure that these SIUs will rise slower than if no competing stimulus were present.

We have now shown that it is possible to simulate empirical findings on face-name interference for PH and normal subjects without modification of the architecture used to simulate cross-domain and within-domain semantic priming. For interference, though, there is a noticeable difference in the sizes of effects over the intact and "lesioned" nets. In the simulation of PH, the interference from an unrelated face distractor appears to be smaller than in the intact net; this is because the "distractor" face has a smaller influence at PIN level due to attenuated FRU–PIN links. This discrepancy in the size of the effect is not observed in the original data. However, as mentioned above, it is impossible to make accurate comparisons of size of effect in the simulations presented here; instead we are limited to ordinal predictions. This is partly because we do not know the nature of the mapping between "cycles" in the model and RT data from subjects (other than that it is monotonic). The ordinal prediction concerning relative difficulty of the different conditions (the unrelated condition will be most difficult both for normals and PH) *is* verified in experimental data.

Other effects from the study of PH

Our characterization of PH's deficit raises an interesting possibility. Given the combinative effects of name and face input on person recognition (shown in the model of interference), might it be the case that name input can aid *face* recognition in a prosopagnosic patient? In a further series of experiments with PH, De Haan, Young, and Newcombe (1991b; see also Young & De Haan, 1991) have observed an increased level of performance in face identification due to processing of a name. PH was simultaneously presented with a face and two names, one of these being the correct name for the face. When asked to choose the correct name in a forced-choice task, PH was able to perform above chance, though far from perfectly (30/40, 27/40, 26/40 and 27/40 correct in four separate runs). The same effect has recently been reported by Sergent and Poncet (1990) with another prosopagnosic patient, PV. In this case, PV chose the correct name in 40/48 trials, though once again her performance was below that of control subjects (who made no errors). Interestingly, neither PH nor PV reported any awareness of scoring above chance in this task. The presentation of names did not induce *overt* recognition of the faces.

This pattern appears to have an analogue in the IAC model. When presented with two names and a face simultaneously (i.e., when two NIUs and one FRU are activated), the PIN receiving input from two sources (name and face) rises faster, and stabilizes at a higher level of activation, than the PIN receiving input from a name only. This occurs both in the "lesioned" and intact model. We

might postulate that in a forced-choice test the subject would choose the person whose PIN has the highest level of activation, or the PIN which is the first to reach threshold. Note that this proposal is independent of the processes which signal awareness, as the NIU–PIN links are unlesioned, and therefore name input is able to produce activation levels for a familiarity judgement at the PINs. The presence of the "unrecognized" face simply contributes to this process.

LIMITS OF THE SIMULATION OF PH

While we have provided an account of some covert recognition effects in normals and PH, we must make clear that there are certain effects which are inaccessible with a model of the present type. In particular, we cannot address the issues of attention or learning using this model.

The problem of attention arises with respect to the interference studies reported above. In the Young, Ellis, Flude, McWeeny, and Hay (1986, Experiment 2) procedure, normal subjects are presented simultaneously with a face and a name, and asked to make a semantic judgement to the name only. However, given that both the name and face are recognizable, how is the subject to discriminate between an SIU which has been stimulated through face input and an SIU which has been stimulated through name input? This discrimination is necessary in order to make the correct response. Given that the two stimuli are spatially separated, and present throughout any given trial, a simple solution would be to assert that active *routes* through the system are available for inspection by some homuncular process. However, this is hardly satisfactory without explication of the homuncular process itself.

In fact, this is a general problem for all interference tasks. It has been the topic of much research into the Stroop effect (Stroop, 1935). One possible solution is to modulate one pathway into the SIUs through attentional control (Logan, 1980). In an attempt to implement such modulation, Cohen, Dunbar, and McClelland (1990) introduce specific "task demand" units into a connectionist model of human performance on the Stroop task. While this approach may provide a solution, the IAC model presented above has no such facility. In order to be clear about the range of phenomena which this model can address, we should point out that we are not in a position to provide an account of selective attention here. Amongst other things, a model incorporating such an account would need to contain representations of spatial location to form the basis of this selective attentional capacity.

Phenomena associated with learning are also inaccessible using this model. A number of studies of covert recognition have used a learning paradigm. For instance, De Haan et al. (1987b, Task 5) examined PH's facility to learn associations between faces and semantic categories. This study was based on a paradigm due to Bruyer et al. (1983) which requires the patient to examine a number of faces of familiar people, and try to learn an occupation for each. The stimuli are

manipulated such that half the associations are veridical and half non-veridical. So in one condition PH was shown the face of Paul Newman, and told that this was the face of an actor. In the second condition he was shown (for example) Geoffrey Boycott's face (an English cricketer), and told that this was a quiz show host. De Haan et al. (1987b) showed an advantage for learning veridical associations.

Couched in interactive activation terms, this result seems to be due to the fact that learning can take advantage of existing, though attenuated, connections between FRUs and PINs. We postulate that forming a new pathway is more trouble than using an existing one. Although the present model allows the possibility of some learning through modification of connection strengths (see Burton et al., 1990), it does not specify a mechanism for the creation of new units or links. There is therefore no account of learning in the normal course of events. This problem is in fact a general one, common to all current functional accounts of face recognition (e.g., Bruce & Young, 1986). We are currently exploring ways of introducing such a facility into the model. In the meantime, we can only note that findings with learning tasks are not inconsistent with the general architecture of our model (De Haan et al., 1987b; Sergent & Poncet, 1990; Young & De Haan, 1988) but cannot be directly simulated by it in its present form.

PROSOPAGNOSIA WITHOUT COVERT RECOGNITION

PH's covert recognition abilities are not typical of *all* cases of prosopagnosia. Whilst several patients showing covert recognition of familiar faces have been reported, there are now also a number of reports in the literature of prosopagnosic patients who do *not* show these effects (Bauer, 1986; Newcombe, Young, & De Haan, 1989; Sergent & Villemure, 1989; Young & Ellis, 1989b). We will now briefly discuss one of these patients, MS (studied by Newcombe et al., 1989), in terms of the functional model presented here.

MS contracted a febrile illness in 1970, at the age of 23, and was given a presumptive diagnosis of herpes encephalitis. He has normal visual acuity, and is able to read without difficulty. However, his colour vision is severely impaired, and there is evidence of some impairment in semantic memory, particularly for living things (Young, Newcombe, Hellawell, & De Haan, 1989). Newcombe and Ratcliff (1974) and Ratcliff and Newcombe (1982) provide a full case description of this patient.

MS is completely unable to recognize familiar faces, scoring 0/20 on tests of both highly familiar and moderately familiar faces (Newcombe et al., 1989). He is also poor on matching photographs of unknown people, with a score of 33/54 on the Benton test of facial recognition (Newcombe et al., 1989). MS also suffers from object agnosia, recognizing only 8/36 line drawings of familiar objects (Ratcliff & Newcombe, 1982).

Newcombe et al. (1989) show that there is no evidence of covert recognition in MS. Unlike PH, he shows no effect of face-to-name semantic priming, though name-to-name semantic priming continues to exist. Furthermore, in a learning task, MS shows no evidence of an advantage for learning "true" name–face associations over "false" associations.

In the terms of the model presented here, MS shows no evidence of activation at the PIN level as a result of face input. This could arise for at least three reasons: (1) the FRU–PIN links have been abolished, or at least more severely attenuated than is the case for PH; (2) the FRUs themselves are in some way damaged, preventing output being passed along the links to PINs; (3) the *input* to the FRUs is damaged; that is, the configural processing leading to FRU activation has been impaired.

Explanation (1) would lead to the pattern observed in this patient. As there are no (or severely attenuated) links between FRU and PIN, activation at FRU would not be passed to PIN, and so a face input would be unable to cause a rise in activation of a PIN necessary for a familiarity decision. In PH, we assume that there is *some* (sub-threshold) activation passed to a PIN; however, in MS, there is no activation passed to these units from FRUs. There will therefore be no face-to-name semantic priming. In this case, however, there will be preserved name-to-name priming, proceeding through the normal route.

Explanations (2) and (3) also imply that there is no activity at FRU to be passed along (possibly intact) links to PINs. Once again, a simulation of this patient in which no activation reaches the PIN should show an intact name-to-name semantic priming effect, but no face-to-name semantic priming, and, of course, no overt recognition of faces.

Disrupted configural processing (explanation 3) would be consistent with MS's general object agnosia, and may provide the most natural account of his particular deficit. Given his poor performance in matching faces in different views, it seems likely that the deficit occurs in the system feeding input to FRUs. This account in terms of higher-order perceptual impairment was the explanation given by Newcombe et al. (1989).

OTHER NEUROLOGICAL DEFICITS OF
PERSON RECOGNITION

We have shown how Burton et al.'s (1990) interactive activation implementation of the Bruce and Young (1986) functional model of face recognition can provide the basis for a principled account of the impairments underlying different forms of prosopagnosia, and the otherwise puzzling phenomenon of covert recognition. However, if the approach is to be of general utility, it should also be able to encompass other forms of neuropsychological deficit affecting person recognition.

One of the interesting features of functional models is that they can be used to predict the existence of types of neuropsychological deficit which have not

previously been observed. A clear example of this arises from the present model. Consider what would happen if the connection strengths between the pool of PINs and the pool of SIUs were reduced. If these links have attenuated strength, then the model would predict intact ability to perform the person familiarity task, whether this is carried out to face or name input, but attenuation of performance in retrieving any semantic information. So, the SIUs will not reach the activation threshold necessary for a semantic decision to be made. The resulting deficit will thus be a domain-independent impairment of access to identity-specific semantic information, with a preserved sense of familiarity. It should be noted that this is quite different from prosopagnosia, since prosopagnosia primarily affects only one input domain (faces), and prosopagnosic patients experience no overt sense of a face's familiarity.

Exactly this predicted pattern of preserved familiarity and impaired access to semantic information has recently been found in a patient, ME, studied by De Haan, Young, and Newcombe (1991). ME has high IQ (verbal IQ 120; performance IQ 125), normal short-term memory, language comprehension, and visuoperceptual abilities. However, she has severely impaired long-term memory. ME is able accurately to rate pictures of faces as familiar or not, scoring similarly to controls on familiarity ratings to a line-up of high-familiar, low-familiar and unfamiliar faces. Similar results hold for her familiarity ratings of names; once again her performance on a name line-up echoes that of controls. The implication of this, couched in terms of the interactive activation model (and in terms of Bruce & Young, 1986), is that the system linking FRUs, NIUs and PINs is intact.

In contrast to this well-preserved ability to make familiarity decisions, ME is unable to retrieve semantic information about familiar people from either names or faces. Occasionally she is able to retrieve a broad occupational category such as "politician" (De Haan et al., 1991a). However, her performance in accessing appropriate identity-specific semantic information is considerably below that of control subjects.

The case of ME provides further evidence for the modifications of the Bruce and Young (1986) model made by Burton et al. (1990). Our characterization of her deficit (i.e., attenuated PIN–SIU links) implies that she should be able to *match* names to faces, despite being unable to retrieve semantic information from either input. This is because the same PIN will rise in response to each input. De Haan et al. (1991a) chose 26 famous people whom ME was able to categorize as familiar, but about whom she was unable to retrieve any semantic information. She was shown each face, and simultaneously presented orally with three names, one being correct, one being the name of a celebrity from the same occupational category, and one being the name of an unrelated person. ME was very accurate on this task, scoring 23/26 correct. From this we may conclude that the functional locus of ME's deficit must lie after the point where the face and name recognition systems converge (i.e., the PINs). So, this case provides support for both of our modifications to Bruce and Young's model: (1) that

familiarity decisions are taken at PINs; and (2) PINs provide gateways to semantic information, rather than storing semantic information themselves.

In addition to re-describing the functional complaint of this patient, the present model has the advantange that it can also make empirical predictions concerning phenomena one might well not think to test—for example, our account of ME's impairment implies that SIUs are active (i.e., above resting state) but below threshold. Thus, for reasons similar to those used above for PH, ME should show some semantic priming both in within-domain and cross-domain variants of semantic priming tasks using the familiarity decision paradigm. It will not necessarily be of the same size as for normal subjects, as the amount of activation passing between PIN and SIU and back to associated PIN will be small. However, it should exist, even if in attenuated form. The ability to make predictions of this type is a powerful feature of the present model.

DISCUSSION AND CONCLUSIONS

We have shown how a model, couched in interactive activation terms, can be used to provide an explanation for different effects observed in patients with impaired recognition of familiar people, both in prosopagnosic and other forms. We have presented demonstrations of observed effects, and proposed possible mechanisms for these. We have also used the model to make empirical predictions about these patients, demonstrating that it has predictive, as well as descriptive, capabilities.

This model provides an advance over previous work in this area. For example, it demonstrates how apparently similar functional deficits can occur for a variety of reasons. So, it is clear that the term prosopagnosia refers not to a single complaint, but to a number of possible deficits, at different locations, each of which lead to different but predictable patterns of behaviour. This much is in fact evident from the empirical papers on which we have drawn, and from the Bruce and Young (1986) functional model. However, the use of a computer implementation has allowed us to progress further in exploring the functional system than did the original unimplemented version. The Bruce and Young (1986) model does not have the same range of predictive power as the present IAC account. As with any modelling exercise, the process of implementation forces one to be explicit about the nature of the elements with which one is dealing. For example, it is not sufficient to specify that FRUs are linked to PINs; instead one must specify exactly what is the nature of these links. For this reason, the unimplemented version could not have predicted the nature of the cross-domain priming effect, or the complex patterns of rising activation in the interference tasks described above.

As we have shown, a simple modification of the Burton et al. (1990) model, involving attenuating the FRU–PIN connections, can provide an effective simulation of the semantic priming and interference effects from "unrecognized"

faces observed in one form of prosopagnosia. Our account of this form of prosopagnosia has similarities to that offered by Young and De Haan (1988), insofar as it places emphasis on defective output from intact FRUs, but it also has considerable advantages over Young and De Haan's (1988) account. Not the least of these is, again, that because it involves a computer implementation we can demonstrate that it has the properties claimed. In addition, it is simpler than Young and De Haan's (1988) account, because all of the necessary properties are achieved without postulating any modification to the basic architecture. In particular, we have demonstrated that the problematic FRU–NIU links proposed by Young and De Haan are unnecessary.

To avoid becoming over-enthusiastic, though, we should be clear about the status of the model presented here. It is clearly a functional model, which has its location at the same level of abstraction as standard box and arrow models of cognition. The fact that we have used one form of connectionism (interactive activation) to implement the model does not commit us to any statement about the neurological hardware in which cognition is implemented. The physical instantiation of a lesion can be a loss of connections between neurones. Such a lesion may have the functional effect of attenuating the information passed from one functional location to another. We suggest, then, that the characterization of prosopagnosia as presented here is not implausible given neurological constraints.

We also need to be clear that, although our simulation takes much of the enigma from covert recognition, and shows how the phenomena involved have their place in the operation of normal or disordered systems organized in the way we have described, it is not intended as a solution to more "philosophical" questions concerning the nature of awareness. Characterizing PH's deficit as a loss of awareness of recognition (De Haan et al., 1987b; Young & De Haan, 1990) remains an adequate description; all we have done here is to reveal something of what might be the underlying mechanism. We do not claim to have solved the problem of what "awareness" is. Our computer is not "aware" of "recognizing" a face just because it passes an arbitrary threshold.

In future work we aim to extend the model to take account of different effects in face recognition. We have mentioned the need to model learning faces, and there is also a need for a name output mechanism to be added. There is considerable evidence accruing that naming is a specialized task, more difficult than retrieval of semantic information, and subject to specific deficit (Brennen, Baguley, Bright, & Bruce, 1990; Flude, Ellis, & Kay, 1989; Hanley & Cowell, 1988; Johnston & Bruce, 1990; McWeeny, Young, Hay, & Ellis, 1987; Young, Hay, & Ellis, 1985; Young, McWeeny, Ellis & Hay, 1986). The model presented here incorporates only name *input* units, and has nothing to say about the process of name *retrieval*. For this reason it is unable to address such issues as the relative difficulty of name retrieval (compared to retrieval of other semantic information; e.g., Johnston & Bruce, 1990; Young, Hay, & Ellis, 1985) or TOT states induced on naming (e.g., Brennen et al., 1990; Hanley & Cowell, 1988). In current work

we are examining how the model presented here might be developed to provide a framework for investigations in these areas (Burton & Bruce, 1992).

ACKNOWLEDGEMENTS

This research was supported in part by the following grants: a SERC (Image interpretation) award to Vicki Bruce and Mike Burton (GR/F 10569); an ESRC programme award for a multi-centred investigation (funded as grants XC15250001 to Vicki Bruce, XC1520002 to Ian Craw at Aberdeen University, XC1520003 to Haydn Ellis at University of Wales, Cardiff, XC1520004 to Andy Ellis and Andy Young, and XC1520005 to David Perret at St Andrews University); and an ESRC grant (R00023 1922) to Andy Young, Rick Hanley and Freda Newcombe. R. A. Johnston was supported by a SERC studentship.

NOTE

1. Semantic priming is sometimes referred to as associative priming. Here we use the terms interchangeably. Similarly, repetition priming is sometimes referred to as identity priming, and once again we use these terms interchangeably.

REFERENCES

Bauer, R. M. (1984). Autonomic recognition of names and faces in prosopagnosia: A neuropsychological application of the guilty knowledge test. *Neuropsychologia, 22,* 457–469.

Bauer, R. M. (1986). The cognitive psychophysiology of prosopagnosia. In H. D. Ellis, M. A. Jeeves, F. Newcombe, & A. Young (Eds.), *Aspects of face processing* (pp. 253–267). Dordrecht: Martinus Nijhoff.

Bodamer, J. (1947). Die Prosop-Agnosie. *Archiv für Psychiatrie und Nervenkrankheiten, 179,* 6–53.

Brennen, T. J., Baguley, T., Bright, J., & Bruce, V. (1990). Resolving semantically induced tip of the tongue states for proper nouns. *Memory and Cognition, 18,* 339–347.

Bruce, V. (1983). Recognising faces. *Philosophical Transactions of the Royal Society, B302,* 423–436.

Bruce, V. (1986). Recognising familiar faces. In H. D. Ellis, M. A. Jeeves, F. Newcombe, & A. Young (Eds.), *Aspects of face processing* (pp. 107–117). Dordrecht: Martinus Nijhoff.

Bruce, V. (1988). *Recognising faces.* Hove, UK: Lawrence Erlbaum Associates Ltd.

Bruce, V., & Valentine, T. (1985). Identity priming in the recognition of familiar faces. *British Journal of Psychology, 76,* 373–383.

Bruce, V., & Valentine, T. (1986). Semantic priming of familiar faces. *Quarterly Journal of Experimental Psychology, 38A,* 125–150.

Bruce, V., & Young, A. (1986). Understanding face recognition. *British Journal of Psychology, 77,* 305–327.

Brunas, J., Young, A. W., & Ellis, A. W. (1990). Repetition priming from incomplete faces: Evidence for part to whole completion. *British Journal of Psychology, 81,* 43–56.

Bruyer, R. (1987). *Les mecanismes de reconnaissance de visages.* Grenoble: Presses Universitaires de Grenoble.

Bruyer, R., Laterre, C., Seron, X., Feyereisen, P., Strypstein, E., Pierrard, E., & Rectem, D. (1983). A case of prosopagnosia with some preserved covert remembrance of familiar faces. *Brain and Cognition, 2,* 257–284.

Burton, A. M., & Bruce, V. (1992). I recognise your face but I can't remember your name: A simple explanation. *British Journal of Psychology, 83,* 45–60.

Burton, A. M., Bruce, V., & Johnston, R. A. (1990). Understanding face recognition with an interactive activation model. *British Journal of Psychology*, *81*, 361–380.

Carr, T. H., McCauley, C., Sperber, R. D., & Parmelee, C. M. (1982). Words, pictures and priming: On semantic activation, conscious identification, and the automaticity of information processing. *Journal of Experimental Psychology: Human Perception and Performance*, *8*, 757–777.

Cohen, J. D., Dunbar, K., & McClelland, J. L. (1990). On the control of automatic processes: A parallel distributed processing account of the Stroop effect. *Psychological Review*, *97*, 332–361.

Damasio, A. R., Damasio, H., & Van Hoesen, G. W. (1982). Prosopagnosia: Anatomic basis and behavioral mechanisms. *Neurology*, *32*, 331–341.

De Haan, E. H. F., Young, A. W., & Newcombe, F. (1987a). Faces interfere with name classification in a prosopagnosic patient. *Cortex*, *23*, 309–316.

De Haan, E. H. F., Young, A. W., & Newcombe, F. (1987b). Face recognition without awareness. *Cognitive Neuropsychology*, *4*, 385–415.

De Haan, E. H. F., Young, A. W., & Newcombe, F. (1991a). A dissociation between the sense of familiarity and access to semantic information concerning familiar people. *European Journal of Cognitive Psychology*, *3*, 51–67.

De Haan, E. H. F., Young, A. W., & Newcombe, F. (1991b). Covert and overt recognition in prosopagnosia. *Brain*, *114*, 2575–2591.

De Renzi, E. (1986). Current issues in prosopagnosia. In H. D. Ellis, M. A. Jeeves, F. Newcombe, & A. Young (Eds.), *Aspects of face processing* (pp. 243–252). Dordrecht: Martinus Nijhoff.

Ellis, A. W., Young, A. W., Flude, B., & Hay, D. C. (1987). Repetition priming of face recognition. *Quarterly Journal of Experimental Psychology*, *39A*, 193–210.

Ellis, A. W., Young, A. W., & Hay, D. C. (1987). Modelling the recognition of faces and words. In P. E. Morris (Ed.), *Modelling cognition* (pp. 269–297). London: Wiley.

Ellis, H. D. (1986). Processes underlying face recognition. In R. Bruyer (Ed.), *The neuropsychology of face perception and facial expression* (pp. 1–27). Hillsdale, NJ: Lawrence Erlbaum Associates Inc.

Flude, B. M., Ellis, A. W., & Kay, J. (1989). Face processing and name retrieval in an anomic aphasic: Names are stored separately from semantic information about familiar people. *Brain and Cognition*, *11*, 60–72.

Hanley, J. R., & Cowell, E. (1988). The effects of different types of retrieval cues on the recall of names of famous faces. *Memory and Cognition*, *16*, 545–555.

Hay, D. C., & Young, A. W. (1982). The human face. In A. W. Ellis (Ed.), *Normality and pathology in cognitive functions* (pp. 173–202). London: Academic Press.

Hécaen, H., & Angelergues, R. (1962). Agnosia for faces (prosopagnosia). *Archives of Neurology*, *7*, 92–100.

Hinton, G. E. & Anderson, J. A. (1981). *Parallel models of associative memory*. Hillsdale, NJ: Lawrence Erlbaum Associates Inc.

Johnston, R. A., & Bruce, V. (1990). Lost properties: Retrieval differences between name codes and semantic codes for familiar people. *Psychological Research*, *52*, 62–67.

Landis, T., Cummings, J. G., Christen, L., Bogen, J. E., & Imhof, H. G. (1986). Are unilateral right posterior cerebral lesions sufficient to cause prosopagnosia? Clinical and radiological findings in six additional patients. *Cortex*, *22*, 243–252.

Logan, G. D. (1980). Attention and automaticity in Stroop and priming tasks: Theory and data. *Cognitive Psychology*, *12*, 523–553.

McCauley, C., Parmelee, C., Sperber, R., & Carr, T. (1980). Early extraction of meaning from pictures and its relation to conscious identification. *Journal of Experimental Psychology: Human Perception and Performance*, *6*, 265–276.

McClelland, J. L., & Rumelhart, D. E. (1981). An interactive activation model of the effect of context in perception, Part 1. An account of basic findings. *Psychological Review*, *88*, 375–406.

McClelland, J. L., & Rumelhart, D. E. (1988). *Explorations in parallel distributed processing*. Cambridge, MA: Bradford Books.

McClelland, J. L., Rumelhart, D. E., & the PDP Research Group (1986). *Parallel distributed processing: Explorations in the microstructure of cognition. Vol II: Applications.* Cambridge, MA: Bradford Books.

McWeeny, K. H., Young, A. W., Hay D. C., & Ellis, A. W. (1987). Putting names to faces. *British Journal of Psychology, 78,* 143–149.

Meadows, J. C. (1974). The anatomical basis of prosopagnosia. *Journal of Neurology, Neurosurgery and Psychiatry, 37,* 489–501.

Newcombe, F., & Ratcliff, G. (1974). Agnosia: A disorder of object recognition. In F. Michel & B. Schott (Eds.), *Les syndromes de disconnexion calleuse chez l'homme* (pp. 317–341). Lyon: Colloque International de Lyon.

Newcombe, F., Young, A. W., & De Haan, E. H. F. (1989). Prosopagnosia and object agnosia without covert recognition. *Neuropsychologia, 27,* 179–191.

Ratcliff, G., & Newcombe, F. (1982). Object recognition: Some deductions from the clinical evidence. In A. W. Ellis (Ed.), *Normality and pathology in cognitive function* (pp. 147–171). London: Academic Press.

Renault, B., Signoret, J. L., DeBruille, B., Breton, F., & Bolgert, F. (1989). Brain potentials reveal covert facial recognition in prosopagnosia. *Neuropsychologica, 27,* 905–912.

Rizzo, M., Hurtig, R., & Damasio, A. R. (1987). The role of scanpaths in facial recognition and learning. *Annals of Neurology, 22,* 41–45.

Rumelhart, D. E., McClelland, J. L., & the PDP Research Group (1986). *Parallel distributed processing: Explorations in the microstructure of cognition, Vol. I: Foundations.* Cambridge, MA: Bradford Books.

Schacter, D. L., McAndrews, M. P., & Moscovitch, M. (1988). Access to consciousness: Dissociations between implicit and explicit knowledge in neuropsychological syndromes. In L. Weiskrantz (Ed.), *Thought without language* (pp. 242–278). Oxford: Oxford University Press.

Sergent, J., & Poncet, M. (1990). From covert to overt recognition of faces in a prosopagnosic patient. *Brain, 113,* 989–1004.

Sergent, J., & Villemure, J. G. (1989). Prosopagnosia in a right hemispherectomized patient. *Brain, 112,* 975–995.

Stroop, J. R. (1935). Studies of interference in serial verbal reactions. *Journal of Experimental Psychology, 18,* 643–662.

Tranel, D., & Damasio, A. R. (1985). Knowledge without awareness: An automatic index of facial recognition by prosopagnosics. *Science, 228,* 1453–1454.

Tranel, D., Damasio, A. R., & Damasio, H. (1988). Intact recognition of facial expression, gender and age in patients with impaired recognition of face identity. *Neurology, 38,* 690–696.

Valentine, T., & Bruce, V. (1986). Recognising familiar faces: The role of distinctiveness and familiarity. *Canadian Journal of Psychology, 40,* 300–305.

Yarmey, A. D. (1973). I recognise your face but I can't remember your name: Further evidence on the tip-of-the-tongue phenomenon. *Memory and Cognition, 1,* 287–290.

Young, A. W. (1988). Functional organization of visual recognition. In L. Weiskrantz (Ed.), *Thought without language* (pp. 78–107). Oxford: Oxford University Press.

Young, A. W., & Bruce, V. (1991). Perceptual categories and the computation of "grandmother". *European Journal of Cognitive Psychology, 3,* 5–49.

Young, A. W., & De Haan, E. H. F. (1988). Boundaries of covert recognition in prosopagnosia. *Cognitive Neuropsychology, 5,* 317–336.

Young, A. W., & De Haan, E. H. F. (1990). Impairments of visual awareness. *Mind and Language, 5,* 29–48.

Young, A. W., & De Haan, E. H. F. (1991). Face recognition and awareness after brain injury. In A. D. Milner, & M. Rugg (Eds.), *The neuropsychology of consciousness.* London: Academic Press.

Young, A. W., Ellis, A. W., Flude, B. M., McWeeny, K. H., & Hay, D. C. (1986). Face-name interference. *Journal of Experimental Psychology: Human Perception and Performance, 12,* 466–475.

Young, A. W., & Ellis, H. D. (1989a). Semantic processing. In A. W. Young & H. D. Ellis (Eds.), *Handbook of research on face processing* (pp. 235–262). Amsterdam: North-Holland.

Young, A. W., & Ellis, H. D. (1989b). Childhood prosopagnosia. *Brain and Cognition, 9*, 16–47.

Young, A. W., Hay, D. C., & Ellis, A. W. (1985). The faces that launched a thousand slips: Everyday difficulties and errors in recognising people. *British Journal of Psychology, 76*, 495–523.

Young, A. W., Hay, D. C., McWeeny, K. H., Ellis, A. W., & Barry, C. (1985). Familiarity decisions for faces presented to the left and right cerebral hemispheres. *Brain and Cognition, 4*, 439–450.

Young, A. W., Hay, D. C., McWeeny, K. H., Flude, B. M., & Ellis, A. W. (1985). Matching familiar and unfamiliar faces on internal and external features. *Perception, 14*, 737–746.

Young, A. W., Hellawell, D., & De Haan, E. H. F. (1988). Cross-domain semantic priming in normal subjects and a prosopagnosic patient. *Quarterly Journal of Experimental Psychology, 40A*, 561–580.

Young, A. W., McWeeny, K. H., Ellis, A. W., & Hay, D. C. (1986). Naming and categorising faces and written names. *Quarterly Journal of Experimental Psychology, 38A*, 297–318.

Young, A. W., McWeeny, K. H., Hay, D. C., & Ellis, A. W. (1986a). Access to identity-specific semantic codes from familiar faces. *Quarterly Journal of Experimental Psychology, 38A*, 271–295.

Young, A. W., McWeeny, K. H., Hay, D. C., & Ellis, A. W. (1986b). Matching familiar and unfamiliar faces on identity and expression. *Psychological Research, 48*, 63–68.

Young, A. W., Newcombe, F., Hellawell, D., & De Haan, E. H. F. (1989). Implicit access to semantic information. *Brain and Cognition, 11*, 186–209.

APPENDIX

All simulations reported here were run using McClelland and Rumelhart's (1988) interactive activation and competition program *iac*. Update functions are given in McClelland and Rumelhart (1988, p. 13). The global parameters were set as follows in all cases:

maximum activation	1.0
minimum activation	−0.2
resting activation	−0.1
decay rate	0.1
estr (strength of external input)	0.4
alpha (strength of excitatory input)	0.1
gamma (strength of inhibitory input)	0.1

In each of the simulations, excitatory connections had weight 1.0, while inhibitory connections had weight −0.1. In the simulation of PH, excitatory connections between FRU and PIN were reduced to 0.5, while all other connections remained unchanged.

Dissociated overt and covert recognition as an emergent property of a lesioned neural network

Martha J. Farah, Randall C. O'Reilly, and Shaun P. Vecera
Carnegie Mellon University, USA

Covert recognition of faces in prosopagnosia, in which patients cannot overtly recognize faces but nevertheless manifest recognition when tested in certain indirect ways, has been interpreted as the functioning of an intact visual face recognition system deprived of access to other brain systems necessary for consciousness. The authors propose an alternative hypothesis: that the visual face recognition system is damaged but not obliterated in these patients and that damaged neural networks will manifest their residual knowledge in just the kinds of tasks used to measure covert recognition. To test this, a simple model of face recognition is lesioned in the parts of the model corresponding to visual processing. The model demonstrates covert recognition in 3 qualitatively different tasks. Implications for the nature of prosopagnosia, and for other types of dissociations between conscious and unconscious perception, are discussed.

In recent years, neuropsychology has seen what Weiskrantz (1990) has called an "epidemic" of dissociations involving the loss of conscious awareness in particular perceptual or cognitive domains. Many of these dissociations involve vision. In such cases, patients may deny being able to see or recognize visual stimuli, and indeed perform poorly on certain direct tests of visual perception, but may nevertheless manifest considerable knowledge of the stimulus on certain other, generally indirect, tests of perception. We defer discussion of most of these syndromes until the General Discussion section and begin with the primary focus of the present article, namely covert face recognition in prosopagnosia.

Psychological Review 1993, Vol. 100, No. 4, 571–588.

Prosopagnosia is an impairment of face recognition following brain damage, which can occur relatively independently of impairments in object recognition and which is not caused by impairments in lower level vision or memory. In at least some cases of prosopagnosia, there is a dramatic dissociation between the loss of face recognition ability as measured by standard tests of face recognition, as well as patients' own introspections, and the apparent preservation of face recognition when tested by certain indirect tests. Our goal is to elucidate the underlying causes of this dissociation and its implications for both the nature of prosopagnosia and for the neural correlates of conscious and unconscious perception.

EVIDENCE FOR COVERT RECOGNITION OF FACES IN PROSOPAGNOSIA

Demonstrations of covert recognition in prosopagnosia have made use of extremely varied methodologies so that it is unlikely that any simple methodological artifact underlies the phenomenon. The relevant research includes psychophysiological measures such as skin conductance responses (SCRs) and event-related potentials (ERPs) as well as behavioral measures such as reaction time (RT) and learning trials to criterion.

In the absence of theories relating psychophysiological indexes to mechanistic accounts of cognition or neural information processing, it is difficult to use the psychophysiological findings to constrain a mechanistic model of covert recognition. Therefore, we focus primarily on the behavioral data implicating covert recognition and provide just a brief review of some representative psychophysiological data here.

Psychophysiological evidence

Bauer (1984) presented a prosopagnosic patient with a series of photographs of familiar faces. While viewing each face, the patient heard a list of names read aloud, one of which was the name of the person in the photograph. This test has been called the *Guilty Knowledge Test* because it is based on a technique used to assess suspects' familiarity with the details of crimes of which they deny knowledge. For normal subjects, the SCR is greatest to the name belonging to the pictured person, regardless of whether the subject admits to knowing that person. Bauer found that, although the prosopagnosic patient's SCRs to names were not as strongly correlated with the names as a normal subject's would be, they were nevertheless significantly correlated. In contrast, the patient performed at chance levels when asked to select the correct name for each face.

In a different use of the SCR measure. Tranel and Damasio (1985, 1988) showed that prosopagnosic patients had larger SCRs to familiar faces than to unfamiliar faces, even though their overt ratings of familiarity versus unfamiliarity did not reliably discriminate between the two.

Renault, Signoret, Debruille, Breton, and Bolger (1989) recorded ERPs to familiar and unfamiliar faces that had been intermixed in different proportions within different blocks of trials. In general, the P300 component of the ERP is larger to stimuli from a relatively infrequent category. They found that a prosopagnosic patient showed larger P300s to whichever type of face, familiar or unfamiliar, was less frequent in a block of trials, even though the patient was poor at overtly discriminating familiar from unfamiliar faces.

Behavioral evidence

The first evidence of covert recognition in prosopagnosia was gathered by Bruyer, Laterre, Seron, Feyereisen, Strypstein, Pierrard, and Rectem (1983) in the context of a paired-associate, face–name relearning task, and this task has become the most widely applied measure of covert recognition in prosopagnosia. Bruyer et al.'s patient was asked to learn to associate the facial photographs of famous people with the names of famous people. When the pairing of names and faces was correct, the patient required fewer learning trials than when it was incorrect, suggesting that the patient did possess at least some knowledge of the people's facial appearance. Unfortunately, this demonstration of covert recognition is not as meaningful as it could be, because Bruyer et al.'s subject was not fully prosopagnosic; he could manifest an appreciable degree of overt recognition on conventional tests of face recognition such as forced-choice, face-naming tests.

Recently, several more severe prosopagnosic patients have been tested in the face–name relearning task, and some have shown the same pattern of faster learning of correct than incorrect face–name associations, despite little or no success at the overt recognition of the same faces. For example, De Haan, Young, and Newcombe (1987b) documented consistently faster learning of face–name and face–occupation pairings in their prosopagnosic subject, even when the stimulus faces were selected from among those that the patient had been unable to identify in a pre-experiment stimulus screening test.

Greve and Bauer (1990) used a different form of learning as evidence of covert recognition in prosopagnosia. They showed a prosopagnosic patient a set of unfamiliar faces and then showed him the same faces, each paired with another face, at which time he was asked the following two questions about each pair: Which of these faces have you seen before? Which of these faces do you like better? Normal subjects tend to prefer stimuli that they have seen previously, whether or not they explicitly remember having seen these stimuli, and this has been attributed to a "perceptual fluency" advantage for previously seen stimuli (Jacoby, 1984). Perceptual fluency refers to the facilitation in processing a stimulus that has already been perceived, which leads to a subjective sense of the stimulus seeming more salient, which may in turn be attributed by the subject to the attractiveness of the stimulus. Although the prosopagnosic patient was unable to

discriminate previously seen from novel faces, he did show a normal preference for the previously seen faces.

Evidence of covert recognition has also come from RT tasks in which the familiarity or identity of faces are found to influence processing time. In a visual identity match task (see Posner, 1978) with simultaneously presented pairs of faces, De Haan et al. (1987b) found that a prosopagnosic patient was faster at matching pairs of previously familiar faces than unfamiliar faces, as is true of normal subjects. In contrast, he was unable to name any of the previously familiar faces. De Haan et al. then went on to show another similiarity between the performance of the patient in this task and that of normal subjects. If the task is administered to normal subjects with either the external features (e.g., hair and jaw line) or the internal features (e.g., eyes, nose, and mouth) blocked off and with instructions to match on the visible parts of the face, normal subjects show an effect of familiarity only for the matching of internal features. The same result was obtained with the prosopagnosic patient.

In another RT study, De Haan et al. (1987a, b) found evidence that photographs of faces could evoke covert semantic knowledge of the depicted person, despite the inability of the prosopagnosic patient to report such information about the person when tested overtly. Their task was to categorize a printed name as belonging to an actor or a politician as quickly as possible. On some trials, an irrelevant (i.e., to be ignored) photograph of an actor's or politician's face was simultaneously presented. Normal subjects are slower to categorize the names when the faces come from a different-occupation category relative to a no-photograph baseline. Even though their prosopagnosic patient was severely impaired at categorizing the faces overtly as belonging to actors or politicians, he showed the same pattern of interference from different-category faces.

A related finding was reported by Young, Hellawell, and De Haan (1988) in a task involving the categorization of names as famous or nonfamous. Both normal subjects and a prosopagnosic patient showed faster RTs to the famous names when the name was preceded by a picture of a semantically related face (e.g., the name "Diana Spencer" preceded by a picture of Prince Charles) than by an unfamiliar or an unrelated face. Furthermore, the same experiment was carried out with printed names as the priming stimulus so that the size of the priming effect with faces and names could be compared. The prosopagnosic patient's priming effect from faces was not significantly different from the priming effect from names. However, the patient was able to name only 2 of the 20 face prime stimuli used.

In summary, a wide variety of methods has been used to document covert recognition of faces in prosopagnosia. Although in some cases fairly coarse-grained discriminations are taken as evidence of recognition (e.g., between familiar and unfamiliar faces, De Haan et al., 1987a; Tranel & Damasio, 1985), in other cases the patients successfully discriminate among unique individuals (e.g., Bauer, 1984; Bruyer et al., 1983; De Haan et al., 1987a, b) or classify

individuals in a way that presumably requires individual recognition (actors vs. politicians, De Haan et al., 1987b). Although we argue that not all viable interpretations of these phenomena have been considered and we urge consideration of a new interpretation, it would seem that the correct interpretation is very unlikely to be any kind of methodological artifact. The investigators in this area have been vigorous in attempting to eliminate possible artifacts in each of the experimental paradigms they have used. Furthermore, the sheer diversity of such paradigms makes an artifactual explanation unlikely. Finally, the absence of covert recognition in some cases (e.g., Etcoff, Freeman, & Cave, 1991; Newcombe, Young, & De Haan, 1989; Sergent & Villemure, 1989) suggests that it is not a result of the experimental paradigms themselves.

INTERPRETATIONS OF COVERT RECOGNITION IN PROSOPAGNOSIA AND THEIR IMPLICATIONS

The foregoing results would appear to indicate that, at least in those cases of prosopagnosia that show covert recognition, the underlying impairment is not one of visual recognition per se but of conscious access to visual recognition. Indeed, all of the interpretations so far offered of covert recognition in prosopagnosia include this assumption.

For example, Tranel and Damasio (1988) said, of their patients' SCRs, that they are "not the result of some primitive form of perceptual process, but rather an index of the rich retro-co-activation produced when representations of stimuli successfully activate previously acquired, non-damaged, and obviously accessible facial records" (p. 248). Similarly, De Haan et al. (1987a) described their subject's prosopagnosia as involving a "breakdown (or disconnection) in the mechanisms that allow people to be aware of what has been recognized [rather] than a breakdown in recognition mechanisms per se" (p. 315). In a recent computer simulation of semantic priming effects, described in greater detail later, this group modeled covert recognition as a partial disconnection separating intact visual recognition units from the rest of the system, again preserving the assumption of intact visual recognition (Burton, Young, Bruce, Johnston, & Ellis, 1991). Bruyer (1991) offered a similar interpretation, in terms of personal (i.e., conscious agent) and subpersonal (i.e., comprising at least the visual recognition system) levels of description: "The conscious subject does not recognize or identify familiar faces, while her/his 'information processing system' does?" (p. 230).

Figure 1 shows a depiction of De Haan et al.'s (1992) conception of the relation between face recognition systems and other systems needed for conscious awareness and the functional lesion responsible for prosopagnosia with covert recognition. According to their model, the face-specific visual and mnemonic processing of a face (carried out within the face-processing module) proceeds normally in covert recognition, but the results of this process cannot access the conscious awareness system because of a lesion at location number 1.

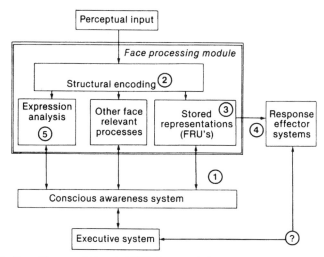

Figure 1. De Haan, Bauer, and Greve's (1992) framework for analysing disorders of face recognition. (Covert recognition in prosopagnosia is thought to result from a functional disconnection at [1] between normally activated stored face representations and the conscious awareness system. FRU = face recognition units. From "Behavioral and Physiological Evidence for Covert Recognition in a Prosopagnosic Patient" by E. H. F. De Haan, R. M. Bauer, and K. W. Greve, 1992, *Cortex, 28,* p. 89. Copyright 1992 by Erminio Capitani. Reprinted with permission of Masson S.p.A.)

A different type of explanation was put forth earlier by Bauer (1984), who suggested that there may be two neural systems capable of face recognition, only one of which is associated with conscious awareness. According to Bauer, the ventral cortical visual areas, which are damaged in prosopagnosic patients, are the location of normal conscious face recognition. The dorsal visual areas are hypothesized to be capable of face recognition as well, although they do not mediate conscious recognition but, instead, mediate affective responses to faces. Covert recognition is explained as the isolated functioning of the dorsal face system. This interpretation is similar to the others in that it hypothesizes some form of intact visual recognition. It is distinctive in that the dissociation between recognition and conscious awareness is not a form of disconnection (functional or anatomical) between the visual recognition system and other brain systems that mediate conscious awareness brought about by brain damage but is the normal state of affairs for the dorsal face recognition system.

These interpretations of covert recognition have implications both for the nature of prosopagnosia and, more generally, for the neural bases of conscious awareness. With regard to prosopagnosia, current interpretations of covert recognition imply that there are at least two kinds of prosopagnosia, with different underlying causes: one in which visual recognition is intact but unavailable to consciousness (in the case of patients with covert recognition) and one in which visual recognition is impaired (in the case of patients without covert recognition).

At a more general level, these interpretations have implications for the broad issue of the neural bases of consciousness, in that they hypothesize distinct stages of processing, and corresponding distinct neural substrates, for face recognition on the one hand and awareness of face recognition on the other. The assignment of separate brain mechanisms to information processing and awareness of information processing has roots as far back as Descartes's writings on the mind–body problem (with the pineal gland subserving awareness in that case), and in the context of modern neuroscience this has been dubbed "Cartesian materialism" by Dennett and Kinsbourne (1992). Perhaps the most general and lucid expression of this idea, applied to a variety of neuropsychological syndromes including covert recognition by prosopagnosic patients, was put forth by Schacter, McAndrews, and Moscovitch (1988). They tentatively proposed that "(a) conscious or explicit experiences of perceiving, knowing and remembering all depend in some way on the functioning of a common mechanism, (b) this mechanism normally accepts input from, and interacts with, a variety of processors or modules that handle specific types of information, and (c) in various cases of neuropsychological impairment, specific modules are disconnected from the conscious mechanism" (p. 269).

AN ALTERNATIVE HYPOTHESIS: RESIDUAL FUNCTIONING OF AN IMPAIRED VISUAL RECOGNITION SYSTEM

We argue that the available evidence on covert face recognition in prosopagnosics is consistent with an impairment in visual recognition per se. This interpretation has implications for our understanding of prosopagnosia in that it dispenses with the necessity of postulating different forms of prosopagnosia that are due to different underlying causes. Instead, cases with covert recognition are hypothesized to have more residual functioning of the visual face recognition system than cases without. It also has implications for our understanding of the neural bases of conscious awareness in that conscious awareness of recognition is not attributed to a distinct neural system from the one subserving recognition per se. Instead, the same neural system subserves both overt and covert recognition.

The primary challenge for such an account is to explain the dissociation between overt and covert recognition given that these two sets of phenomena are hypothesized to rely on the same neural substrates. We argue that the difference between them lies in the robustness to brain damage of performance of the two kinds of tasks, in other words, the degree of preserved neural information processing that is required in each case. Specifically, we argue that lower quality visual information processing is needed to support performance in tests of covert recognition (e.g., to show savings in relearning and the various RT facilitation and interference effects) relative to the quality of information processing needed to support normal overt recognition performance (e.g., naming a face or sorting faces into those of actors and politicians).

One very general way of stating this hypothesis is to say that the covert tests of recognition are more sensitive to the residual knowledge encoded in a damaged recognition system than are the overt tests. Thus, very impaired performance on overt tests might be associated with only moderately or slightly impaired performance on the covert tests. Stating the hypothesis in this way calls attention to two questions important for evaluating the hypothesis: First, what are the precise levels of patient performance on tests of overt and covert recognition, and are they consistent with the hypothesis of a single damaged system being tapped by tests of differing sensitivity? Normal-size covert recognition effects are unlikely to be due to the functioning of a damaged system (although it would not, strictly speaking, be impossible if the "ceiling" on covert performance was very low relative to the ceiling on overt performance). Better than chance performance by prosopagnosic patients on overt tests would also be consistent with residual functioning of the visual recognition system (although, by the same token, there is no logical reason why overt performance could not have its "floor" of chance performance above the floor of the covert tests). Second, is there any independent reason to believe that the covert tests would be more sensitive measures of residual recognition ability in a damaged recognition system?

Empirical evidence relevant to testing the alternative hypothesis

To answer the first question, it is impossible to compare directly the covert recognition performance of prosopagnosic patients and normal subjects on the basis of the evidence currently available, so we cannot know whether their covert recognition is normal or merely present to some degree. In some cases data from normal subjects have either not been reported, as in the P300 study, or would be impossible to obtain, as when familiar faces and names are retaught with either the correct or incorrect pairings. In other cases the problem of comparing effect sizes on different absolute measures arises. In both the SCR and RT paradigms, covert recognition is measured by differences between the dependent measures in two conditions (e.g., familiar and unfamiliar faces). Unfortunately, patients' SCRs are invariably weaker than those of normal subjects (Bauer, 1986), and their RTs are longer (De Haan et al., 1987b). It is difficult to know how to assess the relative sizes of differences when the base measures are different. For example, is an effect corresponding to a 200-ms difference between RTs on the order of 2 s bigger than, comparable to, or smaller than an effect corresponding to a 100-ms difference between RTs of less than a second? The true scaling of RT in any given task is an empirical issue; using proportions may be a better approximation to the scale than linearity, but one cannot a priori know the true scale (see Snodgrass, Corwin, & Feenan, 1990, for a discussion of these issues).

The study that comes closest to allowing a direct comparison of covert recognition in patients and normal subjects is the priming experiment of Young et al.

(1988). Recall that they found equivalent effects of priming name classification for their prosopagnosic patient with either photographs or names of semantically related people. Of course, this fact alone does not imply that the face-mediated priming was normal, as face-mediated priming in this task might normally be larger than name-mediated priming. To address this problem, Young et al. cited their earlier experiment, reported in the same article, in which normal subjects were also found to show equivalent effects of face-mediated and name-mediated priming. Unfortunately, the earlier experiment differed in several ways from the latter, which could conceivably shift the relative sizes of the face-mediated and name-mediated priming effects: Normal subjects in the earlier experiment performed only 30 trials each, whereas the prosopagnosic patient performed 240 trials; items were never repeated in the earlier experiment, whereas they were in the later one; the type of prime was varied between subjects in the earlier experiment, whereas the prosopagnosic patient received both types; different faces and names were used in the two experiments; and the primes were presented for about half as long in the earlier experiment as in the later one. Ideally, to answer the question of whether this prosopagnosic patient shows normal priming from faces, a group of normal control subjects should be run through the same experiment as the patient.

Turning now to the question of whether the prosopagnosic patients who show covert recognition also show some degree of overt recognition, consistent with a damaged but not obliterated visual recognition system, the evidence is similarly difficult to evaluate. For example, some patient's chance performance on overt tasks is consistent with the use of extreme response biases, which would mask any degree of remaining sensitivity. Among the three prosopagnosic patients studied by Tranel and Damasio (1988), two rated almost all faces as unfamiliar, and the one who used a larger portion of the rating scale narrowly missed the .05 significance level in discriminating familiar from unfamiliar faces.

Statistical naivete concerning the concept of chance performance has also led to confusion. In some cases, the term "chance performance" has been used synonymously with poor performance. For example, De Haan et al. (1987a) presented the results of an overt politician–nonpolitician face judgement task with their patient and described the score of 30/48 in a two-alternative, forced-choice task as being at chance. In fact, there is only a .06 probability of achieving such a high score by guessing alone. In other cases, performance is truly not statistically different from chance (e.g., in Young & De Haan, 1988, 12/30 in a three-alternative, forced-choice familiarity task), but the small number of trials makes this a relatively weak test for purposes of obtaining confidence in the null hypothesis. In addition, the ability of this patient and others to occasionally identify a face by name, a task whose "chance level" is difficult to estimate but is certainly close to 0% correct, also indicates that visual recognition has not been entirely obliterated. For example, this same patient was able to identify 2 out of 20 of the faces used in the semantic-priming study of Young et al. (1988).

One way in which investigators have attempted to control overt recognition performance and measure covert recognition in the absence of overt recognition is by testing patients only on faces that were not successfully identified in a screening test. For example, De Haan et al. (1987b) used only the faces that their prosopagnosic patient had failed to recognize in their face-name relearning task. This procedure is certainly a more conservative way of testing for a dissociation between overt and covert recognition than simply pooling the data from all faces. However, there could still be some measurement error in the overt task, which could in principle lead some overtly recognizable faces to remain in the covert test. Perhaps more likely, overt identification could be a less sensitive test of recognition than savings in relearning. That these considerations are not purely academic was demonstrated by Wallace and Farah (1992), who followed the same screening procedure of eliminating successfully identified faces with normal subjects on faces that had been learned 6 months before the experiment and nevertheless found savings in relearning the original face-name associations, relative to new pairings.

Computational rationale for the alternative hypothesis

The empirical data reviewed so far fail to distinguish between the original hypothesis of intact face recognition deprived of access to consciousness and the alternative hypothesis that face recognition is impaired and that covert tasks are more sensitive than overt tasks to detecting residual functioning. Our reason for preferring the alternative hypothesis is based on a consideration of the relative computational demands of the overt and covert tests. To explain how these differ, we first provide a very brief overview of computation in recurrent neural networks. More extensive background can be found in Rumelhart and McClelland's (1986) book on parallel distributed processing models of cognition.

In parallel distributed processing models, representations consist of a pattern of activation over a set of highly interconnected neuronlike units. The extent to which the activation of one unit causes an increase or decrease in the activation of a neighboring unit depends on the "weight" of the connection between them; positive weights cause units to excite each other, and negative weights cause units to inhibit each other. For the network to learn that a certain face representation goes with a certain name representation, the weights among units in the network are adjusted so that presentation of either the face pattern in the face units or the name pattern in the name units causes the corresponding other pattern to become activated. On presentation of the input pattern to the input units, all of the units connected with those input units will begin to change their activation in accordance with the activation value of the units to which they are connected and the weights on the connections. These units might in turn connect to others and influence their activation levels in the same way. In recurrent, or attractor, net-

works, the units downstream will also begin to influence the activation levels of the earlier units. Eventually, these shifting activation levels across the units of the network settle into a stable pattern, or attractor state. The attractor state into which a network settles is determined jointly by the input pattern (stimulus) and the weights of the network (stored knowledge).

Accordingly, much of the behavior of the network depends on the pattern of weights. For example, the weights determine not only which pattern becomes activated in association to an input pattern but they also determine how quickly this pattern becomes stable and how quickly a given unit or set of units reaches some predetermined threshold of activation. Not surprisingly, the current pattern of weights will also determine how many training cycles are needed to teach the network a new association. In ways that we elaborate on shortly, these aspects of network behavior seem closely related to the behavioral measures of covert recognition reviewed earlier: speed of perception (corresponding to settling time), speed of classifying actors and politicians (corresponding to how quickly actor or politician representations reach threshold), and, of course, paired-associate learning (a direct correspondence).

When a network is damaged by eliminating units, it will be less effective at associating the patterns that it knew previously. This can be understood in terms of the idea that knowledge is stored in the weights by viewing unit damage as the permanent zeroing of all weights going into and out of the eliminated units. As more units are eliminated, the ability of the network to correctly associate previously known patterns will steadily decline until it reaches chance levels.

The impetus for our project comes from the following key idea, first set out by Hinton and Sejnowski (1986; see also Hinton & Plaut, 1987): The set of the weights in a network that cannot correctly associate patterns because it has never been trained (or has been trained on a different set of patterns) is different in an important way from the set of weights in a network that cannot correctly associate patterns because it has been trained on those patterns and then damaged. The first set of weights is random with respect to the associations in question, whereas the second is a subset of the necessary weights. Even if it is an inadequate subset for performing the association, it is not random; it has, "embedded" in it, some degree of knowledge of the associations.

Consideration of the kinds of tests used to measure covert recognition suggest that the covert measures might be sensitive to this embedded knowledge. The most obvious example is that a damaged network would be expected to relearn associations that it originally knew faster than novel associations because of the nonrandom starting weights. Less obvious, but nevertheless plausible for reasons to be elaborated on later, the network might settle faster when given previously learned inputs than novel inputs, even though the pattern into which it settles is not correct, because the residual weights come from a set designed to create a stable pattern from that input. Finally, to the extent that the weights continue to activate partial and subthreshold patterns over the nondamaged units in association

with the input, these resultant patterns could prime (i.e., contribute activation toward) the activation of patterns by intact routes. We later discuss these mechanisms in greater detail in the context of the individual simulations. For present purposes, the general implication of these ideas is that as a neural network is increasingly damaged, there might be a window of damage in which overt associations between patterns (e.g., faces and names) would be extremely poor, whereas the kinds of performance measures tapped by the covert tasks might remain at high levels. Note that if this is true, it does more than just undermine the prevailing hypothesis of intact face recognition systems in those prosopagnosic patients who manifest covert recognition. It offers a specific, mechanistic hypothesis explaining the overt–covert dissociations in terms of general principles of computation in neural networks.

To test this hypothesis, we developed a very simple model of face recognition, and explored the effects of damage to visual input units on network performance of three different types of tasks, corresponding to the savings in relearning paradigm, the physical matching paradigm, and the priming paradigm. . . .

THE MODEL

The present model is intended to illustrate some very general, qualitative aspects of the behavior of damaged neural networks in the kinds of tasks used with prosopagnosic patients. It is accordingly very simple. Figure 2 shows the architecture of the model. There are five pools of units. The face input units subserve the initial visual representation of faces, the semantics units subserve representa-

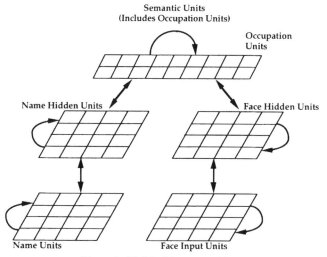

Figure 2. Model of face recognition.

tion of the semantic knowledge of people that can be evoked by either the person's face or name, and the name units subserve the representation of names. In a model of this kind, hidden units are helpful to learn the associations among patterns of activity in each of these three layers. These are located between the face and semantic units, (called the *face hidden units*) and between the name and the semantic units (called the *name hidden units*). Thus, there are two pools of units that make up the visual face recognition system in our model in that they represent visual information about faces: the face input units and the face hidden units.

The connectivity among the different pools of units was based on the assumption that to name a face, or to visualize a named person, one must access semantic knowledge of that person (Young, Hay, & Ellis, 1985). Thus, face and name units are not directly connected, but rather they send activation to one another through hidden and semantic units. The arrows in Figure 2 show the bidirectional connectivity between layers and the within-layer connectivity. Furthermore, each unit had a bias weight that learned the average activation level of that unit (a technique for improving the ability of the network to learn).

Units in this model have a threshold of zero. Thus, when the activation value of a unit is positive, it will activate those units to which it is connected by positive weights and inhibit those units to which it is connected by negative weights, and when its activation value is negative, it will have the opposite effects.

Faces and names are represented by random patterns of 5 active units out of the total of 16 in each pool. Semantic knowledge is represented by 6 active units out of the total of 18 in the semantic pool. The model makes no commitment to any particular form of representation, beyond supposing that the representations are distributed; that is, each face, semantic representation, or name is represented by multiple units, and each unit represents multiple faces, semantic representations, or names. The information encoded by a given unit will be some "microfeature" (Hinton, McClelland, & Rumelhart, 1986) that may or may not correspond to an easily labeled feature (such as eye color in the case of faces). The only units for which we have assigned an interpretation are the "occupation units" within the semantic pool. One of them represents the semantic microfeature "actor" and the other represents the semantic microfeature "politician."

We created 40 distinct individuals, each consisting of a random name, face, and semantic pattern (over the 16 unlabeled semantics units). Ten individuals were actors (i.e., their semantic pattern had the actor unit active in addition to the other five active semantics units), 10 were politicians, and the remaining 20 were not assigned either of these two occupations. These 20 individuals were not tested in the simulations to be reported but were included in training to simulate the fact that subjects know many more people than are ever tested in a given experiment. Of the 10 actors and 10 politicians, 5 of each were not used in training so that we could compare the effects of familiarity on network performance in Simulation 2, resulting in a training set of 30 patterns.

The network was trained to be able to associate an individual's face, semantics, and name whenever one of these was presented, using the contrastive Hebbian learning (CHL) algorithm (Hinton & Sejnowski, 1986; Movellan, 1990; Peterson & Anderson, 1987). The CHL function can be used to train stochastic (e.g., Boltzmann machine, Hinton & Sejnowski, 1986) and deterministic (e.g., mean field networks, Peterson & Anderson, 1987) recurrent networks. It stipulates that the weight change is proportional to the difference between the product of the activations of the two units on either side of the weight in the positive and negative phases, where the positive phase has both input and desired output patterns presented and the negative phase has just the input presented. In this way, the difference between the desired activation state and the one that results from the input is minimized. The specific formulation used here follows Movellan (1990) in the use of the interactive activation and competition (IAC) activation function (McClelland & Rumelhart, 1981), with a step size of .01, maximum of 1, minimum of −1, rest of 0, and decay of 2.

For each training epoch we presented one of the three representations for each individual (face, semantics, or name) and trained the network to reproduce the other two. The learning rate was .01. The network was trained for 320 epochs on the complete set of 30 individuals and for an additional 5 epochs on the set of the 10 individuals to be tested later to ensure 100% accuracy for these individuals in the undamaged network.

Simulation 1: Savings in relearning face–name associations

The primary goal of this simulation was to examine the effects of different degrees of damage to the visual units (face input and face hidden units) on both overt identification of face patterns and on the difference in the number of cycles needed to relearn previously known name–face associations, relative to the number needed to learn to associate the same names and faces paired differently. Hinton and Sejnowski (1986) demonstrated savings in relearning after a variety of types of damage to a recurrent network, including unit ablation. Hinton and Plaut (1987) presented similar findings obtained with a feedforward network. If there is some degree of damage to the face units that can result in poor overt performance while preserving significant savings in relearning, then the savings in relearning observed in prosopagnosic patients need not imply that visual recognition per se has been spared.

Method.   The network was lesioned in two different ways: by eliminating randomly chosen units from the face input pool and from the face hidden unit pool. These are the two pools of units in the model that correspond to visual face recognition. Seven different levels of damage were used, corresponding to removal

of 2, 4, 8, 10, 12, and 14 units from the pools of 16 units, corresponding to 12.5%, 25%, 37.5%, 50%, 62.5%, 75%, and 87.5% damage.

The basic measure of overt recognition, used for comparison with covert performance in all of the simulations to be reported, was the percentage of correct name identifications of faces in a 10-alternative, forced-choice task among the 10 test patterns. A face was considered correctly identified if the resultant name pattern matched the correct name pattern more closely than any of the other 9 test patterns. Degree of match was quantified by the number of units having the same sign (positive or negative). This is a more lenient method of scoring overt recognition than requiring a perfect match, or even a match to within one bit.

In the first simulation, the names and faces for the 10 familiar actors and politicians were paired correctly. In the second simulation, they were paired incorrectly, although never across occupation categories, because this would confound the correct–incorrect distinction with the compatability of the occupation unit pattern. To expedite learning, each network was required to learn only five name–face pairs at a time. These were presented to the network after damage for retraining in separate simulations. To simulate the training procedure used with patients in which they are asked to name the face on each trial rather than select from a multiple-choice set of names, we used the pattern that resulted in the name units of the network following presentation of the face as the simulation's response. This was scored as correct if it matched the target pattern to within 2 units.

To measure savings in relearning for correctly paired names and faces, the damaged network was retrained for 10 epochs, and its performance on overt identification was assessed. This procedure was repeated 10 times with different sets of random lesions to assess the reliability of the results.

Results and discussion.   Table 1 and Figure 3 show the overt identification performance of the network in the 10-alternative, forced-choice task after different amounts of damage to the two pools of visual units. By 50% damage to either pool of units, the network is correct for only about 1 in 4 faces. With higher levels of damage, performance drops further. At 62.5% and 75% damage to face input units, only about 1 in 6 faces are correctly identified. At these same levels of damage to face hidden units, performance is not significantly different from 1 in 10, or chance performance.

Despite the network's poor performance in the overt tasks under damage, it manifests covert knowledge of the faces by relearning correct name–face pairings more quickly than incorrect ones. Table 2 shows the average percentage correct naming, to within a 2-unit matching criterion of the correct name, for each degree of damage to the face input and hidden units after 0 and 10 epochs of learning for correctly and incorrectly paired faces and names. Figure 4 shows the learning curves for the network after 50%, 62.5%, and 75% damage to the face input and face hidden units for the same pairings. Although not all levels of damage lead to equivalent performance for correct and incorrect pairings at

TABLE 1
Overt identification in 10-alternative, forced-choice tasks

	Percentage correct	
Amount of damage (%)	M	SE
Hidden unit damage		
12.5	62	4.9
25.0	43	5.0
37.5	43	4.8
50.0	24	4.3
62.5	14	3.5
75.0	13	3.4
87.5	8	2.7
Input unit damage		
12.5	64	4.8
25.0	56	5.0
37.5	41	4.9
50.0	26	4.4
62.5	17	3.8
75.0	17	3.8
87.5	19	3.9

TABLE 2
Savings in relearning correct relative to incorrect face–name pairings

	Percentage correct							
	Correct pairings				Incorrect pairings			
	0 epochs		10 epochs		0 epochs		10 epochs	
Amount of damage (%)	M	SE	M	SE	M	SE	M	SE
Hidden unit lesion								
12.5	58.0	5.0	98.0	1.4	6.0	2.4	10.0	3.0
25.0	26.0	4.4	82.0	3.9	8.0	2.7	14.0	3.5
37.5	34.0	4.8	62.0	4.9	8.0	2.7	18.0	3.9
50.0	18.0	3.9	50.0	5.1	10.0	3.0	12.0	3.3
62.5	20.0	4.0	36.0	4.8	4.0	2.0	6.0	2.4
75.0	12.0	3.3	36.0	4.8	18.0	3.9	14.0	3.5
87.5	6.0	2.4	24.0	4.3	16.0	3.7	12.0	3.3
Input unit lesion								
12.5	68.0	4.7	98.0	1.4	0.0	0.0	4.0	2.0
25.0	58.0	5.0	96.0	2.0	8.0	2.7	4.0	2.0
37.5	32.0	4.7	72.0	4.5	8.0	2.7	4.0	2.0
50.0	20.0	4.0	74.0	4.4	6.0	2.4	18.0	3.9
62.5	16.0	3.7	18.0	3.9	10.0	3.0	10.0	3.0
75.0	12.0	3.3	46.0	5.0	6.0	2.4	24.0	4.3
87.5	10.0	3.0	18.0	3.9	2.0	1.4	20.0	4.0

(A) Hidden Unit Lesions

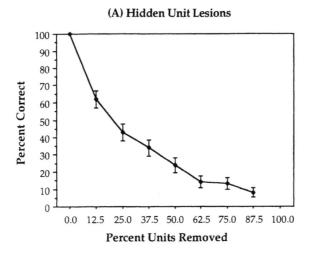

(B) Input Unit Lesions

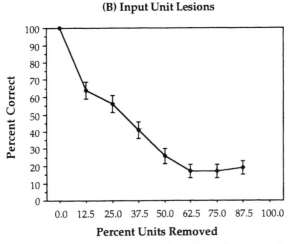

Figure 3. Performance of model at forced-choice naming of faces after varying degrees of damage to (A) face hidden units and (B) face input units.

the outset of training, the learning curve is steeper, that is, learning is faster for the correct pairings in all cases. The chance probability of six out of six cases showing the predicted form of interaction is $(.5)^6$, or .016. Furthermore, the faster relearning is found even with the four cases in which the pretraining performance of the damaged network is comparable for correct and incorrect pairings: 62.5% and 75% damage to face input units and 50% and 75% damage to face hidden units. Tested individually, over the 10 different random lesions,

216

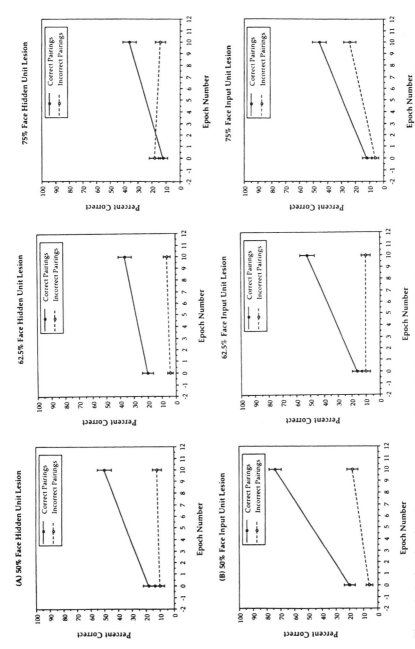

Figure 4. Savings in relearning face–name associations. (Performance of model after varying degrees of damage to [A] face hidden units and [B] face input units, initially and after 10 epochs of training, on correct and incorrect face–name associations.)

TABLE 3
Distances between weight matrix before and after 10 epochs
of learning for correct and incorrect face–name pairings

	Distance[a]			
	Correct pairing		Incorrect pairing	
Amount of damage (%)	M	SE	M	SE
Hidden unit lesion				
12.5	4.84	0.54	19.90	0.60
25.0	7.58	0.76	18.71	0.47
37.5	10.74	0.94	19.57	0.58
50.0	12.67	0.69	19.56	0.68
62.5	15.33	0.77	19.84	0.75
75.0	15.99	0.94	18.13	0.76
87.5	16.14	0.49	15.45	0.71
Input unit lesion				
12.5	2.88	0.65	19.20	0.40
25.0	6.81	0.77	19.38	0.62
37.5	11.19	0.87	19.51	0.78
50.0	14.90	1.17	20.68	0.66
62.5	15.87	1.07	19.87	0.66
75.0	16.71	0.87	21.00	0.74
87.5	20.67	1.13	19.10	0.58

[a] Distance is the total sum of the squares.

these differences in learning rate have chance probabilities of .0004, .0763, .0671, and .0148 by t test, respectively.

Why does the damaged network relearn correct (old) name–face associations faster than incorrect (novel) ones? The answer lies in the ability of the network to incorporate the residual knowledge in the remaining weights into a new pattern of weights that enable it to associate names and faces. This can be verified by comparing the pattern of weights after damage but before relearning with the pattern of weights after relearning correct and incorrect face–name associations. Accordingly, we computed the total sum of the squares (TSS) distance between the weight matrices for the initial damaged network (which is a subset of the original set of weights, specifically all weights except those going into and out of the eliminated units) and both the correct and incorrect face–name associations after relearning. This procedure was repeated for 10 different networks at each lesion size. As shown in Table 3, the pattern of weights in the damaged network before relearning is more similar to (lower TSS) the pattern of weights for the relearned correct face–name pairings than for the incorrect face–name pairings.

Simulation 2: Speed of visual perception

The goal of this simulation was to examine the effect of different degrees of damage to visual units on the speed of visual analysis of face patterns and specifically whether speed of analysis will depend on face familiarity at levels of damage where faces are not reliably identified. This question is of interest primarily because of De Haan et al.'s (1987b) demonstration that their prosopagnosic subject could perform physical same–different matching on faces more quickly when the faces were previously known to him. Presumably, the effect of familiarity on speed in this paradigm is not dependent on same–different matching per se but reflects a difference in the speed of deriving a visual representation that can be used to compare the appearance of the two faces. Therefore, we have not tried to implement a same–different matching paradigm here. The relevant issue is whether visual analysis of a face pattern proceeds more quickly when the face is familiar than when it is unfamiliar.

In the present model, the speed of visual perception is most directly measured by the number of cycles needed for the visual units of the network to settle into a stable pattern after presentation of a face pattern. Note that we need assume only a monotonic relationship between model settling time and human RT to interpret the results of the present simulation. Nevertheless, no transformations of the data are necessary to capture the qualitative pattern of human RTs.

Method.   The model was lesioned as in the previous simulation. The face portion of the 10 actor and 10 politician patterns were then presented to the network. As explained earlier, in the description of the model, the network had been trained on half of these patterns, divided equally into 5 actors and 5 politicians. The number of cycles needed for the visual units (input and hidden) of the network to settle was recorded for each face pattern. The visual units were considered to have settled when the average change in activation of the units in a cycle was less than .001. The face input unit activations were allowed to settle by presenting the input pattern as a component of the net input to each unit, instead of simply clamping the activations (i.e., "soft" clamping). As for the previous simulation, 10 replications were performed with different random patterns of damage.

Results and discussion.   The settling times for familiar and unfamiliar face patterns are shown in Table 4 and presented graphically in Figure 5. At levels of damage causing poor or chance overt performance (see Table 1), the settling time for familiar face patterns is nevertheless faster than for unfamiliar patterns. This pattern is maintained throughout all degrees of damage to the face hidden units and is present with as much as 50% damage to the face input units.

Why should the familiarity of the pattern affect how quickly it settles? In an intact network, a familiar input pattern will roll into an attractor representing the correct pattern of activation to which it should be associated, because the energy

TABLE 4
Settling time for familiar and unfamiliar face patterns

Amount of damage (%)	Familiar face		Unfamiliar face	
	M	*SE*	*M*	*SE*
Hidden unit lesion				
12.5	154.3	6.9	278.1	14.1
25.0	176.5	11.5	256.3	12.8
37.5	170.6	10.2	267.4	13.8
50.0	162.5	10.8	223.5	14.3
62.5	145.0	8.5	191.6	10.1
75.0	124.2	6.9	162.5	8.3
87.5	119.9	12.0	138.3	7.4
Input unit lesion				
12.5	187.4	10.2	284.2	18.4
25.0	222.3	10.8	276.4	15.2
37.5	255.9	14.2	255.7	14.3
50.0	258.3	11.2	306.6	18.1
62.5	255.3	14.4	273.3	15.0
75.0	293.7	14.0	296.6	14.7
87.5	368.9	20.8	359.2	18.8

Number of cycles spans the Familiar face and Unfamiliar face columns.

landscape has been tailored for this purpose. Given that much of the activation space has been shaped by learning, the trajectory of the network when presented with the input portion of an unfamiliar pattern will also tend toward attractors for the familiar patterns. However, because the activation space has not been specifically shaped to bring the unfamiliar patterns into attractors, their trajectories will typically be less direct and more circuitous. For this reason, familiar input patterns will settle faster than unfamiliar input patterns in an intact network.

When the network is lesioned, the loss of units reduces the dimensionality of the space, and the loss of weights distorts the shape of the new, lower dimensional energy landscape. Whereas the new surface will lack some of the topographic features that draw familiar input patterns into the correct attractors, it will retain others, so that at least part of the trajectory of at least some of the familiar patterns will tend to be maintained. In contrast, this will be no more true of unfamiliar patterns after damage than before.

The faster settling of familiar patterns is also relevant to Greve and Bauer's (1990) finding of greater attractiveness ratings for faces seen previously by their prosopagnosic subject, which they interpreted as greater perceptual fluency, or speed of perceptual analysis. With exposure to new patterns, the damaged network will alter its weights to begin to form attractors for those patterns, although it will arrive at the best set of weights more slowly than a network that has a

(A) Face Hidden Unit Lesions

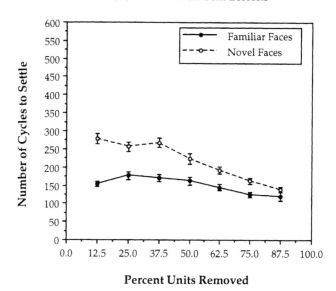

Percent Units Removed

(B) Face Input Unit Lesions

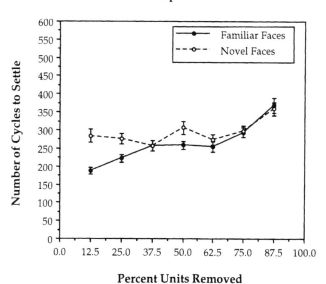

Percent Units Removed

Figure 5. Speed of perception of familiar and unfamiliar faces. (Settling time for [A] face hidden units and [B] face input units after varying degrees of damage, for familiar and unfamiliar faces.)

TABLE 5
Settling time for novel patterns before and after a small
amount of learning

	Number of cycles			
			After training 5 epochs	
	Before learning			
Amount of damage (%)	M	SE	M	SE
Hidden unit lesion				
12.5	376.0	18.8	365.0	21.1
25.0	476.2	26.9	430.9	26.3
37.5	475.3	23.9	419.1	30.0
50.0	513.9	29.2	465.8	25.7
62.5	506.6	24.9	438.3	23.6
75.0	521.6	25.7	467.2	25.3
87.5	669.4	35.0	431.6	18.2
Input unit lesion				
12.5	369.5	22.0	365.8	22.5
25.0	473.3	27.3	446.7	29.3
37.5	464.3	21.4	468.1	33.4
50.0	529.4	31.4	474.3	23.4
62.5	506.3	26.9	462.8	26.6
75.0	538.5	25.3	468.2	21.7
87.5	469.6	22.6	544.2	36.5

larger number of weights (cf., the slower learning of the increasingly damaged networks in Simulation 1). This leads to faster settling times for faces seen postdamage than for completely novel faces, even before the network has learned to accurately recognize the patterns.

Indeed, examination of the settling times for the novel patterns of Simulation 1 (i.e., the novel combinations of faces and names) shows that, at early stages of learning associated with chance overt performance in the damaged network, setting time is nevertheless reduced relative to no learning. As shown in Table 5, at all levels of hidden unit damage and at 4 out of 7 levels of input unit damage, settling time is faster after just 5 epochs of training than before.

Simulation 3: Semantic priming of occupation decisions

The goal of this simulation was to examine the effects of different amounts of damage to the visual units on facilitation and interference caused by a face prime when judging the occupation of a named person. As a related measure of overt performance, the network was presented with the face input patterns alone to classify according to occupation.

Method.   The model was lesioned as in the previous simulations. The name portions of the 5 familiar actor and 5 familiar politician patterns were presented to the network, paired with face patterns from the same group of individuals. Each of the 10 names was presented in three conditions: alone, paired with the nonidentical same-occupation faces, and paired with the different-occupation faces. The number of cycles needed for one of the occupation units, actor and politician, to attain a positive activation value was recorded. (The bias weights, learned during training, were largely inhibitory, leaving the units in a negative state in the absence of input activation.) As usual, 10 replications of the simulation with different random lesions in each of the two pools of units were carried out.

The overt ability of the network to derive occupation information from the face patterns was measured by recording which occupation unit reached threshold (i.e., became positive) after presentation of the face. For trials on which neither unit reached threshold, the network was assumed to guess with probability .5 of being correct. The rationale for scoring performance in this way, rather than taking the larger activation of the two regardless of whether either are positively activated, is that units, like neurons, have a categorical quality to their state. In the present model, there is a categorical difference between the way in which positive- and negative-valued activation in a unit affects the other units to which it is connected. For example, a negatively activated unit will inhibit units to which it is connected by positive weights but will excite them when its activation goes positive. Note that the method of scoring overt categorization was lenient in that we only require the sign of the activation to be correct.

Results and discussion.   The performance of the network on the overt occupation decision for faces is shown in Table 6. With lesions to hidden units or input units of 50% and 62.5%, the network's performance falls in the range of 59%–65% correct. This is roughly similar to the performance of the prosopagnosic patient reported by De Haan et al. (1987a, b), who obtained 55.5% and 62.5% correct in comparable tasks.

Table 7 and Figure 6 show the number of cycles required for the correct occupation unit to become positive after presentation of a name, without an accompanying face, and with faces from the same- or different-occupation category. Fewer cycles are required for the occupation units to attain positive values when the face and name are from the same-occupation category than when they come from different-occupaton categories. The effect of the face is evident at all but the most extreme levels of damage. In particular, it is evident at the levels of damage to input and hidden units whose corresponding overt performance was discussed earlier. The data from the no-face condition suggest that, as in De Haan et al.'s (1987a, b) studies, the effect is primarily one of interference rather than facilitation.

The mechanism by which faces affect performance in the present model is as follows: To the extent that the presentation of a face pattern causes any activation

TABLE 6
Overt occupation categorization

Amount of damage (%)	Percentage correct M	SE
Hidden unit damage		
12.5	85.5	3.1
25.0	77.0	3.3
37.5	74.0	4.4
50.0	62.5	4.5
62.5	59.5	5.1
75.0	53.0	5.0
87.5	51.5	4.5
Input unit damage		
12.5	88.0	1.2
25.0	86.5	2.3
37.5	73.0	3.4
50.0	64.5	4.4
62.5	59.5	4.9
75.0	57.5	4.8
87.5	57.0	5.0

TABLE 7
Time to categorize names according to their occupation alone and in the presence of same- and different-category faces

Amount of damage (%)	No face M	No face SE	Same category M	Same category SE	Different category M	Different category SE
Hidden unit damage						
12.5	50.5	5.5	49.0	4.4	142.8	13.6
25.0	49.8	5.9	75.3	9.1	150.5	12.2
37.5	55.3	5.8	76.1	9.3	110.1	8.9
50.0	70.8	13.3	81.6	8.9	114.0	8.8
62.5	66.6	13.9	59.6	6.5	82.1	6.9
75.0	73.0	15.1	84.0	7.6	98.0	7.8
87.5	62.8	9.1	72.9	9.2	66.9	5.0
Input unit damage						
12.5	52.0	4.4	115.4	9.3	55.3	9.3
25.0	69.6	9.2	101.7	9.2	77.0	16.0
37.5	55.8	5.6	88.9	8.3	96.3	20.2
50.0	101.3	10.4	146.5	13.1	126.9	21.6
62.5	106.0	11.2	131.8	11.3	123.0	24.2
75.0	107.5	10.9	120.6	10.7	130.9	21.9
87.5	76.3	7.6	78.8	6.7	144.0	27.2

Cycles for correct occupation unit to attain positive activation

(A) Face Hidden Unit Lesions

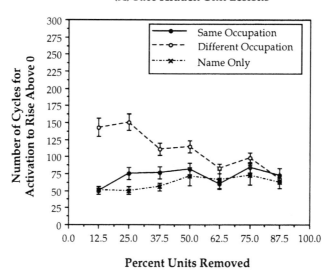

(B) Face Input Unit Lesions

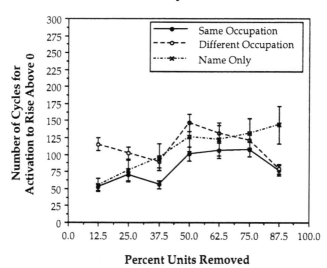

Figure 6. Semantic priming. (Time needed for correct occupation unit to reach threshold when name input is accompanied by face of same occupation, different occupation, or no face, for varying degrees of damage to [A] face hidden units and [B] face input units.)

to propagate into the rest of the network, this activation will influence the activation of the occupation units, even if it is not in itself sufficient to bring them all the way to threshold. At first glance this would seem to predict both facilitation and interference. Facilitation would arise because the face would contribute activation toward its occupation unit, and if the name has the same occupation, less additional activation from the name pattern would be needed for that occupation unit to attain a positive value. Interference would be predicted because the negative correlation between the two occupation units' activations, over the set of known patterns, would have resulted in an inhibitory connection between them having been learned by the network, so that the activation of either occupation unit would tend to inhibit the activation of the other. In effect, the network learns which subpatterns are consistent and inconsistent with which others, and inconsistent subpatterns (e.g., the single-unit actor or the single-unit politician) will tend to inhibit each other. The lack of an observed facilitation effect is attributable to mutual inhibition of the patterns for different individuals in the same-occupation category counteracting the facilitation mechanism just described. That is, some of the units activated by the name, which would normally contribute activation to the occupation unit, are themselves being inhibited by the influence of the face pattern.

A similar account has already been presented by Burton et al. (1991) to explain semantic priming by faces in prosopagnosia. They adapted a model of normal face recognition, developed by Burton, Bruce, and Johnston (1990), which was based on the McClelland and Rumelhart (1981) IAC architecture. In the Burton et al. model, there are three pools of units, face recognition units (FRUs), semantic information units, and name units, all connected by way of personal identity units (PINs), which serve to index the appropriate parts of each individual's representation to one another. They model covert recognition by leaving intact all units, including the FRUs, and attenuating the connections between the FRUs and the PINs. Semantic priming by faces is therefore the result of attenuated activation of semantic and name units coming from intact FRUs, which is insufficient to push semantic or name units over threshold for an overt response but lowers the amount of activation from name inputs needed to reach threshold.

The structural similarities between their model and ours include the three types of units (excluding PINs) and the use of a connectionist architecture. Perhaps more important, both models agree that the basic mechanism for semantic priming after damage involves subthreshold activation of semantic representations. The models differ structurally in that their representations are local, whereas ours are distributed, and their connections are hard wired, whereas ours are set by learning. One of the most obvious consequences of these differences is that our model can attempt to account for savings in face–name relearning (Simulation 1), whereas the hard-wired model cannot. A further, indirect result of the learning process in our model was the development of inhibitory relationships among

patterns for different individuals, which causes the model to evince more inter-ference than facilitation in the occupation semantic-priming task (Simulation 3), just as real human subjects do. Our use of distributed, as opposed to local, representations allowed us to simulate the effects of familiarity within that sys-tem on settling time (Simulation 2). Perhaps most important, in a model with distributed face representations, which undergo "graceful degradation," it seems natural to explore the effects of degrading the face recognition system proper, and this provided the basis for all of our simulations.

The same mechanism proposed here, in principle, explains Young et al.'s (1988) finding of semantic priming of names by associated faces in a name familiarity task. In this case, the relevant locus of priming would not be limited to occupation units but would involve any part of semantics shared by the priming and target individuals. Indeed, Burton et al. (1991) were also able to simulate the two kinds of priming task in the same way.

Simulation 4: Covert recognition of overtly unrecognised faces

In this final section, we demonstrate that the preserved covert recognition ability in the damaged network is not the result of the network's preserved overt re-cognition ability for a subset of the familiar patterns. The demonstration takes the form of a series of existence proofs. For each of the three tasks that were simulated, we tested the covert recognition performance of the network just on the subset of faces that it failed to recognize in the overt recognition tests.

Method. A randomly selected 50% of the face hidden units were damaged, and the resulting network was tested on the overt 10-alternative, forced-choice recognition test. The 2 faces out of 10 that were correctly identified were elim-inated from the set of test faces. For the semantic-priming experiment, only the 5 faces that were not correctly categorized as actors or politicians were retained in the test set. The damaged network was then tested for covert recognition in the three previously described tasks.

Results and discussion. The network relearned the correct associations among the eight faces and names faster than the incorrect: After damage and before learning, it obtained a score of 0% correct for both the correct and incorrect name–face pairs. After 10 epochs of learning, more learning had taken place for the correct pairs: The network obtained a score of 50% correct for the correct pairs and 0% correct for the incorrect pairs.

As before, presentation of a face from the wrong occupation category delayed the relevant occupation unit from reaching threshold when a name was presented. The mean number of cycles to reach threshold was 70.0 when no face was presented, 33.6 when a face from the same category was presented, and 94.9

when a face from the other category was presented. Settling time in the face units was faster for the 8 previously learned faces than for the 10 novel faces, on average 200.8 and 232.2 cycles, respectively.

In summary, the covert recognition abilities displayed by damaged attractor networks does not depend on the presence in the test set of any overtly identified face patterns.

GENERAL DISCUSSION

We have shown that some very general properties of neural networks lead to preserved performance, after network damage, for the types of tasks used to measure covert recognition in prosopagnosia. Specifically, we have simulated in varying degrees of detail three types of behavioral tasks used to document covert recognition. At levels of damage associated with low overt identification and categorization performance of face patterns, the network continues to manifest knowledge of the faces when tested by the covert tasks. Of additional interest is the fact that visual portions of the network were damaged in these simulations, demonstrating that one need not conclude that visual recognition is intact in cases of prosopagnosia with covert recognition. In the remainder of this article, we discuss the implications of these results for our understanding of covert face recognition, other covert visual abilities, prosopagnosia, and consciousness.

Covert face recognition

Previous attempts to explain covert recognition of faces in prosopagnosia have assumed that covert and overt recognition are dependent on at least partly distinct components of the cognitive architecture, somehow disconnected by brain damage, and that the visual recognition component is intact. In contrast, we have shown that the same system may subserve both overt and covet visual recognition and that damage to this system may spare covert recognition relative to overt recognition. This result is another example of how connectionist architectures can provide unified accounts of dissociations that initially appear to imply the existence of separate mechanisms (Rumelhart & McClelland, 1986; Seidenberg & McClelland, 1989).

Of course, the results of our simulations do not prove that our account is correct, merely that it is possible. Nevertheless, we find it plausible for three reasons: First, it follows from a set of independently motivated computational principles. These include the robustness and efficiency of distributing knowledge among a large number of connections (relevant to all simulations, but especially Simulation 1), the notion that there is a degree of fit between a network and any input pattern (relevant to Simulation 2), and the utility of having a threshold for activation flow between units (relevant to Simulation 3). Second, it is consistent with the available data on overt and covert performance in prosopagnosic patients, specifically the occasional success in overt tasks by these patients. Third, it is a

parsimonious account. It is not necessary to invoke separate brain centers for recognition and overt awareness of recognition, and only one face recognition system is hypothesized (cf., Bauer, 1984). Furthermore, consideration of the lesion sites and associated perceptual deficits in cases of prosopagnosia suggest that the visual system is likely to have been damaged.

In our view, the phenomenon of covert recognition in prosopagnosia is no less interesting or important if it is explained in terms of incomplete damage to the face recognition system. The fact that recognition can be manifest in different ways, some of which are accompanied by conscious awareness and others are not, and that this distinction appears to be coextensive with their vulnerability to brain damage, is of obvious high importance to the understanding of perception and the brain. We are merely pointing out that the most straightforward explanation of this dissociation, that the face recognition system is spared and the impairment in overt recognition tasks arises elsewhere, is not the only possibility. In addition to questioning the prevailing hypothesis, we are offering a new one that has the advantage of being more explicit about mechanism.

Covert recognition in other syndromes

In addition to covert recognition in prosopagnosia, there are several other syndromes in which indirect tests of visual perception seem to reveal greater capacities than are apparent on standard overt tests (see Farah, 1994, for a review). Can these dissociations also be explained in terms of a single damaged network capable of supporting performance of some tasks and not others? In principle, they could, although there is no reason to assume that all of the syndromes will have the same explanation. In some cases, there is clear evidence favoring the involvement of at least partially distinct systems subserving overt and covert perception. We briefly review the other syndromes and assess the applicability of the present hypothesis, that covert perceptual abilities reflect the functioning of a damaged, but not obliterated, visual system.

Blindsight. The phenomenon of blindsight, in which cortically blind patients who deny having any visual experience can localize and discriminate visual stimuli, was the first neuropsychological dissociation involving conscious awareness to be studied in detail. Although it was initially subject to much skepticism, two decades of careful research have demonstrated to most people's satisfaction that the dissociation is real, and current efforts center on elucidating the specific neural systems responsible for the nonconscious components of visual perception in blindsight (see Weiskrantz, 1990, for a review). Although it has been suggested that the visual abilities in blindsight may be mediated by residual functioning of spared primary visual cortex (Campion, Latto, & Smith, 1983), there is evidence of disproportionate involvement of the subcortical visual system in at least some of these abilities. For example, asymmetries in the processing of

visual stimuli between nasal and temporal hemifields suggests that the subcortical visual system (which receives disproportionate input from the temporal hemifield) plays a primary role in some of the covert visual abilities in this syndrome (e.g., Rafal, Smith, Krantz, Cohen, & Brennan, 1990). A wealth of other evidence (summarized by Weiskrantz, 1990) suggests that more than one visual pathway may be involved in the preserved abilities of blindsight patients but that the residual functioning of the primary visual cortex is not a necessary factor.

Implicit reading. Another form of visual recognition in the absence of conscious awareness of recognition can be found in certain patients with pure alexia. Pure alexic patients are, by definition, impaired in reading but have roughly normal auditory word comprehension and writing, and their underlying deficit is therefore inferred to be one of visual word recognition. To the extent that they are able to read, they do so by a slow and laborious letter-by-letter strategy, and their reading can therefore be obliterated entirely by presenting words briefly. However, with brief presentations of words, some pure alexic patients are able to derive considerable information from the words, even though they report being unable to recognize the words and even though they cannot name the words (e.g., Shallice & Saffran, 1986; Coslett & Saffran, 1989). For example, with presentations too brief for any explicit reading, these patients are able to discriminate words from orthographically legal nonwords and to classify words as belonging to a certain category (e.g., animals or foods) at levels far above chance. Implicit reading may also be carried out by different systems from those subserving normal explicit reading. The hypothesis of right-hemisphere mediation of implicit reading (in contrast with the predominant role of the left hemisphere in normal reading) is supported by the relative absence of implicit reading for abstract words, function words, and grammatical inflections, and the lack of access to phonology, all characteristics of the right-hemisphere lexicon (Coslett & Saffran, 1989). Nevertheless, it is conceivable that this profile of reading abilities would also emerge from damage to the left-hemisphere reading system, as discussed by Shallice and Saffran (1986). For example, differences between word classes such as word frequency and availability of collateral support from semantic representations may confer different degrees of robustness to damage on them. However, differences in the regularity of mapping among print, meaning, and phonology could also affect the robustness of these mappings in the network after damage and would seem to predict lesser rather than greater vulnerability of phonology relative to semantics.

Unconscious perception of extinguished visual stimuli. Extinction refers to the impairment in perception of a contralesional stimulus when presented simultaneously with an ipsilesional stimulus. Volpe, Ledoux, and Gazzaniga (1979) tested the ability of right parietal-damaged patients to perceive contralesional visual stimuli in two ways. First, the patients were shown a tachistoscopic

presentation of a pair of stimuli (line drawings or words), one on each side of fixation, and were asked to name what they saw. In this task, the patients manifested visual "extinction" of the left stimulus by the right, which is typical of right parietal-damaged patients: the right stimulus was generally named correctly, but the left stimulus was not, and patients sometimes even denied that the left stimulus had been presented. In contrast, the patients performed well in a second kind of task with the same stimuli. When asked whether the two stimuli presented on a given trial were the same or different, the patients were highly accurate, even though this task requires perception of the left stimulus. Volpe et al. interpreted their findings as revealing "a breakdown in the flow of information between conscious and nonconscious mental systems" (p. 724). However, it is possible that these findings can be explained in terms of the residual functioning of a damaged visual system, rather than a dissociation between two types of system, one conscious and one unconscious.

Farah, Monheit, and Wallace (1991) showed that the dissociation observed by Volpe et al. could be obtained in normal subjects simply by placing a translucent sheet of drafting stock over the left half of the display to degrade subjects' perception of stimuli on the left. We also showed that the dissociation could be eliminated in parietal-damaged patients with extinction when the overt and covert tasks were matched for the precision of visual perception required by each. This implies that the dissociation between overt and covert perception after parietal damage is also due to differences in the quality of information needed to support performance in the two types of task, with performance in the covert task again more robust to low-quality information. The nature of the information degradation appears to be different in the two cases, however. In prosopagnosia, what is degraded is the pattern of previously learned associations within the visual recognition system, so that the effects of prior learning on perception are disrupted. In extinction, there is no structural impairment of representations, as evidenced by the ability of patients with extinction to perceive normally in the absence of a simultaneously occuring ipsilesional stimulus. Rather, the locus of degradation appears to be before visual recognition, affecting the input to visual recognition memory. This is consistent with our ability to simulate covert recognition in extinction by degrading the stimulus input to normal subjects.

The most general implication of the present model for the study of covert perception is that it demonstrates another mechanism by which overt and covert processing can be dissociated, beyond those previously considered by neuropsychologists. Schacter et al. (1988) listed three general types of account for overt–covert dissociations: conservative response bias in the overt tasks, disconnection from language (on the assumption that language is more involved in the overt tasks) and truly distinct and thus dissociable processing systems for overt and covert performance. To these we would add a fourth: differential susceptibility to damage of overt and covert performance. We have shown how knowledge can

reside in a damaged network but be inaccessible for most purposes, for reasons quite distinct from either the signal-detection theory concept of bias or a disconnection from other systems. As Hinton and Plaut (1987) showed, savings in relearning reveals the knowledge retained in damaged networks that is not apparent in the overt performance of the network. We have extended these findings to two other measures of covert knowledge in damaged networks: speed of settling and priming.

Prosopagnosia

The finding that some prosopagnosic patients manifest covert recognition and others do not has been taken as an indication that there are two different types of prosopagnosia: one caused by a visual perceptual impairment per se and the other caused by a disconnection of visual recognition and other, conscious, mental systems (e.g., Bauer, 1986; Bruyer, 1991; Burton et al., 1991; De Haan et al., 1992; Newcombe et al., 1989). However, our analysis suggests that these two groups of prosopagnosic patients are more likely to differ in severity than in kind. In particular, the similarity of the effects obtained when we lesioned face input units and face hidden units suggests that the presence of covert recognition may not be a precise way of discriminating different functional loci of damage. In fact, lesions further downstream in our model also showed similar effects to the ones reported here. This is a consequence of the highly interactive nature of the model. The nonlocalizability of errors resulting from damage in interactive models has been discussed in detail by Hinton and Shallice (1991) for their model of reading. This is not to deny that prosopagnosia may be accompanied by, or may even result from, impairments of different levels of visual face processing.

Consciousness

The dissociations between covert and overt perception in prosopagnosia and in other syndromes are of interest independent of the association between overt perception and consciousness. The fact that knowledge may be accessible in certain tasks and not in others is somewhat counterintuitive and promises insights into how information is represented in the brain. Indeed, this has been the focus of the present article. However, it cannot be denied that part of the fascination of these dissociations comes from the involvement of consciousness, specifically the patients' seemingly earnest denials of conscious awareness of stimulus properties of which they show knowledge in certain tasks. On the basis of our research, can we offer any insights into consciousness?

We believe that neuropsychological evidence can indeed answer certain questions about consciousness, specifically those concerning its physical correlates. In the present case, it appears that conscious awareness of recognition is correlated with a certain minimal quality of information representation within the visual

recognition system. Why should the likelihood of conscious awareness depend on the quality of the representation? Kinsbourne (1988) has suggested that stimuli reach conscious awareness only when they are integrated into the global information-processing state of the brain as a whole. He has also suggested that faulty perceptual processing of a stimulus will decrease the likelihood that it will become integrated. This idea is consonant with the dynamics of neural networks, particularly attractor networks such as the one presented here: When a new input pattern is presented, it pulls the network into a new attractor state, with each part of the network taking on new activation values that are integrated in the sense of being mutually compatible. When the input patterns are degraded by damage to perceptual units, they lose their ability to pull the remaining parts of the network into an integrated state consistent with themselves (i.e., semantics and name units no longer take on the patterns corresponding to the presented face), even for levels of degradation at which residual information can be detected by other means (that do not involve propagating information throughout the system). In summary, our model suggests that an important neural correlate of conscious awareness in perception is the quality of perceptual representation, perhaps because perceptual quality limits the ability of perceptual representations to draw other parts of the system into an integrated state with themselves.

ACKNOWLEDGEMENTS

This research was supported by Office of Naval Research (ONR) Grant N00014-91-J1546, National Institute of Mental Health Grant R01 MH48274, National Institutes of Health Career Development Award K04-NS01405, and Grant 90-36 from the McDonnell-Pew Program in Cognitive Neuroscience to Martha J. Farah, an ONR graduate fellowship to Randall C. O'Reilly, and National Science Foundation Grant BNS 88-12048 to J. L. McClelland. We thank M. Gasser, C. Glymour, J. L. McClelland, and three anonymous reviewers for their insightful comments on an earlier draft of this article.

REFERENCES

Bauer, R. M. (1984). Autonomic recognition of names and faces in prosopagnosia: A neuropsychological application of the guilty knowledge test. *Neuropsychologia, 22,* 457–469.

Bauer, R. M. (1986). Aspects of face processing. In H. D. Ellis, M. A. Jeeves, F. Newcombe, & A. Young (Eds.), *The cognitive psychophysiology of prosopagnosia* (pp. 253–267). Dordrecht, The Netherlands: Martinus Nijhoff.

Bruyer, R. (1991). Covert face recognition in prosopagnosia: A review. *Brain and Cognition, 15,* 223–235.

Bruyer, R., Laterre, C., Seron, X., Feyereisen, P., Strypstein, E., Pierrard, E., & Rectem, D. (1983). A case of prosopagnosia with some preserved covert remembrance of familiar faces. *Brain and Cognition, 2,* 257–284.

Burton, A. M., Bruce, V., & Johnston, R. A. (1990). Understanding face recognition with an interactive activation model. *British Journal of Psychology, 81,* 361–380.

Burton, A. M., Young, A. W., Bruce, V., Johnston, R. A., & Ellis, A. W. (1991). Understanding covert recognition. *Cognition, 39,* 129–166.

Campion, J., Latto, R., & Smith, Y. M. (1983). Is blindsight an effect of scattered light, spared cortex, and near-threshold vision? *The Behavioral and Brain Sciences, 3*, 423–447.

Coslett, H. B., & Saffran, E. M. (1989). Evidence for preserved reading in "pure alexia." *Brain, 112*, 327–359.

De Haan, E. H. F., Bauer, R. M., & Greve, K. W. (1992). Behavioral and physiological evidence for covert recognition in a prosopagnosic patient. *Cortex, 28*, 77–95.

De Haan, E. H. F., Young, A. W., & Newcombe, F. (1987a). Faces interfere with name classification in a prosopagnosic patient. *Cortex, 23*, 309–316.

De Haan, E. H. F., Young, A. W., & Newcombe, F. (1987b). Face recognition without awareness. *Cognitive Neuropsychology, 4*, 385–415.

Dennett, D. C., & Kinsbourne, M. (1992). Time and the observer: The where and when of consciousness in the brain. *Behavioral and Brain Sciences, 15*, 183–247.

Etcoff, N. L., Freeman, R., & Cave, K. R. (1991). Can we lose memories of faces? Content specificity and awareness in a prosopagnosic. *Journal of Cognitive Neuroscience, 3*, 25–41.

Farah, M. J. (1994). Visual perception and visual awareness after brain damage: A tutorial overview. In M. Moscovitch & C. Umilta (Eds.), *Conscious and unconscious information processing: Attention and performance XV*. Cambridge, MA: MIT Press.

Farah, M. J., Monheit, M. A., & Wallace, M. A. (1991). Unconscious perception in the extinguished hemifield: Re-evaluating the evidence. *Neuropsychologia, 29*, 949–958.

Greve, K. W., & Bauer, R. M. (1990). Implicit learning of new faces in prosopagnosia: An application of the mere exposure paradigm. *Neuropsychologia, 28*, 135–141.

Hinton, G. E., McClelland, J. L., & Rumelhart, D. E. (1986). Distributed representations. In D. E. Rumelhart & J. L. McClelland (Eds.), *Parallel distributed processing: Explorations in the microstructure of cognition. Vol. 1: Foundations* (pp. 77–109). Cambridge, MA: MIT Press.

Hinton, G. E., & Plaut, D. C. (1987). Using fast weights to deblur old memories. *Proceedings of the Ninth Annual Conference of the Cognitive Science Society*. Hillsdale, NJ: Lawrence Erlbaum Associates Inc.

Hinton, G. E., & Sejnowski, T. J. (1986). Learning and relearning in Boltzmann machines. In D. E. Rumelhart & J. L. McClelland (Eds.), *Parallel distributed processing: Explorations in the microstructure of cognition. Vol. 1: Foundations* (pp. 282–317). Cambridge, MA: MIT Press.

Hinton, G. E., & Shallice, T. (1991). Lesioning an attractor network: Investigations of acquired dyslexia. *Psychological Review, 98*, 74–95.

Jacoby, L. L. (1984). Incidental vs. intentional retrieval: Remembering and awareness as separate issues. In L. R. Squire & N. Butters (Eds.), *The neuropsychology of human memory*. New York: Oxford University Press.

Kinsbourne, M. (1988). An intergrated field theory of consciousness. In A. J. Marcel & E. Bisiach (Eds.), *Consciousness in contemporary science* (pp. 159–182). Oxford, UK: Clarendon Press.

McClelland, J. L., & Rumelhart, D. E. (1981). An interactive activation model of context effects in letter perception: I. An account of basic findings. *Psychological Review, 88*, 375–407.

Movellan, J. R. (1990). Contrastive Hebbian learning in the continuous Hopfield model. In D. S. Touretzky, G. E. Hinton, & T. J. Sejnowski (Eds.), *Proceedings of the 1989 Connectionist Models Summer School* (pp. 10–17). San Mateo, CA: Morgan Kaufman.

Newcombe, F., Young, A., & De Haan, E. H. F. (1989). Prosopagnosia and object agnosia without covert recognition. *Neuropsychologia, 27*, 179–191.

Peterson, C., & Anderson, J. A. (1987). A mean field theory learning algorithm for neural networks. *Complex Systems, 1*, 995–1019.

Posner, M. I. (1978). *Chronometric explorations of mind*. Hillsdale, NJ: Lawrence Erlbaum Associates Inc.

Rafal, R., Smith, J., Krantz, J., Cohen, A., & Brennan, C. (1990). Extrageniculate vision in hemianopic humans: Saccade inhibition by signals in the blind field. *Science, 250*, 118–121.

Renault, B., Signoret, J. L., Debruille, B., Breton, F., & Bolgert, F. (1989). Brain potentials reveal covert facial recognition in prosopagnosia. *Neuropsychologica, 27*, 905–912.

Rumelhart, D. E., & McClelland, J. L. (1986). *Parallel distributed processing: Explorations in the microstructure of cognition. Vol. 1: Foundations.* Cambridge, MA: MIT Press.

Schacter, D. L., McAndrews, M. P., & Moscovitch, M. (1988). Access to consciousness: Dissociations between implicit and explicit knowledge in neuropsychological syndromes. In L. Weiskrantz (Ed.), *Thought without language* (pp. 242–278). New York: Oxford University Press.

Seidenberg, M., & McClelland, J. L. (1989). A distributed, developmental model of word recognition and naming. *Psychological Review, 96,* 523–568.

Sergent, J., & Villemure, J. G. (1989). Prosopagnosia in a right hemispherectomized patient. *Brain, 112,* 975–995.

Shallice, T., & Saffran, E. (1986). Lexical processing in the absence of explicit word identification: Evidence from a letter-by-letter reader. *Cognitive Neuropsychology, 3,* 429–458.

Snodgrass, J. G., Corwin, J., & Feenan, K. (1990). The pragmatics of measuring priming: Applications to normal and abnormal memory. *Journal of Clinical and Experimental Neuropsychology, 12,* 61.

Tranel, D., & Damasio, A. R. (1985). Knowledge without awareness: An automatic index of facial recognition by prosopagnosics. *Science, 228,* 1453–1454.

Tranel, D., & Damasio, A. R. (1988). Nonconscious face recognition in patients with face agnosia. *Behavioral Brain Research, 30,* 235–249.

Volpe, B. T., Ledoux, J. E., & Gazzaniga, M. S. (1979). Information processing of visual stimuli in an "extinguished" field. *Nature, 282,* 722–724.

Wallace, M. A., & Farah, M. J. (1992). Savings in relearning as evidence for covert recognition in prosopagnosia. *Journal of Cognitive Neuroscience, 4,* 150–154.

Weiskrantz, L. (1990). Outlooks for blindsight: Explicit methodologies for implicit processes. *Proceedings of the Royal Society of London, B239,* 247–278.

Young, A. W., & De Haan, E. H. F. (1988). Boundaries of covert recognition in prosopagnosia. *Cognitive Neuropsychology, 5,* 317–336.

Young, A. W., Hay, D. C., & Ellis, A. W. (1985). The faces that launched a thousand slips: Everyday difficulties and errors in recognising people. *British Journal of Psychology, 76,* 495–523.

Young, A. W., Hellawell, D., & De Haan, E. H. F. (1988). Cross-domain semantic priming in normal subjects and a prosopagnosic patient. *Quarterly Journal of Experimental Psychology, 38A,* 297–318.

CHAPTER EIGHT

Simulation and explanation: Some harmony and some discord

A. Mike Burton
University of Glasgow, UK

Andrew W. Young
University of York, UK

This short reply to O'Reilly and Farah (1999) highlights three issues that continue to divide our approaches. We disagree about what needs to be modelled, the theoretical importance of distributed representations, and how to account for provoked overt recognition. However, the exchange has helped to show why different groups favour different approaches, and has highlighted some testable empirical predictions.

INTRODUCTION

O'Reilly and Farah (1999) (henceforth OF) have provided an interesting and spirited defence of their FOV (Farah, O'Reilly, & Vecera) model presented in Chapter 7. They have challenged many of our (Young & Burton, 1999) criticisms of their approach to understanding covert recognition in prosopagnosia, and face recognition in general.

We welcome the fact that OF have developed their model to account for a greater range of effects. We are not surprised that, with extra features, the FOV model can be made to accommodate extra phenomena. For example, the addition of inter-trial decay (whose magnitude is tuned to the particular phenomenon being studied) allows the FOV model to capture some new effects in a way that had previously escaped us. This seems to us a step forward: We see the incremental development of models as a legitimate and even desirable step toward the overall goal of achieving a reasonably realistic simulation of human face recognition.

Cognitive Neuropsychology, 1999, 16(1), 73–79.

235

However, some fundamental points of disagreement remain. In the hope that readers will find a short response more attractive than point-by-point argument, we will focus here on what we take to be the key issues that divide us. For readers interested in more detailed discussion of each of the individual points in dispute, we have provided a short Appendix contesting some of OF's criticisms of the IAC model, which we consider to be unwarranted. The bulk of the article will address more general issues.

WHAT NEEDS TO BE MODELLED?

It is hardly surprising that the approach of different groups diverges when we cannot even agree which phenomena are to be modelled. A fundamental difference between the approaches taken by FOV and by IAC (presented in Chapter 6) is that familiarity is an important component of the IAC model. In contrast, OF write that familiarity is such a little-understood process that they have preferred to avoid it in their simulations. In particular, they prefer not to bring questionable assumptions into the model (O'Reilly & Farah, 1999, p. 52).

Familiarity is indeed a difficult issue, but our own view is that it is essential to any adequate understanding of face recognition—the fact that it is hard to operationalise makes it no less central. In our daily lives we very commonly make judgements involving familiarity. As we walk along a street we may see hundreds of unfamiliar faces, but when we see colleagues or acquaintances we can pick them out routinely and without apparent effort. One of the most common forms of everyday error is to know that a person's face is familiar, but be unable to remember how you know them (Young, Hay, & Ellis, 1985).

As well as being a key aspect of normal face recognition, familiarity seems crucial to prosopagnosia: in prosopagnosia, discrimination of familiar from unfamiliar faces is at chance, and patients complain that even their own face seems unfamiliar when seen in a mirror. We do not understand how it is possible to have a satisfactory model of covert recognition without an operationalisation of familiarity. This is not to say that our particular operationalisation is correct. In fact, in the original statement of the IAC model, Burton, Bruce, and Johnston (1990) went to some lengths to discuss this, and offer various other options, all mechanical, and all using some aspects of the model's state. It is easily possible that our current model of familiarity is mistaken, but we think it unlikely we can make much progress without a model at all.

Finally regarding OF's concern about our use of a threshold, we should point out that a threshold mechanism is natural in most models of this kind. When OF attempt to capture familiarity using the *goodness* of the network's state (O'Reilly & Farah, 1999, p. 52) they implicitly appeal to a threshold beyond which the state is *good enough* to signal familiarity: "Greater familiarity would be associated with larger goodness values" (O'Reilly & Farah, 1999, p. 70, Appendix B). We should note that this characterisation has exactly the same features as our

own which is so roundly criticised by OF: It is arbitrary (of course) and it is external to the workings of the model—it monitors activation change rather than causing it. We are disappointed that OF do not like our attempts to capture familiarity, but we make no apologies for trying to do so explicitly.

DISTRIBUTED REPRESENTATIONS

At the heart of the disagreement between us lies the issue of distributed representations. There are several points of misunderstanding in OF's reply, which show that we need to make our position more clear. In general, we do not object to complicated theories, as long as the complications do not serve only to obscure the properties of the theory.

1. We do not dispute that the brain may use some form of distributed representations.
2. We do not dispute that big things are made up of little things (i.e., that representations are *componential*).
3. We believe that the *particular* learning algorithm used is intimately connected with the *particular* form of distributed representations one derives, but we do not believe this to be an advantage if the learning algorithm used is unrelated to human learning.

We will briefly discuss each of these points.

1. It seems we have misrepresented FOV. We had thought they would accept that there is a difference between psychological and neurophysiological levels of explanation, and that an account which works at the psychological level need not map *directly* onto the underlying physiology (even though there must be some form of mapping). In their reply, though, OF (O'Reilly & Farah, 1999, p. 64) write "FOV, like other connectionist models, has some properties in common with real neural networks, and can therefore be considered a model of the brain". On this matter we simply have to agree to disagree. Our own view is that, whatever its interest at the psychological level, FOV is sufficiently unlike a brain to rule it out as a candidate model of brain function.

To make the connection between FOV and brain function at the neurophysiological level, one has to argue that the two have significant aspects in common. The proffered common aspect is distributed representations. The problem here is that there are many ways in which representations can be distributed, so that any particular method of distributing representations need be no more like another than it is like a local representation. To use the fact that FOV has distributed representations as evidence that it is brain-like, one therefore needs to argue that the *particular type* of distributed representation it uses is like the particular type of distributed representation the brain uses. OF cite various neurophysiological studies implying that the brain uses some form of distributed representations.

However, most of this evidence suggests the use of coarse coding by the brain, not fully distributed representations. With coarse coding, representations are indeed distributed, but there is relatively fine tuning of each distribution. In essence this means that each representation is coded over a small proportion of the available units, rather than each being coded equally across the entire set. This is an important distinction. Systems which use "few-unit", coarse-coded distributed representations behave entirely unlike systems in which all units are used for each representation. Of course, FOV uses the second type of distributed representation, whereas the brain most likely uses the first. As an example of the differences, a brain-like coarse-coded architecture allows simultaneous representation of several patterns whereas the type of representation used in FOV does not. In sum, we do not think there are *general properties* common to all forms of distributed representations, as do OF. This must remain a point of disagreement.

2. There is no dispute between us that representations can be componential. It is clear that complex representations are made up of more fundamental components. Imagine a network representing a lexicon. One approach would be to suggest that there are 26 units corresponding to letters. Representations of words could then be formed by simultaneously activating component letters (this is a simple model, so let us ignore the issue of letter-order for the sake of the example). If this is the sense of distributed representation intended by OF, then we have no quarrel. As they point out, our own model uses this form of distributed representation, as does FOV in assigning occupation.

The problem is that this form of distributed representation lacks attributes generally cited as being among the advantages of fully distributed representations. In particular, it will not show robustness or graceful degradation after damage. Losing a letter representation in such a model would be the same as losing a letter on a typewriter—effectively, a particular component of all (and only) those words that use that component goes missing, rather than every word just being a little less well represented in total. Second, OF want to invoke the general properties of fully distributed representations, but they end up needing representations composed of locally interpretable units (for occupations, etc.). However, it is extremely difficult to get automatic learning algorithms to come up with representations that decompose into symbolically contentful representations. Instead (and usually cited as an advantage) the entire pattern must be taken as a representation, and the individual unit activations cannot be interpreted in isolation. Now, if this is the case, other advantages listed by OF (e.g., accuracy, generalisation) also break down. In sum, we believe, like OF, that representations are made up of representational components. However, when each of these components is itself locally interpretable, this form of representation no longer has the properties attributed to it as "general, emergent properties of distributed representations".

3. Finally, we discuss the issue of learning. OF state that the particular learning algorithm used in their model is not theory-relevant. Instead, it was used

because fully distributed representations are so complex that one has to get them into the model somehow. We objected to the particular algorithm used for several reasons, one being that it is non-monotonic. We do not find very convincing the argument that non-monotonic learning is simply an inconvenience for modellers (i.e. that it only makes it harder for us). Our point is that *in principle* there is no way of knowing when to stop learning if one employs a non-monotonic rule. We accept that people may exhibit forms of non-monotonic learning under certain circumstances, but we would be amazed if people sometimes simply forgot everything they had previously learnt and started to learn again from scratch. The fact that this happens at (in principle) unpredictable stages in the learning process used by FOV seems to us to make it totally unlike human learning.

Having argued that the learning algorithm is theory-irrelevant, OF also state (O'Reilly & Farah, 1999, p. 65) that "not only must learning be used in the set-up of most connectionist models of cognitive end state, it provides insights into that end state". This is exactly the point. In connectionist models using learning, the learning and the final representation are intimately linked. The type of learning determines the type of representation one ends up with. But given this, it seems strange to argue that the type of learning used in a model can be theory-irrelevant. Once again, we must point out that the mere presence of learning in connectionist models is of little value if that learning is unlike human learning. If one does not have a theory of human learning, it seems inappropriate to develop systems with learning regimes that one knows to be unlike the human case.

PROVOKED OVERT RECOGNITION

A good example of the impact of differences between our models comes in OF's treatment of provoked overt recognition—the phenomenon in which prosopagnosic patients (sometimes) manage to recognise some of the faces from a common category if they are presented together. We originally included a discussion of provoked overt recognition in our paper because it strikes us as one of the most challenging phenomena to emerge from research in prosopagnosia. Not only do current models have problems simulating the effect, but it seems clinically important as a faint glimmer of hope for rehabilitation research. We therefore spent some time trying to capture it.

Our failure ran against our original intuitions derived from thinking about the IAC model rather than running it. Intuitively, the model seemed able to deliver this phenomenon, but in practice, we could not get it to give what seemed to us the correct analogue. This is a potentially important failing, and a challenge to researchers to come up with better models. Unfortunately, FOV may not be the answer. In their paper, OF present a model of provoked overt recognition which also fails to simulate what has been observed in prosopagnosia, but for which success is claimed. The key point is that OF presented their model with a set of faces *in sequence*, and could then show behaviour which seems like provoked

recognition. Unfortunately, *sequential* presentation of faces from a common category is a procedure that has never been used with prosopagnosic patients. The provoked recognition effect has only been demonstrated with *simultaneous* presentation of a number of faces. As reported in our original article, the IAC model produces behaviour against the prediction when presented with stimuli simultaneously, though more neutral behaviour is elicited by sequential presentation. Both models therefore at present fail to capture this important phenomenon—or at least to capture it precisely.

This issue runs deep into the heart of the matter. The FOV model, by its very nature, cannot be presented with more than one face at a time. Because the representations are distributed over all face units, each pattern occupies all units. Whether this is something its authors would consider a theory-relevant or a theory-irrelevant detail of the FOV model is unclear to us. However, it strikes us as an important point. The IAC model has no problems with simultaneous presentation of any of its represented faces.

CONCLUSIONS

What can be learn from this exchange? We recognise that our views run counter to prevailing fashion, though a recent collection edited by Grainger and Jacobs (1998) shows that researchers in other fields have similar concerns. It seems that profound differences about the purposes of modelling exist within the research community. It is impossible to judge whether there is a right horse to back at this stage, or whether we will all be left behind when a complete unknown enters the race.

Some of the differences reflect different starting points. FOV and OF are interested in using face recognition as a vehicle for exploring what they see as bigger questions. This broad focus can distract one from the details of empirical phenomena. For example, OF state that sequential associative priming arises when stimuli are semantically related, such as when both are members of Britain's royal family, but the evidence shows that such priming is *not* based simply on category membership—it only arises when both stimuli are also close associates (Young, Flude, Hellawell, & Ellis, 1994). Similarly, we have noted their misdescription of the phenomenon of provoked overt recognition in prosopagnosia. Our own concerns are almost the reverse. We have sought to achieve a detailed account of empirical phenomena found in studies of face recognition, and then considered what implications this might have for broader issues.

As unashamed book-keepers, we still consider that evidence should be the arbiter of what is the more successful account, and our exchange with OF has thrown into relief two points where the models do seem genuinely to differ in what they predict. First, OF make a telling observation (O'Reilly & Farah, 1999, p. 56) that IAC predicts that prosopagnosia (of the form under dispute) should mainly affect familiar faces, leaving unfamiliar face processing relatively

unaffected. This is because the supposed damage occurs at a point downstream of the perceptual representation of faces—although damage to any component of an interactive model will have some consequential impact on all its functions, the impact on unfamiliar face processing should not be so great. However, OF claim (O'Reilly & Farah, 1999, p. 56) that the literature on prosopagnosia shows that "whenever the perception of unfamiliar faces have been carefully tested it has been found to be impaired", which would require an extra site of damage in IAC.

We agree this would not be an elegant solution—though that does not in itself make it incorrect. However, our reading of the literature leads us to be more equivocal than OF. It is true that the majority of prosopagnosic patients show problems in the perception of unfamiliar faces. On difficult tests such as the Benton Test of Facial Recognition (Benton, Hamsher, Varney, & Spreen, 1983) they may be inaccurate, slow, or both. But the issue under discussion concerns only the (at present relatively small) subset of patients who have been demonstrated to show covert recognition. For some of these, there is also impaired perception of unfamiliar faces, but this correlation might simply be due to associated deficits (the inelegant solution noted earlier). The important question is whether *any* cases of prosopagnosia show covert recognition of familiar faces and intact perceptual processing of unfamiliar faces. The literature already reveals this as a distinct possibility. For example, in one of the very first published studies of covert recognition, Bauer (1984) reported normal performance of the Benton test by his patient. At the time, the importance of measuring speed as well as accuracy was not widely appreciated, but a later study by Sergent and Poncet (1990) reported accuracy and speed of performance of the Benton test clearly comparable to that of neurologically normal controls (well within 1 SD). In addition, Sergent and Poncet showed that their patient PV's similarity ratings for pairs of faces showed an equivalent pattern to controls when subjected to multidimensional scaling. Sergent and Poncet took this to indicate that PV could still process the faces' configurational properties—her problems were to do with face memory, not perception per se.

We therefore think that the precise relation of familiar and unfamiliar face processing deficits in cases of prosopagnosia with covert recognition remains a more open question than OF imply. The tests used by Sergent and Poncet (1990) were as thorough, well-chosen and well-documented as for any other case reported in the literature, and did not reveal problems in the *perception* of unfamiliar faces. The fact that deficits affecting the perception of unfamiliar and familiar faces are necessarily related in the FOV but not in the IAC approach provides a useful contrast between the accounts.

A second difference highlighted by our exchange came from the attempts to account for provoked overt recognition, which we still consider problematic for both models. Discussing this with OF has thrown into relief the inability of their model to deal with simultaneously presented faces—it has to process them one

at a time, whereas IAC does not have this limitation. Now dealing with faces one at a time might also be what human beings do, or it might not—we simply do not know at present, but the issue is open to empirical test.

It seems to us that these are good examples of the value of fully implemented, detailed models. They can be used to challenge our assumptions about the processes involved in cognition in a way that unimplemented models cannot (or at least not so readily). We have argued throughout that this is an advantage of the approach we have adopted.

REFERENCES

Bauer, R. M. (1984). Autonomic recognition of names and faces in prosopagnosia: A neuropsychological application of the guilty knowledge test. *Neuropsychologia, 22*, 457–469.

Benton, A. L., Hamsher, K. S., Varney, N., & Spreen, O. (1983). *Contributions to neuropsychological assessment: A clinical manual.* Oxford: Oxford University Press.

Burton, A. M., Bruce, V., & Hancock, P. J. B. (1999). From pixels to people: A model of familiar face recognition. *Cognitive Science, 23*(1), 1–31.

Burton, A. M., Bruce, V., & Johnston, R. A. (1990). Understanding face recognition with an interactive activation model. *British Journal of Psychology, 81*, 361–380.

Burton, A. M., Kelly, S. W., & Bruce, V. (1998). Cross domain repetition priming in person recognition. *Quarterly Journal of Experimental Psychology, 51A*, 515–529.

Burton, A. M., Young, A. W., Bruce, V., Johnston, R. A., & Ellis, A. W. (1991). Understanding covert recognition. *Cognition, 39*, 129–166.

Cabeza, R., Burton, A. M., Kelly, S. W., & Akamatsu, S. (1997). Investigating the relation between imagery and perception: Evidence from face priming. *Quarterly Journal of Experimental Psychology, 50A*, 274–289.

Grainger, J., & Jacobs, A. M. (Eds.). (1998). *Localist connectionist approaches to human cognition.* Mahwah, NJ: Lawrence Erlbaum Associates Inc.

O'Reilly, R. C., & Farah, M. J. (1999). Simulation and explanation in neuropsychology and beyond. *Cognitive Neuropsychology, 16*, 49–72.

Sergent, J., & Poncet, M. (1990). From covert to overt recognition of faces in a prosopagnosic patient. *Brain, 113*, 989–1004.

Young, A. W., & Burton, A. M. (1999). Simulating face recognition: Implications for modelling cognition. *Cognitive Neuropsychology, 16*, 1–48.

Young, A. W., Flude, B. M., Hellawell, D. J., & Ellis, A. W. (1994). The nature of semantic priming effects in the recognition of familiar people. *British Journal of Psychology, 85*, 393–411.

Young, A. W., Hay, D. C., & Ellis, A. W. (1985). The faces that launched a thousand slips: Everyday difficulties and errors in recognising people. *British Journal of Psychology, 76*, 495–523.

APPENDIX

In this Appendix we briefly challenge some of the criticism of the IAC model made by OF.

The ratio of assumptions made to data accounted for (O'Reilly & Farah, 1999, p. 55). This would be a worry if we were truly guilty, but we find the criticism unfounded. Additions to the IAC model have all been documented in the research papers we cited, which show that they were motivated by considerations other than the need to account for specific covert recognition effects. Nothing was added for the purpose of our article. The most recent statement of the model can be found in Burton, Bruce, and Hancock (1999).

IAC predicts intact forced-choice overt recognition prosopagnosia (O'Reilly & Farah, 1999, p. 55). The argument used to support this claim is that familiar faces will always have more activation than unfamiliar faces, despite the fact that both will have sub-threshold activation. This is true. OF further suggest that forced-choice decision processes will have access to sub-threshold activations. This is not a feature of the IAC model. Indeed, as we explicitly discuss in our original article (O'Reilly & Farah, 1999, pp. 18–19) it is a defining characteristic of the model that there is no access to below-threshold activation for the decision mechanism. Hence this is not a prediction of the IAC model.

IAC predicts prosopagnosia is all-or-none (O'Reilly & Farah, 1999, pp. 55–56). The simplifying assumption we have made in all our simulations is that FRU–PIN links are equivalent. That is to say, all faces are equally well known. This is evidently a simplification, and has always been acknowledged as such. As is implicit in our discussion of priming, we recognise that in practice some FRU–PIN links can become stronger than others. This arises naturally through priming, and presumably in the real state through frequency of encounter. If the FRU–PIN links are of different strengths for different individuals, then a particular lesion may take some people into the region where overt recognition cannot be achieved, leaving others able to reach threshold.

In our original statements of the model (Burton et al., 1990; Burton, Young, Bruce, Johnston, & Ellis, 1991) we explicitly discussed and justified this simplifying assumption for simulations. The way to capture a more realistic snapshot of a system would be to have FRU–PIN links of varying strengths, representing the variation in how well people are known. The reason this has not been incorporated into the simulations is that we wish to demonstrate properties of the architecture per se rather than behaviour under any particular set of assumptions. However, it would be trivial to demonstrate that the model does not make this prediction under all but the simplest assumptions.

IAC predicts prosopagnosia is temporary (O'Reilly & Farah, 1999, p. 56). This assertion is based on the idea that FRU–PIN links can be strengthened indefinitely. There seems to be no good reason to make this assertion. In the standard Hebb-like learning rule used, the link update is a sigmoid function so that learning is bounded by the maximum possible link strength. There is no reason to change this in the lesioned net. So, one may get some link strengthening, but there is no need to think this will rise forever, or to its previous maximum. This is a well-known problem with Hebb updates, and is generally solved by bounding the learning with a sigmoid. To our knowledge, nobody has proposed a model with unbounded weight-changes, and we are not intending to do so. We therefore do not agree with this prediction.

Repetition priming should cross domains (O'Reilly & Farah, 1999, pp. 58–59). This is a topic on which we have recently published theoretical and empirical contributions (Cabeza, Burton, Kelly, & Akamatsu, 1997; Burton, Kelly, & Bruce, 1998) whose implications were discussed on p. 26 of our paper. For the reasons given there, in more recent versions of the IAC model the previous two-way links are re-cast as being separate links in each direction. Further, these links are not necessarily equivalent in weight. Experimental results have forced us to make the following alteration to the model of priming. We propose that link updates are made only in the direction of stimulus presentation. So, if a face is presented, only FRU to PIN links are strengthened. As there is no activation from NRUs to PINs (though there is some from PINs to NRUs) there will thus be no strengthening providing later name recognition priming. We note that the bidirectionality of FOV's connections does not allow a similar solution. This may therefore be a further source of differential prediction between the two models.

Studies in language processes

Gillian Cohen

Language processes can be distinguished by source and by modality. Language originating within the individual involves processes of production, and language originating from an external source requires processes of comprehension. Language processes are further distinguished according to modality into spoken language and written language. These distinctions correspond to speech (spoken production), writing (written production), listening (speech comprehension), and reading (written comprehension). Research in all four areas has been very extensive and this section is necessarily selective, sampling two of these domains, speech production and reading, and focusing on salient topics that are of particular interest within them. The selected topics are ones where there is ongoing debate and where both neuropsychology and connectionist modelling are yielding insights.

NEUROPSYCHOLOGY AND LANGUAGE

Cognitive neuropsychology has been especially useful in enriching our understanding of language processes. In normal adults language processes are fluent, rapid and, for the most part, covert and unconscious. The complex operations that are necessary to produce a spoken sentence or to read a written one can only be inferred. Speech production has often been studied by analysing the nature of the errors that are made or by measuring the time taken to produce sentences of varying complexity. Skilled reading is usually automatic and readers have little or no insight into how they have got from print to meaning. Investigation of reading processes also relies on errors and reaction times, on observing the

effects of distorting the written input, and on the pattern of eye movements as the print is scanned. Interpretation of these data is not straightforward and the models of speech and reading that are constructed are controversial.

Neuropsychology can help to resolve the controversies. The complex patterns of impaired performance that are exhibited by brain-damaged patients provide valuable evidence about the covert language processes that cannot be directly observed. The effects of brain injury are assumed to reflect the underlying organisation of these processes and give some indication of how they are sequenced. The modularity assumption is crucial for this reasoning (see p. 251). Modularity is generally considered to hold good for language at the macrostructure level, but the modularity of component operations of language processing at the microstructure level is more controversial. According to traditional theories of language processing, separate independent modules are involved at different stages and, on the basis of these theories, cognitive neuropsychologists have assumed that when one module is damaged the other modules may continue to function as normal. If this account is incorrect, and processes are interactive and non-modular, it is much more difficult to infer the organisation.

WORD RECOGNITION AND READING

Cognitive neuropsychologists studying dyslexia have argued that in brain-damaged patients the reading process breaks down in ways that reveal the component stages of normal reading and the way they are organised. Studies in this section focus on the reading of single words, where different types of dyslexia have been identified and related to existing models of word recognition. There are three main types of central dyslexia (as distinct from peripheral dyslexia in which the problem lies in the visual perception of the letters). These are surface dyslexia, phonological dyslexia, and deep or semantic dyslexia. In surface dyslexia the ability to map the visual form of the printed word directly onto its spoken name is damaged. This is known as the direct route to meaning, whereby a whole word is instantly recognised by the semantic system. In phonological dyslexia the ability to read a word by applying spelling-to-sound conversion rules is damaged. This is known as the indirect route to meaning, whereby the sound of the word is derived from the spelling-to-sound correspondence rules and the sound is recognised by the semantic system. In deep dyslexia there are multiple deficits. Most strikingly, access to the semantic system is impaired so semantic errors (e.g., "night" for "sleep") are typical. These patterns of impairment have been interpreted in terms of a traditional model of reading described by Parkin (1996). This model has separate modules identified as a visual lexicon which stores visual representations of words, a phonological module which stores grapheme-to-phoneme (spelling-to-sound) correspondence rules, and a semantic module which stores word meanings. Each type of dyslexia is characterised by a pattern of errors that is both predictable and explicable in terms of damage

to one of the modules or disconnection of a pathway between them. Note, however, that interpretations of the observed deficits rest on the assumption that language processing mechanisms consist of independent modular components, that the effects of damage are local and that undamaged components continue to function more or less normally.

These assumptions have been challenged by connectionist models in which language processes are nonmodular and interactive. These models have had considerable success in simulating intact human performance, and lesioning the models has been shown to mimic the deficits seen in patients. The modularity assumption has to be reconsidered in the light of these simulations and different interpretations have to be evaluated. This section includes discussion of conflicting explanations of dyslexia (Coltheart et al., Chapter 13; Hinton, Plaut, & Shallice, Chapter 14) and of the phenomenon of covert recognition of words (Mayall & Humphreys, Chapter 15). Covert recognition of words is similar to the covert recognition of objects and faces described in Section I. Patients may display knowledge of a word's meaning without conscious awareness and without being able to name the word overtly. Models that, like some patients, display covert recognition in the absence of overt recognition, have suggested alternative explanations for this phenomenon.

SPEECH PRODUCTION

Neuropsychological studies of patients with spoken language impairments have contributed similarly to our understanding of the processes involved in speech production. These patients display deficits that can be broadly classified into different types of dysphasia and linked to a model of speech production. Traditional theories of speech production have been modular and, as in the case of dyslexia, different deficits appear to reflect damage to different modules or levels within the speech production system. However, it must be emphasised that cases with "pure" deficits are relatively rare, most patients exhibit a mixture of deficits occurring at different levels in the system, and these are particularly difficult to interpret. In this area, too, the modularity assumption has been challenged. In Chapter 12 Martin et al. describe a case of deep dysphasia which they interpret in terms of an interactive model. Deep dysphasics have difficulty in repeating real words that they have just heard and make semantic errors (e.g., substituting "mouse" for "rat"). Martin et al.'s interpretation of this deficit is that activation of the semantic target word is not maintained effectively, whereas modular theorists make the less precise claim that deep dysphasia reflects damage to the semantic module. In Chapter 10, Marslen-Wilson and Tyler describe aphasic patients with Broca's type of agrammatic speech who showed interesting patterns of dissociations in understanding the grammatical inflections that mark plural and past tense forms. This evidence has been used to infer the nature of the underlying neural architecture.

DEVELOPMENTAL DISORDERS

Although cognitive neuropsychology has proved valuable in understanding acquired disorders of language (i.e., impairment resulting from damage to the mature system), its value in providing explanations for developmental disorders of language has been questioned by Bishop (1997). She points out that some of the basic assumptions of cognitive neuropsychology may not be true for the developing language system. Specifically, children typically display very complex patterns of associated impairments rather than highly selective deficits. Because the system is in the process of changing, a snapshot of the system at any one point in time may be misleading, and, in spite of the claim that modules are innate (Fodor, 1983), modularity may only be established as the system matures. The crux of this argument is that similar disruption can produce very different effects in a child and in an adult. An adult with fully developed syntactic, semantic, and reading skills can develop strategies to bypass damage at the stage of auditory analysis of spoken language. A child with damage at this stage may be unable to develop these skills. In developmental disorders clear-cut dissociations are rare: patterns of associated deficits are much more common and much more difficult to interpret theoretically. It is not surprising, therefore, that Chapters 13 and 14 focus on acquired dyslexia rather than developmental dyslexia.

MODELLING REHABILITATION

Modelling the effects of damage by lesioning neural networks is one thing: modelling rehabilitation is the other side of the coin. Linguistic impairment in brain-damaged adults is not necessarily static and may also, like developmental disorders, be in a process of dynamic change. The deficit may deteriorate or improve with or without therapeutic intervention. The causes of these changes are not well understood. In the study of speech production connectionist modellers are working closely with neuropsychologists and are beginning to shed some light on the process of rehabilitation. This is an exciting development which illustrates the way that the two approaches can be used in an integrated fashion that produces new insights. As well as modelling normal cognitive processes and the impaired performance that results from brain damage, connectionist models are being used to simulate the changes that occur during the process of rehabilitation.

Two kinds of recovery have been modelled within two different kinds of architecture. Spontaneous recovery has generally been modelled by interactive architectures (as in the recovery from deep dysphasia reported by Martin et al. in Chapter 12) and recovery that takes place by relearning has been modelled by back-propagation networks (e.g., Plaut, 1996). Once the network has "learned", most connectionist models represent a static system, but models of dynamic

processes are needed to simulate recovery, and can involve modification and reorganisation of the network. Modelling recovery is related to modelling the effects of lesions, because the underlying assumption is that the system moves from a high degree of lesioning to a less severe degree of lesioning as recovery proceeds. Recovery from brain damage is a complex multi-factorial process and theoretical understanding of the underlying mechanisms is weak. The concept of recovery is, in any case, unclear. A return to normal performance is not necessarily mediated by true recovery of function but may be by substitution of different means or by reorganisation of function. Cognitive neuropsychology has been more concerned with understanding the nature of the dysfunction that with the fine-grain dynamics of recovery. However, connectionist modelling has a potential contribution to make in this area and the use of neuro-imaging techniques is also proving informative.

Strikingly interesting findings have emerged. Plaut (1996) lesioned and then retrained a back-propagation model which associated orthographic inputs with semantic outputs. The degree of relearning depended on the site of the lesion. When semantic units had been lesioned, retraining produced better recovery than when the orthographic units had been lesioned. There was also more generalisation of the improvement to items that had not been specifically retrained. This finding mirrors the results with patients relearning to read words. The model of spontaneous recovery from deep dysphasia described by Martin et al. (Chapter 12) provides a possible explanation for the deficit and for the process of rehabilitation. Instead of retraining their network, they varied rate of decay and temporal interval to mimic changes in short-term memory function.

In general, this kind of connectionist modelling of recovery has potential implications for identifying what factors influence the degree of recovery, for generating prognoses, and for indicating the kind of therapy likely to be helpful. Nevertheless, modelling recovery is at an early stage and there are many limitations on it. The correspondence between model and neurology is loose and, to date, only very restricted aspects of language dysfunction are being modelled. Moreover, although models may succeed in discovering the principles that govern relearning in networks, these fail to take account of the pervasive and largely unexplained individual differences in recovery exhibited by patients.

CONNECTIONIST VS SYMBOLIC APPROACHES TO LANGUAGE

In cognitive psychology, information theory had an important impact on theories of memory and attention, and this approach was extended to the use of language. Structural linguists described language in terms of symbols manipulated by a set of rules. Syntax was considered as rules for combining the symbols for words (such as nouns, adjectives, verbs) or phrases (such as noun phrases and verb phrases). Similarly, semantics involved the application of combinatorial rules

to symbols standing for objects, events, and actions. Cognitive psychologists adopted this view of the psychological processes involved in the use of language, considering the mind as a symbol-manipulation machine, operating according to a well defined set of rules.

Connectionist modelling presented an alternative nonsymbolic approach to language. In 1986 Rumelhart and McClelland published an account of a connectionist model which, they claimed, demonstrated that it was not necessary to assume that language learning involved acquiring a system of symbolic rules. They suggested that invoking symbolic rules was merely a *descriptive* convenience. In so doing, Rumelhart and McClelland challenged the fundamental principles on which cognitive psychology had been built—viewing the mind as a symbolic, rule-driven system. Instead, they proposed that parallel, distributed processing (PDP) in associative networks might provide a better and inherently nonsymbolic explanatory framework for understanding cognitive and linguistic processes. They outlined examples of how connectionist models could be used to explain cognitive phenomena. Not surprisingly, many theorists working within the symbolic framework rejected Rumelhart and McClelland's claim that rules were merely a descriptive convenience. They pointed out that there were numerous aspects of linguistic and cognitive processing that the PDP approach failed to address, and that Rumelhart and McClelland's claims were merely promissory rather than being fully realised. Furthermore, they argued that specific connectionist models failed to account for the behavioural data adequately. Seidenberg (1994) has characterised this period as the "linguistics meets Frankenstein" era, during which theoretical linguists thought connectionism had nothing to contribute to understanding language. Many of the criticisms of early models have been met by later developments, but the issue of whether language learning and language use are symbolic, rule-based processes or whether connectionist models can offer an alternative account is still highly controversial and is reflected in the articles in this section.

One of the connectionist models targeted for criticism was Seidenberg and McClelland's (1989) model of reading aloud which is challenged by Coltheart et al. in Chapter 13. Another was Rumelhart and McClelland's (1986) model of past tense formation. In a lengthy critique of the past tense model, Pinker and Prince (1988) detailed a number of important flaws that undermined its claim to offer an account of the developmental sequence of past tense acquisition in young children, and argued convincingly that the model's behaviour did not, in fact, mimic the behaviour of children. Initially, these criticisms were viewed as undermining the PDP approach to language and cognition quite generally, and reinforced the view that the symbolic approach was correct. However, although the original model may have been incorrect in detail, more recent versions of a nonsymbolic connectionist model can, as Marchman argues in Chapter 9, do a good job of explaining the behavioural data.

THE MODULARITY ASSUMPTION: DUAL ROUTE VS SINGLE ROUTE MODELS

The modularity assumption is implicated in this controversy. Single route models are essentially nonmodular whereas dual route accounts imply that different modules are involved. Hence the single route versus dual route controversy is closely related to the debate about modularity. However, single route connectionist models of a particular function, such as word recognition, do not imply that the macro-level organisation of the brain is nonmodular, only that word recognition does not break down into separate independent modules at the micro level. Arguments for and against single and dual route models are presented in several articles in this section. The aim is to assess how far each type of model can simulate the performance of both intact and brain-damaged humans. But a successful simulation is not necessarily decisive and may not resolve the issue. It constitutes what has been called an "existence proof". That is, it shows that this is one possible way to perform the task, but not necessarily the one used by the human brain.

Single route and dual route accounts offer quite different explanations of the nature of the mental representations and processes underlying both reading and the learning of past tenses. They differ in two important respects. The first concerns the allocation of resources. In the case of past tense learning, the single route account assumes that regular and irregular verbs (for example, a regular form like jump/jumped or an irregular form like go/went) share the same processing resources. In a single route connectionist model, these shared resources are the network of connections that inflect the stem of the verb to produce a past tense. More or less all the connections in the network are involved in the inflection of both regular and irregular words. By contrast, the dual route account assumes that different processing resources are involved in the inflection of regular and irregular words. The past tenses of regular verbs are generated by rules: the past tenses of irregular verbs are learned as exceptions and reproduced from associative memory. These processes do not overlap.

In the case of reading, the single route account assumes that both regularly and irregularly spelled words (e.g., spot and yacht) are converted to sound for reading aloud by the same mechanism. The dual route theory includes two separate procedures, a visual route that matches the visual form of the word directly to its sound, and a second, phonological route that uses a system of rules specifying the spelling-to-sound correspondences. Regular words can be decoded by the phonological route because they conform to the rules, but irregular, exception words can only be read by the visual route. It is often assumed that single and dual route accounts have different implications for the localisation of processing in the brain. Single route accounts imply a shared location whereas dual route accounts imply separated locations for the mechanisms underlying the

processing of regular and irregular words. Although this is a perfectly reason-able interpretation of the two accounts, it is not the only one. If we interpret single and dual route accounts as *functional* descriptions of the processing re-sources involved rather than anatomical descriptions, then the implications for localisation in the brain are less obvious.

The second primary difference between the two accounts concerns the type of mental representation underlying regular and irregular words. Again, this applies to both the reading of regular and irregular spellings and to learning past tenses that are regularly or irregularly formed. Consider first the formation of past tenses. On the dual route account, a symbolic rule process takes care of the inflection of regular words and a rote memory process, often called *associat-ive* memory, takes care of the irregular words. The regular route is symbolic because it is impervious to the phonological content of the particular word stem: It simply adds an /ed/ to whatever word it encounters. The irregular route, in contrast, needs to pay attention to the phonological content of the word stem in order to identify whether the current word is a candidate for irregular inflection. Rather than applying a rule, it *associates* that particular word stem with its irregular past tense form. On the single route account, there is no such qualit-ative distinction between the type of mental process underlying regular and irregular inflection. Both regular and irregular words are associated with their past tense forms by the same type of process, namely associative memory. Cor-respondingly, in reading, the dual route model postulates a symbolic rule-based process that operates for regularly spelled words, and a nonsymbolic associative memory mechanism that learns to associate irregularly spelled words with their spoken form. The single route model handles both regular and irregular words by the same associative mechanism. To summarise, the single route connectionist models are interactive, associative, and nonmodular. The dual route accounts are independent, rule-based, and modular. Damaged brains tend to be interpreted in terms of dual route modular mechanisms: connectionist models instantiate single route nonmodular mechanisms.

MODELLING LEARNING

A particular strength of connectionist models lies in their ability to learn. They can learn to recognise words or to formulate past tenses, and the process of modelling reveals the nature of the "experience" that is necessary for learning to occur and the nature of the constraints that have to be built in. However, whether or not the learning mechanisms they employ are the same as for human learners is questionable. In most models a relatively small number of words are presented for hundreds or thousands of trials during the learning sequence. It is extremely unlikely that children need to experience a word for a similarly large number of times in order to learn it, and in many cases children do appear able to learn some aspects of language from a single exposure. Children are thought to be innately

programmed for language learning (Chomsky, 1965), possessing a set of built-in constraints that facilitate their acquisition of language, but there is no reason why models cannot simulate this biological endowment in so far as it is sufficiently well understood. Models of past tense learning have succeeded in replicating the pattern of children's development, but it is not clear whether the learning mechanisms are similar in child and machine.

Although connectionist models have had considerable success in simulating some aspects of human language learning and language use, they are clearly still at a very early stage and many questions are unanswered. Models of word recognition are typically limited to small vocabularies. Could the same mechanism be extended to handle the huge vocabulary of the skilled human reader? Most models are only capable of performing one task. Will it be possible to create a supermodel with linked sets of modules that can read and spell, understand and produce words, operate over long texts rather than just single words, and combine semantic, syntactic, and contextual information? Will models ever be able to demonstrate the full range and versatility of the human language user? Although we do not know the answers to these questions yet, critics of connectionist modelling have learned that they should never say never. Claims that models will "never" be able to do this or that tend to be disproved quite rapidly.

REFERENCES

Bishop, D. M. (1997). Cognitive neuropsychology and developmental disorders: Uncomfortable bedfellows. *Quarterly Journal of Experimental Psychology, 50,* 899–923.

Chomsky, N. (1965). *Aspects of the theory of syntax.* Cambridge, MA: MIT Press.

Fodor, J. A. (1983). *The modularity of mind.* Cambridge, MA: MIT Press.

Parkin, A. J. (1996). *Explorations in cognitive neuropsychology.* Oxford: Blackwell.

Pinker, S., & Prince, A. (1988). On language and connectionism: Analysis of a parallel distributed model of language acquisition. *Cognition, 48,* 21–69.

Plaut, D. (1996). Relearning after damage in connectionist networks: Toward a theory of rehabilitation. *Brain and Language, 52*(1), 25–82.

Rumelhart, D. E., & McClelland, J. L. (1986). On the learning of past tense verbs. In *Parallel distributed processing: Explorations in the microstructure of cognition, Vol. 2: Psychological and biological models* (pp. 216–271). Cambridge, MA: MIT Press.

Seidenberg, M. S. (1994). Language and connectionism: The developing interface. *Cognition, 50,* 385–401.

Seidenberg, M. S., & McClelland, J. L. (1989). A distributed developmental model of word recognition and naming. *Psychological Review, 96,* 523–568.

Speech production: Rules and rehabilitation

Kim Plunkett and Gillian Cohen

This section includes studies of learning, unlearning, and relearning. It focuses on two aspects of speech production. The first three articles are concerned with the acquisition of grammatical forms, that is learning the correct past tense form of verbs. Of course, past tenses are used in writing as well as speech, but almost all the research has been carried out on the spoken forms. This topic is important for a number of reasons. First, it exemplifies long-running theoretical controversies about the underlying mechanisms. These controversies centre on whether there are two different modular mechanisms, a symbolic, rule-based mechanism for regular forms and an associative one for irregular forms, or whether there is a single associative mechanism that can handle both forms. Second, this topic is particularly interesting because it has been investigated using a wide range of different methodologies: neuropsychology, connectionist modelling, and developmental psychology. Children learn to use past tenses correctly over a period of years and the errors they make while learning provide useful clues to the underlying mechanism. More clues are derived from case studies in which brain-injured patients have "unlearned" some past tense forms though they continue to use others correctly.

The second topic in this section is concerned with relearning. The process of recovery during rehabilitation (see pp. 248–249) is important both theoretically and practically. The study selected for inclusion in this volume as Chapter 12 describes a case of deep dysphasia, and shows how connectionist modelling can be used to simulate recovery and to identify the underlying cause of the breakdown. More generally, study of the different types of spoken language impairment, like the study of dyslexia, has shed light on the organisation of language processing. The pattern of selective deficits has provided evidence for models of speech production.

UNIVERSITY OF WINCHESTER LIBRARY

LEARNING PAST TENSE INFLECTIONS

Children's mastery of past tenses shows an interesting developmental pattern. Around the age of 2 years, children start by using the correct grammatical form of some irregular past tenses (e.g., slept or gave); then they go through a stage of over-regularising and make mistakes by applying the regular rule to the same irregular verbs (e.g., sleeped, gived); and finally they learn the correct form for both regular and irregular past tenses. This profile of development is often referred to as U-shaped development because children start out getting the grammatical inflection right, they then get it wrong, and finally they get it right again. A similar pattern is found in children's use of plurals.

Over-regularisations (like gived, or sheeps) were thought to reflect inappropriate use of a rule. Indeed, it is difficult to see how these errors could otherwise occur, as children do not hear such mistakes in their parents' speech. The U-shaped profile of development led researchers to interpret children's behaviour as indicating that the mental representation of inflections involved a dual route mechanism. One mechanism takes care of the irregular forms while the second mechanism embodies knowledge of the regular rule. The dual route theory of inflectional morphology prevailed unchallenged in cognitive psychology for well over 25 years. Indeed, no alternative accounts of this U-shaped behaviour gained acceptance until a radically new approach to the study of cognition surfaced in the mid-1980s. This approach was, of course, connectionism.

CONNECTIONIST APPROACHES

In 1986, Rumelhart and McClelland published their controversial paper on past tense morphology. The paper described a connectionist model that exploited only a single route associative mechanism, yet managed to capture a number of important features of children's acquisition of the English past tense. In particular, the model mimicked the U-shaped profile of development observed in young children. It started off inflecting irregular verbs correctly. The model then went through a phase when it over-regularised irregular verbs before establishing correct performance across the board. There were a number of features that made the model controversial. The most important was that the model did not use a symbolic rule to inflect the regular verbs. Instead of having two routes, a symbolic rule-based route for regular verbs and an associative route for irregulars, it used the same network of connections to inflect regular and irregular verbs alike—hence its characterisation as a single route model. On the single route account, there is no qualitative distinction between the type of mental process underlying regular and irregular inflections. Both regular and irregular past tenses are learned and retained by processes of associative memory.

EXPLAINING DISORDERS OF INFLECTION

There is another type of evidence, besides the pattern of normal development in children, that has the potential to offer important insights into the nature of the mental representations underlying inflectional morphology. The patterns of breakdown observed in individuals who have a language disorder affecting their inflectional systems may also reveal important clues as to the character of the underlying mental representations.

Dual route explanations

The hybrid character of the dual route model suggests clear-cut predictions about disorders in inflectional morphology, whether these are acquired or inherited. The separate and distinct pathways of the dual route account can, in principle, be subject to malfunction, either simultaneously or independently. Hence, it should be possible to observe individuals who suffer malfunction of the symbolic route while the associative route operates normally (i.e., they can inflect irregular words but not regular words) *and* to observe individuals who suffer malfunction of the associative route while the symbolic route operates normally (i.e., they can inflect regular words but not irregular words). A double dissociation of this kind is compatible with the idea that regular and irregular inflection are served by separate mental processes.

In Chapter 9 Marchman points out that double dissociations can be observed in inherited disorders of inflection. For example, children suffering from a disorder known as Specific Language Impairment (SLI) are sometimes reported as having difficulty inflecting regular verbs for past tense, while showing relatively normal behaviour as far as irregular past tense forms are concerned. In contrast, children suffering from Williams syndrome sometimes show the opposite pattern of impairment. They have difficulty inflecting irregular verbs for past tense but do not experience difficulty applying the regular inflection to verb stems. One interpretation of this pattern of deficits is that SLI children have an intact associative memory that enables them to inflect irregular words correctly, but suffer a malfunction of symbolic rule inflection. In contrast, William's children have an intact symbolic past tense rule, but a faulty associative memory. Note, however, Bishop's warnings about the interpretation of developmental deficits (p. 248).

Marslen-Wilson and Tyler have also reported a double dissociation between regular and irregular past tense processing in acquired language disorders (i.e., disorders resulting from brain injuries). They describe the results of a lexical decision task (where individuals have to decide whether a target stimulus is a real word or not) carried out with normals and aphasic patients. On some trials the target words were either regular or irregular verbs preceded by their past tense forms acting as a prime (e.g., jumped–jump or took–take). Normal subjects

showed effective priming (i.e., the prime word speeded up reaction times to the target) for both regular and irregular verbs. However, for some aphasic patients the pattern of results looked very much like a double dissociation between regular and irregular morphology. In some patients regular past tenses primed while irregulars did not. In other patients, irregular past tenses primed while regulars did not. The results are thus entirely compatible with a dual route model of inflectional morphology.

Single route explanations

According to the single route account the same processing resources are involved in the inflection of regular and irregular words, so any damage to these resources should affect both inflectional types simultaneously. We should not expect to observe dissociations between regular and irregular morphology.

However, Marchman describes a series of lesioning experiments that involve removing some of the hidden units from a single route, connectionist network trained on an inflectional process like the English past tense. The lesioning of hidden units is an attempt to mimic the loss of information processing resources that might cause the language impairments described earlier. However, instead of selective damage to qualitatively different processes (symbolic or associative), the lesioning experiments conducted by Marchman involved damaging processing resources of the same type (associative). Furthermore, the lesions damaged hidden units randomly. Her most important finding is that damage to a single route model can have differential effects on regular and irregular morphology. In particular, regular verbs take longer to recover from damage to the network than irregular verbs. Marchman also notes that the extent of recovery from damage depends on when the lesions are performed. By and large, regular verbs are particularly susceptible to damage during the later stages of training, whereas irregular verbs are relatively immune to lesions.

Given that regular and irregular verbs share the same processing route, how do the observed asymmetric effects of damage come about? The simple answer to this question is that the building blocks of the single route, the individual hidden units in the network, do not contribute equally to the processing of regular and irregular verbs. Some hidden units have a *greater* responsibility (but not an *exclusive* responsibility) for processing regular verbs than irregular verbs. Consequently, damage to those hidden units results in greater deficits in performance (and hence longer recovery times) for the regular verbs. Although such models are still considered to be single route, they do seem to blur the distinction between single and dual route models to some extent.

Marchman's lesioning experiments show that single route models of inflectional morphology can provide an explanation for dissociations between regular and irregular verbs. However, the dissociations reported are always in the direction of sparing of irregular words relative to regular words. Marchman does not

report any simulations in which regular words are spared relative to irregular words. In other words, there is no indication of a *double* dissociation in the single route model. The work on SLI children and William's syndrome children, as well as work with aphasic patients, indicates that double dissociations between regular and irregular morphology do occur, even though they may be quite rare. The single route account would, therefore, seem inadequate in accounting for the facts of the matter. In contrast, the dual route account offers a natural interpretation of these language disorders: separate and distinct computational processes underlie the inflection of regular and irregular verbs. These computational processes can malfunction independently of each other, thereby leading to the observed double dissociations.

Searching for double dissociations in a single route model

Marchman trained the network so that irregulars were presented to the network with a higher token frequency (i.e., more often) than the regulars. Furthermore, Marchman chose the irregular words to group together in phonologically coherent patterns. For example, all the verbs (like "hit") that do not change in the past tense end in a /t/ or a /d/. Marchman points out that the combined effects of token frequency and phonological coherence conspire to make the irregular verbs more robust to damage than the regulars (which have the lowest token frequency and no phonological coherence).

In the study described in Chapter 11 Juola and Plunkett examined the effects of lesioning the network for its performance on regular and irregular nouns and verbs. Unlike Marchman, they lesioned the network by targeting specific connections rather than randomly lesioning hidden units. Lesioning was carried out only on the trained networks. The results of their study were quite different from Marchman's. Juola and Plunkett found that irregulars were more susceptible to damage than regulars. This result in itself suggests that differences in the training regimes in the two studies were sufficient to cause the discrepancy. However, both factors, training regime and method of lesioning, may be playing a role.

Furthermore, Juola and Plunkett were able to identify double dissociations between regular and irregular verbs in their single route model. For a small minority of networks, performance on regular verbs was bad while performance on irregular verbs was good *in the same network*. For a larger (but still small) number of networks, performance on irregular verbs was bad while performance on regular verbs was good, again *in the same network*. How could such double dissociations occur in a single route model? The answer to this question is really the same as the answer to why single dissociations occur in the Marchman model. Responsibility for processing regular and irregular words is not equally divided between the connections in the network. If lesions target connections with primary responsibility for regular words, then regular words will suffer, or

vice versa. Note again that this is not the same as claiming that the network has *become* a dual route model because the great majority of connections are involved in the processing of both regular and irregular words (and, of course, there is no symbolic rule).

There is some difficulty in defining a double dissociation. A classic double dissociation is defined as occurring "when subject A performs poorly on task X but within the normal range on task Y, while subject B performs poorly on task Y but within the normal range on task X" but pure cases like this are hard to find. The problem lies in defining what is meant by "normal range". One solution is to offer a *statistical* definition of double dissociation measuring variation in performance across groups of subjects, in order to establish what constitutes normal or deviant performance. Ultimately, this method of defining double dissociations will involve some arbitrary decisions about the cut-off between normal and deviant performance.

It is apparent that both the dual route and the single route accounts can, in principle, explain the pattern of deficits found in developmental and acquired language disorders of inflectional morphology. In particular, each approach offers a different explanation of the source of double dissociations between regular and irregular words. How are we to decide which account is right? In the end, this matter must be decided on empirical grounds. Which approach best explains the available data and which approach makes the most accurate empirical predictions? We have seen that each account makes different predictions about the distribution of double dissociations in the population. The single route account predicts that individuals suffering a deficit in regular morphology will also suffer some deficit in irregular morphology. Only occasionally will the two inflectional types dissociate. The probability of finding a double dissociation will be even smaller. In contrast, the dual route model predicts that deficits in regular morphology need not co-occur with deficits in irregular morphology, or vice versa. Hence, dissociations between inflectional types should be relatively common in disorders of inflectional morphology and double dissociations should not be so hard to find as a single route account would predict. These contrasting predictions would seem to offer a clear-cut way to test the theories. Unfortunately, the issue is not so easy to resolve. Because of the time and effort involved in data collection with language-disordered patients, most of the work in this field is concerned with single case studies and these are few in number. Consequently, it is very difficult to get a picture of the overall distribution of deficits in the disordered population. We, therefore, need to turn to other sources of evidence.

When reporting the double dissociations between regular and irregular priming in their aphasic patients, Marslen-Wilson and Tyler noted that aphasics who did not exhibit priming by irregulars had suffered brain damage to temporal lobe regions of the brain roughly corresponding to Wernicke's area. Likewise, the aphasics who did not exhibit priming by regulars had suffered brain damage to frontal lobe regions of the brain roughly corresponding to Broca's area. Findings

from brain imaging studies (fMRI and PET scans) of normal subjects also indicate that Broca's area and Wernicke's area are implicated in the processing of regular and irregular morphology, respectively. These results fit well with the dual route account of inflectional morphology, if one assumes that each route is located in a different brain region. If Wernicke's area is interpreted as implementing the associative route and Broca's area is interpreted as implementing a symbolic route, the dual route account is entirely compatible with these findings.

However, single route theorists are not necessarily saying that the same brain location is involved in the processing of both regular and irregular morphology. Although in their models irregular and regular inflections share the same processing resources, it is not the case that they share all these resources evenly. Some hidden units and connections have greater responsibility for regular inflections than irregular inflections, and vice versa. Single route accounts would therefore expect to observe differential activity across brain regions for regular and irregular morphology.

APHASIA

Marslen-Wilson and Tyler's patients exhibited a particular kind of language disorder but there are many different kinds of aphasia. Traditional models of speech production (e.g., Levelt et al., 1991) envisage a sequence of distinct modules. Thus word production starts at the level of semantic representation; activation is transmitted to a phonological/morphological level sometimes called the speech output lexicon and then to a lower level where phonemic encoding takes place and finally articulation. Each stage is modular and informationally encapsulated. This type of model has been used to interpret speech errors (slips of the tongue) made by normals.

Types of aphasic disorder can also be explained in terms of damage affecting different stages in a sequence of processing of this kind. However, aphasic disorders are very wide-ranging and can affect almost every aspect of language comprehension and production, so that interpretation is not straightforward. Anomia is characterised by difficulty in finding the right word and may accompany difficulties with grammar and articulation. It can arise at the semantic level, sometimes affecting words for specific categories (see Chapter 1). Alternatively, anomia can arise at the level of the speech output lexicon leaving the semantic representation intact. Anomia tends to be more severe for words that are less frequent in the language and words that were acquired at a later age. Speech is classified as jargon aphasia when output is fluent but contains many neologisms (meaningless nonsense words). Typically, patients are not aware that they are talking nonsense. With this condition the semantic level appears intact, as patients can categorise words and pictures correctly, and the articulation level seems to be unimpaired because many words can be pronounced correctly. The problem has been identified as "derailment" at the phonological speech output level.

Deep dysphasia is diagnosed when patients have difficulty repeating real words. They tend to make semantic errors and are unable to repeat nonwords. There appears to be damage at the level of converting the auditory input of the spoken word to the phonological form for speech output. Other forms of aphasia are apparent when patients try to form sentences. Broca's aphasics produce "telegrammatic" speech which is essentially agrammatic, with short sentences lacking function words and inflections. Wernicke's aphasics speak fluently in well formed sentences that make little sense. The interpretation of these patterns of disorder is complicated because they are rarely "pure". Patients exhibit multiple impairments that are difficult to disentangle. Interestingly, some of the deficits shown by brain-damaged patients can be seen as exaggerations of the kind of slips of the tongue made occasionally by normal speakers. Most people have word finding difficulties at times. Semantic substitutions occur with a word of opposite meaning being substituted (e.g., hot for cold), and phonological errors may involve substitutions of similar sounding words (e.g., ghost for goat) or phoneme misordering as in Spoonerisms. A theoretical model is strengthened when it can encompass both the errors made by normal people and the impaired performance of the brain-injured.

Modular models of speech production have been challenged. Dell (1986) developed a localist interactive model which can also be applied to aphasic disorders. In this spreading activation model, processes are not sequential but are interactive, with activation passing back and forth bidirectionally between conceptual, syntactic, morphological, and phonological levels. This means that the semantic word selection stage may be influenced by phonological information, and phonological segment selection can be influenced by semantic information. Dell's model was developed to explain slips of the tongue, especially malapropisms which are phonologically related errors like *sheep* for *sheet*. Errors of this kind appear to reflect activation spreading from the phonological level to selection of the word and thus provide evidence for interactivity. Mixed errors in which target and substitute words are both semantically and phonologically related like *start–stop* are considered to be the result of convergence of information from both levels and so are also taken to support the interactive position. Dell's model has been used to explain jargon aphasia in terms of abnormally slow spread of activation between levels. Neologisms are produced because top-down semantic constraints operate too slowly and fail to influence the phonological level effectively. Alternatively, another connectionist account (Harley, 1993) has suggested that jargon aphasia is produced by damage to the inhibitory connections that should suppress competing words.

In Chapter 12 the study by Martin et al. employed an interactive architecture based on Dell's spreading activation model to simulate the spontaneous recovery from deep dysphasia shown by a patient, NC. He had extreme difficulty in repeating words and produced a distinctive pattern of errors. Martin et al. monitored his performance at several points along the path of recovery, and

hypothesised that he initially had an abnormally fast rate of decay of activation in auditory-verbal short-term memory and that this slowly returned to a more normal rate. As a direct test of this hypothesis they manipulated two factors in their model, decay rate and the temporal interval between input and output, and found that, in line with their hypothesis, the model reproduced NC's perform-ance. When decay rate was fast, or the temporal interval long, the model made few correct responses and many semantic errors, but performance improved as the decay rate was slowed down and the temporal interval reduced. Thus the computational model allows the dynamics of the spontaneous recovery process to be systematically investigated. To summarise, connectionist models have begun to have some success in identifying possible mechanisms underlying different types of aphasia and the course of recovery. Interactive models are beginning to challenge the modular accounts and offer alternative explanations for aphasic deficits.

REFERENCES

Dell, G. S. (1986). A spreading activation theory of retrieval in language production. *Psychological Review, 93*, 283–321.

Harley, T. A. (1993). Connectionist approaches to language disorders. *Aphasiology, 7*, 221–249.

Levelt, W. J. M., Schriefers, H., Vorberg, D., Meyer, A. S., Pechmann, T., & Havinga, J. (1991). The time course of lexical access in speech production: A study of picture naming. *Psychological Review, 98*, 122–142.

CHAPTER NINE

Constraints on plasticity in a connectionist model of the English past tense

Virginia A. Marchman
University of Wisconsin, Madison, USA

This paper investigates constraints on dissociation and plasticity in a connectionist model undergoing random "lesions" both prior to and during training. When networks were trained only on phonological encodings of stem-suffixed pairs similar to English regular verbs (e.g., *walk* → *walked*), long-term deficits (i.e., "critical period" effects) were not observed, yet there were substantive short-term effects of injury. When training vocabulary reflected the English-like competition between regular (suffixed) and irregular verbs (e.g., *go* → *went*, *hit* → *hit*), the acquisition of regular verbs became increasingly susceptible to injury, while the irregulars were learned quickly and were relatively impervious to damage. Patterns of generalization to novel forms conflicts with the assumption that this behavioral dissociation is indicative of *selective* impairment of the learning and generalization of the past tense rule, while the associative lexical-based mechanism is left intact. Instead, we propose a view of network performance in which the regular–irregular dissociation derives from a *general* reduction in the ability to find a single-mechanism solution when resolving the competition between two classes of mappings. In light of other models in which "regular" and "irregular" forms compete (e.g., Patterson, Seidenberg, & McClelland, 1989), as well as patterns of performance in normal and disordered English speakers (e.g., Pinker, 1991), two general implications are discussed: (1) critical period effects need not derive from endogenously determined maturational change, but instead may in part result from learning history in relation to characteristics of the language to be learned (i.e., entrenchment), and (2) selective dissociations can result from general damage in systems that are not modularized in terms of rule-based vs. associative mechanisms.

Journal of Cognitive Neuroscience 5:2, pp. 215–234 (1993).

INTRODUCTION

A traditional goal of aphasia research has been to outline the nature and organization of the mechanisms involved in language acquisition and processing by exploring how linguistic behavior is or is not altered by brain injury. For example, in the mature speaker/hearer, language abilities typically remain intact following injury to the right hemisphere.[1] Left-hemisphere injury, in contrast, is associated with a variety of deficits that are predictable, in general terms, on the basis of the affected brain areas. Anterior lesions are likely to result in a loss of fluent productive skills in conjunction with spared comprehension; posterior lesions are associated with impaired comprehension and lexical access skills, even though expressive fluency remains relatively intact. Observing linguistic behavior under less-than-optimal conditions like these has been viewed as a unique and potentially powerful source of insight into the neurological basis for language, as well as the character of linguistic systems in normal language users.

However, over the history of the field, it has become apparent that language outcome after brain injury can take a variety of forms in the mature speaker/hearer, some more easily predictable by lesion factors than others (Basso, Capitani, Laiacona, & Luzzatti, 1980; Damasio & Damasio, 1989). In addition, deviations from normal language functioning have been observed *without* known impairment in the brain areas typically associated with language, e.g., Specific Language Impairment (SLI) and Williams Syndrome (WS). Within a single lesion or syndrome group, profiles of language dysfunction are still quite heterogeneous. Several frameworks have been put forth to account for these profiles, varying in whether outcomes reflect the organization of the language faculty in sensorimotor (e.g., production vs. comprehension), linguistic (e.g., lexical semantics vs. grammar), modality- (e.g., functional vs. visual), or processing-based (e.g., automatic vs. controlled) terms. Even controlling for the wide array of artifacts that potentially confound the interpretation of dissociations (e.g., task factors and individual differences) (Shallice, 1988), many patterns of deficit do not appear to be consistent with any of these. Several cases have been discussed that display very specific (rather than system-wide) deficits that are apparently restricted to particular aspects of grammar (e.g., Miceli, Silveri, Romani, & Caramazza, 1989), the lexicon (e.g., Hart, Berndt, & Caramazza, 1985), or language processors (e.g., Tyler, 1988). Further, taxonomies derived from English-speaking subjects often lose their predictive power when applied to language behavior in languages such as Hebrew, Italian, or German (e.g., Bates, Friederici, & Wulfeck, 1987; Menn & Obler, 1990). Hence, identifying a set of core principles that underlie language in aphasic patients as well as normal speakers has, needless to say, proven to be a challenging enterprise. Some researchers have gone so far as to question whether there is any theoretical value at all in grouping subjects in terms of behavioral profile, opting for a single-subject or case-study approach (e.g., Caramazza, 1986; Miceli et al., 1989). [But see Bates, Appelbaum, & Allard

(1991), Bates, MacDonald, MacWhinney, & Appelbaum (1991), and Shallice (1988, 1991) for discussions of the validity and usefulness of group studies.]

Even in the face of this variation within and between individuals, languages, and syndromes, many studies remain consistent with the original goal—language breakdown yields strong insights into the underlying conceptual, and perhaps neurological, organization of the "normal" mind/brain. This enterprise is generally interpreted to be compatible with another prominent theoretical assumption, i.e., linguistic systems are decomposable into isolable subsystems or modules (Fodor, 1983; Pinker, 1991). Deficits in linguistic skill are assumed to reflect the inability of subpart(s) of the system to process information at the level of input and/or output. Hence, breakdown respects the boundaries of the components (or subcomponents) of the language faculty. As Tyler (1992) recently noted, there has also been a tendency to assume a one-to-one mapping between deficit and module—that is, as new behavioral profiles are identified, corresponding modules or submodules are created to account for each new particular syndrome. Debates primarily surround which characterizations are the most explanatory (e.g., functional vs. linguistic), as well as the degree of detail with which specific deficits should map onto specific brain areas. Nevertheless, dissociations in selective deficit and sparing, and more specifically double dissociations,[2] are seen as one of the most powerful pieces of evidence that the language faculty represents information within domain-specific systems of encapsulated modules.

Focusing on the domain of past tense morphology in English, Pinker and colleagues (Pinker, 1991; Gopnik, 1990; Gopnik & Crago, 1991) recently appealed to dissociations as support for a modular, dual-mechanism model of language. Because regular and irregular forms have different representational requirements, language abilities are decomposable into a rule mechanism that is responsible for generating suffixed regular verb forms (e.g., *walk* → *walked*), and an associative mechanism that stores pairs of irregular stems and past tense forms independent of the suffixation process. Regular verbs do not share surface features with other class members, whereas irregular stems demonstrate within-class similarity in the features that are predictive of the type of mapping they undergo. For example, a few irregular verb stems in English are arbitrarily related to their past tense forms (e.g., *go* → *went*), however, the majority form clusters according to the type of vowel change that they undergo from stem to past (e.g., *ring* → *rang*; *sing* → *sang*), or do not change at all if the stem ends in a dental consonant (e.g., *hit* → *hit*; *put* → *put*).

Pinker (1991) cites two acquisition and neuropsychological phenomena in support of the hypothesis that regular and irregular verbs are distinct. First, it is a classic finding that regular and irregular verbs follow different trajectories of acquisition in normally developing children, with irregulars having some advantage early in learning. While this developmental dissociation could reflect separate underlying mechanisms, single-mechanism associative systems (that are similar, although not identical, to that proposed by Pinker) can offer an alternative account

of several past tense acquisition and processing phenomena (e.g., Daugherty & Seidenberg, 1992; Plunkett & Marchman, 1990, 1991; Rumelhart & McClelland, 1987). For example, networks trained on English-like languages are quite successful at learning both regular and irregular past tense forms, especially when vocabulary size expands incrementally (Plunkett & Marchman, 1990).[3] Further, like children learning English, networks produce systematic errors at various points in training, yet can appropriately generalize to novel forms (e.g., *wug* → *wugged*) depending on the size of the training set and learning history. Errors result from the over-application of the suffix to an irregular stem (e.g., *go* → *goed*), as well as irregularizations (e.g., *mend* → *mend*). In these systems, between-class differences in acquisition derive from between-class differences in input characteristics (rather than the structure of the processor), such as token frequency (i.e., number of times an individual stem-past tense form is seen during an epoch of training), type frequency (i.e., number of exemplars in each class), and phonological predictability (i.e., the degree to which the class is predictable by the presence or absence of phonological features).

As a second phenomenon, Pinker notes the contrasting behavioral profiles of subjects with SLI and WS. In a recent Gopnik and Crago (1991) study, several members of a family reported to be afflicted with a form of SLI (originally discussed by Gopnik, 1990) appear to be selectively impaired in their ability to mark tense using the regular past tense suffix, while their ability to store and retrieve irregular past tense forms is seemingly intact, compared to unaffected family members.[4] Gopnik and Crago (1991) state that the SLI subjects demonstrate an inability to "know that individual instances must be seen as evidence for the construction of paradigms that encode morphological regularities; (yet) they appear to have a learning mechanism that sees each word as an independent item that must be learned and entered into a lexicon that specifies its grammatical properties and meaning" (p. 47).

Children with WS are reported to display an opposite profile (Bellugi, Bihrle, Jernigan, Trauner, & Dougherty, 1990). In Pinker's terms, subjects with WS retrieve lexical items from an associative store in a deviant fashion, however, their ability to utilize the rule-governed aspects of language is intact. The latter is evidenced by the tendency for some of these children to overgeneralize irregular past tense forms at a higher-than-expected rate.[5]

Taking the reported profiles of the two populations at face value, a double dissociation in "rule-based" vs. irregular past tense morphology is observed. And, it is clear that Pinker has adopted aphasiology's assumption that such behavioral dissociations comprise unfaltering evidence for the existence of separate, modular, and encapsulated neural systems within the domain of language. As he states:

> because [the model] categorically distinguishes regular from irregular forms, the rule-association hybrid predicts *that the two processes should be dissociable from virtually every point of view*. With respect to implementation in the brain, because regular and irregular verbs are subserved by different mechanisms, *it should be*

possible to find one system impaired while the other is spared. The predictions can be tested with methods ranging from . . . the study of child development to the investigation of brain damage and genetic effects. (p. 532, emphasis added)

Heeding lessons from studies of brain injury, it may be appropriate to exercise caution in interpreting dissociations in this manner (Shallice, 1988, 1991). First, considerable evidence suggests that the character of acquired aphasia, in particular the relationship between brain injury and behavioral outcome, is qualitatively different in children than in adults. It is a classic finding that brain injury is considerably more devastating for adults than children, at least in terms of linguistic performance (Lenneberg, 1967). Of course, some adults do show considerable recovery of language functioning after specific lesions, and at the same time, there is evidence for subtle and persistent effects of brain injury at all ages (e.g., Aram, 1988; Woods & Carey, 1979). A wide array of factors have been seen to contribute to a child's potential for recovery, including age at injury, size/extent of damage, lesion location, and so on (see, for example, papers in Pavao-Martins, Castro-Caldas, Van Dongen, & Van Hout, 1991). Nevertheless, it is generally accepted that children who experience brain injury during the course of acquisition display a degree of plasticity that is observed only rarely in the mature speaker/hearer (e.g., Woods & Teuber, 1978), regardless of lesion factors.

Further, the neurological bases of language appear to be configured in a different fashion (or to a different degree) in the child compared to the adult. For example, several studies have noted the impact of right-hemisphere injury on grammatical abilities in children (Aram, Ekelman, & Whitaker, 1986, 1987; Riva & Gazzaniga, 1986), and there is little evidence for classic patterns of breakdown emerging from lesions in anterior vs. posterior brain regions when brain injury occurs in the pre- or perinatal periods [i.e., prior to any (substantive) language learning] (Thal, Marchman, Stiles, Trauner, Aram, Nass, & Bates, 1991). It appears that the behavioral consequences of most types of brain injury undergo change across the course of development. Yet, the long-term potential for recovery tends to become more constrained outside the "critical period" for language development.

What developmental processes are responsible for changes in the relationship between brain mechanism and language functioning? Why do linguistic systems generally (although not always) demonstrate critical period effects, losing plasticity across the course of acquisition? One possibility is that acquisition is guided by an endogenously determined, maturationally defined set of guidelines which constrain the brain's organization of linguistic abilities. In the case of brain injury, the maturational status of the organism places limits on the ability of the brain to reorient to linguistic input by, for example, constraining the degree to which (1) intact resources are recruited for tasks that were previously carried about by the injured brain area (functional reorganization), and/or (2) intact mechanisms are recruited to solve problems that were previously solved in a different manner (substitution of function).

Although it is not necessary, the view that critical period effects derive primarily from maturationally triggered changes in brain function/structure typically goes hand-in-hand with a modular view of the language faculty of the sort posited by Pinker. The division between, for example, rule-based and associative processes is seen to be maturationally and hence genetically predetermined, developing independently of environmental input (Pinker, 1991). In the hybrid view, neither a rule-based nor an associative system is sufficient and both are necessary, with each mechanism considered to have a unique genetic and neurological basis. In sum, these patterns of dissociation, as well as critical period effects and differences in postinjury outcome, are often attributed to the maturational factors controlling the course of acquisition (e.g., Newport, 1990).

A second body of research relates to the link between language breakdown and the modular status of the language faculty and the appeal to maturational factors in order to constrain that modular organization. Specific and selective patterns of deficit and sparing (similar to those observed in research in aphasia and language disorders) can be derived within systems that are *not* explicitly organized in a modular fashion (see Shallice, 1988 for discussion). Indeed, several connectionist models have already demonstrated that behavioral dissociations need not mirror the explicit componential structure of the underlying mechanisms and processes (Farah & McClelland, 1991; Hinton & Sejnowski, 1986; Hinton & Shallice, 1991; Mozer & Behrmann, 1990; Patterson, Seidenberg, & McClelland, 1989; Plaut, 1991; Plaut & Shallice, 1991; Wood, 1978). In connectionist models, dissociable subcomponents of a task are not exclusively defined with respect to their mechanism or content, but instead gain their structure via the patterns of interconnections over the course of learning. Information is distributed across the units and layers in the network in a highly redundant manner, and hence units can be seen to share, rather than compartmentalize, resources.[6] Such models illustrate that dissociations in output can arise *even when system architecture or patterns of connectivity are not explicitly modular.* If behavioral dissociations provide support for the modular organization of the mind/brain only to the extent that such patterns do not (and cannot) arise in a nonmodular system (Shallice, 1988), these models suggest that patterns of behavioral sparing and deficit after brain injury and the existence of certain syndromes of language disorders are not necessarily evidence for the modular character of the language faculty.

Of course, it might be argued that connectionist models are *implicitly* modular with respect to the particular pattern of breakdown observed. Learning in these nets may be nothing more than the "partitioning" of the task, implemented as the dedication of sets of hidden units to various subparts. As such, networks come to structure themselves in terms of the subcomponents that necessarily constrain successful task performance. To the extent that resulting partitions map onto particular modular views, the organization of the network would be functionally equivalent (at least not different) in principle, to systems in which

such a task decomposition is achieved via constraints on information-flow or representational format (McCloskey, 1991).[7] For example, if a single-mechanism model is incapable of achieving an adequate solution to the English past tense problem unless it represents the qualitative difference between generalization via rules and lexically based association, then one could argue that learning requires explicitly demarcating the differences between regular and irregular forms. Further, a dissociation in the behavior of regular and irregular verbs after injury would merely reflect a selective deficit in one of the component mechanisms provided by the hybrid, dual-mechanism hypothesis.

The studies in this paper seek to demonstrate that behavioral dissociations in regular and irregular past tense forms can be observed within a single-mechanism connectionist system. In addition, it is proposed that the dissociations do not reflect a selective loss of the network's ability to generalize to novel forms vs. to store and retrieve individual lexical items. In light of previous investigations of the English past tense (Rumelhart & McClelland, 1987; Plunkett & Marchman, 1990, 1991; Hare & Elman, 1992) as well as other domains in which mapping types are placed in competition (e.g., Seidenberg & McClelland, 1989), we argue that a strong distinction between regularity and irregularity need not be built into the system architecture in order to account for dissociations in both the learning and breakdown of language abilities.

Before turning to these studies, one last comment is necessary regarding the differences between connectionist approaches and traditional or hybrid models with respect to the appeal to maturational processes to account for critical period effects. As mentioned above, it is traditionally assumed that loss of plasticity is the result of endogenously determined changes in the ability of brain tissue to reorient to different categories of linguistic input. In the absence of constraints deriving from a maturational blueprint, one must appeal to factors related to the learning process itself to account for critical period effects. In backpropagation connectionist nets, learning is the process of configuring a weight-space, encoded in the interconnections between the layers of units, in such a way that the error between the system output and the teacher signal is minimized. Via gradient descent, the net continues to reduce error throughout training. For most training sets, there is a limited class of successful solutions (i.e., those configurations of the weight matrix that conform to the constraints in the input) that is flexible and robust enough to tolerate variability in the ultimate structuring. Studies have shown that the nature of the input set and training regimen has a tremendous impact on the ability of the net to structure (and restructure) that weight space. For example, input parameters may be more or less prone to the establishment of local minima from within which the network finds it difficult to escape. Under conditions of damage, the net may find the old configuration altered and suddenly inadequate, and it must reorganize the weight matrix to support another solution. Plasticity would be observed only to the extent that the net is not entrenched in a particular solution from which it would be too "costly" to

reorganize. In this sense, it is *the act of language learning* itself that constrains the ability of the system to recruit new resources for solving linguistic problems.

Clearly, maturation and entrenchment due to learning must both be involved in constraining plasticity in human children and adults. Yet, the following classic question is worth asking: To what extent is the loss of plasticity and/or changes in the selective patterns of sparing and deficit attributable to maturationally determined changes in brain capacity/mechanism vs. an inflexible organization of resources as a function of quality and quantity of experience? In connectionist models, unlike in children, we are able to pull these two factors apart. In most cases, modelers adopt a "hands-off" approach, allowing the network to dictate its own resource-availability schedule. However, an experimentalist does have direct control over how and when resources can be utilized by imposing changes in the availability of connections or units, mimicking the effects of maturationally determined changes in brain organization (e.g., "sprouting" or "pruning" of synapses). The modeler may also systematically reduce resources that are available to the network by "lesioning" connections from the input to the hidden units, thereby rendering those units inoperative. Studies using this technique have demonstrated that systematic losses in behavior need not be isomorphic with the underlying modular structure of the processing mechanism.

In this paper, we explore a connectionist model of language learning and break-down, focusing on (1) the relationship between behavioral outcome and the modular or nonmodular organization of the language faculty, and (2) the role of learning and entrenchment in accounting for critical period effects in the ability of systems to relearn after injury. More specifically, we investigate the short- and long-term effects of "brain lesions" on the acquisition of the English past tense. In Study I, networks are exposed to sets of mappings similar to the class of English regular verbs. This study assesses the ability of these networks to learn a morphological system that is homogeneous and highly predictable, and serves to establish baseline performance for the regulars. In Study II, the vocabulary is modified to be analogous to the entire system of English past tense morphology, and the network must learn past tense forms for regular, as well as three classes of irregular verbs. Hence, we compare the learning and relearning of various types of morphological mappings in supportive vs. competitive contexts. To assess the ability of the networks to abstract and represent general patterns in ways that are productive, we also examine generalization to three types of novel forms.

All models adopt a developmental perspective. Networks are lesioned both prior to any learning (i.e., "prenatal") and at several points during the acquisition phase (i.e., "postnatal"). Apart from the lesioning procedure, computational re-sources are constant across the course of development. The nets do not undergo any endogenously determined changes in resource availability that might impact on the trajectory of learning/recovery or the types of errors that are produced. Thus, these studies seek to explore how prior learning constrains the immediate and chronic effects of injury in systems that are not undergoing maturational change. It is hoped that the hypotheses generated by these series of simulations

will inform possible constraints on the organization of the language faculty, and suggest areas of future research in normal and aphasic populations, in particular regarding the interpretation of behavioral dissociations.

STUDY I: REGULAR MAPPINGS ONLY

Results

Performance on the training set.   Figure 1 outlines the course of acquisition in networks learning a vocabulary of 433 regular stem-past tense mappings. Trajectories across 25 epochs are presented for intact networks (baseline), as well as networks experiencing 2, 11, 22, 33, and 44% lesions. Focusing first on the intact condition (darkest line), it is clear that this task is quickly and easily mastered. Each of the five baseline networks achieved 100% performance well before training was halted. The steepness of the trajectory indicates that the majority of the learning was accomplished during the first one-third to one-half of training. Over 90% of the items were output correctly by the eighth epoch of training by each network.

Figure 1 also presents learning trajectories in networks undergoing lesions of various sizes prior to the onset of training. Note that the more substantive the lesion, the less steep and less rapid the rate of learning. These data suggest that, in this task, it is the course of acquisition rather than the final level of performance that is affected by amount of initial resources. This relationship between

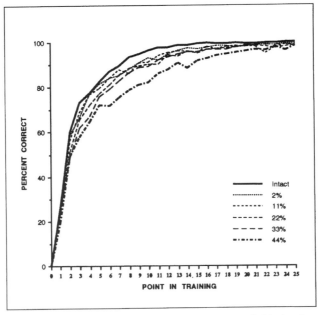

Figure 1. The acquisition of regular verbs in intact and "prenatally" lesioned networks.

lesion size and developmental trajectory can also be expressed as average performance across the 25 epochs: a high average performance is indicative of a steep learning curve, whereas dampened learning is reflected in a lower overall performance averaged across the 25 epochs. Intact networks averaged a relatively high average of 89% correct. In contrast, lesioned networks demonstrated lower average levels of performance, bearing some relationship to extent of damage (2% lesion, 85.1%; 11%, 84.6%; 22%, 83.5%; 33%, 82.9%; 44%, 79.1%). However, a main effect of lesion size only approaches significance using a within-subjects ANOVA [$F(4, 16) = 2.9, p < 0.06$].

Prenatal injury had little effect on the long-term potential to master the regular mappings within the allotted training period. All networks achieved a high level of performance (over 98%), regardless of the sheer amount of "innate" resources available [$F(4, 16) = 0.5$, n.s.]. In general, initial availability of resources does not appear to be related to learning over the long term, but may impact on the exact shape of the learning trajectory. Variations in endowed capacity are likely to play a role in determining the rate at which the systematicities inherent in the set of regular mappings are assimilated.

The steep and rapid course of learning is also evident when examining mean proportion change in performance for each epoch of training. In the intact networks, these nets mastered an average of 25% of the mappings after a single sweep through the training set. Substantive learning also occurs between the first and second epochs of training, as indicated by an improvement of approximately 125%. Performance drastically decelerates over the next few epochs, gradually but steadily approaching ceiling from epoch 5 throughout the remainder of training. This measure can also be used to examine the impact of a lesion on the ability to output appropriate past tense forms measured immediately postinjury. Across the 14 lesion conditions, acute effects are systematically related to the extent of damage [$F(14, 56) = 24.9, p < 0.001$]. However, the *absolute* character of this effect varies with amount of training. For example, early in training, when mappings are being learned at a rapid rate, a sudden reduction in resources is not manifested as a net "loss" in performance—progress is simply slowed down. Lesion size determines the degree to which learning is slowed, but in all cases, the first epochs of training result in positive gains regardless of extent of injury. In contrast, lesions later in training have a clear and observable *negative* impact on performance, with proportional losses in performance increasing for late-occurring lesions. For example, whereas lesions at epoch 2 result in a slight drop in percent correct, on average ($M = -1.8\%$), lesions at epoch 10 resulted in a much greater decrement ($M = -16.5\%$). This relationship is statistically reliable, most importantly, even for those lesions occurring at epoch 4 or later when the majority of the mappings have already been learned. A significant main effect of lesion timing on performance change during this period is noted [$F(14, 56) = 27.01, p < 0.001$], and interacts with lesion size across this latter part of the training [$F(56, 224) = 4.36, p < 0.001$].

In sum, the immediate consequences of damage are related to amount of previous training; however, long-term potential for recovery is independent of size and timing of injury. All networks, regardless of injury status, demonstrate a remarkable ability to master this set of regular mappings. The only exception was that final performance was slightly lower in the 44% lesions ($M = 95\%$) vs. the other lesion sizes ($M = 99.3\%$), resulting in a significant main effect of lesion size on final outcome [$F(4, 16) = 3.84, p < 0.03$]. This effect was identical regardless of whether the lesion occurred early or late in training [$F(14, 56) = 1.2$, n.s.].

Discussion

All networks exhibited considerable plasticity and demonstrated the ability to learn the set of regular mappings during the training period. Nevertheless, the nets were not completely immune from the effects of injury. First, amount of prenatal resources determined the shape of the learning trajectory. Even though all nets ultimately achieved almost-perfect mastery of the task, greater resources enabled more substantive advances during each epoch of training, especially early on. Second, larger and later lesions had a consistently more devastating acute impact on performance. This effect *continued* to increase in severity even after the majority of the mappings (> 80%) were mastered. Consistent with an entrenchment view, then, the weight matrix became increasingly susceptible to injury across training, even though only very small improvements in performance were observed at the behavioral level.

Clearly, the task of mastering a set of regular mappings is fairly simple for these networks, and is not sufficiently representative of the complexities of linguistic systems to allow a realistic comparison to human acquisition and processing. Nevertheless, it is important to keep these baseline results in mind as we train on a more realistic vocabulary comprised of both regular and irregular verbs. In Study II, the network, like the child, must resolve the competition between regular and irregular mappings, learning to form the past tense of some stems by appending a suffix, while others require a vowel change, identity map, or an arbitrary reconfiguration. The items contained in the regular class, as well as network and training parameters, are virtually identical in the two studies. Hence, differences in performance are attributable only to the changes in composition of the language to be learned.

STUDY II: REGULAR AND IRREGULAR VERBS

Results

Performance on the training set. Figures 2a and b present trajectories of learning for irregular and regular verbs, respectively, in intact and lesioned networks. Focus first on the solid dark lines representing acquisition when all resources are available at all points in training. Note that the course of learning

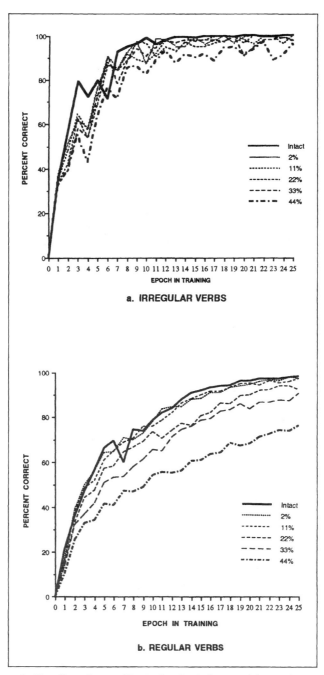

Figure 2. The effect of competition on learning in intact and damaged networks.

is different for the two classes of stems. Irregular mappings (Figure 2a) are learned quickly, with approximately four-fifths of the forms mastered within the first few sweeps through the training set. Performance reaches near-ceiling shortly after epoch 7, and only slight improvements observed with each subsequent epoch of training. Perfect performance is achieved by each of the nets well within the allotted time. The steep learning trajectory is confirmed by the high level of performance averaged across the training period ($M = 90.6\%$).

In contrast, Figure 2b indicates that the learning of regular verbs follows a shallower and less drastic developmental course, extending over a greater portion of training (average $M = 79.3\%$). While very high overall performance is ultimately achieved ($M = 98.2\%$), trajectories are dampened when regular verbs must compete for resources with irregular forms. Recall that the average performance was considerably higher in Study I (89%) *when the same set of regular mappings is learned in isolation*. A significant main effect of verb class on average network performance confirms that regulars and irregulars follow different learning trajectories [$F(1, 3) = 2763.3, p < 0.001$]. This result replicates the effects of the competition between regular and irregular forms previously demonstrated using slightly different vocabulary configurations in Plunkett and Marchman (1991). More importantly, however, is the similarity of this pattern to the developmental dissociations noted in children. It is the less representative, less homogeneous, yet more frequent class (i.e., irregulars) that has the early advantage (Cazden, 1968; Marchman & Bates, 1994; Pinker, 1991).

Figure 2a and b also outlines learning in networks experiencing a reduction in resources prior to the onset of training. Looking first at the irregulars (Figure 2a), learning is somewhat dampened in the lesioned ($M = 82.6\%$) compared to the intact nets ($M = 90\%$, see above), and a systematic relationship between lesion size and average performance is observed [$F(4, 12) = 14.7, p < 0.001$]. Interestingly, the effect of injury is more pronounced for items in the regular class (Figure 2b). Average performance is 75% across all damage conditions (compared to 79% in the intact), and the largest lesions reduce average performance to about 65% across the period. Again, a significant main effect of lesion size is observed [$F(4, 12) = 41.5, p < 0.001$]. Comparison of the two sets yields a significant lesion size by verb class interaction [$F(4, 12) = 55.76, p < 0.001$], confirming that trajectories for regular verbs are more vulnerable than those of the irregulars. Prenatal reductions in resources affect the course of learning in the two classes of verbs differentially in this single-mechanism competitive system.

When injury occurs during the course of training, the potential to master the training set within 25 epochs of training is again only marginally impaired for the irregular verbs in any of the lesion conditions. Averaging across all lesion sizes and times, long-term performance on the irregulars drops slightly to 98.4% (from 100%). Contrary to an entrenchment view then, late lesions do not limit the potential for recovery of this aspect of the language any more or less than early lesions. The relationship between timing of lesion and final performance

approaches statistical significance [$F(14, 42) = 1.77, p < 0.08$], but no interaction between size and timing is found. Hence, drops in final performance are only attributable to the fact that large lesions, regardless of when they occur, are likely to have a greater impact on recovery than smaller lesions [$F(4, 12) = 4.8$, $p < 0.02$]. The effect of lesion size observed here is consistent with models of other linguistic systems using a similar technique (Plaut, 1991).

A different pattern emerges when we examine recovery of regular mappings under the various conditions of injury. Here, damage has a considerable effect on long-term recovery as a function of both size of lesion [$F(4, 12) = 19.6$, $p < 0.001$] and timing of injury [$F(14, 42) = 2.1$, $p < 0.04$]. Compared to the intact condition which achieved 98% final performance, *any type* of brain injury results in an 8 to 10% reduction in the ability of these networks to master the regular verbs in the training set within 25 epochs. However, the consequences of injury were most clearly felt when the injury involved 33% ($M = 87.3\%$) and 44% ($M = 74.7\%$) of the resources available to the network. Again, large lesions were more devastating than small lesions, on average.

Interestingly, especially in networks with extensive damage, a monotonic decrease is observed in the ability of these networks to master the regular verbs within the allotted training time as a function of time of lesion ($r = -.35$ for large lesions). That is, unlike the pattern observed for the irregulars, the recovery of regular mappings became more limited as lesions occurred later in training. To explore this trend further, we divided the time course of training into three major developmental periods: early (Epochs 0 to 4), middle (epochs 5 to 9), and late (epochs 10 to 14). For lesions involving 33% of the hidden units, early lesions limited long-term recovery to 89.2% of the items, mid-occurring lesions resulted in 87.8% recovery, and late lesions restricted performance to only 85% [$F(2, 6) = 6.4, p < 0.03$]. A similar, but even more dramatic pattern is observed for the 44% lesions, with early lesions resulting in 77.2% final performance, middle lesions 74.8%, and late lesions allowing approximately 72% mastery by the end of training [$F(2, 6) = 6.3, p < 0.03$]. No significant decrement in performance was observed for networks experiencing small lesions (early, 96.0%; mid, 96.3%; late, 96.0%). Hence, it is the *interaction* of size and timing of injury that best accounts for this pattern [$F(2, 6) = 7.32, p < 0.03$]. Recall that this performance is clearly different from that observed for the irregular mappings. For those mappings, early, middle, and late lesions only barely disrupted the recovery of the overwhelming majority of the patterns ($M = 98.1\%$, $SD = 2.0$), regardless of size.

Of course, it is possible, and perhaps likely, that the remainder of the regular mappings will be learned eventually if training were allowed to continue. A strong demonstration of critical period effects would require that learning be *impossible* regardless of the amount of continued training. Nevertheless, these simulations do demonstrate that the quantity of prior experience can *alter* the nature of the recovery process for a subset of the patterns in this language. First,

recall that these networks were capable of learning the identical set of regular mappings in isolation under all lesion conditions (Study 1). Second, when the *identical reduction of resources* occurs prior to the onset of training (Figure 2b), recovery is evident throughout the period with 83% mastery attained by the end of 25 epochs. Thus, the same injury has different long-term consequences depending on the "age" of the network. Yet, network "age" is not characterized by endogenously determined changes (either qualitative or quantitative) in the resources available to the network to solve the problem. Rather, we propose that late lesions yield less extensive recovery over the course of training because the nature of the learning process is the dedication of resources to a problem solution (i.e., a particular configuration of weight-space). Limited recovery results from configurations that have become too costly to alter after injury as training continues.

Yet, this monotonic decrease in recovery may be a function not of entrenchment, but of a corresponding monotonic decrease in the amount of training that the networks receive after injury. While this confound cannot account for the dissociation that was observed between regular and irregular forms, it is true that nets undergoing lesions later in training receive fewer exposures to the data set, and hence have fewer opportunities to find a solution that is representative of the entire set of mappings, compared to networks undergoing lesions early in life. To investigate this possibility, we examined performance averaged over 10 epochs postlesion for 14 developmental periods. Figures 3a and b present these results for the irregular and regular verbs, respectively. Note first that for intact networks (dark line), about 80% of the irregular mappings are mastered in the first 10 epochs of training (epoch 0 to epoch 10). Between epochs 6 and 7, for example, virtually 100% performance is achieved for every 10-epoch period after about the middle of training (e.g., epochs 6–16, 7–17, and so on). Under lesion conditions, a similar, though slightly depressed pattern is found for all lesion sizes. That is, consistent with the data reported above, larger lesions affect the steepness of the trajectory, but analogous gains are made on the irregular items in each of the developmental periods for all networks.

Not unexpectedly, Figure 3b indicates that learning trajectories are more drawn out for the regular compared to the irregular mappings. For example, only 60% of regular verbs are acquired in the first 10 epochs, and asymptotic performance is not reached until the end of training. Further, note that lesions of all sizes result in considerable delays in the rate of acquisition, similar to the pattern observed in Figure 2b. For example, a 2% lesion at epoch 1 reduces gains within the first 10 epochs to less than 60% of the data set; a 44% lesion limits learning even further to only 41% of the regular mappings. More relevant to the issue at hand, however, is that the relationship between lesion size and performance *diverges* as lesions occur later in the course of training. The difference in the impact of a small versus a large lesion is greater later in the life than if that same lesion had occurred prior to a considerable amount of training. Thus, controlling

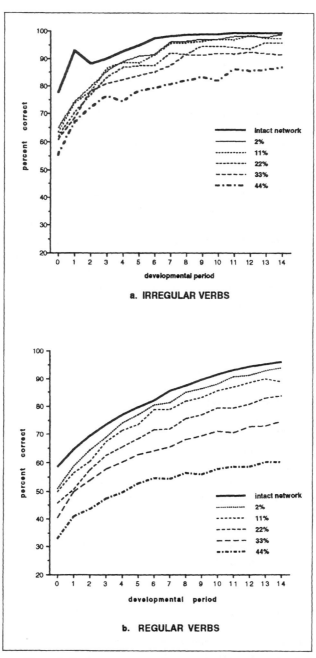

a. IRREGULAR VERBS

b. REGULAR VERBS

Figure 3. Performance averaged across 10 epochs postlesion.

for length of exposure to the training set, it is still the case that late lesions (especially 33% and 44%) are considerably more devastating than those occurring early in training.

Turning briefly to short-term consequences, differences are again observed between the two classes of verbs in the relationship between amount of prior training and performance. While bigger lesions have more substantive immediate consequences than smaller ones for both irregular [$F(4, 12) = 10.71, p < 0.001$] and regular verbs [$F(4, 12) = 86.7, p < 0.001$], entrenchment effects are only observed for the regulars. A significant monotonic increase in acute impact on performance for regular verbs is observed as damage occurs later in life [$F(14, 42) = 3.30, p < 0.001$], which is felt more significantly as lesion size correspondingly increases [$F(56, 168) = 2.5, p < 0.001$]. For example, 44% damage at epoch 3 results in a −37% change in performance, whereas, the same injury at epoch 14 results in more than 60% loss. For the irregulars, in contrast, no main effect of lesion timing is observed, nor is there an interaction of lesion size by time. For example, the effect of a 44% lesion is approximately the same at all points in training ($M = -25\%$). Hence, dissociations between regular and irregular forms are demonstrable for both the short and the long term, even though such a distinction has not explicitly been "built in" to these networks.

Performance on novel stems.   Figure 4 outlines several categories of responses produced by intact networks when presented with three types of novel verbs. Two sets are potential members of the irregular class, i.e., Vowel Changes and Dental Finals. A third, Indeterminates, does not share defining phonological features of any class of irregular verbs. These novel verbs contrast in the degree to which they possess phonological characteristics that are predictive of class membership in this language: Indeterminates (least predictive of irregularity, most predictive of regularity), Vowel Changes (medium), Dental Finals (most predictive of irregularity, least predictive of regularity).

In Figure 4a (Indeterminates), note that the network is able to provide an appropriate response to only a few novel forms at the beginning of training. Responses not classifiable into any error category (possibly not legal strings in the language) comprised 62% of the output at epoch 1. These responses occur at all test points, but averaged less than 14% of the total number of responses, as the ability to generate systematic responses quickly and consistently improves. In particular, the preferred response, suffixation, exceeds 75% by the end of the testing period. A small set of indeterminate novel stems are consistently produced as identity mappings ($M = 3.8\%$). For the Vowel Change novel forms (Figure 4b), the system is again unable to produce systematic responses early on; however, this tendency is quickly overcome by a suffixation strategy. More than 50% of the vowel change novel stems are suffixed with the appropriate past tense allomorph, while approximately 15% are treated as legal vowel changes. Twenty-five percent of responses (not shown) resemble vowel change forms in

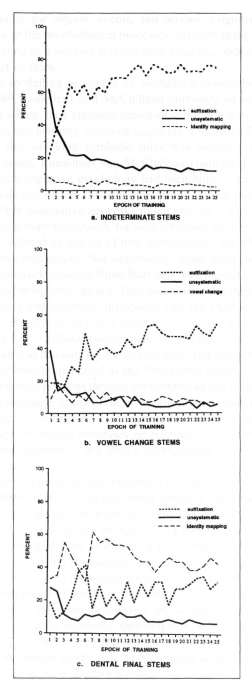

Figure 4. Generalization to novel stems in intact networks.

some respect: illegal vowel changes, legal blends (legal vowel change plus suffix), or illegal blends (inappropriate vowel change plus suffix). Unclassifiable responses comprise fewer than 9% of responses overall. Finally, we see a slightly different pattern for the Dental Final novel forms (Figure 4c). Unsystematic responses are again common early in the testing period, and gradually decrease in frequency ($M = 10.5\%$ overall). Unlike the other novel forms types, however, the preferred response here is to treat novel forms as members of the identity mapping class ($M = 41.5\%$). Suffixation responses do occur throughout ($M = 23.1\%$); however, they are rarely dominant even though they increase slightly over training.

These results indicate that the networks quickly assimilate patterns represented in the input set into a usable form. One or two passes through the data set are all that are necessary for the network to begin to treat novel stems in a systematic fashion by adding a suffix. Further, the tendency to do so intensifies over training. However, these networks also quickly latch onto another characteristic of this artificial language: the association between "dental final" and identity mapping (predictive of approximately 19% of the training set). The pattern of responses to novel forms suggests that both suffixation and identity mapping can be systematically and productively applied, yet *which* response is made to a given novel form varies as a function of the presence or absence of phonological features of the stem. While some members of each class of novel stems are suffixed, the tendency to rely upon this strategy decreases in direct relationship to the type of novel form: Indeterminate stems are suffixed the most, Vowel Change stems an intermediate amount, and Dental Finals, the least. In contrast, the tendency to treat forms as members of the identity mapping class is primarily (although not always) restricted to those stems that possess a dental consonant in final position.

Returning now to the main focus, Figure 5 outlines responses to two categories of novel stems by networks undergoing lesions prior to the onset of training. We hypothesize that if the behavioral dissociations observed over the course of learning and as a function of brain injury outlined in the previous section reflect a selective deficit in the ability to form generalizations based on the input, then we expect that the networks would also be impaired in the ability to generalize to all novel forms. Further, a qualitative difference between generalization and lexically based association would be reflected in terms of *all* types of generalizations (i.e., both suffixation and identity mapping). On the other hand, if the behavioral dissociations derive from the operation of a single associative-based generalization mechanism that is dependent on the presence or absence of features to predict class membership, then it is possible that some generalization abilities would be more vulnerable to injury than others. In this single-mechanism view, an across-the-board (i.e., selective) loss of generalization ability would not be necessary. Instead, patterns of acquisition, deficit, and sparing, as well as generalization skills must all be predictable in terms of the input factors provided by the model.

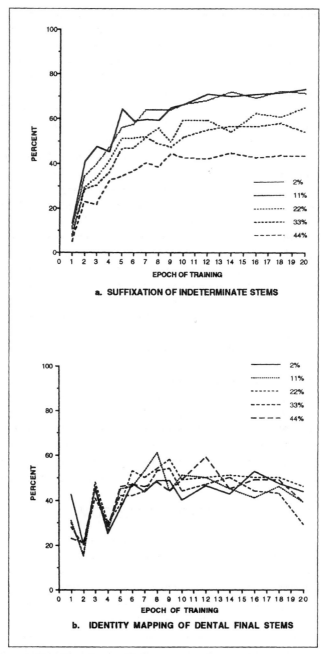

Figure 5. The effect of prenatal injury on appropriate mapping to novel stems.

Figure 5a shows that initial capacity does indeed affect how easily the network learns to add a suffix to indeterminate novel stems. Average trajectories decrease correspondingly as a function of lesion size from 63% for 2% lesions to 39% for the largest lesions. An inverse monotonic increase in unsystematic responses is also observed over the same period (not shown). Thus, consistent with the acquisition of the training set, resource reductions affect the degree to which the network is able to treat indeterminate novel forms in a reasonable fashion. Interestingly, variations in initial capacity do *not* appear to influence the treatment of novel dental final stems as members of the identity mapping class (Figure 5b). Here, we see no systematic relationship between size of lesion and the ability of the network to abstract the general pattern associated with dental final stems and to apply it to novel instances. Hence, reduced resources early in life do not affect the ability to abstract and utilize *all* predictive patterns from the input. In the terms of the single-mechanism model, the effects of resource reduction are restricted to those patterns in the input that are not easily predictable given finite resource constraints. For this English-like language, the most difficult generalization to draw happens to be "add a suffix" because this pattern is (1) representative of a large number of dissimilar stems, and (2) characterized by a lack of phonological cueing. It is these same regular forms, as members of the language to be learned, that are the most vulnerable to lesions over the course of acquisition.

In sum, early capacity reductions disrupt the assimilation of the suffixation pattern, yet the appropriate marking of dental final stems remains relatively impervious to prenatal injury. Hence, these injuries cannot be selectively affecting generalization abilities, per se; nor are the dissociations observed between regular and irregular verbs across acquisition necessarily the result of a selective loss of abstraction and generalization skills. Nevertheless, it is still possible that this dissociation does indeed reflect some type of qualitative difference in underlying mechanism. That is, is the same mechanism guiding the two types of generalization responses, as would be predicted in a single-mechanism view? Or, has the network partitioned its resources in order to functionally distinguish between generalization of the suffix and generalization of identity mapping? While it would be difficult to characterize such a distinction in the terms of the rule-association hybrid model, the behavioral dissociations may nevertheless reflect a partitioning of resources over the course of training.

If the same portion of the network is guiding the productive use of identity mapping and suffixation, then we would expect that both of these processes would exhibit vulnerability under similar injuries. In contrast, if the two processes were functionally differentiated in terms of the resources the network has allocated to each task, then it is less likely that a given injury would affect both processes in an analogous fashion. Our final analysis of the limitations on recovery of generalization abilities for lesions occurring during the postnatal period may shed some light in this regard. Figure 6 presents three types of responses to novel forms that are relevant to this issue.

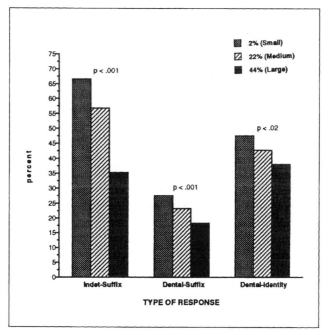

Figure 6. Three types of responses to novel forms as a function of lesion size—postnatal only.

Focus first on the left-most response pattern, which represents the average tendency to generalize the suffix to indeterminate novel stems (Indet-Suffix) during four "snapshots" of training, beginning immediately postlesion and continuing for 10 epochs. Three sizes of lesions are contrasted: Small (2%), Medium (22%), and Large (44%). Hence, while timing of injury is not evaluated here, we have controlled for the amount of training following injury (see also Figure 4a and b). Note first that the tendency to generalize the suffix is inversely related to extent of injury. Consistent with the prenatal findings (Figure 5a), suffixation to novel forms decreases drastically under conditions of extensive injury, for example, 2% lesions ($M = 66.5\%$) compared to 44% lesions ($M = 35.2\%$). This difference is statistically reliable [$F(2, 18) = 126.1$, $p < 0.001$]. The middle panel outlines the proportion of dental novel stems, which were also suffixed. Again, the tendency to do so decreases as a greater portion of the units are damaged [$F(2, 18) = 39.9$, $p < 0.001$]. Thus, the tendency to use the suffix in a productive fashion is reduced incrementally for both categories of novel stems as lesion size expands.

The third set of data presented in Figure 6 outlines the proportion of responses in which dental final stems were produced as identity mappings. Note here that this second generalization process also decreases monotonically as lesions become more extensive [$F(2, 18) = 2.2$, $p < 0.03$]. Hence, even though

this effect differs in magnitude across the three response types (as would be expected given the acquisition results), both types of generalizations are vulnerable to stepwise increases in the extent of lesion. Of course, it is possible that these randomly administered lesions are indeed affecting two separate processes. Yet, these data are consistent with the hypothesis that the mechanisms guiding the two types of generalizations are not explicitly differentiated in these networks. Analyses that would further substantiate this claim (e.g., hidden unit clustering) are left to future endeavors.

Discussion

In summary, these simulations provide several examples of a behavioral dissociation between regular and irregular forms within a single-mechanism connectionist system. Across most conditions of lesion size and timing, the acquisition of irregular mappings was considerably more resilient to both the immediate and long-term consequences of damage, regardless of how much training the network has already experienced. It appears that the solutions available to these networks are relatively unaffected by the types of sudden and drastic changes in the weight-space that we have initiated here. In light of previous models using languages of this type, the ability of the network to maintain this level of plasticity is likely to result from the fact that mappings between irregular stems and past tenses were high in token frequency and were predictable in terms of their phonological features. These input features enabled the nets to organize the weight space using non-costly and robust solutions. The resources available to even the most damaged systems appear to be sufficient to find new solutions to the irregular past tense problem.

In contrast, regular verbs were considerably more affected by injury, especially when lesions involved a substantial portion of the units, both acutely, in terms of immediate losses of performance, as well as by an increasing limitation to recover from late injury. While it is unlikely that plasticity is completely lost, it was nevertheless shown that the effect of an identical injury can change as a function of prior training. Analyses indicated that these entrenchment effects were more strongly associated with the regular verbs and were not attributable to fewer exposures to the training set. Further, each of these dissociations were observed in absence of any explicitly modular organization of the learning architecture or pattern of interconnectivity in terms of rule-based vs. associative mechanisms.

What conclusions can be drawn regarding the underlying mechanisms that guide the processing of regular and irregular forms in these networks? One might be that these dissociations are observable in a system that does not explicitly build such distinctions into the architecture because the network has learned to partition the task into rule versus nonrule components. In other words, achieving an adequate solution to the past tense problem indeed requires that the network allocates some resources to abstracting a general "rule" of the form "add /-ed/,"

while other resources are dedicated to storing exemplars of the disparate set of irregular stem and past tense forms. When systems are damaged, dissociations arise from selective injury to that part of the network devoted to abstracting and storing general patterns, while the portion dedicated to encoding and accessing individual stem-past tense pairs is left relatively intact. Recall that this characterization is similar to that posited within the hybrid account of Pinker (1991) to account for the pattern of deficit exhibited by some individuals with SLI (Gopnik, 1990; Gopnik & Crago, 1991).

The alternative explanation posits that behavioral dissociations between regular and irregular mappings need not derive from a qualitative division between rule-governed generalization and associative mechanisms. Instead, regular and irregular forms are different in degree, not in kind, as defined by several factors, such as type or token frequency and phonological predictability. These factors not only define the differences between regular and irregular classes, but also provide the basis for a single-mechanism system to resolve the competition between regular and irregular forms given a finite amount of resources.

To further evaluate the underlying processes guiding performance in the network, we investigated the abilities of intact and damaged networks to generalize (i.e., produce systematic and reasonable output) when presented with novel verbs. These analyses suggested that the disruption of generalization abilities after injury is not consistent with the suggestion that dissociations arise as a consequence of partitioning resources to derive a qualitative distinction between generalization and association across the learning period. Instead, generalization abilities were not impaired categorically, but were predictable by the degree to which productive application was supported by the input characteristics of the language. Further, similar injuries were found to affect the application of both types of patterns to novel forms.

Taking these results together, we can note that these networks, like children, are sensitive to the phonological shape of stems, a tendency that is reflected in both the production of errors and the manner in which novel items are processed (Berko, 1958; Bybee & Slobin, 1982). This reliance on phonological shape has also been noted for adults, but is generally seen to decrease over the course of development (Marchman & Plunkett, 1991). These patterns are consistent with a single-mechanism solution in which the abstraction of general input characteristics is not restricted to one aspect of the input set (i.e., the regulars). Instead, the network seeks out tendencies across all patterns, using them when they are the most predictive, ignoring them when they are not. Hence, these networks are not motivated to create a division between the abstraction of the regular "rule" and the storage of individual nonregular mappings. In one sense, the goal of the single-mechanism solution is to identify a configuration that *unites*, rather than divides, the disparate set of mappings. In this artificial language, the solution rests on the network organizing the input in terms of the presence or absence of key phonological features.

Interestingly, over the course of training, the tendency to add a suffix to novel forms achieves an increasingly strong "default" status, applied most liberally when irregular phonological features are *absent*, but to some extent, when the form is characteristic of an irregular pattern. This tendency to "over"-overgeneralize the suffix to novel forms is also characteristic of children (e.g., Berko, 1958). Further, it is reported that children overgeneralize more often in elicitation situations than in naturalistic discourse (Marchman, 1988; Marcus, Ullman, Pinker, Hollander, Rosen, & Xu, 1992). For both children and these networks then, tests of nonsense forms may inflate the "productive" nature of the suffix. Indeed, studies show that children sometimes generalize the suffix to novel forms or produce overgeneralization errors even when they are not marking the regular past tense correctly in other contexts. This decoupling of elicited and spontaneous performance has been observed in both normal and disordered populations (e.g., Leonard, Bortolini, Caselli, & McGregor, 1992).

In sum, performance in these networks was similar to that reported for English-speaking children in the following ways: (1) irregular forms are learned early in training, (2) suffixation is the predominant response to novel forms, even when errors are made on known forms, (3) patterns of responses to novel forms are predictable in terms of the phonological characteristics of the stems (e.g., identity mapping forms are resistant to overregularization errors), (4) the tendency to apply a suffix to novel forms acts like a "default" rule, applying to novel forms even when they possess phonological features characteristic of members of the irregular class, and (5) the tendency to suffix novel forms increases across the course of development.

GENERAL DISCUSSION

In these studies, we systematically evaluated constraints on learning and recovery in networks faced with a language of regular and irregular mappings analogous to those in the English past tense. In all networks, there was no explicit differentiation between the computational mechanisms guiding the acquisition of regular versus irregular mappings, nor the corresponding ability to generalize that knowledge to novel forms. The various verb classes used were similar to English in frequency structure and phonological character. Regardless of the difficulties posed by the competition between the various mapping types, all networks successfully learned the input–output pairs which comprised this artificial language. The effects are interpreted within the context of a computational mechanism that is sensitive to these input features and seeks out general patterns in the input to configure a weight matrix so that error is minimized and the maximum amount of input variance is captured.

In networks in which computational resources were reduced via injury, regular mappings were more susceptible to damage than the irregulars, demonstrating behavioral dissociations of regular and irregular forms. Yet, contrary to previous

interpretations of similar dissociations in children and adults with language deficits, the dissociations observed here are seen to derive from systematic differences in the nature of the two classes of mappings, rather than an explicit differentiation in the mechanisms responsible for learning. Assessments of damage on performance with novel forms suggest that the injury did not selectively impair generalization abilities. Instead, the behavioral dissociations are accountable by several aspects of the vocabulary on which the networks were trained. First, while there are considerably fewer examples of irregular stems in the training set, each mapping is seen up to 10 times more often than any given regular mapping (i.e., greater token frequency). Hence, additional exposures to a particular form may assist the network in abstracting a pattern from the input using fewer resources (Plaut & Shallice, 1991). Second, patterns inherent in the irregular verbs are highly predictable by phonological characteristics (e.g., all identity mapping stems end in a final dental consonant). Previous studies (Plunkett & Marchman, 1991) have demonstrated that learning in these networks is greatly facilitated when phonological cues to class membership are provided. Stems that cluster in phonologically predictable, local patterns are more resistant to damage, exhibiting the ability to withstand both the short- and long-term impact of injury. Third, suffixation is characteristic of the largest number of forms in the input, and was identified and utilized early in training (evidenced by generalization to novel forms only after a few epochs of training). Nevertheless, suffixation was also more susceptible to damage and critical period effects as injuries were more likely to interfere with the ability to abstract patterns that are widespread and not supported by local features of the representational system. Yet, the tendency of the system to suffix all novel forms (i.e., a "default" strategy) increased. These results suggest that the default strategy emerges over the course of training when number of exemplars is high and phonological predictability is low. Phonological predictability and token frequency work together in this language to support the identification, abstraction, and appropriate application of patterns to novel forms.

However, this particular English-like combination of frequency and phonological predictability is not characteristic of all natural languages in which regular and irregular mappings coexist. In many cases, classes of regulars are quite small relative to irregular classes. Nevertheless, regular forms are frequently seen to act as the default, e.g., that mapping is applied to new forms that enter the language. These languages, in which regulars are not the most numerous in the language, could be viewed as problematic to the current model. A recent connectionist model of historical change in the past tense system of English (Hare & Elman, 1992) has demonstrated that default behavior can occur even when the regular class size is small. Instead, default behavior relates to the *presence* of clusters of phonological similarity in some classes (i.e., the irregulars), and the *absence* of phonological similarity in others (i.e., the regulars). Further, there are cases in other natural languages (e.g., Finnish) in which among the more than 80 classes of nominal forms, it is difficult to identify a clear default mapping (Thyme,

Ackerman, & Elman, 1992). The default behavior observed in English (and these networks) may be an artifact of the structure of the input, and represents one end of a continuum of language typology. A strong, in principle, division between rule (i.e., default) and associative mechanisms would be incompatible with such a degree of variability in the structure of linguistic systems.

Other systems in which regular and irregular patterns coexist have also been shown to demonstrate dissociations between regular and irregular verbs as a function of injury to network connections. For example, Patterson, et al. (1989) used a similar technique to mimic errors in phonological to orthographic correspondences, similar to those that are characteristic of some types of dyslexia. It is interesting to note that in these systems, the most resilient class of mappings was the regulars. In contrast to the pattern of results reported here, it was the irregular mappings that were the most vulnerable to injury, manifesting the greatest disruption in network performance.

To resolve these apparently conflicting findings, we must again look at the structure of the input languages that the networks were required to learn. In the English orthographic system, regular words are similar to each other in terms of the degree to which surface features are predictable of output form. In contrast, the irregular forms comprise isolated examples that do not possess within-category phonological predictability. In that system, then, irregularity is defined by the *lack of similarity to other forms*, whereas, regular forms share surface features with other members of the set (i.e., "neighborhoods") (Seidenberg & McClelland, 1989). Across training, the network must learn to identify and use those features in the task of categorizing items according to their phonological–orthographic relationship. It is exactly the opposite situation in the case of the English past tense. Here, the lack of within-class similarity is characteristic of the regular, rather than the irregular forms. Thus, the same combination of input characteristics that are responsible for the robustness of the irregular verbs under conditions of damage in the English past tense system allow the regulars the same advantage in the system of English orthography.

Across linguistic domains, then, there is evidence for a double dissociation between regular and irregular forms in systems in which no such distinction is explicitly represented. However, how is it possible to account for a double dissociation *within the same linguistic domain*, similar to the contrasting profiles between WS and SLI subjects reported by Pinker (1991), in a model that is dependent on features of the target input that are presumably constant for all speakers of a given language? Clearly, the existence of both patterns of deficit (e.g., regulars intact, irregulars damaged for SLI subjects; regulars intact, irregulars damaged for WS subjects) provides the strongest evidence for distinct underlying processors in the neuropsychological literature. At least one possibility derives from work already conducted with models of this type. Using an incremental learning paradigm, Plunkett and Marchman (1990) demonstrated that the rate at which networks were presented with new vocabulary items affected (1) the degree

to which irregular past tense forms have an early advantage, (2) the proportion of irregulars subject to overregularization during training, and (3) the overall mastery of the vocabulary. Hence, individual differences across networks that are independent of representational format and processing mechanism can demonstrate distinct profiles of learning within the same learning system. Outlining the degree to which these profiles can be mapped onto known processing limitations in children is hoped to be a fruitful area of future study.

Finally, while the learning of all forms exhibited a remarkable degree of plasticity after damage, critical period effects were observed in these networks. Mastery of the regular verbs became increasingly constrained as the damage became more extensive and lesions occurred later in training. Recall that the more devastating effects of later injury cannot be attributed to qualitative changes in the learning mechanism or resources that the network had available for solving the mapping problem in different developmental periods. Thus, these studies demonstrate one way in which the act of learning itself initiates change in the effects of brain injury immediately after injury, as well as in the long-term prospects for recovery.

In conclusion, the developmental and neuropsychological dissociations between irregular and regular forms observed here strongly reflected the characteristics of the target language. Crosslinguistic research in acquisition and aphasia also suggests that the variability observed across languages is a primary factor in determining the course of both learning and breakdown. Hence, the results presented here support the notion that dissociations in behavior do not necessarily reflect differences in underlying mechanism that are moderated by maturational changes in the organism. Instead, predicting the course of language learning, breakdown, and recovery may be better achieved by examining the linguistic and developmental facts of the task to be learned within the context of a highly interactive associative learning mechanism.

METHOD

Overview

Deriving from previous work (Plunkett & Marchman, 1990, 1991), three-layer connectionist networks were trained to learn the past tense morphological system of an artificial language. Considerable care was taken to structure the vocabulary to approximate English in terms of the (1) relative size of the regular and irregular classes, (2) token frequency of regular (low) vs. irregular (high) verbs, and (3) predictability of class membership by phonological features of the verb stem. All results represent performance averaged across several networks that vary in initial conditions and training parameters. In both Studies I and II, the networks were subjected to artificial reductions in resources (i.e., "lesions") at key points prior to and during training. Lesions randomly eliminated connections between the input and hidden layer, affecting from 2% to just under half (44%)

of the units. Network performance is evaluated both before and after injury as a function of size and timing of lesion. Comparisons focus on trajectories of correct performance for regular and irregular verbs in the intact (i.e., no lesion) vs. damaged (i.e., lesioned) networks. Performance on a set of novel forms is assessed before and after damage by presenting legal stems that were not members of the training set. The impact of brain injury on both learning and generalization is evaluated as a function of size and timing of lesion in the following ways:

1. Learning Trajectory: Shape of the trajectory of learning across the life-span (across 25 epochs).
2. Long-Term Potential for Recovery: Mean final performance after training is completed (after 25 epochs).
3. Acute Impact: Mean percentage change in correct output immediately after lesion, as a function of the proportion of the task already mastered [(% correct postlesion – % correct prelesion)/% correct prelesion].
4. Short-Term Recovery: Mean performance averaged over 10 epochs of training postlesion.

Vocabulary

The vocabulary was randomly compiled from an artificial language consisting of approximately 1000 stem–past tense pairs analogous to English regular (e.g., *walk → walked*) and irregular verbs (e.g., *go → went, ring → rang*). Each stem is three phonemes in length, configured in a fixed-length format as either consonant–vowel–consonant (CVC), consonant–consonant–vowel (CCV), or vowel–consonant–consonant (VCC) strings. All stem and past tense forms conform to conventions of English pronunciation and are hence possible, but frequently nonsense, English words (e.g., /vIp/ → /vIpt/, /sku/ → /skud/, or /ebt/ → /ebt/). All vowels, consonants, and suffixes are encoded across 15 units using a distributed featural representation involving phonological feature contrasts, such as ±voice, ±nasal, etc. This representation is a modified version of the one used in earlier models,[8] revised by Alan Prince and Kim Plunkett.

In Study I, the training vocabulary consisted of 433 regular verbs randomly chosen from the one-thousand word vocabulary. Forming past tenses involved appending one of three possible suffixes as a function of the voicing of the final phoneme in the stem, analogous to the allomorphic variation in English. If the stem ended in a voiced consonant or vowel, the suffix was encoded as the voiced dental stop consonant /d/. If the final phoneme was an unvoiced consonant, the suffix was encoded as the voiceless dental stop /t/. Approximately 13% of the regular stems in the training set ended in the dental stop consonants /t/ or /d/. For these verbs, the suffix is analogous to the English blend of a schwa (/ˆ/) and voiced dental stop (/d/) (as in *pad → padded*, i.e., /pæd/ → /pædˆd/). This past

tense allomorph is presented to the network as the single-phoneme suffix /D/. All stem–past tense mappings were presented to the system with equal frequency, once per epoch of training (i.e., token frequency = 1).

In Study II, the training vocabulary consists of a total of 500 unique stems, including the identical 433 regular verbs used in Study I. The additional 67 stem–past tense pairs were irregular, classified either as Arbitrary ($N = 2$) (i.e., no apparent relationship between stem and past tense form), Identity mapping ($N = 40$) (i.e., past tense forms are identical to their corresponding stems), or Vowel Change ($N = 25$) (i.e., stems and past tense forms differ only in terms of the vowel). These type frequencies (i.e., class sizes) were chosen so that the entire vocabulary configuration would approximate the relative proportion of regular to irregular verbs in English (see Plunkett & Marchman, 1991).

While regular verbs represent the largest class of past tense forms in English, it is the irregular verbs that are the most commonly used. To capture this between-class difference in token frequency, a given irregular form is presented to the network *up to 15 times more often* than a given regular form. Following Plunkett and Marchman (1991), arbitrary stems were presented with a token frequency of 15; identity mapping stems had a token frequency of 5; and vowel change mappings were presented 10 times during each epoch. In contrast, dental final regular forms were presented with a token frequency of 3 and nondental final regulars had a token frequency of 1. Thus, during each epoch of training in Study II, networks were presented with a total of 1025 stem–past tense pairs. While this distribution approximates the relative token frequencies of English regular and irregular verb classes, it is of course unrealistic to assume that *all* members of a given class are encountered in the input equally frequently (or equally infrequently). It is acknowledged that a more realistic configuration would involve constructing distributions *within* classes in which individual items vary in token frequency, ideally based on the frequency of actual English forms (e.g., Daugherty & Seidenberg, 1992). Nevertheless, the configuration used here serves to capture differences among the *average* token frequencies of the various verb classes of English.

One hundred percent of identity mapping verbs end in a dental stop consonant, however, approximately 13% (56 of 434) of the regular stems do also. Hence, the phonological shape of a verb stem is predictive, but not defining, of membership in both the identity mapping and vowel change classes. All vowel change stems possessed one of seven vowel–consonant endings. No restrictions were placed on the stem-initial phoneme in the string. One vowel–consonant cluster was represented once (/Ul/ → /ul/); three clusters comprised two (/ɛm/ → /Om/), three (/Is/ → /æs/), and four (/is/ → /ɛs/) exemplars; and three vowel-change subtypes were represented by 5 exemplars (/iz/ → /ɛz/; /of/ → /Uf/; /ul/ → /ol/). Approximately 10% of all nonvowel change stems also met these phonological criteria. Again, these phonological features characterize but do not exclusively define membership in the vowel change class.

Network configuration and training

All networks consisted of three-layers: 45 input units (three 15-unit phonemes), 45 hidden units, and 60 output units (four 15-unit phonemes). All layers and units were completely interconnected, configured in a strictly feed-forward manner. Training utilized a standard back propagation learning algorithm (TLEARN, Center for Research in Language, UCSD) in which weighted connections are adjusted in response to a discrepancy between the actual and desired output of the network (i.e., the teacher signal). Weight updating occurred on a pattern-by-pattern basis where error is propagated back through the network after each input presentation, rather than summed over a set of patterns. A "massed" training procedure was used in which training on all stem–past tense pairs occurred during each epoch, in contrast to a incremental procedure in which vocabulary size is gradually increased across learning (Plunkett & Marchman, 1990; Elman, 1991). The order of presentation within epoch was randomized within and across simulations.

In Study I, five identically configured networks were trained in each experimental condition. In Study II, four networks were used. (Data from a fifth network were eliminated due to technical difficulties.) In both studies, a set of baseline networks was presented with the identical vocabulary for a maximum of 25 epochs (i.e., 25 presentations of the complete training set). The nine individual networks differed *only* in (1) the order of the presentation of the items within each epoch of training, determined by random seed, (2) the configuration of the weight matrix prior to training (i.e., initial conditions), also determined by random seed, and (3) the values of network parameters that determine the impact of a given error signal. In Study I, momentum values ranged from 0.5 to 0.75; the values for learning rate ranged from 0.1 to 0.2. In Study II, momentum ranged from 0.1 to 0.2; learning rate varied between 0.05 and 0.2. These learning parameters were varied across the two studies due to the demands of the different vocabulary sizes and complexity of the task.

Lesioning procedure

To assess the effects of injury on learning and recovery, each network was lesioned to various extents, randomly rendering 2, 11, 22, 33, or 44% of the hidden units inoperative. Some of the lesions were performed "prenatally," prior to the beginning of training. Note that evaluating the impact of prenatal lesions of various sizes is equivalent to comparing performance in networks initially configured with different numbers of hidden units. Lesions were also administered at various points after the onset of training. These "postnatal" lesions were administered at every epoch through 14 epochs of training. Prior to each lesion, the network was trained using the "normal" configuration of 45 hidden units. At the point of lesion, some of the hidden units were rendered inoperative and training was subsequently resumed in this "damaged" network.

A within-networks, fully crossed factorial design was used. That is, each of the nine networks (5 in Study I and 4 in Study II) experienced all sizes of lesions at each of the 14 points in training. Initial weight matrix configurations, randomized orders of presentation, and network parameters varied across networks, but were held constant across lesion conditions.

Evaluation of network performance and generalization to novel forms

After each epoch, the ability of the network to produce each past tense form in the training vocabulary was tested. Performance was evaluated using a "closest fit" procedure on a phoneme-by-phoneme basis. That is, the network received credit for producing a past tense form correctly if and only if all phonemes represented on the output signal (including the suffix) were closest, in Euclidean space, to each and every target phoneme. Scores of "% correct" for regular and irregular (identity, arbitrary and vowel change) stems were derived after every epoch of training, and errors were classified (e.g., additions of a suffix, blends, unsystematic responses).

A set of 142 novel verb stems was used to assess each network's ability to productively produce past tense forms that were not included in the training set. Twenty of these ended in a dental stop consonant (Dentals), 20 were potential members of one of the seven vowel change subclasses (Vowel Changes), and 102 did not possess phonological features characteristic of irregular verbs (Indeterminates). The output generated for each of these novel stems was evaluated using the closest fit procedure (described above), and output tendencies were categorized with respect to the set of target mappings.

ACKNOWLEDGEMENTS

This work was conducted with the support of a postdoctoral fellowship from the San Diego McDonnell-Pew Foundation Center for Cognitive Neuroscience and the Center for Research in Language at the University of California, San Diego. Additional support was received from the John D. and Catherine T. MacArthur Research Network on the Transitions from Infancy to Childhood. I am deeply indebted to Georgina Justice and Paul Smith for programming assistance and support, as well as to Jeff Elman for computational guidance. A special thanks to Elizabeth Bates, Clay Helberg, Art Glenberg, Will Langston, Mark Seidenberg, and the members of the PDPNLP discussion group at the University of California, San Diego.

NOTES

1. While performance on traditional tests of grammar is not generally affected by injury to the right hemisphere, such injuries have been shown to affect the processing of discourse-level, pragmatic, and/or nonliteral aspects of language (e.g., Joanette & Goulet, 1990; Van Lancker, 1988; Van Lancker & Kempler, 1987).

2. Note that the neuropsychological data on double dissociations are necessarily derived from analyses between (rather than within) subjects or subject groups. That is, Patient A (or Syndrome A) displays a behavioral profile in which X is spared and Y is damaged, whereas Patient B (or Syndrome B) displays sparing in the abilities associated with Y, yet tests of the abilities associated with X yield poor performance. Hence, it is difficult to control for individual difference factors such as premorbid learning history or neurological organization across populations of subjects.

3. See Plunkett and Marchman (1990, 1991) for a discussion of vocabulary configurations and expansion regimens in which learning in these networks is *not* successful.

4. In a commentary on Gopnik (1990), Vargha-Khadem and Passingham (1990) comment that this family also displays a severe articulation disorder. In light of this report, it is interesting to note that five of the six experimental tasks reported by Gopnik and Crago (1991) in which differences were observed between the affected and nonaffected family members involved some type of production task (e.g., sentence-completion for plurals, derivational morphology, tense marking, or the production of a narrative) or measure of speaking rate (i.e., time to complete their response). The one remaining test involved grammaticality judgments of tense, person, and number, and also required subjects to provide a verbal correction of ungrammatical sentences. No differences were observed in the other nine measures, all of which involved receptive language processing. It is possible that articulation deficits may make the accurate interpretation and coding of responses more difficult, especially with respect to stem-final suffixes, and surely interferes with the subjects' fluency and rate of production.

5. It is important to note that the tendency to be "hypergeneralizers" has not been observed in all cases of WS. Further, like normally developing children, certain tasks may overestimate the proportion of incorrect forms that a subject might produce.

6. Clearly, connectionist models are not *by definition* antimodular or antinativist (e.g., Jacobs, Jordan, & Barto, 1991; Jordan, 1990). Modular structure can be "built in" to a network prior to any learning taking place by, for example, structuring patterns of interconnectivity, restricting learning in certain portions of the network, and/or varying input/output representational formats as a function of task or location.

7. Several techniques have been developed (e.g., hidden unit clustering, principle component analyses) to assist in the interpretation of network performance in theory-relevant terms, i.e., analyse the ways in which the network modularizes its resources over the course of training (see Hanson & Burr, 1990 for discussion).

8. In earlier models, suffixes were encoded nonphonologically across two output units (i.e., 00, 01, 10, and 11). Adopting a similar phonological representation for phonemes belonging to the stem and the suffix blurs an imposed distinction between base forms and bound morphemes, while at the same time increases the salience of the phonological features that condition the allomorphic variation.

REFERENCES

Aram, D. M. (1988). Language sequelae of unilateral brain lesions in children. In F. Plum (Ed.), *Language, communication and the brain*. New York: Raven.

Aram, D. M., Ekelman, B. L., & Whitaker, H. (1986). Spoken syntax in children with acquired unilateral hemisphere lesions. *Brain and Language, 27*, 75–100.

Aram, D. M., Ekelman, B. L., & Whitaker, H. (1987). Lexical retrieval in left and right brain lesioned children. *Brain and Language, 31*, 61–87.

Basso, A., Capitani, E., Laiacona, M. & Luzzatti, C. (1980). Factors influencing type and severity of aphasia. *Cortex, 16*, 631–636.

Bates, E., Appelbaum, M., & Allard, L. (1991). Statistical constraints on the use of single-case studies. *Brain and Language, 40*(3), 295–329.

Bates, E., Friederici, A., & Wulfeck, B. (1987). Grammatical morphology in aphasia: Evidence from three languages. *Cortex, 23*, 545–574.

Bates, E., MacDonald, J., MacWhinney, B., & Appelbaum, M. (1991). Maximum likelihood procedures for the analysis of group and individual data in aphasia research. *Brain and Language*, *40*(2), 231–265.

Bellugi, U., Bihrle, A., Jernigan, D., Trauner, D., & Dougherty, S. (1990). Neuropsychological, neurological, and neuroanatomical profile of Williams Syndrome. *American Journal of Medical Genetics*, *6*, 115–125.

Berko, J. (1958). The child's learning of English morphology. *Word*, *14*, 150–177.

Bybee, J., & Slobin, D. I. (1982). Rules and schemas in the development and use of the English past tense. *Language*, *58*, 265–289.

Caramazza, A. (1986). On drawing inferences about the structure of normal cognitive systems from the analysis of patterns of impaired performance: The case for single-patient studies. *Brain and Cognition*, *5*, 41–66.

Cazden, C. B. (1968). The acquisition of noun and verb inflections. *Child Developments*, *39*, 433–448.

Damasio, H., & Damasio, A. (1989). *Lesion analysis in neuropsychology*. New York: Oxford University Press.

Daugherty, K., & Seidenberg, M. (1992). Rules or connections? The past tense revisited. In *Proceedings of the 14th annual meeting of the Cognitive Science Society*. Hillsdale, NJ: Lawrence Erlbaum Associates Inc.

Elman, J. (1991). *The importance of starting small*. Center for Research in Language (Technical Report No. 9101), University of California, San Diego, La Jolla, CA.

Farah, M., & McClelland, J. (1991). A computational model of semantic memory impairment: Modality specificity and emergent category specificity. *Journal of Experimental Psychology: General*, *120*(4), 339–357.

Fodor, J. (1983). *Modularity of mind*. Cambridge, MA: MIT Press.

Gopnik, M. (1990). Feature-blind grammar and dysphasia. *Nature (London)*, *344*, 715.

Gopnik, M., & Crago, M. B. (1991). Familial aggregation of a developmental language disorder. *Cognition*, *39*(1), 1–30.

Hanson, S. J., & Burr, D. J. (1990). What connectionist models learn: Learning and representation in connectionist networks. *Behavioral and Brain Sciences*, *13*, 471–489.

Hare, M., & Elman, J. (1992). Connectionist account of English inflectional morphology: Evidence from language change. In *Proceedings of the 14th annual meeting of the Cognitive Science Society*. Hillsdale, NJ: Lawrence Erlbaum Associates Inc.

Hart, J., Berndt, R. S., & Caramazza, A. (1985). Category specific naming deficit following cerebral infarction. *Nature (London)*, *316*, 439–440.

Hinton, G., & Sejnowski, T. (1986). Learning and relearning in Boltzmann machines. In D. Rumelhart, J. McClelland, & the PDP Research Group (Eds.), *Parallel distributed processing: Explorations in the microstructure of cognition, Vol. 1: Foundations*. Cambridge, MA: MIT Press.

Hinton, G., & Shallice, T. (1991). Lesioning an attractor network: Investigations of acquired dyslexia. *Psychological Review*, *98*(1), 74–95.

Jacobs, R. A., Jordon, M. I., & Barto, A. (1990). Task decomposition through competition in a modular connectionist architecture: The what and where vision tasks. *Cognitive Science*, *15*(2), 219–250.

Joanette, Y., & Goulet, P. (1990). Narrative discourse in right brain-damaged right-handers. In Y. Joanette & H. H. Brownell (Eds.), *Discourse ability and brain damage*. New York: Springer Verlag.

Jordan, M. I. (1990). A non-empiricist perspective on learning in layered networks: Commentary on Hanson and Burr, Connectionist learning and representation. *Behavioral and Brain Sciences*, *13*(3), 497.

Lenneberg, E. H. (1967). *Biological foundations of language*. New York: Wiley.

Leonard, L., Bortolini, U., Caselli, M. C., & McGregor, K. K. (1992). Morphological deficits in children with specific language impairment: The status of features in the underlying grammar. *Language Acquisition*, *2*, 151–179.

Marcus, G. F., Ullman, M., Pinker, S., Hollander, M., Rosen, T. J., & Xu, F. (1992). Overregularization in language acquisition. *Monographs of the Society for Research in Child Development, 57*(4), Serial No. 228.

Marchman, V. (1988). Rules and regularities in the English past tense. *Center for Research in Language Newsletter, 2*(4), San Diego.

Marchman, V., & Bates, E. (1994). Continuity in lexical and morphological development: A test of the critical mass hypothesis. *Journal of Child Language, 21*, 339–366.

Marchman, V., & Plunkett, K. (1991). *Irregularization.* Paper presented at the 16th Annual Boston University Conference on Language Development. Boston, Massachusetts, October 1991.

McCloskey, M. (1991). Networks and theories: The place of connectionism in cognitive science. *Psychological Science, 2*(6), 387–395.

Menn, L., & Obler, L. K. (1990). *Aggrammatic aphasia: Cross-language narrative sourcebook.* Amsterdam: John Benjamins.

Miceli, G., Silveri, M., Romani, C., & Caramazza, A. (1989). Variation in the pattern of omissions and substitutions of grammatical morphemes in the spontaneous speech of so-called aggrammatic aphasics. *Brain and Language, 36*, 447–492.

Mozer, M., & Behrmann, M. (1990). On the interaction of selective attention and lexical knowledge: A connectionist account of neglect dyslexia. *Journal of Cognitive Neuroscience, 2*(2), 96–103.

Newport, E. (1990). Maturational constraints on language learning. *Cognitive Science, 14*(1), 11–28.

Patterson, K. E., Seidenberg, M. S., & McClelland, J. L. (1989). Connections and disconnections: Acquired dyslexia in a computational model of reading processes. In R. G. M. Morris (Ed.), *Parallel distributed processing: Implications for psychology and neurobiology.* London: Oxford University Press.

Pavao-Martins, A., Castro-Caldas, H., Van Dongen, H., & Van Hout, A. (Eds.). (1991). *Acquired aphasia in children.* NATO ASI Series, D. Kluwer Academic Press.

Pinker, S. (1991). Rules of language. *Science, 253*, 530–535.

Plaut, D. (1991). *Connectionist neuropsychology: The breakdown and recovery of behavior in lesioned attractor networks* (Technical Report No. CMU-CS-91-195). Carnegie Mellon University, Pittsburgh, PA.

Plaut, D. C., & Shallice, T. (1991). Effects of word abstractness in a connectionist model of deep dyslexia. In *Proceedings of the 13th annual meeting of the Cognitive Science Society.* Hillsdale, NJ: Lawrence Erlbaum Associates Inc.

Plunkett, K., & Marchman, V. (1990). *From rote learning to system building: Acquiring verb morphology in children and connectionist nets.* Center for Research in Language (Technical Report No. 9020), University of California, San Diego.

Plunkett, K., & Marchman, V. (1991). U-shaped learning and frequency effects in a multi-layered perceptron: Implications for child language acquisition. *Cognition, 38*, 43–102.

Riva, D., & Gazzaniga, M. (1986). Late effects of unilateral brain lesion sustained before and after age one. *Neuropsychologia, 24*(3), 423–428.

Rumelhart, D., & McClelland, J. (1987). Learning the past tenses of English verbs: Implicit rules of parallel processing. In B. MacWhinney (Ed.), *Mechanisms of language acquisition.* Hillsdale, NJ: Lawrence Erlbaum Associates Inc.

Seidenberg, M., & McClelland, J. (1989). A distributed, developmental model of word recognition and naming. *Psychological Review, 96*, 523–368.

Shallice, T. (1988). *From neuropsychology to mental structure.* Cambridge: Cambridge University Press.

Shallice, T. (1991). How neuropsychology informs an understanding of normal function—author's response. *Behavioral and Brain Sciences, 14*(3), 429–437.

Thal, D. J., Marchman, V., Stiles, J., Aram, D., Trauner, D., Nass, R., & Bates, E. (1991). Early lexical development in children with focal brain injury. *Brain and Language, 40*, 491–527.

Thyme, A., Ackerman, F., & Elman, J. (1992). *Finnish nominal inflection: Paradigmatic patterns and token analogy*. Paper presented at the 21st Annual UWM Linguistics Symposium on The Reality of Linguistic Rules. Milwaukee, WI, April 1992.

Tyler, L. K. (1988). Spoken language comprehension in a fluent aphasic patient. *Cognitive Neuropsychology, 5*(3), 375–400.

Tyler, L. K. (1992). *Language disorders: A psycholinguistic account of language comprehension deficits*. Cambridge, MA: MIT Press.

Van Lancker, D. (1988). Nonpropositional speech: Neurolinguistic studies. In A. W. Ellis (Ed.), *Progress in the psychology of language* (Vol. III). Hove, UK: Lawrence Erlbaum Associates Ltd.

Van Lancker, D., & Kempler, D. (1987). Comprehension of familiar phrases by left- but not right-hemisphere damaged patients. *Brain and Language, 32*, 265–277.

Vargha-Khadem, F., & Passingham, R. E. (1990). *Nature (London), 346*(6281), 226.

Wood, C. C. (1978). Variations on a theme of Lashley: Lesion experiments on the neural model of Anderson, Silverstein, Ritz and Jones. *Psychological Review, 85*, 582–591.

Woods, B. T., & Carey, S. (1979). Language deficits after apparent clinical recovery from childhood aphasia. *Annals of Neurology, 6*(5), 405–409.

Woods, B. T., & Teuber, H. (1978). Changing patterns of childhood aphasia. *Annals of Neurology, 3*, 273–280.

CHAPTER TEN

Rules, representations, and the English past tense

William Marslen-Wilson
MRC Cognition and Brain Sciences Unit, Cambridge, UK

Lorraine K. Tyler
University of Cambridge, UK

The significance of the English past tense in current cognitive science is that it offers a clear contrast between a potentially rule-based system—the procedures for forming the regular past tense—and an unpredictable and idiosyncratic set of irregular forms. This contrast has become a focus for a wide-ranging debate about whether mental computation requires the use of symbols. Highly regular combinatorial phenomena, such as the regular past tense, are prime candidates for rule-based symbolic computation. Earlier research concentrated on the evidence for this during language acquisition, looking at how children learned the English regular and irregular verb systems. Over the last five years attention has shifted towards the properties of the adult system, and we review here some recent research into the neural correlates of the two types of procedure. The evidence suggests that there are divergences in the neural systems underlying the generation and perception of regular and irregular forms. Regular inflected forms seem to involve primarily combinatorial processes, while irregular forms appear to have a hybrid status, sharing their semantic properties with the regular forms but diverging in the phonological domain, where their form representations are stored as complete units. This indicates that the regular and irregular past tenses may not, after all, provide a clean contrast in the types of mental computation they implicate.

A fundamental issue in the cognitive sciences is to determine the nature of mental computation. Over the last decade the focus of this debate has been the contrast between classical views of mental computation, seen as the rule-based manipulation of strings of symbols with a syntax, as opposed to more distributed systems, operating subsymbolically and without syntax. Despite the pervasive and crucial nature of this debate, it has nonetheless been hard to find specific

Trends in Cognitive Sciences–Vol. 2, No. 11, November 1998

domains where empirical evidence could be generated that might decide between these two broad classes of views. The English past tense, perhaps surprisingly, offers one of the few cases where this seems to be true. Protagonists on both sides of the debate generally agree that the mental representation of the regular and irregular past tense of the English verb is a crucial test case. In this brief essay, we begin by explaining why this should be so, and then go on to focus on the recent emphasis, in our own work as well as in the work of others, on the neural correlates of the cognitive systems supporting the English past tense, and on the resulting claims for the neurological as well as functional dissociability of these underlying systems in the brain.

THE ENGLISH VERB

The significance of the English verb is that its procedures for forming the past tense offer an unusually sharp contrast, within the same cognitive domain, between a highly regular procedure and a highly irregular and idiosyncratic set of exceptions. The great majority of English verbs, numbering 10,000 or more, form their past tense by adding the regular [-d] affix to an otherwise unchanged stem. Depending on the final segment of the stem, this affix is realized as /d/, /t/ or /ed/, as in verbs like *jump/jumped, agree/agreed, state/stated*. This is an apparently paradigmatic example of a rule-based process, applying across the board to almost all the verbs in the language, and which functions as the default procedure for all new verb formations. The only exceptions are about 160 English verbs, many of them among the most common words in the language, which have irregular past tense forms, and which do not employ the regular affixing procedure. These are verbs like *give/gave, tell/told* and *buy/bought*, where the past tense form is idiosyncratic and phonologically unpredictable.

Because of these unpredictabilities, it is unlikely that the acquisition of irregular forms involves the acquisition of rules of any sort, and it is widely agreed that they are learned and stored by some form of pattern-association process. The key theoretical issue, instead, is how to characterize the mechanisms underlying the regular past tense, and whether, in particular, the explanation of this classically rule-like procedure requires the postulation of an internal symbolic rule.

During the "cognitive revolution" of the 1960s, the acquisition profile for the English past tense played an important role in establishing the view of mental computation as rule-based manipulation of symbol systems (Chomsky, 1959). Children learning English seemed to move from an early stage of rote-learning of individual past tense forms to the induction of rule-based representations, as reflected in over-regularizations such as *goed* and *bringed* (Berko, 1958; Ervin & Miller, 1963; Kuczaj, 1977). These followed an initial period when *went* and *brought* were used appropriately, and *goed* and *bringed* did not occur. It was argued that these anomalous forms could not be explained in terms of non-cognitive accounts of the acquisition process—for example, through some form

of imitation, or through Skinnerian reinforcement procedures—because the child would never be exposed to these forms in the environment (Brown & Bellugi, 1964; McNeill, 1966). Their occurrence seemed to implicate strongly the child's induction of a linguistic rule—in this case, governing the formation of the regular past tense—with the subsequent misapplication of this rule to verbs which had irregular past tenses, and where, crucially, the child had previously used these irregular and highly frequent forms correctly.

This familiar and widely accepted argument from acquisition was fatally undermined by Rumelhart and McClelland's well-known demonstration that a simple two-layer connectionist network could apparently simulate the crucial characteristics of the learning sequence attributed to human learners (Rumelhart & McClelland, 1986). In particular, this network moved from an early period of correct generation of irregular past tense forms to a phase of over-regularization, where these irregular forms were regularized in ways analogous to the child's errors. The network could not possibly be said to have learnt a symbolically stated rule. The fact that it could, nonetheless, exhibit apparently rule-governed behaviour, including apparent over-extension of these "rules", has proved enormously influential in subsequent attempts to argue for (or against) a view of mental computation as rule-based and symbolic. Not surprisingly, it has also triggered an extensive and forceful debate.

Without discussing in detail the contents of this debate, it is fair to say that the controversy between connectionist and symbolic accounts of the acquisition process for the English past tense has effectively reached stalemate as far as the observable properties of the process are concerned. Early criticisms (Pinker & Prince, 1988) of the Rumelhart and McClelland model did pinpoint important flaws in this specific model, but subsequent work—for example by Plunkett and Marchman (1993)—has gone a long way towards meeting these criticisms (for a dissenting view, see Marcus, 1995). Arguably, both connectionist learning models and accounts in terms of symbolic mechanisms each seem able to explain the qualitative and quantitative properties of the acquisition of the past tense by the human child.

To distinguish the two types of account it is necessary to look, in addition, at other aspects of the mental representation of English regular and irregular past tenses. Attention has shifted, accordingly, to the properties of the "end state"—the manner in which regular and irregular forms are mentally represented by the adult native speaker of English. Current views of this, most prominently through the influence of Steven Pinker and his colleagues, have crystallized into the contrast between a single-mechanism approach, arguing for a complete account of mental computation in terms of current multi-layer connectionist networks, and a dual-mechanism approach, arguing that while connectionist accounts may be appropriate for the learning and representation of the irregular forms, a symbolic, rule-based system is required to explain the properties of the regular past tense, and, by extension, the properties of language and cognition in gen-

eral (Pinker, 1991). Again, however, it is fair to say that current behavioural research, using the techniques of experimental cognitive psychology to probe the properties of these types of representation, has not come to a clear resolution. Evidence that regular and irregular past tenses behave differently, for example, in some priming tasks (Marslen-Wilson, Hare, & Older, 1993), is not necessarily inconsistent with connectionist learning models of the underlying representations (Hare & Marslen-Wilson, 1997).

Potentially more decisive evidence comes from examining the properties of the neural systems that underlie adult processing and representation of these two types of linguistic material. This can be done either by using imaging techniques to study patterns of neural activity in the intact system, or by neuropsychological research examining the effects of damage to these systems through injury to the brain. We describe below some recent neuropsychological work of our own, and then relate this to other neuropsychological work and to research looking at brain activity in the intact system.

NEUROPSYCHOLOGICAL DISSOCIATIONS

The logic of the neuropsychological approach is relatively straightforward (Shallice, 1988). If regular and irregular forms are mentally represented and processed in fundamentally the same way, then both should be affected in similar ways by damage to the brain that disrupts morphological processing systems, and should show equivalent deficits in the appropriate experimental tests. But if there are two separate underlying systems, engaged, respectively, by the regular and irregular morphology, then it should be possible to find dissociations in performance between these two morphological domains.

To probe these possibilities we initially tested two aphasic patients (JG and DE) with well-documented difficulties in the comprehension and production of inflected forms in English. Both patients had typical "agrammatic" speech, which is hesitant and rarely contains inflected words. In tests of their ability to interpret inflected words, they were able to access the stems of such words, but had consistent difficulties in interpreting the combination of the stem with an inflectional affix—as, for example, in forms like *jumps* or *smiling* (decomposable, respectively, into {jump} + {-s} and {smile} + {-ing}). We expected them to also have problems in the access and interpretation of regular past tense forms like *jumped* or *smiled*, which again involve the combination of a stem with a regular inflectional affix. The crucial question, however, was whether they would show the same kinds of problems for irregular forms like *gave* or *taught*, where the morphological relation between stem and past tense does not involve the same type of combinatorial operation. These irregular forms do not have any internal morphological structure, and must be accessed as whole forms.

In order to bypass many of the problems inherent in testing the language abilities of such patients (e.g., reading difficulties and production problems) we

focused on tasks involving the comprehension of spoken words. The patients were tested in a priming task, where a spoken target word is immediately preceded by a spoken prime word, and where the listener makes a timed lexical-decision response to the target stimulus ("Is this a word or not?"). For unimpaired listeners, responses to a target word are speeded up when it is preceded by a morphologic-ally related prime word (as in the prime/target sequence *jumped/jump*) or by a semantically related prime (as in *swan/goose*), but not when the relationship is purely phonological (as in *gravy/grave*). Earlier studies confirmed that the patients could perform this task and that they showed normal levels of semantic priming —that is, they responded faster to a word like *goose* when it was preceded by a semantically related prime, such as *swan*, than by an unrelated word.

The results were clear-cut (Marslen-Wilson & Tyler, 1997). The control sub-jects, consistent with results for other groups of unimpaired adults in spoken priming tasks, showed significant priming for both regular and irregular past tense forms, with no interaction between regularity and priming. The aphasic patients (JG and DE), in contrast, exhibited a striking dissociation between regular and irregular morphology. They showed positive priming effects only for the irregular past tense, and not for the regular past tense. At the same time, like the controls, they showed significant priming for the semantically related pairs. This suggests a closer relationship between the processing of semantic primes and irregular past tense primes than between semantic and regular primes.

This relationship was sustained in testing of a third patient (TS), also classi-fied as "agrammatic", but with some right- as well as left-hemisphere damage. TS produces the opposite pattern to that shown by DE and JG, with normal performance on the regular past tense and no priming for the irregular past tense, accompanied by a failure of semantic priming. This double dissociation for the regular and irregular morphology is plotted in Figure 1, together with the pattern of semantic priming effects.

The pattern of results across the three aphasic patients, showing a close relationship between priming for semantically related words and for irregularly inflected words, is supported by data from a very different kind of patient, the semantic dementia patient ES, who has a severe and progressive semantic im-pairment (Moss & Tyler, 1997). This patient's semantic deficit is demonstrated by her poor performance on tasks such as picture naming, defining words, word–picture matching, and property verification. When tested on the same priming experiment as the aphasics, she showed significant priming for the regularly inflected words but not for the semantically related words and the irregularly inflected pairs.

This overall pattern of results for the four patients has significant implications for the functional and neural architectures underlying the representation and processing of regular and irregular past tense forms in English. We now explore these.

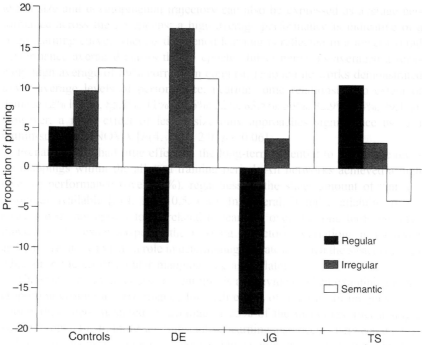

Figure 1. Repetition priming. Effects across patients (DE, JG, TS) and control subjects for regular and irregular past tense primes and for semantic primes. Priming effects are expressed as response proportions (mean priming effect for each condition as a proportion of mean control RT for that condition) to normalize for differences in base reaction-time between subjects. Reprinted with permission from *Nature*. Marslen-Wilson, W. D. & Tyler, L. K. (1997). Dissociating types of mental computation, *Nature*, *387*, 592–594. Copyright © (1997) Macmillan Magazines Limited.

NEURAL ARCHITECTURE

The most salient feature of the above results is the neurological dissociation of the regular and irregular past tenses, with the appropriate on-line tasks showing deficits in the access of regular but not irregular inflected forms for DE and JG, and the converse effect for TS and ES. These dissociations, together with the dissociations observed in other patient populations (Ullman et al., 1997), allow us to develop more specific hypotheses about the different brain regions that underlie the representation and processing of the different types of past tense. It is generally assumed that left posterior frontal cortex (Broca's area) is involved in the processing of grammatical information. Damage to this area often goes hand-in-hand with syntactic impairments and problems with inflectional morphology. The neuropathological data from the two agrammatic patients, DE and JG, are consistent with this picture, as both have extensive damage to Broca's area. JG had a large perisylvian lesion involving most of the region supplied by

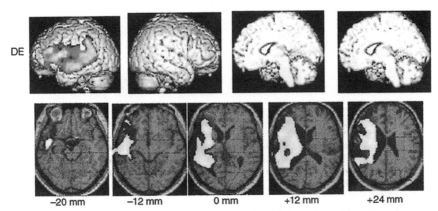

DE

−20 mm   −12 mm   0 mm   +12 mm   +24 mm

Figure 2. Extent of DE's left hemisphere lesion. Using the technique of voxel-based morphometry (Wright et al., 1995), it is possible to reconstruct from a structural MRI scan the 3D volume corresponding to the areas of DE's brain damaged by his middle cerebral artery stroke. . . . The upper four images, from left to right, show the damaged areas rendered onto the surfaces of the left and right hemispheres, followed by two medial sections, oriented to left and right. The bottom five images are transverse sections through DE's brain, showing the lateral extent of the missing or damaged tissue at five different levels (using Talairach co-ordinates). Note the extensive frontal and temporal damage, but with sparing of inferior temporal cortex and no sign of any right hemisphere involvement.

the left (L) middle cerebral artery, including the L temporo-parietal cortex and L inferior and middle frontal cortices (Price et al., 1998). DE also had extensive damage in the L fronto-parietal-occipital regions (see Figure 2). In both patients, there was extensive L posterior frontal damage (Broca's area) while ventral temporal cortex was relatively spared.

Although TS showed some linguistic deficits that are typical of agrammatism— slow, hesitant speech and comprehension problems—he also had a relatively severe semantic deficit, which is atypical in agrammatism. Moreover, TS's neuropathology differed from that of JG and DE in that he had a large right-hemisphere (RH) lesion resulting from a middle cerebral artery stroke in 1995. A CT scan in October 1996 revealed RH inferior parietal and temporal damage and changes to the frontal and occipital lobes, as well as patchy ischaemic damage in left frontal, parietal and temporal areas. Thus, TS may have sustained mild damage to left-hemisphere (LH) posterior frontal cortex but, in addition, he clearly has bilateral temporal lobe damage as well. The temporal lobes are typically involved in tasks involving semantics (Vandenberghe et al., 1996) and damage to the temporal lobes has been associated with semantic deficits in cases of semantic dementia (Hodges et al., 1992; Snowden, Goulding, & Neary, 1989) and category-specific deficits for living things (Gainotti et al., 1995). The fact that TS has damage to the temporal lobes may account for both his semantic deficit and for the lack of priming for irregularly inflected words. This analysis is supported by our fourth patient, ES, who is severely semantically impaired

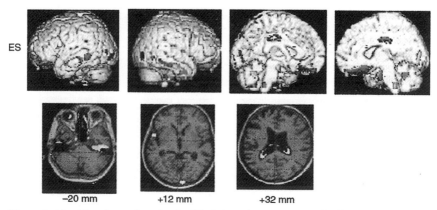

Figure 3. Voxel-based morphometry for ES. Subsequent to a structural MRI scan, voxel-based morphometry was used to determine the damaged areas in ES's brain, caused by progressive brain disease. . . . Although there is widespread minor damage, the principal lesions are in the inferior temporal lobes. The upper four figures show the rendered surfaces of the left and right hemispheres, followed by medial sections oriented to left and right. Damage is clearly most advanced in the inferior surface of the right temporal lobes. As with DE (see Figure 2), a number of transverse sections are also included, showing the extent of the lesions at three levels.

and who also shows no priming for the irregularly inflected pairs. She has substantial damage to the inferior temporal lobes, more extensive on the right, as determined by voxel-based morphometry of her MRI scan (courtesy of Dr Cathy Price; see Figure 3). Broca's area was essentially intact, with only a tiny region (too small to be detected by radiological examination) identified by voxel-based morphometry as being damaged. Thus, both TS and ES had relatively extensive temporal lobe damage accompanied by mild damage in Broca's region, and both showed the same behavioural pattern of a semantic deficit going hand-in-hand with problems with the irregular past tense and with normal priming of the regular past tense.

The relationship between the patient data and their neuropathology provides evidence for the role of posterior frontal brain regions in the processing of the regular past tense and of the left ventral temporal lobe in the processing of the irregular past tense. These claims are supported by a recent neuroimaging study by Jaeger et al. (1996) using PET, in which unimpaired adults were asked to produce either regular or irregular past tense forms. Jaeger et al. found increased activation in the left prefrontal cortex only during the production of regular past tense forms, and more activation in temporal and temporo-parietal regions only during the production of irregular past tenses. Although the interpretation of this study has to be qualified by doubts about uncontrolled differences in the difficulty of producing irregular and regular forms, the neuroimaging data and the patient neuropathology nonetheless present a consistent picture of the irregular and regular past tense being associated with different neural structures.

FUNCTIONAL ARCHITECTURE

Turning to the underlying functional architecture, the results for these patients suggest that the two morphological categories ally themselves with different domains of mental computation. DE and JG's deficits for the regular past tense are consistent with earlier evidence that these patients have marked deficits in combinatorial operations involving morphologically complex words—though note that recent evidence from our laboratory suggests that this deficit is restricted to the inflectional morphology; processes involving derivational morphology seem to be intact (Tyler & Marslen-Wilson, 1997). The irregular past tenses, in contrast, which are relatively spared for DE and JG, seem to accord with the evidence that these patients are relatively intact in their ability to access the semantic properties of morphologically simple words (Ostrin & Tyler, 1995; Tyler & Ostrin, 1994). TS and ES, in contrast, who show no semantic priming, also show no sparing of the irregular past tense relative to the normal levels of priming they achieve for the regular past tense.

What are the functional implications of this neuropsychological association between intact semantic priming and intact irregular priming? What does it have to say about possible differences in the mental representation of regular and irregular forms, and how does this bear on the claims about types of mental computation that have motivated much of the interest in this research? We will consider two possible accounts, each of which corresponds to a "dual mechanism" account in the broad sense that (1) different neural structures seem to be involved for regular and irregular past tense forms, and (2) that the way in which aspects of these forms are mentally represented seems to be qualitatively distinct. The first of these accounts explores the possibility that the priming relation between irregular past tense forms and their stems is primarily a semantic relationship, which parallels the priming relation between semantically related but morphologically unrelated words, such as *swan* and *goose*. For pairs like this, semantic priming reflects the spread or overlap of activation between two distinct lexical elements each with their own semantic representation. The possibility raised by the results here is that this also holds true for irregular past tense forms and their stems, so that *brought* and *bring*, for example, would be represented underlyingly as if they were two different words, with distinct semantic representations.

This would be a fundamentally different view of the relationship between an inflected form and its stem than is generally assumed to hold for the regular inflectional morphology. Here it is assumed that inflectional variants like *jump*, *jumped*, *jumps*, etc., do not correspond to separately represented underlying lexical elements, each with its own semantic representation. Rather, there is a single underlying representation, of the morpheme {jump}, capturing its abstract semantic, syntactic, and phonological properties. This morpheme has a number of inflectional variants, expressed phonologically as the stem plus an inflectional

TABLE 1
Experimental contrasts for delayed
repetition experiment

	Prime–target relationship		
	Regular	Irregular	Semantic
Prime	called	gave	white
Target	call	give	black

affix, but these are not separately represented in the mental lexicon. Priming effects, for these morphologically related words, are the consequence of repeated activation of the same underlying morpheme, and are not the result of spreading activation between distinct representations, as we established in earlier research looking at the basis for morphological priming in English (Marslen-Wilson et al., 1994).

This semantic account, based on the properties of the damaged system, seems inconsistent, however, with research we have been recently conducting into the properties of the intact system. One piece of evidence comes from a study using delayed repetition priming, where young adults make lexical decisions to spoken words presented one at a time, at intervals of two or three seconds, and where several words may intervene between the prime word and its related target. Note the contrast with the immediate repetition task used in the research with patients, where primes and targets are presented in pairs, and the gap between them is of the order of 250 ms. The reason for using the delayed repetition task here is that semantic priming drops away sharply over time but morphological priming does not. If the relationship between irregular past tense forms and their stems is more like the relationship between two separate but related lexical representations, then irregulars should pattern with the semantically related pairs, rather than with regularly related inflected pairs (see Table 1).

In our experiment the materials were presented with 12 items intervening between prime and target (approximately 35 seconds), and the outcome was unequivocal (see Figure 4). There is no semantic priming at all at these long delays, but equally strong and significant priming for both regular and irregular primes. This is strong evidence that the underlying relationship between past tense form and stem is a morphological one in both cases, involving repeated access to the same underlying lexical element—in the case of these stimuli, the morpheme corresponding to the verb stem.

This alignment of the irregulars with regulars rather than with semantically related pairs is confirmed by a further study looking at the electrophysiological correlates of priming. Unimpaired young adults carried out cross-model priming tasks, where an auditory prime is immediately followed by a visual target, while event-related scalp potentials (ERPs) were measured using a high-density

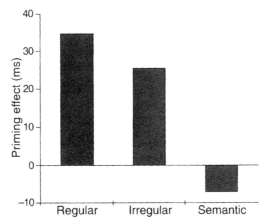

Figure 4. Delayed repetition priming. Listeners made lexical decisions to primed and unprimed targets, and the difference (in ms) is plotted for each condition. No priming was found at these long lags for purely semantically related targets, but significant and equally strong priming was found for targets preceded by both regular and irregular morphologically related primes.

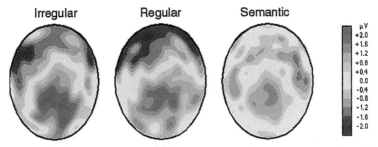

Figure 5. ERP responses to primed targets. The interpolated difference waves are shown for each condition, computed by measuring the difference in electrical activity in scalp responses, over 128 electrode sites, when subjects were responding to primed as opposed to unprimed visual targets. Activity is summed here over the period 340–400 ms after the onset of the target. The targets were preceded either by unrelated spoken control words, or by semantically or morphologically related primes (see Table 1). This study was carried out at the MRC Cognitive Development Unit, in collaboration with Gergely Csibra, Harry Hatzikis and Mark Johnson.

128-channel system. The subjects were tested with the same contrasts as in Table 1, covering regular and irregular pairs and semantically related pairs. Figure 5 plots the interpolated difference waves for the three critical conditions, showing the differences in responses to primed as opposed to unprimed targets. All three priming conditions have in common a central positivity, peaking in a time-frame of 340–400 ms after the onset of the visual target. This is the N400 effect standardly observed in semantic priming (Holcomb & Anderson, 1993), as well as many other processing situations (Kutas & Hillyard, 1984). Both regular and irregular, however, diverge from the semantic case, in that in addition they

each show significant left anterior negativities, typically associated with linguistic processing (Penke et al., 1997). Thus, although there may be differences in detail in the pattern of activation for targets primed by regular as opposed to irregular primes, it is nonetheless the case that the irregulars globally parallel the regulars rather than the semantic pairs.

The outcome of these two studies indicates that the underlying relationship between an irregular past tense and its stem is more like the morphological relationship between a regular inflected form and its stem than it is like the relationship between pairs that are just semantically related. This, in turn, means that we cannot explain the neuropsychological results simply in terms of the semantic account sketched earlier, where the joint sparing of semantic priming and irregular priming is attributed to underlying parallels in their representational relationships. We are left, instead, with a view where the irregular form, like the regular form, maps onto the same underlying morpheme, and that it is repeated activation of this morpheme which gives rise to priming effects.

To explain why regular and irregular forms do, nonetheless, dissociate under some circumstances, we need to focus on the differences in the phonological representations of these forms. As noted earlier, we assume that regular inflectional forms are not stored as such, but are generated as required, as combinations of stems and inflectional affixes (*jump + s*, *jump + ed*, etc.). The recognition of these forms, where the underlying morpheme is activated by the incoming speech stream, requires a converse process of phonological parsing, where the spoken input is disassembled into stem and affix. This representational claim can be contrasted with those for monomorphemic forms, like *speed*, *elbow*, *table*, and so on. Here we assume that production and recognition involves the access of a stored full form, so that no process of phonological parsing is required in order to access this representation. The crucial claim here is that irregular inflected forms are also stored as full-form representations, with no internal phonological structure as combinations of stems and affixes. Again, access to these representations does not require them to be phonologically parsed.

This points to an alternative explanation of why irregular primes pattern with semantic primes for the patient populations, and why these can remain intact when regular priming is disrupted. One of the defining features of agrammatic patients like JG and DE is that they have problems with processes of phonological assembly, especially where this involves the domain of "morphosyntax"— that is, where words combine with syntactic elements, such as tense markers and plurals, to form inflectionally complex words. The spoken output of these patients is markedly lacking in regular inflected forms, and there is little doubt that they have comparable problems on the input side, in the phonological disassembly, or parsing, of inflected complex forms. This would lead to on-line impairments in the processing of regularly inflected words (such as the regular past tense), hence making these less effective as primes in the auditory–auditory immediate priming task. But for inputs that do not require this kind of phonological

disassembly, including both monomorphemic words and irregular past tenses, there would be no on-line impairment, allowing prime words of this type to contact their underlying representations with normal efficiency and rapidity, so that subsequent priming, whether based on semantic overlap or on repeated access to the same morpheme, can also proceed normally.

What is less straightforward for this account is to explain why regular inflected forms can remain effective as primes when semantic priming and priming from irregular past tense forms is disrupted. If failure of semantic priming is due to underlying disruptions in storage of left infero-temporal semantic representations, and this also disrupts priming from irregular past tenses, then priming from regular past tenses should also be disrupted, given the argument we have just made for the underlying similarities in the way regular and irregular inflected forms connect to their stems. A phonological account would have to argue, instead, that the access routes via full-form representations and those that require phonological disassembly are qualitatively distinct and neurologically dissociable. Thus, when the full-form route is disrupted, reducing the effectiveness of both monomorphemic and irregular past tense primes, the listener is still able to access underlying lexical representations via intact fronto-temporal systems supporting phonological parsing and morphosyntactic analysis. Additional research is needed, however, to evaluate these speculations.

DISSOCIATING TYPES OF MENTAL COMPUTATION?

The neuropsychological data from a variety of sources indicate that it is possible to dissociate at least some aspects of the neural systems supporting the perception and generation of regular as opposed to irregular past tense forms. This seems to follow directly from the predictions of a dual mechanism approach, and presents at least apparent difficulties for a single mechanism approach. However, the fact of dissociation itself is insufficiently constraining to discriminate among these approaches—there are, for example, developmental connectionist accounts which allow for the possibility that different cortical areas can recruit to themselves different aspects of the same processing domain, depending on the kinds of computational resources they require (Elman et al., 1996; Quartz & Sejnowski, 1997). Learning the regular rule may differ from learning irregular exceptions in just this kind of way.

Additional constraints come from a functional analysis of how the facts of association and dissociation, in both the damaged and the intact system, point to more specific hypotheses about the underlying differences in the representation and processing of regular and irregular forms. We looked at two accounts, one semantic and one phonological, both of which had in common the assumption that regulars and irregulars differ along the dimension of what linguists would call "listedness" (DiSciullo & Williams, 1987)—that is, whether the underlying

representation is stored as a whole unit, or whether it is generated, in a combinatorial manner, when required.

In the semantic domain, we evaluated the possibility that irregular past tense forms were separate lexical entries, rather than being linked to a verb stem in the same way as the regular forms, where these are assumed not to have separate representations. Alternatively, in the phonological domain, we considered the possibility that it is the form representation of the irregular that is stored as a separate entity, again contrasting with the regular inflected forms, which are assumed not be stored in the same manner. Neither account seems completely satisfactory on its own, and it is likely that they are complementary rather than mutually exclusive—especially given the special developmental history of the English irregular past tense (Clark, 1993; Marcus et al., 1992). Children initially learn forms like *took* and *brought* as forms in their own right, and analyse them as separate verb roots. It is only later, in a process that can take several years to complete, that they fully re-analyse *took* as part of the verb *take*, *brought* as part of the verb *bring*, and so on. These processes of analysis and reanalysis may give the irregular past tense its apparent hybrid status in the adult representational system, with listed phonological forms, but with their semantic and syntactic properties subsumed under those of the verb stems to which they are linked.

These arguments suggest an "end state" with complex functional and neurological properties. The regular inflected forms do not have an independent representational status but are generated and parsed as required, depending on neural systems with a primarily LH frontal distribution. An important function of these systems is to support the processes of phonological assembly and disassembly which subserve the crucial domain of morphosyntax, where inflectional morphemes knit together strings of lexical morphemes into higher-order phrasal and clausal structures. Irregular past tense forms must also link into this domain, ultimately serving the same grammatical and interpretative functions as their regular counterparts. They seem to do so, however, through the involvement of somewhat different functional and neural subsystems, reflecting the listedness of their phonological representations, where there is no requirement to invoke combinatorial processes of phonological assembly. These subsystems seem to overlap substantially with those involved in the access and representation of morphologically simply forms, implicating the inferior temporal lobes in particular.

Within this framework, it is doubtful that an all-or-none computational dissociation between single and dual mechanisms will be a plausible outcome. It is becoming clear, both functionally and neurologically, that at least two, if not more, separable systems are involved. But any account of the computational properties of these systems, and any decision about the possible contrasts between them, is going to have to be firmly rooted, unlike most current models, in specific and testable proposals about the functional and neural architectures of the relevant cognitive and linguistic domains.

OUTSTANDING QUESTIONS

- It is likely that the contrast in English between regular and irregular past tenses is cross-linguistically unusual, and provides an inadequate basis for claims about the universal properties of cognitive computation. A start has been made at looking into these questions in other languages, suggesting that there are interesting cross-linguistic variations—for example, between English, German (Clahsen, Eisenbeiss, & Sonnenstuhl-Henning, 1997) and Italian (Orsolini & Marslen-Wilson, 1997). These are issues that need to be pursued across a wider range of language types.

- We raised the possibility that access routes via full-form representations and those that require phonological parsing are qualitatively distinct and neurologically dissociable. Are there other types of patient data that bear on this, and what differences might we predict in behavioural tasks?

- There is some evidence that patients who have difficulties with inflectional morphology have relatively spared derivational morphology. Does this relate to differences in the phonological aspects of these two types of morphology, or does it suggest a dissociation between different types of lexical combinatorial process?

- The work we report here is with isolated words. Would similar patterns of impaired and preserved performance emerge if we looked at processing of regular and irregular forms in more natural utterance contexts?

- Irregular past tenses in English are phonologically unpredictable, in the sense that the language learner cannot predict, given a stem, whether or not it has an irregular past tense, and, if it is irregular, what form it might take. This has to be learnt, on a case-by-case basis, for every irregular verb in the language. Nonetheless, there are subsets of irregular verbs that share phonological properties—for example, the verbs showing the *ing–ung* variation (as in *fling/flung*, *ring/rung*, *sing/sung*, etc.). These phonological sub-regularities play a role in generalization to new stems (Prasada & Pinker, 1993), and may well have influenced the historical evolution of the English system to its current state (Hare & Elman, 1995). On the appropriate tests, would these more "regular" irregular verbs behave like regular verbs in terms of their representation and access?

ACKNOWLEDGEMENTS

This research was supported by an MRC programme grant held by L.K.T. and W.M.-W., and by ESRC grants held by W.M.-W. We thank Dr Cathy Price of the Wellcome Functional Imaging Laboratory for her advice and help in providing voxel morphometry data for the patients DE and ES. We also thank Mike Ford, Paul deMornay-Davies, Lianne Older and Christiaan Morgan for their help in carrying out the studies described in this review.

REFERENCES

Berko, J. (1958). The child's learning of English morphology. *Word, 14*, 150–177.

Brown, R., & Bellugi, U. (1964). Three processes in the child's acquisition of syntax. In E. Lenneberg (Ed.), *New directions in the study of language*. MIT Press.

Chomsky, N. (1959). A review of B. F. Skinner's "Verbal Behavior". *Language, 3*, 26–58.

Clahsen, H., Eisenbeiss, S., & Sonnenstuhl-Henning, I. (1997). Morphological structure and the processing of inflected words. *Theoretical Linguistics, 23*, 201–249.

Clark, E. V. (1993). *The lexicon in acquisition*. Cambridge University Press.

Di Sciullo, A. M., & Williams, E. (1987). *On the definition of word*. MIT Press.

Elman, J., Bates, E.-A., Johnson, M. H., & Karmiloff-Smith, A. (1996). *Rethinking innateness*. MIT Press.

Ervin, S. M., & Miller, W. R. (1963). Language development. In H. W. Stevenson (Ed.), *Child psychology: The sixty-second yearbook of the National Society for the Study of Education, Part I*. University of Chicago Press.

Gainotti, G., Silveri, M.-C., Daniele, A., & Giustolisi, L. (1995). Neuroanatomical correlates of category-specific semantic disorders: A critical survey. *Memory, 3*, 247–264.

Hare, M., & Elman, J. L. (1995). Learning and morphological change. *Cognition, 56*, 61–98.

Hare, M., & Marslen-Wilson, W. D. (1997). Past tense priming in an auto-associative network. In *Proceedings of the 19th annual conference of the Cognitive Science Society* (p. 945). Lawrence Erlbaum Associates Inc.

Hodges, J., et al. (1992). Semantic dementia: Progressive fluent aphasia with temporal lobe atrophy. *Brain, 115*, 1783–1806.

Holcomb, P. J., & Anderson, J. E. (1993). Cross-modal semantic priming: A time-course analysis using event-related potentials. *Language and Cognitive Processes, 8*, 379–411.

Jaeger, J. J., et al. (1996). A positron emission study of regular and irregular verb morphology in English. *Language, 72*, 451–497.

Kuczaj, S. A. (1977). The acquisition of regular and irregular past tense forms *Journal of Verbal Learning & Verbal Behavior, 16*, 589–600.

Kutas, M., & Hillyard, S. (1984). Brain potentials during reading reflect word expectancy and semantic association. *Nature, 307*, 161–163.

Marcus, G. F. (1995). The acquisition of inflection in children and multi-layered connectionist networks. *Cognition, 56*, 271–279.

Marcus, G. F., Ullman, M., Pinker, S., Hollander, M., Rosen, T. J., & Xu, F. (1992). Overregularization in language acquisition. *Monographs of the Society of Research into Child Development, 57*.

Marslen-Wilson, W. D., Tyler, L. K., Waksler, R., & Older, L. (1994). Morphology and meaning in the English mental lexicon. *Psychological Review 101*, 1–31.

Marslen-Wilson, W. D., Hare, M., & Older, L. (1993). Inflectional morphology and phonological regularity in the English mental lexicon. In *Proceedings of the 15th annual meeting of the Cognitive Science Society* (pp. 693–698). Lawrence Erlbaum Associates Inc.

Marslen-Wilson, W. D., & Tyler, L. K. (1997). Dissociating types of mental computation. *Nature, 387*, 592–594.

McNeill, D. (1966). Developmental psycholinguistics. In F. Smith & G. Miller (Eds.), *The genesis of language*. MIT Press.

Moss, H. M., & Tyler, L. K. (1997). A category-specific semantic deficit for non-living things in a case of progressive aphasia. *Brain and Language, 60*, 55–58.

Orsolini, M., & Marslen-Wilson, W. (1997). Universals in morphological representation: Evidence from Italian. *Language and Cognitive Processes, 12*, 1–37.

Ostrin, R. K., & Tyler, L. K. (1995). Dissociations of lexical function: Semantics, syntax, and morphology. *Cognitive Neuropsychology, 12*, 345–389.

Penke, M., Weyerts, H., Gross, M., Zander, E., Muente, T., Thomas, F., & Clahsen, H. (1997). How the brain processes complex words: An ERP study of German verb inflection. *Cognitive Brain Research 6*, 37–52.

Pinker, S. (1991). Rules of language. *Science, 253*, 530–535.

Pinker, S., & Prince, A. (1988). On language and connectionism: Analysis of a parallel distributed processing model of language acquisition. *Cognition, 28*, 73–193.

Plunkett, K., & Marchman, V. (1993). From rote learning to system building: Acquiring verb morphology in children and connectionist nets. *Cognition, 48*, 21–69.

Prasada, S., & Pinker, S. (1993). Generalisation of regular and irregular morphological processes. *Language and Cognitive Processes, 8*, 1–56.

Price, C. J., Moore, C. J., Humphreys, G. W., & Wise, R. J. S. (1998). A functional neuroimaging description of two deep dyslexic patients *Journal Cognitive Neuroscience, 10*, 303–315.

Quartz, S., & Sejnowski, T. J. (1997). The neural basis of cognitive development: A constructivist manifesto. *Behavioral Brain Sciences, 20*, 537–596.

Rumelhart, D., & McClelland, J. (1986). On learning the past tense of English verbs. In J. L. McClelland, D. E. Rumelhart, & the PDP Research Group (Eds.), *Parallel distributed processing: Explorations in the microstructure of cognition, Vol. 2, Psychological and biological models* (pp. 216–271). MIT Press.

Shallice, T. (1988). *From neuropsychology to mental structure.* Cambridge University Press.

Snowden, J. S., Goulding, P. J., & Neary, D. (1989). Semantic dementia: A form of circumscribed cerebral atrophy. *Behav. Neurol, 2*, 167–182.

Tyler, L. K., & Marslen-Wilson, W. D. (1997). Disorders of combination: Processing complex words. *Brain and Language, 60*, 48–50.

Tyler, L. K., & Ostrin, R. K. (1994). The processing of simple and complex words in an agrammatic patient: Evidence from priming. *Neuropsychologia, 32*, 1001–1013.

Ullman, M., Corkin, S., Coppola, M., & Hickock, G. (1997). A neural dissociation within language: Evidence that the mental dictionary is part of declarative memory and that grammatical rules are processed by the procedural system. *Journal Cognitive Neuroscience, 9*, 266–276.

Vandenberghe, R., Price, C., Wise, R., Josephs, O., & Frackowiak, R. S. J. (1996). Functional anatomy of a common semantic system for words and pictures. *Nature, 383*, 254–256.

Wright, I. C., et al. (1995). A voxel-based method for the statistical analysis of gray and white matter density applied to schizophrenia. *Neuroimage, 2*, 244–252.

CHAPTER ELEVEN

Why double dissociations don't mean much

Patrick Juola and Kim Plunkett
University of Oxford, UK

The conventional interpretation of double dissociations is that they are almost irrefutable evidence of distinctions in both function and type of mental processes, or of separation of cognition into modules. We present a connectionist model that demonstrates apparent double dissociations within a single-route, single-mechanism network and argue that these apparent dissociations are simply the expected tails of a standard bell curve describing network performance. We conclude that within a connectionist model, the appearance of double dissociations may not be evidence for functional or mechanistic separation, and that similar caveats apply to the interpretation of double dissociations in human cognitive behaviour.

INTRODUCTION

Dissociations, and specifically double dissociations, are widely considered to be one of the more powerful tools in a cognitive neuropsychologist's arsenal. This phenomenon occurs when "[cognitive psychologists] can find one patient who can perform task A but not task B and a second patient who can perform task B but not task A" (McLeod, Plunkett, & Rolls, 1998, p. 254). The philosophical position is simple, but far-ranging. By examining behaviour, and specifically how behaviour breaks down, the goal is to fractionate the components of cognition into their logical and behavioural constituents. If two styles of processing are logically and behaviourally separable (for example, the recognition of people by their faces and the person-independent recognition of facial expressions), one is tempted to conclude that the two processes are independent and don't rely on one another. Furthermore, if the two processes appear to do radically different things, or to do things in radically different ways, one can argue for a complete

Proceedings of the Cognitive Science Society, 1998, 1–6.

processing difference. This can further be argued to be not just a difference between separate systems doing the same sort of processing, but between separate systems doing completely different kinds of processing, as the needs of the separate constituents demand—for example, the basic features relevant to facial recognition are different from the basic features for expression recognition, and so there's reason to think that the two processes operate in completely different ways.

Inflectional morphology in English has been a fruitful area for this sort of study and analysis. It is relatively easy to fractionate, for example, the process of inflection into two separate processes of regular and irregular inflection. Even within a single syntactic category, the inflection of regular forms (e.g., *house* → *houses*) seems intuitively different from the inflection of irregular forms (*mouse* → *mice*). Regular inflections appear to generalize easily to novel or nonword forms, to unusual productions, and even to word forms that are usually irregular but are used in unusual or atypical ways. In contrast, irregulars seem to generalize significantly less when they generalize at all (few people are tempted to produce **hice* as the plural of *house*).

Daugherty and Seidenberg (1992) have demonstrated that irregular forms are much more sensitive to frequency effects in reading aloud than are regular forms. Prasada and Pinker (1993) have shown differences in similarity effects between regular and irregular forms in terms of generalization performance levels. The crowning piece of evidence for some sort of separation, or against any theory of a unified mechanism, should be the production of case studies showing a double dissociation—for example, studies of Williams syndrome patients (Bellugi, Hoeck, Lillo-Martin, & Sabo, 1988) seem to show that regular forms are relatively preserved (in comparison with performance on irregular forms), while studies of SLI patients (Gopnik & Crago, 1994) show that *irregular* forms are relatively preserved. Finally, Marslen-Wilson and Tyler (1997) present a case of two aphasics with different lexical decision performances on regular and irregular words, and claim, specifically, that "this is evidence for functional and neurological distinctions in the types of mental computation that support these different aspects of linguistic and cognitive performance". This is the classic form and conclusion of a double dissociation.

This argument, we claim, is incorrect. Plaut and Shallice (1994) have produced a connectionist network that does show functional separation between various sets of units, and thus damage to one particular set of units (or interconnecting weights) produces predictably different error patterns than damage to other sets. Similar effects could be expected to be found in, for instance, the (Mareschal, Plunkett, & Harris, 1995) model of object permanence or the (Miikkulainen, 1993) model of story understanding. In general, any of the generalized pipe-fitting complex connectionist models show as much functional separation between their units and connections as the box-and-arrow diagrams that underly them and are often used to explain their functioning. Despite this degree of functional separation, however, this sort of structure does not provide evidence for "distinctions in the

types of . . . computation", as the type of processing is the same for all units within this type of network.

We present here a model and associated connectionist simulation that may explain some forms of double dissociation as simple variance from a stochastic norm within a single-system, single-mechanism, associator. In this model, the effects of damage are unpredictable, and further, these effects may differentially affect different words or word categories. Our experiments show, for example, that a single network can be damaged randomly in such a way as to have very good performance on a particular class of words, or very bad performance, despite the level of damage being the same in either case. We argue that the mere observance of a double dissociation, particularly as a rare or pathological case, is not sufficient evidence to conclude a separation of processing, especially in cases where the damage itself can only be observed crudely and the function lost is highly complex.

SIMULATION

Network definition

The network that we chose to damage is a standard connectionist simulation, constructed as a multi-layer perceptron network using backpropagation of error (Rumelhart, Hinton, & Williams, 1986). The simulation was built using the PlaNet simulator (Miyata, 1991) using 130 units for the input layer, 160 units for the output layer, and 200 units as the hidden layer.

Five random sets of starting weights were trained over a gradually expanding corpus of training data eventually encompassing 2280 noun types and 946 verb types of varying frequencies representing their token frequencies as found in the Brown corpus (Kučera & Francis, 1967). The training data for the simulations were taken from the CELEX corpus (Baayan, Piepenbrock, & Rijn, 1993); we extracted from this database all words which were monosyllabic, which contained no "foreign" sounds in their pronunciation (according to the Moby Pronunciator database (Ward, 1997)), and for which we had evidence that they could be used as nouns or verbs. This yielded a total corpus of 2626 stems, which encompassed 3226 total inflected types (2280 nouns and 946 verbs). Of these types, 26 were irregular nouns and 122 were irregular verbs. For these words, we took the corresponding token frequencies (of the stems) from the Brown corpus (Kučera & Francis, 1967) as a rough measure of token frequencies in running speech. The token frequencies of words were individually tabulated as nouns and verbs, then the function $\log_2(freq^2 + 1)$ applied to these frequencies to flatten them into something more presentable to the network. The final variance was between 1 and 21 tokens/inflected type, meaning that the most frequent words appeared just over twenty times as often as the least. These token frequencies were also heavily dominated by nouns. Of the 17,129 tokens in the training set 13,045 were noun tokens (204 of them irregular) and 4084 were verb tokens (997 of them irregular).

The training corpus was prepared by converting the Moby symbolic pronunciation (Ward, 1997) into a large binary vector using a modification of the PGPfone alphabet representation (Juola & Zimmermann, 1996). Each phoneme was represented as a cluster of 16 binary phonetic features including aspects such as place, manner, and height of articulation. Each word was divided into onset–nucleus–coda constituents and right-justified within a CCCVVCCC template (e.g., the word "cat" (/kAt/) would be represented by the training pattern ##k#A##t, where "#" represents an absent sound). To this 128-bit pattern, two additional bits were appended representing the syntactic form to be inflected into, either the past tense (of a verb) or the plural (of a noun). The desired outputs were a similar encoding of the phonology of the inflected form, including an optional epenthetic vowel and final consonant. An incremental training regime was applied, where training started out with a small number (20 types) of high frequency words. The training set was then gradually expanded (5% type expansion per epoch) to include words of decreasing frequency until the entire corpus is absorbed. This training schedule is intended to capture the distinction between input to and uptake by the child (Plunkett & Marchman, 1993).

Each of the five starting points yielded a unique weight configuration after 115 training increments and was used as the basis for the lesioning experiments. Increment 115 is the earliest point at which the network had been exposed to the entire training corpus and, as might be expected, is the point with the worst overall performance on the training corpus. Because of the high error rate under "normal" circumstances, it is reasonable to assume that it would be the most sensitive to damage and therefore an appropriate time to lesion in search of interesting error patterns. The acquisition and loss profiles can be briefly summarized by the results that nouns are, in general, superior to verbs and regulars superior to irregulars, in keeping with their relative frequencies within the corpus. We focus here not on the average level of loss, but instead on the variation in loss.

Analysis

Each (lesioned) subject network was presented with the training corpus and the outputs interpreted by taking the closest phoneme string to the output units' activation pattern. This pattern was simply evaluated as "correct" or "incorrect," and the number of correct types of each category (e.g., regular nouns, irregular nouns, regular verbs, and irregular verbs) was taken as a measure of network performance.

We first note that the level of performance is "random", in at least the limited sense of not entirely predictable. Because of this unpredictability, we therefore can "expect" unexpected behaviour, both unexpectedly good and unexpectedly bad.

To confirm this, we performed 1065 separate lesions, all at the 97% level (in other words, leaving a random 97% of the connections intact) of one of the

networks developed in the prior experiment. In a medical context, this might represent an exploration of the range of damage that could be expected after a particular patient received an injury of some particular severity.

Some degree of normalization is necessary, as the training set itself only included 26 irregular noun types but 2254 regular noun types—and the undamaged networks correctly inflected a higher percentage of regular noun tokens than irregular ones. (The network, for example, achieved 99% on regular nouns, 97% on regular verbs, but only 90% on irregular verbs and only 77% [20 out of 26] on irregular nouns. This is typical for all networks we studied.) We therefore normalized performance by calculating it as a percentage of "baseline" performance of the undamaged network used as a base for each subject. Because in many cases, especially for irregular nouns and verbs, the baseline performance included errors, it occasionally happened that the performance of an individual subject on an individual category would exceed the baseline, resulting in apparently paradoxical performance levels that exceed 100%. In other words, under certain circumstances, damage not only does not degrade performance, but will actually increase it.

Results

Figure 1 presents a histogram of the performance level on the inflection of regular verb types. Even after variation in patient and physical severity of damage have been controlled for, the outlines of a skewed bell curve can be seen. In other words, depending upon the exact nature of the lesion, an individual network/patient may display "little" impairment or "severe" impairment, relative to the expected performance level, although most networks will display "moderate" or "average" impairments. A similar curve, although with a different mean and

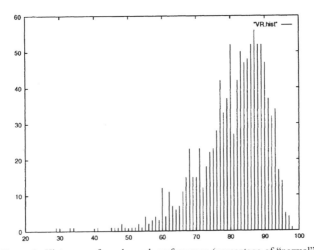

Figure 1. Histogram of regular verb performance (percentage of "normal").

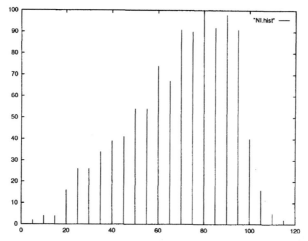

Figure 2. Histogram of irregular noun performance (percentage of "normal").

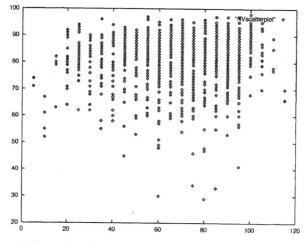

Figure 3. Scatter plot of irregular noun vs. regular verb performances (percentages).

median level of impairment, can be seen in Figure 2, showing the same lesions' performance on irregular noun types.

Furthermore, these performance levels, although correlated, are at least partially independent, as can be seen on the scatter-plot (Figure 3). Obviously, the lesions at the upper left corner of the graph will display an apparent dissociation of performance on irregular nouns relative to regular verbs, and the converse holds for the lesions in the lower right. However, *these represent identically-severe lesions for the same network*! These lesions demonstrate a "double dissociation" within the same, unified-route, unified-mechanism processor. . . .

DISCUSSION

This argument, then, may explain both the occurrence as well as the rarity of some neurological impairments. If one considers the case of a neurologist sitting in an emergency ward and examining patients as they come in, it should be evident that most "closed head injury patients" will not present with an interesting collection of symptoms. The patients that receive interest (and journal writeups) are somewhat rare examples that show how things *can* go wrong, and not necessarily how they are expected to go wrong. In particular, the change in output behaviour of a sufficiently complex system might not appropriately be described as just a performance "loss". A better description would be a change or alteration in performance; as we describe above, sometimes the change can improve (some aspects of) performance by eliminating factors that have contributed to errors. There appears to be no hard and fast boundary between routes, or modules, such that the module fails to function—instead, the outputs are subtly altered (by the insertion of unpredictable "noise") and the noisy outputs themselves may be subject to further noisy processing.

In particular, this model demonstrates that double dissociations may be possible, even in the absence of specific modular differences in type and function of processing. These double dissociations are instead the result of stochastic processes. The appearance of such a dissociation may not be sufficient evidence to conclude that such a separation exists. By extension, this sort of evidence *in humans* may not be sufficient evidence to conclude that an equivalent functional or neurological separation exists.

CONCLUSIONS

We have presented a model and explanation for some kinds of double dissociation that does not require a different method of processing or even a functional separation between modules in the underlying processing. We argue instead that, because the effects of damage to as complex a system as inflectional morphology are somewhat unpredictable, in some cases "random" damage will result in surprisingly good performance on some aspects of a task and surprisingly bad performance on other aspects, merely as a result of the task complexity exceeding our understanding of the system underlying it. Specifically, because we are unable to understand the exact differences between the representation of one type and another in connectionist networks, the differences in representation may occasionally conspire (under damage) to produce variance among some representational groups, whether these groups are "irregular nouns" or "words with even parity". These apparent conspiracies will (stochastically) produce double dissociations at the extreme tails of the probability distribution, irrespective of the functional and computational makeup of the system.

This argument might be extended as a suggestion against the extensive use of individual case studies in the general psychological literature; if connectionist

networks are regarded as complex, how much more so is the human brain? It would be unusual indeed if we could predict the exact behavioural result from a particular injury or genetic makeup, meaning that in some cases, the results will be surprisingly devastating, while in other cases (or other tasks) the results will be surprisingly preserved. By sorting through enough patients or networks, one can "expect" that one's expectations will sometimes be woefully misleading. So the appearance of individual cases, absent some analysis of how characteristic or uncharacteristic they are, may not be significant in the fractionating of cognition. Paradoxically enough, then, the double dissociations produced by neural networks *may* actually be better evidence for how mental processes might break down, because the network developers can lesion the same network over and over until the results can be described, not in terms of idiosyncratic cases, but in terms of means and expectations.

ACKNOWLEDGEMENT

This work was supported by a research project grant from the ESRC to Kim Plunkett.

REFERENCES

Baayan, H., Piepenbrock, R., & van Rijn, H. (1993). *The CELEX lexical database (CD-ROM)*. University of Pennsylvania, PA: Linguistic Data Consortium.

Bellugi, U., van Hoeck, K., Lillo-Martin, D., & Sabo, H. (1988). Dissociation between language and cognitive function in Williams syndrome. In D. Bishop & K. Mogford (Eds.), *Language develoment in exceptional circumstances*. Edinburgh: Churchill Livingstone.

Daugherty, K., & Seidenberg, M. S. (1992). Rules or connections? The past tense revisited. In *Proceedings of the fourteenth annual conference of the Cognitive Science Society*. Hillsdale, NJ: Lawrence Erlbaum Associates Inc.

Gopnik, M., & Crago, M. (1994). Familial aggregation of a developmental language disorder. *Cognition, 39*, 1–50.

Juola, P., & Zimmermann, P. (1996). Whole-word phonetic distances and the PGPfone alphabet. In *Proceedings of the International Conference on Spoken Language Processing (ICSLP-96)*, Philadelphia, PA.

Kučera, H., & Francis, W. N. (1967). *Computational analysis of present-day American English*. Providence, RI: Brown University Press.

Mareschal, D., Plunkett, K., & Harris, P. (1995). Developing object permanence: A connectionist model. In J. D. Moore & J. E. Lehmann (Eds.), *Proceedings of the seventeenth annual conference of the Cognitive Science Society* (pp. 170–175). Hillsdale, NJ: Lawrence Erlbaum Associates Inc.

Marslen-Wilson, W. D., & Tyler, L. K. (1997). Dissociating types of mental computation. *Nature, 387*, 582–4.

McLeod, P., Plunkett, K., & Rolls, E. T. (1998). *Introduction to connectionist modelling of cognitive processes*. Oxford, UK: Oxford University Press.

Miikkulainen, R. (1993). *Subsymbolic natural language processing: An integrated model of scripts, lexicon, and memory*. Cambridge, MA: MIT Press.

Miyata, Y. (1991). *A user's guide to PlaNet version 5.6: A tool for constructing, running, and looking into a PDP network*.

Plaut, D., & Shallice, T. (1994). *Connectionist modelling in cognitive neuropsychology: A case study*. Hove, UK: Lawrence Erlbaum Associates Ltd.

Plunkett, K., & Marchman, V. (1993). From rote learning to system building: Acquiring verb morphology in children and connectionist nets. *Cognition, 48,* 21–69.

Prasada, S., & Pinker, S. (1993). Generalizations of regular and irregular morphology. *Language and Cognitive Processes, 8,* 207–296.

Rumelhart, D., Hinton, G., & Williams, R. (1986). Parallel distributed processing: Explorations in the microstructure of cognition. In *Psychological and biological models* (Vol. 2, pp. 318–362). Cambridge, MA: MIT Press.

Ward, G. (1997). *Moby pronunciator.* 3449 Martha Ct., Arcata, CA, USA. (Also available at *http://www.dcs.shef.ac.uk/research/ilash/Moby/index.html*)

CHAPTER TWELVE

Recovery in deep dysphasia: Evidence for a relation between auditory–verbal STM capacity and lexical errors in repetition

Nadine Martin and Eleanor M. Saffran
Center for Cognitive Neuroscience, Temple University, USA

Gary S. Dell
Department of Psychology and Beckman Institute, University of Illinois, USA

This study investigates the changes in auditory–verbal short-term memory (AVSTM) and error patterns in repetition observed in a Wernicke's aphasic, NC, over a period of about 2 years following the onset of a left middle cerebral artery aneurysm. When first tested, NC demonstrated deep dysphasia, a disorder characterized by the production of semantic errors in repetition and a severe disability in repeating nonwords. At this stage, his AVSTM span, assessed in a pointing task, was less than one item. As NC recovered somewhat, his performance on AVSTM tasks improved (span increased to two items), and his pattern of error in word repetition changed (fewer semantic errors, more formal paraphasias and neologisms). Other features of his span performance after some recovery resembled patterns associated with STM-based repetition impairments (reduced recency effects and reduced word length effects). In a series of computer simulation and empirical studies, we show that NC's repetition performance can be accounted for by varying two parameters of an interactive activation model of repetition adapted from Dell and O'Seaghdha's (1991) model of production: decay rate and temporal interval. These results provide support for the view that AVSTM performance depends on storage capacities intrinsic to the language processing system. Such a model allows deep dysphasia and STM-based repetition disorders to be seen as quantitative variants of the same underlying disturbance.

Brain and Language 52, 83–113 (1996).

329

INTRODUCTION

Disorders of repetition in aphasia encompass a broad range, from failure at the single word level to limitations in span performance, and include a number of qualitatively different error patterns. Thus, for example, characterizations of repetition in conduction aphasia have emphasized features which implicate disruption to the phonological assembly system: omissions, insertions, and transpositions of phonemes and syllables. Shallice and Warrington (1977) (see also Shallice, 1988) identified another form of repetition impairment that is characterized by decreased span and an error pattern that includes phonologically accurate paraphrases of sentence input (e.g., Saffran & Marin, 1975). This deficit has been attributed to a selective impairment in auditory–verbal short-term memory (AVSTM) (e.g., Vallar & Shallice, 1990). Perhaps the most remarkable impairment of single word repetition is deep dysphasia, a relatively rare disorder distinguished by the presence of semantic errors in word repetition as well as a disability in repeating nonwords. Subjects with deep dysphasia also tend to have a restricted AVSTM, and it has been proposed that this restriction may contribute to the repetition deficit in this syndrome (Katz & Goodglass, 1990; Martin & Saffran, 1992).

The possibility that deep dysphasia represents a severe form of an STM-based repetition disorder was considered but rejected by Shallice (1988). Although the auditory–verbal span associated with deep dysphasia is frequently only a single item, one such patient, MK, was shown to have a matching span of four digits (Howard & Franklin, 1990), a performance seemingly difficult to reconcile with a STM account of this disorder. However, good matching span performance may not be reason enough to dismiss the possibility that the repetition impairment in deep dysphasia is related to a restricted STM. The matching span task (judging the identity of two serially presented strings of items) requires recognition but not recall of the input string, as is required in repetition. Furthermore, recent evidence indicates that short-term storage of linguistic input occurs at all levels of linguistic representation (see Shiffrin, 1993 for recent discussion of this issue). Thus, it is likely that STM requirements vary as a function of the demands of the task (e.g., recognition vs. reproduction) as well as the characteristics of the items to be encoded (e.g., frequency, word class, lexical status, etc.). To establish a relationship between storage capacity and a particular cognitive function, it would seem appropriate to use a measure of STM that taps the capacity as it would be deployed in the cognitive function being investigated. In the case of repetition, one such task would be reproduction span assessed with a pointing response (to eliminate confounding verbal output difficulties).

In this paper, we reconsider the possibility that deep dysphasia and STM-based repetition impairments are related disorders, differing primarily in their severity. We report a longitudinal investigation of a patient, NC, whose pattern of error in single word repetition evolved from one associated with the syndrome deep dysphasia to a more typical span limitation, and we offer a theoretical account of the relationship of these two performance patterns.[1]

When first studied by Martin and Saffran (1992), NC's single word repetition was severely impaired as was his auditory-verbal span (less than a single digit or word, whether responding by pointing or repetition). Errors in repetition included semantic paraphasias, formal paraphasias (sound related word substitutions) and nonword errors (phonemic paraphasias and neologisms). Martin and Saffran (1992) proposed an account of the most unusual feature of NC's error pattern, semantic errors in repetition, within the framework of Dell's (1986; Dell & O'Seaghdha, 1991) interactive spreading activation theory of language processing. They argued that the occurrence of semantic errors in repetition could be explained by a pathological increase in the rate of decay of activated nodes in the phonological–lexical–semantic network. Dell's model of lexical retrieval was originally developed as an account of language production. Figure 1 depicts an adaptation of Dell's model that is essentially reversed to deal with input processes (in this figure, lexical retrieval in repetition). A full account of this model and the effects of a decay rate impairment are detailed in Martin and Saffran (1992). In brief, Dell's model postulates two parameters, connection strength and decay rate, that operate in conjunction with temporal parameters and noise in the system to maintain activation levels of linguistic nodes during processing of utterances. Assuming connection strength at normal levels, a global and uniform increase in decay rate has a more devastating effect on lexical nodes primed early in the lexical selection process than nodes primed later. In repetition, these are the target (Lt) and phonologically related competitors (Lp). The effect of increasing decay rate is to shift the probability of lexical selection in favor of semantically related competitors (Ls) primed at a late stage of lexical selection by feedback from primed semantic nodes. This account of NC's production of semantic errors in repetition was supported by computational simulations demonstrating that the increase in decay rate increases the probability of semantic errors relative to other types of lexical errors in word repetition (see summary below and Martin, Dell, Saffran, & Schwartz, 1994).

Notable features of NC's recovery included an increase in his AVSTM capacity, as assessed by pointing span, and an alteration in his repetition error pattern: a decrease in semantic errors relative to formal paraphasias and neologisms. We were able to simulate this change in repetition error pattern by reducing the decay rate from a pathologically rapid level towards a normal rate (see Martin et al., 1994, and summary below). The relationship between a decrease in decay rate and an increase in AVSTM capacity is a straightforward consequence of the view of STM that we have adopted here; with further resolution of decay rate toward normal, we would expect a further increase in span and a change in error patterns as that capacity increases. As we will show, the patterns of change that did occur in NC are predicted by the interactive activation model.

In what follows we describe additional studies of NC's repetition and AVSTM that indicate both quantitative and qualitative correspondences in the recovery of these two functions. We take these studies as support for the view that repetition and AVSTM exploit storage capacities that are intrinsic to the language processing

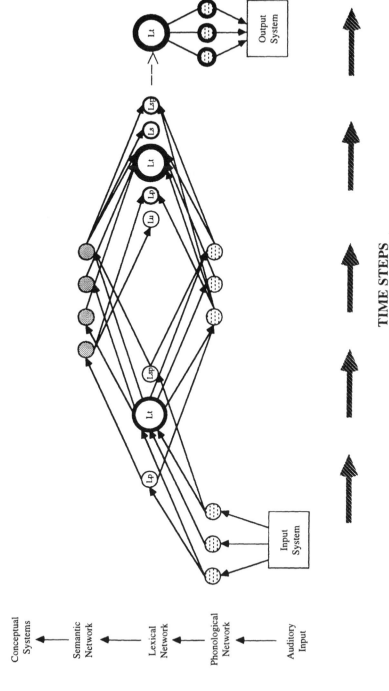

Conceptual Systems

Semantic Network

Lexical Network

Phonological Network

Auditory Input

TIME STEPS

Figure 1. A single pass through Dell's model of lexical retrieval subserving input processes that depict priming activity leading to selection of the target or a related lexical node in repetition.

system. Additionally, we suggest that NC's recovery pattern is indicative of a continuum of impairment underlying error patterns in deep dysphasia and STM-based repetition disorders.

CASE DESCRIPTION

NC, now 30 years old, suffered a ruptured left middle cerebral artery aneurysm in November, 1989 which was surgically clipped. A post-operative CT scan revealed a periventricular dense area and a more recent CT scan (March, 1991) indicated involvement of the mid to posterior portions of the superior temporal gyrus and small portions of the supramarginal gyrus.

A full report of NC's input and output language processing is reported in Martin and Saffran (1992). Since that time, NC has shown improvement in most aspects of language function. Below, we summarize changes in performance on tasks that pertain to the present study: repetition and auditory–verbal STM.

Repetition

In Table 1, specific changes in repetition performance are outlined. These changes include not only an increase in overall correctness, but also a change in error pattern. Semantic errors are present in single word repetition at acute stages of NC's aphasia, but drop out of his error pattern as he recovers. Nonword repetition remains difficult for him even after recovery, but his errors show a tendency to be words rather than nonwords.

TABLE 1
Assessment of NC's repetition at 0–3 months post-CVA and
12–18 months post-CVA

0–3 months post-CVA	*12–18 months post-CVA*
	Words
.30 correct ($n = 80$)	.85 correct ($n = 80$)
Hi-Image > Lo-Image	Hi-Image > Lo-Image
Errors: neologisms	Errors: neologisms
formal paraphasias	formal paraphasias
semantic paraphasias	
	Nonwords
.10 correct ($n = 30$)	.10 correct ($n = 30$)
Errors: .19 lexicalizations	Errors: .58 lexicalizations
	Sentences
Not formally tested	Short sentences (3 open class words) are repeated accurately.
(Task was too difficult for NC)	Repetition of longer sentences preserves gist (e.g., The waitress is serving the man. → The waitress took food to the man.) Sentences from Saffran and Marin (1975) with 4–6 open class words: 15/20 repetitions preserving, in part, the gist of the sentence.

Auditory–verbal STM

Span was initially assessed 2 months post-onset with tape-recorded sequences of digits or words of varying lengths (1–4 items). In one condition, NC responded by repeating the list in serial order. In another condition, he responded by pointing to the sequence on a test plate with either nine digits or nine object pictures that was not visible until the sequence was complete. Ten test plates with randomly varied arrangements of the digits or words were used in rotation to prevent NC from employing any spatial encoding strategies to aid in recall. NC's span for digits or words was less than 1 item. His best performance was on single words with a pointing response (.90 correct). Performance was better when tested with visual input (2–3 digits).

Figure 2 shows NC's performance on the same test described above, but at 20 months post-onset. NC's span at that time was 2–3 items (digits and words, pointing response) and his serial position curve was characterized by primacy effects (better retention of the initial than subsequent items) but loss of recency (end of the list) information. The reduced recency effect is characteristic of span performance in most of the patients reported with STM-based repetition impairments (Shallice & Vallar, 1990).

Effects of word length on span.   Word length has been shown to reduce span performance in normals (Baddeley, Thompson, & Buchanan, 1975), a finding consistent with the notion that coding in STM is phonological. Patients with a STM-based repetition impairment frequently fail to show normal effects of word length in span, implicating a deficit at the level of phonological representations (Shallice & Vallar, 1990). NC was tested on a repetition span task that varied syllable length (one vs. two) of high frequency, concrete words. For lists of two words, NC recalled (in serial order) .90 ($n = 40$) of the one-syllable words and .83 of the two-syllable words ($n = 40$). In repeating 3 word lists, he recalled .77 ($n = 60$) of the one-syllable words and .73 ($n = 60$) of the two-syllable words. Although NC consistently retains more one syllable words than two-syllable words, the difference is insignificant for 2 word lists [$\chi^2(1) = .421$] and 3 word lists [$\chi^2(1) = .044$]. Thus, like other patients with STM-based repetition impairments, NC shows reduced effects of word length in span performance.

Computer simulation studies of NC's error patterns in naming and repetition

Simulation of early pattern of error.   Although in the present study we are concerned with NC's repetition error pattern, earlier studies focused on his unusual error pattern in naming as well as repetition (Martin & Saffran, 1992; Martin et al., 1994). Therefore, by way of introduction to the current studies, we will briefly summarize the computational studies of NC's naming and repetition error patterns.

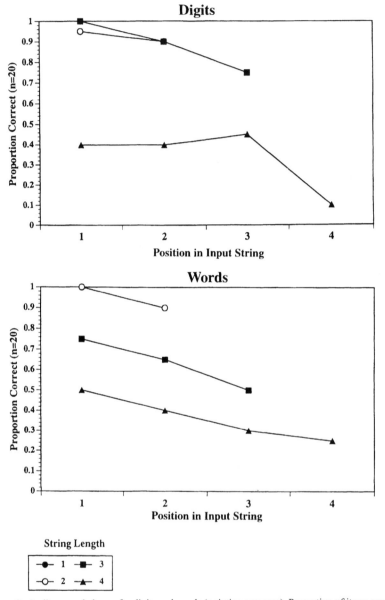

Figure 2. Auditory–verbal span for digits and words (pointing response). Proportion of items recalled accurately and in serial order as a function of string length and position in input string.

Martin and Saffran (1992) proposed that NC's naming and repetition error patterns could be accounted for within Dell's (1986) interactive spreading activation model by assuming a lesion affecting the decay rate of activated nodes uniformly throughout the semantic–lexical–phonological network. This account was verified by computational studies which simulated NC's naming and repetition error patterns (Martin, et al., 1994). By error patterns, we mean the relative proportions of semantic paraphasias, formal paraphasias, neologisms and other types of errors. In attempting to "name" or "repeat" a word, the model (and simulation) will potentially produce any or all of these errors (due to noise). It is the pattern of error, however, that varies depending on the settings of the parameters connection strength and decay rate as well as the time interval between input and output.

The network model used was a slightly modified form of that described in Dell and O'Seaghdha (1991) (see Appendix). Before investigating the effects of lesions on error patterns, parameter values that simulated normal naming accuracy and error patterns (based on investigations of normal speech errors such as Garnham, Shillcock, Brown, Mill, & Cutler, 1982) were established: connection weight = .1 and decay rate .4. To simulate NC's error pattern in naming, the strength of the connection weights was held constant (at the "normal" rate) and the decay rate was raised to .92.

Simulation of NC's repetition error pattern was accomplished using the same parameter settings established for naming, but reversing the flow of spreading activation (as in Figure 1). Thus, while input activates semantic nodes first in naming, phonological nodes are primed first in repetition. The critical result of this simulation was the demonstration that an increase in the decay rate to a level of .92 increased the relative probability of semantic errors in repetition (which is virtually zero in the normal case). Thus, global impairment—increase of decay rate throughout the network—generated essential features of NC's error pattern in both naming and repetition.

Simulation of error patterns after some recovery.   During the period of recovery, NC showed some evidence of improvement in naming and repetition tasks as well as other language functions. The most notable aspect of NC's improved performance, in addition to an increase in correct responses, was a change in error patterns. In naming, the rate of formal errors dropped considerably, while the rate of semantic errors remained the same and dominated the error pattern. In repetition, semantic errors dropped out of his pattern almost entirely. Formal paraphasias decreased in number but remained the dominant lexical error type in repetition (Martin et al., 1994). These changes in NC's naming and repetition error patterns were simulated by decreasing the decay rate parameter toward normal levels. Thus, it was possible to account for two different error patterns and changes in those patterns over the course of recovery by varying a single parameter (decay rate) in the interactive activation model. In the

computational and empirical studies described below, we report additional investigations of NC's repetition and STM performance as his recovery continued.

EXPERIMENT 1. TEMPORAL EFFECTS ON REPETITION: PREDICTIONS OF THE INTERACTIVE ACTIVATION MODEL

The simulations of NC's single word repetition at early and later stages of his recovery showed a direct relationship between decay rate and the probability of semantic errors in repetition. This relationship was explored with the temporal parameter (number of time steps elapsing between input and response selection) held constant. At a given decay rate, however, the effects of decay on relative activation levels of nodes in the network are magnified with each time step. When decay rate is reduced toward normal levels (as in the simulation of NC's recovery above), the strength of the target node's activation is increased relative to that of semantically related competitors primed by feedback, resulting in more correct repetitions and fewer semantic errors in word repetition.

The model predicts that under less extreme decay rate settings (such as those used in simulating NC's recovery), a longer interval between stimulus and response should have two effects on repetition: accuracy should decrease and the rate of semantic errors should increase. This is because a less extreme (but still abnormal) decay rate should affect activated nodes in the network in the same way, i.e., it will be more detrimental to nodes primed early in lexical selection (the target and phonologically related lexical nodes) than nodes primed later (semantically related lexical nodes). It will take more time, however, for that effect to result in a shift in selection probability that favors semantically related nodes. This prediction is demonstrated in the simulation described below.

Method

The model was the same as that used in Martin et al. (1994) and is detailed in the Appendix. The network contained 10 semantic feature nodes per word and word nodes for the target *cat*, a semantically related word, *dog*, which shared 1 semantic feature with *cat*, two phonologically related words, *mat* and *hat* and two words that were phonologically related to a semantically related word, *log* and *fog*.[2] Additionally, the network contained phoneme nodes corresponding to these words.

Three simulations were run with 1000 trials each. Connection weights (p) were set at .1 (the normal weight) and decay rate (q) was set at .86. This decay rate is lower than that used to simulate NC's single word repetition (.92) at acute stages of his disorder (Martin et al., 1994). Under the assumption that recovery had affected this parameter by shifting it toward a normal decay rate ($q = .4$), the lower, but still abnormal rate seemed appropriate. What was varied across these three simulations was the number of time steps (k) before selection occurred.

Simulation 1 ran for 8 time steps before selection, simulation 2 for 9 steps, and simulation 3 for 10 steps.

Results

In Table 2 we show the results of three simulations which vary only in the number of time steps which passed before selection. The table shows the proportion of responses in each response category selected at two levels of output, lexical and phonological. The simulations capture two essential features of the interaction of temporal and decay parameters. First, as time steps increase, the proportion of correct repetitions decreases. Second, error patterns change as time passes: the proportion of semantic errors increases while the proportion of formal paraphasias decreases. This pattern is similar to the lexical error pattern observed in single word repetition when the decay rate was set at .92 (to simulate NC's repetition before recovery). The reduced, but still abnormal decay rate of .86 has the same effect as the higher rate, but only after more time has passed. That is, semantically related lexical nodes primed by late stage feedback from the target word's semantic features show less decay than phonologically related lexical nodes primed earlier by phonological input to lexical activation. As time passes, the activation of late primed semantically related lexical nodes increases relative to the target node and phonologically related lexical competitors, shifting the probability of lexical error in favor of semantically related competitors. In this simulation, then, we have shown that time passage interacts with decay rate to determine the relative influences of phonological input and semantic feedback on lexical activation.

Our claim is that NC originally made semantic errors in word repetition and had a span of less than one item because activation in the phonological–lexical semantic network decayed too rapidly. After some recovery, span increased

TABLE 2

Simulation of temporal effects on word repetition when decay rate is increased and semantically related lexical nodes share one feature: Proportion of responses in each response category as a function of number of time steps before selection

Time steps	Level of output	C	S	F	N	S→F	S→N
k = 8	Lexical	0.590	0.000	0.410	—	0.000	—
	Phonological	0.555	0.000	0.431	0.014	0.000	0.000
k = 9	Lexical	0.515	0.004	0.480	—	0.000	—
	Phonological	0.429	0.004	0.485	0.082	0.000	0.000
k = 10	Lexical	0.413	0.052	0.482	—	0.027	—
	Phonological	0.242	0.036	0.356	0.298	0.052	0.016

Parameters: Connection strength, $p = .1$. Decay rate, $q = .86$. $k =$ time steps. Dog/cat share 1.5 semantic features. $N = 1000$ trials. C = correct; S = semantic errors; F = formal paraphasias; N = neologisms.

somewhat and the semantic errors in single word repetition essentially disappeared, suggesting that the decay of activation is now not quite so severe. However, the model predicts that semantic errors should reemerge under conditions in which more time elapses before the repetition response. That is, *adding more time* to the repetition task should result in a pattern of performance that mimics NC's "pre-recovery" state. In the experiments described below, temporal parameters were manipulated in the repetition task in two ways: (1) by increasing the number of items to be repeated and (2) by imposing a delay between onset and repetition of a single word.

EXPERIMENT 2: SINGLE WORD AND WORD PAIR REPETITION

In this experiment, we examined NC's repetition of single words and pairs of words varied for frequency and imageability. In keeping with his "recovered" repetition performance noted above, NC's single word repetition should result in few semantic errors relative to formal paraphasias and neologisms. His error pattern on the word pair repetition task, which increases the time between stimulus and response, should reflect effects of increased time passage demonstrated by the model. That is, semantic errors that were present in single word repetition in NC's early profile, but not his later profile, should re-emerge. Furthermore, the model demonstrated that as time passed before lexical selection, semantic influences on lexical activation increased relative to phonological influences. Thus, semantic errors should be more likely at the second list position, assuming a longer delay for production of the second word than the first.

Method

Materials.   NC's repetition was tested on a set of 240 single two- and three-syllable words varied for frequency (Kučera & Francis, 1967) and imageability (Paivio, Yuille, & Madigan, 1968) and 240 word pairs comprised of the same two- and three-syllable words. The 240 single words were combined into 120 word pairs which were presented twice with the order of the members of each pair reversed on the second administration. For both single words and word pairs, there were 60 stimuli from each of four frequency-imageability combinations (HiF-HiI; LoF-HiI; HiF-LoI; LoF-LoI). Frequency and imageability type were held constant within word pairs.

Procedure.   Test words in the single word and word pair conditions were presented auditorily and only a single presentation was allowed. In the single word condition, NC was asked to repeat the words immediately after hearing the word. In the word pair condition, the first word of the pair was presented and this was followed immediately by the second word. NC was instructed to repeat the sequence of words in the order presented immediately after the sequence was

complete. Only one presentation of the word or word pair was allowed and lip cues were not provided. All responses were audio-taped and transcribed by two research assistants. Any discrepancies between the two transcripts were resolved by one of the authors (NM).

Data analysis.   The data were analyzed for effects of serial position, frequency and imageability on accuracy of repetition and on the occurrence of semantic and formal paraphasias. Errors were coded on the basis of their relation to target words (semantic, phonological, neologism, etc.) and according to the criteria outlined in Martin et al. (1994). Analyses of NC's performance in the word pair condition were carried out with respect to serial order unless otherwise indicated.

Results

Single words

Repetition accuracy.   Overall, NC repeated .66 of the 240 words correctly. Table 3 shows NC's performance on single words as a function of frequency and imageability. Repetition accuracy was affected by both frequency [$\chi^2(1) = 9.02$, $p < .01$] and imageability [$\chi^2(1) = 36.07$, $p < .001$].

Error analyses.   Although a number of error types were produced, most errors fall into the categories of semantic paraphasias, formal paraphasias, or nonwords (phonemic paraphasias and neologisms) and it is the occurrence of these error types as a function of frequency and imageability that will be the concern of these analyses. Errors that were not analysed included mixed errors, morphological errors, unrelated lexical errors, and no responses, all of which occurred at low rates. The data were first collapsed across imageability conditions to determine effects of frequency on error patterns and then were collapsed across frequency conditions to examine effects of imageability on error patterns. Figure 3a shows the proportion of errors that were semantic paraphasias, formal paraphasias or nonwords as a function of frequency of the target word, and Figure 3b shows the same group of errors distributed over error types as a function of imageability. As Figure 3 indicates, there is a low rate of semantic errors irrespective of the frequency or imageability of the target. Formal paraphasias and nonword responses dominate the error pattern.

TABLE 3
Effects of frequency and imageability on
accuracy of single word repetition:
Proportion of correct repetitions

	Frequency	*Imageability*
High	0.76	0.85
Low	0.57	0.48

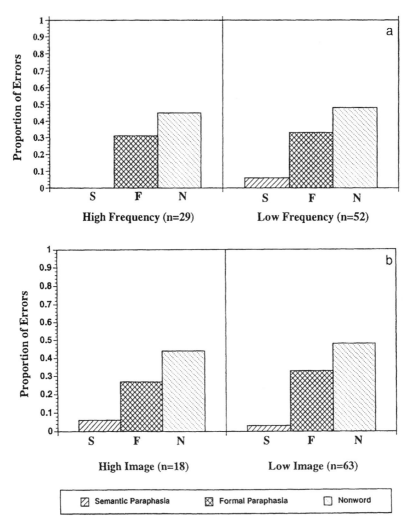

Figure 3. Single word repetition: Proportions of error responses that were semantic paraphasias (S), formal paraphasias (F), or nonword (N) responses as a function of (a) target frequency and (b) target imageability.

Word pairs

Serial position effects. As predicted, NC repeated more items accurately from Position 1 than Position 2 whether serial order was taken into account (.60 vs. 31) or not (.65 vs. .53). Figure 4 shows the proportion of words repeated accurately and in serial order from Positions 1 and 2 of the word pairs as a function of frequency (4a) and imageability (4b). NC's better performance on initial list items corresponds with the serial position curve in his span performance (primacy effect, loss of recency effect).

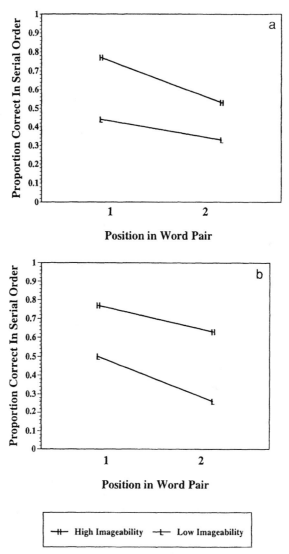

Figure 4. Word pair repetition: Proportion of words from Position 1 and Position 2 repeated accurately and in serial order as a function of (a) target frequency and (b) target imageability.

Effects of frequency and imageability. Frequency affected the total number of words repeated correctly and in serial order from Position 1 [$\chi^2(1) = 25.16$, $p < .001$] and Position 2 [$\chi^2(1) = 9.80$, $p < .01$]. Imageability also affected accuracy of NC's word repetition from both positions in the word pair, Position 1 [$\chi^2(1) = 17.24$, $p < .001$] and Position 2 [$\chi^2(1) = 31.24$, $p < .001$].

Error analysis across serial positions.   Occasionally, NC would not attempt to repeat both items of the pair or would reverse the order of the input string in his response. The error analysis across serial positions includes only those responses in which there was a clear attempt to repeat both items of the pair in their serial position. Overall, nonword responses were most frequent, followed by formal paraphasias and then semantic paraphasias. Frequency had no effect on the occurrence of any particular error type in either position. Imageability had an interesting effect on error patterns, in particular on the occurrence of semantic errors. The error data, therefore, are presented as a function of imageability of the target. Figures 5a and 5b show the proportion of *errors* that are semantic paraphasias, formal paraphasias or nonword responses to target words from Positions 1 and 2 as a function of the target word's imageability. Errors made in response to Position 1 (Figure 5a) targets distribute across error types in a pattern similar to the distribution observed in the single word repetition condition: relatively fewer semantic errors (HiI: .07, LoI: .08) than formal paraphasias (HiI: .25, LoI: .24) and neologisms (HiI: .67, LoI: .63).

In Position 2 (Figure 5b), errors distribute across error types differently than errors made either in single word repetition or in response to Position 1 targets. For those errors made on high imageability target words, there is a sharp rise in the proportion of semantically related errors (.36) and a decline in the proportion of formal paraphasias (.11) and neologisms (.36). Imageability influenced the occurrence of semantic errors in Position 2 [$\chi^2(1) = 6.10, p < .05$], but not formal paraphasias. The error pattern for LoI words is similar across Positions 1 and 2 except for a decline in the rate of neologisms in Position 2.

Temporal analysis of responses on the word pair repetition task

As was shown in the simulation of temporal effects on error patterns in repetition under conditions of abnormally high decay rate, the increase in semantic errors is a direct consequence of the temporal interval between input and lexical selection. If NC's tendency to produce more semantic errors in response to the second target word is related to the temporal course of lexical retrieval in the way that the model predicts, then his response latency to Target 2 should be greater than it is to Target 1. To test this hypothesis, we compared the mean temporal distance between the onsets of Target 1 and Response 1 and between the onsets of Target 2 and Response 2.

Method.   The tape recordings of the target word pairs and NC's subsequent responses were digitized on a Macintosh computer using the Sound Edit program. The sound spectrographs of these recordings were analysed to determine the time lapse between onset of the target word and onset of NC's response to each target word. As was noted in the error analysis above, NC occasionally failed to

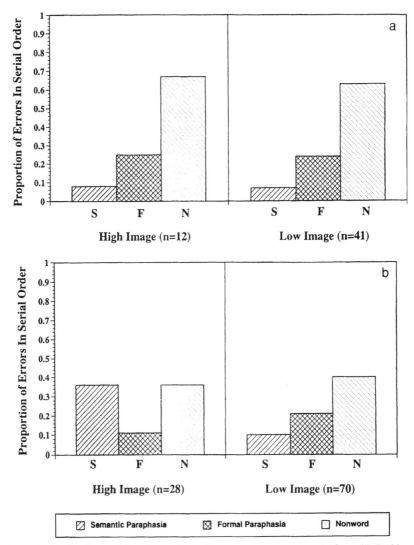

Figure 5. Word pair repetition: Proportions of error responses to targets from (a) Position 1 and (b) Position 2 that were semantic paraphasias (S), formal paraphasias (F), or nonword (N) responses as a function of target imageability.

repeat both items of the pair or reversed the order of the word pair in his response. These responses were excluded from this analysis. The time intervals between targets and responses were averaged across all target-response pairs.

Results. The mean latency of Response 2 (3.43 seconds) measured from Target 2 was found to be greater than that between Target 1 and Response 1 (2.12 sec.). This finding lends additional support to the account of NC's error

pattern on the interactive model. That is, it is consistent with the model's demonstration that the increase in semantic errors on Position 2 targets is related, at least in part, to an increased latency between input and lexical selection.

Summary.   The results of the single word and word pair repetition studies confirmed our prediction that semantic errors would re-emerge as a dominant lexical error in NC's repetition pattern if the temporal interval between stimulus and response was increased. Presumably, under conditions of rapid node decay, as time steps pass before lexical selection, the strength of the phonological trace that supports veridical repetition is reduced, particularly for items at the end of the input string. As the phonological trace becomes less available, the activation of the target word's lexical node (and consequently, its retrieval) becomes more dependent on feedback from primed semantic nodes. That feedback also primes semantically related lexical nodes which compete with the target lexical node. Although primed semantic nodes are also decaying rapidly, their input to lexical activation is relatively less affected by the cumulative effects of rapid decay. This is because in repetition, semantic nodes are activated subsequent to the activation of phonological nodes, and the effects of the rapid decay, which accumulate over time, are more detrimental to those nodes primed earliest, the target and phonologically related lexical nodes.

One final point to consider is that the influence of primed semantic features on lexical activation appears to vary in relation to the target word's imageability. That is, semantic features of highly imageable words appear to be more influential on lexical activation than semantic representations of abstract, less imageable words. This conclusion stems from our finding that the increase in semantic errors in response to the second word of the target pair was observed primarily on pairs of highly imageable words.

[...]

EXPERIMENT 4: EFFECTS OF IMAGEABILITY ON LEXICAL ACTIVATION AND SEMANTIC ERRORS IN REPETITION

Although imageability has been shown to influence lexical retrieval in normals (e.g., Kroll & Merves, 1986), the nature of semantic representations which underlie that effect is a matter of debate. One possibility is that the referents of highly imageable words are specific and vary little from one context to another, whereas the meanings of abstract words are variable and depend more on the context in which they are used (e.g., Saffran, Bogyo, Schwartz, & Marin, 1980). Additionally, highly imageable words have been assumed by a number of authors to have "richer" semantic representations than low imageability words, which might provide stronger semantic support for lexical activation (e.g., Martin & Saffran, 1992; Plaut & Shallice, 1993). That "richness" of representation may be

related to the number of semantic features associated with a word (Plaut & Shallice, 1993), the overlap of its semantic features with those of other semantically related words, or both of these factors.

Our studies of NC's repetition show that imageability has two effects on his performance: highly imageable words are more likely to be repeated accurately, but at the same time, are more likely to elicit semantic errors than low imageability words. How can these two seemingly contradictory effects be reconciled? Although the increase in accuracy may be due in part to stronger semantic input to lexical activation, this factor alone cannot account for the effect on the occurrence of semantic errors (but see Plaut & Shallice's, 1993 account of abstractness effects in a model with a different architecture). In an interactive model, error-specific effects of imageability derive, at least in part, from the relationships among representations of words. When two lexical nodes share many semantic features, they tend to activate each other more than lexical nodes that share few semantic features. For example, if the target is *cat*, sharing features with *dog* boosts the activation of both *cat* and *dog*. This increases the strength of the target node's (*cat*) activation relative to other competitors primed by phonological activation (formally related lexical nodes like *hat* and *mat*). At the same time, it increases the probability that *dog* will be selected, though that increase is small in comparison to the gain in the target's activation. Thus, increased sharing of semantic features should increase *both* the probability of a correct response and the probability of a semantic error.

Although our implementation of imageability in the computational study below implies that this variable is related to the degree with which a word's semantic features overlap with those of other words, we do not offer this account as a theory of how imageability is represented. Rather, we claim that whatever that theory is, it will be the case that there will be more overlap or similarity of the representational elements for highly imageable words. This could be due to the greater number or different kinds of features associated with highly imageable words (e.g., visual features) or to some interaction between representational elements and the context dependency of abstract words. Given the assumption that highly imageable words tend to share more semantic features than abstract words, it essentially would be trivial to demonstrate that the model has a greater tendency to activate semantic neighbors of high-imageability words. What would not be trivial, however, would be a demonstration that a tendency to activate semantic neighbors leads to greater accuracy and to more semantic errors at the same time.

Simulation of imageability effects on the occurrence of semantic errors in repetition

The network used to test temporal effects on lexical retrieval in repetition (see earlier computational study) was used here as well, but with one modification. The original network contained 10 semantic feature nodes per word. The word nodes for the target, *cat*, and a semantically related word, *dog*, shared 1 semantic

TABLE 4

Simulation of temporal effects on word repetition when decay rate is increased and semantically related lexical nodes share three features: Proportion of responses in each response category as a function of number of time steps before selection

Time steps	Level of output	C	S	F	N	S → F	S → N
k = 8	Lexical	0.672	0.005	0.323	—	0.000	—
	Phonological	0.563	0.006	0.327	0.104	0.000	0.000
k = 9	Lexical	0.587	0.044	0.366	—	0.003	—
	Phonological	0.415	0.039	0.340	0.198	0.003	0.005
k = 10	Lexical	0.460	0.113	0.389	—	0.038	—
	Phonological	0.247	0.065	0.240	0.360	0.040	0.048

Parameters: Connection strength, $p = .1$. Decay rate, $q = .86$. k = time steps. Dog/cat share 3 semantic features. $N = 1000$ trials.

feature. To simulate the effects of imageability on lexical retrieval the number of semantic features shared by the two word nodes, *cat* and *dog*, was increased to 3. Three simulations were run with 1000 trials each. Connection weights (p) were set at .1 (the normal weight) and decay rate (q) was set at .86. The results of three simulations of repetition with *cat* and *dog* sharing 3 semantic features are outlined in Table 4 which shows the distribution of responses across all response categories at the lexical level and phonological level. In order to simulate the effects of temporal parameters on single word and word pair repetition, we varied the number of time steps (k) which passed before selection of the word node and before selection of the phonological nodes. Simulation 1 (single word repetition) ran for 8 time steps before selection, simulation 2 (response to Target 1 of the word pair) for 9 steps and simulation 3 (response to Target 2) for 10 steps. As in the earlier simulation, time passage had the effect of reducing the probability of a correct response and increasing the probability of a semantic error.

Figure 6 shows a direct comparison of the proportions of correct responses and semantic errors produced at the lexical level when *cat* and *dog* share 1 semantic feature and when they share 3 semantic features. As the figure shows, an overlap of 3 semantic features between *cat* and *dog* results in more correct responses and more semantic errors made at the lexical level than an overlap of 1 semantic feature. Thus, as both the simulation and NC's data indicate, increased semantic input to lexical activation associated with high imageability increases not only the probability of an accurate response, but also the relative probability of a semantic error.

GENERAL DISCUSSION

In this study of the evolution of NC's repetition and AVSTM performance as he recovered, we have focused on two related questions which bear on the functional organization of language and STM: (1) What is the relationship between NC's AVSTM and repetition impairments? and (2) Can the syndrome known as deep

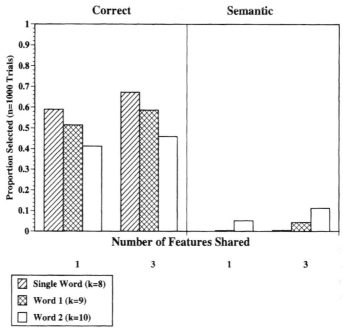

Figure 6. Proportion of correct responses and semantic errors generated in simulations of repetition as a function of number of shared semantic features between two lexical nodes. Connection weight (p) = .1 and decay rate (q) = .86. The number of time steps (k) before lexical selection is varied (8, 9, or 10 steps).

dysphasia be viewed as a quantitative variant of STM-based repetition impairments? The data reported here provide some insight into each of these questions.

Repetition and AVSTM impairment

Aphasic disorders are frequently accompanied by a restriction in STM span, but one form of repetition disturbance has been associated specifically with an isolated impairment of phonological STM processes (see Shallice, 1988 for discussion). The assumption that STM can be selectively impaired derives from the more general assumption of some memory models that STM is a discrete subsystem dedicated to short-term storage and isolable from other cognitive systems (as in the working memory model of Baddeley & Hitch, 1974).

To date, most patients found to have phonologically based STM deficits also demonstrate language impairments ranging widely in severity and affecting both output (word-finding and phonemic paraphasias) and input (sentence comprehension) (Vallar & Shallice, 1990). Consequently, neuropsychological arguments for an isolable STM system have generally turned on demonstrations of the independence of the language and STM impairments present in a single patient.

For example, cases have been reported that show reduced AVSTM but intact phonological processing capabilities (e.g., Vallar & Baddeley, 1984; Butterworth, Campbell, & Howard, 1986) and the reverse pattern, impaired speech perception but normal auditory–verbal span (R. Martin & Breedin, 1992), indicating that phonological processing deficits and STM impairments are dissociable. Although such evidence suggests that STM deficits are not linked to language impairments, the fact remains that language processing is not entirely normal in patients with restricted spans. In particular, performance on metalinguistic tasks involving controlled manipulation of linguistic representations seems most vulnerable to a reduction in STM capacity (Caplan & Waters, 1990). While this observation does not preclude the independence of linguistic and STM functions, it does suggest that the two are related in some way. In the present study, we are concerned with the relation between retrieval and temporary storage of linguistic units in repetition. On the account outlined below, it follows, in fact, that these two components of the repetition task are closely intertwined.

The co-occurrence of an increase in NC's AVSTM span (as measured with a pointing response) and his repetition span indicates a relation between the STM and repetition impairments, but is not sufficient evidence to demonstrate that a common mechanism mediates storage and retrieval of lexical items in repetition. Presumably an STM system that operates independently of the language system would support an increase in repetition span as its capacity increased. The essential finding that implicates a common process underlying retrieval and storage components of repetition is the change in NC's error pattern that coincided with his increasing STM span. Semantic errors present at acute stages of NC's disorder, when span was at most one item, diminished in frequency as his span increased (Martin et al., 1994). In the present study, semantic errors re-emerged in NC's error pattern when the limits of his AVSTM are stressed, indicating that storage capacities affect qualitative as well as quantitative aspects of repetition.

Recent investigations of language impairment and STM performance provide additional evidence of a qualitative relationship between these two processes. Martin, Shelton, and Yaffee (1994) have shown, for example, that semantic impairment and phonological impairment have specific effects on the retention of semantic vs. phonological information as assessed by performance on STM tasks. Lexical–semantic and phonological impairments also appear to have different effects on serial position curves in span performance; lexical–semantic impairment is associated with loss of primacy and phonological impairment with loss of recency (Saffran & Martin, 1990; Martin & Saffran, 1990). These findings support a linkage between processing and storage of linguistic information at least to the extent that there is a predictable co-occurrence of performance patterns in STM and language tasks.

Models that view the short-term store as a separate, isolable process operating over phonological representations generated by the language system would have difficulty accounting for semantic influences on NC's span performance

(imageability effects and semantic errors) which are generally attributed to long-term (or "secondary") memory (e.g., Shallice & Warrington, 1970). The presence of semantic errors in NC's span performance and especially in response to the second words in the target pair (akin to the final positions of the normal serial curve typically attributed to the short-term store) suggest that semantic representations have a direct influence on the contents of short-term memory. Thus, the notion that phonological representations are the exclusive domain of short-term memory seems untenable.

Associations between language and STM impairments such as those described above can be realized in models that impute storage functions to language processing mechanisms (Craik & Lockhart's, 1972; Monsell, 1984; Barnard, 1985). In the framework of Dell's (1986) interactive activation model of language production, processing and temporary storage are mediated in part by the operation of two parameters of the language network, connection weight and decay rate, which together operate over time to keep targeted nodes (those representing an intended utterance) more active than other nodes primed by spreading activation. Extending this model to input processes, it would be predicted that AVSTM would be compromised by any language impairment that decreases the ability of lexical nodes to remain active (e.g., Saffran, 1990; Saffran & Martin, 1990; Martin & Saffran, 1990).

This account of the relation between storage and processing in an interactive model does not dispute the possibility that these two components are dissociable, but does claim that they are *distributed* properties of the cognitive system that mediates language performance. Processing of linguistic input, then, should be affected by an impairment to storage functions only if a task requires that representations of that input be maintained for *any* amount of time longer than decay properties allow.[3] Conversely, processing impairments are most likely to disrupt temporary maintenance of activated input if the linguistic representations affected by that impairments are the *only* units being stored in a particular task. Lower level representations affected by a processing deficit (e.g., phonological representations) should have little effect on storage functions in tasks that exploit higher levels of representation (lexical and semantic) if processing at these levels is intact. Thus, for example, a patient, MP, recently reported by Martin and Breedin (1992) exhibited a severe phonological processing deficit but normal AVSTM performance. Span capacity may not have been compromised in this case because lexical processes were sufficiently functional to maintain auditory input at the word level. In fact, Martin and Breedin (1992) propose an account of MP's performance along these lines.

In NC's case, we have hypothesized a global impairment to the decay rate parameter that affects persistence of node activation in the phonological-lexical-semantic network. The link between a global decay impairment and the occurrence of semantic errors in repetition depends on the basic assumption that the influences of phonological and semantic representations on lexical activation

occur over time.[4] In repetition, phonological nodes are primed before lexical nodes which are primed before semantic nodes. As nodes at each level are primed, they send activation to the next level of representation and then decay at a certain rate until their activation is reinforced by feedback from subsequently primed levels of representation. The feedforward-feedback cycles modulated by the ongoing decay function continue until lexical selection is initiated. As discussed in the Introduction and elsewhere (Martin & Saffran, 1992), this model accounts for the semantic errors in NC's single word repetition (at acute stages of his disorder) by assuming a grossly abnormal decay rate which over time affects nodes primed earlier (phonological and lexical) more than nodes primed later (semantic nodes). Thus, semantically related lexical nodes primed by feedback become more active relative to the target and phonologically related lexical nodes than they would under normal conditions.

Under the assumption that NC's recovery entailed reduction of the pathologically high decay rate toward normal, the model demonstrated that such a reduction would result in greater accuracy and fewer semantic errors in immediate repetition of single words (Martin et al., 1994), a pattern that simulated NC's performance in repeating single words as he recovered. In the present study, we confirmed the model's prediction that semantic errors will recur, as decay rate recovers somewhat, if the decay parameter is given more time to produce its effect. That is, the likelihood of a semantic error in repetition is related to an interaction between the amount of increase in decay rate and the interval between input and lexical selection. The re-emergence of semantic errors in NC's repetition of single words after a delay and in response to words from Position 2 of the words pairs can be explained on this account.

The primary focus of the experiments reported in this paper concerns temporal effects on error patterns in repetition. The data from Experiments 1 and 2 indicate that imageability, a variable affecting relative strength of semantic input to lexical activation, also affects word repetition. Highly imageable words were repeated correctly more often, but at the same time, elicited more semantic errors than abstract words. This pattern parallels the effects of imageability/concreteness and abstractness on reading errors in deep dyslexia; visual errors occur more often in response to abstract words and semantic errors more in response to concrete words (Plaut & Shallice, 1991, 1993). Here, we demonstrated that the imageability effect on repetition can be accounted for, at least in part, by assuming that highly imageable words share more semantic features than abstract words.

The effects of time passage and imageability on error patterns in repetition are but two factors that need to be considered in developing a model in which language and short-term memory functions exploit a common mechanism dedicated to temporary storage. We have not addressed other important considerations such as the representation of sequence in auditory–verbal STM or effects on the target's activation level that could be attributed to the number of items being

held in memory. The need to consider this latter point is illustrated by the fact that NC made more semantic errors in repetition of two words that repetition of one word after a delay. These issues remain for future investigation.

Deep dysphasia and STM-based repetition impairment

The second major issue that these experiments address is the relationship of deep dysphasia to repetition disorders that have been linked to a specific impairment of STM processes. The evolution of NC's error pattern in repetition suggests that his early and late profiles (deep dysphasia, STM-repetition disorder) represent two points on a functional continuum of repetition impairment rather than two distinct syndromes, a notion that parallels recent views of the relationship between deep and phonological dyslexia (Sartori, Barry, & Job, 1984; Laine, Niemi, & Marttila, 1990; Glosser & Friedman, 1990). NC's AVSTM span after recovery was similar in capacity 2–3 items) and character (loss of recency, reduced effects of word length) to that of most patients with a phonological STM-based repetition impairment reported in the literature. NC's error pattern in single word and sentence repetition has also evolved to approximate that of some STM-impaired patients (e.g., IL reported by Saffran & Marin, 1975). In particular, he produces partial or full paraphrases in sentence repetition. Although NC still produces semantic errors in single word repetition (not a characteristic of STM-impaired patients) they are much less frequent.

Although NC's current profile is similar to that of patients with STM-based repetition disorders, our account of his impairment departs from the traditional view that assumes a disturbance involving *only* the phonological short-term store. We have posited a global decay impairment in NC; within a distributed model of temporary storage, this would be interpreted as an impairment affecting the phonological, lexical and semantic short-term stores. In recovery, we have assumed a global decrease in decay rate, rather than a complete return to a normal decay rate at all linguistic levels except the phonological level.

To reconcile the account of NC's repetition disturbance and that of other patients with STM-based repetition disorders, two possibilities can be considered. One is that some or all of the patients with impairment to a phonological short-term store in fact have global decay impairments that are milder than NC's (thus no semantic errors in single word repetition) but severe enough to restrict span performance and repetition of very long sentences. This would account for semantically related errors in sentence repetition, but would also predict the occurrence of semantic errors in list repetition.

The second possibility is that a decay rate impairment limited to the phonological level could account for the performance of at least some patients with STM-based repetition impairments. However, when disturbances of decay rate are selective (i.e., affect at least one, but not all levels of linguistic representation),

their impact on lexical retrieval will depend on whether activation levels of target lexical nodes can be maintained by input from unaffected levels of representation. For example, Harley and MacAndrew (1992) demonstrated on a production model similar to Dell's interactive model that an elevated decay rate affecting lexical nodes, but not semantic or phonological nodes, did not reduce the target lexical node's activation level relative to competing lexical nodes. Thus, in an interactive activation model, a decay impairment affecting only phonological node activation would have to be very severe in order to result in reduced accuracy and semantic errors in word repetition (as in NC). This is because semantic feedback, presumably unaffected by the rapid phonological decay, would keep the activation of the target lexical node active despite loss of phonological support. Nonetheless, a severe disturbance at this level might compromise the ability to maintain a veridical representation of an input stimulus particularly as the amount of time that passes between stimulus input and response initiation increases.

Various combinations of functional loci of impairment and severity will result in a number of different performance patterns, and it may seem that it would be a formidable task to establish associations between underlying impairment and behavioral patterns on a language model that postulates a distributed storage function. However, such a model has the potential to account for the varied language profiles among patients with a common STM impairment without assuming that the differences are necessarily related to independent disturbances to the language system. The important point is that deep dysphasia and STM-based repetition impairments can be explained as fundamental disturbances of the same property of the linguistic system, the ability of nodes to persist in activation. The two "syndromes" may or may not differ in the locus of disturbance, and they certainly differ in severity. Nevertheless, the data from NC and other patients with similar repetition impairments indicate a common impairment that involves the ability to temporarily store linguistic information. A language processing model which postulates a distributed storage function can account for the similarities and differences among these patients.

ACKNOWLEDGEMENTS

The work was supported by grants from the James S. McDonnell Foundation (90-42) to the first author, from the National Institutes of Health to the first author (DC01924) and to the second author (DC 00191), and from the National Science Foundation (BNS-8910546) to the third author.

NOTES

1. NC was also deficient in repeating nonwords. This is one of the cardinal features associated with the syndrome deep dysphasia, but is also present in other repetition disorders. In our study, we focus on changes in error patterns that occur in word repetition. Semantic errors in single word

repetition are unique to deep dysphasia. Thus, it is the change in this feature of the repetition error pattern that will be critical in drawing a connection between deep dysphasia and other repetition disorders.

2. This configuration differs from the network used in Dell and O'Seaghdha (1991) which had a semantic/phonologically related word, *rat*. In this network, we eliminated the semantic/phonologically related word, *rat* and created a second purely phonologically related word, *hat*. This was done to create a more realistic neighborhood, as few words have semantic/phonological neighbors. *Rat* was made into *hat* by eliminating the connection between the semantic feature shared by *cat*, *rat*, and *dog* and the *rat* word node, and relabeling the phoneme node *r* as *h*.

3. This prediction entails that input cannot be effectively refreshed or recycled by articulatory rehearsal.

4. If the decay rate impairment was applied locally to the phonological nodes, for example, one might predict that semantic errors would result. However, in the case of a phonologically specific decay impairment semantic input to lexical activation would be unaffected and would be sufficient to maintain the target word's activation level. In such a case, imageability effects on repetition would be expected and semantic errors would be rare. The predominant error types should be target-related nonword errors and formal paraphasias (Martin & Saffran, 1997).

REFERENCES

Baddeley, A. D., & Hitch, G. J. (1974). Working memory. In G. H. Bower (Ed.), *The psychology of learning and motivation* (Vol. 8). New York: Academic Press.

Baddeley, A. D., Thompson, N., & Buchanan, M. (1975). Word length and the structure of short-term memory. *Journal of Verbal Learning and Verbal Behavior, 14,* 575–589.

Barnard, P. (1985). Interacting cognitive subsystems: A psycholinguistic approach to short-term memory. In A. W. Ellis (Ed.), *Progress in the psychology of language* (Vol. 2). Hove, UK: Lawrence Erlbaum Associates Ltd.

Butterworth, B., Campbell, R., & Howard, D. (1986). The uses of short-term memory: A case study. *Quarterly Journal of Experimental Psychology, 38A,* 705–737.

Caplan, D., & Waters, G. S. (1990). Short-term memory and language comprehension: A critical review of the neuropsychological literature. In G. Vallar & T. Shallice (Eds.), *Neuropsychological impairments of short-term memory.* Cambridge: Cambridge University Press.

Craik, F. I. M., & Lockhart, R. S. (1972). Levels of processing: A framework for memory research. *Journal of Verbal Learning and Verbal Behavior, 11,* 671–684.

Garnham, A., Shillcock, R. C., Brown, G. D. A., Mill, A. I. D., & Cutler, A. (1982). Slips of the tongue in the London-Lund corpus of spontaneous conversation. *Linguistics, 19,* 805–817.

Dell, G. S. (1986). A spreading activation theory of retrieval in sentence production. *Psychological Review, 93,* 283–321.

Dell, G. S., & O'Seaghdha, P. G. (1991). Mediated and convergent lexical priming in language production: A comment on Levelt et al. (1990). *Psychological Review, 98,* 604–614.

Glosser, G. & Friedman, R. B. (1990). The continuum of deep/phonological alexia. *Cortex, 28,* 343–359.

Harley, T. A., & MacAndrew, S. B. G. (1992). Modelling paraphasias in normal and aphasic speech. In *Proceedings of the 14th annual conference of the Cognitive Science Society* (pp. 378–383). Bloomington, IN.

Howard, D., & Franklin, S. (1988). *Missing the meaning? A cognitive neuropsychological study of the processing of words by an aphasic patient.* Cambridge, MA: MIT Press.

Katz, R., & Goodglass, H. (1990). Deep dysphasia: An analysis of a rare form of repetition disorder. *Brain and Language, 39,* 153–185.

Kroll, J. F., & Merves, J. S. (1986). Lexical access for concrete and abstract words. *Journal of Experimental Psychology: Learning, Memory and Cognition, 12,* 92–107.

Kucera, H., & Francis, W. N. (1967). *Computational analysis of present-day American English.* Providence, RI: Brown University Press.

Laine, M., Niemi, J., & Marttila, R. (1990). Changing error patterns during reading recovery: A case study. *Journal of Neurolinguistics, 5,* 75–81.

Martin, N., Dell, G. S., Saffran, E. M., & Schwartz, M. F. (1994). Origins of paraphasias in deep dysphasia: Testing the consequences of a decay impairment to an interactive spreading activation model of lexical retrieval. *Brain and Language, 47,* 609–660.

Martin, N., & Saffran, E. M. (1990). Repetition and verbal STM in transcortical sensory aphasia: A case study. *Brain and Language, 39,* 254–288.

Martin, N., & Saffran, E. M. (1992). A connectionist account of deep dysphasia: Evidence from a case study. *Brain and Language, 43,* 240–274.

Martin, N., & Saffran, E. M. (1997). Language and auditory–verbal short term memory impairments: Evidence for common underlying processes. *Cognitive Neuropsychology, 14,* 641–682.

Martin, R. C., & Breedin, S. (1992). Dissociations between speech perception and phonological short-term memory deficits. *Cognitive Neuropsychology, 9*(6), 509–534.

Martin, R. C., Shelton, J., & Yaffee, L. (1994). Language processing and working memory: Neuropsychological evidence for separate phonological and semantic capacities, *Journal of Memory and Language, 33,* 83–111.

Monsell, S. (1984). Components of working memory underlying verbal skills: A "distributed capacities" view. In H. Bouma & D. G. Bouwhuis (Eds.), *Attention and performance X: Control of language processes.* Hove, UK: Lawrence Erlbaum Associates Ltd.

Paivio, A., Yuille, J., & Madigan, S. (1968). Concreteness, imagery and meaningfulness values for 925 nouns. *Journal of Experimental Psychology Monograph, 76*(1, Pt. 2).

Plaut, D. C., & Shallice, T. (1991). Effects of word abstractness in a connectionist model of deep dyslexia. *Proceedings of the 13th annual meeting of the Cognitive Science Society* (pp. 73–78). Chicago, IL.

Plaut, D. C., & Shallice, T. (1993). Deep dyslexia: A case study in connectionist neuropsychology. *Cognitive Neuropsychology, 10,* 377–500.

Saffran, E. M. (1990). Short-term memory impairment and language processing. In A. Caramazza (Ed.), *Advances in cognitive neuropsychology and neurolinguistics.* Hillsdale, NJ: Lawrence Erlbaum Associates Inc.

Saffran, E. M., Bogyo, L. C., Schwartz, M. F., & Marin, O. S. M. (1980). Does deep dyslexia reflect right hemisphere reading? In M. Coltheart, K. Patterson, & J. C. Marshall (Eds.), *Deep dyslexia* (pp. 381–406). London: Routledge.

Saffran, E., & Marin, O. S. M. (1975). Immediate memory for word lists and sentences in a patient with deficient auditory short-term memory. *Brain and Language, 2,* 420–433.

Saffran, E. M., & Martin, N. (1990). Neuropsychological evidence for lexical involvement in short-term memory. In G. Vallar & T. Shallice (Eds.), *Neuropsychological impairments of short-term memory.* Cambridge: Cambridge University Press.

Sartori, G., Barry, C., & Job, R. (1984). *Phonological dyslexia: A review.* Boston: Martinus Nijhoff.

Shallice, T. (1988). *From neuropsychology to mental structure.* Cambridge: Cambridge University Press.

Shallice, T., & Vallar, G. (1990). The impairment of auditory-verbal short-term storage. In G. Vallar & T. Shallice (Eds.), *Neuropsychological impairments of short-term memory.* Cambridge: Cambridge University Press.

Shallice, T., & Warrington, E. K. (1970). Independent functioning of verbal memory stores: A neuropsychological study. *Quarterly Journal of Experimental Psychology, 22,* 262–273.

Shallice, T., & Warrington, E. K. (1977). Auditory-verbal short-term memory impairment and conduction aphasia, *Brain and Language, 4,* 479–491.

Shiffrin, R. M. (1993). Short-term memory: A brief commentary. *Memory and Cognition, 21,* 193–197.

Vallar, G., & Baddeley, A. D. (1984). Phonological short-term store: Phonological processing and sentence comprehension. *Cognitive Neuropsychology, 1,* 121–141.

UNIVERSITY OF WINCHESTER
LIBRARY

Vallar, G., & Shallice, T. (Eds.). (1990). *Neuropsychological impairments of short-term memory.* Cambridge: Cambridge University Press.

APPENDIX

Network used to simulate normal naming error patterns and also as the basis of lesion studies reported here and in Martin et al. (1994)

The network contains 10 semantic feature nodes per word and word nodes for the target *cat*, a semantically related word, *dog*, two phonologically related words, *mat* and *hat*, and two words that were phonologically related to a semantically related word, *log* and *fog*. Additionally, the network contains phoneme nodes corresponding to these words.

Selection of a word node (in production) involves activation of semantic features followed by a spreading process that ultimately activates a lexical node and phonological segments. The spreading process occurs over *k* time steps. During each time step, any node with activation greater than zero sends a portion of its activation (connection strength, *p*) to all nodes to which it is connected thus adding to the overall activation level of those nodes. Additionally, at each time step, a node's activation decays by some percentage (*q*) toward a resting level which is 0 for all nodes. Connection strength and decay rate are each set at some value between 0 and 1. Each word node is connected to 10 semantic features and semantically related words share 1 of these features. The word nodes are also connected to corresponding phonological segment nodes, and phonologically related words share two out of three segments. The activation function is completely linear and there are no thresholds or saturation points.

To simulate naming, one hundred units of activation were given to the semantic features of *cat* (10 per semantic feature). This activation was allowed to spread through the network according to the following rules:

(1) *Updating function:* $a(j,t) = a(j,t-1)(1-q) + Input\ (j,t)$. In this standard linear activation function, $a(j,t)$ is the activation of unit *j* at time *t*, *Input* (j,t) is the input to *j*, and *q* is the decay rate.

(2) *Input function:* $Input\ (j,t) = w(i,j)\ a(i,\ t-1)$. In this standard weighted sum rule, $w(i,j)$ is the weight from unit *i* to unit *j*. All weights, with the exception noted below, are equal to *p*, $0 < p < 1$, and summation is over all units.

(3) All connections are bidirectional.

(4) *Noise:* $X_1 + X_2$ is added to each node for every time step. X_1 (intrinsic noise) is a value sampled from a normal distribution of mean $= 0$ and $SD = S_1$, X_2 (noise related to activation level) is sampled from a normal distribution of mean $= 0$, and $SD = S_2 \cdot a(j,t)$.

After *k* time steps, the lexical node with the highest activation level was selected. It was given another jolt of activation (100 units) and after *k* more time steps the most activated phonological nodes were selected. A single onset, vowel, and coda node were chosen, constituting the model's encoding of the target word.

To simulate normal naming, five parameters were set: *p*, *q*, *k*, *S*1, and *S*2. The first three, *p*, *q*, and *k*, were set as in Dell and O'Seaghdha's (1991) second simulation and were not varied: $p = .1, q = .4$, and $k = 8$ time steps. *S*1 and *S*2 were allowed to vary in an attempt to approximate normal performance. Also, the connection weight between the semantic feature common to *cat* and *dog* and the word node for *dog* was allowed to vary. After some exploration of the parameter space, *S*1 was set at .01, *S*2 was set at .18, and the common semantic feature/dog weight was set at 1.5 *p*.

Reading: Modelling the deficits

Peter Naish

INTRODUCTION

The ability to use language is arguably the most complex aspect of human cognition. Other components of our cognitive toolbox are certainly complex too, and indeed some, such as perception and memory, must play a part in language processing, but they are not uniquely human. Many animals, although less sophisticated than ourselves, are highly effective at perceiving and recognising sounds, objects, or even specific individuals; it is their ability to communicate that is so rudimentary.

The use of language is a symbolic process, in the sense that words are *representations* of objects and ideas. It is perhaps no accident that language development in children begins to blossom at the same time as they start using objects to represent other things when playing. Not many years after learning the elements of their language, although while still relative novices, children are taught to read. This in some respects is an even more remarkable process, as the marks on a printed page are symbols that represent the spoken word which, as explained, is itself a symbol. Thus, reading employs symbols of symbols, and the processing required to link the written word with the original concept has been considered by some to be so complex that if we could understand fully how it took place we would effectively understand the whole of human cognition.

Connectionism attempts to model all of cognition, so proponents have naturally attempted to show that parallel networks can give good accounts of the reading process. A central tenet of connectionism is that complex processes are performed by large numbers of uniform, simple, interconnected elements working in parallel,

rather than by a series of complex, specialised units. Traditional models of the reading process have often been represented in "box-and-arrow" fashion, encapsulating the notion that the system actually comprises a serial (non-parallel) connection of special processing sub-systems. Such a view does not fit easily with the connectionist approach, but before the advent of PDP it seemed obvious that complex cognitive processes had to take place in a series of discrete steps. One of the costs of using that kind of segmentation is that it requires a degree of "hard wiring"; in other words the brain would need to have evolved in such a way that the necessary neural circuitry was in place to perform each step. In evolutionary terms, written language is very young, so it seems hardly plausible that special neural circuitry could have developed to enable us to read and write. It must be supposed that reading takes place by building on existing language structures; if they were themselves built from discrete components, then reading too would have a modular quality. Thus, the question of whether language processing is likely to be modular must be addressed.

At a global level it has been known for a long time that the brain is modular. Thus, many components of visual processing (and hence part of the reading process) take place at the rear of the brain, and language, for most people, is dealt with in the left hemisphere. Within the language area itself, recognition is primarily handled in the posterior region, while production takes place towards the front. Connectionism has never claimed that the brain is an amorphous mass of identical, parallel-connected neurons; it is accepted that there are broad divisions of labour between different regions. The claim for uniformity applies within a region, where the system is said to be nonmodular, with no further specialisation and no genetically determined hard wiring. Perhaps the strongest way of expressing this is to say that although humans have evolved large areas of cortex that will be ready for language processing, the actual neural interconnections available at birth are no more set up for that task than they are in, say, a new-born chimpanzee. This claim would not be acceptable to linguists adopting Chomsky's claim that there are underlying structures that have evolved to enable humans to analyse the grammar to their languages. A strong advocate of connectionism once reminded me that we are supposed to have about 99% of genes in common with chimpanzees. He went on to say that he saw sufficient differences between himself and a chimp to keep that remaining 1% busy, so that he could not imagine any spare genes left over to encode the complexities of grammar! The chapter by Marchman in this volume (Chapter 9) shows that at least some elements of English grammar can be acquired by a nonmodular neural net, and that damage to the net produces very much the same sorts of errors as are sometimes found in patients known to have brain damage. Although not irrefutable evidence, observations like these suggest that the systems that underpin human language processing may be far less modular than has hitherto been supposed.

MODULARITY EFFECTS IN READING

It was stated earlier that elements of reading might be modular if they were built on a modularised language structure. Although there is now reason to question whether language processing is modular, there remain aspects of the reading process where the argument for some kind of separation of processing pathways is quite strong.

At the time children start learning to read they can already perform two very relevant tasks: (1) look at an object (or picture) and speak its name, and (2) understand the meaning of spoken words that they hear. Either process could form the basis for reading. The first is very direct, simply requiring the child to look at the pattern of a printed word and speak its "name". The second mechanism uses the correspondence between letters and the sounds they represent, so that the pronunciation of the word can be derived and hence understood, just as if the spoken form had been heard. Of course, in either case there is no need actually to speak the word; internal recognition would be sufficient. These two pathways from word to understanding are sometimes referred to as the visual route and the phonological route. As one makes strong use of object recognition mechanisms, while the other is closely linked with auditory processes, it seems inescapable that the two routes would have to use quite different neural circuits. Moreover, the underpinning *mechanisms* could be described as being different. Thus, the so-called visual route would be an associative process, in which words were *associated* with their printed forms. In contrast, the phonological mechanism would be rule based, generating specific outputs for specific groups of letters. Is there evidence that these two routes actually exist?

Clearly reading by a visual route does take place, because that is the only way to read an ideogram. Printed Chinese cannot be "sounded out" in the way that English children are often taught to read; the many different ideograms have to be remembered as visual patterns. For readers of English the visual route must be employed with mathematical symbols (the "equals" sign bears no clue to its pronunciation), or highly irregular words such as "sleigh" or "colonel". Another class of word needing visual checking, even when regularly spelled, is the homophone (a word that sounds exactly like another with different spelling). If words were understood purely from their sounds, then it would not be possible to distinguish between say "pear" and "pair". In spoken language context helps to remove such ambiguity, but sentences can be formed where even context fails. Consider the question "Are beeches often found by the sea?". That can be answered correctly only after *visual* recognition of the crucial word; beech trees are not a common coastal feature.

In addition to coping with beaches we can also answer questions such as "Does *gote* sound like an animal?". Such a written question would be impossible in Chinese. Although pronounceable, "gote" is an invented nonword; an invented

ideogram would be both unpronounceable and meaningless, as it could not evoke any visual recognition. English readers cannot be familiar with "gote" visually, so recognising it by sound suggests that a phonological route exists. Numerous experiments (often formal versions of these examples) with accomplished readers have reinforced the belief that two reading routes do exist. People with reading difficulties have also been investigated, in a search for dissociations. The concept of dissociation is described in earlier sections; it will be recalled that finding patients with complementary patterns of deficit and functionality is taken to be strong evidence for the existence of separate processing pathways. This appears to be the case with the reading disabilities known as dyslexia; the various types are described in the introduction to Section II.

A sufferer from phonological dyslexia would not be able to suggest any pronunciation at all for *gote*, although *goat* and even irregular words such as *choir* might be read perfectly successfully. Interestingly, in response to *goat* some deep dyslexics might respond with "sheep", a semantically related word. This kind of error will be considered again later, in the context of connectionist modelling of these conditions.

For surface dyslexics, reading *goat* or *gote* would present no difficulty, but *choir* might be rendered as something like "chair". Thus, irregularly spelled words are regularised in surface dyslexia, suggesting that there is no visual recognition. All letter strings seem to be forced through the phonological route. Consequently, phonological and surface dyslexias offer a convincing double dissociation, supporting the claim that there are two ways of getting from text to meaning. It should be pointed out that many of these descriptions focus very much on the ability or failure to find *pronunciations* for letter strings. That is not necessarily equivalent to finding their meanings, a distinction worth bearing in mind when some of the connectionist models are considered. Connectionists have risen to the challenge of trying to model reading, and there have been attempts to demonstrate dissociation effects in nonmodular networks.

MODELLING THE READING PROCESS

One of the first reports of modelling was by Seidenberg and McClelland (1989). Many of the concepts discussed in this early approach were not actually implemented in the working model; their neural net was restricted to producing a pronunciation in response to a presented letter string, using just one route. In fact the network did not literally produce speech: it output a set of phoneme (speech sound) representations, using a coding system that was simple enough to make the system manageable. Just as Marchman (Chapter 9) demonstrated that a single neural net could deal with both regular and exception past tenses, so Seidenberg and McClelland were able to train theirs to handle regular and irregular pronunciations. This demonstration rather undermined the belief that words with regular spelling could be analysed by a phonological system, which had learned the

spelling-to-sound rules, while irregular words would have to use a different "visual" route. One explanation of the demonstration would be that Seidenberg and McClelland had succeeded in creating a "Chinese" network: it had learned to pronounce all the words "visually". The test of this would be to give the network a pronounceable nonword. As explained earlier, a purely visual route cannot find a sound for a shape that it cannot recognise, whereas a phonologically derived sound can be deduced for any legal letter string, simply by applying rules. It turned out that the Seidenberg and McClelland network was able to produce pronunciations for nonwords, although it was not particularly good at it. The lack of clear-cut success leaves the model open to criticism (see Coltheart, Curtis, Atkins, & Haller in Chapter 13), but it does seem clear that the system was able to go some way to extracting the regular aspects of spelling-to-sound conversion. In a sense it had learned the spelling-to-sound rules, while also being able to deal with exceptions, so it appears to have developed rule-like behaviour, although the system was an associative network, rather than being formally rule-based.

Even if the Seidenberg and McClelland model were deemed a success, the fact that a single network was shown to deal with all classes of word (and nonword) does not necessarily mean that the process is carried out in the same way by the human brain. There are many subtleties of human function (and dysfunction) that would have to be demonstrated by a model, before critics of the connectionist approach could reasonably be satisfied. Coltheart et al. cite examples of studies of developmental and acquired dyslexias, with combinations of symptoms that the model either did not explain, or did not mimic closely. A particularly interesting case is the patient known as WB (see pp. 381–382), who was phonologically dyslexic (could not read nonwords at all), could read real words, but appeared to have imprecise semantic representations of words and objects. Thus, WB would not have been able to pronounce *grush*. He would have been able to read *brush* aloud, but if asked to find a matching picture he might well have selected one of a comb. This case is of particular relevance to the Seidenberg and McClelland model, as part of the structure that they proposed (although did not implement) was a route that linked orthographic input directly to semantic representation, which was itself linked to phonological output. With such a circuit it would be possible for a patient who had lost the direct letter-to-sound route to find the meaning of the word instead. Having done so, the meaning–sound link would be used to speak the word. This account would neatly explain how some patients can pronounce words of irregular spelling, yet cannot pronounce simple nonwords; the latter have no meaning to find. However, the explanation is inadequate for WB, whose meaning representations were imprecise. If he could not clearly distinguish the *meanings* of semantically related items, then the Seidenberg and McClelland model would predict that he should say "comb" when shown the word *brush*; in fact he could say "brush" correctly.

Part of the difficulty when seeking explanations for these kinds of findings is that the distinction between word *naming* and word *understanding* sometimes

becomes blurred. WB's responses are a clear indication that the sound of a word can be produced accurately, without the reader having an accurate understanding of its meaning. The Seidenberg and McClelland network produced pronunciations without *any* understanding of meaning, although their complete model showed how a meaning-mediated pronunciation might be derived. This would constitute yet another possible route from spelling to sound. It is a plausible route, as reading is usually engaged in to derive the *meaning* of the words, not to speak them aloud without understanding. Similarly, words for speaking are most often derived direct from meaning: that is what we do in conversation. Given these two, well-practised activities, it is quite likely that print-to-speech would often take place via meaning, rather than by using a less frequently practised direct translation route. Connectionist implementations can produce counter-intuitive, non-programmed results (generally seen as one of their strengths), so it is unwise to draw strong conclusions from a model that has not been implemented; the real thing may produce surprises. Thus, among the weaknesses of the Seidenberg and McClelland model, the absence of a fully implemented meaning strand was a significant shortcoming.

In Chapter 15 Mayall and Humphreys describe a neural net that does implement a component to represent meaning, although it lacks the semantic–phonological link that was postulated in the Seidenberg and McClelland model. Nevertheless, the Mayall and Humphreys approach was successful in demonstrating that a network could simultaneously derive meaning and pronunciation from the same set of input letters. Additionally, by lesioning their network they were able to demonstrate a dissociation; words could not be spoken at all (alexia) although some knowledge of meanings was preserved. In other words, Mayall and Humphreys had demonstrated a form of covert recognition which, as with the covert recognition of faces, means that although the stimulus (in this case a word) cannot be named overtly, nevertheless it must be recognised at some level for meaning to be accessed.

It is possible that the poor word production performance, following lesioning of the network, would have been less bad had there been a link from the relatively preserved semantic units to the phonological units, as the Seidenberg and McClelland model had proposed but not implemented. An alternative approach was adopted by Hinton and Shallice (1991) who also developed a network that could derive meanings for words. An account of their work can be found in Chapter 14 by Hinton, Plaut, and Shallice. In designing the more elaborate network they improved on another weakness of the earlier models. Seidenberg and McClelland had used a simple network which, as already explained, activated a series of output modes (representing phonemes), in response to an input (representing the printed word). With networks of this type the output pattern appears as quickly as the computer that implements the model can perform the calculations; all outputs take the same length of time to appear. This is not representative of human behaviour, where the time to respond to a word depends on

factors such as the word's frequency. With so many human experiments depending on reaction time measures, it is unfortunate if networks that are claimed to model human behaviour cannot reproduce reaction times. The solution adopted by many researchers, including Seidenberg and McClelland, has been to use the preciseness of the output pattern as an analogue of reaction time. If, for example, it is very clear which phoneme units are "on" (i.e., highly active), and which are not, this is equated with the system being "sure" of the word and an answer being produced quickly. If, on the other hand, the active units do not produce a very high activity level, and if the weaker units continue to be relatively active, then it is taken as equivalent to a human taking longer to reach a decision. This method produces plausible results, but is clearly unsatisfactory as a model of human behaviour. Hinton et al. avoided this difficulty by developing what is known as an attractor network.

Attractor networks use internal loops of connections, so that one unit activates or inhibits another, then the final level of activity from that second unit is linked back to the first. The result is a spiral of activity, as the mutual influence is continually fed back and forth between the elements. Of course, these are not the only connections involved; activity from other parts of the network will also contribute to the overall activation levels of a given set of circularly connected units. An analogy for this activity is to be found in the behaviour of a depressed person, who tends, because of the sense of unhappiness, to focus on unhappy events in his or her life. The result is to exacerbate the feelings of depression, and so the vicious circle continues. (Perhaps this behaviour is underpinned by neural feedback loops linking mood and memory representations.) In an attractor network the spiral of activity, whether up or down, eventually stops. How long the system takes to settle depends on the particular input that started the process, and on the prior learning history of the net. Measuring the number of cycles around the loop before settling is a far better equivalent to reaction time than looking at output "certainty", because in an attractor network the eventual outputs are all equally definite; they simply vary in how long they take to reach the state. Why might a neural net require this kind of circuitry? It clearly will not do to implement it in a model simply because it happens to mimic reaction times. The answer is that it is a very effective way of producing rather distinct outputs from not very distinctive inputs. The networks do not have only one possible end state; the spiralling process can lead to many different outcomes, depending on the initial input. Quite similar initial inputs can be distinguished by this means, so, for example, *hat* and *bat* are visually very similar words, but on reading them they should evoke very different semantic concepts. The networks that achieve this are referred to as attractors, because the cyclic process pulls the initial activity towards a definite outcome, like a vessel approaching a whirlpool. The units in the network that form part of the feedback loop are sometimes called "clean-up" units, because they transform what would have been a rather indistinct, "muddy" output (such

as achieved by Seidenberg and McClelland) into a sharply defined, "clean" pattern of activity.

Hinton and colleagues used an attractor network, which apart from the clean-up circuitry was similar to that of Seidenberg and McClelland. However, the output units of the net represented "sememes" instead of phonemes. Sememes are units of semantic information, and just as phonemes can be assembled to represent a word, so sememes can be combined to represent its meaning. Some of the sememes for a dog might be *living*, *has legs*, and *mammal*. As will be appreciated, the list is potentially very long; the researchers used 68 possible descriptors for the 40 words that their network learned. The system learned successfully, and was then tested after lesioning. To a large extent the results mirrored those of human patients, including the exhibiting of combined semantic and visual errors. This particular effect is another example of a single network producing results that might have been ascribed to problems in two different circuits. If a patient were to read *hat* as "bat" the result would be described as a visual error. If they were to read *cat* as "dog" that would be classed as a semantic error; the wrongly produced word is visually quite distinct, but is clearly semantically very similar. Patients who make semantic errors often produce visual errors too, and this could well be ascribed to damage in two different pathways. From the numbers of each error type produced by a patient it is possible to calculate how many "double" errors might be committed, such as reading *cat* as "rat". This word is both semantically and visually related to the proper word, so if there were damage in two regions it would be expected that occasionally this type of error would occur. However, in practice the "rat" error type is encountered far more frequently than would be expected from the chance combination of errors in two independent pathways. The Hinton et al. network, which of course had only one route, produced a very patient-like pattern of single and combined error types, once again suggesting that many effects in humans can be explained without having to postulate multiple pathways.

This study demonstrated the value of using attractor networks, showing that a form of meaning representation could be accessed directly from a letter-based input, this being an unimplemented component of the earlier Seidenberg and McClelland model. Plaut, McClelland, Seidenberg, and Patterson (1996) revisited the old model, and they too introduced feedback circuits, to form an attractor network. Among other improvements they also found a way of mimicking (although not actually implementing) the presence of semantic information. The result was a circuit that performed far better than its predecessor, and went a long way towards addressing the criticisms of their earlier paper, although the results of lesioning experiments still remained less clear-cut than with human patients. A particularly interesting development in the Plaut et al. investigation concerned their use of semantic information. The authors reasoned that the sememe–phoneme link would become stronger as the meanings of words became better activated by their visual presentation. On this basis, as the words were

repeatedly presented during training, an ever-growing additional input was applied to the pronunciation units, as if coming from a semantic (sememe) region. The result of this manipulation was revealing. After training, the original route, which in the old model dealt with regular and exception words alike, had become principally concerned with the regular words; that is, a phonological route had developed. The exception words were handled largely by the "meaning" route, so appearing to vindicate dual-route protagonists who had always claimed that exception words could only be pronounced by "looking them up" in an internal lexicon (dictionary). This model will not quite deal with WB, who could not access meanings accurately, but this explanatory shortcoming exists only if the visual lexicon is taken to be synonymous with the semantic unit.

CONCLUSIONS

It would appear that the human experimentalists and the connectionists are beginning to produce convergent accounts, although the latter (as represented by Plaut et al.) are keen to point out that their version of two routes is not exactly that described by traditional dual-route theorists. At present the combined data seem to point to the possibility of three routes: one largely phonological, one derived through visual access of the lexicon/semantic store, and perhaps another that is visual, but does not depend on accessing meaning. All the research with human subjects reveals that they are remarkably flexible in their response strategies, and suggests that if there *is* a possible route, then it will probably be used in at least some circumstances. On the other hand, the connectionist approach has demonstrated beyond doubt that it can be unwise to proliferate proposals for routes, because many results can be accounted for with as little as a single network circuit. The final "truth" will not be found through recent brain mapping methodology, which is insufficiently fine-grained to detect the subtleties of lexical neural circuitry. If a definitive answer is possible, it is likely to be derived from continued accurate observing of brain-damaged patients, and from the use of ever more powerful computers, able to implement all the putative elements of a large-vocabulary word recognition system.

REFERENCES

Hinton, G. E., & Shallice, T. (1991). Lesioning an attractor network: Investigations of acquired dyslexia. *Psychological Review, 98*, 74–95.

Plaut, D. C., McClelland, J. L., Seidenberg, M. S., & Patterson, K. (1996). Understanding normal and impaired word reading: Computational principles in quasi-regular domains. *Psychological Review, 103*, 56–115.

Seidenberg, M. S., & McClelland, J. L. (1989). Distributed, developmental model of word recognition and naming. *Psychological Review, 96*, 523–568.

Models of reading aloud: Dual-route and parallel-distributed-processing approaches

Max Coltheart, Brent Curtis, Paul Atkins, and Michael Haller
Macquarie University, Sydney, Australia

It has often been argued that various facts about skilled reading aloud cannot be explained by any model unless that model possesses a dual-route architecture (lexical and nonlexical routes from print to speech). This broad claim has been challenged by Seidenberg and McClelland (1989, 1990). Their model has but a single route from print to speech, yet, they contend, it can account for major facts about reading that have hitherto been claimed to require a dual-route architecture. The authors identify 6 of these major facts about reading. The 1-route model proposed by Seidenberg and McClelland can account for the first of these but not the remaining 5. Because models with dual-route architectures can explain all 6 of these basic facts about reading, the authors suggest that this remains the viable architecture for any tenable model of skilled reading and learning to read. The dual-route cascaded model, a computational version of the dual-route model, is described.

The fundamental property of dual-route models of reading (see, e.g., Baron & Strawson, 1976; Behrmann & Bub, 1992; Berndt & Mitchum, 1994; Coltheart, 1978, 1985; Coslett, 1991; Forster & Chambers, 1973; Frederiksen & Kroll, 1976; Funnell, 1983; Kay & Bishop, 1987; Marshall & Newcombe, 1973; Mitchum & Berndt, 1994; Morton & Patterson, 1980; Paap & Noel, 1991; Patterson & Morton, 1985; Patterson & Shewell, 1987) is the idea that skilled readers have at their disposal two different procedures for converting print to speech. These are, roughly speaking (for more precise characterizations, see the following paragraphs) a dictionary lookup procedure and a letter-to-sound rule procedure.

Psychological Review 1993, Vol. 100, No. 4, 589–608.

By this view, any word the reader has learned is represented as an entry in a mental dictionary or internal lexicon, and such words can be read aloud by accessing the word's lexical entry from its printed form and retrieving from that entry the word's pronunciation. This is generally described as the lexical route for reading aloud.

Readers can, of course, read aloud pronounceable letter strings that they have never seen before: nonwords, for example. Nonwords do not possess lexical entries. Therefore, dual-route theorists claim, the reader must also have available a nonlexical route for reading aloud: a system of rules specifying the relationships between letters and sounds in English. This nonlexical route allows the correct reading aloud of pronounceable nonwords and of words that obey the spelling-sound rules of English, but it delivers incorrect translations of the "exception" or "irregular" words of English, words like *pint* or *colonel*, that disobey the rules.

In summary, then, the lexical route will succeed when the input string is a word but will deliver no output when it is a nonword, whereas the nonlexical route will deliver correct output when the input string is a nonword or a regular word and will deliver an incorrect output (a "regularization error") when the input string is an exception word.

Models of this general class have enjoyed considerable popularity because they have succeeded in accounting for various facts about normal reading (both in skilled readers and in children learning to read) and about abnormal reading (both acquired and developmental dyslexias). However, this general conception of the architecture of the reading system has not gone unchallenged. For example, both Glushko (1979) and Marcel (1980) have argued that nonwords are read aloud by some form of analogy process. This involves a nonword activating the lexical entries for words that are orthographically similar to it, and so nonword reading is not nonlexical here and is not based on explicit rules. Other ways in which aspects of dual-route models have been challenged are discussed in Humphreys and Evett (1985) and the commentaries following that article.

It was difficult to evaluate these challenges to the dual-route model because none of the alternative models were explicitly formulated. Dual-route theorists have been explicit about the architecture of the model, displaying it in box-and-arrow diagram form so that the specific submodules of the system are made clear. Analogy theorists, to take one example, did not do this. So it was not possible to investigate how well such alternative models might be able to account for the range of facts about reading to which the dual-route model has been successfully applied.

This situation has now changed, with the development of an explicit model of reading that does not have a dual-route architecture: the parallel-distributed-processing (PDP) connectionist model of Seidenberg and McClelland (1989) and the development of an explicit model of reading by analogy (Sullivan, 1991;

Sullivan & Damper, 1992). Both models are explicit in the strict sense that they are computer programs that accept as input letter strings and produce as output some form of phonological representation.

Hitherto, dual-route theorists have identified certain facts about reading that, they asserted, could only be explained by positing the existence of separate lexical and nonlexical routes. Seidenberg and McClelland (1989) argued that a model with only a single route can also explain such facts. For example, "our model, and others like it, offers an alternative that dispenses with this two-route view in favor of a single system that also seems to do a better job of accounting for the behavioral data" (p. 564) and "a key feature of the model we propose is the assumption that there is a single, uniform procedure for computing a phonological representation from an orthographic representation that is applicable to exception words and nonwords as well as regular words" (p. 525).

Our aim in this article is to consider how well the one-route PDP model does account for the behavioral data. We also consider briefly the analogy model referred to earlier.

ONE, TWO, OR THREE ROUTES?

If there are distinct lexical and nonlexical procedures for reading aloud, how does the lexical procedure work? Is it a matter of a direct pathway from visual word recognition to spoken word production, or is the pathway less direct, going from visual word recognition to a semantic system (we must have such a pathway because we can understand printed words) and then from semantic system to spoken word production (we must have such a pathway because we can speak spontaneously)? In some versions of the dual-route model (e.g., Morton & Patterson, 1980; Patterson & Shewell, 1987), both of these lexical pathways are proposed. We also adopt this view; reasons for doing so are given later. One might refer to this kind of model as a triple-route model, but it is vital to not overlook the fact that such a model is still based on the fundamental distinction between lexical reading (not available for nonwords) and nonlexical reading (which will incorrectly transcode exception words), the basic distinction characteristic of all dual-route models of reading and rejected by the PDP and analogy approaches referred to earlier.

There is a potential confusion here that we must clarify. The quotations given earlier from pages 525 and 564 of the Seidenberg and McClelland (1989) article refer to their model as having a single system rather than two routes; yet page 559 of their article says this: "Ours is a dual-route model, but it is not an implementation of any previous model." They say this because, in addition to the (implemented) pathway linking the orthographic input system to the phonological output system, they also discuss an (unimplemented) pathway that runs from the orthographic system to a semantic system and then on from this semantic system to the phonological system.

In the present article, what we mean by the term dual-route model is a model that has a route that can read words but cannot read nonwords and another route that can read nonwords and regular words but misreads exception words by regularizing them. Given this terminology, the Seidenberg and McClelland model is not a dual-route model, whereas the alternative to it that we discuss is. This is a terminological, not a substantive, point.

The substantive point is this: Does the human reading system contain a processing procedure that can correctly translate both exception words and nonwords from print to phonology? Seidenberg and McClelland (1989) say yes; dual-route modelers say no. This conflict is the subject of our article.

SIX QUESTIONS ABOUT READING

What are the important questions about reading that one might expect any serious model to attempt to answer? We propose six such questions. They are important because dual-route theorists have regarded the answers that the dual-route model gives to these questions as providing some of the major empirical support for the model and because Seidenberg and McClelland (1989) explicitly considered how their model might provide answers to each.

Question 1: How do skilled readers read exception words aloud?

According to dual-route theory, any tenable answer to this question requires the postulation of a lexicon containing word-specific representations, the argument being that many exception words contain unique mappings from letters to sounds, such as the vowel phoneme in *pint* or the first vowel phoneme in *colonel*. The claim of dual-route theory is that general rules about print-to-speech conversion cannot help here; word-specific representations are needed.

Question 2: How do skilled readers read nonwords aloud?

According to dual-route theory, just as the reading of exception words requires the postulation of a system of whole-word representations, the reading of nonwords requires the postulation of a system of rules. This rule system is loosely referred to as the letter-sound rule system, but this is imprecise because a number of the relevant rules mapping letters to individual phonemes involve more than one letter: Two-letter, three-letter, and even four-letter rules exist (such as the rules for *th*, *igh*, and *eigh*. To make the terminology precise, we need a term to refer to any letter or letter group that corresponds to a single phoneme; some have used "grapheme" for this purpose. Thus, the rule system is termed the grapheme-phoneme correspondence, or GPC, system.[1]

Question 3: How is the visual lexical-decision task performed?

The dual-route model offers the following explanation: Because all words are represented as entries in an internal lexicon, and no nonwords are, the decision as to whether a visually presented letter string is a word or not is made by consulting the lexicon. If a representation of the stimulus is found there, respond "Yes." If not, respond "No."

Question 4: How does surface dyslexia arise?

Surface dyslexia is a form of acquired dyslexia (reading impairment caused by brain damage in a previously literate person) in which the reading aloud of nonwords (and regular words) is selectively preserved relative to the reading aloud of exception words, and exception words are often read as the GPC rules specify. For example, *glove* may be read as if it rhymed with "cove," or *flood* as if it rhymed with "mood"; such responses are referred to as regularization errors. This acquired dyslexia was first described by Marshall and Newcombe (1973), and a number of other cases have been reported in the past 10 years (see, e.g., the book on this disorder by Patterson, Marshall, & Coltheart, 1985). Extreme cases include KT (McCarthy & Warrington, 1986), whose reading of nonwords was normal in accuracy but who misread, with regularization errors, many exception words. Even with very high frequency exception words, he could only achieve an accuracy of 47%, whereas reading accuracy with regular words of comparable frequency was 100%. Once again, the interpretation of this form of acquired dyslexia in terms of the dual-route model is very straightforward: The lexical route is damaged and the nonlexical route is relatively spared (in cases like KT, it is even intact).

Question 5: How does phonological dyslexia arise?

Phonological dyslexia is a form of acquired dyslexia in which the reading aloud of nonwords is selectively impaired relative to the reading aloud of words. A number of cases have been described since the original report by Beauvois and Derouesne (1979), with the most severe case being that described by Funnell (1983). Her patient, WB, scored around 90% correct in various tests requiring words to be read aloud (including long, uncommon, affixed, abstract words such as *satirical* or *preliminary*). In contrast, he was entirely unable to read any nonwords aloud, not even simple monosyllabic nonwords such as *nust*, *cobe*, or *ploon*. When stimuli were just single printed letters, he could give their names (10 of 12 correct) but not their sounds (0 of 12 correct), even though he could repeat these sounds. The interpretation of this form of acquired dyslexia in terms of the dual-route model is of course very straightforward: The nonlexical route

is damaged and the lexical route is relatively spared. In the case studied by Funnell (1983), the nonlexical route is completely destroyed, whereas the lexical route is almost entirely intact.

Question 6: How does developmental dyslexia arise?

Everyone agrees that there are various different patterns or subtypes of developmental dyslexia. The dual-route account of this (see, e.g., Coltheart, 1984; Harris & Coltheart, 1986; Marshall, 1984) is as follows. The skilled reader possesses a reading system consisting of a number of separate modules such as a letter-identification system, a visual word recognition system, a GPC system, and so on. Some of these modules belong to the lexical route for reading, some belong to the nonlexical route, and some (e.g., the letter-identification system) belong to both. A child has to acquire all of these processing modules at a normal rate if learning to read is to progress normally. There can be selective difficulties in acquiring specific modules of the system; these correspond to different subtypes of developmental dyslexia. In particular, some children have a difficulty that selectively affects acquiring the grapheme–phoneme rule system: This is developmental phonological dyslexia (Temple & Marshall, 1983). Some others have a selective difficulty in acquiring the lexical procedure for reading: This is developmental surface dyslexia (Coltheart, Masterson, Byng, Prior, & Riddoch, 1983; Holmes, 1973). These are two of the subtypes of developmental dyslexia.

Here, then, are six important questions about reading. We have shown that dual-route theorists have offered answers to all six questions. So have Seidenberg and McClelland (1989): That is, they have asserted that their PDP model can give an account of all six of these questions about reading and hence that none of the facts about reading that these questions refer to requires the postulation of a dual-route architecture for the reading system.

Because a number of their arguments depend on the specific architecture of their model, we need to describe the model in some detail before we can consider how successful it is in providing answers to these six questions.

THE SEIDENBERG–McCLELLAND MODEL

The structure of the implemented model is depicted in Figure 1. This model is a standard three-layer feed-forward network. All 400 orthographic units are connected to all 200 hidden units (80,000 connections), and all 200 units are connected to all 460 phonological units (92,000 connections). In addition, there are 80,000 connections from the hidden units back to the orthographic units. The connections initially have random weights, so that the network initially computes random pronunciations for orthographic inputs. The network is trained using backpropagation, and the consequent adjustments of weights produces progressively increasing accuracy of the patterns of activation across the phono-

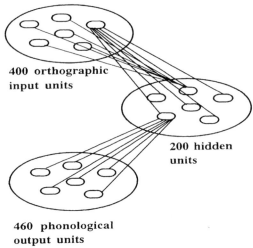

400 orthographic input units

200 hidden units

460 phonological output units

Figure 1. Outline of the implemented part of the Seidenberg–McClelland model of reading aloud. (Only some of the connections are shown. All units in any layer are connected to all units in the next layer, and all the hidden units have backward-operating connections to all input units. (From "A Distributed, Developmental Model of Word Recognition and Naming" by M. S. Seidenberg and J. L. McClelland, 1989, *Psychological Review*, 96, p. 527. Copyright © 1989 by the American Psychological Association. Adapted with permission.)

logical units in response to orthographic inputs: That is, the network learns (see Figures 3 and 7 in Seidenberg & McClelland, 1989).

Orthographic units

When designing a connectionist model of reading aloud, one might first think of an architecture in which each input unit represents a letter, and indeed this option has sometimes been taken (e.g., McClelland & Rumelhart, 1981; Rumelhart & McClelland, 1982). This option, however, encounters two serious problems: letter duplications and anagrams. If there is just one unit for the letter *o* and just one for the letter *f*, then the words *of* and *off* would have identical input representations (the *f* and *o* units on, all others off) and so they could not be pronounced or understood differently. Anagram sets like *apt*, *tap*, and *pat* would also have identical representations at input; therefore, they could not have different pronunciations at output. The solution to this problem adopted by McClelland and Rumelhart (1981) was to have a full set of letter detectors for each position in a word. Seidenberg and McClelland (1989) tried a different tack.

In Seidenberg and McClelland's model, each of the 400 input units has the following structure. The unit can be thought of as consisting of a list of 10 possible first characters, a list of 10 possible second characters, and a list of 10 possible third characters. The character vocabulary consists of all the letters of the alphabet plus a word-boundary symbol, and the tables of characters are assembled entirely at random except for the sole constraint that the word-boundary character is not

allowed in the list of possible second characters.[2] Thus, each orthographic unit specifies 1,000 possible character triples. An input string turns on an orthographic unit if that string contains a sequence of three consecutive characters that is 1 of the 1,000 triples in the unit's repertoire. So, for example, if we denote the word-boundary symbol by #, then the word *made* will turn on any unit that includes any of the triples *#ma*, *mad*, *ade*, or *de#*. On average, any three consecutive characters in the input string activate about 20 orthographic units. With this setup, the probability that two different input strings would activate exactly the same set of orthographic units is effectively zero, so all input strings should be discriminable at the input level (even anagrams and strings with repeated letters).

Phonological units

Similar problems of repetitions and anagrams (anaphones?) would arise at this level if the output units represented phonemes. The option adopted by McClelland and Rumelhart (1981) to confront the input problem (a full set of units for every position in a word) was adopted by Lacouture (1989) to confront this output problem; Lacouture proposed a full set of phoneme feature units for each possible phoneme position in a spoken response (limiting himself to words with seven phonemes or fewer). Seidenberg and McClelland (1989) instead used an output system that, like their input system, coded sequential information by using triples.

Each of the 460 output units in Seidenberg and McClelland's model represents just a single triple (not a large set of triples, as with the input coding scheme), and these triples were selected systematically (not randomly, as with the input coding scheme). The output scheme they adopted was in fact that used by Rumelhart and McClelland (1986) in their model of the acquisition of the past tenses of English verbs. This output scheme derives from the concept of the Wickelphone: a sequence of three consecutive phonemes. Each Wickelphone corresponds to a set of Wickelfeatures, where a Wickelfeature is a sequence of three phonetic features, one from each of the three consecutive phonemes of the Wickelphone. Given the phoneme coding scheme used by Rumelhart and McClelland (1986), there are 1,210 possible different Wickelfeatures. An output system containing this many units was computationally too intensive for Rumelhart and McClelland (1986), so they reduced the number of output units from 1,210 to 460 by discarding every Wickelfeature in which the first and the third features referred to a different phonetic dimension. No rationale for this way of eliminating Wickelfeatures was given. Note that many of the retained Wickelfeatures are phonotactically illegal (e.g., stop–stop–stop or nasal–nasal–nasal), and so there are units that will never be used for output; also note that many of the discarded Wickelfeatures are phonotactically legal (e.g., stop–vowel–unvoiced as in "cat" or nasal–vowel–fricative as in "mouse") and so would be used for output if they had been retained.[3]

How does one know whether a response by the model is correct?

The correct pronunciation of the input string is specified as a string of phonemes, but because the model's output is not a string of phonemes, deciding whether the output is correct by comparing desired and produced phoneme strings is not possible. The computed output consists of an activation level on each of the 460 output units. Could one, perhaps, judge correctness by determining whether all the units representing Wickelfeatures that are present in the desired response are on (activation 1.0) and all the other units are off (activation 0.0)? No, because the logistic activation function that the network uses does not permit activations to get as high as 1.0 or as low as 0.0. Therefore, whenever the network produces a response, every output unit has some activation. It is clear, then, that the problem of assessing correctness of response is nontrivial. Yet, of course, this is absolutely critical for the evaluation of the model.

One method by which responses can be roughly evaluated is described on pages 530 and 532 of the Seidenberg and McClelland (1989) article. Target outputs are defined as an activation value of 0.9 for all the output units that should be on and an activation value of 0.1 for all the output units that should be off. The target output vector of 460 values is compared with the network-computed output vector of 460 values, and an error score is calculated (mean squared error [MSE] between corresponding elements of the two vectors). The smaller this MSE is, the more accurate the network's output is. How small, however, does the MSE have to be for the response to be counted as actually correct rather than just close? This was decided as follows: For a particular word like *hot*, where the desired output is the Wickelfeature representation of the syllable "/hot/," all the possible three-phoneme sequences that differed by one phoneme from the target sequence were formed, and the correct output pattern for each of these possible sequences was determined. Then the pattern that the network actually generated was compared with all of these possible outputs plus the target output. A response was counted as correct if the network's output yielded a smaller MSE when compared with the target output than when compared with all of the other output patterns considered. The general procedure, then, was to assemble a set of potential target outputs, of which the desired output was one, and determine whether the network's output was closer to the correct target than to all the other one-phoneme-different possibilities. This is the BEATENBY criterion: A response is judged incorrect by this criterion if the correct target is beaten by any incorrect alternative.

The use of the BEATENBY criterion only puts a lower bound on the model's error rate in pronouncing a particular set of stimuli. When the computed response is not beaten by any of the incorrect potential target outputs, this does not guarantee that the computed response would not be beaten by any incorrect potential output; there might be a potential output that matches the computed

output very closely but is not in the list of potential outputs generated by the BEATENBY procedure. The BEATENBY procedure offers as alternatives only responses that differ by a single phoneme from the desired response, but the computed response might contain more than one incorrect phoneme. Indeed, sometimes the computed response can even contain the wrong number of phonemes. Rumelhart and McClelland (1986) evaluated the performance of their past-tense learning model (which uses the same phonological output system as the Seidenberg and McClelland model) by comparing the output computed by the network with much larger sets of possible alternatives. Their Table 18 gives examples where the computed output differs from the desired output in the number of syllables (e.g., the network said "membled" when it should have said "mailed," and "toureder" when it should have said "toured"). Thus, the model is capable of making errors that would not be included in the list of possible errors generated by BEATENBY. That is why the BEATENBY analysis gives only a lower bound to the model's error rate.

THE SEIDENBERG AND McCLELLAND MODEL AND THE SIX QUESTIONS ABOUT READING

Reading of exception words

Seidenberg and McClelland (1989) used the BEATENBY criterion to evaluate the model's success in reading; of the 2,897 words in the model's training set, only 77 (2.7%) were wrongly read, judging by this criterion. Most of these errors are with low-frequency exception words, as would be the case in data collected from human subjects in naming-latency experiments. Hence, both quantitatively and qualitatively the model succeeds in simulating exception-word reading.

Nonword reading

As Seidenberg and McClelland (1989) repeatedly emphasized, their model is meant to perform well on exception words, regular words, and nonwords; hence, we need to know whether it can indeed read nonwords correctly. Seidenberg and McClelland reported some results concerning the effect of stimulus variables on the size of the output error score with nonwords as input, but they did not report any data that tell us what proportion of nonwords the network can actually read correctly (as assessed by their BEATENBY criterion, for example). This kind of analysis of accuracy of nonword reading using the BEATENBY criterion was, however, carried out by Besner, Twilley, McCann, and Seergobin (1990). With the nonwords from Experiment 2 of Glushko (1979), the model was correct 65% of the time. With two other sets of nonwords, the model scored 59% and 51%, human subjects yielding scores of 94% and 89% in these two conditions (even under speeded-naming conditions). Thus, the model cannot in fact read nonwords aloud as well as it can read words; its performance is far below that of the skilled readers whose performance it is intended to simulate.

Seidenberg and McClelland (1990) replied to Besner et al. (1990) by conceding that their model reads nonwords less well than people do. Their explanation for this is as follows:

> The principal difference between the model and people is that whereas people's vocabularies are on the order of 30,000 words, the model's vocabulary is 2,897 ... Nonword performance therefore depends on vocabulary size. The model's performance reflects which words did or did not happen to be included in the training corpus ... People are able to pronounce nonwords like DOWT on the basis of their knowledge of words; the model performs similarly, within the restrictions of the training corpus. It is important to understand the limits of the current simulation; it is also important to ask how well a person would pronounce nonwords if the person's vocabulary were limited to 2,900 words. (pp. 447–448)

The argument here is that the model's low accuracy on nonword reading reflects a deficiency of the training set, not a deficiency of the model: The training set just does not contain all the information about orthographic–phonological relationships that needs to be learned to produce a system that reads nonwords as well as people do.

The implication is clear: No learning algorithm, trained only on the 2,897 words in the Seidenberg–McClelland corpus and then tested on the Glushko (1979) nonwords, could achieve accuracies of nonword reading in excess of 90% (as people do), simply because the information necessary for this level of performance cannot be learned from the Seidenberg–McClelland database.

We show later in our article that this is not so. The learning algorithm we have developed, when trained on the Seidenberg–McClelland database and then exposed to the Glushko (1979) nonwords, reads these nonwords aloud correctly with an accuracy of 98%. Therefore, the necessary information is in the database; so the poor performance of the PDP model in reading nonwords is a defect not of the database but of the model itself.

Lexical decision

As Figure 1 indicates, there are feedback connections from the hidden units to the orthographic units in the one-route model. The function of these units is to perform visual lexical decision.[4] Once the model has been fully trained, it uses these connections to perform lexical decision as follows. After a letter string is submitted to the input units and activation of the hidden units is computed, the feedback connections compute a representation back at the orthographic units, and this computed representation is compared with the input representation, the comparison yielding an orthographic error score (a measure of the difference between the original input pattern and its recreation via the feedback connections). This orthographic error score is a kind of measure of the familiarity of the input pattern, and the subject applies a criterion to it to make lexical decisions: If the orthographic error score is below the criterion value, respond "Yes," otherwise,

respond "No." Calculations by Besner et al. (1990) revealed that with the words and nonwords used by Waters and Seidenberg (1985), a criterion that would yield the error rate to word stimuli the latter observed (6.1%) would yield an error rate to nonword stimuli of over 80%. Similarly high error rates by the model were obtained by Besner et al. in analyses of other published lexical-decision experiments. Thus, the PDP model is much poorer than people are at lexical decision.

Seidenberg and McClelland (1989) have responded to this problem by suggesting that, when the words and the nonwords in a visual lexical-decision experiment are difficult to distinguish in terms of orthographic properties, subjects might seek to perform the task phonologically. The architecture of the model would need to be embellished to try to accommodate this kind of processing:

> The phonological representation computed by our existing orthography → phonology pathway can be seen as an input pattern over the phonological units. If this pattern were passed through a set of hidden units reciprocally connected to the phonological units and trained through experience with the sounds of words, the difference between the incoming phonological stimulus and this feedback could serve as the basis for a familiarity judgment. (Seidenberg & McClelland, 1989, p. 552)

Several points may be made here. First, it remains to be seen whether the addition of this new set of units and these two new sets of connection to the model would in fact increase its lexical-decision accuracy to the level exhibited by people; only simulations with a new model implementing the additional architecture could determine this, and these are not available. Second, the point we make in Note 4 can be reiterated: These new units and connections would have a sole function—to improve the model's lexical-decision performance; taking them away would not affect any other reading task. Third, it is very hard to see why this proposal would solve the problem. What would this new model do in a lexical-decision task in which all the words were orthographically unusual (*waltz*, *yacht*, *oasis*), all the nonwords were orthographically orthodox, and every item was, phonologically, a word (i.e., all the nonwords were pseudohomophones)? Here, provided that the model is competent at computing phonology for nonwords, which it is meant to be, the computed phonological representation could not assist in lexical decision because it is always that of a word, regardless of whether the input is a word or not; the computed orthographic representation will be of very little use too because the nonwords are, orthographically, more wordlike than the words. Of course, human subjects will not be error free in such circumstances, but it seems extremely unlikely that they would be as prone to error as the new model would be.

Another way in which the PDP model might attempt to perform the lexical-decision task is to use the unimplemented pathway from orthography to meaning; if meaning is activated, the input string must be a word. Once again, however, it is by no means clear that this would work at all. A highly wordlike nonword such as *sare* would surely produce considerable activation in the meaning

system because it would produce considerable activation in the orthographic system. Could we be sure that a highly unwordlike word such as *hymn* would produce a greater degree of activation in the meaning system? Only detailed simulations could tell us this.

Acquired dyslexia

Seidenberg and McClelland (1989) said, "The model also provides an account of certain forms of dyslexia that are observed . . . as a consequence of brain injury" (p. 525). The two forms of acquired dyslexia they considered are surface dyslexia and phonological dyslexia.

Surface dyslexia. The model's account of surface dyslexia is given in Patterson, Seidenberg, and McClelland (1989) and Patterson (1990). Those authors took the trained network and "lesioned" it in several ways in an attempt to produce a damaged network that showed the symptoms of surface dyslexia.

This attempt was not successful. For example, specific regularization errors, the essential type of error in surface dyslexia, were not observed with any of the damaged versions of the network. In their article reporting comparisons between data from two surface dyslexic patients and data from the lesioned model, Patterson et al. (1989) noted,

> The patients appear to differentiate among the various options at each level, selectively favouring the pronunciation corresponding to the exact regularization. For the model, on the other hand, all alternatives within each level seem to be more or less equivalent: the regularization has no special status. (p. 169)

Further work of this sort is reported by Patterson (1990). After training, the model was lesioned by setting to zero the activation values of 20 randomly chosen units of the model's 200 hidden units. The reading of this damaged model was compared with the reading of two surface dyslexic patients, MP (Bub, Cancelliere, & Kertesz, 1985) and KT (McCarthy & Warrington, 1986). The results are shown in Table 1.

As will be seen, the performance of the lesioned model with the four types of words is similar to the data of MP, though very different from the data of KT. Patterson (1990) noted that an obvious step here to try to simulate KT's performance more closely would be to lesion a greater number of hidden units; however, this will not do because, as Patterson (1990) pointed out, "the model's performance on regular words begins to decline when larger proportions of hidden units are eliminated" (p. 96) and hence "thus far, our lesioning explorations have not reproduced the dramatic pattern of performance shown by KT" (p. 96). This lesioning study did succeed in generating regularization errors. The patients' errors on exception words consisted of pure regularization errors about 85% of the time; about 50% of the model's errors were regularization errors.

TABLE 1
Word-naming performance (percentage correct) on high- and
low-frequency regular and exception words by two surface
dyslexic patients

	Word type			
	High frequency		Low frequency	
Patient	Regular	Exception	Regular	Exception
KT[a]	100	47	89	26
MP[b]	95	93	98	73
PDP model[c]	93	86	93	78

PDP = parallel-distributed-processing.
    [a] Subject from McCarthy and Warrington (1986).   [b] Subject from Bub,
Cancelliere, and Kertesz (1985).   [c] From Patterson (1990). The model had
20% of its hidden units "lesioned."

There is no obvious way of increasing the rate at which the model produces regularization errors so that a simulation of the patients' regularization error rates might be achieved. Lesioning a large number of hidden units will not do the job for the reason noted earlier.

In any case, attempting to simulate surface dyslexia would seem to be a premature endeavor. In the purest cases of surface dyslexia, nonwords are read very well. For example, MP read correctly 95.5% of 44 nonwords, with a mean naming latency of 818 ms (Behrmann & Bub, 1992); KT scored 96.5% correct in a test of reading 86 nonwords (McCarthy & Warrington, 1986). The unlesioned Seidenberg and McClelland model only achieves nonword reading accuracies between 51% and 65%, as reported earlier. Only if the unlesioned model's nonword reading accuracy were comparable to the nonword reading accuracy of these surface dyslexic patients would it seem appropriate to attempt to simulate surface dyslexia by lesioning the model.

Phonological dyslexia.   No attempt has been made to account for phonological dyslexia with the implemented model, but Seidenberg and McClelland (1989) indicated that if future developments of the model were to address questions about reading comprehension, then a second route (from orthography to semantics to phonology) could be added. If such a model was successfully implemented, then phonological dyslexia "would follow if the patient's capacity to compute pronunciations from orthography were impaired but the indirect route from orthography to meaning to phonology were not" (p. 558). The idea here is that, as long as reading through meaning is preserved, the patient will be able to read words, even if nonwords cannot be read; that is, the phonological dyslexic is dependent on semantic mediation for the processing of single words.

Exactly this idea had already been investigated by Funnell (1983) with her phonological dyslexic patient WB. She concluded that "WB is not dependent upon semantic mediation for the processing of written words" (p. 170). Seidenberg and McClelland (1989) did not mention Funnell's work or her conclusion, but it merits an account here in view of its relevance to their explanation of phonological dyslexia. Funnell studied WB's performance on semantic tasks with written words precisely because "a significant deficit in semantic tasks, relative to reading aloud, would be incompatible with the notion that the reading performance of WB is mediated by semantic processing strategies" (Funnell, 1983, p. 167).

A first point is that WB was significantly worse at naming pictures than at reading aloud the corresponding picture names. There was no evidence that this was due to any problem in picture recognition, and the difference clearly was not due to the use of letter-sound rules to assist the reading of words, because WB could not use such rules at all: He scored 0% correct when asked to read aloud nonwords. Because it is almost universally accepted that pictures can only be named by means of semantic mediation, this superiority of reading aloud over picture naming implies that WB's reading aloud was not dependent on semantic mediation. To strengthen this conclusion, Funnell (1983) carried out experiments directly assessing WB's semantic processing of printed words. Two results are important here:

1. When a spoken word (e.g., "brush") was presented and WB had to choose which of two pictures (the target and a semantically related picture such as one of a comb) matched the target, he made a number of errors (7 of 36 incorrect), whereas when the distractor picture was unrelated (target "brush," pictures of a brush and a mug), he made no errors. This indicates that he had a semantic impairment: His semantic representation for "brush" is degraded in such a way that, though still distinguishable from the semantic representation for "mug," it is not distinguishable from the semantic representation for "comb." If so, and if WB's reading was semantically mediated, he would make the same kinds of errors when target and distractor are printed words; that is, with the spoken target "brush" and the printed words *brush* and *comb*, he will behave just as he did with pictures. This was not so; on the printed-word version of this task, he made no errors at all. So he must be doing this reading task nonsemantically; he knows the pronunciations of the two printed words and the pronunciation of the target word he has just heard, so he can do the task by phonological matching. To achieve error-free performance using this strategy of course requires error-free conversion from print to speech for words.

2. Next WB was given trios of printed words. His task was to decide which of Word 2 and Word 3 was closest to Word 1 in meaning. With trios like *bough—twig/branch* or *toast—cake/bread*, where precise semantic knowledge of the printed words is needed to perform the task, he did badly: 13 of 16 and 11 of 16 on two occasions, where chance would be 8 of 16. With trios like *bough—*

cake/branch or *toast—nail/bread*, where imprecise semantic knowledge of the printed word would suffice, he performed significantly better: 15 of 16 on both occasions.

In summary, then, these tests showed that WB could read words aloud precisely while knowing their meanings only imprecisely. Therefore, he could not have been relying solely on semantic mediation when he read aloud. This refutes the suggestion by Seidenberg and McClelland (1989) that the explanation of phonological dyslexia is in terms of reading through a semantic route. Therefore, even the unimplemented version of their model cannot offer a tenable account of phonological dyslexia.

An alternative approach to the attempt to reconcile phonological dyslexia with the Seidenberg and McClelland model has been suggested by Patterson (personal communication, March 1992). This is based on ideas advanced by Hillis and Caramazza (1991). Perhaps a patient with an impaired semantic system, who therefore makes semantic errors in reading comprehension and who also has a severely impaired nonsemantic reading system, could avoid making semantic errors in reading aloud by making use of even very poor information about the pronunciation of a word yielded by the nonsemantic reading system. The semantic system may no longer be able to distinguish the concept *orange* from the concept *lemon*; however, to avoid semantic error in reading aloud, all the nonsemantic route needs to deliver is just the first phoneme of the written word, not a complete representation of its phonology. However, this argument does not succeed in reconciling Funnell's (1983) data with Seidenberg and McClelland's model, because WB's nonsemantic reading route was not just severely impaired, it was completely abolished. He scored 0% correct in reading nonwords; he even scored 0% correct when asked just to give the individual phonemes corresponding to single printed letters (even though he could repeat these phonemes). Hence, one cannot argue that WB was making use of partial information from a nonsemantic reading route to avoid making semantic errors in reading aloud (while making them in reading comprehension). Thus, the data reported by Funnell remain as evidence against the Seidenberg and McClelland model.

Another study of phonological dyslexia, that of Coslett (1991), also provides data that conflict with this model. Coslett's patient, WT, read words aloud well, scoring over 90% correct in several tests of word reading; in contrast, his ability to read aloud short nonwords was poor (25% of such nonwords read correctly). Could this be because he was using semantic mediation to read aloud? No, because Coslett showed that WT had a semantic impairment selectively affecting abstract words and yet could read such words aloud well. In writing words to dictation, WT did well with concrete words but did poorly with abstract words; the same effect was observed in tests of word repetition. In contrast, his reading aloud was very good with abstract words. However, reading comprehension was

poor for abstract words. It is clear, then, that if WT was reading aloud semantically, he should have been poor at reading abstract words aloud, and he was not. However, if he was reading aloud by the direct orthography-to-phonology route in the Seidenberg–McClelland model, the important feature of which is that it is meant to read words and nonwords equally well, he should have been as good a reader of nonwords as of words, and he was not.[5]

It is therefore clear that answers to two of our six questions about reading, the two questions about acquired dyslexia, have not been provided by the one-route model of Seidenberg and McClelland, and so suggestions that the model "provides an account of certain forms of dyslexia that are observed ... as a consequence of brain injury" (Seidenberg & McClelland, 1989, p. 525) or can "perform like several patients in the literature when damaged" (Seidenberg & McClelland, 1990, p. 451) are without justification.

Developmental dyslexia

Seidenberg and McClelland (1989) said that "the model ... provides an account of certain forms of dyslexia that are observed developmentally" (p. 525). Developmental dyslexia was simulated by training a version of the model that had only 100 hidden units rather than 200. The result was that, at training asymptote, exception words were read less accurately than regular words, even when these words were high in frequency (i.e., had been presented very frequently during training). Seidenberg and McClelland (1989) observed that

> These results capture a key feature of the data obtained in studies of poor readers and dyslexics. These children exhibit *larger* regularity effects than do good readers; they continue to perform poorly in naming even higher frequency exception words. At the same time, their performance shows that they have learned some generalizations about spelling-sound correspondences: for example, they are able to pronounce many nonwords correctly. (p. 547)

This form of developmental dyslexia, a selective difficulty in reading aloud exception words, is known as developmental surface dyslexia (Coltheart et al., 1983; Holmes, 1973). In the early case of CD (Coltheart et al., 1983), nonword reading was also not very good. If that is characteristic of developmental surface dyslexia, then the account of this condition offered by the Seidenberg–McClelland model would be superior to the account offered by the dual-route model. The analysis of developmental dyslexias offered by the dual-route model (see, e.g., Coltheart, 1984; Harris & Coltheart, 1986; Marshall, 1984) is that, just as each of the two routes can be selectively affected by brain damage with the other remaining intact, it is possible for a child to have difficulty acquiring one of the routes, with the other being acquired at a normal rate. Hence, there should be developmental dyslexics who are abnormally poor at reading exception words while in the normal range at nonword reading. In contrast, although Seidenberg

and McClelland (1989) did not report any data on the nonword reading of their simulation of surface dyslexia, we can be sure that this would not have been very good: The error scores for reading of regular words were about twice as large in the 100-unit network than in the 200-unit network, and the reduction in the number of units could hardly help nonword reading if it harmed regular word reading.

It turns out that the early case of developmental surface dyslexia, CD, was an impure case, just as the early cases of acquired surface dyslexia (Holmes, 1973; Marshall & Newcombe, 1973) were. These acquired cases were not normal at reading nonwords, but eventually cases of acquired surface dyslexia in which nonword reading was normal were found (such as the cases MP and KT discussed earlier), and the same thing has happened with developmental surface dyslexia. Castles and Coltheart (1993) collected a sample of 53 developmentally dyslexic boys (who were of at least average intelligence, were at least 18 months behind their chronological age in reading, and had no evident difficulties with spoken language) and gave these children exception words and nonwords to read aloud. The same materials were given to a matched control group of normal readers.

Ten dyslexic children were identified whose accuracy in reading exception words was grossly abnormal relative to the control group but whose nonword reading accuracy was within the normal range. The existence of this pure form of developmental surface dyslexia is inconsistent with the Seidenberg–McClelland account of developmental dyslexia but is predicted by the dual-route account.

Seidenberg and McClelland (1989) very briefly discussed developmental phonological dyslexia (reading of nonwords selectively impaired relative to reading of words). They suggested that this might be simulated by altering the input or output architecture of the model, or the condition might correspond to a major impairment of the implemented pathway from orthography to phonology in their model, with the child relying on reading via the (unimplemented) pathway through semantics. We have already argued that acquired phonological dyslexia cannot be explained by the model in this way, and we see no reason why the explanation would be any more suitable for developmental phonological dyslexia. In contrast, the dual-route model's analysis of developmental phonological dyslexia predicts that some children should have great difficulty in learning grapheme–phoneme rules even though acquiring a sight vocabulary at a normal rate. The result would be children with grossly defective nonword reading but normal accuracy at reading exception words. Castles and Coltheart (1993) found 8 such children in their sample of 53 dyslexics. We argue, then, that the dual-route model provides a good account of patterns of developmental dyslexia, whereas the Seidenberg–McClelland model does not.

We have now considered all six of the questions about reading posed earlier in this article. The dual-route model offers a satisfactory answer to all six questions; the Seidenberg–McClelland model offers a satisfactory answer to only one. Their model, after training to asymptote, reads exception words well; how-

ever, it cannot read nonwords as well as people can, it cannot perform lexical decision as well as people can, it cannot be used to explain acquired dyslexias (surface dyslexia and phonological dyslexia), and it cannot be used to explain developmental dyslexias (surface dyslexia and phonological dyslexia).

A DUAL-ROUTE CASCADED (DRC) MODEL OF READING

The PDP model of Seidenberg and McClelland has two highly desirable features that the dual-route model currently lacks: The model is computational, and it learns. We agree with Seidenberg and McClelland that it is desirable that any model of cognition be computational and that it offer an account of how the cognitive skill in question is acquired, rather than simply presenting a static picture of the mature system; for this reason, we have begun work on the development of a dual-route model of reading that has these two properties. Its name comes from the fact that it has dual routes for proceeding from print to speech, a lexical route and a nonlexical route, and that processing stages pass on information in a cascaded rather than in a thresholded way (see the following paragraphs for a further discussion of this). A sketch of the architecture of the DRC model is given in Figure 2; it follows architectures that may be found in figures in Morton and Patterson (1980), Coltheart (1985), and Patterson and Shewell (1987). One computational realization of the dual-route model has already been described by Reggia, Marsland, and Berndt (1988). There are two main differences between their approach and ours. First, in their model, the common input stage for the two routes is a level of graphemes, not letters, where grapheme means the written representation of a phoneme (thus, e.g., the word *sheep* is composed of the three graphemes *sh*, *ee*, and *p*). In our approach, the concept of grapheme is relevant only to the nonlexical route. The common first stage for the two routes is a level of letters, and this stage feeds the visual word recognition stage of the lexical route and the grapheme–phoneme conversion stage of the nonlexical route. Processing in the latter stage includes a process of *graphemic parsing* (Coltheart, 1978), that is, converting a letter string into a string of graphemes. Second, we have required our model to learn the GPCs of English: In the Reggia et al. approach, these are built into the model, having been determined from a statistical analysis of a corpus of word spellings and pronunciations.

Because the components of the DRC model are meant to be truly modular, it is possible to work independently on computational models of the various modules of the system; most of our work so far has been on the nonlexical rule system. The algorithm we have developed is one which, when exposed to the printed forms of words and their pronunciations, learns the grapheme–phoneme rules embodied in the training set of words and then is able to apply these rules to new letter strings it has not seen before, "reading them aloud" in the sense of outputting a string of phonemes for each input string of letters.

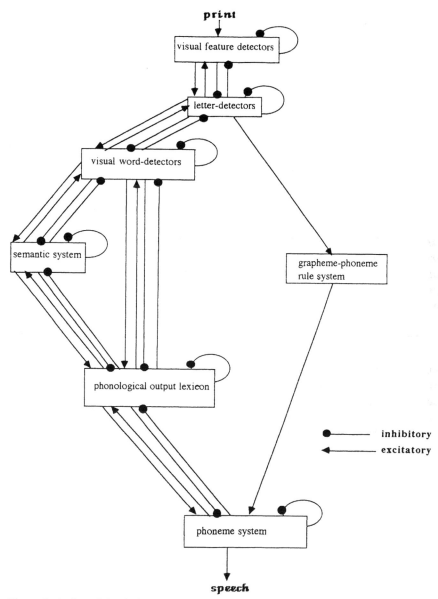

Figure 2. Outline of the dual-route cascaded model: a computational version of the dual-route model of reading.

LEARNING AND APPLYING GPC RULES

Learning the rules

The nature of the rules.   The nonlexical route of the DRC model translates letter strings to strings of phonemes. This translation is done using GPC rules; that is, the right-hand side of a rule is always only a single phoneme (the left-hand side can be any number of letters; for English, it happens that no grapheme larger than four letters exists; by the term grapheme we mean the written representations of a phoneme). These GPC rules were not specified a priori by us. Instead, they were automatically learned, from exposure to the spellings and pronunciations of real words (these being the 2,897 words that Seidenberg & McClelland, 1989, used when training their model). Some GPC rules are context sensitive (e.g., the rules for initial *c* and initial *g*, where the pronunciation assigned to a letter depends on the following letter, or the rule that is applicable to the letter sequence *qu*, where what needs to be learned is that $u \rightarrow$ /w/ when the letter preceding the *u* is *q*). Some GPC rules are position specific (e.g., there are three different rules for the letter *y*, one for initial positions as in *yet*, one for medial positions as in *gym*, and one for final positions as in *sky*).

The GPC algorithm learns as follows. Words are presented in a random order, the spelling of each word being presented jointly with its phonetic transcription. For each word, the algorithm attempts to infer all the GPC rules that describe the relationship between that word's spelling and its pronunciation, and the inferred rules are used to update the rules in the current rule base (or to add new rules to this rule base if any rule inferred from the word is not present in the rule base). So, for a word like *mint* with its pronunciation /mint/, the rules $m \rightarrow$ /m/, $i \rightarrow$ /i/, $n \rightarrow$ /n/, and $t \rightarrow$ /t/ would be inferred, and the frequencies of these rules in the rule base would be incremented by 1 (or if any of these rules did not yet exist in the rule base at the time when the word *mint* was encountered, these new rules would be introduced and given an initial frequency of 1). In the case of an irregular word like *pint*, a different rule for the grapheme *i*, the rule $i \rightarrow$ /I/, would be inferred and added to the rule base.

Each rule created carries with it a rule type that indicates the position of the grapheme within the word from which the rule was created. We identify three positions: a grapheme that begins a word, a grapheme that ends a word, and a medial grapheme. For the *mint* example earlier, the $m \rightarrow$ /m/ rule will have the rule type "b", the $t \rightarrow$ /t/ rule will be given the rule type "e", and the rules for *i* and *n* will each be given a rule type "m", indicating that these rules originated between the first and last graphemes of a word.

Learning single-letter rules.   In the examples *mint* and *pint* given earlier, the number of letters in the word is equal to the number of phonemes. For any word with this property, the algorithm infers rules by assuming a simple one-to-one mapping of letters to phonemes, and in this way it acquires single-letter rules

(rules whose left-hand sides are single letters). However, of course, one of the complexities of English orthography is that a large number of English words contain many-to-one mappings from letters to phonemes, that is, these words instantiate multiletter grapheme-to-phoneme rules.

Learning multiletter rules.   If a word has more letters than phonemes, then this simple one-to-one mapping strategy will not yield coherent information: There will be one or more left-over letters to which no phonemes can be assigned. Whenever a word is encountered for which this happens, then, clearly, somewhere in the word there must be a correspondence between letters and phonemes involving more than one letter, so the learning procedure must seek to discover which letters are involved in this multiletter correspondence; that is, they must try to create a multiletter rule that maps more than one letter onto a single phoneme. The algorithm does this by using the single-letter rules it has already learned[6] to account for as many single-letter–phoneme pairs contained in the word and its phonetic transcription as possible. Whatever remains unaccounted for is used to form the multiletter rule.

As an example, consider the word *eel*, pronounced /El/. Here there are more letters than phonemes, so the word must embody at least one multiletter GPC rule. To discover which phonemes are generable by single-letter rules and which are involved in multiletter rules, the algorithm successively disregards single letters from the spelling of the word and applies single-letter rules to the remaining letters, comparing the resulting pronunciation with the correct pronunciation of the whole word. So it begins by disregarding the first letter from *eel* (an *e*) and then checks each of the remaining letters (*el*) to determine whether they can be mapped onto the phonemes in /El/; that is, the single-letter rules are examined to determine whether *e* is pronounced /E/ and *l* is pronounced /l/. The letter combination *el* is given a score that is based on the number of matches between single letters and phonemes found. Following this, the second letter (also an *e*) is disregarded and the process is repeated, and finally the *l* is disregarded and the two-letter combination *ee* is scored. The scoring of *el* proceeds as follows:

$$e \rightarrow /E/, \quad \text{no match;}$$
$$l \rightarrow /l/, \quad \text{match;}$$
$$\text{score: 1.}$$

The second *el* will of course score the same, and *ee* will receive a score of zero:

$$e \rightarrow /E/, \quad \text{no match;}$$
$$e \rightarrow /l/, \quad \text{no match}$$
$$\text{score: 0.}$$

The maximum score obtained is for *el* and indicates that one of the two phonemes in /El/ was accounted for by one of the two letters in *el* by applying the single-

letter rules. The information gained from this phase is used to eliminate those components of the word's spelling and pronunciation that can be accounted for by the single-letter rules: Each matching letter–phoneme pair is removed from the word and its phonetic transcription, and a multiletter rule is formed from the residual components. The orthographic residue that remains from *eel* is *ee*. The phonological residue that remains from /El/ is /E/. Thus, the multiletter rule *ee* → /E/ is discovered.

This procedure will succeed in learning all those multiletter rules in which exactly two letters map onto a single phoneme. However, it will fail when a rule contains more than two letters, as in *blight*, where the rule *igh* → /I/ occurs. When the procedure just described in relationship to the example *eel* fails, it must be the case that a multiletter rule involving more than two letters is present, and so the learning procedure must seek such a rule. It does this by disregarding not all possible single letters but all possible pairs of letters in an effort to work out what three-letter grapheme maps onto a single phoneme in this word. There are 15 different four-letter combinations that can be generated by disregarding all possible letter pairs from *blight*. Applying single-letter rules to the corresponding four-letter strings and scoring these for letter–phoneme matches indicates that the strings *blht* and *blit* score highest (scoring 3; when there is a tie, as here, either example may be chosen). For *blit*, the letters *b*, *l*, and *t* match phonemes in the word's pronunciation; hence, the unmatched letters *igh* must correspond to the unmatched phoneme /I/. Thus, the multiletter rule *igh* → /I/ is discovered.

For the few words of English where four letters map to a single phoneme (e.g., *eight*) this procedure does not yield coherent results; so a procedure in which all possible trios of letters are disregarded is tried. This discovers the rule *eight* → /A/ and any other four-letter rules.

One complication about the multiletter GPCs of English is that the letters making up a multiletter grapheme need not be adjacent, as in *gate*, where the rule is *a_e* → /A/ (the underscore standing for "an intervening letter"). We were very surprised to find that the procedure described earlier that finds the two-letter rule in *eel* (where the two letters are adjacent) works just as well for finding two-letter rules where the letters are separated by an intervening grapheme. Thus, nothing new needed to be added to the learning procedure to enable it to learn multiletter rules in which the letters in the grapheme were nonadjacent.

If the reader applies all of the procedures we have been describing to the word *shout* (or any other word that contains within it more than one example of a multiletter rule), it can be seen that no situation ever arises in which the phonological residue is a single phoneme. The algorithm is only interested in this situation because it is only interested in learning which letters or letter combinations correspond to single phonemes. If this situation never arises when a word is being processed (and it will never arise for a word containing more than one multiletter rule), then the word is abandoned as a source of useful information; the algorithm shrugs its shoulders and moves on to the next word.[7]

Given this, consider words with geminate consonants, such as *buff*. Here there is a two-letter rule *ff* → /f/ that the algorithm must discover. In the course of applying the procedure described earlier in relation to the word *eel*, a situation will arise in which the phonological residue is too small rather than too large: When either of the last two letters is discarded, applying the single-letter rules to the orthographic residue *buf* will account for all of the phonemes in the word. This must, of course, mean that a "silent letter" is present: a letter that contributes to the word's spelling but not to its pronunciation. The algorithm then behaves as follows: When a letter does not contribute to pronunciation in this way, a rule is formed consisting of this letter plus the one preceding it, mapped to the phoneme corresponding to this preceding letter. In this way, such rules as *ff* → /f/ and *wh* → /w/ are formed. If there is no letter preceding the silent letter (i.e., the silent letter is the first letter in the word), then a rule is formed that maps the silent letter and the letter following onto the initial phoneme: In this way, such rules as *kn* → /n/ (*knife*), *wr* → /r/ (*write*), and *gn* → /n/ (*gnu*) are formed. These rules as well as the rule *wh* → /w/ (*when*) become initial rules, whereas the rule *ff* → /f/ (*buff*) automatically becomes a final rule.

Context sensitivity. Our discussion of the *mint* and *pint* examples earlier indicated that for a given grapheme more than one rule can be formed. Words like *cyst* will contribute to the rule *c* → /s/; words like *cost* will contribute to the rule *c* → /k/. So the algorithm will end up with at least two different rules for *c*. How is this conflict resolved?

In general, it is done by the obvious method of discarding, after learning, all but the most frequent rule within each set of conflicting rules. If this was the only method of dealing with this situation, however, the rules could never succeed with words like *cyst* and *cost* because there could only be one rule for initial *c*. Clearly, there are rules that can correctly describe these words: *c* before *e*, *i*, or *y* is /s/ and otherwise it is /k/. This is a context-sensitive GPC rule. The algorithm needs to discover such rules and does so as follows.

In the dialect of the Seidenberg and McClelland database, words like *ham* end with the pronunciation /am/, whereas words like *harm* end with the pronunciation /orm/. Because for both types of words there are equal numbers of letters and phonemes, the algorithm will learn two different single-letter rules: *a* → /a/ (this rule accumulates a frequency of 169) and *a* → /o/ (this rule accumulates a frequency of 48, from exposure to words containing the letter sequence *ar*). If the algorithm simply discarded the less frequent of these two rules, it would never be able to pronounce correctly any of the words containing the letter sequence *ar*, and there are a lot of these words in the database (more than 60).

So, before discarding all but one of a set of conflicting rules, the relative and absolute frequencies of these rules are inspected. If any rule that is not the most frequent one of a set has an absolute frequency of at least *x* (we have used 5, but one could experiment with this value) and a frequency relative to the most

frequent rule of at least y (we have used 0.20, but, again, one could experiment with this), the algorithm studies all words embodying this less frequent correspondence and tabulates the single letters immediately preceding or following the relevant letter. Whenever a particular context letter greatly predominates in this tabulation, a context-sensitive rule is formed. For our example, the algorithm discovers that in almost all of the words where $a \rightarrow /o/$, the a is followed by an r and that in almost none of the words where $a \rightarrow /a/$ is this the case. It therefore forms the context-sensitive rule: $< (f) \ ar \rightarrow /o/ >$ (which reads "following context: a when followed by r is $/o/$." This procedure identifies 15 context-sensitive rules from the Seidenberg and McClelland database, including such highly productive rules as $< (p) \ qu \rightarrow /w/ >$, where p stands for "preceding context." However, the context-sensitive rule for c is not learned because at present the algorithm only learns context-sensitive rules from words with the same number of letters as phonemes, and the Seidenberg and McClelland database contains only two such words with a ce, ci, or cy in them: the words *cent* and *cyst*.

Rule consolidation. Consider the grapheme *oo*. The Seidenberg and McClelland database contains no words beginning with *oo* but does have words with *oo* in medial or final positions. So the algorithm learns only medial and final rules of the form $oo \rightarrow /U/$. If nothing further was known about *oo*, nonwords like *oob* could not be pronounced by the learned rule set, even though nonwords like *voob* or *voo* could be. This potential limitation is overcome as follows: If the rule set contains, for any grapheme, two of the three types of rule (initial, medial, and final) and these two rules specify the same phoneme, and if there is not a conflicting rule for the third case, then rule consolidation occurs for that grapheme: an A rule (A = all positions) replaces the two position-specific rules. In our example, although only medial and final rules for *oo* are extracted from the database, these will be generalized to an A rule because there is no conflicting initial rule. The resulting rule set will correctly pronounce nonwords beginning with *oo*, even though it has never seen any word beginning with *oo* during training.

X. Our endeavor to restrict ourselves solely to rules at the level of the grapheme and the phoneme met with only one problem: the letter x. There is no getting around the fact that x corresponds to a two-phoneme sequence, not a single phoneme. We decided to tackle this problem in a general way, consistent with how other rules are learned. Any word that would otherwise contain the same number of phonemes as letters but contains an x will have fewer letters than phonemes; in English, this only happens for words containing an x. The presence of a single-letter-to-multiple-phoneme correspondence is shown by this property. When a word is identified as possessing this property, identifying the actual rule proceeds in much the same fashion as the identification of multiletter rules: The single-letter rules are used to account for as much of the spelling–sound correspondence as possible, and whatever remains unaccounted for represents

the new rule. The only difference here is that the orthographic residue will consist of one letter and the phonological residue will consist of two phonemes, so a single-letter-to-multiple-phoneme rule is added to the rule list.

Applying the rules

We have described so far the procedure by which the algorithm learns a set of GPC rules (including position-specific, context-sensitive, generalizable, and multiletter rules) from a database of spellings and pronunciations. The algorithm can also apply these rules to any string of letters to produce a string of phonemes. Whether a rule is applied depends on a critical frequency value, which can be set as the user desires. This is absolutely necessary for good performance. Consider the word *coup*, pronounced /ku/. The learning procedure described earlier will infer two rules here: $k \rightarrow$ /k/ and *oup* $\rightarrow$ /u/. It will not encounter the correspondence *oup* $\rightarrow$ /u/ again, so this rule will have a frequency of 1. Now when rules are applied to a nonword like *voup*, because larger rules are applied before smaller rules, the rule that one would want applied (*ou* $\rightarrow$ /W/) will be blocked by the larger rule *oup* $\rightarrow$ /u/, and the nonword will be pronounced /vu/, which is not what human subjects do. We prevent this by using a minimum rule frequency (generally around 5, but even 2 works well) during the application of rules.

Because of the existence in English of graphemes that consist of more than one letter, a rule-conflict problem needs to be dealt with when the GPC rules are being applied to a letter string. In a word like *chip*, the otherwise invaluable rules $c \rightarrow$ /k/ and $h \rightarrow$ /h/ must not be applied because the pronunciation /khip/ is not desired. Our GPC application procedure achieves this as follows. When confronted with a letter string for translation, it seeks to apply the rules to the string from left to right, starting with the longest possible rule that could accommodate that string. For the word *chip*, it would start with the four-letter rules, looking for a rule that maps the letters *chip* onto a single phoneme. No such rule will be found in the rule base. So a rule corresponding to the first three letters *chi* is sought; none will be found. The search for a rule for the first two letters *ch* (*ch* $\rightarrow$ /C/) will, however, be successful. If a two-letter rule had not been found, the context-sensitive, single-letter rules would have been interrogated and finally the remaining single-letter rules, looking for a rule that maps a single *c* onto a phoneme.

When a match is found (as for *ch* in *chip*), the portion of the string that was matched is absorbed, and the process is restarted for the remaining part of the string. This continues until all letters in the string have been translated.

Performance of the GPC-learning algorithm on various types of words

In its present form, the learning algorithm produces a set of GPC rules that allow it to translate correctly 78.17% of the 2,897 words it was trained on. It is, of course, essential to appreciate that this percentage should be well below 100%,

because the GPC rules are supposed to make errors with exception words and the database contains numerous examples of these. Thus, as far as these GPC rules are concerned, 21.83% of the words in the Seidenberg and McClelland database are irregular or exception words. It is a mark of the robustness of the learning procedure that it can learn the rules even when almost a quarter of the words on which it is trained violate these rules and when even among the regular words those containing more than one multiletter rule do not contribute to learning, as discussed earlier.

We have looked at the performance of this GPC system on various types of letter strings, with the following results.

Exception words.   As indicated earlier, we expect the GPC system to score 0% correct on these words, even though they are words on which it has been trained. However, performance was not quite as low as expected: 5 of the 47 words labeled as exceptions by Seidenberg and McClelland (1989) are correctly read by the GPC system. Inspection of these successes here reveals why: Seidenberg and McClelland's definition of exceptionality is not that the word must disobey standard GPC rules but instead that the pronunciation of its "body" or "rime," the part of a monosyllabic word that follows its initial consonant or consonant cluster, must not be the most common one. Hence, they classify *shall*, *doll*, *spook*, and *plow* (though also *bowl*) as exception words, even though all the GPCs in these four words are the most common ones, and it is just these exception words that the GPC system reads correctly. The fifth exception word correctly read was *were* (pronounced /wer/ in the Seidenberg–McClelland database. The system got this right by using the rule *re* → /r/ in final position.

Regular inconsistent words.   These are words like *moth*; they are regular (i.e., they obey the GPC rules) but inconsistent because there is a word that has the same body or rime but a different pronunciation of it (in this case, the word *both*). There are 54 words thus labeled in the Seidenberg and McClelland database;[8] the GPC system should get all of these words right because they are classified as regular. However, it incorrectly pronounced 12 of them. In six cases, the word concerned is clearly not regular by a GPC definition of regularity (*cook*, *small*, *roll*, *grow*, *moth*—note that the database pronunciation of this word is /m*T/ not /moT/—and *here*; see the discussion of *were* in the preceding paragraph). Four other cases involved the grapheme *s*. This is pronounced /s/ in many words and /z/ in many other words. The more common pronunciation is /s/, and there are no orthographic context sensitivities that can be used to decide when /z/ should be used instead. Therefore, any word that has *s* → /z/ is not regular. To put this another way, it cannot be the case that both *dose* and *pose* are regular or that both *cheese* and *geese* are both regular because different pronunciations of the grapheme *s* are used in these words. That is why the GPC procedure gets *jays*, *goes*, *days*, and *pose* wrong: In all cases, it translates the

TABLE 2
Proportion correct nonword reading by the parallel-
distributed-processing (PDP) model, the analogy model, and
the grapheme–phoneme correspondence (GPC) procedure
for the 133 different nonwords used by Glushko (1979)

PDP model (Seidenberg & McClelland, 1989)[a]	Analogy model (Sullivan, 1991; Sullivan & Damper, 1992)	GPC procedure
.68	.71[b]	.98

A correct response to a nonword is defined as a response that was made by any 1 of the 20 subjects of Sullivan (1991) when reading aloud the Glushko nonwords, except that, for the five nonwords with the pattern [vowel + *r*], the postvocalic pronunciation of the /r/ is not counted as incorrect for the models trained with North American pronunciations.

[a] From Besner, Twilley, McCann, and Seergobin (1990). These data are from responses to a 52-item subset of the 133 Glushko nonwords.

[b] Highest accuracy of the various orthographic analogy modules explored by Sullivan (1991).

grapheme *s* to the phoneme /s/. Thus, 10 of the 12 errors by the GPC procedure here are in fact regularization errors in response to words that in GPC terms are not in fact regular. The other two errors (*go* → /go/ and *taste* → /taste/) arise because the rules *o* → /O/ in final position and *a_e* → /A/, which would allow these regular words to be read correctly, do not have a high enough frequency to be applied (because there are too few words in the Seidenberg–McClelland database embodying these two rules).

Regular consistent words. These are words like *vent*, which are not only regular but in which the orthographic body or orthographic rime (in this case, -*ent*) has the same pronunciation in all the words that contain it. There are 21 words thus labeled in the Seidenberg and McClelland database; the GPC system misread one of these, reading *health* as /hEIT/. In GPC terms, of course, *health* is an exception word because it violates the rule *ea* → /E/, and indeed the system's reading of the word is a regularization error.

These results from word reading indicate that the GPC procedure behaves with words as it should. More important, however, is its performance when, after training with the 2,897 words of the McClelland database, it is tested without further training on nonwords. How well does it generalize? We have used the nonwords from Glushko (1979) to assess this, with the results shown in Table 2.

Overall, the GPC system correctly pronounced all except 3 of these 133 nonwords, that is, it scored 97.7% correct. Thus, the GPC procedure closely

TABLE 3

Proportion correct nonword reading by the parallel- distributed-processing (PDP) model, human subjects, and the grapheme–phoneme correspondence (GPC) procedure for the 80 pseudohomophones and 80 control nonwords from Besner and McCann (1987)

Reader	Pseudohomophones	Controls
PDP model (Seidenberg & McClelland, 1989)	.590	.510
Humans (Besner, Twilley, McCann, & Seergobin, 1990)	.943	.886
GPC procedure	.900	.900

approximated human performance here, whereas the PDP model and the analogy procedure did not.

Table 3 reports the performance of the PDP model, human subjects, and the GPC procedure in the reading of the 80 pseudohomophonic and 80 control nonwords devised by McCann and Besner (1987). These are considerably more complex than the Glushko (1979) nonwords of Table 2. The PDP model, people, and the GPC procedure all do worse with the Table 3 nonwords. However, once again the GPC procedure's level of performance is much better than the performance of the PDP model and is similar to the performance of human subjects.

The errors made by the GPC procedure here are instructive. Seidenberg and McClelland (1990) have drawn attention to nonwords like *jinje* in these materials and pointed out that the relevant orthographic–phonological correspondences here are not all represented in the training database, which is perfectly true: The GPC procedure did not learn the rule *je* → /J/ because it saw no words instantiating that rule, and so it could not pronounce *jinje* correctly. Similarly, the orthographic pattern at the end of the nonword *plaie* is illegal in English, so it would not be learned no matter how many English words were in the training set. However, there are very few such examples, so the poor performance of the PDP model here cannot be explained in this way (if it could, then the GPC procedure would have been equally limited).

The very high levels of accuracy that the GPC procedure can attain in reading nonwords after being trained on the 2,897-word database on which the PDP model was trained indicate definitively that this database does contain sufficient information about letter–sound relationships to permit excellent generalization to the task of pronouncing novel, untrained stimuli. Therefore, the poor generalization exhibited by the PDP model must be a consequence not of deficiencies in the database but of deficiencies in the PDP model. Perhaps it might be argued here that if the PDP model was trained on a much larger database, it might do much better. This is not, however, a practical possibility. The model is trained on monomorphemic monosyllables because of the extra complications of letter–sound relationships that are introduced by morphemic or syllabic boundaries. To

expand its training regimen appreciably one would need many more mono-morphemic monosyllabic words, and these simply are not available; almost all such words that exist in English are already included in the Seidenberg and McClelland database.

Graphemes versus bodies

As noted earlier, Seidenberg and McClelland (1989) classified *spook* as an irregular word (and words such as *look*, *cook*, and *book* as regular). This is appropriate if the orthographic unit being considered is the orthographic body (because the most common pronunciation of *-ook* is as in *look*) but wrong if the orthographic unit being considered is the grapheme (because the most common pronunciation of *oo* is as in *spook*). A similar pattern is *-ind*. For most words ending in *-ind*, the pronunciation is as in *mind*, but the most common pronuncia-tion of the single grapheme *i* is as in (the meteorological sense of) *wind*. Hence, *look* and *mind* are regular as far as bodies are concerned but irregular as far as GPCs are concerned; so, of course, our GPC procedure reads *spook* correctly and assigns a short-*i* pronunciation to *wind* but misreads such words as *look* or *mind*.

What about skilled readers? Do they process patterns such as *-ook* or *-ind* at the body level or at the grapheme level? This can be studied by giving them nonwords to read that end in these sequences and observing which pronuncia-tions they choose. Kay (1982, cited in Patterson & Morton, 1985) found that 80% of her subjects pronounced *jook* to rhyme with *spook*; Patterson and Morton (1985) found that 93% of their subjects gave the *spook* pronunciation for *jook*. Similarly, 72% of Kay's subjects read *nind* with a short *i*; every one of Patterson and Morton's 60 subjects read *lind* with a short *i*. Thus, the overwhelming effect here is processing at the grapheme rather than at the body level. The GPC procedure pronounces such nonwords differently from the way an analogy pro-cedure or other procedure that operates at the body level does; these results show that the pronunciations that skilled readers choose are generally those that the GPC procedure chooses.

Acquired dyslexics, specifically surface dyslexics, are also relevant here. They have selective difficulty with irregular words. Therefore, if words like *look* or *mind* are regular, such words should be correctly read by surface dyslexics; the patients should not produce the *spook* or short-*i* pronunciations. If, instead, the appropriate orthographic unit is the grapheme, then these words are irregular and so will be liable to misreadings: specifically regularization errors that here would be *spook*-type or short-*i* pronunciations. In the error corpora for the very pure surface dyslexic patient MP (Behrmann & Bub, 1992; Bub et al., 1985), there are four words ending with *-ook* (*cook*, *shook*, *crook*, and *hook*); MP pronounced all four as rhyming with *spook*. There are seven words in the corpora ending with *-ind* (*kind* [twice], *hind*, *blind*, *find*, *grind*, and *mind*); MP pronounced all

seven with the short-*i* pronunciation. Once again, it is the graphemic level rather than the body level that is supreme here.

Other dialects and other languages

The GPC learning and GPC application procedures were developed solely by working with the Seidenberg and McClelland database, in which the pronunciations are in one particular dialect of American English. However, the principles involved—concepts such as grapheme–phoneme rule, position specificity, and context sensitivity—are meant to apply to alphabetic orthographies in general. Hence, the algorithm ought without any modifications to work equally well for other dialects of English and indeed for languages other than English as long as they are written alphabetically. We have tried the algorithm with a database of 3,917 monosyllabic words where the pronunciations are those of a particular dialect of British English. Having learned a set of GPC rules from this database, it could then pronounce 75.9% of the words in that database correctly, a figure very similar to that achieved with the American English database. So nothing new needed to be added to the algorithm to make it capable of learning the GPC rules of British English. We are currently applying it to an Australian English database and to a French database, French being like English in having many exception words. Italian, Spanish, and Hungarian differ from English and French in that they are reputed to have no exception words; if that is true, after training on database from one of these languages the algorithm should be able to read all words in that language correctly, rather than the 75% it achieves with American or British English.

Other aspects of the DRC model

We have nothing yet to report concerning our work on the implementation of the second of the DRC model's two routes, the lexical route, but it seems worth indicating what direction this work will take and, in particular, how the ultimately implemented model should explain some of the other data on reading that Seidenberg and McClelland (1989) discussed in their article. Two of the major components of the DRC lexical route for reading are a visual word recognition system and a spoken word production system, so we will need to implement systems for carrying out these two functions.

   We hope not to have to start from scratch in this endeavor. It would be deeply regrettable if, after at least 30 years work by cognitive psychologists on how the visual word recognition system might work, it was the case that our simulation of visual word recognition in the model could not draw on anything in the previous literature. Fortunately, the opposite appears to be the case. There is already a computational model of visual word recognition that does an excellent job of explaining the results of many studies of visual word recognition: It is the interactive-activation model of McClelland and Rumelhart (1981) and Rumelhart

and McClelland (1982). In the hope that cognitive science is a cumulative enterprise, our first move has simply been to plug this model (or, rather, the recent stochastic version of it described by McClelland, 1991) into the overall model described in Figure 2. That is, the components labeled *visual feature detectors*, *letter detectors*, and *visual word detectors* are the three levels of the interactive–activation model, and these levels are connected as specified in that model.

Similarly, we have not attempted to develop our own computational module for spoken word production but have used instead a development of the already existing spreading-activation model of spoken word production that is due to Dell (1986). This model explains very well a variety of phenomena seen in spoken word production, particularly slips of the tongue. If our use of these models and our developing of an interface between the model of visual word recognition and the model of spoken word production[9] are successful, it will follow that all of the many facts about word recognition and spoken word production that these two models are demonstrably able to explain will also be explainable by the DRC model of reading.

How might the DRC model simulate the effects of regularity, neighborhood size, and consistency on rapid letter-string naming by skilled readers?

Our analysis here depends on a crucial property of the DRC model, namely, *cascaded processing*. When a letter string is presented to the interactive-activation model of visual word recognition, activation in entries in the visual word recognition system will begin to rise, and these activations will approach their final values over time; in typical implementations of the model, perhaps 70 processing cycles will elapse before the system settles into its final state. What does not happen is the letter-identification system settling into its final state and then passing activation on to the word level. As soon as there is any activation at the letter level, activation will be passed on to the word level. Because, in the DRC model, each unit in the visual word recognition module is connected to a corresponding entry in the spoken word production module, it follows that as soon as there is any activation at the level of the visual word recognition system, this will be passed on to the spoken word lexicon, and in turn this will be passed on to the phoneme system. This is what is meant by cascaded processing, and it will occur throughout the various processing stages of the lexical route of Figure 2. This has some profound implications for ways in which the model behaves.

Regularity.   With an exception word like *pint*, the two routes of the model produce different outputs at the phoneme level, and these will have to be reconciled; we propose to do this by a lateral inhibition process. For each of the positions in an utterance, there is a set of units representing all the possible phonemes, and these are fully interconnected with inhibitory connections.

Exception words will generate conflict at the phoneme level that can be resolved by the operation of this inhibitory network. When there is conflict at the phoneme level, it takes time to resolve; that is, it will take longer for the system to build up to a critical activation level than it would if there was no conflict. Here we have a potential mechanism for explaining why under certain conditions naming latency is longer for exception words (where there is time-consuming conflict) than for regular words (where there is not). This explanation would not work if the nonlexical route operated so slowly that its input never reached the phoneme system until after the activation of the phoneme system from the lexical route had reached its full value. So we must assume that this is not the case.

The rate at which activation rises throughout the lexical route is proportional to word frequency because, in the interactive-activation model, the rise of activation in any unit of the visual word recognition system depends on a bias parameter, which is a function of that word's frequency. Hence, in the DRC model, the more common a word is, the sooner it will begin activating its appropriate phonemes in the phoneme system. Therefore, a parameterization of the model exists such that, for common words, activation of the phoneme system by the lexical route is complete before much activation gets to that system from the nonlexical route, whereas for less frequent words there will be competition between lexical and nonlexical activation in that system. The result is that exception words will not show a naming-latency delay if they are of high frequency but will show this delay if they are of low frequency.[10] It is clear, then, how the dual-route model, once implemented, could simulate the interaction between frequency and regularity, which has been observed in a number of naming-latency studies cited by Seidenberg and McClelland (1989).

Neighborhood size. As a measure of the degree to which letter strings (whether these be words or nonwords) are similar to words, Coltheart, Davelaar, Jonasson, and Besner (1977) introduced the variable *N*: the number of real words that differ by a single letter from the letter string, taking position in the string into account. These real words are called the *neighbors* of the letter string. Various studies have demonstrated effects of *N* on visual lexical decision and on word and nonword naming. The largest and most consistent effects are on responses to nonwords in the lexical-decision task: The higher a nonword's *N* value, the slower and less accurate are subjects in responding.

To simulate lexical-decision data with the implemented DRC model, the model will have to be able to perform the task. This was simple with the discrete-processing version of the model: A nonword would not produce any output from the visual word recognition system, and a word would; this was what told a subject whether to say "No" or "Yes" when performing lexical decision. With the cascaded version, this will not do. Preliminary studies that we have done suggest that, although a nonword does produce activations of various words in the model's word recognition system, particularly activations of the

nonword's neighbors, no entry is activated to a value that is as high as the value to which a real word activates its own representation. Hence, the model can perform lexical decision by using a criterion: If any entry has an activation value greater than X, respond "Yes"; otherwise, respond "No."

This account of lexical decision was introduced by Coltheart et al. (1977). They pointed out two problems. The first was that, because activation rises over time, the fact that no entry has reached an activation level of X at a particular moment does not mean that this will not happen at the next moment. The solution they proposed was a *deadline*: If at deadline time T a value of X has not been reached, respond "No." The second problem was that this deadline decision procedure would yield the same response time for all nonwords, high N or low N, which is not what is observed. So Coltheart et al. proposed that a *variable deadline* is being used: As activation is rising, the deadline is shortened if overall activation is rising very slowly (which will happen in response to a low-N stimulus) and lengthened if it is rising rapidly (which will happen in response to a high-N stimulus). It is easy to see how this variable-deadline decision procedure can be implemented as a method for simulating lexical decision in the DRC model: The deadline value is expressed as a particular number of processing cycles, and while a letter string is being processed the deadline value can be lengthened or shortened as a function of how rapidly the total activation of the visual word recognition system is rising.

It is very difficult to know just what effect N will have on naming latencies for words and nonwords in the implemented model (simulations are essential to determine what the model predicts here), though it seems likely that the effects will depend on whether all the neighbors of a letter string have pronunciations consistent with its pronunciation, because this will determine the extent of conflict within the phoneme system.

Consistency. Glushko (1979) and others have studied two types of regular words (i.e., words that obey the grapheme–phoneme rules of English): There are regular-consistent words such as *mail* (all words ending with *-ail* have the same pronunciation of this body or rime segment) and there are regular-inconsistent words such as *maid*; there is a word (*said*) in which the pronunciation of the final segment is inconsistent with its pronunciation in *maid*. The same distinction applies to nonwords (cf., *zail* vs. *zaid*). Various studies have shown that inconsistency slows naming latency. This is often cited as evidence against dual-route models, especially the nonword result: If all nonwords are read aloud solely by applying GPC rules, how could the word *said* possibly exert any influence on the processing of the nonword *zaid*?

Well, suppose, for example, the stimulus is *zaid*. This is not a word. Nevertheless, it will produce some activation in the visual word recognition system; it will turn on the letter units for *a*, *i*, and *d* in the second, third, and fourth positions, respectively, and because of this all words ending in *-aid* will receive

considerable activation (and some inhibition too because of inhibitory connections from the letter unit for *z* in the first position). Because the whole system
works in cascade, the partial activations of various word units in the visual word
recognition must cascade forward to these units' analogues in the spoken word
lexicon, and activation must then cascade on to the phoneme units in the phoneme system corresponding to the pronunciations of these activated entries in the
spoken word lexicon. Therefore, there will be some activation at the phoneme
level that is generated by the lexical route even when the stimulus is not a word.
This is not an ad hoc assumption; it follows directly from the fact that the model
operates in a cascaded fashion. Because *zaid* excites both *said* and *paid* in
the visual word recognition system, there will be some activation for competing
second-position phonemes in the phoneme system. This competition will not
occur with consistent nonwords such as *zail*. Because competition increases
naming latency, this is a way in which a pure dual-route model can explain consistency effects on nonword (and word) naming latency. Of course, only genuine
simulations can tell us how important these partial activations could be for
explanatory purposes; however, it does seem highly likely that there will exist a
set of parameters that will yield quantitatively what, at a qualitative level, appear
to be effects that the model should generate.

In earlier versions of the dual-route model that viewed the lexical procedure
as operating by means of discrete (thresholded) rather than cascaded processing,
the lexical route was viewed as making no possible contribution to nonword
reading aloud, simply because a nonword would generate zero output from the
visual word recognition system. Now that presentation of a nonword to the
model is going to generate, through the lexical route, some phonological activation at the phoneme stage, through activation of various visually similar words
at the visual word recognition level, might it be argued that nonwords could be
read aloud correctly via this route, making a second (viz., GPC) route redundant? This is a version of "analogy theory" (Marcel, 1980), and if this process of
multiple partial activations from the lexical procedure could actually generate
the correct phonemic representations for nonwords, this would be a devastating
blow to dual-route modeling.

We can explore this in our simulations, but theoretical considerations already
make it seem extremely unlikely that these partial activations would generate
correct pronunciations for nonwords (and the data from the analogy model that
are reported in Table 2 support this suggestion). Take the nonword *bi*. Its word
neighbors (words of the same length differing in one letter) are *be* and *pi*. If
these are the entries in the visual word recognition system that are partly excited
by the nonword, then by means of cascaded processing there will be two candidate first-position phonemes excited in the phoneme system, /b/ and /p/, and two
candidate second-position phonemes, /E/ and /I/. How could it be determined
which is the correct pairing? How would the reader know whether to say /bE/,
/bI/, /pE/ or /pI/? The nonword *vub* has five neighbors but none begin with the

phoneme /v/, so how could the lexical route generate this phoneme? The perfectly pronounceable nonword *kwiv* has no neighbors at all. Such examples illustrate why we believe that, in our simulations, output from the lexical route will be able to influence nonword reading but will not be able to accomplish it unaided. The simulations will have to be done, of course, if this is to become more than a belief.

How might the DRC model simulate acquired dyslexia?

If the nonlexical route of Figure 2 was removed, we would have a system that could read all words but no nonwords. Approximations to this pattern are seen in patients with the acquired dyslexia known as phonological dyslexia; the patient reported by Funnell (1983), for example, could not read any nonwords at all after his stroke but scored up to 90% correct on various tests of the reading of words. At least at a qualitative level, it is obvious how the dual-route model simulates this acquired dyslexia: More stringent tests of the simulation will have to await more detailed quantitative studies of phonological alexia.

If the lexical route of Figure 2 was removed, we would have a system that could read nonwords and regular words but no exception words; the errors in reading exception words would be regularization errors, reading the exception words as the rules prescribe. Approximations to this pattern are seen in patients with the acquired dyslexia known as surface dyslexia. No reported surface dyslexic has been unable to read all exception words, but there are cases (e.g., Bub et al., 1985; McCarthy & Warrington, 1986) in which the reading of nonwords and regular words was normal, whereas the reading of exception words was very impaired, with abundant regularization errors.

In the case reported by Bub et al. (1985), the probability that the patient could correctly read an exception word declined monotonically with word frequency. We intend to simulate this quantitatively by various manipulations at the level of the visual word recognition system. The most promising to try initially would be to subtract a constant from the word frequency bias value of each entry in that system. This would mean that activation from the lexical route would arrive later at the phoneme system. The larger this constant is, the more words would reach the phoneme system after their phonological representations from the nonlexical route reach that system. The lateral-inhibition structure of the phoneme system produces a winner-take-all result; so if the lexical activation arrives second, the word will be read nonlexically, which, if the word is an exception word, will mean a regularization error. Bub et al. have published detailed data on the relationship between the probability of correct reading and word frequency; we will see whether we can simulate this function quantitatively by manipulation of the bias parameter in the visual word recognition system. Both Bub et al. and McCarthy and Warrington (1986) have collected extensive error

corpora from their patients. We will submit words from such error corpora to our lesioned dual-route model and compare what it says with what the patients said in response to each word.[11]

CONCLUSIONS

We have shown that many important facts about reading that are discussed by Seidenberg and McClelland (1989) cannot be explained by their PDP model but can be explained by the dual-route model. Our critique of their model has many points of resemblance to the critique by Pinker and Prince (1988) of the PDP model of past-tense learning developed by Rumelhart and McClelland (1986). In these two linguistic domains, reading aloud and producing the past tenses of verbs, the PDP modelers have argued in the same way. They have pointed out that previous theorists have taken the facts as demanding a model that incorporated the notion of rule and the notion of (local) lexical representation, and they have attempted to rebut such claims by arguing that the facts can be explained by PDP models that use neither rules nor local representations: "Naming is simulated without pronunciation rules, and lexical decisions are simulated without accessing word-level representations" (Seidenberg & McClelland, 1989, p. 523). We concur with Pinker and Prince's conclusion that the PDP model of past-tense learning does not offer a tenable explanation of what is known about that aspect of human language. We have argued that the situation is the same with respect to the PDP model of reading aloud.

If these claims are correct, then the conclusion continues to seem inescapable: Our ability to deal with linguistic stimuli we have not previously encountered (to coin a new past tense or to read a nonword aloud) can only be explained by postulating that we have learned systems of general linguistic rules, and our ability at the same time to deal correctly with exceptions to these rules (to produce an exception past tense or to read an exception word aloud) can only be explained by postulating the existence of systems of word-specific lexical representations.

ACKNOWLEDGEMENTS

This work was supported by Grant AC8932386 from the Australian Research Council and by a Macquarie University Research Grant. Some of this work was presented at the Psychonomic Society Meeting in San Francisco, November 1991.

We thank Michael McCloskey, Steven Pinker, Karalyn Patterson, Martin Davies, Ken Paap, and Derek Besner for valuable discussions and Ken Seergobin and Robert McCann for assistance. Part of this research was completed while Max Coltheart was a visiting scientist at the Medical Research Council Applied Psychology Unit, Cambridge, England; the use of their facilities is gratefully acknowledged.

NOTES

1. There are data suggesting that the rule system might also use orthographic units larger than the grapheme (see, e.g., Kay & Lesser, 1985; Patterson & Morton, 1985). This is an important question for dual-route models, but it is not relevant here because a nonlexical route that used units larger than the grapheme (e.g., rules for orthographic "bodies" such as -*ook*) would still be a nonlexical route. In any case, as we argue later, processing of orthographic units larger than the grapheme is far less influential than processing at the grapheme level, as far as the nonlexical route is concerned.

2. Why choose character triples at random? This procedure guarantees that many of a unit's 1,000 triples will never be seen in the input; there is even a nonzero probability that none of a unit's triples will be orthographically legal, in which case that unit would never play any role in reading. Seidenberg and McClelland (1989) did not explain what disadvantages there would have been in allowing only orthographically legal triples in the orthographic input units. Surely this would have greatly reduced the size and number of input units and therefore the computational load on the whole system.

3. There are many other unusual properties of this phonological output scheme (for further discussion, see Pinker & Prince [1988], all of whose points about the Rumelhart–McClelland past-tense learning model also apply to the Seidenberg and McClelland reading model because of the latter's use of the former's output scheme).

4. This appears to be the sole function of these connections; their removal would not affect the model's ability to read aloud. This seems to us to be a dubious architectural motivation. In contrast, the dual-route model's ability to perform lexical decision depends on something that is an essential constituent of the model, something without which it could not function adequately at all: the lexicon.

5. Perhaps his good reading of abstract words was achieved by combining imperfect output from the semantic route and imperfect output from the other route, as discussed earlier. Coslett (1991) considered this and rejected it on the ground that nonword writing and nonword repetition were impaired to the same level as nonword reading; hence, if the output of the route that is used for reading nonwords is adequate, when combined with imperfect semantic output, to produce good reading of abstract words, similar processes should have been able to produce good writing and good repetition of abstract words.

6. At present, the rules are learned in two passes through the database: Single-letter rules only are learned in the first pass, and multiletter rules are learned in the second pass. We do not believe that this is essential; we judge that all rules could be learned in a single pass but have not yet investigated whether this is in fact the case.

7. Of course, the fact that such words as *shout* do not contribute to the learning of the GPC rules does not mean at all that the eventual GPC rule set cannot cope with these words. The *sh* rule is learned from words like *shot* and *shut*. The *ou* rule is learned from words like *out* and *sound*. Hence, the rules needed to pronounce *shout* correctly will be learned, though not from this word itself.

8. Their definition of regularity appears in fact to be inconsistent: The word *brood* is classified as regular, yet in their database the most common pronunciation of the body/rime -*ood* is /u/ as in *good*, *hood*, *stood*, and *wood*.

9. Why not fold these two stages into one because there is a complete one-to-one mapping between the units at the word-detector level (the last stage in the input model) and the units at the morpheme level (the first stage of the output model)? The answer is because the cognitive–neuropsychological data indicate that these stages are two separate systems, despite this one-to-one correspondence.

10. Effects reported by Perfetti and Bell (1991) and Perfetti, Bell, and Delaney (1988) are critically important here. Their backward-masking studies suggest that, in as little as 40 ms, phonological

representations of printed stimuli can be generated by the nonlexical route and can affect recognition of a subsequently presented word. DRC simulations will have to account for such effects with parameter values that also allow the lexical route to generate the pronunciations of high-frequency words before phonological information from the nonlexical route reaches the phonemic output stage.

11. Reggia et al. (1988, pp. 538–540) also discussed how their model could simulate phonological and surface dyslexia if it was damaged in various ways.

REFERENCES

Baron, J., & Strawson, C. (1976). Use of orthographic and word-specific knowledge in reading words aloud. *Journal of Experimental Psychology: Human Perception and Performance, 2,* 386–393.

Beauvois, M. F., & Derouesne, J. (1979). Phonological alexia: Three dissociations. *Journal of Neurology, Neurosurgery and Psychiatry, 42,* 1115–1124.

Behrmann, M., & Bub, D. (1992). Surface dyslexia and dysgraphia: Dual routes, single lexicon. *Cognitive Neuropsychology, 9,* 209–251.

Berndt, R. S., & Mitchum, C. C. (1994). Approaches to the rehabilitation of "phonological assembly": Elaborating the model of nonlexical reading. In G. W. Humphreys & M. J. Riddoch (Eds.), *Cognitive neuropsychology and cognitive rehabilitation.* Hove, UK: Lawrence Erlbaum Associates Ltd.

Besner, D., & McCann, R. S. (1987). Word frequency and pattern distortion in visual word identification and production: An examination of four classes of models. In M. Coltheart (Ed.), *Attention and performance XII: The psychology of reading* (pp. 201–219). Hove, UK: Lawrence Erlbaum Associates Ltd.

Besner, D., Twilley, L., McCann, R. S., & Seergobin, K. (1990). On the connection between connectionism and data: Are a few words necessary? *Psychological Review, 97,* 432–446.

Bub, D., Cancelliere, A., & Kertesz, A. (1985). Whole-word and analytic translation of spelling to sound in a nonsemantic reader. In K. E. Patterson, J. C. Marshall, & M. Coltheart (Eds.), *Surface dyslexia: Neuropsychological and cognitive studies of phonological reading* (pp. 15–34). Hove, UK: Lawrence Erlbaum Associates Ltd.

Castles, A., & Coltheart, M. (1993). Subtypes of developmental dyslexia. *Cognition, 47,* 149–180.

Coltheart, M. (1978). Lexical access in simple reading tasks. In G. Underwood (Ed.), *Strategies of information processing* (pp. 151–216). San Diego, CA: Academic Press.

Coltheart, M. (1984). Theoretical analysis and practical assessment of reading disorders. In C. Cornoldi (Ed.), *Aspects of reading and dyslexia* (pp. 117–126). Padua, Italy: Cleup.

Coltheart, M. (1985). Cognitive neuropsychology and the study of reading. In M. I. Posner & O. S. M. Marin (Eds.), *Attention and performance XI* (pp. 3–37). Hillsdale, NJ: Erlbaum.

Coltheart, M., Davelaar, E., Jonasson, J. T., & Besner, D. (1977). Access to the internal lexicon. In S. Dornic (Ed.), *Attention and performance VI* (pp. 535–555). Hillsdale, NJ: Lawrence Erlbaum Associates Inc.

Coltheart, M., Masterson, J., Byng, S., Prior, M., & Riddoch, J. (1983). Surface dyslexia. *Quarterly Journal of Experimental Psychology, 35A,* 469–495.

Coslett, H. B. (1991). Read but not write "idea": Evidence for a third reading mechanism. *Brain & Language, 40,* 425–443.

Dell, G. S. (1986). A spreading activation theory of retrieval in sentence production. *Psychological Review, 93,* 283–321.

Forster, K. I., & Chambers, S. M. (1973). Lexical access and naming time. *Journal of Verbal Learning and Verbal Behavior, 12,* 627–635.

Frederiksen, J. R., & Kroll, J. F. (1976). Spelling and sound: Approaches to the internal lexicon. *Journal of Experimental Psychology: Human Perception and Performance, 2,* 361–379.

Funnell, E. (1983). Phonological processes in reading: New evidence from acquired dyslexia. *British Journal of Psychology, 74*, 159–180.

Glushko, R. J. (1979). The organization and activation of orthographic knowledge in reading aloud. *Journal of Experimental Psychology: Human Perception and Performance, 5*, 674–691.

Harris, M., & Coltheart, M. (1986). *Language processing in children and adults.* London: Routledge & Kegan Paul.

Hillis, A. E., & Caramazza, A. (1991). Mechanisms for accessing lexical representations for output: Evidence from a category-specific semantic deficit. *Brain and Language, 40*, 106–144.

Holmes, J. M. (1973). *Dyslexia: A neurolinguistic study of traumatic and developmental disorders of reading.* Unpublished doctoral dissertation, University of Edinburgh, Edinburgh, Scotland.

Humphreys, G. W., & Evett, L. (1985). Are there independent lexical and non-lexical routes in word processing? An evaluation of the dual route theory of reading. *Behavioral and Brain Sciences, 8*, 689–739.

Kay, J. (1982). *Psychological mechanisms of oral reading of single words.* Unpublished doctoral dissertation, University of Cambridge, Cambridge, UK.

Kay, J., & Bishop, D. V. M. (1987). Anatomical differences between nose, palm and hand, or, the body in question: Further dissection of the processes of sub-lexical spelling-to-sound translation. In M. Coltheart (Ed.), *Attention and performance XII: The psychology of reading* (pp. 449–469). Hove, UK: Lawrence Erlbaum Associates Ltd.

Kay, J. M., & Lesser, R. (1985). The nature of phonological processing in oral reading: Evidence from surface dyslexia. *Quarterly Journal of Experimental Psychology, 37A*, 39–83.

Lacouture, Y. (1989). From mean square error to reaction time: A connectionist model of word recognition. In D. Touretzky, G. Hinton, & T. Sejnowski (Eds.), *Proceedings of the 1988 Connectionist Models Summer School* (pp. 371–378). San Mateo, CA: Morgan Kauffman.

Marcel, A. J. (1980). Surface dyslexia and beginning reading: A revised hypothesis of the pronunciation of print and its impairments. In M. Coltheart, K. Patterson, & J. C. Marshall (Eds.), *Deep dyslexia* (pp. 227–258). London: Routledge & Kegan Paul.

Marshall, J. C. (1984). Toward a rational taxonomy of the developmental dyslexias. In R. N. Malatesha & H. A. Whitaker (Eds.), *Dyslexia: A global issue* (pp. 211–232). Dordrecht, The Netherlands: Martinus Nijhoff.

Marshall, J. C., & Newcombe, F. (1973). Patterns of paralexia: A psycholinguistic approach. *Journal of Psycholinguistic Research, 2*, 175–199.

McCann, R. S., & Besner, D. (1987). Reading pseudohomophones: Implications for models of pronunciation and the locus of word frequency effects in word naming. *Journal of Experimental Psychology: Human Perception and Performance, 13*, 14–24.

McCarthy, R., & Warrington, E. K. (1986). Phonological reading: Phenomena and paradoxes. *Cortex, 22*, 359–380.

McClelland, J. L. (1991). Stochastic interactive processes and the effect of context on perception. *Cognitive Psychology, 23*, 1–44.

McClelland, J. L., & Rumelhart, D. E. (1981). An interactive activation model of context effects in letter perception: Part 1. An account of basic findings. *Psychological Review, 88*, 375–470.

Mitchum, C. C., & Berndt, R. S. (1994). Diagnosis and treatment of the non-lexical route in acquired dyslexia: An illustration of the cognitive neuropsychological approach. *Journal of Neurolinguistics.*

Morton, J., & Patterson, K. (1980). A new attempt at an interpretation, or an attempt at a new interpretation. In M. Coltheart, K. Patterson, & J. C. Marshall (Eds.), *Deep dyslexia* (pp. 91–118). London: Routledge & Kegan Paul.

Paap, K. R., & Noel, R. W. (1991). Dual route models of print to sound: Still a good horse race. *Psychological Research, 53*, 13–24.

Patterson, K. E. (1990). Alexia and neural nets. *Japanese Journal of Neuropsychology, 6*, 90–99.

Patterson, K. E., Marshall, J. C., & Coltheart, M. (Eds.). (1985). *Surface dyslexia: Neuropsychological and cognitive studies of phonological reading.* Hove, UK: Lawrence Erlbaum Associates Ltd.

Patterson, K. E., & Morton, J. (1985). From orthography to phonology: An attempt at an old interpretation. In K. E. Patterson, J. C. Marshall, & M. Coltheart (Eds.), *Surface dyslexia: Neuropsychological and cognitive studies of phonological reading* (pp. 335–359). Hove, UK: Lawrence Erlbaum Associates Ltd.

Patterson, K., Seidenberg, M. S., & McClelland, J. L. (1989). Connections and disconnections: Acquired dyslexia in a computational model of reading processes. In R. G. M. Morris (Ed.), *Parallel distributed processing: Implications for psychology and neurobiology* (pp. 131–181). London: Oxford University Press.

Patterson, K. E., & Shewell, C. (1987). Speak and spell: Dissociations and word-class effects. In M. Coltheart, G. Sartori, & R. Job (Eds.), *The cognitive neuropsychology of language* (pp. 273–294). Hove, UK: Lawrence Erlbaum Associates Ltd.

Perfetti, C. A., & Bell, L. (1991). Phonemic activation during the first 40 ms of word identification: Evidence from backward masking and masked priming. *Journal of Memory and Language, 30,* 473–485.

Perfetti, C. A., Bell, L., & Delaney, S. (1988). Automatic (prelexical) phonetic activation in silent word reading: Evidence from backward masking. *Journal of Memory and Language, 27,* 59–70.

Pinker, S., & Prince, A. (1988). On language and connectionism: Analysis of a parallel distributed processing model of language acquisition. *Cognition, 28,* 73–193.

Reggia, J. A., Marsland, P. M., & Berndt, R. S. (1988). Competitive dynamics in a dual-route connectionist model of print-to-sound translation. *Complex Systems, 2,* 509–517.

Rumelhart, D. E., & McClelland, J. L. (1982). An interactive activation model of context effects in letter perception: Part 2. The contextual enhancement effect and some tests and extensions of the model. *Psychological Review, 89,* 60–94.

Rumelhart, D. E., & McClelland, J. L. (1986). On learning the past tenses of English verbs. In D. E. Rumelhart & J. L. McClelland (Eds.), *Parallel distributed processing: Vol. 2. Psychological and biological models* (pp. 216–271). Cambridge, MA: MIT Press.

Seidenberg, M. S., & McClelland, J. L. (1989). A distributed, developmental model of word recognition and naming. *Psychological Review, 96,* 523–568.

Seidenberg, M. S., & McClelland, J. L. (1990). More words but still no lexicon: Reply to Besner et al. (1990). *Psychological Review, 97,* 447–452.

Sullivan, K. P. H. (1991). *Synthesis-by-analogy: A psychologically-motivated approach to text-to-speech conversion.* Unpublished doctoral dissertation, University of Southampton, Southampton, UK.

Sullivan, K. P. H., & Damper, R. I. (1992). Novel-word pronunciation within a text-to-speech system. In G. Bailly, C. Benoît, & T. Sawallis (Eds.), *Talking machines: Theories, models and applications.* Amsterdam: Elsevier.

Temple, C. M., & Marshall, J. C. (1983). A case study of developmental phonological dyslexia. *British Journal of Psychology, 74,* 517–533.

Waters, G. S., & Seidenberg, M. S. (1985). Spelling-sound effects in reading: Time course and decision criteria. *Memory & Cognition, 13,* 557–572.

CHAPTER FOURTEEN

Simulating brain damage

Geoffrey E. Hinton
University of Toronto, Canada

David C. Plaut
Carnegie Mellon University, USA

Tim Shallice
University College, London, UK

Adults with brain damage make some bizarre errors when reading words. If a network of simulated neurons is trained to read and then is damaged, it produces strikingly similar behavior.

In 1944 a young soldier suffered a bullet wound to the head. He survived the war with a strange disability: although he could read and comprehend some words with ease, many others gave him trouble. He read the word *antique* as "vase" and *uncle* as "nephew".

The injury was devastating to the patient, G.R., but it provided invaluable information to researchers investigating the mechanisms by which the brain comprehends written language. A properly functioning system for converting letters on a page to spoken sounds reveals little of its inner structure, but when that system is disrupted, the peculiar pattern of the resulting dysfunction may offer essential clues to the original, undamaged architecture.

During the past few years, computer simulations of brain function have advanced to the point where they can be used to model information-processing pathways. We have found that deliberate damage to artificial systems can mimic the symptoms displayed by people who have sustained brain injury. Indeed, building a model that makes the same errors as brain-injured people do gives us confidence that we are on the right track in trying to understand how the brain works.

We have yet to make computer models that exhibit even a tiny fraction of the capabilities of the human brain. Nevertheless, our results so far have produced

Scientific American, *October 1993*, 58–65.

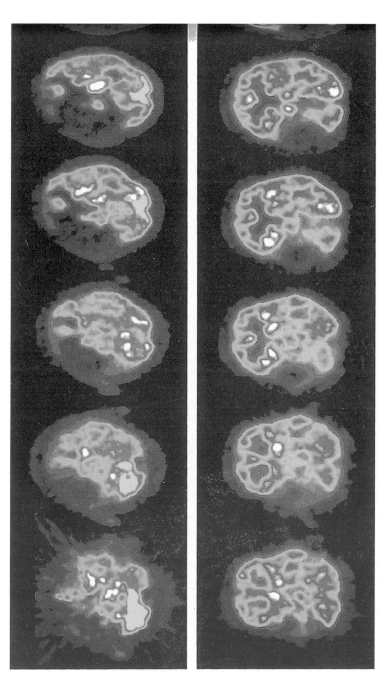

Brain images show damage to the language-processing areas of patients with acquired dyslexia, which can now be modeled by artificial neural networks. (These positron-emission tomography scans, made by Cathy J. Price and her colleagues at the MRC Cyclotron Unit in London, measure activity of the brain in successive horizontal slices, starting at the top of the brain.) Patient A (*top row*) has lost almost all function in the left hemisphere of the cerebral cortex, except for the most posterior regions. Patient B (*bottom row*) has sustained damage to the parietal and temporal lobes of the left hemisphere, regions generally believed to be crucial for processing language.

410

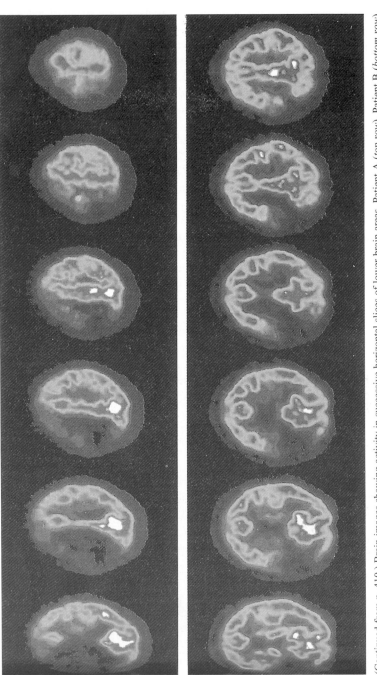

(Continued from p. 410.) Brain images showing activity in successive horizontal slices of lower brain areas. Patient A (*top row*). Patient B (*bottom row*).

unexpected insights into the way the brain transforms a string of letter shapes into the meaning of a word.

When John C. Marshall and Freda Newcombe of the University of Oxford analysed G.R.'s residual problems in 1966, they found a highly idiosyncratic pattern of reading deficits. In addition to his many semantic errors, G.R. made visual ones, reading *stock* as "shock" and *crowd* as "crown". Many of his mis-readings resembled the correct word in both form and meaning; for example, he saw *wise* and said "wisdom".

Detailed testing showed that G.R. could read concrete words, such as *table*, much more easily than abstract words, such as *truth*. He was fair at reading nouns (46 percent correct), worse at adjectives (16 percent), still worse at verbs (6 percent) and worst of all at function words, such as *of* (2 percent). Finally, he found it impossible to read wordlike nonsense letter strings, such as *mave* or *nust*.

Since then, clinicians have studied more than 50 other patients who make semantic errors in reading aloud, and virtually all of them show the same strange combination of symptoms. In 1973 Marshall and Newcombe described two contrasting types of acquired dyslexia. So-called surface dyslexics misread words that are pronounced in an unusual way, often giving the more regular pronunciation; a surface dyslexic might read *yacht* as "yatched". In contrast, a "deep" dyslexic patient like G.R. might read *yacht* as "boat".

To explain the existence of these two types of dyslexia, Marshall and Newcombe proposed that the information processed in normal reading travels along two distinct, complementary routes. Surface dyslexics retain the phonological route, which relies on common spelling-to-sound correspondences. Deep dyslexics, meanwhile, retain the semantic route, which allows the meaning of a word to be derived directly from its visual form (when it can be derived at all).

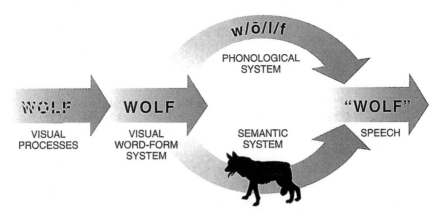

Two pathways in the brain are responsible for the mental processing and pronunciation of written words. One (the phonological route) derives pronunciation from spelling, the other (the semantic route) from meaning. Deep dyslexics have lost the phonological route completely and have suffered damage to the semantic route as well.

A person reading words aloud via the semantic route derives pronunciation entirely from meaning.

According to Marshall and Newcombe, the errors produced by deep dyslexics reflect how the semantic route operates in isolation. Later empirical findings suggest that this account is oversimplified, but the notion of a semantic route is still generally accepted. It now seems likely that deep dyslexics not only lose their phonological route but have damage somewhere along the semantic one as well.

The hypothesis that reading depends on multiple routes that can be separately damaged has proved fruitful in classifying patients but less useful in understanding the precise nature of their injuries. Max Coltheart of Macquarie University in Australia and Eleanor M. Saffran of Temple University have both proposed, for example, that the reading of deep dyslexics may bear a strong resemblance to that of patients who have only the right hemisphere of their brain functioning.

This explanation, however, provides little insight into the highly characteristic pattern of errors that typically occurs in acquired dyslexia. Any detailed explanation of how errors arise and why they form consistent patterns requires a model of how that information is processed in each route—and of how this processing goes wrong when the neural circuitry is damaged. Psychologists often use abstract, algorithmic descriptions of the way that the brain handles information. These descriptions obviously cannot be subjected to the kinds of injuries that brain cells may incur.

As a result, we have turned to neural networks—idealized computer simulations of ensembles of neurons. We have developed networks that perform the role of the semantic route, and then we have selectively removed connections between neurons to see how their behavior changes. A few years ago we designed a simple network to mimic the semantic route and found that damaging any part of it could reproduce several of the symptoms of deep dyslexia. We have since made more detailed models to learn which aspects of neural-network architectures were responsible for this behavior. We have also extended the approach to account for additional symptoms of deep dyslexia.

Our models of the semantic route consist of interconnected units representing neurons. Each neuron unit has an activity level (between 0 and 1) that depends on the inputs it receives from other neurons. Connections between units have an adjustable weight that specifies the extent to which the output of one unit will be reflected in the activity of the unit it is feeding. These weights, along with the pattern of connections among neurons, determine the computation that the network performs.

The first version of our network consisted of three sets of units: "grapheme" units, each of which represented a particular letter in a specific position within the word; "sememe" units that represented the meanings of words; and a layer of intermediate units that make it possible to learn complex associations. A completely general network would require 26 grapheme units for each position within

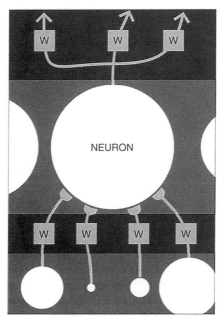

Idealized neuron is the basis for artificial neural networks. It sums the weighted inputs that it receives from other neurons (*bottom*) and generates an activation level between 0 and 1. It then passes this activation (through weighted connections) to other neurons. The set of weights and connections in a neural network determines its behavior. © Boris Starosta. Reproduced with permission.

a word, but we used a simplified vocabulary that permitted a smaller number. The grapheme units in the first position were all consonants, for instance, and those in the second, all vowels.

The sememe units do not correspond directly to individual word meanings but rather to semantic features that describe the thing in question. The word *cat* activates such units as "mammal", "has legs", "soft", and "fierce". Units representing such semantic features as "transparent", "tastes strong", "part of limb", or "made of wood" remain quiescent. Our network has 68 sememe units representing both physical and functional attributes of a word's definition. Each word that we chose was represented by a different combination of active and inactive sememe units.

To make our neural network produce the correct pattern of semantic features for each word, we had to set the weight on each connection to the appropriate value. These weights are set not by hand but rather through a learning procedure —an algorithm for programming neural networks. To teach a network a task, one starts with random weights and then presents the network repeatedly with a "training set" of input patterns (in this case, letters in specified positions). The algorithm adjusts the weights after each training run to reduce the difference between the network's output and the "correct" response.

Neural-net workers have known since the 1950s how to adjust weights in simple, two-layer networks, but training networks with a greater number of layers is more difficult. In particular, it is not immediately obvious how to set the weights on the connections from the input units to the intermediate units because there is no way to determine, a priori, which intermediate units should be active for any given input and output.

During the 1980s, however, neural-net researchers developed a number of different methods for training multi-layer networks. These methods apportion changes to the connection weights of each layer according to their contribution to the error. Over the course of many training cycles, the resulting weights converge to yield a network that produces the correct results. Depending on the initial random weights, learning may result in any of a number of sets of weights, each of which leads the network to produce correct answers for its training inputs. (For further details of the learning procedure, see "How Neural Networks Learn from Experience," by Geoffrey E. Hinton; *Scientific American*, September 1992.)

In theory, these learning procedures can get stuck in so-called local minima— configurations of weights that are incorrect but for which any small change would only make the network's errors worse. In practice, however, a network almost always learns nearly optimal solutions. In addition, some of the learning procedures are more biologically plausible than others, but our results do not seem to depend on which method we use. We suspect that even if the brain uses a quite different learning procedure, the resulting neural circuitry will still resemble the structure that our network develops. Thus, our explanation of what happens when the network is damaged may be correct even if its learning procedures are not.

Although our initial network, with one intermediate layer, could learn to map word-forms to their semantic features, it was not really satisfactory. It had a strong tendency to map very similar inputs (such as *cat* and *cot*) to similar outputs unless subjected to excessively long training. We addressed this problem by adding another layer of "cleanup" neurons. If the original set of connections produces a sloppy answer, the new units will change it to produce exactly the correct semantics. The number of word meanings is limited, so the pathway from the input need only get the activities of the sememe units closer to the correct meaning than to any other. The same learning techniques that succeed on networks with a single intermediate layer can direct the learning of nets containing multiple intermediate layers or even networks whose units are connected in cyclical fashion.

The most natural way to implement this cleanup mechanism is with a feedback loop. The output of the sememe units goes to the cleanup units, and their output goes to the inputs of the sememe units. Each time activity flows around the loop, the influence of the cleanup units on the sememe units (and vice versa) will yield a pattern of semantic features that is closer to the correct one.

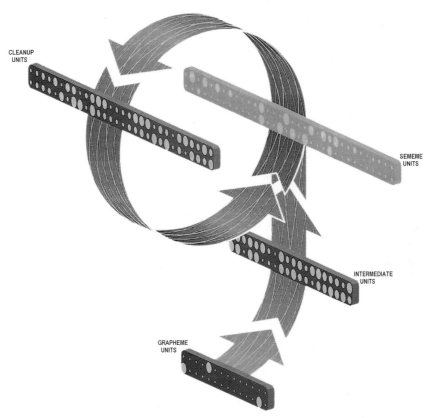

Neural network for reading contains four layers. The first responds to the letters in each word. Connections between input and intermediate units and between intermediate and "sememe" units convert the word-form to a representation in terms of semantic features, such as size, edibility or aliveness. "Cleanup" units are connected to sememe units in a feedback loop that adjusts the sememe output to match the meanings of words precisely. © Boris Starosta. Reproduced with permission.

The feedback loop introduces a new characteristic into the behavior of our neural network. The original network was static—any given input would cause the network to produce a corresponding output pattern, and that pattern did not change as long as the input stayed constant. The output of the new network, however, is dynamic; it settles gradually into a stable pattern.

Consequently, we have found it useful to think of the network's output not just as a list of active semantic features but rather as motion through a multidimensional "semantic space", whose coordinates are defined by all the semantic features that the network can represent. Every point in the space corresponds to a specific pattern of activity among the sememe units, but only a few of those patterns correspond to valid meanings. The correct meanings of words are points in semantic space.

The first three layers of the network, seen according to this perspective, take a word-form and convert it to a position somewhere in semantic space. Activity in the cleanup layer then draws the output of the network to the point corresponding to the closest meaning. The region around each word is what physicists and mathematicians know as a point attractor—whenever the network's initial output appears within a certain region, the network's state will inexorably be drawn to one position within the region.

This notion of a semantic space dotted with attractors representing the meanings of words has proved valuable for understanding how our network operates and how it can make the same semantic errors that dyslexics do. If we damage the network by randomly changing the weights in the cleanup mechanism, for example, the boundaries of the attractor for each word will change. As a result, if the network is in a region in semantic space where it was previously drawn to one word, it may now be drawn to a semantically related one instead. Alternatively, if we disrupt the pathway coming from the input, the network's initial output may be closer to the meaning of a semantically related word than to the meaning of the word originally presented.

This result clears up one of the first puzzles presented by deep dyslexia: why damage to any part of the brain's semantic route produces an essentially similar pattern of misreadings. Neurologists and others had wondered how damage near the input—the visual part of the reading system—could cause semantic errors. According to our models, these errors arise naturally as the cleanup neurons use semantic information to try to make sense of the output of the damaged earlier stages.

The notion of attractors helps to explain another anomaly in the data as well. Almost all patients who make semantic errors also make some visual errors— they confuse a word like *cat* with a visually similar word like *cot*. They do not, however, make the sounding-out errors of surface dyslexics ("loave" for *love* or "deef" for *deaf*). This invariable connection between semantic errors and visual errors is odd. Some patients must have damage solely to the later stages of their processing systems, and one would intuitively expect them to make only semantic errors.

After implementing our neural-network model, we discovered to our great surprise that damage to the semantic cleanup circuit sometimes caused visual errors. Retrospectively, we can understand why: the earlier layers of an undamaged network can afford to produce somewhat similar semantic outputs for the words *cat* and *cot* because the cleanup circuit will steer each to its proper meaning. But when the cleanup circuit is damaged and the shapes of each attractor change, the output of the sememe units may fall into the attractor for a visually similar but semantically unrelated word.

This explanation did not initially occur to us because it relies on the idea that the boundary of the attractor for *cat* can come very close to the one for *cot* even though the two words are semantically dissimilar. One would expect the attractors

for many other meanings to come between those for *cat* and *cot*. In a two-dimensional space this intuition is correct: if we choose 40 points at random to represent word meanings and construct fairly compact attractors around each point, the attractors for dissimilar meanings will not come anywhere near one another.

It is very dangerous, however, to assume that the same is true in spaces that have many dimensions. Our network represents 68 semantic features in its sememe units, and so the attractors for each of its 40 words reside in a 68-dimensional space. It turns out that in 68 dimensions, the midpoint between any two randomly chosen points is almost certainly closer to each of those points than it is to any of 38 other random points. Consequently, the attractors for *cat* and *cot* can have a common border without any other attractors getting in the way. Avoiding obstacles is easy in 68-dimensional space.

Although our network was able to mimic both the correct and dysfunctional mapping of word-forms to meanings, that does not mean its architecture is the only possible one for the brain's semantic processing route. To determine the range of possible alternatives, we investigated the effects of damage on several different architectures, each designed to evaluate one aspect of the original network design.

We programmed versions of the neural network that contained connections among the sememe units and ones that lacked such connections; we also programmed some networks so that each neuron in one layer was connected to every neuron in the succeeding layer and others whose connections were sparse. In addition, we moved the cleanup units so that they performed their work ahead of the sememe units, and we combined the cleanup units with the intermediate layer. We even changed the arrangement of neurons in the input layer to alter the way that words were represented and added an output network that converted meanings to strings of phonemes, so that the system actually spoke.

Most of the architectural details are irrelevant. The specific way the visual input is represented is not important as long as words that resemble each other visually produce similar patterns of activity in the input layer. The only crucial ingredient is the existence of attractors—if there are no cleanup units "downstream" of the damage, the network does not exhibit the pattern of errors characteristic of deep dyslexia.

Interestingly enough, our network not only reproduces the obvious visual and semantic errors of deep dyslexia, it also mimics some of the subtler characteristics of the disorder. For instance, patients occasionally make "visual then semantic" errors, in which a semantic confusion seems to follow a visual one. G.R. would read *sympathy* as "orchestra" (presumably via *symphony*). Our networks also produce these errors—sometimes reading *cat* as "bed", via *cot*.

Semantic space has many dimensions, corresponding to the semantic features. The meanings of particular words are points in semantic space. When the

authors' neural network reads a word, interaction between sememe and cleanup units causes any word-form that is mapped into a region of semantic space near the meaning of a word to converge on that meaning. If the network is damaged so that the boundaries of these so-called attractors shift, a word can be misread as a semantically similar one—"cot" for *bed*, for example. Semantic errors may also occur if damage causes a word-form to be mapped to a slightly different point in semantic space. Such a network can make visual errors because visually similar words will initially be mapped to nearby points in semantic space, even if the stable points of the attractors they fall into are quite distant.

When severely damaged, our network also exhibits a strange effect that occurs when patients have a lesion so large that their semantic representations are distorted beyond recognition and they cannot find a word at all. Such patients are unable to identify the word they are trying to read, but they can often still decide which category it falls into, say, "animal" versus "food". Under similar circumstances, our network no longer stabilizes at the attractor corresponding to a particular word—indeed, the attractors for several words may have merged. Nevertheless, the network's output does stabilize within a larger volume of semantic space wherein the correct word and its relatives once resided. Consequently, the word's category can still be determined.

One symptom of deep dyslexia that our models did not initially address is the way in which patients have more trouble reading abstract words than concrete ones. This phenomenon appears to be an integral part of the syndrome because abstractness—a semantic property—increases the probability of visual errors. Furthermore, when patients make such misreadings, the responses they come up with tend to be more concrete than the original word presented.

We based our approach to simulating this effect on the proposal, made by Gregory V. Jones of the University of Warwick in England and others, that concrete words are easier for deep dyslexic patients because they evoke a more consistent and detailed meaning. In terms of our network, a concrete word has more semantic features than does an abstract one. For example, *post* has 16 features ranging from "size between one foot and two yards" to "used for games or recreation". In contrast, *past* has only two features: "has duration" and "refers to a previous time". We designed a new vocabulary containing 20 pairs of four-letter words differing by a single letter, one concrete and the other abstract. On average, the concrete words had about four times as many semantic features as did the abstract ones.

After the network had been trained to pronounce the words, we found that lesions to any part of the network "upstream" of the cleanup units reproduced the effects of abstractness. The concrete words cause fewer errors because there is more redundancy in their semantic activity patterns. Hence, there is more structure that the cleanup units can use to make the network converge on the proper meaning. The abstract words, which have less redundancy in their semantic

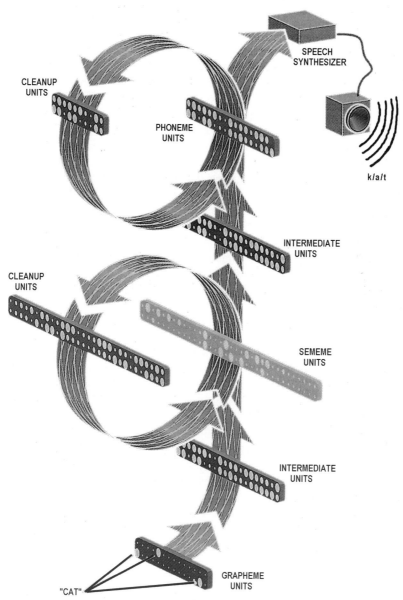

Speaking network adds another set of three layers to the original reading neural net. It converts sequences of letter shapes to semantic representations and maps those in turn to sequences of phonemes that can be fed to a speech synthesizer. This network is particularly useful because it does not require researchers to make potentially biased judgments about what word (if any) corresponds to a perturbed pattern of semantic features, as may be generated when the network is damaged to simulate dyslexia. © Boris Starosta. Reproduced with permission.

420

patterns, must rely more heavily on the feed-forward pathway, where visual influences are the strongest.

Because correct recognition of concrete words relies more on the cleanup circuit, severe damage there leads to a surprising reversal: the damaged network reads concrete words less well and produces more visual errors than with abstract words. This type of lesion and pattern of performance are consistent with what is known about the single, enigmatic patient with "concrete-word dyslexia", studied by Elizabeth K. Warrington at National Hospital in London. Not only did he have much more trouble reading concrete words than abstract ones, he also did better matching spoken abstract words with pictures. This consistency suggests that his problem lay at the level of the semantic system.

Our account of the error pattern of deep dyslexia relies on the properties of a neural network that transforms one representation (a visual word-form) into another, arbitrarily related representation (a set of semantic features). One would expect similar error patterns to result from damage to other cognitive processes that involve an arbitrary transformation to or from a semantic space. Moreover, neuropsychologists have already described somewhat similar error patterns in deep dysgraphia, a disorder of writing, and deep dysphasia, a disorder of word repetition.

This additional evidence suggests that our model may have a wider validity than we originally supposed. More important, however, it marks the successful use of a new technique for understanding how the brain works. Our work differs from other explanations for deep dyslexia (and, with few exceptions, other explanations for neuropsychological phenomena in general) in the kinds of hypotheses that we frame. Instead of verbally characterizing each component in a complex neural mechanism and relying on intuition to tell us how damage will affect its behavior, we simulate that mechanism, damage it and watch to see what happens. We have found that many of our hunches were wrong. This discovery suggests that detailed computer simulations will play a crucial role in furthering understanding of how the brain normally processes information about language and of how that function is disrupted by injury or disease.

CHAPTER FIFTEEN

Covert recognition in a connectionist model of pure alexia

Kate Mayall and Glyn W. Humphreys
University of Birmingham, UK

Covert recognition, apparent knowledge without consciousness, has been described in several cognitive disorders, including pure alexia. Patients have been documented who cannot name briefly presented words, but can make semantic categorisation and lexical decisions to a degree of accuracy above chance. Here, we describe a simple connectionist model which, when lesioned, demonstrates many of the performance characteristics of pure alexia, including covert recognition. It is concluded that covert recognition can be explained in terms of the functioning of a damaged processing system, and it is not necessary to assume a disconnection of a normally functioning system from conscious expression.

COVERT RECOGNITION

In many areas of Cognitive Neuropsychology, there have been reports of patients with an apparent loss of conscious awareness in a particular cognitive domain (see Schacter et al., 1988, and Young & De Haan, 1990, for reviews). For example, patients have been described who appear, and claim, not to be able to see or to process visual stimuli fully, but who show knowledge of the stimulus when information is tapped covertly. Examples of disorders in which covert recognition has occurred include blindsight, prosopagnosia, alexia, hemineglect, amnesia and aphasia. In some, but not all, patients suffering from these impairments, covert tests can demonstrate existence of knowledge which is not apparent when the knowledge is tested overtly. We shall briefly review all of the above impairments, then describe in more detail the covert abilities which have been demonstrated in prosopagnosia and pure alexia, for which explanations have been

Neural Modelling of Brain and Cognitive Disorders, 1996, pp. 229–247.

offered in terms of connectionist models. Other interpretations of patterns of overt and covert ability will be discussed at the end of this section.

Blindsight and visual attention disorders

Investigations of blindsight constituted the first systematic studies of apparent loss of conscious awareness of perception or cognitive processing in neurological patients (Pöppel, Held, & Frost, 1973; Weiskrantz et al., 1974). The term "blindsight" was first used by Weiskrantz et al. (1974) to describe the apparently unconscious awareness of stimuli within an area of cortical blindness or "scotoma". Pöppel et al. (1973) tested ex-servicemen who were suffering from visual field defects. When a brief flash of light was presented within an area of scotoma, patients reported that they could not see it. However, when they were told to guess at its position, their eye movements tended to be towards the position of the flash. Weiskrantz and his colleagues (1974, 1980, 1986, 1987) studied in depth a patient, DB, who could point relatively accurately to the position of a flash of light presented within his scotoma, despite claiming he was unable to see it. He could distinguish static from moving light, and could make simple orientation and shape discriminations.

Similar findings have been reported concerning neuropsychological patients demonstrating spatial "extinction". These patients are able to detect a single stimulus presented anywhere within their field of vision. However, if two stimuli are presented simultaneously, one in the left and one in the right visual field, they tend to ignore the stimulus presented in the visual field contralateral to their brain lesion. Volpe et al. (1979) described four patients who demonstrated spatial extinction when presented with two stimuli, but, when asked if the two stimuli presented were the same or different, patients were remarkably accurate.

Covert processing has also been demonstrated in visual neglect, with patients showing knowledge of items presented on the left which they cannot report when requested to do so directly (Berti & Rizzolatti, 1992; Marshall & Halligan, 1988). For example, Marshall and Halligan (1988) documented a patient who reported that she could see no difference between pictures of a plain house and pictures of the same house with flames coming from its left-hand side. Despite this, when asked which house she would prefer to live in, she consistently chose the house which was not on fire.

These three types of patient have in common the fact that they appear on the face of things to be unable to see, or attend to, particular visual stimuli or parts of stimuli. However, in each case, stimuli have been shown to have been processed at least to some extent. (See Milner, 1995, for a discussion of covert recognition in the domain of vision.)

Loss of conscious awareness in non-visual impairments

Covert recognition has also been reported in non-visual impairments. Examples have been found in both amnesia and aphasia. Some amnesic patients have been shown to recover memories when tested implicitly, but not when tested explicitly (Warrington & Weiskrantz, 1968, 1970). In early cases, the amnesic patients tested by Warrington and Weiskrantz (1968, 1970) were facilitated at a fragmented picture and word identification task the second time they attempted it. This occurred despite the patients claiming to have no memory of attempting the task before.

There have also been reports of covert recognition in both Broca's and Wernicke's aphasia. Broca's aphasics produce slow effortful speech, and function words in sentences are often omitted, producing a "telegraphic" style of speaking. Wernicke's aphasics, in contrast, produce relatively fluent speech, but it tends to be full of lexical selection and grammatical errors. Andrewsky and Seron (1975) asked a Broca's aphasic to read or complete sentences with words which could be read as either content words or function words, depending on the context. When the words appeared as function words they tended to be omitted. But when the same words appeared as content words they tended to be included in the aphasic's sentences. Tyler (1989) reported a similar patient who, despite having a syntactic processing deficit which was apparent in free speech, was slower to respond to a target word embedded in a syntactically disrupted sentence than to the same word within acceptable, or semantically disrupted, sentences. Both of these patients appear to have some residual implicit knowledge of grammar.

Wernicke's aphasics, tested by Milberg and Blumstein (1981), performed poorly on a semantic relatedness judgement task, which overtly tested semantic knowledge. However, when tested on a lexical decision task, the aphasic patients were facilitated on word judgements if the word followed a semantically related prime. This suggests an implicit knowledge of the semantics of the words on which they were tested.

One further example of loss of conscious awareness is anosognosia, the denial of suffering from a disability. This impairment is slightly different from the others discussed, since there are no covert tests to indicate that knowledge does in fact exist. However, it certainly reflects a form of lack of conscious awareness, and reviewers have tended to group it with the other deficits (Young & De Haan, 1990). An example of anosognosia is the existence of patients who suffer from both hemiplegia and hemianopia, but are aware of only one of the disorders (Bisiach et al., 1986). Bisiach et al. (1986) described a patient who claimed to move his left arm, for example, when in fact the left side of his body was completely paralysed.

Covert recognition in prosopagnosia

Prosopagnosia is the inability to recognise faces which were once familiar, e.g., those of family, friends and famous celebrities. Prosopagnosic patients can generally perceive and describe facial features, but cannot recognise people from the features, and rely on other cues, such as voice, for recognition. However, evidence exists for covert knowledge of face identity in some patients. Several different experiments have been reported in the literature and are described below.

Firstly, psychophysiological indications of face identity knowledge have been demonstrated in prosopagnosics (Bauer, 1984; Tranel & Damasio, 1985, 1988). Bauer (1984) used the "Guilty Knowledge Test" to demonstrate that, for pictures of faces which could not be named by his prosopagnosic patient, skin conductance responses were greater when the picture was presented with the correct name as opposed to an incorrect name. Tranel and Damasio (1985, 1988) further showed that skin conductance responses were greater when familiar faces were presented to prosopagnosic patients, as opposed to unfamiliar faces.

Using indirect behavioural assessments of face identity knowledge, De Haan et al. (1987a, b) demonstrated that, in a test of whether two faces were the same or different, their prosopagnosic patient, PH, was faster at responding to familiar faces. Further, he was slower to classify names (as politicians or actors) if the name was accompanied by an incorrect picture. PH's response time was slightly faster if, for example, the name of a politician was accompanied by another politician rather than by a picture of an actor. PH also demonstrated associative priming effects from pictures he could not name, on the task of classifying a written name as famous or non-famous (Young, Hellawell, & De Haan, 1988). For example, he was faster to respond to the name "Diana Spencer" if it followed a picture of Prince Charles than if it followed a picture of an unrelated person.

In summary, a variety of tasks presented to certain prosopagnosic patients all appear to have generated the same findings. When tested indirectly these patients indicate knowledge of face identities, which, when tested directly, they cannot recognise.

Covert recognition in pure alexia

The final area for which a significant amount of evidences has been provided for covert recognition is pure alexia. The most notable characteristic of this disorder is that reading can be literally "letter-by-letter": the word CAT may be read, either silently or aloud, "C . . . A . . . T . . . cat". The argument for letter-by-letter reading is supported by evidence that reading latencies increase linearly with word length (Warrington & Shallice, 1980) and are abnormally long.

Landis et al. (1980) described the first case of covert word recognition in alexia. Their patient could correctly point to objects corresponding to briefly presented words he could not name. A number of pure alexic patients have been reported subsequently who are able to make correct lexical decision and semantic

categorisation judgements on words presented too briefly to be named overtly (Coslett & Saffran, 1989, 1992; Coslett et al., 1993; Shallice & Saffran, 1986). For example, the pure alexic patient, ML (Shallice & Saffran, 1986), performed significantly above chance when asked to answer questions such as "Is it an author or a politician?" or "Is it pleasant or unpleasant?" for briefly presented words he could not read. All four patients reported by Coslett and Saffran (1989) were able to report, to a proficiency above chance level, whether a briefly presented word was an "animal" or not, or whether it was a "food" or not. Further, Coslett and Saffran (1992) showed that their patient could match a briefly presented word to one of two pictures with an accuracy rate above chance.

Theories of covert recognition

There are three main groups of theories of covert recognition. The first is that the particular information processing module being tapped is undamaged, but is no longer linked to higher cognitive processes which support consciousness (Schacter et al., 1988; Young & De Haan, 1990). The second is that there are (at least) two separable systems capable of achieving the task in question (Bauer, 1984; Coslett & Saffran, 1989, 1992; Shallice & Saffran, 1986; Weiskrantz, 1986). One of these, which is connected to consciousness, is damaged and cannot be used. A second system, which does not have an output to consciousness, is undamaged and is used by the patient. The third set of theories suggest that individual modules are damaged, but that indirect tasks can tap the residual processing of the module (Farah, O'Reilly, & Vecera, 1993; Mayall & Humphreys, 1996).

Young and De Haan (1990) argue that the dissociation between overt and covert face recognition in prosopagnosia is caused by a disconnection of output from an adequately functioning face processing system to processes which support awareness of recognition. They also explain the other disorders mentioned above as a disconnection from consciousness. Schacter et al. (1988) agree that covert recognition is caused by a disconnection of a processing module from a conscious mechanism, although they do concede that "some of these phenomena may turn out to be related to one another only superficially" (p. 243).

Bauer (1984), in discussing prosopagnosia, suggested that there may be two neural systems for face recognition, only one of which is linked to consciousness. It is suggested that both ventral and dorsal visual areas are capable of face recognition, but only processing by the ventral system can lead to conscious expression. The dorsal system, which is relied on by those prosopagnosics who demonstrate covert recognition, normally mediates affective responses to faces. Further evidence is provided by Tranel et al. (1995) who report the opposite dissociation following frontal lobe damage. Weiskrantz (1986) provided a similar interpretation for blindsight. He suggested that the disorder could be explained by use, not of the geniculo-striate pathway, but of one of the other branches of the optic nerve which project to the midbrain or subcortical areas.

Interpretations of covert recognition in pure alexia have included suggestions of a disconnection of a normally functioning word recognition system from consciousness, but also of right hemisphere reading (Coslett & Saffran, 1989, 1992; Shallice & Saffran, 1986). This is comparable to the explanations of blind-sight and covert recognition in prosopagnosia which suggest that there are two functionally and anatomically separate systems involved, one used for overt and one for covert recognition (Bauer, 1984; Weiskrantz, 1986).

Finally, covert recognition may reflect residual processing in a damaged system. Farah et al. (1993) and Mayall and Humphreys (1996) suggest that covert recognition in prosopagnosia and pure alexia, respectively, can be explained in this way. They provide simple connectionist models which suggest that covert effects can be found in a single system without recourse to a disconnection from consciousness or the use of second processing system.

FARAH ET AL.'S MODEL OF COVERT RECOGNITION IN PROSOPAGNOSIA

Farah et al. (1993) have suggested that covert recognition in prosopagnosia can be explained in terms of residual processing in a damaged face processing system. The support they provided for this argument included the fact that prosopagnosics who display covert recognition can score above chance on overt tasks (though not as highly as on covert tasks), thus suggesting that the face recognition system is not completely obliterated. In order to demonstrate that covert recognition can emerge from a damaged system, Farah et al. developed a connectionist model of the face processing system, which when lesioned could perform better on "covert" than on "overt" tasks.

The model

Farah et al.'s (1993) model consisted of a set of face units, a set of name units and a set of semantic units. Both the face units and the name units were connected to the semantic units via a set of hidden units specific to the type of input. The network was recurrent, and the output of each set of units fed back into itself. Representations of names and faces were random and distributed. Representations of semantics were also distributed and random, except for 2 units, one of which referred to the occupation "actor" and one to the occupation "politician". The model was trained on five "actors", five "politicians" and twenty "other people" using the contrastive Hebbian learning algorithm. Training consisted of 320 epochs on the set, with each epoch consisting of one of the three representations (name, face or semantics) being presented and associations with the other two being learned. The model was lesioned by removing varying numbers of face input units or hidden units from the visual input to the semantic units.

The simulations

Three main sets of simulations with lesioned versions of the model were conducted to compare performance with that of prosopagnosic patients who display covert recognition. Firstly, the lesioned model's ability to relearn face–name pairs was examined. After damage, the number of correct names produced for faces was reduced. Relearning was tested by giving the model 10 learning epochs, in one condition with correct face–name pairs and in a second condition with incorrect face–name pairs. For all types and size of lesion, the model was better at relearning the correct pairings than at learning the incorrect pairings.

In the second simulation, Farah et al. tested whether visual analysis of a face pattern proceeded more quickly if the face was familiar than if it was not. After lesioning, the face representations of the five "actors" and five "politicians" taught to the network, plus another five "actors" and five "politicians", were presented to the model. The number of iterations for the visual units to settle was recorded for each face. On the whole, the lesioned models needed fewer cycles to settle for familiar than for unfamiliar faces. If it is assumed that number of iterations is comparable with reaction times, the lesioned model shows the same pattern as the prosopagnosic patient studied by De Haan et al. (1987b) who was faster at classifying familiar faces as same or different, than unfamiliar faces.

The third simulation considered semantic priming on occupation decisions. Names were presented in three conditions: individually, paired with different faces from the same occupation category, and paired with different faces from the other occupation category. The number of cycles for one of the occupation units to attain a positive activation value was recorded. Fewer cycles were required when the face accompanying the name was from the same category compared to when it was from the other category. This suggests that the model possessed covert semantic knowledge, as faces from the incorrect category produced interference.

Farah et al. concluded from their modelling work that it is possible for a damaged face recognition system to exhibit covert recognition. A disconnection from conscious expression is thus not the only possible interpretation of the results found with these prosopagnosic patients. It was suggested that, while this was not necessarily the case with covert recognition in all disorders, covert recognition in prosopagnosia could reflect residual processing in a damaged system.

A CONNECTIONIST MODEL OF PURE ALEXIA

We (Mayall & Humphreys, 1996) have developed and lesioned a simple model of word recognition in an attempt to demonstrate that covert recognition in pure alexia could result from residual processing in a damaged word recognition system, and so also does not necessarily need to be explained in terms of a disconnection of the word recognition system from conscious expression. In this section we will describe the model and the experiments performed with simulated lesions.

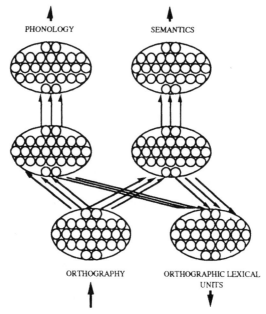

Figure 1. Architecture of the Mayall and Humphreys (1996) model.

General framework of model

The Mayall and Humphreys (1996) model does not stand as an attempt to model all aspects of word recognition and identification, but was developed to study covert recognition in word naming and to test two assumptions: (1) that there are separable routes to access phonology and semantics; and (2) that words resemble each other more than do letters, and that both are represented within the same visual recognition system. It is intended that the model simulates lexical processing, and, when lesioned, it simulates residual word recognition rather than the use of any compensatory letter-by-letter reading strategy. This is a simple exploratory model, and as such, was only tested with one set of initial weights and one type of lesion (the complete removal of processing units). As a previous smaller model with the same general architecture produced similar results, and as dissociations within the current model were robust over lesion sizes, we argue that the pattern of results is not simply an artefact of an overly small network (see Bullinaria & Chater, 1995).

Specific architecture

The model is of the form shown in Figure 1. Input units represent orthography, and output units represent phonology and semantics. The input units and the hidden units are fully interconnected, however, only half of the hidden units are

connected to the phonological output units and half are connected to the semantic output units. Evidence from neuropsychology suggests that phonological or semantic information can be retrieved in isolation (Coltheart, 1980; Coslett & Saffran, 1989; Schwartz, Saffran, & Marin, 1980; Shallice & Saffran, 1986; Warrington & Shallice, 1979). We recognise that, in a more complete model, semantic and phonological units would also be connected to allow spontaneous speech to occur.

The tasks we used to examine the model included not only naming and semantic categorisation, but also lexical decision. This is of interest as some pure alexic patients have demonstrated a level of performance above chance on lexical decision when words are presented too briefly to be named overtly. Besner and McCann (1987) argued that lexical decisions involve a familiarity check in which the orthographic familiarity of a string contributes to decision making. Seidenberg and McClelland (1989) used a similar assumption in their connectionist model of word recognition. Lexical decisions were carried out in their model by a form of auto-association in which the orthographic description of a string was reconstructed by feedback from hidden units. A familiar string was judged to be one where the reconstructed orthographic representation was similar to the original input representation; an unfamiliar string was taken as one for which the reconstructed representation was dissimilar to the input. We incorporated a similar procedure here. Orthographic input values were mapped through the two sets of hidden units (phonological and semantic) to a set of "orthographic lexical" units, which during the training phase had values matching the input units (and so led to auto-associative learning of input values). Lexical decision could then be based on comparing activation values over the orthographic lexical units for words and nonwords. (The criterion for a word response was taken as the error score where the two distributions crossed.)

Seidenberg and McClelland's model has been criticised for the way in which it simulates lexical decision, as performance by the unlesioned model is not as good as that by normal humans (Besner et al., 1990). However, in our unlesioned model there is no overlap in the distributions of orthographic lexical errors scores for words and nonwords. Therefore the unlesioned model performs "lexical decision" perfectly. Secondly, we do not claim that an orthographic familiarity check is the only process involved in lexical decision. Phonological and semantic information influences the orthographic lexical units through the hidden units.

Hidden units in the model can be thought of as lexical units from which phonology and semantics are derived. The orthographic lexical units can then be assumed to constitute an orthographic output lexicon, which can be used to produce orthographic outputs from other input modalities, or as a familiarity check for use in lexical decision.

The model consisted of 16 input units, 90 hidden units (45 phonological and 45 semantic) and 74 output units (29 phonological, 29 semantic and 16 orthographic lexical). It was trained on 69 words and 10 letters.

Representations

Orthography, phonology and semantics in the model were represented by distributed patterns of 1s and 0s. There was no representation of constituent letters within words. Our intention here was not to capture details of how orthography is presented in skilled readers, but only of how similarity influences performance in a damaged system. Letters and words were represented over the same set of input units, as representations of single letters, having specific pronunciations, may only differ from those of words in terms of semantics (see Arguin & Bub, 1994). The same number of units were used to represent letters and words, as the model was intended to be of a lexical system which processes words as single wholes.

The difference between letters and words was represented in terms of the similarity of orthographic representations, with words having more similar representations than letters. In modelling orthography in this way we made the following assumptions. Printed letters are, visually, relatively simple representations; there are only 52 different lower and upper case forms and these are made up of distinguishing stroke features. Words, on the other hand, are more complicated being made up of several letters. There are many more words than letters, and many contain letters in the same positions making them visually more similar to one another. Many studies of word processing have shown interference between multiple letters presented in words (e.g., Bouma, 1971), whilst we know of no comparable evidence indicating interference between multiple features presented in letters.

Phonology was represented by a 29-bit vector pattern of fourteen 1s and fifteen 0s. The phonology of letters and words was of identical construct, as the spoken form of words and letters is fundamentally the same (indeed, some letters and words are homophones, e.g., b and bee; c and sea; t and tea).

Semantic representations were subdivided into two sets of units: "category units", which were identical for words within the same category (e.g., all animals), and "individuating units" which differed between each word. Of the 29 semantic units, 14 represented the super-ordinate category, whilst the remaining 15 differentiated the word from others in the same category. All semantic units of letters had activation values of 0, based on the assumption that individual letters hold negligible semantic information. Word imageability was also represented within the semantic units. (See Mayall & Humphreys, 1996, for discussion of imageability representations and effects.)

Training and testing the network

All weights in the model initially were assigned random values of between −0.1 and 0.1. To ascertain whether a particular representation over output units (e.g., a phonological representation) was correct firstly a "thresholding" procedure was undertaken where units below 0.2 were rounded down to 0, and units above 0.8 were rounded up to 1. Output units with a value of between 0.2 and 0.8 were

taken as "undetermined". Using the values which were determined, the response was taken as the word (or letter) whose target output had the greatest overlap in activation values with the actual output. Whilst our model does not include feedback loops, the process by which an output is assessed includes a simple notion of "attraction" (Hinton & Shallice, 1991; Plaut & Shallice, 1993; Plaut & McClelland, 1993), as responses are taken as the word or letter with the closest known representation. An advantage of using our procedure is that exact responses can be generated so that we can measure when the system fails to produce a response and when it produces a correct response.

The model was trained via standard back propagation (Rumelhart, Hinton, & Williams, 1986). During training, the model was run through 50,000 iterations of the training set. The number of occurrences of a word within the training set was a function of its Kucera and Francis (1967) word frequency. Items were divided into four relative frequency bands, and the number of occurrences of the word in the training set were 4:3:2:1 across the four frequency bands. (See Mayall & Humphreys, 1996, for a discussion of frequency effects in the model.)

Having been trained to near perfect performance on all stimuli, the model was lesioned to varying degrees of severity. Four different lesions of 33%, 50% and 67% of the hidden units were undertaken. (Input unit lesions were also investigated but are not discussed here, see Mayall & Humphreys, 1996.) The lesions were designed to overlap as little as possible. (Throughout this chapter the four lesions of the same size are referred to as A, B, C, and D. For example, the 50% lesions are referred to as 50A, 50B etc.)

Here we will discuss three simulations with lesioned versions of the model: a comparison of word and letter naming, which is crucial to modelling pure alexia, and comparisons of semantic categorisation and lexical decision with word naming, which are of interest in terms of covert recognition. Further simulations using the model are described by Mayall and Humphreys (1996).

Simulation 1: Letter and word naming

Alexic patients are usually not perfect at letter naming, but their performance at letter naming is substantially superior to that of word naming; hence they may adopt a letter-by-letter reading strategy. Figure 2 shows the percentage of letters and words correctly named by the model. At the 33% and 67% lesions, there was superior letter naming over word naming performance [*33% lesions*—75% (30/40) correct letter naming vs. 49.61% (127/256)[1] correct word naming, $\chi^2 = 7.96$, df = 1, $p < 0.01$; *67% lesions*—27.5% (11/40) correct letter naming vs. 12.5% (32/256) correct word naming, $\chi^2 = 5.12$, df = 1, $p < 0.05$]. When lesion 50A was removed from the calculations, there was also superior letter naming over word naming for the 50% lesions [40% (12/30) correct letter naming vs. 27.60% (53/192) correct word naming, $\chi^2 = 6.86$, df = 1, $p < 0.01$]. Lesion 50A shows the reverse effect with better word naming than letter naming

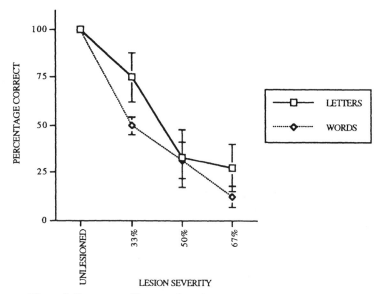

Figure 2. Percentage of letters and words correctly "named" by the model.

[10% (1/10) correct letter naming vs. 42.19% (27/64) correct word naming]. Interestingly, there has been a deep dyslexic patient reported in the literature who, similarly, is surprisingly good at word naming whilst performing poorly at letter matching (Howard, 1987). This apparent double dissociation in the model is discussed in detail by Mayall and Humphreys (1996).

As the number of hidden units was reduced, the model became less capable of discriminating between input patterns. As inputs for words were more similar to each other than those for letters, words became indiscriminable first after damage. When the activations of hidden units were studied it was noted that letters had more hidden units highly activated than words (mean number of hidden units with activation values greater than 0.8: Letters—10.7, Words—8.56). This difference is likely to render letters more robust to damage than words, as a random lesion is less likely to remove the necessary proportion of highly activated units to produce the correct output. It is possible that the greater visual distinctiveness of letters compared to words similarly leads to the superior performance of pure alexic patients on letter naming compared to word naming.

Simulation 2: Word naming vs. semantic categorisation

Several pure alexic patients have been described who are able to perform above chance on forced choice semantic categorisation tasks, when words are presented too briefly to be named overtly (Coslett & Saffran, 1989, 1992, 1993; Shallice &

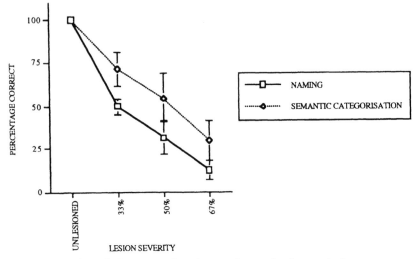

Figure 3. Percentage of words correctly named and categorised.

Saffran, 1986). A comparison between these tasks was therefore made for the model. More correct responses over semantic category units than over phonology units were produced by the model for all lesion severities (see Figure 3).

It must be taken into consideration, however, that as there are 79 phonological representations known to the model but only 14 semantic categories, the level of chance report is greater for semantic categorisation than for naming (7.14% vs. 1.27%). Guesses were corrected by assuming that the network either "knew" the correct response or "guessed". Thus:

$$p(correct) = p(know) + (1 - p(know)) \times p(guess)$$

so:

$$p(know) = \frac{p(correct) - p(guess)}{1 - p(guess)}$$

where p(correct) is the observed correct performance across equivalent conditions (lesion instances), p(know) is the probability that the network knows the correct response, and p(guess) is the chance correct rate. Comparing across the lesion instances, p(know) for semantic categorisation was reliably higher than p(know) for naming (*33% lesions*—t(3) = 14.49; *50% lesions*—t(3) = 5.53; *67% lesions*—t(3) = 5.07, all *p* < 0.05).

The fact that the model produced more correct semantic categorisations than correct phonological name responses is likely to be due to the semantic category units receiving more reinforcement during learning. In most cases five words share the same semantic category, so the model received more exposure to the semantic category representations than to the phonological representations. There

are also fewer alternative semantic category representations with which the target must compete. As applied to human neuropsychological patients, this is consistent with semantic categorisation benefiting because it is based on a reduced number of response alternatives (Shallice & Saffran, 1986).

Word naming vs. lexical decision

The model was tested on 20 "nonwords" in addition to the words it had been taught. Nonwords had orthographic and phonological representations of similar structure to the known words, but the semantic units were all assigned 0s. As lesion severity increased, so the distributions of orthographic lexical error scores for words and nonwords overlapped further, reducing lexical decision ability. Measures of d' were calculated for the results of each lesion. d' provides a measure of discrimination sensitivity and has been used to quantify the lexical decision ability of neuropsyehological patients. At the 33% lesion level performance was significantly above chance, but after 50% and 67% lesions the difference was not significant [*33% lesions*—69.38% (247/356) correct, $\chi^2 = 26.99$, df = 1, $p < 0.001$; *50% lesions*—54.49% (194/356) correct, $\chi^2 = 1.267$, df = 1, NS; *67% lesions*—52.53% (187/356) correct, $\chi^2 = 0.360$, df = 1, NS].

It should be noted that at the 33% lesion level word naming was also relatively good (49.61% correct word naming vs. 69.38% correct lexical decision). As chance level for lexical decision is 50%, lexical decision performance is not greatly superior to word naming performance. We suggest that this may be because the orthographic lexical units, whose activation values are used in lexical decision, receive equal input from both phonological and semantic hidden units. If lexical decision in the lesioned model was based only on input from semantic hidden units, performance may improve (as semantic categorisation performance is superior to word naming performance following lesions). If pure alexic patients have difficulty in retrieving phonology from briefly presented words, their lexical decisions under these conditions are more likely to be based on visual and semantic information than phonological information.

GENERAL DISCUSSION

We have described a very simple model of the word recognition system. When lesioned, it is intended that the model simulates residual word recognition capabilities, as opposed to any letter-by-letter reading strategies, which may be resorted to by pure alexic patients. The model produces significantly better performance on a "semantic categorisation" task than on a "word naming" task, as is found with patients who demonstrate covert recognition (Coslett & Saffran, 1989, 1992, 1993; Shallice & Saffran, 1986). It also performs lexical decisions at an accuracy level above chance, at least after 33% hidden unit lesions, and we have suggested how this performance in the lesioned model could be improved.

In addition to the simulations described above, the Mayall and Humphreys (1996) model successfully simulated several other performance characteristics of pure

alexia, e.g., frequency effects, imageability effects, the production of mainly visual errors plus a few semantic errors and a case mixing × task interaction. Further, predictions were made for super vs. sub-ordinate categorisation, category specificity effects and the naming of category headings compared to category members.

Two important points to note about the model are, firstly, that a single network has simulated many different performance characteristics of pure alexia, and, secondly, that it models aspects of covert recognition. Correct semantic categorisations, and to some extent, lexical decisions, have been made by the model even when naming is incorrect. The model provides an existence proof that it is possible to explain the dissociation in the reading of pure alexic patients in terms of architecture and processes. Hence, as argued by Farah et al. (1993) with regard to prosopagnosia, it is not necessary to conclude that covert recognition is a manifestation of a disconnection of consciousness from a normally functioning reading system. Neither is it necessary to argue that covert recognition reflects right hemisphere reading. The present model has no representations that can easily be linked to right as opposed to left hemisphere processing.

In conclusion, the above model has provided more weight to the argument that covert recognition does not necessarily have to be explained in terms of undamaged processing modules that have been disconnected from consciousness, or even in terms of two separable systems capable of the same processing. The Farah et al. (1993) and Mayall and Humphreys (1996) models both provide examples of processing systems which, when lesioned, can demonstrate "covert" without "overt" recognition. The fact that not all prosopagnosic or pure alexic patients demonstrate covert recognition may suggest that the type or size of the lesion may influence whether covert recognition occurs or not. While it appears possible to explain covert recognition in pure alexia and prosopagnosia in terms of damage to the relevant processing system itself, we would not wish to claim that this extends to all disorders which display covert recognition. Nevertheless, it is plausible that at least some other examples of covert recognition, for instance those in amnesia and aphasia, could similarly be explained in terms of damage to a normal processing system, and could be simulated in connectionist terms, as we have described above.

NOTE

1. Only 64 words were tested for each lesion, as 5 word phonologies were not "learned" during training.

REFERENCES

Andrewski, E. L., & Seron, X. (1975). *Cortex, 11*, 379–390.

Arguin, M., & Bub, D. N. (1994). In M. Farah & D. N. Bub (Eds.), *The neuropsychology of high-level vision*. Hillsdale, NJ: Erlbaum.

Bauer, R. M. (1984). *Neuropsychologia, 22*, 457–469.

Berti, A., & Rizzolatti, G. (1992). *Journal of Cognitive Neuroscience, 4*, 345–351.

Besner, D., & McCann, R. S. (1987). In M. Coltheart (Ed.), *Attention and performance XII*. Hove, UK: Lawrence Erlbaum Associates Ltd.

Besner, D., Twilley, L., McCann, R. S., & Seergobin, K. (1990). *Psychological Review, 97*, 432–446.

Bisiach, E., Vallar, G., Perani, D., Papagno, C., & Berti, A. (1986). *Neuropsychologia, 24*, 471–482.

Bouma, H. (1971). *Vision Research, 11*, 459–474.

Bullinaria, J. A., & Chater, N. (1995). *Language and Cognitive Processes, 10*, 227–264.

Coltheart, M. (1980). In M. Coltheart, K. E. Patterson, & J. C. Marshall (Eds.), *Deep dyslexia.* London: Routledge & Kegan Paul.

Coslett, H. B., & Saffran, E. M. (1989). *Brain, 112*, 327–359.

Coslett, H. B., & Saffran, E. M. (1992). *Brain and Language, 43*, 148–161.

Coslett, H. B., Saffran, E. M., Greenbaum, S., & Schwartz, H. (1993). *Brain, 116*, 21–37.

De Haan, E. H. F., Young, A. W., & Newcombe, F. (1987a). *Cortex, 23*, 309–316.

De Haan, E. H. F., Young, A. W., & Newcombe, F. (1987b). *Cognitive Neuropsychology, 4*, 385–415.

Farah, M. J., O'Reilly, R. C., & Vecera, S. P. (1993). *Psychological Review, 100*, 571–588.

Hinton, G. E., & Shallice, T. (1991). *Psychological Review, 98*, 74–95.

Kucera, H., & Francis, W. N. (1967). *Computational analysis of present-day American English.* Providence, RI: Brown University Press.

Landis, T., Regard, M., & Serrat, A. (1980). *Brain and Language, 11*, 45–53.

Marshall, J. C., & Halligan, P. W. (1988). *Nature, 336*, 766–767.

Mayall, K. A., & Humphreys, G. W. (1996). *British Journal of Psychology, 87*, 355–402.

Milberg, W., & Blumstein, S. E. (1981). *Brain and Language, 14*, 371–385.

Milner, A. D. (1995). *Neuropsychologia, 33*, 1117–1130.

Plaut, D. C., & McClelland, J. L. (1993). In *Proceedings of the 15th Annual Conference of the Cognitive Science Society.* Hillsdale, NJ: Lawrence Erlbaum Associates Inc.

Plaut, D. C., & Shallice, T. (1991). *Cognitive Neuropsychology, 5*, 377–500.

Pöppel, E., Held, R., & Frost, D. (1973). *Nature, 243*, 295–296.

Rumelhart, D. E., Hinton, G. E., & Williams, R. J. (1986). In J. L. McClelland & D. E. Rumelhart (Eds.), *Parallel distributed processing.* Cambridge, MA: MIT Press.

Schacter, D. L., McAndrews, M. P., & Moscovitch, M. (1988). In L. Weiskrantz (Ed.), *Thought without language.* Oxford: Oxford University Press.

Schwartz, M. F., Saffran, E. M., & Marin, O. S. (1980). In M. Coltheart, K. E. Patterson, & J. C. Marshall (Eds.), *Deep dyslexia.* London: Routledge & Kegan Paul.

Seidenberg, M. S., & McClelland, J. L. (1989). *Psychological Review, 96*, 523–568.

Shallice, T., & Saffran, E. M. (1986). *Cognitive Neuropsychology, 3*, 429–458.

Tranel, D., & Damasio, A. R. (1985). *Science, 228*, 1453–1454.

Tranel, D., & Damasio, A. R. (1988). *Behavioral Brain Research, 30*, 235–249.

Tranel, D., Damasio, H., & Damasio, A. R. (1995). *Journal of Cognitive Neuroscience, 7*, 425–432.

Tyler, L. K. (1989). *Cognitive Neuropsychology, 6*, 333–356.

Volpe, B. T., Ledoux, J. E., & Gazzaniga, M. S. (1979). *Nature, 282*, 722–724.

Warrington, E. K., & Shallice, T. (1979). *Brain, 102*, 43–63.

Warrington, E. K., & Shallice, T. (1980). *Brain, 103*, 99–112.

Warrington, E. K., & Weiskrantz, L. (1968). *Nature, 217*, 972–974.

Warrington, E. K., & Weiskrantz, L. (1970). *Nature, 228*, 628–630.

Weiskrantz, L. (1980). *Quarterly Journal of Experimental Psychology, 32*, 365–386.

Weiskrantz, L. (1986). *Blindsight: A case study and implications.* Oxford: Oxford University Press.

Weiskrantz, L. (1987). *Brain, 110*, 77–92.

Weiskrantz, L., Warrington, E. K., Sanders, M. D., & Marshall, J. (1974). *Brain, 97*, 709–728.

Young, A. W., & De Haan, E. H. F. (1990). *Mind and Language, 5*, 29–48.

Young, A. W., Hellawell, D., & De Haan, E. H. F. (1988). *Quarterly Journal of Experimental Psychology, 38A*, 297–318.

Overview

Gillian Cohen

This book has explored a number of areas of human cognition and has illustrated the contributions made by both cognitive neuropsychology and connectionist modelling in each area. This section attempts an assessment of how useful these approaches are. Traditionally cognitive psychologists have relied on observation and experiment to try to understand the mechanisms of cognitive processes. Neuropsychology and computational modelling have provided additional research tools and enable researchers to use converging evidence from different sources to build, test, modify, and confirm or disconfirm their theories. The new approaches have benefited cognitive theorising in two particularly valuable ways. First, they have added a lot of fine-grain detail to the prevailing broad-brush accounts of cognitive processes. Second, they have added many important constraints to these models by showing what is, or is not, possible; what can be done and what cannot be done. Neuropsychological studies of damaged brains can reveal which modules are essential for normal function and which are not. Computational models can challenge established cognitive theories by showing that it is possible to simulate human performance using a different system. However, the concept of simulation rests on the idea that brains and machines are in some ways analogous: the rationale for cognitive neuropsychology rests on the idea that intact brains and damaged brains are analogous.

ANALOGIES AND LEVELS OF EXPLANATION

In order to evaluate these methodologies it is necessary, therefore, to confront the issue of the goodness of the analogy. That is, how far can we accept that the functioning of the damaged brain is analogous to the intact brain? How far is the

computer model analogous to the human brain? Obviously the equivalence is not exact, so we need to ask at what level the analogy holds.

COMPUTERS AND BRAINS

Marr (1982) identified three different levels of explanation that can be applied to cognitive processes. At the highest level, the computational level, the explanation is in terms of an abstract description of the task that the system is performing. At an intermediate level, the algorithmic level, the explanation consists of the set of representations and operations required to perform the task. At the lowest level, the level of physical implementation, the explanation is concerned with the hardware that performs the task. These three levels can be broadly characterised as functional, psychological, and neurophysiological. The question then arises as to the level of equivalence between connectionist models and the human brain. Is there functional equivalence, psychological equivalence, or neuronal equivalence?

Parallel distributed models have been thought to have particular power to yield insights into human cognition because of their resemblance to the structure of the brain. However, most researchers (e.g., Smolensky, 1988) agree that, in spite of being known as neural networks, connectionist models do not have neuronal equivalence. The units in a connectionist model have some properties in common with neurons. They derive activation from other units and pass on activation to more units as neurons do. Concepts such as rates of firing and thresholds are common to connectionism and to neurophysiology but the reality is different. Connectionist models are dynamic mathematical constructions and it is generally agreed that the structure and operations of the neurons in the human brain are quite different. However, the wish to claim neuronal equivalence lingers on. Burton and Young in Chapter 8 took up this issue in their debate with Farah, O'Reilly, and Vecera. Farah et al. claimed that their model "has some properties in common with real neural networks, and can therefore be considered as a model of the brain". Burton and Young disagree. They point out that having distributed representation does not necessarily make a model equivalent to the brain, as there are many different kinds and extents of distributedness.

If neuronal equivalence can be dismissed, there is general agreement that equivalence at the computational, functional level does hold, at least for some tasks. Connectionist networks may not be very similar to the neural networks in the brain but they carry out computations in a similar way. It has yet to be established whether connectionist networks will eventually prove able to simulate the full range of human cognitive abilities or whether functional equivalence is restricted to a limited repertoire. In any case, although the abstract specification of the task may be the same for both the human brain and the connectionist model, equivalence at this level is not very informative. The really important debate centres on the psychological level.

So what about psychological equivalence? There are strong grounds for claiming equivalence at this level. As we have seen in many specific examples in this book, models can be trained to perform cognitive tasks in the same way as humans, exhibiting the same patterns of error (as in Martin et al.'s model of word repetition in Chapter 12), or the same performance deficits (as in Coltheart et al.'s model of dyslexic reading in Chapter 13). Models may simulate the same phenomena, such as the covert recognition of faces or words, or category specificity. (see Chapters 2, 3, and 7). Their performance can be influenced by the same factors such as familiarity (Burton & Young, Chapter 8), imageability (Martin et al., Chapter 12), or regularity (Marchman, Chapter 9). Nevertheless, claims of psychological equivalence are not always accepted. Broadbent (1986) considered that McClelland and Rumelhart's (1986) model of word recognition was not analogous to human performance at a psychological level but only at the level of algorithmic microstructure. His view can be understood in the light of Smolensky's (1988) distinction between three levels of processing. Smolensky distinguished a top level of conscious rule processing, as in reasoning and much of language use. Below this, at an intermediate level, the intuitive processor operates in perception, skilled motor performance, and fluent language use. These are the well learned automatic processes carried out without conscious thought. His third level, like Marr's, is the neural level. According to Smolensky, connectionist models operate at the intermediate level, simulating the intuitive processor. This account raises the issue of whether psychological equivalence can be achieved by a model that lacks the level of conscious rule processing. Broadbent thought not. The confusion arises because the notion of what constitutes a psychological level breaks down into different levels of analysis. What the models appear to offer is a partial form of psychological equivalence which does not include the higher levels of conscious thought that are usually encompassed by the term "psychological".

Arguments about the level of analogy prove to be more complex and confused than at first sight but it is clear that connectionist models are at least as psychological as most of the box-and-arrow models of cognitive psychologists and can provide working simulations of these that add a fine-grain microstructure to the crude macrostructure of the original theory. Most importantly, working implemented models can show where the theories may be incomplete or wrong. Dual route theories of reading (Coltheart et al., Chapter 13) and two system accounts of past tense learning (Marslen Wilson & Tyler, Chapter 10) have been effectively challenged by models that demonstrate that a single route or a single system might be able to produce a similar pattern of performance. Similarly, a simulation of covert word recognition (Mayall & Humphreys, Chapter 15) has shown that a damaged system can produce the observed results, so that it is not necessary for a theoretical account to assume a disconnection below the level of consciousness. The IAC model developed by Burton et al. to account for face recognition, person recognition, and naming illustrates the way such a model

goes beyond the earlier flow chart type of theory proposed by Bruce and Young (1986) and explains a wider range of phenomena. The box-and-arrow type of models are constrained by the available experimental data and by logical reasoning. It is clear that these constraints are not always sufficient to exclude alternative explanations or to specify component mechanisms in detail. Connectionist models are proving immensely valuable in filling these gaps. Nevertheless, Kinsbourne (1994) has argued that simulations need to have quantitative equivalence not just qualitative similarity to human performance. In his view, connectionist models are flawed because they are "so unconstrained that a simulation could hardly fail" (p. 73).

DAMAGED BRAINS AND INTACT BRAINS

According to Ellis and Young (1997) cognitive neuropsychology has two basic aims. One is to understand and explain the patterns of impairment seen in brain-injured patients as being due to damage in one or more of the components postulated by a model that is based on experimental investigation of normal performance. The second aim is to confirm or develop theories of normal cognitive functioning on the basis of the observed patterns of deficit in the brain-injured. Both of these aims rest on the assumption of an analogy between intact and damaged brains. How far is this justified? Saffran (1982) pointed out that cognitive neuropsychology relies on the assumption of subtractivity—that the performance of the damaged brain reflects the normal intact cognitive system minus those components that have been damaged. Related to this, the assumption of transparency (see p. 7) claims that undamaged areas will continue to function normally. Both of these assumptions are relying on an analogy between damaged and intact brains. A further assumption is that, by looking at patterns of impairment in brain-damaged patients, it is possible to infer which processes are independent of each other, which are organised so that they are dependent, and which are downstream of each other in a sequence of processing operations. These inferences are based on existing theoretical models and on assumptions about the modularity of processes within the system. Nonmodular connectionist models have challenged these assumptions. Some researchers have adopted fully interactive models and others admit that modularity is a matter of degree with some unspecified amount of interaction between components (Farah, 1994, p. 17). This weaker version of the modularity assumption makes it much more difficult to sustain strong claims about the organisation of processing operations. And, once it is conceded that interactions may occur, it is much harder to maintain the assumptions of subtractivity and transparency.

The validity of generalisations from single case studies or groups of patients has also been questioned. There must be reservations about drawing general theoretical conclusions about normal brains from groups composed of nonhomogeneous patients. Groups that are labelled as, for example, deep dyslexics, do not exhibit absolutely uniform patterns of deficit. Inferences based on single cases are also

worrying given the extent of individual variation and because the effects of compensatory strategies that patients adopt can easily obscure the nature of the damage they have suffered. Should we conclude, for example, that the case of NC described by Martin et al. in Chapter 12 is typical of deep dysphasia? (See Shallice, 1991, for a detailed discussion of these problems). However, in many areas converging evidence carefully built up has begun to accumulate and provide justification for extrapolating from damaged brains to normal ones. In many cases the neuropsychological findings converge with those derived from experimental studies of normals. For example, both sources confirm the existence of separate short-term stores for auditory-verbal memory and for visual short-term memory, and the separability of phonological and semantic information in reading.

Inferences about organisation in the intact brain rely heavily on the discovery of double dissociations, as, for example in the acquisition of regular and irregular past tenses (see Marchman, Chapter 9, and Marslen-Wilson & Tyler, Chapter 10, for a discussion). However Juola and Plunkett (Chapter 11) have challenged this assumption by showing that an appearance of dissociation between two independent modules can arise from a single mechanism, and, as Plunkett and Cohen point out (p. 260), the definition of a double dissociation is itself imprecise. Even when double dissociations are apparent, as for recognising living versus nonliving things (Forde & Humphreys, Chapter 1), the interpretation of the dissociation is far from being straightforward. Detailed analysis of the tasks may reveal that it is not necessarily the case that they are subserved by different modules, and computational models have proved to be a useful corrective to overly hasty conclusions by demonstrating that alternative explanations are possible.

It is worth noting, also, that rehabilitation of damaged systems poses a threat to the strong version of the assumption of transparency (see p. 7). The view that the operation of the intact brain can be inferred from the damaged brain rests on the assumption that the damage has not caused the system to function in an essentially different way. If rehabilitation involves radical reorganisation of operations, this assumption will be incorrect. Indeed, if reorganisation is sufficiently radical, it may also undermine the weak version of transparency, according to which post-traumatic processing may still be understood in terms of normal processing, even if it has changed. It is clear, in the light of these considerations, that the analogy between damaged and intact brains is far from being straightforward.

DAMAGED BRAINS AND DAMAGED MODELS

The rationale of lesioning models rests on assuming that the performance of the damaged model is analogous to the performance of the brain-injured patient, and that inferences about the nature of the damage in the brain can be made from knowing the nature of the damage in the model. A note of caution needs to be sounded here. There are a considerable variety of ways in which a model can be "lesioned". One method is to reduce the weights and so weaken the connection strengths between units (e.g., Burton et al.'s IAC model, Chapter 6). Another

method is to add noise to the system. A third method of lesioning a model is to remove units (e.g., Mayall & Humphreys, Chapter 15) and yet another is to add or remove connections (Devlin et al., Chapter 3; Hinton et al., Chapter 14). Lesioning frequently involves a process of tinkering with the model until the required performance deficits are obtained. The degree of severity of the lesion can be manipulated by varying the type and amount of damage inflicted on the model.

The extent to which these manipulations are analogous to the type of damage sustained by patients is questionable. It is not at all clear which, if any, of these methods is equivalent to the lesions incurred by patients. Damage to the human brain probably involves all of the types of lesion just described. That is, some neurons are lost, some are disconnected, and the injury causes added noise in the system. The majority of brain-damaged patients suffer from focal lesions but some of the methods of lesioning models, such as adding noise produce diffuse "lesions". A further problem is that different patients seldom, if ever, sustain identical damage. So which individual is the lesioned model simulating? The analogy between the performance of the lesioned model and a patient tends to be superficial and confined to relatively few tasks. Nevertheless, lesioning can be a valuable experimental tool. A useful technique involves selectively damaging different parts of a system in order to test a theory about the involvement of each part in performing a given task. Farah and McClelland (Chapter 2) used this method to damage visual and functional units selectively, and succeeded in simulating selective impairment in recognising living and nonliving things. Lesioning models does provide insight into the ways observed patterns of deficit could arise and the ways a lesioned system could repair itself during recovery (Martin et al., Chapter 12).

STRENGTHS AND WEAKNESSES

Computational models have two major advantages over the box-and-arrow models of cognitive psychology. First, as we have already noted, they can instantiate the microstructure of a hypothesised mechanism. Second, they can model dynamic behavioural change. Where cognitive theories are static, computational systems can model the way responses change during learning, during the loss of learning caused by damage, and during the relearning that takes place in recovery. This ability to model change allows developmental processes to be simulated (as in the studies of children's past tense learning), and can make important contributions towards understanding what is happening during the recovery of function and what kinds of therapy might be most effective. However, the question arises of, whether models are genuinely productive. That is, whether they can generate new predictions or only test existing theories.

Computational models do sometimes produce unexpected and surprising findings. Hinton et al. (Chapter 14) wrote that "we simulate a mechanism, damage it and watch to see what happens". Their model of deep dyslexia obtained the

predicted pattern of errors and, additionally, produced errors that had not been anticipated but which were nevertheless consistent with patients' behaviour. The network unexpectedly produced visual errors when the semantic circuit was lesioned and, by a process of manipulating the network and observing the effects of the manipulations, the researchers were able to narrow down and identify a possible mechanism. Existing models of reading were both confirmed and extended by these findings.

In Burton et al.'s IAC model, weakening the connections between the Face Recognition Units and the Person Identity Nodes produced the expected phenomena of covert recognition but also had the unexpected result of slowing down decisions about the familiarity of names. This had not been predicted because the name judgements did not involve the weakened links, but it showed that lesions within a system can have far-reaching effects and is consistent with a general slowing of response observed in patients.

Computational modelling has proved to be valuable both in confirming existing theories and also in challenging them by showing that alternative explanations are possible. However, cases are beginning to accumulate where two different computational models offer different explanations for a particular cognitive phenomenon. Different models of reading—Seidenberg and McClelland's single route model and the Dual-route Cascaded model proposed by Coltheart et al.— have different architectures but both can account for some aspects of the performance of human readers. Similarly, both Burton and Young's IAC model and Farah et al.'s distributed model can reproduce covert recognition of faces. At present, it is difficult to decide between competing models of this kind. Burton and Young suggest that the model that can account for the widest range of performance is to be preferred, but most models are in a state of continuous evolution, with researchers increasing their scope and power with add-ons so that Model A may widen its range and overtake Model B at any time. The development of good criteria for adjudicating between competing models is urgently needed. At present modular and interactive models co-exist uneasily and the issue is unresolved.

Connectionist modelling and neuropsychology may inform and invigorate ongoing debates and controversies in cognitive psychology. Detailed studies of patterns of impairment from cognitive neuropsychology have greatly influenced thinking about the nature of consciousness. The phenomena of blindsight, and the covert recognition of faces, objects, and words, reinforce the idea that cognitive operations can take place below the level of conscious awareness, and support a theory that recognises different levels of consciousness. Computational approaches to consciousness have been put forward (e.g., by Johnson-Laird, 1988) but are strongly disputed as many people are unwilling to attribute consciousness to computer-based systems. According to Smolensky (1988), connectionist networks simulate unconscious, rather than conscious, processes. Nevertheless, the fact that connectionist models can produce both covert recognition and overt

recognition can be seen as suggesting that they can model different levels of consciousness. On the other hand, people who have sustained brain damage struggle consciously and effortfully to develop strategies for continuing to perform the tasks impaired by the damage. This is very different from the residual function displayed by lesioned models.

Methodological constraints impose limitations on both neuropsychology and connectionist modelling but there is some reason to believe that these are not insuperable. Neuropsychology has been immensely strengthened by the development of neuroimaging techniques and by the accumulation of converging evidence that makes it easier to identify commonalities between cases. Connectionist models have been limited by being small-scale models of the performance of single tasks, which weakens their analogy with brains capable of performing many different tasks. (The question here is whether a machine that can only wash the dishes can significantly resemble one that can wash the clothes and make toast as well.) However, this objection is likely to be overcome in the near future by the development of multi-task models. Certain types of cognitive operations such as rule-based linguistic processes, conscious planning, and reasoning are difficult to represent in connectionist models, but it is already clear that researchers are finding ways to overcome what seemed initially to be fundamental limitations. The full potential of connectionist models has only been glimpsed so far and the new discipline that has been called "connectionist neuropsychology" (Plaut & Shallice, 1993) is flourishing.

REFERENCES

Broadbent, D. E. (1986). A question of levels: Comment on McClelland and Rumelhart. *Journal of Experimental Psychology: General, 114*, 189–192.

Bruce, V., & Young, A. W. (1986). Understanding face recognition. *British Journal of Psychology, 77*, 305–327.

Ellis, A. W., & Young, A. W. (1997). *Human cognitive neuropsychology*. Hove, UK: Psychology Press.

Farah, M. J. (1994). Neuropsychological inference with an interactive brain: A critique of the 'locality' assumption, *Behavioral and Brain Sciences, 17*, 43–104.

Johnson-Laird, P. (1988). *The computer and the mind: An introduction to cognitive science*. Cambridge, MA: Harvard University Press.

Kinsbourne, M. (1994). Do neuropsychologists think in terms of interactive models? *Behavioral and Brain Sciences, 17*, 72–73.

Marr, D. (1982). *Vision*. San Francisco: W. H. Freeman.

Plaut, D. C., & Shallice, T. (1993). Deep dyslexia: A case study of connectionist neuropsychology. *Cognitive Neuropsychology, 10*, 352–377.

Saffran, E. M. (1982). Neuropsychological approaches to the study of language. *British Journal of Psychology, 73*, 317–337.

McClelland, J. L., & Rumelhart. D. E. (1986). Distributed memory and the representation of general and specific information. *Journal of Experimental Psychology: General, 114*, 159–188.

Shallice, T. (1991). From neuropsychology to mental structure. *Behavioral and Brain Sciences, 14*, 429–437.

Smolensky, P. (1988). On the proper treatment of connectionism. *Behavioral and Brain Sciences, 11*, 1–74.

Glossary

Acquired dyslexia: reading difficulties resulting from brain damage, e.g., from trauma, stroke, or disease and occurring after acquisition of normal reading skill.

Agrammatic speech: typical of patients with Broca's aphasia. Speech consists of a string of nouns and verbs with no articles or prepositions and no grammatical structure.

Alexia: the loss or disruption of ability to understand written language due to brain damage.

Alzheimer's disease (DAT): dementia resulting from pathological degeneration of cortical and possibly subcortical brain areas.

Aneurysm: an aneurysm is caused when a weakness in an artery wall balloons out. It may rupture and cause haemorrhage.

Anomic aphasia: patients with anomic aphasia have word-finding difficulty, especially for the names of things.

Apperceptive prosopagnosia and associative prosopagnosia: a distinction between impairment of face recognition due to perceptual deficits (apperceptive prosopagnosia) and one due to difficulty in retrieving information from memory about a face that has been adequately perceived (associative prosopagnosia).

Association cortices: areas of cortex that do not receive direct projections from sensory systems but receive information from other cortical regions.

Attractor networks: attractor networks are ones that can settle into stable states. The time taken to settle into an attractor state has been taken to simulate reaction time. Attractor networks are relatively less affected by noisy input.

Auditory-verbal short-term memory (AVSTM): short-term memory for speech.

Backpropagation: a technique for training networks using a measure of the output error to adjust the connection weights.

Benton and van Allen test: this is a test of facial recognition that assesses ability to recognise unfamiliar faces. The task in each case is to select from six possible choices the photograph(s) that represent the same person as the stimulus photograph. The matching photographs are either identical front views, front views taken under different lighting conditions, or side views of the same person.

Boston Diagnostic Aphasia Examination: the BDAE is a comprehensive and detailed battery for assessing language functions in people with aphasia. It incorporates rating of speech samples, as well as structured tests of auditory comprehension, oral expression, comprehension of written language, and writing.

Boston Naming Test (BNT): this test assesses the ability to name objects pictured in line drawings which are presented one at a time. The 60 items include both common and rarely encountered objects. For items that are not named spontaneously, first a semantic and then a phonemic cue is given to determine whether cueing facilitates performance.

Broca's area: the area in the left frontal cortex which is associated with severe difficulty in speech production and agrammatism.

Cascade approach: with a cascade approach, processes do not occur in a strictly linear sequence of stages. Instead a later stage can begin before an earlier one is completed. This means that activation at the earlier stages of processing can influence subsequent stages.

CAT or CT scans: CAT stands for Computerised Axial Tomography, sometimes just written as CT scan. Tomography is a method of displaying "slices" through the body or brain, i.e., showing cross-sectional information. X-rays are used, but not in the more usual way where only a simple silhouette is produced. The CAT technique revolves the X-ray machine on an axis around the body (or head) taking multiple images from different directions. A computer uses these "flat" pictures to derive a 3-dimensional image.

Cerebral hemisphere: the two cerebral hemispheres are the two regions of the cortex of the forebrain. Left and right cerebral hemispheres are separated by a fissure, but connected by the corpus callosum. In general, in right-handers, the left is specialised for language, and abstract and symbolic processing, the right for nonverbal, spatial, and holistic processing.

Cerebrovascular accidents (CVAs): strokes resulting from a blockage of blood supply in the brain (infarct) or haemorrhage.

Clamping: during training of an interactive network the output nodes are held (i.e., clamped) at the desired activation level rather than letting them find their own levels, as is the case in normal use.

Clean-up units: these operate in a loop to adjust an imprecise output and yield a more precise one.

Coarse coding: Burton and Young are distinguishing between different types of distributedness. They argue that the brain uses a coarse coding form of distribu-

tion, with representations distributed across a small set of units as opposed to being distributed across all units.

Conduction aphasia: characterised by impaired ability to repeat back spoken words or sentences.

Configural processing (of faces): processing the whole face including the relationships between the features.

Conservative response bias: when there is a conservative response bias the patient or subject does not respond unless there is strong evidence or high-quality information.

Content words or function words: there are a few words that can be either content or function words depending on context, e.g., the French word "car" meaning either "for" (a function word) or "coach" (a content word).

Contralesional and ipsilesional stimuli: stimuli presented to the opposite (contralesional) or to the same (ipsilesional) side as the side of the brain lesion, e.g., if a patient with right side damage is presented with a face in the left visual field this would be contralesional.

Contrastive Hebbian learning: normal Hebbian learning (named from the neurophysiologist Hebb) is a method of calculating weight changes. Input units are connected to output units via simulated synapses. The connection weights of the synapses are determined by multiplying together the levels of activity of the two units on either side of the connection. *Contrastive* Hebbian learning performs a similar multiplication, but between the levels of activity in two separate phases: one when the system is allowed to produce its own output, the other when a training signal is forcing the output to what it should be.

Critical period: a brief period of time during development, in which learning is programmed to take place.

Cycles: in an interactive network the activity in one component influences the activity in another which in turn can re-influence the first. An initial input can give rise to a whole sequence of changes, but eventually the system settles down into a steady unchanging state. When this process is simulated in a computer it has to be broken down into a series of steps: all the initial activities are used to calculate all the influences, then those are used to calculate what the new activities would be, then the new activities are implemented. This sequence is repeated again and again until there are no further changes. Each repetition is called a cycle.

Deep dysphasia: a rare form of aphasia in which the patient tends to make semantic errors when repeating real words and cannot repeat meaningless nonwords.

Delta rule: a training procedure for nodes in neural nets. A node produces activity when driven by other nodes connected to it. The amount of activity depends on the weights (or strengths) of these connections. A node is trained by adjusting the weights in such a way that the magnitude of its output will more nearly approach the target level. When the delta rule is used, the size of

the adjustment is made proportional to the size of the discrepancy between actual and desired activity: the closer the goal the smaller the adjustment.

Dental finals: in a verb such as "hit" the final consonant is a dental, i.e., the sound is made with the tongue against the teeth.

Deterministic networks: in a deterministic system changes are not random (as in stochastic networks), but are purposefully calculated as being "moves in the right direction".

Developmental dyslexia: failure to develop normal reading skill in childhood due to an inborn defect.

Distractor: a distractor is any stimulus that is not the target stimulus. In most cases it causes interference. In Chapter 4, in the "no distractor" condition only the name that requires a response is presented. In the other conditions this target name is accompanied by a distractor which is either (A) the face of the named person; (B) a different but related face; or (C) a different and unrelated face. However, in normal usage of the term (A) would not be considered a distractor as it might be helpful.

Dot product: once a net has been trained, a particular pattern of activity at its input will give rise to a specific (but generally different) pattern at its output. Thus, a series of facial characteristics represented at the input may lead to a pattern representing the name at output. The transformation from input to output is produced by the nature of the interconnections. Their various weights can be represented as a table of numbers. Similarly, the inputs and outputs can be defined numerically. A field of mathematics known as matrix algebra shows how the output pattern can be derived from calculations involving the input numbers and weights table. The technique involves repeatedly multiplying pairs of numbers and summing the results; the resulting figures are termed dot products.

EEG, electroencephalography: measurement of electrical activity in the brain by means of electrodes placed on the scalp at different locations. It is used to study normal and abnormal cognition.

Embedded knowledge: knowledge is embedded in a network when a set of weights has been established by training.

Emergent property: a characteristic of a simulation which has not been anticipated and has not been explicitly built in (so surprising the modellers!).

Entrenchment: a network is said to be entrenched when a particular pattern of organisation has stabilised.

Epenthetic vowel: an optional additional vowel.

Evoked potentials: also known as event related potentials, these are measured by averaging wave forms in successive EEG (electroencephalogram) recordings of brain activity taken by placing electrodes on the scalp, and can be used to map which parts of the brain are active in response to particular stimuli.

Existence proof: a demonstration that something *could* be the case, e.g., that a model is possibly, but not necessarily, correct.

Feedforward networks: a feedforward network is the simplest type possible. It has connections from input to output but no interactive connections leading back again. Neither does it use links between units within a layer.

Frontal lobe: the two lobes of the frontal cortex of the brain comprise one third of the total cortex, contain the primary motor cortex, and have a complex role controlling and monitoring ongoing activity. Damage to the frontal lobes causes distractability and also perseveration.

Geminate consonants: doubled consonants like the "f" in "buff".

Global aphasia: impairment of a wide range of language abilities.

Hemineglect: unawareness and failure to respond to stimuli in the side of space opposite to the side of the brain lesion.

Hemiplegia and hemianopia: hemiplegia is one-sided paralysis involving one arm, leg, and side of the face. For hemianopia, *see* homonymous hemianopia.

Hidden units: a layer of units intervening between the input units and the output units, hence "hidden".

Hierarchy vs heterarchy of processing stages: in a hierarchical model, processing stages are organised in an ordered sequence with a linear flow of control. In a heterarchical model there is no fixed order of stages and the flow of control is multidirectional.

Hippocampus: posterior part of the temporal lobes implicated in memory formation.

Homonymous hemianopia: a hemianopia is a visual field defect in which vision is lost in one half of each visual field. A homonymous hemianopia affects the visual half field of both eyes contralateral to the side of a cerebral lesion, e.g., a lesion on the right side affects all vision to the left of a central fixation point: a lesion on the left would affect vision to the right of the fixation point.

Homuncular process: a higher-level supervisory mechanism, literally a "little man" (homunculus) acting as controller.

Implicit reading: this is the same as covert recognition of words described in Chapter 15.

Inflectional morphology: examples of inflectional morphemes are suffixes added to the verb stem such as "s" (plural), "ed" (past tense), and "ing" (present continuous tense).

Inhibitory links (and excitatory links): activity in one unit may either excite or inhibit activity in other units to which it is linked.

Interactive activation architecture: neural networks using this architecture employ additional connections between components of the network. Unlike a simple network in which the output follows rather directly from the input, in an interactive system the internal links may cause one unit to influence another and may be influenced itself as a result. These interactions delay the final output until the system settles into a steady state.

Ischaemic damage: follows insufficient blood supply to the brain caused by narrowing or blocking of an artery.

Lateral ventricle: the ventricles are cavities or canals within the brain through which cerebrospinal fluid flows. The pair of lateral ventricles are in the forebrain.

Left anterior negativities: this refers to characteristics of the evoked potentials. These show changes in amplitude over time, forming peaks that have either positive or negative polarity.

Left temporal hypometabolism: failure of metabolism in the left temporal lobe.

Lesioning: lesions are areas of tissue damage and if they occur in the brain, impairment of function generally results. The process of lesioning can be mimicked in a neural net by disrupting the functioning of some of the units; this may be achieved by adding noise to input values, by reducing the weights on the links, or by removing units.

Lexical decision response: in lexical decision tasks people are presented with a mixed set of real words and nonwords and have to respond "yes" to real words.

Lexical route: the visual route whereby a word is read by accessing the corresponding entry in the mental lexicon where its pronunciation is stored.

Logogen model: a model of word recognition in which units that respond to individual words have thresholds that vary with factors such as frequency and recency of use.

Macrostructure and microstructure of the system: a system can be described in terms of its general main features (macrostructure), or in terms of the detailed structure of its component representations and mechanisms (microstructure).

Macula: the macular region is the area of high visual acuity in central vision.

Meningioma: a tumour that is not of brain substance but of the meninges, the layers of tissue that protect the brain and spinal cord.

MMSE, Mini Mental State Examination: a short test used to assess mental state and detect signs of dementia.

Modality-specific semantic systems: according to this view there are separate semantic systems for the visual modality (visual semantics accessed by vision) and the verbal modality (verbal semantics accessed by language) which can be independently impaired.

Monomorphemic forms: words that consist of only one morpheme. Such words do not have affixes like "ed" or "ing".

Monotonic relationship: in a monotonic relationship, values of two variables are correlated. The relationship between the position of a volume control and the loudness of the music is monotonic. In contrast, the relationship between the position of the tuning knob and the loudness of the radio station is non-monotonic, because the loudness first increases as the tuning becomes more accurate, but then decreases as the station is left behind.

Morphological processing systems: the systems that process inflectional morphemes (*see* inflectional morphology).

Multi-layer perceptron network: A feedforward network that, in addition to the inputs and outputs, includes hidden layers of nodes.

Nasal and temporal hemifields: the visual field of each eye is divided into a nasal half (nearest the nose) and a temporal half (the outer half).

Natural kinds: living things.

Neologism: a nonsense word.

'Neologism' means 'a newly coined word' in the dictionary. Not a nonsense word.

Neuritic plaques: areas of pathological cortical tissue caused by neuronal degeneration and characteristic of Alzheimer's disease.

Nonlexical route: the phonological route whereby grapheme-to-phoneme conversion rules (GPCs) are used to derive pronunciation.

Occipital lobe: most posterior part of the cerebral cortex, devoted to vision.

P300 component: this is a component wave form in the evoked potential that is related to frontal lobe mechanisms and is elicited by attention, e.g., to a novel stimulus.

Paraphasia: paraphasias are speech production errors that can be semantic (a semantically related word is substituted) or phonemic (intrusions or substitutions of the wrong sounds).

Perisylvian lesion: a lesion of the perisylvian language area, which includes Broca's area.

Periventricular area: region in the language area of the left cerebral hemisphere.

PET: the PET (positron emission tomography) scan measures the uptake of glucose by brain tissue during a specific activity such as reading or speaking. It produces a map of brain function.

PDP models: connectionist models with paralled distributed processing, i.e., distributed representations are processed in paralled.

Phonetic features: these distinguish between different phonemes according to the way they are produced, and include place of articulation (position of the tongue); manner of articulation (the flow of air during sound production); and voicing (involvement of the vocal chords).

Phonotactically illegal: combinations of sounds that are impossible to produce.

Plasticity: the extent to which ability (or disability) can be modified. Children show much greater recovery from the effects of brain damage than adults.

Point attractor: in an interactive network, activity cycles around the units until a stable position results which leads to no further changes. In general, there will be a number of possible activity states that could satisfy this "no further change" condition. The cycling process will lead from a given start state to the nearest stable state rather like a ball on a bumpy surface finding its way into the nearest hollow. Because these stable states "draw" the activity patterns towards themselves they are called attractors: each one in the set is a point attractor.

Premorbid differences: differences present prior to brain damage.

Progressive aphasia: impairment of language ability worsening over time.

Provoked overt recognition: recognition that occurs in particular circumstances that support it (such as recognising an item when it is presented with other similar items), but fails without this support.

Repetition priming effects: repetition priming occurs if a response to a stimulus (e.g., a word or face) is facilitated when the same word or face has been recently presented.

Rime: the part of a monosyllabic word that follows the initial consonant or consonant cluster so that in "shall" the body of the word is "all": in "spook" it is "ook".

Schonell graded reading test: this forms one of a series of standardised attainment tests for use in educational settings. It is designed to provide an assessment of the level of attainment reached by school pupils in recognising and reading single words. It consists of a set of 100 words of gradually increasing difficulty, which are read aloud to the tester. The number of words read correctly can be used to calculate a Reading Age (RA).

Scotoma: a region of total blindness.

Semantic priming effects: semantic priming occurs if a response to a stimulus (e.g., a word or face) is facilitated when a stimulus with a similar meaning has been recently presented, e.g., a response to a politician's face if another politician's face was seen immediately before.

Semantic route: this is a visual route from the word directly to its meaning. Pronunciation is then derived from the meaning. It is not, therefore, the same as the lexical route described by Coltheart et al. in Chapter 13. The lexical route is also visual but goes directly from the visual form of the word to its pronunciation (i.e., not via the meaning).

Skin conductance: the Galvanic Skin Response (GSR) tracks the electrical conductivity of the skin, which increases with emotion. Heightened emotion increases the amount of sweat and the salty fluid is a good conductor of electricity. Consequently, changes in emotional state lead to changes in how well the skin conducts, a change known as the Galvanic Skin Response. The effect has been used in so-called lie detectors.

Skinnerian reinforcement: on the Skinnerian principle a response is learned if it is rewarded when it is made (positive reinforcement). In this case, the "wrong" past tense forms like "goed" and "bringed" could not have been learned by reinforcement because they are not rewarded. Indeed they tend to persist in spite of being corrected repeatedly, which constitutes negative reinforcement.

Slips of the tongue: speech errors, e.g., Spoonerisms, such as "bake my tike" for "take my bike". Errors may be anticipatory, reversals, or blends.

Somatosensory information: sensory information about the body.

Specific Language Impairment (SLI): where language fails to follow a normal developmental course for no obvious reason, and the language impairment is seen in the context of otherwise normal development. Children with SLI have good nonverbal abilities, which are not reflected in their use of language, and their poor language skills cannot be attributed to causes such as hearing impairment, general learning disability, or emotional disturbance.

Speech analysis: refers to the ability to use lip-reading to assist speech recognition.

Standard bell curve: a distribution of values in which the majority cluster around the average, and roughly equal numbers lie above and below the average. When plotted a bell-shaped curve results.

Stochastic networks: stochastic networks are random in nature. Changes in a stochastic network are analogous to those occurring in evolution where completely random changes are selected or not, depending on how well the resultant organism fits the environment. Compare this with deterministic networks.

Stochastic norm: the average outcome of a large number of random events.

Stroop effect: a test of ability to focus attention and resist distraction. Reaction time to name the colour of the ink used to write a word is slowed if the word is the name of a different colour, e.g., "Red" written in blue ink. Patients with frontal lobe damage have greater distractibility than normals and do poorly on the Stroop test.

Structurally similar and structurally dissimilar: according to this view objects belong to either structurally similar or structurally dissimilar categories. Structurally similar categories have the roughly the same overall shape. Members of structurally dissimilar categories have a good deal of visual diversity.

Subcortical visual system: optic pathways such as those involving the superior colliculus but not involving the striate cortex.

Synaptic junctions (synapses): junctions between neurons.

Temporal gyrus and supramarginal gyrus: surface landmarks in the language area of the brain.

Temporal lobe: brain region with many functions including audition, vision, memory, and language. The inferior surface is implicated in object recognition. The role of the left temporal lobe differs from the right temporal lobe due to hemispheric specialisation of function. In most right-handers it is the left temporal lobe that is specialised for language.

Temporo-parietal tumour: the parietal lobes are specialised for sensory and perceptual activity. In this case the tumour involves both temporal and parietal lobes.

Threshold: a fixed level such that a response is triggered whenever activation exceeds this level.

Token frequency: a token is the representation of the stimulus to be applied to the input of a neural net. The token frequency is a measure of how many times that particular token will be presented to the net during the training

phase. This is directly analogous to word frequency which is a measure of how often a word is encountered in everyday use. Type frequency refers to the number of times a type, or class, of item is presented.

Training epochs: typically, neural net simulations train the system by presenting a series of sample "stimuli" each paired with a target output pattern which represents what the net should produce if it were fully trained and performing perfectly. Generally the net will not have learned very well after being presented with the list just once, so it is presented again and again, probably thousands of times. Each time through the list is called a training epoch.

Vector pattern: a pattern created by an ordered set of numbers which may be constituted by an input to a network in the form of a series of 0s and 1s.

Visual agnosia: loss of ability to recognise or identify previously known stimuli.

Visual masking: occurs when a target stimulus is followed by visual noise which interferes with perception.

Vowel changes: some verbs change the vowel in the past tense form, e.g., swim–swam.

Voxel-based morphometry: voxel morphometry is a way of measuring shape. A voxel is a small 3D element of volume, usually a cube. A digitised representation of shape can be created in terms of voxels.

WAIS test: Wechsler Adult Intelligence Scales (WAIS, WAIS-R, WAIS-III). These widely used scales are designed to measure general intellectual functioning (IQ). The revised WAIS incorporates six verbal and five performance subtests which yield verbal, performance, and full-scale (combined) IQ scores.

Williams syndrome (WS): this is a rare abnormality of calcium metabolism. In mild form, it can be controlled by dietary restriction of calcium and vitamin D, so that physical and mental development proceeds normally. In severe form, it results in moderate or severe learning disability. People with Williams syndrome have a characteristic elfin-like facial appearance. Despite their low IQ, they tend to have relatively good linguistic skills.

Author index

Subject index

UNIVERSITY OF WINCHESTER
LIBRARY